Introduction
to Computers
and
Programming:
P a s c a l

Peter P. Smith

Southern Utah State College

Wadsworth Publishing Company
Belmont, California
A Division of Wadsworth, Inc.

To Rip

Computer Science Editor: Frank Ruggirello
Editorial Assistant: Reita Kinsman
Production Editor: Sandra Craig
Managing Designer: Merle Sanderson
Print Buyer: Ruth Cole
Text and Cover Designer: Christy Butterfield
Copy Editor: Evelyn Mercer Ward
Technical Illustrator: Raychel Ciemma
Cover: Richard Diebenkorn, Ocean Park #54, 1972, oil on canvas, 100 × 81". San Francisco Museum of Modern Art; gift of friends of Gerald Nordland.

Printed in the United States of America   19

1 2 3 4 5 6 7 8 9 10—91 90 89 88 87

Library of Congress Cataloging-in-Publication Data

Smith, Peter P., 1947–
   Introduction to computers and programming.

   Includes index.
   1. PASCAL (Computer program language)   I. Title.
QA76.73.P2S6   1987   005.13′3   86-24759
ISBN 0-534-07194-5

Contents

This book is a one-year introduction to computer science at the college or university level. The material covered in the text is based on the recommended curriculum for the CS1/CS2 courses developed by the **ACM** (*Communications of the ACM*, October 1984 and August 1985). The purpose of this text is to provide thorough coverage of fundamental concepts and techniques in computer science in a readable, pleasant, and nonthreatening fashion.

My motivation for writing this book stems from my experiences in teaching computer science to beginning students. This text is designed with such students in mind and is intended to provide a basic understanding of computers along with problem-solving and programming skills sufficient for continued study in the discipline. I have gone to considerable effort to reduce the opportunities for despair frequently encountered by novice programmers. Explanations are detailed and complete, and enough support is provided to allow students to surmount the initial difficulties and enable them to continue with more advanced courses. The coverage of material is sufficiently thorough so that anyone who completes a course based on this text will have a strong foundation upon which to build professional expertise in computer science.

A number of principles and techniques are incorporated into the text to make learning this material as easy as possible for students. The primary elements include the following:

CONSISTENT USE OF THE TOP-DOWN APPROACH

The key underlying assumption on which this text is based is that the top-down approach is the best method for solving most computer-oriented problems, including not only typical computer problems/solutions (How do I generate a program that will correctly track inventory?) but more general problems as well (How can I learn to write computer programs?). Consequently, the top-down approach permeates the text so that it will come to be seen by students as the natural way to proceed in approaching any task. Students thus develop good programming and problem-solving habits from the beginning. Manifestations of the top-down approach can be seen in the organization of the text, in the problem-solving methodology, and in the syntax presentation.

Text organization. The text itself is divided into three parts: first principles, control structures, and data structures. Each section is previewed and then subdivided further, making sure that students are not offered too much detail too soon. For most topics, students are presented with a motivation followed by a description of what material is to be explained. Thus every detailed description is preceded by a more general description so that students can proceed in an orderly and logical fashion and can retain more knowledge.

Problem-solving methodology. A five-phase problem-solving paradigm that embodies the principles of top-down program development is presented early and used repeatedly throughout the text. In fact, there is a complete chapter on program development, a rarity in current books. Also, in order to reinforce the concept of modularity and to provide students with better tools for implementing top-down design, procedures and functions are introduced early, even before control structures.

Syntax presentation. Another way the top-down approach is used in the text is in the presentation of specific language elements. This is done via the concept of productions in a context-free language, as used in theory to define grammars. This is similar to standard BNF descriptions but is somewhat less formal. The method provides an elegant and easy-to-understand description of various Pascal syntax elements. Of course, it has been modified for use in this beginning text, but the concept is valid and very useful since it embodies the ideas of the top-down approach. Also, students are thereby introduced to a formalism that will be useful to them in future studies.

EMPHASIS ON PROBLEM SOLVING AND PROGRAM DEVELOPMENT

This text is intended to teach students how to use the computer as a tool to solve problems. Consequently, the emphasis in the text is on *problem solving* and not on learning the Pascal programming language. The underlying assumption here is that learning a computer language in detail is *not* the way to learn good programming techniques. This text, therefore, uses the Pascal programming language as a vehicle rather than as an end in itself. Many fine (but exotic) language capabilities are totally ignored; only what is needed to teach fundamental programming concepts and techniques is used.

At the core of the emphasis on problem solving is the five-phase program development process, which is essentially an algorithm for writing algorithms. This process is introduced in its own chapter and is then used throughout the text in every example. The five phases are understand the problem, plan the solution, code the solution, check out the program, and document the solution.

As a further aid to program development, a very English-like pseudocode, rather than flowcharts, is used to describe and develop algorithms. This natural way of expressing high-level algorithms makes it possible to take full advantage of the top-down approach to solution planning.

EARLY INTRODUCTION OF PROCEDURES AND FUNCTIONS

To emphasize the top-down approach, permit procedural abstraction, and allow students to take advantage of physical modularity, procedures and functions are covered early. Further, this introduction includes parameter passing and local variables so that the full power of this Pascal feature can be used for the rest of the text. Once introduced, procedures are used liberally throughout the text.

NUMEROUS PROGRAMMING EXAMPLES

Students learn as much (and probably more) from examples as they do from reading text material. Consequently, this book contains many programming examples, and each new topic or concept is demonstrated via a complete example chosen for its relevance to the concept, its applicability to the real world, and an appropriate level of difficulty. The guiding principle is that examples should reflect as much as possible the types of problems that will be encountered in real-life situations. For example, binary decision is demonstrated by using complex overtime pay calculations rather than the more abstract determination of the largest of three integers. Loops are demonstrated using progressive income tax calculations rather than the more common method of calculating a disembodied average of some type. Further, these examples are all generated in accordance with the program development process explained in the first part of the text to reinforce the concepts and activities associated with modular programming. Finally, as the text progresses, the level of difficulty of the examples increases to keep up with the interest and abilities of the students.

GRADUATED PROBLEMS AND EXERCISES

A large number of problems is included to provide students with interesting exercises and to allow instructors ease and flexibility in choosing assignments. A substantial effort has been made to use problems typical of those that students will encounter in later endeavors. All of the chapters include one to three categories of exercises intended to provide students with review and practice. The first category, Concepts, includes questions about facts and principles that students should understand. As anyone who has ever learned anything knows, however, the abil to recite ideas and the feeling that an intuitive grasp has been achieved do not mean that the material has been mastered. For this reason, a second category of problems, Tools, is included. These problems focus on a single programming concept, such as the summation of array elements, giving students the opportunity to use the ideas and techniques that have been presented without being distracted by other aspects of the program development process. The last category, Problems, includes exercises in which a complete solution to a realistic problem must be found. These exercises use the current programming concepts being investigated but require that those concepts be integrated into a complete programming solution.

ACKNOWLEDGMENTS

Writing a textbook is a team project, and I would like to acknowledge all those persons who contributed so much to converting an idea into a reality. First and foremost, I would like to thank the reviewers, who conscientiously read and reread the material, making invaluable suggestions and uncovering numerous errors: August "Al" Bauer, San Francisco; Lionel E. Deimel, Allegheny College; Robert Del Zoppo, Jamestown Community College; William J. Eccles, University of South Carolina; Judith L. Gersting, Indiana University/Purdue University; Clarence Krantz, Mansfield University; James Lea, Middle Tennessee State University; Robert R. Little, Clemson University; Jane Wallace Mayo, University of Tennessee; Ronald D. Peterson, Weber State College; David A. Petrie, Cypress College; Seymour V. Pollack, Washington University; Douglas Re, San Francisco City College; Tom Richard, Bemidji State University; Richard Rinewalt, University of Texas at Arlington; Darrell Turnidge, Kent State University; Lynn R. Ziegler, Michigan Tech University.

Second, I would like to express my appreciation to the staff at Wadsworth, especially Frank Ruggirello, who gently (and sometimes not so gently) guided the work and organized the project. Thanks also are due to Sandra Craig, who joined up late but nonetheless worked with impossible schedules and changes. Others who contributed to the book (and my well-being) include Karen Rovens, Terry Baxter, Reita Kinsman, and Serina Beauparlant. I also want to mention and thank Evelyn Ward, who probably learned more about computers than she really wanted to.

My colleagues at Southern Utah State College, especially Bob Jones and Steve Heath, are to be congratulated on their patience and understanding, even when it seemed that all the dark forces of the universe were allied together to keep me from completing the book.

Finally, I would like to thank the members of my family, who graciously consented to do without Daddy for a significant amount of time: to Katie, who chose to be born prematurely, right in the middle of the final draft; to Sarah, who more than once said, "Don't work on your 'puter, Daddy!"; to Chad, who ended up taking care of the horses and many of the domestic chores; and especially to my wife, Judy, who was understanding and generous in making sure I had the time to work on and complete the book.

Peter Smith

List of Programming Examples

1

Overview I:

An Initial Perspective on Computers

*C*omputers, for all their achievements and widespread fame, are actually *very* stupid. A favorite story about computers concerns the person who received a computerized charge account statement in the amount of zero dollars and zero cents. Thinking this was just his final statement, he ignored it. However, the next month he again found in his mailbox a bill for $0.00, with a short note stating that no payment had been received the previous month. Again choosing to ignore the bill, he subsequently received yet another statement, which included a curt warning to the effect that if he did not make a payment soon, action would be taken against him. Shortly thereafter he received a letter stating that his account was very delinquent and would be turned over to a collection agency.

In desperation the fellow returned the bill with a check for zero dollars and zero cents. He was rewarded with a statement saying his account was now paid in full!

How and why do such things happen? Stories like this tend to make people shake their heads and say, "Yes, computers really are stupid." As it turns out, this conclusion is correct, although in a different sense than the above story suggests. For the most part, computers know how to carry out only a small number of elementary tasks, such as addition and subtraction. These manipulations are usually mastered by humans in early childhood, and any adult who could perform only these tasks would be considered simple indeed. However (and this is a big however), computers can do these simple things extremely fast. It generally takes a computer on the order of one-millionth of a second to perform an addition. In other words, a computer can add a million numbers a second, which is considerably faster than a human can do it. Therein lies part of the secret: computers are really stupid, but they can do simple things so fast that they give the *appearance* of intelligence.

Let us begin the process of understanding computers by developing, in this chapter, an initial perspective that can be expanded as we progress through the text. We will start with a formal definition of a computer and two very important consequences that follow logically from this definition. We will then look at, in an abstract way, the kinds of things a computer is able to do. Finally, we will review a brief history of computing that will provide a chronological understanding of the development of the field.

1-1 *Definition of a Computer*

We begin by presenting a conceptual and highly abstract definition of a computer:

> A **computer** is an electronic device designed to carry out any arbitrary task that can be presented in terms of a sufficiently detailed sequence of simple instructions.

In other words, a computer is intended to be able to carry out any tasks or solve any problems whose solutions can be expressed in terms of simple instructions. An example is found in the process of multiplying two multidigit numbers (such as 134 and 712). Neither a human nor a computer can carry this operation out without knowing the required steps, which include shifting and carrying digits from one column to the other.

The above definition leads to two important consequences, which should always be kept in mind by students of computer science:

1. A computer cannot do anything but follow instructions given to it by some person: A COMPUTER CANNOT THINK.

2. In the absence of electronic or mechanical failure, instructions and calculations are always done correctly: A COMPUTER CANNOT MAKE A MISTAKE.

These two rules need to be appreciated fully. Let us examine each of them in more depth.

A COMPUTER CANNOT THINK. There is a tendency to believe that because computers can, in some instances, display characteristics normally associated with human intelligence, they can also think. Consider, for example, computer chess programs. These programs have become so highly sophisticated that they can be beaten by only a handful of human grandmasters. Anyone who has been defeated and humbled by such a chess program cannot help but feel awed. Nonetheless, during a chess match the computer is merely carrying out a set of instructions given to it by a human. Theoretically, if someone gave you this set of instructions and you followed it exactly, you could quite possibly win against a world champion chess player, even if you had never played a game of chess before in your life. Following this set of instructions would not be easy, and you would be unable to play in tournament time (in fact, it's doubtful that you would even live long enough to finish the game). Still, ignoring the time factor, you could do as well as the computer.

A COMPUTER CANNOT MAKE A MISTAKE. This is one rule that many people find hard to accept, especially in light of anecdotes such as the one that began this chapter. However, this rule is nonetheless true. If a mechanical or electronic failure occurs, then of course the computer will make mistakes; however, such failures are usually *very* obvious because the machine probably will not be functioning at all. But, barring electronic or mechanical failure, computers always follow their instructions properly and carry out their mathematical operations correctly. The "computer errors" one hears about can almost always be traced back to some human mistake. The billing problem referred to in the above story could have come about because a programmer asked the computer to send bills to anyone whose balance was greater than or equal to zero rather than to those whose bills were greater than zero. In fact, the computer's insistence on carrying out its instructions *to the letter* can cause much grief to the sloppy programmer, as we will see later. This is summed up in the following "old computer science adage":

A computer does what you TELL it to do, not what you WANT it to do.

Having looked at some of the things computers cannot do, we are in a position to ask: What *can* computers do? We will consider this question next.

1-2 *Functions of Computers*

As our earlier definition of a computer suggests, computers carry out predefined tasks of one kind or another. These tasks invariably involve data (which can be thought of as known or perceived facts), and the refining of data into information (which can be considered to be new knowledge derived from older facts). The conversion of **data** into **information** is usually termed **data processing**. Since data processing is not a new concept, the term **electronic data processing** (or **EDP**) is sometimes used to refer to such processing when it is carried out by computer.

DATA PROCESSING

Examples of data and data processing can be found everywhere there are living things: one could say that where there is life, there is data processing. Data processing is something humans do every moment of their lives and for which they are very well designed. When you take a walk, you are processing data—your eyes collect visual data on the surrounding terrain, your inner ear collects data on your position relative to the surface, and so on. This data is then processed by your brain and results in information that you use to make decisions: What direction will you walk? How fast will you walk? This data processing keeps you from walking into trees, falling off cliffs, or otherwise doing damage to yourself.

Some other examples of human data processing include the activities of a payroll clerk writing checks for company employees or of a handsome young man striking up a conversation with a good looking woman. In each case data is taken in (hour and wage figures, the woman's features), processed into information (gross and net dollar amounts, the sensation of attraction), and a decision is made (produce a check for the given amount, ask the woman for a date). Life can be considered a continual task of processing data.

Similarly, examples of electronic data processing include a computerized payroll system or the flight of a space shuttle. Again, data is taken (hour and wage figures, the coordinates and planned trajectory of the flight), processed into information (gross and net dollar amounts, the thrust and direction provided by the rocket engines), and a decision is made (produce a check for the given amount, open the fuel and oxygen valves to a certain point).

The basic idea is that data is processed into information and decisions are made. In this sense information has a higher value than data. Consider, for example, an agricultural study of fertilizers versus plant yields. The data would consist of tables containing types of fertilizers, rate of application, plant yields, water conditions, and so on. A statistical analysis (data processing) would yield information about which fertilizers, rates, water conditions, and so forth result in the highest plant productivity. On the basis of this information, a plan for actual farming could be generated and implemented.

Note that the distinction between data and information is not hard and fast. Rather, the terms are relative and define a continuum; one person's data could be somebody else's information. Further, information produced by one program might very well be data for another; it is possible to continue the process indefinitely. As noted above, information has a higher value than data, and this is really what computers are all about. Computers are a means of producing information—a very valuable commodity. We will next briefly examine how information is produced by a computer.

OPERATION OF A COMPUTER

Figure 1-1 gives a *very* schematic view of a computer system. Note that the successful operation of a computer system requires more than just the machine itself; people also play a prominent role. One of these people, the **programmer**, must write a program. What is a program? A **program** can be considered a set of instructions (a recipe if you will) that the computer can understand and carry out (the "sufficiently detailed instructions" referred to earlier). For example, in a payroll application, the programmer would tell the computer that in order to figure gross wages, the number of hours worked must be multiplied by the hourly rate of pay. This must be written in such a way that the computer can, in some sense, understand it. After the program is written, it must be entered into the computer before the machine can use the program to carry out the required task.

A second person necessary for this operation is the user—the person who wishes the computer to perform a task. The programmer and the user may be one and the same, but that does not alter the relationship of computer to user. The user provides data, which in this case may be hour and wage figures for company employees. Data can be considered the ingredients that the cook (computer) will use when following the recipe (program). As with the program, the data must also be entered into the computer.

Once the program and the data have been generated and

Figure 1-1

A Schematic Representation of the Elements Comprising a Complete Computer System

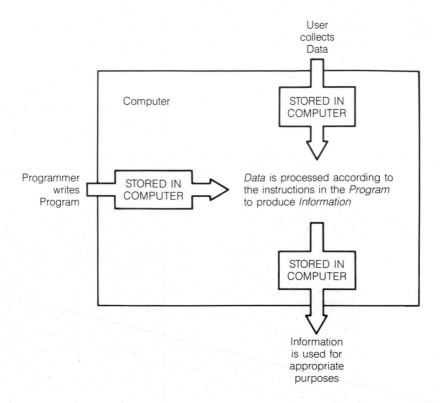

the computer processes the data according to the instructions of the program to produce information (the cake, if we are to extend the recipe analogy). In the case of a payroll problem, information would consist of an actual amount to be paid to the employee. When first generated, this information is still inside the computer; it must somehow be removed in order to be useful. The computer could print out a check for the amount, which the employee could then use in making financial decisions: Should the check be spent on a trip to Hawaii or for repairing the car?

Having briefly discussed what a computer does, we are now ready to consider the final question of this chapter: How did we get here from there?

Figure 1-2

Typical Microprocessor: A Complete Computer on a Single Chip
(Courtesy Intel Corporation)

Actual size of
chip:

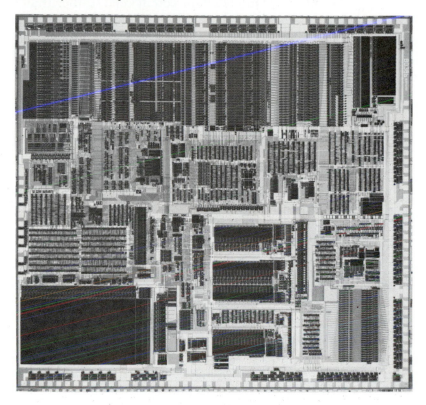

1-3 *A Historical Viewpoint*

The beginning of the *electronic* computer era dates back only to 1946, although there were many nonelectronic advances that preceded this and made the development of modern computers possible. The very first computer was named ENIAC, which is an acronym for Electronic Numerical Integrator and Calculator. It was the first programmable electronic device ever created. It took seven years to build, weighed 30 tons, and occupied 15,000 square feet of floor space. Compared to present-day machines, ENIAC was an unwieldy monster. A modern microprocessor (essentially a complete computer) is pictured in Figure 1-2. The typewriter-sized "computer" that this microprocessor normally fits into is necessary only for the convenience of humans, who are used to large keyboards. The computing power, versatility, and utility of this tiny device far exceed those of ENIAC.

ENIAC was a military project designed for the purpose of generating ballistic firing tables. Once the potential of electronic computers was demonstrated, commercialization followed quickly. In 1951 the first computer intended for commercial (rather than military or scientific) applications, the UNIVAC I, was placed in service with the U.S. Census Bureau. Shortly thereafter, in 1953, IBM came out with the IBM 701, the first practical computer intended to be used for business purposes.

Most noteworthy and unprecedented in the history of humankind is the speed at which developments in the computer industry took place. Not only did the processing speed and power of computers increase exponentially but the cost of computers simultaneously decreased in the same proportion. If the automobile industry had been able to match the record of computers, you could now buy a new car that would get thousands of miles per gallon and pay only a few dollars for it!

Traditionally, the history of computers is divided into generations based on the type of circuitry used. First generation computers used vacuum tubes, once described as "funny glass things that glow in the dark." Although the tubes work well enough, they do have a number of drawbacks: they consume considerable power, are large and bulky, and are not particularly dependable. In addition, they are very slow, because the physical components are separated by (relatively speaking) large distances and it therefore takes a long time for the electrical signals to travel from point to point. It might seem odd that electrical signals, which flash along at the speed of light (186,000 miles per second), can do anything "slowly." However, given a constant speed, the distance that must be traveled determines the time required to complete the action. For instance, if one had to complete all business deals in person but could travel anywhere in the United States in a jet plane at 550 miles per hour, the time required to complete a given task would be a function of the distance between points; it would take considerably longer to complete a New York/Los Angeles deal than a New York/Boston deal. Analogously, the bigger the computer, the greater the area over which messages must be sent, and thus the longer it takes the computer to complete a given task.

Second generation computers used transistors as the major electronic component. Transistors are smaller than vacuum tubes, require considerably less power, and are more dependable. As a result, second generation computers were faster, smaller, and less expensive.

Third generation computers began with the introduction of **integrated circuits (ICs)**, or chips, onto which varying amounts of electronic circuitry could be placed. Using ICs, the power consumption of the computer is next to nothing, the speed is astounding, and reliability is excellent. Because ICs are so small, they must be made photographically rather than mechanically. The necessary circuit diagrams are drawn and then successively reduced photographically to a very small size. Prints of the diagram are then etched onto semiconductor material.

It is generally accepted that we are currently in the fourth generation of computers, although no one is sure just when that happened. It is related to the development of **VLSI** circuitry, which stands for very large scale integration. Utilizing the techniques for making ICs, all of the circuitry necessary for the operation of an entire computer can be placed in a single chip. However, the minimum size of these chips is determined by physical limits related to the properties of light. It is impossible to reduce anything photographically and end up with a picture smaller than the wavelength of the light being used. Consequently a limit has been reached using this process.

There are two other technologies that may, if developed successfully, usher in a new era of compactness and speed (and consequently another generation of computers). The first uses the Josephson junction, which is essentially a superconducting molecule-sized switch. If such a switch can be adequately developed, it will represent considerable progress in miniaturization. A compartment to hold the device at a temperature near absolute zero (in order to allow the superconducting material to work) is necessary, but even with this compartment, the container for the computer would only be a few feet on a side. This computer would have more than three times the amount of memory and would be about twenty times faster than the best computers manufactured today.

A second technology, on which considerable effort is being expended especially in Japan, is that of the Fifth Generation Computer System. Such systems are complex combinations of advanced hardware, artificial intelligence, and data base systems (collections of facts) that can automate large chunks of the problem-solving/data-manipulation process itself. These systems would allow persons with little computer training to use powerful processors to solve difficult problems.

SUMMARY

In this chapter the term *computer* was defined and we examined two of the logical conclusions derived therefrom, namely, *computers cannot think* and *computers do not make mistakes*. We went on to explore the concept of data processing and how it is carried out in the computer. We finally reviewed the history of computers as represented by successive generations.

EXERCISES

CONCEPTS

1. Define or explain and give examples of the following:

   Computer
   Data
   Information
   Data processing
   IC
   VLSI

2. What two generalizations should be remembered when dealing with computers?

3. What is the "old computer science adage"?

4. Describe the conditions that must exist for a computer to carry out a data processing task.

5. Briefly describe the distinguishing characteristics of the five (actual or planned) generations of computers.

2

Systems, Hardware, and Software:

Toward a Deeper View of Computers

*I*n the last chapter we examined, in a very general way, what a computer does and how it does it. In this chapter, these concepts will be expanded. Of special concern here are the components that make up a computer system—how they interact and how they can be used to solve problems.

2-1 *Computer Systems*

We will start with the concept of a **system**, which can be defined as a collection of separate entities whose interactions and functions are co-ordinated, frequently for some purpose. One example of a system is our solar system. The solar system's entities are the sun and the planets and their moons, and the functional interactions of the entities are controlled by gravitation. A human being is an example of a biological system; the various organs, fluids, and electrical signals all work together to ensure the survival of that individual. Human social systems are comprised of collections of individuals; the purpose of these systems is the perpetuation of a given culture.

We can extrapolate the idea of system to include computer systems, which also involve coordinated interactions of constituent components. Obviously, there can be no computer system without a computer. Many people mistakenly consider the computer itself as the computer system. However, this is not really the case. The actual machine (which you can kick and occasionally swear at) is, of course, a primary component of a computer system, but it is in fact an important subsystem, not the system itself. There are *five* components of a complete computer system, as follows:*

1. Hardware
2. Software
3. Data
4. People
5. Procedures

Hardware is the first component of a computer system. **Hardware** is the actual physical device. Advances in hardware technology have to date developed fastest and to the fullest extent.

Software comprises the second facet of a computer system. **Software** is also called **programs.** Many people feel software is the most important and challenging aspect of computer systems. Software can be defined as a set of instructions that directs the actions of the hardware. Software is traditionally stressed most in computer science classes, and it is the aspect that requires the most effort to teach and learn.

Data is thought of as individual elements of some kind, such as

---

* From David M. Kroenke, *Business Computer Systems: An Introduction*, 2d ed. (Santa Cruz, CA: Mitchell Publishing, 1984), pp. 22–29.

hours worked and pay rates for payroll applications, limits of integration for mathematical uses, or statistical tables (such as for the fertilizer study mentioned earlier). However, data is much more complex than this definition implies. Since the processing of data is *the* thrust of computer science, **data structures** (the organizing of individual data items to make processing easier) constitute a very important aspect of computer science.

People are another important part of a computer system, one that is often implicitly recognized but never actually stated. We have already mentioned the programmer and user, and there are other important people involved. The ability to work well with people is an ever-increasing requirement for being a successful computer person. In the "good old days" of computer science, a computer programmer was considered a necessary but pretty much independent resource. In general, computer people liked to be left to themselves to work individually. Since programmers were few and far between and since the computers at that time could not do too many complex things anyway, programmers could work in isolation. However, the nature of today's problems and the programs needed to solve them require that many people cooperate on such projects. Team programming efforts are becoming more popular and more successful. In a very real sense, more people are interested and have a say in the successful outcome of a given project. If you want to write a successful billing program, you must involve the business manager, the billing clerk, the shipping department, the computer department, and the **end users** (those who will use the finished product). The best programmers will be those who can coordinate well with other people involved and who can write the kind of programs that will satisfy everybody. Also, cooperative effort can save time: whereas a lone programmer might take years to write a very complex program, team programming can reduce this time considerably.

Procedures refer to a final aspect of computer systems that is often overlooked completely and is use here to mean simply that you must do the right thing at the right time. (Later, this term will be used in a different, more technical programming sense.) For example, one should not run a program that can change important data until assured that the program works correctly. A more complex example can be found in the process of program generation itself (see Chapter 3), where a distinct sequence of steps must be followed to ensure correct results. The entirety of the system should always be kept in mind; a good computer scientist or programmer is one who has such an overview.

Since software is the primary concern of this book and since an understanding of hardware is necessary to the ability to write software, we will examine both in more detail.

2-2 Hardware

The hardware of a computer consists of its physical components. These components can be classified according to function, as follows:

Peripheral devices	Input (Keyboard part of terminal)
	Output (CRT part of terminal , and the printer)
Central processing unit (CPU)	Arithmetic/Logic unit (Processor)
	Control
Storage	(Main memory)
Auxiliary storage	(Disk)

These components are shown schematically in Figure 2-1, along with a number of busses (the big, fat arrows). A **bus**, for all practical purposes, is a bunch of wires that connects the various components and carries signals between them. Let us now consider each component separately.

Input. As the name implies, an **input device** allows you to enter items (such as programs and data) *into* the computer. There are many kinds of input devices that can be used, and the type chosen depends on the job to be done. A very common input device is the **keyboard**, which is normally part of the computer terminal. Letters and numbers are typed in using the keyboard as if it were a typewriter and then sent automatically to the computer. Another input device (though used less frequently these days) is the card reader. Other types of input devices include disks, magnetic tape, magnetic ink, optical scanner, paper tape, and signals from inertial guidance systems.

Output. Output devices, on the other hand, take the information that is already in the computer and convert it into something readable or usable by people or other machines. A common output device often linked with a keyboard in a computer terminal is the **CRT** (which stands for cathode ray tube), a television-like screen. Another output device is the **printer**, which produces a printed paper output. Other output devices include the card punch, paper tape punch, disks, magnetic tape, and flight con-

Figure 2-1

Schematic Diagram of a Typical Computer

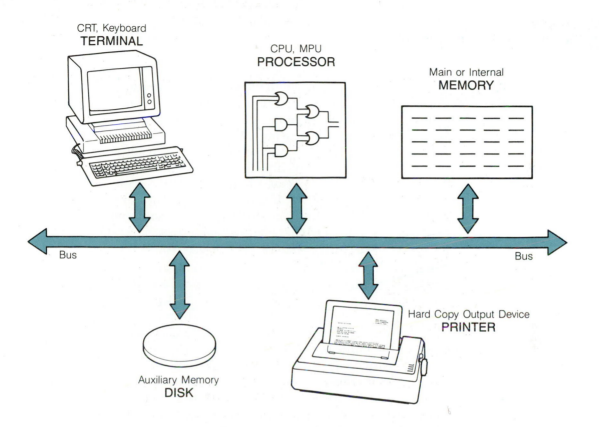

trol systems. Input and output (commonly called **I/O devices**) are together classified as **peripherals** because, in general, they are not an integral part of the computer but rather are attached to it by cables; that is, they are on the periphery of the computer.

CPU. The next two sections of the hardware, namely the **arithmetic/logic unit (ALU)** and the **control unit,** together make up the **central processing unit (CPU)**. This is the heart of the computer, where all the work is actually done. The ALU, as its name indicates, carries out arithmetic and logical operations. The former include addition, subtraction, multiplication, and division. The latter include, among other things, comparisons, which can be used to make tests of various conditions (for example, one might want to check the room temperature to see if it is over 100 degrees). This logic capability allows the computer to make decisions, a very powerful ability when processing data. The second part of the CPU is the control unit. This is the section that coordinates the activities of all the other parts of the computer. The control unit sends appropriate signals to initiate I/O and ALU operations, undertakes data transfers, and figures out what operations are to be done next. It is the real "brain" of the system.

Storage. This component is also referred to as **memory,** main memory, primary storage, and sometimes core (although this latter name actually refers to a particular technology that is mostly obsolete). **Storage** is where programs and data *must* be stored before any processing can be carried out. Memory is sometimes classified as a part of the CPU, but in actual practice it invariably consists of additional components far removed (relatively speaking, since we are dealing on the scale of a computer chip) from the CPU. It should be noted, however, that the CPU actually does have, in small quantity, some special fast memory that it uses to carry out its tasks: these special memory locations are termed **registers**.

Auxiliary Storage. This is almost always a disk unit of some kind. **Auxiliary storage** (or memory) is sometimes counted as a sixth hardware component and sometimes considered a part of one of the other sections. It can, for example, be an I/O device, since it can be written to and read from quite easily. On the other hand, as the name implies, it can also be used as an aid to main memory, which can, as a result, be expanded by many orders of magnitude. But auxiliary memory is really not one of these components because it has characteristics that make it different. Thus, these other classifications should be recognized as useful but not applied too rigidly.

After this brief introduction to hardware, we move on to the next aspect of a computer system—software.

2-3 *Software*

Software can be defined (as we mentioned earlier) as a set of instructions that directs the action of the hardware. Most frequently these instructions take the form of a program. Where do programs come from? They must be developed, and the development of a program is a complex task, replete with artistic and intellectual difficulties. The process will be discussed in considerable detail in the next chapter, but for now we will simply present a program for consideration and demonstration purposes:

```
Program PAYROLL (Input, Output);
Const SSRate = 0.067;
      FedTaxRate = 0.25;
Var   Hours, Rate, Gross,
      FICA, FedTax, NetPay : Real;
BEGIN
  Readln (Hours);
  Readln (Rate);

  Gross := Hours * Rate;

  FICA := Gross * SSRate;
  FedTax := Gross * FedTaxRate;

  NetPay := Gross - FICA - FedTax;

  Writeln (Hours, Rate, Gross, FICA, FedTax, NetPay)
END.
```

This program has the interesting (and highly desirable) property of telling you pretty much what its intended purpose is. Even if you've never seen a computer program before, it is possible to understand both the purpose of this program and how the purpose is to be carried out. The ability to write such programs is a skill that must be learned and practiced and is addressed throughout the text. The above program in fact does a simplified payroll calculation; it multiplies rate times hours to get the gross pay and then goes on to figure FICA, or Social Security deductions, federal withholding (in a *very* simplified manner), and finally the net pay. The results are then printed out and the program terminates. Note the very English-like nature of the program.

Let us next examine, in a schematic way, how such a program would be run, or executed (that is, how the instructions would be carried out), using a computer. The following description is intended to give you an intuitive feel for what goes on when a program is executed and to introduce a number of important concepts that should be kept in mind when writing programs. Technically speaking, however, the ensuing description does *not* accurately reflect what occurs in a typical computer, although many microcomputers (such as, for example, the Apple II) do in fact operate in a mode similar to that described here.

With that disclaimer, let us begin. When the computer is first started up, there is of course no program in memory. The control unit (hereafter referred to simply as control) alternately twiddles its thumbs (figuratively speaking) and checks the input device to see if anything is there.

Before any program can be run, of course, it *must* reside in the computer's memory. Let us assume that a programmer now approaches the input device in order to enter the payroll program described above. The programmer begins by typing in the first line of the program, for instance,

```
Program PAYROLL (Input, Output);
```

This action on the part of the programmer is then noticed by control. Since the statement begins with the word `Program`, control concludes that a sequence of instructions is about to be entered. Control activity from this point on simply involves shuttling such statements from the terminal to appropriate memory locations. This situation is shown in Figure 2-2.

The process continues, statement after statement, until the programmer enters the last line, `END`. Now this particular `END.` has a special meaning: it tells control that the last of the program has been entered. Consequently, no more statements belonging to the particular program called `PAYROLL` can be expected. At this point the entire program is in memory and control resumes twiddling its thumbs and looking in the mail box, as it did initially.

The programmer is now ready for action and types in the magic words `Run PAYROLL`. During the normal course of events, control

Figure 2-2

Getting the Program into Main Memory

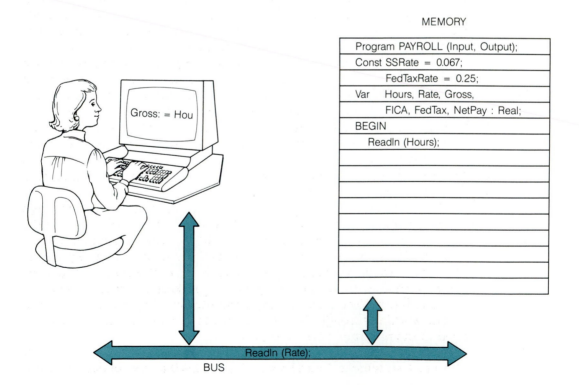

checks the terminal for input, finds something there, and reads it. After examining this most recent statement, control determines that a program called PAYROLL is to be executed. It looks through memory and finds just such a program. Control then goes to the first statement of that program and begins doing exactly what each of the instructions, or statements, requests. Note that this is the very *first* time that the instructions are examined for meaning; when the programmer previously entered the instructions into the computer, control merely transferred them from the terminal to main memory.

Control begins the task by examining the line immediately following the Program PAYROLL heading statement, and encounters the word Const. This tells control that the program is going to contain some constants that will have specific values and also will be given names. In this program there are two such constants, SSRate and FedTaxRate. By **constants** we mean that the values of these entities will not be changed in the program but can nonetheless be used by the program at any time. (As will be discussed further in Chapter 4, there are a number of reasons for using constants. Primarily, they make the program easier to read and understand and also easier to change. In this program we are dealing with taxes, and since tax rates have a bad habit of rising frequently, this can be a very important reason for using a constant.) Control must keep track of the names and values of these defined constants, and it does so by using some of the remaining main memory. Figure 2-3 shows what is in the computer after the constants have been processed. Note the pointer (the arrow in the figure) that marks the position of the *next* statement to be examined.

Having completed the Const statement, control continues on down through the program and finds, at the very next statement, the word Var. This tells control that a list of all the **variables** to be used by the program follows and that space in memory must be reserved for them. (A variable is the name of a memory location in the computer that stores values computed by the program.) In order to reserve space, control must go through the list and allocate memory locations for each variable named. The situation that exists after the variables have been processed is shown in Figure 2-4.

After completing variable allocation, control continues on through the program and comes to the word BEGIN, which tells control that the executable portion of the program starts here. The executable portion of the program consists of all statements (instructions) that require the computer to actually do some sort of work. Up to this point, all that the computer had to do was bookkeeping, that is, keeping track of variables and constants. Now, however, the computer can begin the actual process of working through the instructions to accomplish the tasks as defined in the program by the programmer.

The first executable instruction in the program is the Readln (Hours) statement. Readln stands for READ a LiNe of data, and is a

Figure 2-3

Memory After the Constants Have Been Processed

MEMORY

Program PAYROLL (Input, Output);
Const SSRate = 0.067;
FedTaxRate = 0.25;
Var   Hours, Rate, Gross,
FICA, FedTax, NetPay : Real;
BEGIN
Readln (Hours);
Readln (Rate);
Gross := Hours * Rate;
FICA := Gross * SSRate;
FedTax := Gross * FedTaxRate;
NetPay := Gross – FICA – FedTax;
Writeln (Hours, Rate, Gross,
FICA, FedTax, NetPay);
END.
SSRate   > 0.067
FedTaxRate   > 0.25

request for the computer to fetch data from the terminal. In this case the data consists of a number representing the hours worked. It is important to understand that the computer really does not have any idea what Hours means; as far as control is concerned, it is merely the name of a memory location. The name Hours is significant only to the programmer, *but it is a significance of extreme importance,* since it describes something about what the program is doing. The choice of variable names is related to good programming practice, as will be discussed in Chapter 4.

Figure 2-4

Memory After the Variables Have Been Processed

MEMORY

Program PAYROLL (Input, Output);
Const SSRate = 0.067;
FedTaxRate = 0.25;
Var Hours, Rate, Gross,
FICA, FedTax, NetPay : Real;
BEGIN
ReadIn (Hours);
ReadIn (Rate);
Gross := Hours * Rate;
FICA := Gross * SSRate;
FedTax := Gross * FedTaxRate;
NetPay := Gross − FICA − FedTax;
Writeln (Hours, Rate, Gross,
FICA, FedTax, NetPay);
END.
SSRate > 0.067
FedTaxRate > 0.25
Hours >
Rate >
Gross >
FICA >
FedTax >
NetPay >

Control must now fetch a piece of data and place it in the memory location named Hours. In order to get the data, control alternates between looking for something new at the terminal and waiting, as it had to do when the program was being entered. Let us assume that the programmer now types in the number 40, which is subsequently found by control at the terminal. The computer instruction currently under consideration says that this number is to be Hours; therefore, the value is transferred from the terminal to the particular location named Hours, where it resides until further notice.

Figure 2-5

Memory After the First Readln *Has Been Executed*

MEMORY

Program PAYROLL (Input, Output);
Const SSRate = 0.067;
FedTaxRate = 0.25;
Var   Hours, Rate, Gross,
FICA, FedTax, NetPay : Real;
BEGIN
Readln (Hours);
Readln (Rate);
Gross := Hours * Rate;
FICA := Gross * SSRate;
FedTax := Gross * FedTaxRate;
NetPay := Gross − FICA − FedTax;
Writeln (Hours, Rate, Gross,
FICA, FedTax, NetPay);
END.

SSRate	> 0.067
FedTaxRate	> 0.25
Hours	> 40.0
Rate	>
Gross	>
FICA	>
FedTax	>
NetPay	>

Let's now take a look at the resulting situation, which is pictured in Figure 2-5. The program is still undisturbed, but the memory location named Hours now has the value 40 in it. Note the very important distinction between the *name* of a memory location and the *value* residing in that memory location: the former tells *where* the information is and the latter tells *what* the information is. The relationship is similar to the *address* of a home and the *occupants* of that home. In fact, memory locations are generally referred to by addresses. Also, notice in Figure 2-5 that the pointer marks the instruction to be executed next: the instruction Readln (Hours) has been taken care of, and the one about to be carried out is Readln (Rate), the one being pointed to.

Figure 2-6

Memory After the Second Readln *Has Been Executed*

MEMORY

Program PAYROLL (Input, Output);
Const SSRate = 0.067;
FedTaxRate = 0.25;
Var   Hours, Rate, Gross,
FICA, FedTax, NetPay : Real;
BEGIN
Readln (Hours);
Readln (Rate);
Gross := Hours * Rate;
FICA := Gross * SSRate;
FedTax := Gross * FedTaxRate;
NetPay := Gross − FICA − FedTax;
Writeln (Hours, Rate, Gross,
FICA, FedTax, NetPay);
END.
SSRate   > 0.067
FedTaxRate > 0.25
Hours   > 40.0
Rate   > 5.50
Gross   >
FICA   >
FedTax   >
NetPay   >

Continuing on, control examines the next instruction to be carried out, the one being pointed at, namely Readln (Rate). This is similar to the first Readln in that it is necessary to go to the terminal for data. Assume the programmer enters 5.50; the number would quickly be found at the terminal by control and sent to the memory location named Rate. The new situation is shown in Figure 2-6.

We are now ready for the third instruction, which says Gross := Hours * Rate. The asterisk * represents *multiplication*. This instruction, as written, looks a lot like an equation; however, don't be fooled by appearances. It is *not* an equation in the algebraic sense, because *no equality is implied*. It is, in fact, a *computer instruction*, which means the following: take the value from the location called Hours, multiply that by the value to be found in the location called Rate, and place the product obtained by multiplying these together into the location named Gross.

When control sees this instruction, it will fetch the required values and send them to the ALU with an order to multiply them together. It will then wait until ALU signals that the operation is complete and the results are in hand. Control will then take the result obtained by the ALU, namely 220, and place it in the location named Gross. Similar actions will be taken for the next three instructions; the result in main memory is shown in Figure 2-7.

Figure 2-7

Memory After All Computations Have Been Completed

MEMORY

Program PAYROLL (Input, Output);
Const SSRate = 0.067;
FedTaxRate = 0.25;
Var   Hours, Rate, Gross,
FICA, FedTax, NetPay : Real;
BEGIN
Readln (Hours);
Readln (Rate);
Gross := Hours * Rate;
FICA := Gross * SSRate;
FedTax := Gross * FedTaxRate;
NetPay := Gross − FICA − FedTax;
Writeln (Hours, Rate, Gross,
FICA, FedTax, NetPay);
END.
SSRate   > 0.067
FedTaxRate   > 0.25
Hours   > 40.0
Rate   > 5.50
Gross   > 220.0
FICA   > 14.75
FedTax   > 55.00
NetPay   > 150.25

The last actual instruction, Writeln (Hours, Rate, Gross, FICA, FedTax, NetPay), is an *output* operation; Writeln stands for WRITE a LiNe of output. Control will begin to fetch the values from the appropriate memory locations and send them to the printer. After all of the indicated information is printed out, control moves on to the next instruction.

The final line of the program, END., is now encountered. This tells control that execution of the program is to be terminated. Even if there were more instructions (which there are not in this case and in fact never should be), control would ignore them. Control then resumes its process of alternately waiting and looking at the terminal for something to show up. At this point the programmer could request that the program be run again, start to enter a different program, or turn off the computer.

The above description is *very* schematic; the processes involved are actually much more complex than this. One process that was left out entirely is that of compilation. Normally, a computer cannot tell the difference between a payroll program and the Gettysburg Address. Any program must first be translated to a language the computer can understand by a special software program called a **compiler**. The compilation process is fairly routine and easy to use without necessarily understanding how it is done. A complete discussion of program translation will be deferred until Chapter 4.

More important, however, the schematic description above presents a number of significant concepts relating to the methods by which a computer carries out tasks and provides a conceptual framework for writing programs. Specifically:

1. Both the program and the data *must* reside within the memory of the computer. The idea of having both inside the computer was, in fact, one of the outstanding conceptual breakthroughs leading to the development of modern digital computers. However, a fair amount of effort must be expended in order to get both data and program into the computer.

2. Programs consist of a series of instructions that are executed sequentially in the absence of directives to the contrary. In general, the control unit of a computer fetches one instruction after another, carrying each out as directed. This is why computers are considered unable to think; they merely plod along doing one thing after another in a predetermined order.

3. Variables are merely the symbolic names of memory locations. They are similar to, and share some properties with, algebraic variables.

Now that we have a little conceptual background concerning what goes on in a computer, let's see how programs are assembled and entered on a practical level.

Figure 2-8

Procedures Necessary to Get a Program to Execute

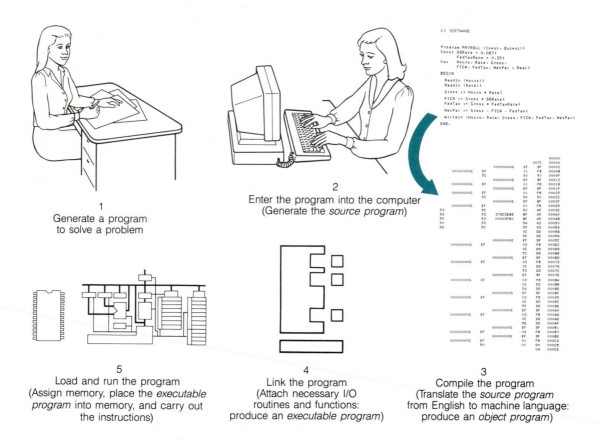

1
Generate a program
to solve a problem

2
Enter the program into the computer
(Generate the *source program*)

5
Load and run the program
(Assign memory, place the *executable
program* into memory, and carry out
the instructions)

4
Link the program
(Attach necessary I/O
routines and functions:
produce an *executable program*)

3
Compile the program
(Translate the *source program*
from English to machine language:
produce an *object program*)

2-4 *Entering and Running Programs*

The detailed procedures that must be followed in order to get a program up and running on a computer depend greatly on your available computer facilities. Therefore, in this section we will only examine, in an abstract way, what must be done. The necessary procedures for executing a program are outlined in Figure 2-8.

First, a hand-written version of the program must be generated; this process, which is quite extensive, is covered in Chapter 3. After the program is written, it must be entered into the computer. This is usually done interactively at a terminal by using an **editor**, which is a program that treats the keyboard much as if it were a typewriter and saves whatever is entered onto a disk.

Once the program is in the computer, it is called a **source program**. However, before it can be executed, it must be translated from the English-like programming language we have been using to a very different, numeric-type language called **machine language**. Machine language is the only language a computer really understands. The translation process is carried out by using a very special piece of software (which, as explained earlier, is actually just another, although very complex, program) called a compiler. (The compiler of interest to us in this book is Pascal.) The initial source program is scanned by the compiler, producing an **object program**, which is the numeric machine language equivalent of the source program. Figure 2-9 shows the machine language equivalent of the PAYROLL program used in this chapter, as compiled for a specific computer, the VAX-11. (More material on languages will be presented in Chapter 4.)

Figure 2-9

Machine Language Version of the PAYROLL Program

```
PAYROLL
Generated Code            VAX-11 Pascal V2.4-277
                                                   00000
                                           007C    00000
                          00000000G    EF    9F    00002
          00000000G    EF              01    FB    00008
                       5C              50    50    0000F
                          00000000G    EF    9F    00012
          00000000G    EF              01    FB    00018
                          00000000G    EF    9F    0001F
          00000000G    EF              01    FB    00025
                       52              50    50    0002C
                          00000000G    EF    9F    0002F
          00000000G    EF              01    FB    00035
  53                   5C              52    45    0003C
  54                   53    374C3E89  8F    45    00040
  55                   53    00003F80  8F    45    00048
  50                   53              54    43    00050
  56                   50              55    43    00054
                                       0C    DD    00058
                                       5C    DD    0005A
                          00000000G    EF    9F    0005C
          00000000G    EF              03    FB    00062
                                       0C    DD    00069
                                       52    DD    0006B
                          00000000G    EF    9F    0006D
          00000000G    EF              03    FB    00073
                                       0C    DD    0007A
                                       53    DD    0007C
                          00000000G    EF    9F    0007E
```

Figure 2-9 continued

00000000G	EF			03	FB	00084
				0C	DD	0008B
				54	DD	0008D
		00000000G	EF	9F	0008F
00000000G	EF			03	FB	00095
				0C	DD	0009C
				55	DD	0009E
		00000000G	EF	9F	000A0
00000000G	EF			03	FB	000A6
				0C	DD	000AD
				56	DD	000AF
		00000000G	EF	9F	000B1
00000000G	EF			03	FB	000B7
		00000000G	EF	9F	000BE
00000000G	EF			01	FB	000C4
		50		01	D0	000CB
					04	000CE

An object program, however, is not yet ready to be executed by the computer; there are a number of necessary appendages that must be added, such as instructions detailing input and output operations from within the program and mathematical functions such as sine, cosine, or exponential if needed. These additional functions are added during **linking**. (Frequently, this phase is coupled with the compile phase so that it is unnecessary to worry about it. However, it must be done, either explicitly or implicitly, as a part of the compilation process.) Linking produces a complete program that is ready to be executed.

When a request is made for the computer to execute a previously compiled and linked program, the linked version (called the **executable program**) is assigned space in main memory, and control is transferred to the beginning of that program. At this point the description of what occurs is very similar to the process described in detail for our conceptual model of the computer. Input will be requested and then processed according to the instructions; and finally the output will be generated.

SUMMARY

We have extended the concepts introduced in Chapter 1 by looking at computer systems and their components. We first considered hardware, which is the actual physical and electronic devices. We next examined software, also called programs, which contains the instructions necessary to permit a computer to carry out a task. We traced the execution of a typical program to see how the software and hardware performed and interacted with each other. We then concluded this chapter by examining how programs and instructions can be communicated to a computer.

EXERCISES

CONCEPTS

1. Define or explain the following terms:

ALU	Keyboard
Auxiliary storage	Linking
Bus	Memory
Compiler	Object program
Constants	Output device
Control	Peripheral devices
CPU	Registers
CRT	Software
Editor	Source program
Executable program	System
Hardware	Variables
Input device	Values

2. What are the five components of a complete *computer system?*

3. What are the *hardware* parts of a computer?

4. Briefly describe the process a program must go through in order to be executed.

TOOLS

5. Get the simple payroll program described in this chapter to successfully execute on your computer system.

PROBLEMS

6. Trace the following Pascal program. A *trace* means that you should pretend to be a computer and execute the program in a manner similar to that detailed in the text for the simple payroll. Carry out all the instructions and keep track of all the variables and show what output will be produced. Input a value of 5.0 for the radius.

```
Program SPHERE (Input, Output);
Const Pi = 3.14159;
Var   Radius, Volume : Real;
BEGIN
  Readln (Radius);
  Volume := 4.0 / 3.0 * Pi * Radius * Radius * Radius;
  Writeln (Volume)
END.
```

Note: The symbol / signifies division.

7. Trace the following program and show what output will be produced. Input a value of 8.78375 for the DecimalTime.

```
Program TIME (Input, Output);
Var DecimalTime,
    Hours, Minutes, Seconds,
    AmtLeft, Temporary           : Real;
BEGIN
  Readln (DecimalTime);
  Hours := Trunc (DecimalTime);
  AmtLeft := DecimalTime - Hours;
  Temporary := 60 * AmtLeft;
  Minutes := Trunc (Temporary);
  AmtLeft := Temporary - Minutes;
  Seconds := 60 * AmtLeft;
  Writeln (Hours, Minutes, Seconds)
END.
```

Note: The term Trunc used in this program is a special function, which takes the value following it in parentheses and drops off (that is, truncates) everything to the right of the decimal point. For example, Trunc (15.95) would be just 15. Note that this does *not* round the number; it cuts it off.

3

The Program Development Process:

A Top-Down Approach

One of the primary goals of any computer science course is to teach students how to write good programs. Writing computer programs is a skill that takes time and effort to learn and one that requires a combination of artistic and analytical concepts and methods. Even though many possible ways of generating programs exist, there are a number of widely accepted principles that should be applied to guide the process. These principles are presented in this chapter. Since the program development process is one of the most important aspects of computer science, we will discuss it in considerable detail. At the conclusion of the discussion, we will apply the principles to a specific problem.

3-1 *The Five Development Phases*

There are five general phases that should be considered and worked through when writing programs. These are

1. Understand the problem

2. Plan the solution (write an algorithm)

3. Code the solution (write the program)

4. Check out the program

5. Document (make the program understandable)

The organization of this list is not hard and fast; there will be some shifting of the order, and in some cases two or more of the items may be worked on simultaneously. Nevertheless, the general progression should be from the first to the fifth phase. For example, you may spend a great deal of time on the first phase trying to understand a given problem only to discover that during the check out phase you have completely misunderstood a particular aspect. Frequently, a fuller understanding evolves during the planning of the solution, when the details must be attended to. In addition, it is important to remember that documentation should be an ongoing process; the very act of producing a program is part of the documentation.

Notwithstanding the strong relationships among these items, a fuller understanding of each is needed. We will examine each in detail and at the same time point out the relationship of one to the other.

UNDERSTAND THE PROBLEM

Although a complete understanding of a given problem may not be possible until the project is almost complete, it is still necessary to have a pretty firm grasp of what is required before much can be done. Take, for example, the following problem:

> Write a program that will solve the Schroedinger Equation for hydrogen-like atoms in three dimensions using spherical coordinates.

Most people would have no idea what this means or where to begin. A programmer must have at least some understanding of what is required before proceeding farther.

There are a number of techniques that can be used as aids in understanding any problem. One of these techniques is to write down in detail *exactly* what data is initially required by the program to correctly solve the problem (the *input*) and what information is to be generated by the program when it executes (the *output*). Writing down this information gives you a place to begin and a destination to head for. It's somewhat like telling you to drive from Salt Lake City to Denver; once you know the terminus points of the journey, you can plan a rational route between them. It's very important to understand that there are any number of possible routes that will work. One could, for example, drive south on I-15 until it intersects I-70, then head East. But, there are always other possible routes you could take. It's possible to go to Denver from Salt Lake City via Tacoma, Washington, if you want, although that may not be the best way to go. Similarly, when you write a computer program, the best "route" can often be determined by knowing where to start and where to end.

To better demonstrate this, consider the PAYROLL program. The scope of the problem, and consequently the level of difficulty of the solution, can often be delimited by a knowledge of the inputs and outputs. For example, we may ask: Should the input consist merely of the hourly rate of pay and the total number of hours worked, or should it include name, address, exemptions, health insurance, and retirement information? Similarly, we could ask: Does the output consist simply of a check and a voucher, or are records for quarterly reports, annual reports, and accounting also needed? Such an analysis will provide us with a pretty good picture of what will be required in the solution of a particular problem.

A second method to help determine the full extent of requirements for a given problem is to ascertain what relationship, if any, the problem has to other programs. In general, the following principle holds true: *programs do not exist in a vacuum.* This particular aspect is difficult for those in introductory programming classes to fully appreciate, because rarely, if ever, does the beginner have the opportunity to write a program that must coordinate with other programs. Nonetheless, in the "real world" (a place we all hope to enter someday), such complex relationships are quite common. For example, assume you have been assigned the task of writing a program that calculates and prints checks and vouchers for a payroll application. This sounds pretty straightforward, but an examination of the entire system reveals some additional operations that must be considered, namely,

Enter/update of employee records. Someone must have a program that will allow changes to be made in the employee records. People quit or are fired, new people are hired, some move or get raises, and some change their status in one way or another. You, as the writer of the check production phase, must coordinate with the records person so that you both are dealing with the same type of data.

Posting to accounts. When somebody gets paid, the money has to come from somewhere; so when the payroll is run, the appropriate amounts must be subtracted from the correct accounts. Your part of the program must, at the very least, produce a report that can be used for such a process or have the program itself make the changes.

Information for internal, state, and federal reports. A great deal of paperwork is associated with payroll; quarterly reports and annual reports (including W-2s at the end of the year) must be prepared for a number of agencies, such as social security, the IRS, the state tax office, and the unemployment office. Your program must therefore be able to save the information necessary for generating these reports.

The point is, it is helpful to understand the *entire* process, even if you are directly concerned only with a part of it.

PLAN THE SOLUTION

Planning is without doubt *the most difficult part of writing a program* and where the most effort should be expended. It is also the phase that many beginning students tend to slight, primarily because the first few programs that are assigned in introductory courses tend to be rather simple. It is easy to fall into the trap of just sitting down and writing the final program directly or, heaven forbid, just typing it in at the terminal as the first step. PLEASE DON'T DO THIS! First of all, if you use this method much, you will find that, sooner or later (and certainly sooner than you think), you will be *unable* to write the "final program" this way. Be assured, your program will be far from final. Second, the more time you spend planning, the less time you will spend on all the other phases. This is not simply a linear relationship; for every unit of energy or time expended at this step, you can save several units on the other phases.

The goal of this second phase of the program development process is the production of something called an **algorithm**, which can be defined as follows:

> An algorithm is a set of step-by-step, unambiguous instructions that, when followed exactly, will always solve the problem.

In a commonly used analogy, an algorithm can be likened to a recipe. If the problem is to make a cherry pie for dessert, the algorithm for its solution would be a recipe for a cherry pie. The instructions in the algorithm should be detailed enough so that anyone can follow them. That is, the instructions should not be open to misinterpretation and should work under *any* conditions.

So, how do we go about getting an algorithm? Our primary method is to use **top-down design**:

Top-down design is a method of generating an algorithm in which you first write down a very *general* description of your solution to the problem and proceed, one step at a time, to a more *specific* description of the solution to your problem.

In other words, *divide and conquer.* (This method is sometimes referred to as *stepwise refinement.*) In order to carry out this method more easily, we must make it modular. **Modularity** is the process of breaking up a large, complex task into a number of smaller, simpler subtasks. We can combine the concepts of top-down design and modularity to come up with an orderly method for producing algorithms. Basically, we proceed as follows:

1. Write a general solution to the problem.

2. Break up the solution reached in step 1 above into smaller sections (that is, modules).

3. Break up each of the modules produced via step 2 above into even smaller modules.

4. Continue this process until a specific, detailed solution to the problem is reached.

Let us demonstrate this with an example. Assume we wish to write a payroll program such as the one demonstrated in the previous chapter. Our first very general description might be

Description 1

Do the Payroll

This is very general, but at least we've delimited the problem. Next, we need a description that divides this task into smaller (but not too many) sections. Hence, we might come up with

Description 2

Do the Payroll
   Get the Inputs
   Do the Calculations
   Do the Outputs

What we essentially have here is a rough outline of the solution. Note that the form, because of the indentations, *looks* just like an outline. Using the outline format helps a great deal and is an important aspect of writing readable programs. (In passing let us note that many problems can be reduced to this form, namely input, calculations, output. In fact a whole language, RPG, is dedicated to solving just such problems.) However, it is obvious we need more detail in our solution. Consider the first step, Get the Inputs. Our understanding of the problem to be solved is that it requires only a bare minimum of input, namely the hours and the rate. Hence we can incorporate these to get

Description 3

Do the Payroll
    Get the Inputs
        Read Hours
        Read Rate
    Do the Calculations
    Do the Output

Take a moment to notice several things. First, each successive description incorporates more detail. Second, the algorithm is structured, or modular, as in an outline: each section can be viewed (within limits) as a separate entity or as a subsection of a larger entity. Third, we are actually doing documentation: the description of the solution is easily understood, and the names of the data (that is, the variable names) make sense. We could have, for example, used the names Fred and Betty for the input data, but nobody would have understood what those meant. The terms "Hours" and "Rate" are very precise and have meaning not only for the programmer but for the reader of the program as well.

Progressing further, let us consider the next item, "Do the Calculations." What calculations need to be done? Well, we need to calculate the gross wages, any deductions, and finally the net wages. Adding these details, our algorithm becomes

Description 4

Do the Payroll
    Get the Inputs
        Read Hours
        Read Rate
    Do the Calculations
        Compute the Gross Wages
        Compute any Deductions
        Compute the Net Pay
    Do the Output

At this point we realize the calculations section needs more work. We need to identify the deductions and how to get them. Since the particular problem we wish to solve requires only that FICA and federal tax be calculated, we can amend the description to read

Description 5

Do the Payroll
  Get the Inputs
    Read Hours
    Read Rate
  Do the Calculations
    Compute the Gross Wages
    Compute any Deductions
      FICA
      Federal Tax
    Compute the Net Pay
  Do the Output

We are now in a position to work on the output. What do we need there? Well, we want to echo the input, namely the hours and the rate, and print out the calculated values of gross wages, FICA, federal tax, and net pay. Hence

Description 6

Do the Payroll
  Get the Inputs
    Read Hours
    Read Rate
  Do the Calculations
    Compute the Gross Wages
    Compute any Deductions
      FICA
      Federal Tax
    Compute the Net Pay
  Do the Output
    Print Hours, Rate,
    Gross Wages,
    FICA, Federal Tax,
    Net Pay

The only thing left to do now is to fill in the arithmetic details as follows:

Description 7

Do the Payroll
  Get the Inputs
    Read Hours
    Read Rate
  Do the Calculations
    Compute the Gross Wages
      Gross $\leftarrow$ Hours $\times$ Rate

```
        Compute any Deductions
           FICA ← Gross × SSRate
           Federal Tax ← Gross × FedTaxRate
        Compute the Net Pay
           Net ← Gross − FICA − Federal Tax
     Do the Output
        Print Hours, Rate,
        Gross,
        FICA, Federal Tax,
        Net
```

The left-pointing arrows used here mean that the value computed on the right side of the arrow should be stored in the variable named on the left side.

This, then, is our final algorithm. Note that it does in fact conform to our definition of an algorithm: it is a set of step-by-step instructions, it is unambiguous (you cannot misinterpret any of the steps), and when followed it will produce the correct results.

This may seem like a very laborious process to go through for such a simple problem, but it is the process itself we wish to emphasize here. When you are actually generating an algorithm by hand, especially after a little practice, the process will go faster. Also, since things normally aren't quite this neat, you must avoid being in too much of a hurry and losing sight of the general process.

Another worthwhile thing to remember when writing algorithms is that being "schizophrenic" in your approach helps. This is to say, solve the problem by hand but watch yourself work through the solution as if you were observing somebody else. Let one part of your mind work through the problem by hand and let the other part of your mind (the programmer part) watch what the first part is doing. For example, in order to get the gross, you would multiply the hours times the rate; the programmer part of you would be watching this multiplication. Having observed this, the programmer part would write down that particular calculation step as

Gross ← Rate × Hours

That's basically the idea: watch yourself carry out the solution and then write a step-by-step description of it that is simple enough so that you could almost give it to your eight-year-old brother and have him work it correctly. Remember, computers are only fast, *not* bright, and they must be shown how to do *everything*.

Another question that might be asked is: Is this English-looking outline-type form, which is called **pseudocode**, the best way to represent an algorithm? And are there other ways to write it? Besides pseudocode, there is another commonly utilized method called **flowcharting**.

The flowchart description of the solution to our payroll problem is shown in Figure 3-1. There has been some discussion in computer circles about which of these two methods is better, and there has gradually been a consensus that pseudocode is superior. Flowcharts were developed before the advent of modern structured languages, and suffer from the limitation that there is not a high correlation between an algorithm expressed as a flowchart and the final program, as written in a structured language. However, when pseudocode is used, the correlation between an algorithm and its corresponding program is very high. (Compare, for example, the finished program as written in the last chapter with the pseudocode and flowcharting algorithms presented here.)

The primary difference between pseudocode and flowcharting can be stated thus: a flowchart stresses *logic*, whereas pseudocode stresses *structure*. Logic shows you how the program gets from one place to another so that you can follow the flow of the program more easily. Structure lets you see the relationships between the various components of your program and how they work together. In other words, pseudocode

Figure 3-1

Flowchart Solution to the PAYROLL *Problem*

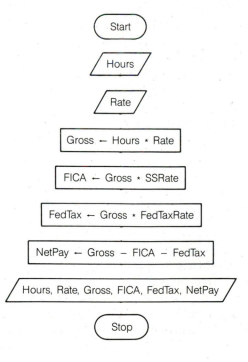

stresses *what* the program does, whereas flowcharting stresses *how,* on a relatively very low level, the program carries out the task.

The ability to write programs that are *structured* is one of the goals we're after. Consequently, this book is written exclusively using pseudocode for algorithm generation and expression.

CODE THE SOLUTION

In contrast to the previous difficult step of generating an algorithm, the coding step should be the *easiest* of the five phases. If you've written a properly structured algorithm, coding the solution should be very straightforward and simply involve rewriting the algorithm to conform to the rules of the language. When this step is carried out you finally have a **program**:

> A program is an algorithm implemented in a computer language.

A program is very much like an algorithm (at least it had better be!), and the only difference is that the program must conform exactly to the rules of the computer language you are using. Compare the PAYROLL program used in the previous chapter with the algorithm for the same problem described in this chapter and you will see the similarity. In order to produce the program from the algorithm, a knowledge of the language rules is required. The language rules for Pascal are the topic of the next chapter.

CHECK OUT THE PROGRAM

The point of this phase is to make sure that the program works and that it *works correctly.* Although programs rarely work right the first time they are run, the amount of time and effort required to eliminate any problems discovered in the program can be substantially reduced if the first two phases, understanding and planning, are carried out properly. THIS CANNOT BE STRESSED STRONGLY ENOUGH! It is tempting to quickly pass through the first few phases and then concentrate on finding and eliminating all the **bugs** (that is, errors) that a program contains. This is a very poor technique. Remember what happened to all those people before the Wright brothers who tried to "debug" their flying machines after they were built rather than planning problem-free vehicles from the start.

Even so, the best programmers using the best techniques often find that their programs are not doing quite what was intended. Hence, developing an understanding of the types of errors that can appear and how to deal with them is worthwhile. A full chapter (Chapter 5) is dedicated to error detection and recovery, but we will briefly introduce the topic here.

One class of errors commonly encountered is **clerical errors**. These are normally of two types: those the compiler can detect and those the compiler cannot detect. An example of the former would be

```
Gross + Hours * Rate
```

The plus sign is obviously a mistake, and the replacement sign (that is, :=) is apparently intended. As the statement stands, however, it makes no sense to the computer, and the compiler will flag it with an error message.

A second example would be

```
Gorss := Hours * Rate
```

Here the variable name on the left is misspelled; the computer would *not* recognize it as a correct variable and would mark it as an error.

Consider an example of a clerical error that would *not* be detected by the computer. Suppose a programmer was writing a program to calculate the roots of quadratic equations and had in the algorithm the following:

$$Det \leftarrow \sqrt{b^2 - 4ac}$$

$$r_1 \leftarrow (-b + Det) / (2a)$$

$$r_2 \leftarrow (-b - Det) / (2a)$$

If these equations were converted incorrectly, the Pascal statements would be

```
Det := Sqrt (A * A - 4.0 * B * C);
Root1 := (- B + Det) / (2.0 * A);
Root2 := (- B - Det) / (2.0 * A);
```

Given these statements, the results would, more often than not, be wrong. This is because the program as written from the algorithm is incorrect in that the *a* and the *b* are transposed in the calculation of the determinant. *The computer will detect no error*, but the program will more often than not produce the wrong answer. (It is important to note that the program would *not always* produce incorrect answers; if by chance *a* and *b* in the equation happened to have the same value, the error would be neutralized and the program would, in fact, produce correct results. This can complicate things grievously.) As the statement stands, it does make sense to the computer, so the computer will not recognize the error. Further, it may take a long time for the programmer to discover the mistake because of the way humans perceive things of this sort. Since the programmer knew what was intended, he or she may continue to see the intended formula rather than the one actually written. Under these circumstances, no matter how hard you look, two plus two will continue to make five.

The second, and more difficult, class of error is **logic errors**. The ability to find and correct this type of error is *the* characteristic that separates the wheat from the chaff. This type of error causes 99 percent of the grief experienced in writing programs.

Let's look at a specific example. Suppose you are a programmer at a school where students can be members in one or more of three organizations, The Athletic Club (TAC), The Dean's Persons (TDP), and The Social Strata (TSS). Further, suppose you are given the following assignment:

> From a complete list of *all* students (which contains, among other things, their organizational affiliations), produce the names of those students who are not members of at least one of the student organizations.

This problem will require a program that will go through the entire student list and examine the record of each student to decide whether a given student meets the criterion. If a particular student does meet the necessary conditions, then the name of that student should be printed out. This will require that a test condition of some sort be applied to each student. After thinking for a little while about what this test ought to be, it is likely that you (the programmer) will decide

If this student is not in TAC or not in TDP or not in TSS, then print the name of this student.

In fact, this test is absolutely incorrect and will *not* yield the names of students who are not members of at least one of the organizations but rather *the names of students who are not in all three of the organizations simultaneously.* The correct test is as follows:

If this student is not in TAC and not in TDP and not in TSS, then print the name of this student.

If you find this somewhat confusing, welcome to the club. This is one of those situations that seems to become murkier rather than clearer the more you think about it. (A full description of logical expressions will be presented in Chapters 9 and 10.) However, situations of this type crop up over and over, and you must be very careful to ensure that the logic used is correct. Again, note that the computer program will run just fine with the original (incorrect) test; it will simply not produce the list that was intended.

As a final word in this section, please be aware that it takes the new computer science student time and experience to develop a method of searching for and recognizing the sources of errors. Such an ability constitutes a large part of the "art" of computer science. As with just about everything else in computer science, however, there are a number of useful techniques that can be employed, at least initially, in an attempt to find such "bugs." These will be discussed at length in Chapter 5.

DOCUMENT

Chronologically, this item should not really be the last and final phase of the program developmental process. You should not find yourself saying "Well, I've got the program working now, and, darn it, I have to go through and document it." **Documentation** (the process of making sure the program is understandable) should proceed along with the development of the program itself. Each of the preceding four phases contains elements that can aid in the documentation process. For example, in your attempt to understand the problem, you should have developed a sufficiently detailed set of notes (such as the input and output lists mentioned earlier) of the various aspects of the problem. Your pseudocode algorithm should explain very well to any reader what you are doing and how you are accomplishing the work. The actual program should be easily readable. All of these constitute parts of the documentation and should become a natural part of the program generation process.

The program itself should be the best documentation, that is, the program should be "self-documenting." The following techniques can help you use the program as documentation:

Use descriptive variable names. When writing the PAYROLL program, the following very descriptive statement was used:

```
Gross := Hours * Rate;
```

Anybody reading this statement will immediately know what the statement is doing and what the program is all about. A statement that accomplishes the same thing could also be written as

```
AMX357 := KK8OPL * AFV45;
```

This statement, however, gives no indication of what is going on and requires much effort by a reader to determine the purpose of the program.

Also, when deriving variable names, be careful not to make them too short, for example:

```
G := H * R;
```

These abbreviations will be easy to identify at the time you are working on the program. However, when you come back six months or a year later, or even worse, if somebody else needs to work on the program, it will take a great deal of (wasted) time to figure out what these abbreviations stand for. A programmer in a prominent U.S. business once explained that whenever any programmer left the company, his programs would die because somebody else had to rewrite them from scratch if any changes were required!

Making variable names too long can also be a problem; it can become tedious to write out long names over and over. For example:

```
TheGrossWagesForThisPerson :=
    TheTotalNumberOfHours Worked * TheHourlyRateOfPay;
```

It wouldn't take long to get tired of this, not to mention the danger of misspelling the names.

Include succinct comments in the program. A **comment** is a line or two of text embedded in the program that gives additional information about difficult-to-understand parts of the program. As with variable names, comments should be neither too short nor too long. If they are too short (or nonexistent), they provide little help; if they are too long, nobody will read them. An example of a good comment to place in a program section that calculates the roots of equations might be

```
(* This section calculates roots using Newton's method *)
```

The fact that Newton's method rather than, say, successive bisection was being used might not be obvious at first glance, and this simple comment complements the code. (It may not even be obvious that the code section calculates roots, for that matter.)

Too many comments are as bad, or worse, than none at all. Too much text all crammed together tends to be skipped over by a reader. Also, if such a great deal of explanation is required, it may be an indication that the program is not written as well as it could be.

Make sure the structure stands out. Block out the program using lots of blank lines and indentation so that "paragraphs" representing the logical structure stand out. From a distance a program should look more like Figure 3-2a than Figure 3-2b.

Figure 3-2

Examples of a (a) Well-Presented, Structured Program and a (b) Poorly Presented Program

a.

```
xxxxxxx xxxxx x xxxxxx xxxxxx x x

 xxx xx xx x x xxxxxxx x
       xx x xxxxxxx x

xxxxx
xxxxx xxx xxx xx
  xxxxx
  xxxxxx x x x x
  xxxxxxxx x
  xxx xxxx xx x xxx x xx
       xxxxx
       x xx x x x x xxx x x x
       xx xxx xxxx xxxxxxxxx
       xxx x
  xx xx xxxx
       xxxxxxx x xxxx x xx xxxxxx x
  xxxx
       xxxxxxx x xxxx x xx xxx xxxxxx x
  xxx
  xxxx
```

b.

```
xxxxxxx xxxxx x xxxxxx xxxxxx x x
xxx xx xx x x xxxxxxx x
xx x xxxxxxx x
xxxxx
xxxxx xxx xxx xx
xxxxx
xxxxxx x x x x
xxxxxxxx x
xxx xxxx xx x xxx x xx
xxxxx
x xx x x x x xxx x x x
xx xxx xxxx xxxxxxxxx
xxx x
xx xx xxxx
xxxxxxx x xxxx x xx xxxxxx x
xxxx
xxxxxxx x xxxx x xx xxx xxxxxx x
xxx
xxxx
```

We are now ready to go through, in detail, the analysis and solution for a complete problem to demonstrate the entire program development process. We will go through this process many times in the remainder of this text, but since this is the first time, we will include considerable detail.

Hal's Hamburgers

Let us say that you are hired by

> HAL'S HAMBURGER HEAVEN
> Home of 2001 Smiles
> (Computerized for Your Convenience)

to write a program to automate the billing process. The system is to operate as follows: a clerk takes an order from a customer, enters it into the computer, and the computer produces an itemized list of the customer's order and the total amount due. The customer pays for the order, and the amount paid is also entered into the computer. Next, the computer prints out how much change is due the customer. Finally, the order is prepared and presented to the customer. The menu at Hal's contains the following items:

Boggle Burger	$1.75
Bitsy Burger	.80
Shimmy Shake	.60
Flaky Fries	.50
Kwita Kola	.40

This is the statement of the problem, as received from the management of Hal's. Where do we go from here?

STEP 1: UNDERSTAND THE PROBLEM

First, let us list in detail what we need to use as input and what we wish to produce as output. The statement of the problem says we are to input the customer's order and produce an itemized list, with prices, of the order. That means we cannot simply treat the system like a cash register and enter merely the individual prices of the food items; we must provide information about the items themselves.

The input, certainly, should consist of at least the quantities of each menu item ordered. For example, a customer may order one Boggle Burger, one Bitsy Burger, and two Kwita Kolas. But we still need to ask if there is anything else that should be included.

You might be tempted to input the names and prices of each item as well, but stop for a moment and think: these items are always the same, and entering them each time will only waste time. It is easier to let the computer keep track of such things. However, we must remember that the customer is going to pay for the order, and part of the problem is to input the amount of money handed over by the customer (the amount tendered). The situation here is a little different from that of the payroll problem, since we must input information at *two different times* during execution of the program. We must do this because the second input depends to some extent on the results of calculations derived from the first input. We require, therefore, two lists of input, which can be described as follows:

Input Required for Program (Order Phase)

    The number of Boggles
    The number of Bitsys
    The number of Shakes
    The number of Fries
    The number of Kolas

Input Required for Program (Change Phase)

    Amount Tendered (Amount paid by customer)

We now turn our attention to the output. We want, as described above, to print out a description of the order along with the cost of each item, the total cost for the items (called the subtotal), the tax due, and finally the grand total amount due. After this we would like to print out the amount tendered and the amount of the change. Summarizing this in the output list would look as follows:

Output from Program (Order Phase)

    The number of Boggles and the cost of those Boggles
    The number of Bitsys and the cost of those Bitsys
    The number of Shakes and the cost of those Shakes
    The number of Fries and the cost of those Fries
    The number of Kolas and the cost of those Kolas

    The subtotal (total of the individual costs)
    The amount of tax
    The grand total

Output from Program (Change Phase)

    The amount tendered
    The change due the customer

A very useful and concise way to represent this would be to draw up an example of *exactly* how we would like a typical bill to look. This not only makes it easier to understand the output but will also aid in writing the output part of the program later. Using our aesthetic sense, we might produce the following:

HAL'S HAMBURGER HEAVEN
(OUT OF THIS WORLD)

BOGGLES	2	3.50
BITSYS	1	.80
SHAKES	2	1.20
FRIES	1	.50
KOLAS	3	1.20
SUBTOTAL		7.20
TAX		.36
TOTAL DUE		7.56
AMT TENDERED		10.00
YOUR CHANGE		2.44

THANK YOU

With these items completed, we can now begin to outline the solution. We know *exactly* what we have to start with and *exactly* what we want produced as output. We therefore move on to the next step.

STEP 2: PLAN THE SOLUTION

As we did with the payroll problem, we will go through and write successively more detailed algorithms. The first one would be simply

Generate a Bill

Then, thinking about this a little more, we could come up with

Generate a Bill
    Get the Order Phase inputs
    Do the Order Phase calculations
    Do the Order Phase outputs
    Get the Change Phase inputs
    Do the Change Phase calculations
    Do the Change Phase outputs

Look familiar? We develop the next version of the algorithm by asking: If I were doing this by hand with a pencil and paper, what would I do? This line of thinking should lead to an algorithm similar to the following (using the abbreviation #Boggles to mean Number of Boggles and so forth):

Generate a Bill
   Get the Order Phase inputs
      Read #Boggles, #Bitsys, #Shakes, #Fries, #Kolas
   Do the Order Phase calculations
      CostBoggles ← #Boggles × PriceBoggles
      CostBitsys ← #Bitsys × PriceBitsys
      CostShakes ← #Shakes × PriceShakes
      CostFries ← #Fries × PriceFries
      CostKolas ← #Kolas × PriceKolas

      Subtotal ← CostBoggles + CostBitsys + CostShakes
                         + CostFries + CostKolas

      Tax ← Subtotal × TaxRate

      Total ← Subtotal + Tax

   Do the Order Phase outputs
      Print #Boggles, CostBoggles
      Print #Bitsys, CostBitsys
      Print #Shakes, CostShakes
      Print #Fries, CostFries
      Print #Kolas, CostKolas
      Print Subtotal
      Print Tax
      Print Total

   Get the Change Phase inputs
      Read AmtTendered
   Do Change Phase calculations
      Change ← AmtTendered − Total
   Do the Change Phase outputs
      Print AmtTendered
      Print Change

This, then, is our final algorithm. It gives us sufficient detail to solve the problem, what it does is obvious, and it is documented. Note also that it is *completely general*—the actual prices and tax rates are not used in the solution. This allows us to change prices and tax rates easily and at will. However, our algorithm, although it does solve the problem, does not address itself specifically to how we can get the output of the program to look exactly like our mock-up of the typical bill. Accomplishing this requires a little knowledge about I/O and how it is handled on a computer. In addition, we will need to go over elements of Pascal in order to carry out the remaining steps of the development process. So, we will defer completion of this problem until we cover these points near the end of Chapter 4.

SUMMARY

In this chapter we have presented the five developmental phases that should be executed to develop a complete program. These steps consist of understanding the problem, planning the solution, coding the solution, checking out the results, and documenting. We also began to develop the solution to a complete problem.

EXERCISES

CONCEPTS

1. Define or explain the following terms:

Algorithm	Modularity
Clerical error	Program
Documentation	Pseudocode
Flowchart	Stepwise refinement
Logic	Structure
Logic error	Top-down design

2. List and explain the five phases of program development.

TOOLS

3. The following are some common activities carried out by human beings; generate an algorithm for each of them. These can be especially difficult because, for the most part, people tend to perform these actions without thinking much about *how* they do them. However, they are good practice items in that you must think carefully about what actually goes on when you carry out these tasks.

    a. Make a phone call
    b. Play a phonograph record
    c. Change an automobile tire
    d. Make a hamburger
    e. Wash a dog
    f. Buy a car
    g. Take a test
    h. Build a campfire

4. Derive explicit lists of input and output at various levels of difficulty for the following problems. For example, in the PAYROLL program described previously, the simplest included only the rate and hours as input and the gross as output, whereas very complex problems could include insurance, retirement, and so forth for the input and all manner of reports for the output.

a. Jack and Jill want to buy a new house. How much will it cost them?

b. Generate checking account statements for the Bank of Burbank.

c. Print up student tuition statements for South Succotash State College.

d. Estimate the cost of constructing a new skyscraper in Apple City.

e. Determine the shortest highway trip between Akron and Greensburg in terms of (a) miles and (b) time.

f. Balance the federal budget.

PROBLEMS

5. Write an algorithm that will generate a credit card statement. Input should consist of the client's name, previous balance, new charges for the month, and the payment for the month. Calculate an interest charge by taking 1.75 percent of the difference between the previous balance and the payments. Calculate a new balance by subtracting the payments from the previous balance and then adding the new charges and the interest. Print out a statement that includes the name, previous balance, charges, payments, interest, and new balance. The following is typical data:

Name	MILDRED M. MILQUETOAST
Previous Balance	$183.25
New Charges	$ 13.75
Payment	$ 10.00

6. The managers of Home and Auto Enterprises (HAUTE) wish to have a program written that will produce a monthly profit-and-loss statement. The store operates two departments, namely the home and the auto departments. The input data consists of the gross sales and the expenses for each department. For a typical month it might look like this:

	Auto Dept	Home Dept
Gross Sales	$10,372	$ 7,981
Expenses	$ 8,575	$ 7,138

The managers would like to get a report containing the following information at the end of the month: gross profit from each department, gross profit for the whole store, percent profit based on sales from each department, percent profit based on sales for the whole store, percent of gross profit coming from each of the departments. Write an algorithm that will solve this problem.

7. Although rarely employed now, in the past banks made loans using the discount method. A customer would borrow a certain amount of money, and the bank would figure out the interest on that amount, based on an annual interest rate. If the money was to be borrowed for three years, for example, the interest would be computed as the interest rate times three times the amount of the loan. The interest would then be subtracted from the face value of the loan (that is, the loan would be discounted) and the proceeds, or the amount left over, turned over to the borrower. The borrower would then be obligated to return the *original* amount of the loan in equal monthly payments over the term of the loan. Write an algorithm that will figure out the interest, the proceeds, and the monthly payments on such a loan. Assume that the loan amount and term (time) of the loan are variable but that the interest rate is fixed.

8. Write an algorithm that calculates final grades by taking a weighted average of all coursework. For this problem let us assume that the grades to be averaged consist of grades for three exams, one quiz average, and one homework average. Each of the exams counts 25 percent, the quizzes count 15 percent, and the homework, 10 percent. The weights should be a part of the program, but the grades should all be entered separately.

9. Honest O'Henry's Used Car Heaven pays its salespeople a commission of 18 percent on all cars sold plus a flat fee of $100 a month. Write an algorithm that will input the total value of cars sold and calculate the proper gross pay.

4

First Elements of Pascal:

Communicating with the Computer

A necessary condition for completing the program development process for the Hal's Hamburgers problem begun in the last chapter is that we be able to communicate our algorithm to the computer. The vehicle for doing this is, of course, language, and we must learn a language that the computer can, in some sense, understand. We will now learn something about the nature of languages in general and the Pascal computer language in particular.

4-1 *Language and Syntax*

In any language, natural or computer, rules exist that define permissible ways to combine elements of the language into meaningful units. This collection of rules is called the **syntax** of the language. For the most part, applying syntax rules correctly comes naturally and seems automatic when you are using your native language. For example, the following sentence is easily understood:

The girl wrote a wonderful computer program.

On the other hand, the sentence

Believed apple a the about sometimes quiver sustain.

is completely meaningless because it fails to comply with the syntax of the English language. An interesting example of a sentence that does comply with the syntax but is nonetheless meaningless is this one:

Another curbinet flassled beyond the grivult.

This sentence is in fact "understandable" in some sense because the rules of syntax are used correctly. The reason the sentence doesn't completely make sense is that many of the individual units of the sentence, the words themselves, have no real meaning (although they do have a syntactical meaning). The words "another," "beyond," and "the" are completely understood. The remaining words, although they seem like they should be comprehensible, are not. "Curbinet" and "grivult" for example, are obviously nouns: the former is the subject of the sentence and the latter is the object of the preposition "beyond." Similarly, "flassled" is a verb, the past tense of the infinitive "to flassle." You can decipher that much of the meaning because you understand the syntax of the English language: you can understand the structure of this sentence, if not its content. (A good example of this kind of writing can be found in "Jabberwocky" by Lewis Carroll.)

As with natural languages, every computer language also has its own syntax. In general, computer languages are easier to learn than natural languages, although they are more rigid and tend to be less forgiving of mistakes. It is entirely possible to learn enough of a computer language to be able to "communicate" with a computer in just a few days, whereas it takes much longer to be able to do the same with a natural foreign language. One of the nice things about computer languages is that, although your grammatical flexibility is limited, you are pretty much able to give the "words" whatever meaning you wish.

One thing to bear in mind about computer languages is that they interpret the "meanings" of sentences very strictly, and ambiguities are never allowable. In English, for example, you may be able to say something like this:

That sure was a hot dish you had last night!

This sentence could have a number of meanings: you had a spicy meal for dinner, or the temperature of your dinner was very high and you burnt your tongue, or you had a good-looking date. With a computer language you can *never* be ambiguous; you must state *exactly* what you mean, because the computer will always interpret it in one standard way.

Languages, both natural and computer, also have dialects. The same language will be "spoken" somewhat differently in different places. For example, English usage in Great Britain is not identical with that of the United States. In fact, differences can appear from one region of a country to another: a bag may be called a sack or a poke, depending on where you are.

Because of this, the Pascal language we will be using may not be, in fact, probably *will* not be, the same from one computer installation to another. However, in general you can always find a subset of the language that *will* work on any computer. Therefore, the description of Pascal language elements used throughout this book will be a "standardized" subset. If the version at your installation has useful enhancements, then by all means take advantage of them. However, if you stick to just the elements presented in this text, you should have no difficulty whatsoever in understanding any of the presentations or completing any of the assignments here.

4-2   *Computer Languages*

Computer languages have gone through an evolutionary process similar to that of computer hardware. The analogy is actually quite remarkable in that there have been three generations of languages (the third is most commonly used), with a fourth currently evolving. Let's look at each, briefly, in turn.

First generation languages. These languages are the same as the machine languages we mentioned in the last chapter. Their elements correspond to operations the machine itself can do and are all strictly numeric. It is very difficult for humans to work with first generation (or machine) languages. On the other hand, **machine language** can be thought of as the computer's natural language: programs written in other languages must be translated into machine language. Also (and this is a big minus), each and every machine has a different machine language. Hence, although a Pascal program could theoretically run on a DEC or an IBM computer, a DEC machine language program could *never* run on an IBM computer.

Second generation languages. As you might expect, these are intermediate languages between first and third generation languages and are normally called **assembler languages**. The elements of such languages still correspond to the operations the machine can do, but instead of being numeric, they are symbolic (that is, they use English-type mnemonics). They are harder to work with than third generation languages, but the process of translation into machine language is correspondingly much easier. The assembler language equivalent of the PAYROLL program is shown in Figure 4-1 (compare this with Figure 2-9, the machine language equivalent of the same program).

Third generation languages. Pascal and in fact all of the modern languages (such as FORTRAN and BASIC) commonly in use are called third generation languages (3GLs). These are relatively high-level languages (that is, they can be read and easily understood by humans) and are called **procedure oriented languages**, which means you have to tell the computer exactly *what* to do and *how* to do it. If you wanted to take an average, for example, you couldn't simply say "take an average," but rather you would have to direct the computer to add up all of the elements and divide by the total number.

Fourth generation languages. Fourth generation languages or 4GLs are said to be nonprocedural, which means they can figure out how to carry out the task you request. Not many 4GLs exist; those that do have usually been designed for specific applications. Using a 4GL in the averaging example used in the previous paragraph, you could simply say "take an average" and the computer would in fact know what to do.

4-3   *Structuring Concepts of Pascal*

Let us now turn our attention specifically to the Pascal computer language. We have been stressing the importance of *structure* in program design from the outset and shall continue to do so throughout the remainder of the text. One of the main advantages of using Pascal is that it encourages (one could almost say forces) the programmer to write programs that are structured. Although it is possible to write unstructured programs in *any* language, Pascal just makes it very, very difficult to do so. Pascal keeps you headed in the right direction, whether you want to or not, and minimizes the number and intensity of bad programming habits you might pick up. Such guidance from the language is extremely important for the novice programmer, who generally has only a vague idea of what structured programming is all about. Once an understanding of and an ability to write structured programs are acquired, even the use of nonstructured languages normally presents no difficulty other than inconvenience.

Figure 4-1

Assembler Language Version of the PAYROLL *Program*

```
                                              VAX-11 Pascal VS.4-277

            .TITLE  PAYROLL
            .IDENT  \01\
            .PSECT  $CODE,PIC,CON,REL,LCL,SHR,EXE,RD,NOWRT,2
PAYROLL:    .WORD   ^M<R2,R3,R4,R5,R6>
            PUSHAB  PAS$FV_INPUT
            CALLS   #1,PAS$READ_REAL_F
            MOVF    R0,HOURS
            PUSHAB  PAS$FV_INPUT
            CALLS   #1,PAS$READLN2
            PUSHAB  PAS$FV_INPUT
            CALLS   #1,PAS$READ_REAL_F
            MOVF    R0,RATE
            PUSHAB  PAS$FV_INPUT
            CALLS   #1,PAS$READLN2
            MULF3   RATE,HOURS,GROSS
            MULF3   #^F6.7E-02,GROSS,FICA
            MULF3   #^F0.25,GROSS,FEDTAX
            SUBF3   FICA,GROSS,R0
            SUBF3   FEDTAX,R0,NETPAY
            PUSHL   #12
            PUSHL   HOURS
            PUSHAB  PAS$FV_OUTPUT
            CALLS   #3,PAS$WRITE_REALE_F
            PUSHL   #12
            PUSHL   RATE
            PUSHAB  PAS$FV_OUTPUT
            CALLS   #3,PAS$WRITE_REALE_F
            PUSHL   #12
            PUSHL   GROSS
            PUSHAB  PAS$FV_OUTPUT
            CALLS   #3,PAS$WRITE_REALE_F
            PUSHL   #12
            PUSHL   FICA
            PUSHAB  PAS$FV_OUTPUT
            CALLS   #3,PAS$WRITE_REALE_F
            PUSHL   #12
            PUSHL   FEDTAX
            PUSHAB  PAS$FV_OUTPUT
            CALLS   #3,PAS$WRITE_REALE_F
            PUSHL   #12
            PUSHL   NETPAY
            PUSHAB  PAS$FV_OUTPUT
            CALLS   #3,PAS$WRITE_REALE_F
            PUSHAB  PAS$FV_OUTPUT
            CALLS   #1,PAS$WRITELN2
            MOVL    #1,R0
            RET
            .END
```

The previously discussed concepts of top-down design and modularity are very important in Pascal. This methodology is used to generate algorithms, and the programs themselves contain both these properties. Besides encouraging these qualities, Pascal can even be defined in a top-down, modular format. The term "modular" implies that a large task is broken up into a number of smaller tasks, or conversely, that a large structure can be thought of as being built up of smaller structures, each of which can in turn be thought of as being made up of even smaller pieces. Each piece represents a logical, distinct unit that can be examined or worked with independently; but each unit is also a subunit of a larger, also logical, independent unit, and so on.

Figure 4-2

PAYROLL *Program with Structure Emphasized*

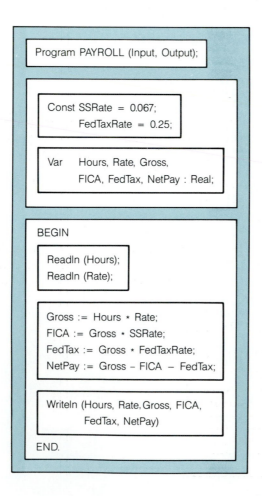

```
Program PAYROLL (Input, Output);

    Const SSRate = 0.067;
          FedTaxRate = 0.25;

    Var   Hours, Rate, Gross,
          FICA, FedTax, NetPay : Real;

BEGIN
    Readln (Hours);
    Readln (Rate);

    Gross := Hours * Rate;
    FICA := Gross * SSRate;
    FedTax := Gross * FedTaxRate;
    NetPay := Gross - FICA - FedTax;

    Writeln (Hours, Rate, Gross, FICA,
             FedTax, NetPay)
END.
```

The Pascal language is defined this way, and algorithms and programs *should* be constructed this way to provide maximum efficiency in design and execution. The algorithm for our PAYROLL program, for example, can be presented in such a way as to emphasize its structure (see Figure 4-2). Note how each section can be viewed separately or as a part of a larger whole. This method of looking at the program on any level and still seeing logical units is what **structured programming** is all about.

The Pascal language will be presented in a manner consistent with the top-down philosophy. We begin by looking at the largest unit of organization, the program, and then dividing it into its constituent parts, constantly working our way down to more and more detail. (Note how structure permeates this entire process.)

At this time we will not attempt to present all of the available subblocks that are permitted within any given larger block. As we study more of the language and techniques of program writing, these subblocks and other elements will be presented as they occur in the structured categories we will now define.

4-4 *The Pascal Program*

In Pascal, the largest unit of organization is the **program**. This contains everything that is needed to complete a task. A program can be defined as follows:

program → heading-section
              declaration-section
              executable-section

This definition shows that a program consists of a heading section followed by a declaration section followed by an executable section. In other words, a program can be divided into three subunits or sections that fit together as shown below:

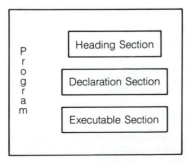

Each of these sections can, in turn, be defined in a similar fashion. Let us now look at each of these in more detail.

HEADING SECTION

The **heading section** consists only of a single statement, which contains the name of the program and lists any files to be used by the program. (Files are the names of places from which input is obtained or to which output is sent; see Chapter 7.) The definition of heading section is given by

heading-section → **program** identifier (**input**, **output**);

The words in bold type (program, input, and output) must appear exactly as they are. The word "program" marks the beginning of a program, "input" indicates that input is to be accepted from the keyboard during execution of the program, and "output" says that the program will send information or results to the terminal during execution. Strictly speaking, the words "input" and "output" are just file names and, to be absolutely correct, are not required. However, if there were no input or output, you wouldn't be writing a program in the first place. In fact the majority of programs you come across (in this text and elsewhere) will include input and output.

 Those words not in boldface type are category names for things that you must supply. In this section, the only nonbold word is "identifier." We ask therefore: What is an identifier, and how is a specific example chosen? The answer is: an **identifier** is essentially just a name; it is a word used to identify something somewhere in the program. In the case of the heading section, we may choose a single identifier that is the name of the program. In our payroll example the name was PAYROLL. A good identifier should be meaningful to whoever reads it. Another example of an identifier can be found in what we have been referring to as a variable, or variable name. However, the concept of identifier is much broader and can include such things as the names of subprograms, the names of functions (such as sine, cosine, logarithm), or even the names of constants (such as the Greek letter pi).

 So how do we construct an identifier? An identifier consists of a letter of the alphabet followed by any number (including zero) of letters or digits. It's that simple. The following are examples of identifiers:

```
X               Y             Amount
TimeExceeded    Alternate32   A13B655
Rate            Payroll       ROBOT
```

Note that any combination of upper- and lowercase letters is acceptable; Pascal makes no distinction based on case. The following identifiers are considered identical:

```
NowDue    nowdue    NOWDUE
```

In contrast, the following are NOT valid identifiers:

```
Flask#25  :  Contains something other than letters and digits.
ID Number :  Contains a space.
357Class  :  Begins with a digit.
@Home     :  Begins with something other than a letter.
```

Again, it is important to choose identifiers that are meaningful.

Since the identifier may be arbitrarily long, you are not limited to the kind of bizarre abbreviations that were necessary with many older programming languages. For example, if you are writing a program concerning tuition and you need a variable for the number of credit hours for which a particular person is registered, you may write, in Pascal,

```
CreditHours
```

instead of the more obtuse

```
CRDHRS
```

as would be necessary with FORTRAN IV, or even worse yet, something like the name

```
C8
```

which would be the best you can do in minimal BASIC. Please take advantage of the flexibility inherent in these variable names. A generation of programmers has become accustomed to short, six-character variable names and has paid a high price in loss of program readability.

A word about the semicolon: it is ubiquitous in Pascal because it is the fundamental way of separating one statement from another. This is important because, in general, you are not limited to one statement per line in a program. You may, if you want, write a complete program on a single line. (Of course you would never *want* to do that, but it's nice to know the flexibility is there to structure the appearance of your program however you see fit.) You may have several statements on one line, or conversely, you may have one statement spread over several lines. The goal is to achieve the best readability.

As we work our way through descriptions of the three sections of a Pascal program, we will look at examples that can help clarify and demonstrate the use of these program parts. The end of this chapter will present a complete example of program construction that uses all of the program sections.

Let's now look at examples of headings. A good place to start would be with the payroll program we've already worked on. We have been writing it as

```
Program PAYROLL (Input, Output);
```

However, we could have written it many different ways, for example,

```
PROGRAM Payroll      (  Input, Output  )    ;
```

```
program payroll (input, output);
```

```
ProGram PayRoll (InPut, OutPut  )  ;
```

or even

```
Program
Payroll
(Input
Output)
     ;
```

You have a great deal of flexibility in Pascal; use this flexibility to write more readable programs!

Here is another example:

```
Program ReactionRates (Input, Output);
```

In this case, the identifier that refers to the program name is ReactionRates, and the program uses both input and output. (Note that although the program codes used in this text could have been written in any style or format—all capital letters, capital and lowercase letters, all lowercase letters—the codes in this text are written with capital and lowercase letters for consistency.)

We are now ready to move on to the next program section.

DECLARATION SECTION

This next section tells, or *declares* to the computer, what kind of data is going to be used by the program. *Every variable and constant that is to be used by the program MUST be declared in this section.* The **declaration section** of a program may be defined as follows:

declaration-section → constants
                               variables

As in the previous examples, this means that the declaration section can be divided into two parts, constants and variables. This can be represented pictorially as follows:

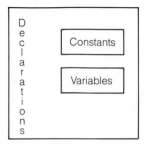

Again, let's break this structure up and look at each component individually.

Constants. The constants subsection is defined as follows:

constants → **const** constant-definition-list
             | nil

That is, the constants subsection may consist of the word "Const" followed by the list of constants to be defined, or it may be Nil. (You don't *have* to declare constants if you don't want to.) The vertical bar means that you may choose any one of the alternatives.

The constant definition list consists of a list of one or more constant definitions whose form is given by

constant-definition → identifier = value;

Note that these are *constants*. Once defined in this section, they can never ever be changed anywhere in the program. An example of a constant list is

```
Const Pi = 3.14159;
        e = 2.71828;
```

In a program that defines these constants you can write

```
V := 4.0 / 3.0 * Pi * r * r * r;
```

but you may NEVER write

```
e := 17.5;
```

because e has already been defined as a constant.

Also note that constants do NOT have to be numeric; it is permissible to write

```
Const Star = `*`;
```

You don't ever have to define constants if you don't want to; however, there are good reasons for doing so:

1. It makes the program easier to read, for example, referencing Pi instead of 3.14159.

2. It makes the program easier to change. If, for example, you are writing a payroll program that uses the rate of social security withholding, it is better to use the constant SSRate rather than the actual number 0.072. This way, when the withholding rate changes next year, all you need to do is change a single line of the program to take care of it rather than searching the program for any and all occurrences of the number 0.072.

It is important to bear in mind that *these are not variables!* They are symbolic constants; that is, instead of using the actual value in the program, you refer to that value by a name, or identifier. You cannot change the values during the course of the program. Note that the name and value are connected by the equal sign: this is to imply that the name and value are, for all practical purposes, one and the same.

Variables. We next come to the variables subsection, which consists of the following:

variables → **var** variable-definition-list

The variable definition list is a list of all the variables that will be used in the program. The variable definition list consists of a list of variable definitions, whose form is given by

variable-definition → var-list : type;

Var-list is a list of one or more identifiers (variable names), which are separated by commas if there is more than one. In any var-list, the variables must all be of the same type. Recall from previous discussions that a variable is the name of a memory location inside the computer and the contents of this location can be changed at will. A variable name must be a valid identifier, but other than that, it can be made to be anything the programmer desires. The important point is that names be chosen so as to enhance the readability of the program. For example

Good Name	Poor Choice of a Name
Payment	P
LoanAmount	A, L
AnnualRate	I, R
Term	T, Y

An important characteristic of a variable is its **type**. The type of the variable restricts the kind of data that may be contained in the memory location that bears its name. We will, for now, look at a subset of four of the types of variables available in Pascal:

type → **integer** | **real** | **boolean** | **char**

Again, the vertical bars in the definition mean that you can choose *any* of the indicated items. Also, Pascal permits you to define your own data types. Although this is a little confusing at first, it can make many programming solutions much easier. The method by which additional data types may be defined is introduced in Chapter 13. The concept of defining new data types is further extended in Appendix A, where you will see that it is possible to make up your very own data types! However, for now we will consider only the above four predefined types.

Now let's see some typical variable definitions:

```
Var x,y,z : Real;
    i,j,k : Integer;
```

We could have, if we'd wanted, written these all out separately, for example,

```
Var x : Real;
    y : Real;
    z : Real;
    i : Integer;
    j : Integer;
    k : Integer;
```

Another allowable way to write these would be

```
Var x : Real; y : Real; z : Real;
    i : Integer; j : Integer; k : Integer;
```

As mentioned previously, a *variable* is the name of a memory location somewhere inside the computer, and the *type* of that variable specifies what kind of information it can contain. With that in mind, let us look more specifically at the data types introduced so far.

`Integer.` **Integer** (sometimes called fixed point) type variables are those that can hold integer values. An integer value is a number that does NOT contain a decimal point; that is, a whole number with no fractional part. Integers can be positive or negative. Examples of integer numbers are

```
100    −3    0    1583    −13
```

Integers are used in those places where an exact number or count is required, such as in keeping track of the number of students registered for a course or in counting the number of times an operation needs to be repeated.

`Real.` **Real** type variables are sometimes referred to as floating point variables. Real values are numbers that DO contain a decimal point, and they are used to represent objects that can have fractional values as well as whole values. These, too, can be positive or negative. Examples of real numbers are

```
25.36    −0.0006    1583.091    −100.2    95.0
```

Note that a real number is not *required* to have a fractional part, but it can. An alternative method for specifying these numbers is the E notation, which is very similar to scientific notation. Take, for example, Avogadro's number, which is

$$602,350,000,000,000,000,000,000.0$$

It would be messy, to say the least, to have to write this out in the long fashion above; however, using scientific notation, we can denote it as

$$6.0235 \times 10^{23}$$

In Pascal, this can be abbreviated to

```
6.0235E23
```

In this case, the E stands for 10 to the power in the scientific notation format. Some other examples are

Scientific Notation	E format
1.954×10^{-5}	`1.954E-5`
-3.01×10^{7}	`-3.01E7`
-5.75×10^{-17}	`-5.75E-17`
4.0×10^{3}	`4.0E3`

In the last item above, it is also permissible to write the number as 4E3, but this latter form is not as understandable and is discouraged. Also please note that if a decimal point *is* used in Pascal, *at least one digit* must be written on each side of the decimal point. For example, the number ˌ25 would be invalid because there is no digit to the left of the decimal point. The correct way of expressing this quantity would be 0ˌ25. In a similar fashion, the number 95ˌ would be incorrect, whereas the number 95ˌ0 would be correct.

Boolean. **Boolean** variables can hold logical values; this particular type gets its name from a famous British mathematician, George Boole, who did considerable work in logic. Boolean variables are very simple, because they can have one of only two values, namely, True or False. These two words are, believe it or not, the actual values permitted for Boolean variables and are used as such. Naturally, they may be written in any combination of upper- and lowercase desired, and the words TRUE, True, and true are all the same. These kinds of variables are used frequently in testing conditions, and Boolean variables with names such as SortComplete or TooBig (which seem to suggest the idea of true or false) are not uncommon.

Char. This is short for character, and **character** variables of this type can hold a single character. For our purposes, a character can be defined as anything you can type on the keyboard. Each character must be delimited by single quotes. Examples of characters are

`'A'      'g'      '?'      '7'      '*'`

The character `'7'` is NOT the same as the integer 7; you CANNOT do any arithmetic with `'7'`, whereas you can with 7.

Two rather interesting characters are

`' '` —The blank character
`''''` —The single quote character

The first is the character "blank." Even though it looks as if there is nothing there, there is in fact something there, which is the blank. Since you can type a blank on the keyboard, it is in fact a character and can be used as such. You may wonder how you represent a single quote, since it is used as the delimiter for all other characters; the second item above (four single quotes in a row) is how you do it.

Characters are useful in programming, especially when you string them together; then you can do interesting things such as store names and addresses. For now, though, we will simply store individual characters.

Let us give one more example of variable declarations. Suppose we wished to have two integer locations named Count and Max; three real locations named FullAmt, Partial, and Leftover; a character variable called Symbol; and a Boolean variable, AllFinished. This would be declared in Pascal as follows:

```
Var  Count, Max : Integer;
     FullAmt, Partial, Leftover : Real;
     Symbol : Char;
     AllFinished : Boolean;
```

This collection of statements would declare to the compiler that the variables `Count` and `Max` could contain only integer numbers; that `FullAmt`, `Partial`, and `Leftover` could contain only real numbers, that is, numbers with decimal points; that `Symbol` could contain any individual character; and that `AllFinished` could have only values of `True` or `False`. The distinctions are real (no pun intended) and play an important part in the writing of good programs.

Finally note that, as with the constant subsection, the word `Var` is used only once, but that as many variables and types may be declared as needed.

Let's now go on to the third and last section of a Pascal program, the executable section.

EXECUTABLE SECTION

This last section contains the actual instructions that must be carried out in order to solve the problem. The general form of the **executable section** is as follows:

executable-section → **begin**
                executable-statement-list
       end.

This section MUST start with the word "begin" and finish with the word "end" with a final period. The executable statement list (as you undoubtedly are beginning to suspect) is a list of executable statements. If there are two or more statements in this list, they must be separated by semicolons. For example, we might have

```
Begin
  Statement1
End.
```

or we may have (more likely)

```
Begin
  Statement1 ;
  Statement2 ;
  Statement3 ;
  Statement4
End.
```

Note that a semicolon is used to separate the executable statements one from another but NOT to separate the Begin or the End, from these statements; there is no semicolon before the first statement or after the last statement! This is because the very words Begin and End, themselves delimit the statements.

There are many, many different kinds of executable statements. In this chapter we will examine only three of them, namely,

executable-statement → assignment-statement
                       | input-statement
                       | output-statement

Assignment statements. Given that we can define our variables as described above, the question now becomes: How do we get information into these variable memory locations? One way to accomplish this is via the **assignment statement**. The general format for this statement is:

assignment-statement → variable := expression

where the assignment operator := (that is, a colon followed immediately by an equal sign) is used to signify that the value on the right-hand side is to be placed into the location signified by the name on the left-hand side.

Since we already know what a variable is, we need only discover what an expression is in order to completely understand the assignment statement. An **expression** may consist of anything from an individual constant or variable to a complex combination of mathematical calculations and operations, for example,

```
Count := 37;
NewAmt := OldAmt;
Area := Length * Width;
```

In each of these, the expression on the right is evaluated to yield a single value, which is then assigned to (that is, placed into) the memory location named on the left. In fact, this is close to being the actual definition of expression, which is as follows:

An expression is a combination of constants, variables, and operators that can be reduced to a single value.

Note that this definition applies to each expression example above: 37 is already a value, OldAmt contains a value, and Length * Width means to multiply the value in `Length` by the value in `Width` to produce a single new value, the product.

Note also that each of the variables above MUST have been previously declared correctly, that is, `Count` must have been declared to be an integer; `Area`, `Length`, and `Width` must have been declared as real; and `NewAmt` and `OldAmt` must have been declared to be the same type (whatever type that may be).

Let's look at each of the above examples in a little more detail. The first says to place the integer value `37` into the memory location named `Count`. The second says to take whatever value is currently in `OldAmt` and place that in `NewAmt`. It is VERY IMPORTANT to understand that, in taking a value from one location to another, the value in the first location *is not disturbed in any way!* After this second statement is executed, `NewAmt` AND `OldAmt` will have the exact same value, namely, whatever it was that `OldAmt` had in it initially. The third assignment statement says to take the value in the memory location named `Length`, multiply that by the value currently in the memory location named `Width`, and move the product of that calculation (that is, assign it) to the memory location named `Area`.

The above assignment statements look very much like algebraic equalities. However, they are definitely *not* algebraic equalities; in fact, the operator `:=` is purposely used instead of an equal sign to aid in differentiating the two. A complete understanding of the exact function of the assignment operator in such statements is very important and cannot be stressed enough. The **assignment operator** represents a *computer instruction* and does NOT IN ANY WAY represent the concept of algebraic equality. For example, in algebra one may write

$$2y + 3 = 5y - 7$$

In this case actual equality is implied. That is, the left and right sides of this equation are identical. If you were to write this as a Pascal statement, that is,

```
2 * y + 3 := 5 * y - 7
```

it would make absolutely no sense, because the left side of this statement is not a variable. When you employ the assignment operator in a computer program, you are not using it to state equality but instead writing a formula that is actually a set of instructions to the computer. Further, in algebra, an equation of the type

$$i = i + 1$$

is meaningless; there is no number such that the number equals itself plus one. However, such an expression in Pascal,

```
i := i + 1
```

is perfectly valid. It means take the contents of the memory location named i, add one to it, and store the result back in the memory location named i. In essence, i is being incremented by one. This technique is very useful in keeping running totals, as we shall see later.

Let us pursue the concept of expressions more fully. A great deal of the power of computers resides in their ability to do computations quickly and accurately. However, we need some way to tell the computer what calculations are to be done. In Pascal (but certainly not in all languages) this is done via an algebra-like method of writing formulas, where variables and constants are combined with **operators** (symbols that represent specific mathematical operations). There are a number of operators available in Pascal, namely,

Operator	Operation Specified
+	addition
–	subtraction
*	multiplication
/	Real division
DIV	Integer division
MOD	remainder on integer division

A sad fact is that in Pascal there is no exponentiation operator, which can make certain computational tasks somewhat awkward. Be that as it may, let's look at some examples of expressions using the operators we do have:

4 + 5; Take the integer value 4 and add to it the integer value 5; the result is the integer value 9.

3.7 + 2.9; Take the real value 3.7 and add to it the real value 2.9; the result is 6.6.

7 – 9; Take the integer value 7 and subtract the integer value 9 from it; the result is integer value −2.

3.7 * 14.2; Multiply the two real numbers 3.7 and 14.2; the result is 52.54.

14.0 / 4.0; Take the real value 14.0 and divide it by the real value 4.0; the result is 3.5.

14 DIV 4; Take the integer value 14 and divide it by the integer value 4; the result is integer value 3, and not 3.5: INTEGER DIVISION TRUNCATES THE RESULT! All fractional parts are simply dropped.

14 MOD 4; Take the integer 14, divide it by 4, and *keep the remainder*, NOT the quotient; the result is the integer 2.

Now a word on mixing up values and operators. You may wonder what would happen, for example, if you wrote down something like

```
2.36 * 15
```

or

```
18 /16
```

or even, heaven forbid,

```
263.45 MOD 145.86
```

The rule for dealing with these expressions is relatively simple: if any part of an expression (either data or operators) is real, then the result is also real. Hence, in these examples the first would be evaluated *as if* it were 2.35 * 15.0 and would produce the result 35.25; the second example would be evaluated as if it were 18.0 / 16.0 and would yield 1.125. Pascal would regard the last example as a serious violation, and possibly a nasty error message would result. This is because the MOD operator is not defined for real numbers (which basically means that Pascal cannot determine what you intend by the operator). The best way to avoid difficulty is to not mix types. There is always some way to get around mixing types, and doing so will save you grief.

Arithmetic expressions that contain a single operator (of which the above examples are typical) are fairly easy to comprehend. However, what is to be done with an expression such as this:

```
2 + 5 * 7 - 3
```

How would this be evaluated? A possible, even logical, solution might be the following: add 2 and 5 to give 7; take this result and multiply it by 7, yielding 49; last, subtract 3 from this result to yield a final answer of 46.

This solution, however, is wrong.

Although some computer languages do in fact solve the problem in this way, Pascal does not. The Pascal language takes into account something called **operator precedence** when evaluating arithmetic expressions. Operator precedence means that not all operators are created equal. The rule is

> Rule 1 — First do: *   /   DIV   MOD
>   Last do: +   −

Basically, the rule states that you do multiplication-type operations first and addition-type operations last.

This explanation still does not totally disambiguate the process. For example, suppose we have an expression such as

```
14 * 50 DIV 17
```

What should we do first? To address such situations, we have a second rule:

> Rule 2 — If you have operators of equal precedence, carry them out in the order they appear, from left to right.

Hence, in the above expression we would take 14, multiply it by 50 to yield 700, and then divide that by 17 (integer arithmetic) to yield a final answer of 41. (Note that if we evaluated this expression backward, that is, divide first and then multiply, we would get an incorrect answer of 28.)

Applying these rules to our original expression can be shown as

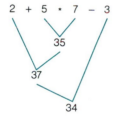

Read this diagram as follows: first multiply 5 by 7 to give 35; next, add 2 to this result, yielding 37; finally, subtract 3 to obtain the final answer of 34.

Next, let's try a somewhat tougher example:

```
3 + 8 - 4 * 3 * 3 + 12 DIV 6
```

The answer to this is −23, which is obtained as follows:

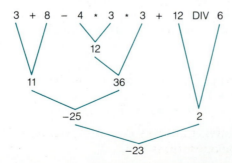

You may possibly find this rigidity in evaluating expressions rather frustrating. Suppose that when you say 4 + 3 * 7, you actually *mean* that you wish to add 4 to 3 and then multiply the result by 7. There *is* a way to express this. If you want to alter the order in which operations are carried out, you may use parentheses. When parentheses are used in an expression, operations within parentheses are carried out first (subject, of course, to operator precedence) followed by operations outside the parentheses. For example, the above expression may be rewritten as

(4 + 3) * 7

This will give the desired result. A more complete example, with the solution, is

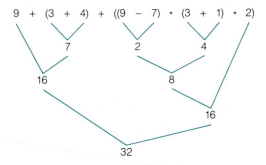

Up to this point, all the examples we've seen have involved only constants. However, variables are perfectly valid and in fact are infinitely more useful than simple constants. For example, the expression Rate * Hours means to take the contents of the location named Rate and multiply this by the contents of the location named Hours. Notice how much more useful this is than saying 7.75 * 40.0. In the former case, any combination of rates and hours may be used, but in the latter case we are stuck with one combination and one result. This is where the usefulness of a computer comes in: by writing an expression (or program) that is a *general* solution to a problem and by giving the variables specific values, we can obtain specific solutions.

We will now look at complete examples of assignment statements in which a variable is assigned the value of an arithmetic expression, for instance,

```
AreaTriangle := Alt * Base / 2.0;
AveTime := (Run1 + Run2 + Run3) / 3.0
VolSphere := 4.0 / 3.0 * Pi * r * r * r;
```

Note that the algebraic-like quality of these statements makes them easy to comprehend.

Let's go on to examine another way of placing values into variables, namely, the input statement.

Input statements. Input statements allow the user to place different values into allocated memory locations *while a program is executing.* This ability to alter the contents of a memory location from outside is one of the properties that gives computers such power. The format of the **input statement** is as follows:

input-statement → **read** (input-list)
                  readln (input-list)
                  readln

An **input list** is a list of variables, each separated by commas. Essentially, during an input operation, the computer gets information from the keyboard (or other input device) and places it into the correct storage locations. It is, in a sense, very similar to the simple assignment statement.

As you can see, there are two input statements, "Read" and "Readln" (pronounced read line). These are differentiated as follows:

Read: Get the data requested and place it in the appropriate memory location(s).

Readln: Get the data requested, place it in the appropriate memory locations, *but then skip to the beginning of the* next *input line.*

What this means is that you may do several Reads from a particular input line (be it from the terminal or other device), but you can only do a Readln from a particular input line *once*. This allows you to control how much material you input to the program from your input devices. Consider, for example, the following program segment:

```
Var Balance, Payments : Real;
BEGIN
  Readln (Balance, Payments);
  Balance := Balance - Payments;
```

When this segment is executed, the computer will request from the terminal (or whatever) a real value to be placed in the memory location called Balance and a real value to be placed in the memory location called Payments. The computer doesn't actually make a polite request

("Dear operator, would you please enter two real numbers?") but instead expects to find such values at the input device. Whoever is running the program might enter these values:

```
1526.78 50.00
```

The memory locations named Balance and Payments would be given the values 1526.78 and 50.00, respectively. Note that the values to be read in are separated by *spaces* and NOT by commas! You may in fact have as many spaces (and returns, for that matter) as you like, because the computer will continue to search the input, line after line, until values for *all* of the variables in the list have been located. For example, the person running the program could enter the numbers on two lines as follows:

```
1526.78
50.00
```

The computer would have no trouble at all locating these numbers.

No matter how the data is actually placed and located on the input line, once the input operation has been completed, the computer will continue by executing the next line of the program segment. In the example we are considering, the next step would be the evaluation of an expression. The value in Payments (in this case 50.00) is subtracted from the value in Balance (1526.78) to yield the value 1476.78, which is then stored in location Balance (thus destroying the value of Balance that had been there previously).

There is one major exception to the rule that Pascal searches until it finds the "data"—namely, those cases in which Char variables are being read. In this situation *the very next character on the input line is read regardless of what it is*. The reason is, of course, that any character at all is character data to the computer! For example, if we had the following Pascal segment:

```
Var First, Second, Third, Fourth : Char;
...
Readln (First, Second, Third, Fourth);
```

and the input line

```
T F R K
```

then the data would be read as follows: First would get the value T because it is, in fact, the first thing on the line. However, the variable

Second would get the value ' ' (blank) because *it is the very next character on the input line.* Pascal does NOT skip over blanks when reading characters as it does when reading numbers! Third would get the value F and Fourth would get another ' ' (blank). Note that if the first character on the line was a blank, the value obtained by the variable First would in fact be a blank; this is because when it reads a character, the computer never searches but simply takes what is there.

Look once again at the definition of input statement and notice that it is possible to use a Readln that has no list; this corresponds to reading no data. The purpose of such a statement is to permit the machine to skip over any data that might be on the input line but is not needed by the program.

The concept of input needs further refinement, as there is sometimes a certain amount of confusion about what goes on when the program itself is entered into the computer versus what goes on when the program is executed. The program is in fact entered through an input device (frequently at the keyboard using an editor). However, it is during *program execution* that the instructions are actually carried out. If the instruction under consideration by the computer is a Read, it is not until *execution time* that the computer requests data (input) from the terminal to be used in bringing about the solution to the problem. Only at this time is the information that is entered used by the program. Specific values of the variables are taken by the computer to produce the appropriate results. The program is, at long last, *using* the data to produce information.

Let's next differentiate Read and Readln a little more. It is worth noting that the input operation mentioned above could have been written instead as

```
Read (Balance);
Read (Payments);
```

or

```
Read (Balance);
Readln (Payments);
```

The data itself could still be entered either on one line or on two, using any of the specific orderings of the Reads and Readlns mentioned thus far. However, if the program was written like this:

```
Readln (Balance);
Readln (Payments);
```

the data *would have to be written on two separate lines!* This is because the first Readln would take one item of data and skip to the next line, regardless of what remained on the first line.

In order to clarify this a little more, let's look at the following two examples:

Version 1	**Version 2**
`Var Min, Max : Integer;`	`Var Min, Max: Integer;`
`BEGIN`	`BEGIN`
`Read (Min);`	`Readln (Min);`
`Read (Max);`	`Readln (Max);`

Assume that the input was presented on two lines, as follows:

```
25      50
75      100
```

What values would be placed into the locations Min and Max for each of these two cases? The answer is

> Version 1 — Min would contain 25,
>   Max would contain 50
> Version 2 — Min would contain 25,
>   Max would contain 75

Here is the reason: in Version 1, for the first Read the computer would fetch the first value of 25 for the variable Min, but the computer would remain on that first input line. When the second Read came along, the computer would simply pick up on the same line at the same place it left off and fetch the value of 50. In Version 2, the computer would (still) fetch the value of 25 on the first Readln; however, after having done this, the computer would move down to the *next* line. Hence, when the second Readln is carried out, the first value on the *second* line (in this case 75) would be placed into the program.

Finally, notice that Readln may also be used *without* any list at all! It merely skips one line of input, a capability that is occasionally useful.

This covers the basic input operations. Let's now move on to output statements.

Output statements. The output operation allows information produced by the computer to be sent out of the computer in a form understandable to humans, usually as a terminal screen image or as printing on paper. The **output statement** is similar to (and in fact quite symmetric with) that of the input instruction and can be defined as

```
output-statement → write (output-list)
              | writeln (output-list)
              | writeln
```

As with input, either a single variable or a number of items may be included in the output list. As is true for input statements, the difference between a "Write" and a "Writeln" (pronounced "write line") is what happens after the output operation is completed. With a `Write`, the device remains at the same position on the output line, but with a `Writeln` the device skips to the beginning of the *next* output line.

There is also a difference in the list items permitted. For input, the list items MUST be variables; for output, however, the list items can be any valid expression. Hence, you can write output statements such as

```
Writeln (Amt, Due, Total / 12.0);
```

Also note that, as in the case of `Readln`, no list is necessary; a lone `Writeln` skips a line on the output device, which can be used to make your output look aesthetically pleasing.

Let's consider the following program sections as examples:

Version 1	**Version 2**
`Var Big, Little : Integer;`	`Var Big, Little : Integer;`
`BEGIN`	`BEGIN`
`Big := 1000;`	`Big := 1000;`
`Little := 3;`	`Little := 3;`
`Write (Big);`	`Writeln (Big);`
`Write (Little);`	`Writeln (Little);`

The results from each of these would be as follows:

Version 1		**Version 2**
1000	3	1000
		3

Note that in Version 1 both results are printed on the same line, whereas in Version 2 they are printed out on separate lines. The former can be very useful in concatenating output, that is, in constructing one line from two or more output statements located at different places in the program.

Another difference between the `Read` and `Write` statements is that, in addition to variables and expressions, you may also use string constants in your output statements. **String constants** can be anything that you want, such as short phrases, special characters, and so forth. They are used to make the output more understandable. Let us consider a simple example. Suppose you want to print out the weight of an object in pounds and ounces. We could easily do something like

```
Writeln (Pounds, Ounces);
```

This statement would produce as output (assuming these values are in memory) the following:

```
25        8
```

This result may seem fine, but it certainly is not very understandable. By using string constants, we can "explain" the output a little better, and this statement can be improved to read

```
Writeln ('The weight is ', Pounds, '# and ', Ounces,
        ' oz.');
```

This statement would result in the following output line:

```
The weight is        25# and        8 oz.
```

This explanation is obviously *much* better. Aesthetically, however, it still leaves something to be desired. There is a lot of blank space in front of each number. Isn't there something we can do about that? Indeed there is: we can format our output. Formatting output allows you to specify exactly what the output should look like. In Pascal you may specify the total number of spaces into which a number must fit when it is displayed or printed. This is done by tacking on to the variable name in the output list an integer representing the total number of such spaces. For example, we can again change the output statement to this:

```
Writeln ('The weight is ', Pounds:4, '# and ',
        Ounces:2, ' oz.');
```

In this case we are specifying that exactly *four* spaces be used in printing the value in Pounds and exactly *two* spaces be used in printing the value in Ounces. The output line would now look like this:

```
The weight is   25# and  8 oz.
                ↑          ↑
            four spaces  two spaces
```

It is only slightly more difficult to format real numbers. Instead of specifying one number, you may specify two: the first tells the *total* number of spaces allotted, and the second tells how many spaces are to be used to the *right* of the decimal point. For example, this program segment

```
AmtDue := 345.85 / 2.0;
Writeln ('Total amount due is $', AmtDue:8:2);
```

would produce the following output:

```
Total amount due is $__172.92
```
← *eight total spaces allotted, including the decimal point*

-- ← *two spaces to the right of the decimal point*

Note a couple of things here:

1. The decimal point itself takes up one of the allotted spaces.

2. The number is rounded (as opposed to truncated) when it is finally printed out.

Another nice thing about output in Pascal is that it can be very forgiving; if you do not allocate enough space on the output for a number, the computer will stretch it until the format specification fits. That way your program won't "bomb" if there is an output field width error; it just won't look quite as nice.

Another use of output is, believe it or not, to make input easier. When you ran your first program (hopefully the simplified PAYROLL program in Chapter 2), you were probably frustrated by the fact that there was no indication given at the terminal, during computer execution of the Read statements, that the computer was in fact waiting for you to enter the information of the Hours and the Rate. A natural question is "Why can't the computer indicate when it requires input and what kind of input it needs?"

The computer can be programmed to indicate its needs by using prompts. A program that requires input should be written in such a way that the computer sends out a request or asks an appropriate question whenever input is desired; such a request or question is termed a **prompt**. The prompt should be unambiguous and easily understood. For example, in the simple payroll problem, it would be possible to use prompting for the input by writing

```
Write ('How many hours have been worked? ');
Readln (Hours);
Write ('What is the rate of pay?');
Readln (Rate);
```

When the first section of code is executed, the following question will appear on the CRT screen:

```
How many hours have been worked?
```

The person at the terminal then knows that a number corresponding to the `Hours` variable is needed and can respond appropriately by typing in, for example,

```
How many hours have been worked? 40.0
```

Note that the use of a `Write` instead of a `Writeln` for the prompt allows the operator to enter the information on the same line as the prompt was issued!

After the computer completes this input operation, the next prompt will appear:

```
How many hours have been worked? 40.0
What is the rate of pay?
```

To which the operator again can easily respond

```
How many hours have been worked? 40.0
What is the rate of pay? 3.75
```

Note how much easier and efficient this is than just sitting around waiting and hoping the computer is ready for the input!

There is one more aspect of Pascal programs we need to examine—presentation. Presentation is very useful in making a program self-documenting, and it should be utilized fully.

PRESENTATION

As mentioned earlier, one of the nice things about Pascal statements is that they can be placed anywhere on a given line and can be spread out as much as desired. Several statements may appear on one line, or one statement can be written over several lines. For example, the following statements are perfectly valid:

```
Sum := 0;   Total := 0;   Maximum := Default;
GrandTotal := GeneralRate * AmtSection1
            + LocalRate * AmtBasic
            - DiscountRate * Total;
```

This latter is considered by Pascal to be a single statement, even though it takes up three lines. Remember that, in Pascal, statements are delimited by semicolons, Begins, and Ends, and NOT by their relative location in the program.

Also, it is sometimes useful or necessary to include in the program those statements that are NOT instructions to the computer but that instead describe or explain aspects of the program. These descriptive statements are called comments and may be placed almost anywhere within a Pascal program. They are set off from the rest of the program by left brace { and right brace } or by the symbols (* and *). For example,

```
{This is a Pascal comment!}
    (* And so is this, *)
```

As we mentioned in the last chapter, comments are useful but should not be overused. Short, succinct comments that help in understanding the program are desired. One of the goals you should have in writing programs is to make your programs easily understandable, not only for you now and later on but also for anybody else who might use them. There is nothing more frustrating than finding that you can't make heads or tails of a program you yourself wrote earlier. A well-written program that includes good comments is the sign of a good programmer.

We have now seen enough of the Pascal computer language to satisfy our present needs. We will conclude this chapter by completing the Hal's Hamburger problem we started in the last chapter.

Hamburger Heaven Revisited

As you recall from Chapter 3, we finished step 2 of the program development process, "Plan the Solution." We were ready to move on to step 3, "Code the Solution," but had to interrupt the process until we learned sufficient Pascal for the task. We have done that and are now in a position to translate the algorithm into Pascal.

STEP 3: CODE THE SOLUTION

As mentioned earlier, this particular phase should be the easiest of all in the development process. Once a good algorithm is generated, turning it into a program should be very straightforward. All that is required is an understanding of the computer language elements and syntax. Comments should be inserted, as appropriate, and the structure of the algorithm should be preserved.

The complete coded solution is shown in Figure 4-3. Note that the program follows the algorithm closely but not slavishly. There is a certain amount of license that you may take in carrying out this transformation from algorithm to program, usually because there are specifics required by the language that don't need to be considered during the algorithm development phase. However, none of the logic will be lost in this transformation.

This program has a number of general characteristics that should be noted. First, the block structure of the program is evident; each section is delimited visually and introduced with brief comments. Second, prompts are used to make it easier to run and use the program. And third, it is possible to understand what the program does and how it does it by simply reading it as if it were a story. The program rather closely follows the logic described in the algorithm.

Figure 4-3

The Completed HAL *Program, Including a Sample Run*

HAL.PAS

```
1       Program HAL (Input, Output);
2
3       (*
4           This program inputs a single order for Hal's Hamburger Heaven,
5           tallies the bill and prints it out, inputs the amount paid,
6           and computes and prints the change,
7       (*)
8
9       Const PriceBoggle = 1.75;   (* These constants make up  *)
10            PriceBitsy  = 0.80;   (* the menu and the current *)
11            PriceShake  = 0.60;   (* price list               *)
12            PriceFries  = 0.50;
13            PriceKola   = 0.40;
14
15            TaxRate = 0.0575;
16
17      Var NumBoggles, NumBitsys, NumShakes, NumFries, NumKolas,
18          CostBoggles, CostBitsys, CostShakes, CostFries, CostKolas,
19          SubTotal, Tax, Total,
20          AmtTendered, Change : Real;
21
22      BEGIN
23
24          (* Input the Order *)
25
26          Writeln;
27          Write ('Number of Boggles?'); Readln (NumBoggles);
28          Write ('Number of Bitsys? '); Readln (NumBitsys);
```

Figure 4-3 continued

```
29          Write ('Number of Shakes?   '); Readln (NumShakes);
30          Write ('Number of Fries?    '); Readln (NumFries);
31          Write ('Number of Kolas?    '); Readln (NumKolas);
32
33             (* Figure Up Totals *)
34
35          CostBoggles := NumBoggles * PriceBoggle;
36          CostBitsys  := NumBitsys  * PriceBitsy;
37          CostShakes  := NumShakes  * PriceShake;
38          CostFries   := NumFries   * PriceFries;
39          CostKolas   := NumKolas   * PriceKola;
40
41          SubTotal := CostBoggles + CostBitsys + CostShakes
42                    + CostFries + CostKolas;
43
44          Tax := SubTotal * TaxRate;
45
46          Total := SubTotal + Tax;
47
48             (* Output the Bill *)
49
50          Writeln;
51          Writeln ('Hal's Hamburger Heaven');
52          Writeln ('Out of this World)');
53          Writeln;
54          Writeln ('Boggles   ', NumBoggles:4:0, CostBoggles:8:2);
55          Writeln ('Bitsys    ', NumBitsys:4:0, CostBytsys:8:2);
56          Writeln ('Shakes    ', NumShakes:4:0, CostShakes:8:2);
57          Writeln ('Fries     ', NumFries:4:0, CostFries:8:2);
58          Writeln ('Kolas     ', NumKolas:4:0, CostKolas:8:2);
59          Writeln;
60          Writeln ('SubTotal  ', SubTotal:12:2);
61          Writeln ('Tax       ', Tax:12:1);
62          Writeln ('Total Due ', Total:12:2);
63          Writeln;
64
65             (* Get the Amount Paid by Customer *)
66
67          Write   ('Enter amount of payment --> '); Readln (AmtTendered);
68
69             (* Figure Up, Print Out Change *)
70
71          Change := AmtTendered - Total;
72
73          Writeln;
74          Writeln ('Your Change ', Change:9:2);
75          Writeln;
76          Writeln ('Thank You!');
77          Writeln
78
79       END.
```

Figure 4-3 continued

```
$run hal

Number of Boggles? 2
Number of Bitsys?  1
Number of Shakes?  2
Number of Fries?   1
Number of Kolas?   3

Hal's Hamburger Heaven
(Out of this World)

Boggles     2.    3.50
Bitsys      1.    0.80
Shakes      2.    1.20
Fries       1.    0.50
Kolas       3.    1.20

SubTotal          7.20
Tax               0.41
Total Due         7.61

Enter amount of payment --> 10.00

Your Change       2.39

Thank You!
```

Also, a number of more specific items have been included in the program. Constants are used for the prices of the items; this makes it easier to change them when necessary. The use of constants eliminates the necessity of searching through the program to track down prices and then change them one by one. It also precludes unforeseen and hazardous changes in the program itself (such as, for example, leaving one of the old prices the same). The variables are also declared in a structured way so that they also give information about the program.

An additional item of interest is the output section of code, starting at line 48. How in the world can you find a proper way to arrange this? The trick is to use the output description you prepared earlier as a part of the "Understanding" phase. Once you know what the output is supposed to look like, it's a simple matter to write the appropriate code. Note, in passing, how an empty Writeln (that is, one that has nothing to write) may be used to skip lines on the output.

STEP 4: CHECK OUT THE PROGRAM

We must next check out the program to ensure that it produces correct results. There are a number of techniques available to assist in this process.

The first technique is to run the program with some fairly typical data for which you already have the correct answers. It is important that you figure out the correct answers *before* you run your program, otherwise you may bias your results. (It's too easy to trust the computer's answers if it goes first). If such typical data works properly, then you should next test the program with borderline data—data that stretches your understanding of the problem. For example, if you are working on payroll, make sure you attempt to use data that will cause the FICA yearly limit to be exceeded to see if the program handles it correctly. Be a devil's advocate and *try* to make your program fail. You'll be a lot happier if you uncover the problems yourself rather than having some other user discover your program's flaws. The question of what to do if an error is discovered will be examined in the next chapter.

STEP 5: DOCUMENT

At this point the fifth phase, "Documentation," is also complete. The algorithm, I/O descriptions (generated during the Understand the Problem phase), and the program itself contain all the **internal documentation** (that is, documentation regarding the program itself, not how to run it) required. If this program was written for use by somebody other than the writer, you would have to produce **external documentation** as well. This consists primarily of instructions for what is needed to run the program, enter data, and perhaps interpret the results. For the most part, external documentation is unnecessary at our current beginning level of computer programming, but you should at least be aware of its existence.

This completes the description of program development, including the complete HAL example. Everyone has to develop his or her own style, and this takes a lot of time and practice. You should work on problems of your own devising in addition to those assigned by your instructor, because the problems you pick will motivate you more than assigned ones will. If you're taking a chemistry or physics course, use the computer to work up your lab results. If you are in some other field, take advantage of the computer's powers. It may not save you much time, especially at this point, but it will give you more practice and will quite likely be more fun than working out the problems by hand!

SUMMARY

In this chapter we covered a substantial amount of material about Pascal and its syntax. We observed the overall structure of a Pascal program and defined its various parts, specifically, the heading, declaration, and executable sections. We examined how constants and variables are declared and looked at the executable statements of assignment, input, and output. Finally, we completed the program development process begun in the previous chapter.

EXERCISES

CONCEPTS

1. Define or explain the following terms:

Assignment operator   Identifier
Comments   Natural language
Computer language   Presentation
Constant   Syntax
Dialect   Type
Executable statement   Variable
Expression

2. Briefly differentiate the four generations of languages.

3. Name and briefly describe four data types available for use in Pascal.

4. Indicate which of the following are valid identifiers:

```
#55                     ThisIsOneVeryLongVariableName
EndofFile               Z104
MX                      $FIVE
Operation775            mmmmmmmmmmmmm
128X                    w34917v6
Stop It                 Twenty%
```

5. Indicate which of the following are valid constants and, of these, what their type is:

```
1.258E-16               'hello'
1984                    125E2
```

```
'75,125'              Zap
,5                    OEO
1966746110            12,
` ` `                 15,479
00                    000,025
true                  F
' = '                 $
```

6. Show how the following expressions would be evaluated by Pascal. Assume the following values:

$$a: 2.56 \quad b: -17.0 \quad c: 0.25 \quad d: 11.11$$
$$i: 0 \quad k: 12 \quad m: -5 \quad n: 100$$

a. `a + b + c + d`
b. `a + k DIV m`
c. `(((a / b) + (k * m)) / (c * c) - n) / 2`
d. `k DIV m * m`
e. `i MOD k * k`

7. Assume the following data is to be input into a program:

```
 5   16  -22    0
15   99    7   -2
 1    2    3    4
```

What values will be read into k, m, n, and p for each of the following?

a. `Read (k,m,n,p);`
b. `Readln (k,m,n,p);`
c. `Read (k,m);`
   `Read (n,p);`
d. `Readln (k,m,);`
   `Readln (n,p);`
e. `Read (k);`
   `Readln (m);`
   `Readln (n);`
   `Readln (p);`

8. What exactly will be printed out by Pascal when the following statements are executed?

a. `Count := 15 ;`
   `Total := 146,97;`
   `Writeln ('The count is ', Count:4);`
   `Writeln ('And the total is ', Total:8:1);`
b. `Write ('The character is ');`
   `A := '$';`

```
Writeln (A);
A := '%';
Writeln;
Writeln('Now it has been changed to ', A);
```

9. Describe some methods for verifying that a program works correctly.

TOOLS

10. Generate valid Pascal constants subsections for the following groups of constants, using appropriate names for the constants:

  a. Operators ' + ', ' − ', ' * ', ' / '
  b. A largest allowed value of 256 and a smallest allowed value of 1.
  c. An asterisk, the integer 1024, and the real number one-half.

11. Generate valid Pascal variable declarations subsections for the following groups of variables, using appropriate names for the variables.

  a. For evaluating mathematical formulas: a, b, c, x, y, z.
  b. A count of animals on a farm, and individual counts of horses, cows, chickens, and pigs.
  c. A starting time, an ending time, and an elapsed time, all expressed in hours and minutes.
  d. The average rates of growth for two comparable fields of wheat treated with different rates of fertilizer application.
  e. Variables indicating the end of an operation and the fact that a maximum count has been exceeded.

12. Generate valid assignment statements, using appropriate variable names, for the following:

  a. The total distance traveled is equal to the rate of travel multiplied by the time actually traveled.
  b. The temperature in degrees centigrade is equal to five-ninths of what you get by subtracting thirty-two from the temperature in degrees Fahrenheit.
  c. $k = \dfrac{[c]\,[d]}{[a]\,[b]}$
  d. $y = x^2 - 4x + 7$

13. Generate a prompt and a `Read` statement that will ask for the dimensions of a rectangular solid and read them all in however the user chooses.

14. Generate a prompt and `Read` statement that will input a letter of the alphabet and a number between one and ten.

15. Generate output statements that will take the variables `BeginningBalance`, `Interest`, `Payments`, and `Ending-Balance` and will print them out as follows:

```
The beginning balance was               $ 286.32

You made payments of                       50.00

And were charged interest
  in the amount of                          5.72

Leaving a final balance of              $ 242.04 ***
```

PROBLEMS

16. Trace the `HAL` program manually, using a calculator. Pay particular attention to the output section to ensure that you understand how the formatting works.

17. Choose a problem from among the Problems listed at the end of the previous chapter. Write an algorithm for it (if you have not done so already) and convert your algorithm into a complete and correct Pascal program. Finally, get this program to execute successfully on your computer.

18. Test the program that you wrote in problem 17 above with different kinds of data to assure yourself that it works correctly.

19. Simultaneous linear equations can be solved using determinants. If the equations are

$$a_1x + b_1y = c_1$$
$$a_2x + b_2y = c_2$$

then the solutions can be written as

$$x = \frac{\begin{vmatrix} c_1 & b_1 \\ c_2 & b_2 \end{vmatrix}}{\begin{vmatrix} a_1 & b_1 \\ a_2 & b_2 \end{vmatrix}}$$

$$y = \frac{\begin{vmatrix} a_1 & c_1 \\ a_2 & c_2 \end{vmatrix}}{\begin{vmatrix} a_1 & b_1 \\ a_2 & b_2 \end{vmatrix}}$$

In general a determinant of the form

$$\begin{vmatrix} i & j \\ k & m \end{vmatrix}$$

can be evaluated to the value $im - kj$. Using this information, write a program to solve general linear simultaneous equations in two unknowns.

20. Test your program from problem 19. Are there any cases where the program does not work properly?

5

The Debugging Process:

Locating and Correcting Errors

*S*ooner or later, in fact quite likely from the very first program you work on, you will run into the problem of bugs, the fly (so to speak) in the ointment of computer science. **Bug** is a term that refers to an error in a program. Bugs are a fact of life that will have to be dealt with as long as you are writing programs. One of the primary reasons for using the program design and development process discussed in the previous chapter is that, when used conscientiously, it significantly reduces the number and intensity of errors that will occur. Unfortunately, it does not eliminate them entirely. In that regard it is like insect repellent—it keeps the bugs from biting but does not necessarily keep them at a respectful distance. Consequently, programming bugs will occur, and some techniques are required to deal with them.

Errors are not unique to computer science, but are common to all aspects of life and are a manifestation of the laws of thermodynamics that say that the universe tends to become disordered in the normal course of events. Under the right conditions, order can prevail. Although it takes a great deal of energy to achieve perfect order, it can be done. Writing a computer program is the production of perfect order, that is, the creation of a computer-understandable algorithm that carries out a specific task.

The problem of errors is so general that procedures similar or identical to those described in this chapter for dealing with program bugs may be employed to solve a wide variety of noncomputer problems. For example, repairing a car engine that is making a funny noise, replacing a blown fuse, and diagnosing an illness all require similar methods of approach, analysis, and solution.

In this chapter we will consider a four-phase process for eliminating bugs that is analogous to the five-phase process presented in Chapter 3 for developing programs. Then, the kinds of errors that may occur will be categorized and methods presented for dealing with each specific type. Finally, we will demonstrate the methods and techniques using a complete example.

5-1   The Four Debugging Phases

There are four general phases that should be considered and worked through when debugging a program. These are

1. Determine exactly what the error is.

2. Locate exactly where the error is.

3. Alter the program (and possibly the algorithm) to remove the error.

4. Test to ensure that the error has been eliminated.

As was the case with the five phases of program development, these four steps need not necessarily be carried out sequentially, and in fact a certain amount of shifting from step to step may be done, depending on the kind of problem to be solved. However, all steps need to be followed. As we did in Chapter 3, let's look at each of these phases in turn.

Determine what the error is. The first thing you must do is determine *what* the error is. Sometimes the computer is helpful with this, and sometimes it is not. Many errors will generate a message for you, but these may or may not be understandable. For example, suppose you enter the following line in your program:

```
Result := 3 + * Number;
```

Quite likely the computer will tell you something like

```
Error - Consecutive operators
```

This message is very specific and there is no question about what the problem is. However, consider the following statement and resulting error message:

```
If A < 3 Then
    B := A * 2;
Else
    B := A / 3;
Error - No matching If with Else
```

This message appears to be incorrect, since we *do* in fact have an If for the Else. However, a closer inspection reveals that a semicolon is used after the If clause; Pascal would interpret that to mean the end of the If. Consequently, when it bumps into the Else, it thinks there is no If to go along with it!

Consider another possibility. Suppose you are executing a program and you get the message

```
Error - Division by zero attempted in line 35
```

Now the error message is quite specific. However, the actual cause of the problem is likely to be far removed from this statement since, hopefully, there was no purposeful intention to divide by zero. In this case an error has been detected and reported, but the indicated error does not represent the actual problem.

There is an even worse situation. Suppose you are computing monthly loan payments and the program comes up with a payment of $376,984.35 on a loan of $25,000. Obviously, this is incorrect, but the computer gives you no indication that an error of some kind has occurred. Again, an error has been detected, but the actual cause of the error is probably far removed from the output statement where it shows up.

The exact methods used to determine the nature of an error are a function of the category of error that has occurred, so we will look at specifics when we examine error types.

Determine where the error is. The next step is to determine exactly *where* the error is, which is, unfortunately, often inextricably tied to *what* the error is. Sometimes the computer can be helpful, and sometimes it will not be. Normally, the computer reports when an error has occurred, but the location of such a report may or may not be close to the location of the actual problem. For example, in the "divide by zero" error mentioned above, the computer indicates the line number where the error occurred, but the actual problem is somewhat removed from that location. Even for relatively straightforward errors, the location may not be easy to pinpoint. For example, suppose you entered the following statements:

```
A := B + C * D;
E := M / N

(* Now finish it up *)

R := M * B;
```

If you enter it this way, quite likely the computer will respond with something like

```
A := B + C * D;
E := M / N

(* Now finish it up *)

R := M * B;
^

Error - Semicolon expected
```

You might think "Why would I want a semicolon right before the R?" In fact you wouldn't. However, note that a semicolon *is* missing right *after* the N four lines back. The compiler couldn't determine that it was missing until it ran into the start of a new statement, which doesn't occur until four lines later.

Of course, with errors such as the $376,984.35 payment on the $25,000 loan, you get neither an indication of what the error is nor an indication of where it is. Again, the exact nature of the error determines, to a large extent, what you can do to locate it. Procedures for determining the nature of errors will be discussed in the sections on each individual error type.

Alter the program. Once you think you know *what* and *where* the error is, you must alter the program (and/or algorithm) to reflect the new knowledge and eliminate the bug. For example, the bug expressed in the example

```
If A < 3 Then
    B := A * 2;
Else
    B := A / 3;
Error - No matching If with Else
```

can be corrected by removing a semicolon so that it reads

```
If A < 3 Then
    B := A * 2
Else
    B := A / 3;
```

The error indicated as

```
A := B + C * D;
E := M / N

(* Now finish it up *)

R := M * B;
^
Error - Semicolon expected
```

can be corrected by *adding* a semicolon so that it reads

```
A := B + C * D;
E := M / N;

(* Now finish it up *)

R := M * B;
^
```

Of course, the more complex errors like division by zero and overly large monthly payments will likely require more extensive corrections.

Test the correction. Once you feel you have removed the error, the program must be tested again to ensure that you have succeeded. In general, you should test for the specific error that caused the problem and go on to see if the correction affects any other parts of the program.

Now that we have an understanding of how to deal with errors, let's examine in detail the kinds of errors that can occur and the specific methods that can be used to deal with them. We will begin by dividing errors up into categories that are based on *how* an error manifests itself and *when* the manifestation occurs.

5-2 *How and When Errors Occur*

We mentioned in Chapter 3 the existence of two categories of bugs that arise in computer programming: clerical and logical. (Interestingly, the original "bug" from which the common term for a programming error was derived really was an insect. A moth got into the computer circuitry and ruined the operation. Such bugs are, however, rare.) The two categories of clerical and logical errors are very broad, but they encompass most of the kinds of bugs that are typically encountered. When trying to uncover errors, however, two overlapping classification schemes are useful. The first scheme is based on the point in the process where the error appears and the second on the way an error manifests itself. These schemes can be summarized as follows:

Temporal

1. Compile-time errors (also known as syntax errors)

2. Run-time errors

Manifestations

1. A direct message from the computer

2. Incorrect output from the program

Let's explain these schemes a little more before examining them in detail. **Compile-time errors** are *always* revealed by a direct message from the computer. Compile-time errors are relatively straightforward, and with a little practice, you can find them quickly and easily. The existence of a **syntax** (compile-time) **error** is always obvious, and some indication of its location and cause is usually present (although this may be more approximate than you might like). Syntax errors are called compile-time errors because they turn up during compilation, when your program is being translated into machine language.

Run-time errors can be errors of the first *or* second manifestation. The primary difference between the two categories is that with run-time errors of the first manifestation the computer points out a location and problem description, whereas with run-time errors of the second manifestation you must discover the problem yourself.

With run-time errors, things get more interesting. Such errors may be easy to correct, but as a general rule they tend to be more difficult to pin down. They can be frustrating because they may be **intermittent**, that is, sometimes you see them and sometimes you don't. Occasionally, you will spend significant amounts of time just trying to reproduce an error so you can track it down. But this is all part and parcel of computer science, and your efforts in this area will be repaid many times.

Using these schemes to help categorize errors, let's examine specific error types and how to deal with them.

5-3   *Syntax Errors*

Let's begin by looking at compile-time, or syntax, errors. These, on the whole, are the easiest to correct. Syntax, as you recall, is the set of rules

Figure 5-1

Typical Compiler Listing with Syntax Errors and Messages

```
BUGS                                              VAX Pascal V3.0-2
Source Listing

00001           Program BUGS (Input, Output);
00002
00003           Const pi = 3.14159
00004
00005           Var  Circumference, Diameter : Real;
                1
%PASCAL-E-SYNSEMI, (1) Syntax: ";" expected
00006
00007           BEGIN
00008               Write ('Enter the diameter...);
                                                   1
%PASCAL-E-QUOBEFEOL, (1) Quoted string not terminated before end of line
00009               Readln (Diameter);
                    1
%PASCAL-E-SYNPARMLST, (1) Syntax: actual parameter list
00010               Circumference := pi * * Diameter;
                                 1
%PASCAL-E-SYNILLEXPR, (1) Syntax: ill-formed expression
00011               Area = pi * (Diameter * Diameter / 4.;
                    1    2                              3 4
%PASCAL-E-UNDECLID, (1) Undeclared identifier AREA
%PASCAL-E-SYNASSIGN, (2) Syntax: ":=" expected
%PASCAL-E-ERREALCNST, (3) Error in real constant: digit expected
%PASCAL-E-SYNRPAREN, (4) Syntax: ")" expected
00012               Writeln ('The circumference is ', Circumference:6:2);
00013               Writeln ('The area is ', Area:6:2)
00014           END
                1
%PASCAL-W-SYNPERIOD, (1) Syntax: "." expected


COMPILATION STATISTICS

  Warnings:       1
  Errors:         8
```

that defines how language elements may be legally combined. If language elements are not combined correctly, the compiler will, while examining the program, note such errors and issue appropriate messages. An example of a program with syntax errors is shown in Figure 5-1. A good compiler will have well-written messages, which are a big help in making the correction process easy. The epitome of poor error messages can be found in some BASIC languages, where all syntax error messages consist of the single phrase

SYNTAX ERROR

The compiler messages shown in Figure 5-1 are much better than this limited error message.

Let's examine the program listing shown in Figure 5-1 a little more closely. In general, the compiler tells what the error is and where it is. Note, however, that these error messages are still subject to interpretation. The very first error message reads

```
(1) Syntax: ";" expected
```

This is pretty straightforward. Apparently, a semicolon was expected by the compiler; that is, one is missing somewhere. Also, the number 1 indicates where the error is, in this case at the word VAR in the program.

But wait. . . . Why would we want a semicolon sitting on top of the Var? Well, we wouldn't. This is the *approximate* location of the error. In fact, the compiler is telling us that a semicolon was expected just when it ran into the Var, which means it should come right *before* the Var. This means it belongs immediately *after* the preceding statement, which is in this case the constant definition. Note that the semicolon *is* missing from that location. The point is, the messages and locations must be taken with a grain of salt. Some compilers are better at indicating location accurately than others.

Moving along in the listing, we next come to the message

```
(1) Quoted string not terminated before end of line
```

Looking at the indicated location we see that a single quote should have closed the string used in the output list; that is, we have an invalid string. Not too tough.

But just when you thought it was easy to read and interpret error messages, we come to the next one:

```
(1) Syntax: actual parameter list
```

HUH??? There is apparently nothing wrong with the Readln statement that this error message indicates, and the error message itself is not exactly enlightening. What's going on here?

Well, this is an example of a **spurious error**, an error that does not really exist but was generated as a result of another error somewhere else in the program. These errors can be very frustrating. The best way to deal with them, however, is to ignore them; that is, if you run across an error that seems to have no basis in fact, and there are lots of other errors in the program, then go ahead and correct the ones you recognize and understand and then recompile the program. Chances are, all of those strange and bizarre errors will disappear. If they haven't, well, you will have to consider them again; however, they will most likely just fade away.

We next come to

```
(1) Syntax: ill-formed expression
```

Not exactly specific, but apparently there is something wrong with an expression. Looking more closely, we see that an extra * was used in the multiplication.

    The next error message is

```
(1) Undeclared identifier AREA
```

This is straightforward and to the point. Looking at the Var section of the program we see that we did, in fact, forget to include Area in the list of variables.

    Moving on, we have

```
(2) Syntax: ":=" expected
```

It seems the compiler wanted to see the assignment operator and it did not. A closer look at the statement (where the number 2 is located) reveals that instead of the assignment operator := we have only an equal sign—a typo or oversight.

    And then

```
(3) Error in real constant: digit expected
```

This message is pointing to the constant 4. Recall that when we defined constants we said that if a number contains a decimal point there must be a digit on both sides. The compiler is telling us we forgot to include the additional digit.

    Proceeding further, we read

```
(4) Syntax: ")" expected
```

We have obviously left out a right parenthesis; looking at the expression indicated by the error message, we see that a left parenthesis was used to bracket the diameter operation but was not closed at the end with a matching right parenthesis.

    Finally, we have

```
(1) Syntax: "." expected
```

We recognize this immediately as the missing period at the end of the program; recall that Pascal programs must be terminated with END. (period!).

    Making the corrections indicated by the compiler messages (excluding the spurious "actual parameter list"), we see that everything is fine and cleared up, as shown in Figure 5-2.

Figure 5-2

Corrected Program

```
BUGS                                                    VAX Pascal V3.0-2
Source Listing

00001          Program BUGS (Input, Output);
00002
00003          Const Pi = 3.14159;
00004
00005          Var  Circumference, Diameter, Area : Real;
00006
00007          BEGIN
00008             Write ('Enter the diameter...');
00009             Readln (Diameter);
00010             Circumference := Pi * Diameter;
00011             Area := Pi * (Diameter * Diameter) / 4.0;
00012             Writeln ('The circumference is ', Circumference:6:2);
00013             Writeln ('The area is ', Area:6:2)
00014          END.
123
```

There are, unfortunately, other possible errors that can considerably complicate the process described above. An example of a program containing such errors is shown in Figure 5-3. In most of these instances, the exact nature of the error is not at all obvious and is such that the message is far removed from the actual error. As we did with the previous example, let us go through this listing error by error to see what turns up. The first error is

```
(1) Program Parameter OUPUT is not declared as a variable
at the outermost level
```

Whew! What in the world does *that* mean? It means that the computer really has no sense. If you look at the error position indicated, you will note that `Output` is simply *spelled wrong*. However, the computer had no way of recognizing the word as being almost `Output` (only the `t` was missing) and assumed it was the name of an external file that was not properly declared! As we already mentioned, error messages are subject to interpretation.

The next error message is

```
(1) Undeclared identifier REEL
```

Again we have a misspelling, but again the computer could not recognize that the word was *almost* the data type `Real`.

Proceeding, we find

```
(1) OUTPUT not declared in heading
```

Figure 5-3

A Listing with Somewhat Harder-to-Interpret Error Messages

```
WORSE                                          VAX Pascal V3.0-2
Source Listing

00001              Program WORSE (Input, Ouput);
                                            1
%PASCAL-E-PROPRMLEV, (1) Program parameter OUPUT is not declared as a variable
at the outermost level
00002
00003              Const Pi = 3.14159;
00004
00005              Var  Circumference, Diameter, Area : Reel;
                                                          1
%PASCAL-E-UNDECLID, (1) Undeclared identifier REEL
00006
00007              BEGIN
00008                Write ('Enter the diameter...');
                         1
%PASCAL-E-OUTNOTDECL, (1) OUTPUT not declared in heading
00009                Readln (Diamater);
                            1
%PASCAL-E-UNDECLID, (1) Undeclared identifier DIAMATER
00010                Circumference := Pi Diameter;
                                         1
%PASCAL-E-SYNSEMI, (1) Syntax: ";" expected
%PASCAL-E-NOTAFUNC, (1) DIAMETER is not declared as a PROCEDURE or FUNCTION
00011                Area := Pi * Diameter * Diameter / 4.0;
00012                Writeln ('The circumference is ',Circumference:6.2);
                         1                                            2
%PASCAL-E-OUTNOTDECL, (1) Output not declared in heading
%PASCAL-E-FLDWDTHINT, (2) Field-width expression must be of type INTEGER
00013                Writeln ('The area is ', Area:6.2)
                         1                       2
%PASCAL-E-OUTNOTDECL, (1) OUTPUT not declared in heading
%PASCAL-E-FLDWDTHINT, (2) Field-width expression must be of type INTEGER
00014      00   END.


COMPILATION STATISTICS

 Warnings:       0
 Errors:        10
```

Same problem. This error message is a spurious result of the misspelling of Output. The computer did not *see* output mentioned in the heading and thus says it cannot do any output. Errors of this sort can be extremely frustrating.

Next we have

```
(1) Undeclared identifier DIAMETER
```

But wait, you say . . . this was declared properly! However, a close look shows that you intended to declare it but did not. More misspellings.

The next two errors are real winners, namely,

```
(1) Syntax: ";" expected
(1) DIAMETER is not declared as a PROCEDURE or FUNCTION
```

What in the world is happening now? Obviously, there are no missing semicolons, and nobody has even mentioned procedures or functions. What gives?

The problem is that the multiplication operator * is missing. The compiler interpreted the fact that two identifiers were adjacent to mean that two statements were intended, hence the missing semicolon message. Also, since what the computer interpreted to be the second statement (had it been so intended) consisted only of the single word Diameter, it assumed this was a procedure, since that is the way procedures are used. And no such procedure had been declared!

Welcome to Wonderland, Alice.

There are two more OUTPUT not declared in heading error messages, with which we have already dealt. The final error message (of which there are two) says

```
(2) Field-width expression must be of type INTEGER
```

The problem appears to be an output format specification, which merely states that we want a real number (not an integer!) to have six total spaces with two to the right of the decimal. What's so wrong about that? What's wrong is that the separator must be a *colon*, not a period. The compiler interpreted what is written to be a real number format specification, *not* a single specification.

Now that we have seen syntax errors and how to deal with them, let's increase the level of difficulty and move on to the next category.

5-4   Run-Time Errors

Well, if those were the easy errors, what in heaven's name will the tough ones be like? Please continue to keep in mind that debugging is a necessary, but difficult, process that must be learned over time. With a little practice, good techniques will be developed and debugging can be an interesting and challenging aspect of program generation.

With that in mind, let us examine how run-time errors present themselves and the methods for correcting them. To demonstrate, we will work through an example that contains run-time errors and deal with them as they occur.

Atomic Spectroscopy

This is a problem from atomic physics; however, don't be intimidated by that. The solution to the problem is quite straightforward, and a little bit of background should make it understandable. (We will abbreviate the program development process just a little in order to concentrate on the debugging aspect.)

What we would like to do is write a program that inputs two energy levels of an atom and produces as output the wavelength (color) of the light that will be generated from it. Let's see how this works.

STEP 1: UNDERSTAND THE PROBLEM

Whenever any kind of material is heated sufficiently, it gives off light. This is the principle of the incandescent light bulb, and the sun, for that matter. More often than not, the light that is produced covers the full visible spectrum; that is, all possible colors are generated. If the generated light is viewed through a prism (or a sufficiently moist atmosphere), a complete rainbow will be produced.

However, many substances do not produce all colors of light but only certain specific colors. This is because the electrons in the substance can move up and down in their orbits only by certain specific amounts. Each electronic jump from one orbit to another generates exactly one color. Since each of these orbits has a certain energy associated with it, one should be able to calculate this energy. Since energy is related to frequency, frequency is related to wavelength, and wavelength determines the color, it should be possible to calculate the colors (wavelengths) of the light produced! This is something that is done frequently in physics, and programs to carry out such calculations are quite common.

Proceeding to specifics: the energy of an electron in any orbit is given by

$$E = \frac{me^4Z^2}{8p^2n^2h^2}$$

where p = the permeativity constant (related to how positive and negative charges attract each other)

m = the mass of an electron

e = the (negative) charge on the electron

Z = the atomic number of the substance (that is, which substance it is)

$n =$ the orbit number

$h =$ Planck's constant (a number, much like π, that Max Planck discovered)

To get the energy produced in going from one orbit to another (the transition energy), you just need to calculate E for the two levels and subtract them:

$$E_t = E_1 - E_2$$

Once you have E_t, you can compute the frequency of the light by using

$$v = \frac{E_t}{h}$$

And finally, you can get the wavelength by the formula

$$\lambda = \frac{c}{v}$$

where λ = wavelength

v = frequency

c = the speed of light

STEP 2: PLAN THE SOLUTION

This program basically requires inputs, calculations, and outputs. We can write an algorithm quickly and easily as

Get the energy levels
  Read n_1
  Read n_2
Compute the energy of the levels

$$E_1 = \frac{me^4Z^2}{8p^2n_1^2h^2} \qquad E_2 = \frac{me^4Z^2}{8p^2n_2^2h^2}$$

Compute the transition energy

$$E_t = E_1 - E_2$$

Compute the frequency of the resulting light

$$v = \frac{E_t}{h}$$

Compute the wavelength of the resulting light

$$\lambda = \frac{c}{v}$$

Print out the results
  Write $E_1, E_2, E_t, v, \lambda$

Figure 5-4

Initial Version of the Spectroscopy Program

```
ENERGY                                                VAX Pascal V3.0-2
Source Listing

00001          Program ENERGY (Input, Output);
00002
00003          Const p = 8.850E-12;        (* Permeativity constant *)
00004                m = 9.109E-28;        (* Mass of the electron *)
00005                e = 4.803E-10;        (* Charge on an electron *)
00006                h = 6.625E-27;        (* Planck's constant *)
00007                c = 3.000E10;         (* Speed of light *)
00008                F = 1.238E-20;        (* Conversion factor to ensure proper units *)
00009
00010          Var   n1, n2 : Integer;    (* Index to energy levels *)
00011                    Z : Integer;     (* Atomic number of isotope *)
00012                E1, E2 : Real;        (* Energy of the levels *)
00013                   Et : Real;         (* Energy of the transition *)
00014                 v, l : Real;         (* Frequency, wavelength of emitted light *)
00015
00016                    R : Real;         (* Rydberg constant *)
00017
00018          BEGIN
00019
00020             Write ('Enter the lowest level........');
00021             Readln (n1);
00022             Write ('Enter the highest level.......');
00023             Readln (n2);
00024             Write ('Enter the atomic number.......');
00025             Readln (Z);
00026
00027             R := m*e*e*e*e*Z*Z / 8*p*p*h*h * F;
00028
00029             E1 := R*(1 / (n1 * n1));
00030             E2 := R*(1 / (n2 * n2));
00031
00032             Et := E1 - E2;
00033
00034             v := Et / h;
00035             l := c / v;
00036
00037             Writeln ('The energy of the first level is    ', E1);
00038             Writeln ('The energy of the second level is   ', E2);
00039             Writeln ('The energy of transition is         ', Et);
00040             Writeln;
00041             Writeln ('The frequency of emitted light is ', v);
00042             Writeln ('The wavelength of emitted light is ', l)
00043
00044          END.
```

STEP 3: CODE THE SOLUTION

All of the above items have been taken into account in converting the above algorithm to the program shown in Figure 5-4. Note a couple of additional items in the program:

1. In order to make the computations a little easier to see, something called the Rydberg constant has been introduced. This is not really a constant but rather a number that remains the same for any given material (and hence must be computed only once).

2. The program can be easily run, because prompts are included for all inputs.

3. There are no errors! The Pascal compiler has completely accepted the program.

We are therefore ready for . . .

STEP 4: CHECK OUT THE PROGRAM

When the program is actually run, the events depicted in Figure 5-5 take place, and a significant run-time error occurs.

So, how to proceed? Following the four debugging phases, our first task is to determine *what* the error is and *where* it is. At first glance, we appear to have that information, because the computer says what the error is (division by zero) and exactly where it occurs (in line 35). However, this is not much help; nobody purposefully divides by zero, but the computer says that the frequency v has a value of zero! We must therefore resort to other methods to make these determinations.

The problem manifested itself right at line 35, but obviously something had to have gone wrong prior to this. The problem becomes one of finding exactly where in the program things begin to go awry. Frequently, the incorrect values themselves will lend a clue as to where the error is. If you are developing a payroll application, and your FICA (social security tax) computation works correctly except when the yearly maximum tax limit is exceeded, then you know where in your program to begin searching for the error. For the most part, however, finding the location of the error requires the ability to examine the contents of the

Figure 5-5

Sample Run of the Initial Spectroscopy Program

```
$ run energy

Enter the lowest level.......2
Enter the highest level......3
Enter the atomic number......1
%SYSTEM-F-FLTDIV_F, arithmetic fault, floating divide by zero at PC=000003A5,
%TRACE-F-TRACEBACK, symbolic stack dump follows
module name       routine name                    line      rel PC      abs PC

ENERGY            ENERGY                           35     00000091    000003A5
```

computer's memory, specifically, the values stored in the variables. The process then becomes one of finding the point in the program where the variables exhibit incorrect values.

There are a number of methods for finding this point. One way is to step through the program one statement at a time, watching how the values of the variables change as each step of the program is executed exactly as written. Another way is to progressively isolate the section of the program wherein the error resides, perhaps noting that everything is fine at line 25 but wrong at line 40. This would tell you that the problem is between lines 25 and 40 and that you can disregard the rest of the program. The former method is useful for shorter programs and the latter for longer and more complex programs.

There are also, as might be expected, a number of ways of "looking at" or examining memory locations. The first involves simulating the program execution by hand. This is especially useful if the program is not too long and involved. You sit down with a copy of the program, a pencil, and a calculator and *you* pretend that you are the computer: you carry out the program instructions and see what happens. This is called a **hand trace**. Frequently, the problem will present itself to you. There is one difficulty with a hand trace, however. Since you yourself wrote the program, you are intimately aware of what it is *supposed* to do, and sometimes, exactly for that reason, you will do what you expect it should do rather than what the program actually says to do. No matter how many times you add it up, two plus two will continue to make five. One way around this is to ask somebody else to look at the program. Since this other person will not have been working on the program, he or she will not have your built-in prejudices and can often see things you cannot.

The other methods of pinpointing the problem location all involve using the computer itself to help you look at the values of the variables. Some of these methods are more sophisticated and easier to use than others, but they are essentially the same in principle. The best method is to use what is termed a symbolic debugger, which enables you to control the step-by-step execution of your program and examine memory locations at will. If you have such a debugger on your system, by all means learn how to use it. A second method of examining the contents of memory locations is the memory dump, in which *everything* in the computer memory, including programs, variables, and garbage, is presented for your perusal. This is an older method, now seldom used.

The middle course, and the one we will present and use throughout this book, makes use of **diagnostic output statements**. The method involves placing additional `Write` statements at selected places in your program so that you can follow the progression of variable values as the program executes. You will then likely spot the location where things go awry. The advantages to this method are that it is easy to use and that you get an accurate report of events from the computer. The disadvantage is that the program must be physically altered and recompiled.

The diagnostic version of the program is shown in Figure 5-6. Note that print statements are placed after the input, to ensure that they have been read in properly, as well as after each set of calculations. Also, the diagnostic print statements are written in all uppercase to make them easy to identify (and remove) later on.

The output generated when this program is run is shown in Figure 5-7. An examination of this output leads to the conclusion that the problem lies in line 30 of the diagnostic program; the input has been read in correctly, *but R should definitely not be zero.*

So, now we ask: How did R get to be zero? If we look at the expression in line 30 more closely, we see that it has not been written properly: the calculation that we specified in the program is, algebraically speaking, the following:

$$r = \frac{me^4 Z^2 p^2 h^2 F}{8}$$

It is not, as was intended, the expression

$$r = \frac{me^4 Z^2 F}{8 p^2 h^2}$$

(Recall the hierarchy of operators discussed in Chapter 4.)

Now that we have located the error, the next step of the debugging process is to make the indicated corrections. If we do that, we end up with the program shown in Figure 5-8. We confidently run this newly corrected program according to step four of the debugging process and get the output shown in Figure 5-9.

We are absolutely devastated! We *still* get a "divide by zero" error, but this time it shows up even earlier, in line 27 instead of line 35! Life is not fair.

So, we begin the debugging process again. We first look at the denominator of the expression in line 27, and we see it involves the subexpression 8*P*P*h*h. However, these are all defined as constants. Could something have gone wrong with the values of the constants somewhere? Well, when in doubt, check. Diagnostic output statements placed immediately before this calculation show (in Figure 5-10) that there is nothing wrong with the constants.

Desperately seeking solutions, we crank out this subexpression by hand on a calculator. So doing yields a value of 2.75E-74. This is extremely small, but not zero . . .

Or is it?

We have here an example of an extremely subtle error in this program. Whenever a real value gets smaller than a certain point, *it is considered by the computer to be zero!* But wait, you say, computers never make mistakes. Is this not a mistake? In point of fact it is not, because

Figure 5-6

Spectroscopy Program with Included Diagnostic Outputs

```
ENERGY                                                          VAX Pascal V3.0-2
Source Listing


00001              Program ENERGY (Input, Output);
00002
00003              Const p = 8.850E-12;         (* Permeativity constant *)
00004                    m = 9.109E-28;         (* Mass of the electron *)
00005                    e = 4.803E-10;         (* Charge on an electron *)
00006                    h = 6.625E-27;         (* Planck's constant *)
00007                    c = 3.000E10;          (* Speed of light *)
00008                    F = 1.238E-20;         (* Conversion factor to ensure proper units *)
00009
00010              Var   n1, n2 : Integer;      (* Index to energy levels *)
00011                         Z : Integer;      (* Atomic number of isotope *)
00012                    E1, E2 : Real;         (* Energy of the levels *)
00013                        Et : Real;         (* Energy of the transition *)
00014                     v, 1 : Real;          (* Frequency, wavelength of emitted light *)
00015
00016                       R : Real;           (* Rydberg constant *)
00017
00018              BEGIN
00019
00020                 Write ('Enter the lowest level.......');
00021                 Readln (n1);
00022                 Write ('Enter the highest level......');
00023                 Readln (n2);
00024                 Write ('Enter the atomic number......');
00025                 Readln (Z);
00026                 WRITELN ('N1 = ',N1);
00027                 WRITELN ('N2 = ',N2);
00028                 WRITELN ('Z  = ',Z);
00029
00030                 R := m*e*e*e*e*Z*Z / 8*p*p*h*h * F;
00031                 WRITELN ('R = ',R);
00032
00033                 E1 := R*(1 / (n1*n1));
00034                 E2 := R*(1 / (n2*n2));
00035                 WRITELN ('E1 = ',E1);
00036                 WRITELN ('E2 = ',E2);
00037
00038                 Et := E1 - E2;
00039                 WRITELN ('ET = ',ET);
00040
00041                 v := Et / h;
00042                 WRITELN ('V = ',V);
00043                 1 := c / v;
00044
00045                 Writeln ('The energy of the first level is     ', E1);
00046                 Writeln ('The energy of the second level is    ', E2);
00047                 Writeln ('The energy of transition is          ', Et);
00048                 Writeln;
00049                 Writeln ('The frequency of emitted light is    ', v);
00050                 Writeln ('The wavelength of emitted light is   ', 1)
00051
00052              END.
```

Figure 5-7

Sample Diagnostic Run

```
$ run energy

Enter the lowest level.......2
Enter the highest level......3
Enter the atomic number......1
N1 =           2
N2 =           3
Z  =           1
R  = 0.00000E+00
E1 = 0.00000E+00
E2 = 0.00000E+00
ET = 0.00000E+00
V  = 0.00000E+00
%SYSTEM-F-FLTDIV_F, arithmetic fault, floating divide by zero at PC=000005A0,
%TRACE-F-TRACEBACK, symbolic stack dump follows
module name   routine name                        line      rel PC    abs PC

ENERGY        ENERGY                               43       0000024C 000005A0
169
```

Figure 5-8

Corrected Version of the Spectroscopy Program

```
ENERGY                                                          VAX Pascal V3.0-2
Source Listing

00001          Program ENERGY (Input, Output);
00002
00003          Const P = 8.850E-12;        (* Permeativity constant *)
00004                m = 9.109E-28;         (* Mass of the electron *)
00005                e = 4.803E-10;         (* Charge on an electron *)
00006                h = 6.625E-27;         (* Planck's constant *)
00007                c = 3.000E10;          (* Speed of light *)
00008                F = 1.238E-20;         (* Conversion factor to ensure proper units *)
00009                                       (* of emitted light *)
00010          Var   n1, n2 : Integer;      (* Index to energy levels *)
00011                   Z : Integer;        (* Atomic number of isotope *)
00012                E1, E2 : Real;         (* Energy of the levels *)
00013                   Et : Real;          (* Energy of the transition *)
00014                 v, l : Real;          (* Frequency, wavelength of emitted light *)
00015
00016                    R : Real;          (* Rydberg constant *)
00017
```

Figure 5-8 continued

```
00018          BEGIN
00019
00020             Write ('Enter the lowest level........');
00021             Readln (n1);
00022             Write ('Enter the highest level......');
00023             Readln (n2);
00024             Write ('Enter the atomic number......');
00025             Readln (Z);
00026
00027             R := m*e*e*e*e*Z*Z / (8*p*p*h*h) * F;
00028
00029             E1 := R*(1 / (n1*n1));
00030             E2 := R*(1 / (n2*n2));
00031
00032             Et := E1 - E2 ;
00033
00034             v := Et / h;
00035             l := c / v;
00036
00037             Writeln ('The energy of the first level is ', E1);
00038             Writeln ('The energy of the second level is   ', E2);
00039             Writeln ('The energy of transition is         ', Et);
00040             Writeln;
00041             Writeln ('The frequency of emitted light is   ', v);
00042             Writeln ('The wavelength of emitted light is  ', l)
00043
00044          END.
282
```

Figure 5-9

Sample Run of the Corrected Spectroscopy Program

```
$ run energy

Enter the lowest level........2
Enter the highest level......3
Enter the atomic number......1
%SYSTEM-F-FLTDIV_F, arithmetic fault, floating divide by zero at PC=000003A9,
%TRACE-F-TRACEBACK, symbolic stack dump follows
module name      routine name                   line       rel PC      abs PC

ENERGY           ENERGY                          27       00000095    000003A9
```

Figure 5-10

*Sample Run of the Spectroscopy Program, with Diagnostic Outputs
for the Constants*

```
$ run energy

Enter the lowest level........2
Enter the highest level.......3
Enter the atomic number.......1
M   =   9.10900E-28
E   =   4.80300E-10
P   =   8.8500E-12
H   =   6.62500E-27
F   =   1.23800E-20
%SYSTEM-F-FLTDIV_F, arithmetic fault, floating divide by zero at PC=000004E4,
%TRACE-F-TRACEBACK, symbolic stack dump follows
module name      routine name                        line      rel PC      abs PC

ENERGY           ENERGY                               32      000001A8  000004E4
```

this specific computer was designed, and intended, to make this specific approximation. This error might not have occurred on a different computer. Although painful, this is something that must be recognized and occasionally expected.

So what do we do about it? Well, we need to balance the calculations (alter the program) so as not to let things get so far out of hand. One solution is shown in Figure 5-11, where computational groupings are made so that any intermediate calculation remains (relatively) large. Compiling and executing (testing) this new program yields the correct output, as shown in Figure 5-12.

The process of successively narrowing down the error location, as demonstrated above, is the key to relatively easy debugging. The same principles can be used on run-time errors of the second category of "manifestations"; the only difference is that, instead of receiving a message from the computer that something is wrong, you must recognize that the results are incorrect yourself.

Now that the program works correctly, we may resume the program development process.

STEP 5: DOCUMENT

The program is well documented; variables and constants are explained with comments, and the visual presentation makes the structure stand out.

This concludes the demonstration of run-time error debugging. The errors were fairly subtle, but they illustrate the kinds of things that can go wrong and the techniques for dealing with them.

Figure 5-11

Final Version of the Spectroscopy Program

```
ENERGYOK                                              VAX Pascal V3.0-2
Source Listing


00001             Program ENERGY (Input, Output);
00002
00003             Const p = 8.850E-12;      (* Permeativity constant *)
00004                   m = 9.109E-28;      (* Mass of the electron *)
00005                   e = 4.803E-10;      (* Charge on an electron *)
00006                   h = 6.625E-27;      (* Planck's constant *)
00007                   c = 3.000E10;       (* Speed of light *)
00008                   F = 1.238E-20;      (* Conversion factor to ensure proper units *)
00009
00010             Var   n1, n2 : Integer;   (* Index to energy levels *)
00011                        Z : Integer;   (* Atomic number of isotope *)
00012                   E1, E2 : Real;       (* Energy of the levels *)
00013                       Et : Real;       (* Energy of the transition *)
00014                     v, l : Real;       (* Frequency, wavelength of emitted light *)
00015
00016                        R : Real;       (* Rydberg constant *)
00017
00018             BEGIN
00019
00020                Write ('Enter the lowest level.......');
00021                Readln (n1);
00022                Write ('Enter the highest level......');
00023                Readln (n2);
00024                Write ('Enter the atomic number......');
00025                Readln (Z);
00026
00027                R  := m / (8*p*p)*(e*e/h)*(e*e/h) * F;
00028
00029                E1 := R*(1 / (n1*n1));
00030                E2 := R*(1 / (n2*n2));
00031
00032                Et := E1 - E2;
00033
00034                v  := Et / h;
00035                l  := c  / v;
00036
00037                Writeln ('The energy of the first level is   ', E1);
00038                Writeln ('The energy of the second level is  ', E2);
00039                Writeln ('The energy of transition is        ', Et);
00040                Writeln;
00041                Writeln ('The frequency of emitted light is  ', v);
00042                Writeln ('The wavelength of emitted light is ', l)
00043
00044             END.
126
```

Figure 5-12

Output from the Correct Version of the Spectroscopy Program

```
$ run energy

Enter the lowest level.......2
Enter the highest level......3
Enter the atomic number......1
The energy of the first level is    5.45549E-12
The energy of the second level is   2.42466E-12
The energy of transition is         3.03083E-12

The frequency of emitted light is   4.57483E+14
The wavelength of emitted light is  6.55762E-05
```

SUMMARY

In this chapter we have categorized the kinds of errors that can occur and presented general and specific methods for dealing with them. Four debugging phases, similar in nature to the five developmental phases, can be used to advantage here. In general, errors can be divided up into syntax errors and run-time errors, depending on when they occur. The former are usually easier to deal with because they are not as subtle as the latter.

EXERCISES

CONCEPTS

1. Define or explain the following terms:

Clerical errors	Logic errors
Diagnostic output statement	Run-time errors
Hand trace	Spurious errors
Intermittent errors	Syntax errors

2. What are the four phases that should be utilized during debugging?

3. Briefly explain the ways in which errors may manifest themselves.

4. Explain the difference between finding an error via a sequential search versus successive isolation.

TOOLS

5. Identify and correct the errors in the following program:

```
00001             Program MUCKEE;
00002
00003             Var x,v,a,t : Real;
00004
00005             BEGIN
00006                 Write ('Enter acceleration : ');
                         1
%PASCAL-E-OUTNOTDECL, (1) OUTPUT not declared in heading
00007                 Read (a);
                         1
%PASCAL-E-INPNOTDECL, (1) INPUT not declared in heading
00008                 Write ('Enter total time : ');
                         1
%PASCAL-E-OUTNOTDECL, (1) OUTPUT not declared in heading
00009                 Readline (t);
                         1
%PASCAL-E-UNDECLID, (1) Undeclared identifier READLINE
00010
00011                 x := x0 + v0 t + 1/2 a t t;
                         1    2  3         4 5
%PASCAL-E-UNDECLID, (1) Undeclared identifier X0
%PASCAL-E-UNDECLID, (2) Undeclared identifier V0
%PASCAL-E-SYNSEMMODI, (3) Syntax: ";", "::", "^", "," or "[" expected
%PASCAL-E-SYNSEMI, (4) Syntax: ";" expected
%PASCAL-E-NOTAFUNC, (4) A is not declared as a PROCEDURE or FUNCTION
%PASCAL-E-SYNIVPRMLST, (5) Syntax: illegal actual parameter list
00012
00013                 Writeln ('The new location is ', x:6.2)
                         1                                 2
%PASCAL-E-OUTNOTDECL, (1) OUTPUT not declared in heading
%PASCAL-E-FLDWDTHINT, (2) Field-width expression must be of type INTEGER
00014         END.
```

6. Identify and correct the errors in the following program:

```
00001             Progam YUCK (Input, Output);
                     1
%PASCAL-E-SYNPROMOD, (1) Syntax: PROGRAM or MODULE expected
00002
00003             Var A,B,C;
                           1
%PASCAL-E-SYNCOMCOL, (1) Syntax: "," or ":" expected
00004
00005             BEGIN
                     1
%PASCAL-I-MISSINGEND, (1) No matching END, expected near line 11
00006                 Print ('Enter a value for A : ');
                         1
%PASCAL-E-UNDECLID, (1) Undeclared Identifier PRINT
00007                 Read (A);
00008                 B = 5 . 75 * A / 2;
                         1 2
%PASCAL-E-SYNASSIGN, (1) Syntax: ":=" expected
%PASCAL-E-SYNNEWSTMT, (2) Syntax: start of new statement expected
00009                 C = A + -B * (A * B);
                         1       2
```

```
%PASCAL-E-SYNASSIGN, (1) Syntax: ":=" expected
%PASCAL-E-SYNILLEXPR, (2) Syntax: ill-formed expression
00010              Print ('The results are ', B:5, C:5)
                                            1      2
%PASCAL-E-SYNCOMRP, (1) Syntax: "," or ")" expected
%PASCAL-E-SYNCOMRP, (2) Syntax: "," or ")" expected
00011            EMD.
                 1    2
%PASCAL-E-SYNSEMI, (1) Syntax: ";" expected
%PASCAL-E-UNDECLID, (1) Undeclared identifier EMD
%PASCAL-E-SYNIDENT, (2) Syntax: identifier expected
%PASCAL-E-SYNEXPR, (2) Syntax: expression expected
%PASCAL-E-SYNILLEXPR, (2) Syntax: ill-formed expression
%PASCAL-E-SYNPERIOD, (2) Syntax: "." expected
```

PROBLEMS

7. Debug the following program; a sample run is shown after the listing.

```
00001 Program BREAKEVEN (Input, Output);
00002
00003 (* This program determines the breakeven point for any
00004    manufactured item *)
00005
00006 Var OperatingExpenses, UnitLabor, UnitMaterial : Real;
00007    SalesExpenses, UnitPrice : Real;
00008
00009    N (* Number to break even *) : Real;
00010
00011 BEGIN
00012    Write ('Enter Operating Expenses : '); Readln (OperatingExpenses);
00013    Write ('Enter Unit Labor Cost : ')   ; Readln (UnitLabor);
00014    Write ('Enter Unit Material Cost : '); Readln (UnitMaterial);
00015    Writeln;
00016    Writeln;
00017    Write ('Enter Sales Expenses : ');     Readln (SalesExpenses);
00018    Write ('Enter Unit Price : ');         Readln (UnitPrice);
00019
00020    N := (SalesExpenses + OperatingExpenses) /
00021         (UnitPrice - (UnitLabor + UnitMaterial));
00022
00023    Writeln ('The breakeven number is ', N:6:0)
00024 END.


$ run breakeven

Enter Operating Expenses : 1250
Enter Unit Labor Cost : 18.50
Enter Unit Material Cost : 7.75

Enter Sales Expenses : 425
Enter Unit Price : 26.25

%SYSTEM-F-FLTDIV_F, arithmetic fault, floating divide by zero at PC=000004B2
%TRACE-F-TRACEBACK, symbolic stack dump follows
module name     routine name          line      rel PC      abs PC

BREAKEVEN       BREAKEVEN              20     0000011F   000003B3
```

8. Debug the following program; a sample run is included. The output from this run is grossly in error.

```
00001  Program INCREASE (Input, Output);
00002
00003  (* This program computes dollar amounts after a given time
00004   using simple interest.*)
00005
00006  Var InitialAmt, NewAmt, Time, InterestRate : Real;
00007
00008  BEGIN
00009     Write ('Enter initial amount of investment : ');
00010     Readln (InitialAmt);
00011     Write ('Enter Annual Interest Rate : ');
00012     Readln (InterestRate);
00013     Write ('Enter Number of Years : ');
00014     Readln (Time);
00015
00016     NewAmt := InitialAmt * InterestRate * Time;
00017
00018     Writeln ('The new amount is $', NewAmt:4:1)
00019  END.


$ run increase

Enter initial amount of investment : 1536.84
Enter Annual Interest Rate : 11.8
Enter Number of Years : 5
The new amount is $90673.65
```

6

Procedures and Functions:

Building Blocks and Physical Modularity

*T*hroughout this text the concept of *modularity* has been stressed. Further, we have discussed and demonstrated the advantages of using top-down design and stepwise refinement in problem solving. In generating and implementing algorithms, we divide the total problem into conceptual sections so that each part can be dealt with easily. We then continue this process until a sufficiently detailed solution is reached. Recall, for example, the development of the Hal's Hamburger solution in Chapter 3. The complete solution was accomplished by breaking down the whole problem into a number of smaller problems, each of which had a simpler solution than the original.

In this chapter we will extend and formalize the concept of modularity to include **physical modularity,** whereby subtasks are separated not only logically by program or algorithm presentation but also physically by isolating the subtask section in terms of location and execution sequence. We will begin by demonstrating the usefulness of physical modularity and then show how it can be utilized in Pascal.

6-1 *Physical Modularity*

Physical modularity enhances even further the advantages of the modular approach and is manifested in the concept of subprograms, which are defined as follows:

> A **subprogram** is a section of code designed to carry out a specific subtask, but it is also a named unit and is physically removed from the point in the program where the task it performs is actually carried out.

In general, the existence of subprograms implies the existence of a **main program,** which is a special program unit in which execution commences. In Pascal the main program corresponds to the executable section of a program.

This more involved concept of modularity can be illustrated with the typical audio system shown in Figure 6-1. Here, a stereo amplifier is connected to an open-reel tape recorder, a record turntable, an AM/FM radio receiver, and a cassette tape player. At any time the amplifier can call on any of the other devices to provide the signal, which will be transmitted at audio frequencies through the air. This same principle can be used in modular program design: a particular subtask can be written as a subprogram and called on at an appropriate place in the main program. Thus, in keeping with our analogy, the amplifier corresponds to the main program and the audio input units to subprograms.

Pursuing this analogy, let us consider some of the advantages of modularity. If there is something wrong with one of the modules (including the main program), it can be removed and tested, corrected or replaced relatively easily, without affecting the other units or the entire system. Also, *it is not necessary for the entire system to be assembled and functioning before one of the parts is altered or improved.* This is an extremely important consideration.

Let us consider another example of modularity, this time specifically regarding computer programming. Suppose, as part of the solution to a problem, that you must alphabetize a list of names. You can accomplish this by including in the middle of the algorithm (or pro-

Figure 6-1

A Component Stereo System Presents a Good Example of Modularity

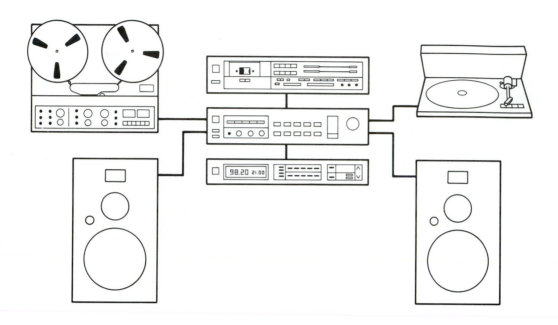

gram) a sequence of steps to order the names; however, because the program sections are intertwined (not physically modular), testing and debugging this section depend on knowing that the rest of the program functioned properly. Otherwise, errors could not necessarily be isolated in the alphabetization section. Worse yet, suppose that a better alphabetizing method was found. Introducing this change into the entire program would be difficult and could lead to more errors.

Further, suppose that the full solution to this problem requires that (1) a list of names be alphabetized near the beginning of the program and (2) a list of identification codes be alphabetized near the end. This could, in fact, be done by writing the alphabetization sequence twice, once for the names and once for the ID codes. Obviously there has to be a better way. In fact, a physically separate module that does nothing but alphabetization would take care of both tasks quite nicely!

A potential difficulty arises here, however: since subprograms are, in fact, physically separate from the main program, we must consider how one is to get *to* the subprogram and back again. Figure 6-2 presents a schematic depiction of how this is done for a program (such as the above) that carries out alphabetization via a separate routine (module). Note that the main program and alphabetization routine are physically separate. Execution proceeds through the main program until it is nec-

Figure 6-2

Control Flow Through a Modular Program That Includes a
Subprogram for Alphabetization

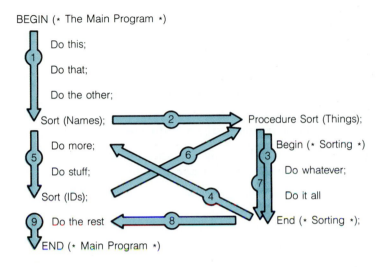

essary for the names to be sorted (that is, alphabetized). At this point execution is transferred away from the main program to the sort routine, where the names are alphabetized. This is termed a **call** to the subprogram. At the conclusion of the sort, control moves *back* to the main program at the point *immediately following the subprogram transfer;* this is a **return.** Execution then continues normally through the main program until it encounters the next required sort (this time of ID codes), whereupon control again is transferred to the alphabetization routine. Then, on completion of the task, control returns to the main program, where it continues until the end of the program is reached.

The sequence of events associated with the execution of a main program and attendant subprograms is very similar to what humans follow in executing a task. For example, suppose you are putting up walls as a part of the process of building a house. You first nail together the frame and then stand it up in a vertical position. Your next tasks are to nail sheetrock to the frame, then apply plaster, and finally paint the walls. But before you can do these three operations, you must suspend your activities until the electricians install the wiring. In this case you would be the main program, which stops temporarily until the subroutine (the electricians) completes its assigned task. After the electricians have finished, you would resume activity from the point at which you stopped, namely, nailing on the sheetrock.

Given this initial presentation, it can be seen that explicit physical modularity in computer programs, stereo systems, construction projects—in fact in any complex system—has a number of advantages, as follows:

1. **Structure.** The structure of the entire system is enhanced and more readily evident.

2. **Temporality.** The solution of a subtask can be worked on independently at a later, more convenient time and need not interrupt work on the remainder of the main program.

3. **Repetition.** A particular task need be implemented only once, even if it must be carried out several times in different places.

4. **Decoupling.** Changing the specifics of a particular subprogram can be done easily without affecting the remaining components.

5. **Testing.** Each subprogram can be tested individually without having to first ensure that the entire system is functioning properly.

6. **Generalization.** The subprogram can be general, that is, it needn't be written only for the specific considerations of the problem at hand.

Basically, subprograms substantially enhance the advantages we sought earlier with the conceptual (rather than physical) isolation of subtasks. However, a mechanism must exist that permits moving back and forth from one program unit or task to another, and this takes a toll in terms of execution time and computer memory required by the program. Nonetheless, the advantages of physical modularity generally outweigh the disadvantages and allow the programmer to do some interesting new things.

We have been thus far considering generic subprograms, but in fact there are two specific categories of subprograms that are widely utilized: **functions** and **procedures.** Although the two types have many characteristics in common, each has properties that make it particularly well suited to solving different kinds of problems. The next section introduces both functions and procedures.

6-2   *Types of Subprograms*

We will first look at functions. The primary characteristic of a function is that its assigned task, no matter how complex, must be such that it presents, or returns, *exactly one single result* to the program section that invoked the function. A function cannot return nothing, and it cannot return two or more items. The name *function* in fact is related to the mathematical term in which some operations are carried out and a single value generated. More often than not, functions are mathematical or numerical in nature and are such that they provide a result that can be used in an expression. A simple example can be found in the square function, that is, the function that multiplies a number by itself. This function can be expressed mathematically as

$$f(x) = x^2$$

This defines a function of x that returns the square of x, that is, the result obtained by multiplying a number (designated as x, in this case) by itself. Note that exactly one unambiguous answer is generated!

In mathematical terminology, x is called a **parameter,** and it is something used to define the function. This is important: *parameters do not really exist;* they are merely a way of expressing the *definition of the function.* In order to evaluate the function, an **argument** must be supplied. An argument is a for-real, honest-to-goodness value that is substituted for the parameter in the function definition. The indicated computations are then carried out on the argument, and a resultant value is calculated.

An example can help clarify these definitions. Using the above definition of the square function, we could substitute the *argument* 5 for the *parameter x* in the definition of $f(x)$. Having done this, we would compute $f(5)$, which according to the definition is 5 times 5, and return the result 25.

Now, having defined $f(x)$ to be x squared, we could use this function in further calculations. For example, we might have

```
3.6 * f(angle) / delta
```

We can evaluate this expression as follows (assuming angle has a value of 0.47 and delta has a value of 2.5):

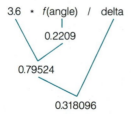

Note that the idea of a function fits in neatly with the idea of expression and in fact extends the concept.

Procedures are a second type of subprogram that is more general than a function. A procedure may be constructed to return any arbitrary number of results, from zero to anything less than infinity (in practice actually much less than infinity). The nature of procedures is such that they may *not* be used in expressions. An example of a procedure is the Sort, or alphabetization, routine mentioned earlier. This procedure sorts a list of unalphabetized names and returns it in alphabetical order. As is true for functions, procedures are defined in terms of parameters, and arguments are used to actually carry out the task. In the case of the Sort procedure, the argument would consist of the unalphabetized list and the procedure would return an alphabetized list (more than one value!).

With this brief introduction, let's look at each of the subprogram types in detail.

6-3 *Functions*

Functions, as we saw, are often mathematical in nature and can return only a single value. In Pascal there are two kinds of functions: those available as a part of the language (the so-called **predefined functions**) and those you can define yourself (termed **programmer-defined** or **user-defined** functions). Predefined functions are a good way to ease into the concept of subprogram, so let us begin with those.

PREDEFINED FUNCTIONS

Predefined functions are functions used so frequently that they are supplied as a part of the Pascal language. You needn't worry about writing them, because they have already been implemented for you. In order to use them, you need only reference them. A partial list of the predefined functions available in Pascal is given in Figure 6-3. Function references always have the same format, namely,

function-name (argument-list)

The argument list more often than not consists of a single argument, although there is no rule that states this must be so. In fact, some functions may have two or more arguments. Also note that the functions listed in Figure 6-3 are very specific with regard to the data types you can use as arguments and the types of results that are returned. A function reference can be used anywhere within the executable section of a program that a constant can be used.

Figure 6-3

Some Predefined Pascal Functions

Function	Description	Argument Type	Result Type	Example
sqr	Square; multiply a number by itself	Real	Real	sqr(2.5) → 6.25
		Integer	Integer	sqr(4) → 16
sqrt	Square root of a number	Real	Real	sqrt(13.69) → 3.7
		Integer	Real	sqrt(5) → 2.236
sin	Sine of an angle; angle must be in radians	Real	Real	sin(0.785) → 0.707
		Integer	Real	sin(3) → 0.141
cos	Cosine of an angle; angle must be in radians	Real	Real	cos(1.05) → 0.498
		Integer	Real	cos(6) → 0.960
arctan	Arctangent; result is an angle in radians	Real	Real	arctan(0.75) → 0.643
		Integer	Real	arctan(2) → 1.107
ln	Natural logarithm, to the base e	Real	Real	ln(2.5) → 0.916
		Integer	Real	ln(10) → 2.303
exp	Exponential, e to a power; inverse of ln	Real	Real	exp(0.455) → 1.576
		Integer	Real	exp(3) → 20.085
abs	Absolute value	Real	Real	abs(-7.3) → 7.3
		Integer	Integer	abs(3544) → 3544
round	Round a number	Real	Integer	round(5.43) → 5 round(5.5) → 6 round(-7.3) → -7 round(-4.9) → -5
trunc	Truncation; all fractional parts are dropped	Real	Integer	trunc(5.75) → 5 trunc(-4.9) → -4 trunc(25.1) → 25

Radar Tracking

In order to demonstrate predefined functions, let us develop an application that uses them. Consider a radar installation that is in the process of tracking an airplane. In general, the radar returns only two pieces of information: the range between the antenna and the plane and the angle of the plane relative to the ground. This situation is shown in Figure 6-4a. However, people tend to want different information, specifically, ground distance from the installation, altitude, actual velocity, ground speed, and the rate at which the plane is gaining or losing altitude (rise). The first two of these require a single radar reading, but the rest require two successive readings and the amount of time that has passed between those readings. The problem to be solved, then, is to write a program that inputs two sets of range and angle information from the radar and computes the desired information. Let us go through the program development process for this.

STEP 1: UNDERSTAND THE PROBLEM

The first thing to do is to list the inputs and outputs. These can be written directly from the above description as

Input: Range1, Angle1, Time1, Range2, Angle2, Time2

Output: Distance, Altitude,
            Velocity, Ground Speed, Rise

It appears, then, that what is to be done is quite clear. The trick is to find appropriate calculations that generate the requisite output. Actually, the solution relies almost entirely on plane (not airplane) trigonometry. The first outputs can be calculated directly from the inputs as

Distance ← Range × Cosine (Angle)

Altitude ← Range × Sine (Angle)

We can use either the first or the second set of radar inputs to compute these quantities, but the second would, of course, be more current.

The remaining three items (namely, velocity, ground speed, and rise) require *two* sets of distances and altitudes, along with the time elapsed between readings. This complicates things somewhat, but given the four quantities of initial distance and altitude and final distance and altitude, the remaining information can be computed.

The ground speed can be calculated easily. Since both distances and

Figure 6-4

(a) Typical Airplane-Radar Configuration and (b) Velocity
Relationships of a Moving Airplane

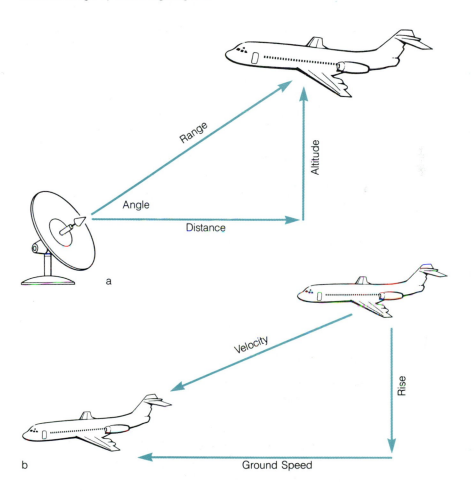

the time are known, the average ground speed is just the distance covered divided by the elapsed time, that is,

$$\text{Ground Speed} \leftarrow \frac{\text{Second Distance} - \text{First Distance}}{\text{Elapsed Time}}$$

The rise is exactly the same thing, only in a vertical direction, and hence can be expressed as

$$\text{Rise} \leftarrow \frac{\text{Second Altitude} - \text{First Altitude}}{\text{Elapsed Time}}$$

The velocity is a little tougher, in that it is computed on the distance between the first plane location and the second. However, trigonometry again comes to the rescue because that distance (let us call it Travel, as shown in Figure 6-4b) is given by

$$\text{Travel} \leftarrow \sqrt{(\text{2nd Alt} - \text{1st Alt})^2 + (\text{2nd Dist} - \text{1st Dist})^2}$$

Therefore, the velocity becomes simply

$$\text{Velocity} \leftarrow \frac{\text{Travel}}{\text{Elapsed Time}}$$

STEP 2: PLAN THE SOLUTION

Now that we have all the formulas, we need only convert them to an algorithm. As always, let's start with a very general algorithm:

Get the First Radar Readings of Range, Angle, and Time
Get the Second Radar Readings of Range, Angle, and Time
Compute the First Distance and First Altitude
Compute the Second Distance and Second Altitude
Compute the Velocity, GroundSpeed, and Rise
Output the Results

Filling in the computational details generates our second algorithm:

Get the First Radar Readings of Range, Angle, and Time
   Read Range1, Angle1, Time1

Get the Second Radar Readings of Range, Angle, and Time
   Read Range2, Angle2, Time2

Compute the First Distance and First Altitude
   Distance1 ← Range1 × Cos (Angle1)
   Altitude 1 ← Range1 × Sin (Angle1)

Compute the Second Distance and Second Altitude
   Distance2 ← Range2 × Cos (Angle2)
   Altitude2 ← Range2 × Sin (Angle2)

Compute the Velocity, GroundSpeed, and Rise

   ElapsedTime ← Time2 − Time1

   $\text{Travel} \leftarrow \sqrt{(\text{Distance2} - \text{Distance1})^2 + (\text{Altitude2} - \text{Altitude1})^2}$

   $\text{Velocity} \leftarrow \dfrac{\text{Travel}}{\text{ElapsedTime}}$

   $\text{GroundSpeed} \leftarrow \dfrac{(\text{Distance2} - \text{Distance1})}{\text{ElapsedTime}}$

$$\text{Rise} \leftarrow \frac{(\text{Altitude2} - \text{Altitude1})}{\text{ElapsedTime}}$$

Output the Results
  Write Distance2, Altitude2, Velocity, GroundSpeed, Rise

There is one other problem with this algorithm as it stands, namely, all the distances are in *miles* and all the times are in *seconds*. This means that the altitude will be in miles and the various speeds will be in miles per second. This is not normally the way these quantities are expressed. Altitude should be in feet, air speed and ground speed should be in miles per hour, and the rise should be in feet per second. This can be taken care of easily by using appropriate conversion factors, in this case 5,280 ft/mi and 3,600 sec/hr (these factors are actually constant and can be defined and used as such). Making these additions yields a final algorithm of

Get the First Radar Readings of Range, Angle, and Time
  Read Range1, Angle1, Time1

Get the Second Radar Readings of Range, Angle, and Time
  Read Range2, Angle2, Time2

Compute the First Distance and First Altitude
  Distance1 ← Range1 × Cos (Angle1)
  Altitude1 ← Range1 × Sin (Angle1)

Compute the Second Distance and Second Altitude
  Distance2 ← Range2 × Cos (Angle2)
  Altitude2 ← Range2 × Sin (Angle2)

  Height ← Altitude2 × FtPerMi

Compute the Velocity, GroundSpeed, and Rise
  ElapsedTime ← Time2 − Time1

$$\text{Travel} \leftarrow \sqrt{(\text{Distance2} - \text{Distance1})^2 + (\text{Altitude2} - \text{Altitude1})^2}$$

$$\text{Velocity} \leftarrow \frac{\text{Travel}}{\text{ElapsedTime}} \times \text{SecPerHr}$$

$$\text{GroundSpeed} \leftarrow \frac{(\text{Distance2} - \text{Distance1})}{\text{ElapsedTime}} \times \text{SecPerHr}$$

$$\text{Rise} \leftarrow \frac{(\text{Altitude2} - \text{Altitude1}) \times \text{FtPerMi}}{\text{ElapsedTime}}$$

Output the Results
  Write Distance2, Height, Velocity, GroundSpeed, Rise

Note that we had to add the variable Height to simplify the altitude calculation, since both altitudes are used a great deal throughout the algorithm.

This completes the algorithm, and we may move on to the next step.

STEP 3: CODE THE SOLUTION

This final step results in the program shown in Figure 6-5. Note that this program requires the use of the predefined functions Sin, Cos, Sqr, and Sqrt.

Figure 6-5

Complete RADAR *Program with Sample Run*

RADAR.PAS

```
 1    Program RADAR (Input, Output);
 2
 3    (*
 4        This program simulates the operation of a radar installation
 5        tracking an airplane. Input consists of the range (distance)
 6        of the object from the radar antenna as well as the angle of
 7        the object with respect to the antenna. Two such sets of
 8        measurements are then used to generate information regarding
 9        the speed, direction, and altitude of the aircraft.
10    *)
11
12    Const SecPerHr = 3600;       (* Conversion factors *)
13          FtPerMi  = 5280;
14
15    Var Range1, Angle1, Time1,   (* First set of measurements from antenna *)
16        Range2, Angle2, Time2,   (* Second set *)
17
18        Distance1, Distance2,                (* Computed quantities for *)
19        Altitude1, Altitude2, Height,        (* the aircraft being tracked *)
20        Travel, ElapsedTime,
21        Velocity, GroundSpeed, Rise : Real;
22
23    BEGIN
24
25    (* Get the radar readings *)
26
27        Readln (Range1, Angle1, Time1);
28        Readln (Range2, Angle2, Time2);
29
30    (* Compute the corresponding distances and altitudes *)
31
32        Distance1 := Range1 * Cos (Angle1);
33        Altitude1 := Range1 * Sin (Angle1);
34
35        Distance2 := Range2 * Cos (Angle2);
36        Altitude2 := Range2 * Sin (Angle2);
37
38        Height := Altitude2 * FtPerMi;
39
40    (* Compute the air speed, ground speed, and rise *)
41
42        ElapsedTime := Time2 - Time1;
43
44        Travel := Sqrt (Sqr (Distance2 - Distance1) +
45                        Sqr (Altitude2 - Altitude1));
46
```

Figure 6-5 continued

```
47      Velocity := Travel / ElapsedTime * SecPerHr;
48
49      GroundSpeed := (Distance2 - Distance1) / ElapsedTime * SecPerHr;
50
51      Rise := (Altitude2 - Altitude1) * FtPerMi / ElapsedTime;
52
53   (* Print this stuff out *)
54
55      Writeln; Writeln;
56      Writeln ('Distance = ', Distance2:8:1,   'mi');
57      Writeln ('Altitude = ', Height:8:1,      'ft');
58      Writeln ('GroundSp = ', GroundSpeed:8:1, 'mph');
59      Writeln ('Velocity = ', Velocity:8:1,    'mph');
60      Writeln ('Rise     = ', Rise:8:1,        'fps')
61
62   END.
```

```
$ run radar

38.39 0.123837 0.0
37.99 0.124029 2.5

Distance =     37.7 mi
Altitude = 24814.9 ft
GroundSp =  -572.9 mph
Velocity =   576.1 mph
Rise     =   -89.1 fps
```

STEP 4: CHECK OUT THE PROGRAM

Included with the actual program of Figure 6-5 are a test run and output. An examination of the resulting numbers shows that they are correct.

STEP 5: DOCUMENT

The program as written is easily understood.

This concludes our introduction to predefined functions, and we are ready to move on to programmer-defined functions.

PROGRAMMER-DEFINED FUNCTIONS

The following example illustrates the use of, and the need for, programmer-defined functions. It also illustrates the benefits of program modularity in reducing the effort required to derive the solution.

Ace Trucking Company

Suppose you work for the Ace Trucking Company (ATC). ATC is a delivery service in Cart City. Customers call ATC and request a truck to pick up goods at one location and deliver them to another. The cost of the service is based on the weight of the cargo and the total distance traveled by the ATC truck. For any section of the journey, the cost is computed as written:

$$Cost \leftarrow DistanceTraveled \times (BaseRate + CargoWeight \times Cost\,per\,Unit\,Weight)$$

Naturally, the cost of going from the ATC office to the customer with an empty truck would be different than for traveling with a loaded truck from the customer to the destination. These factors must be taken into account when computing the cost of each of the three "legs" of the journey, namely,

1. From ATC office to customer (empty)

2. From customer to destination (full weight)

3. From destination back to ATC office (again empty)

You, as a programmer for ATC, are asked to write a program that will use as input the weight of the cargo, the address of the customer, and the address of the destination, and will then compute the total cost of the delivery.

STEP 1: UNDERSTAND THE PROBLEM

The first step, as always, is to get a handle on exactly how this problem is to be solved. A good place to start is to define the input and the output, so let us begin there:

Input Required for the Program
  Cargo Weight
  Customer Address
  Delivery Address

We also need the base rate and the cost per unit weight of the cargo, but we assume that they are constants and will treat them as such. (Making these items constants will permit them to be more easily changed should the need arise.) We also presume that ATC is not a fly-by-night outfit, and that it has a fixed and known address.

Unlike the examples we have seen so far, exactly how these inputs are to be represented is not self-evident. The primary problem is how the addresses are to be specified. How can we represent them?

Since Cart City is of relatively recent origin, the city designers have planned the streets carefully. The center of town is located at the intersection of Main and Center Streets, and the roads extend from these to the North, South, East, and West at exactly one-block intervals. The blocks are numbered in units of 100, so that an address of 250 East Main Street corresponds exactly to two-and-a-half blocks East of the center of town. The general street map is shown in Figure 6-6. Also, the city distances are such that there are exactly six blocks to the mile.

Next, we need some way to represent addresses in Cart City. An easy way to do this is to represent them as pairs of numbers, where the first number gives the East-West part of the address and the second number gives the North-South part of it. Since we only want to use two numbers, we can assign positive values to the East and North distances and

Figure 6-6

Street Map of Cart City

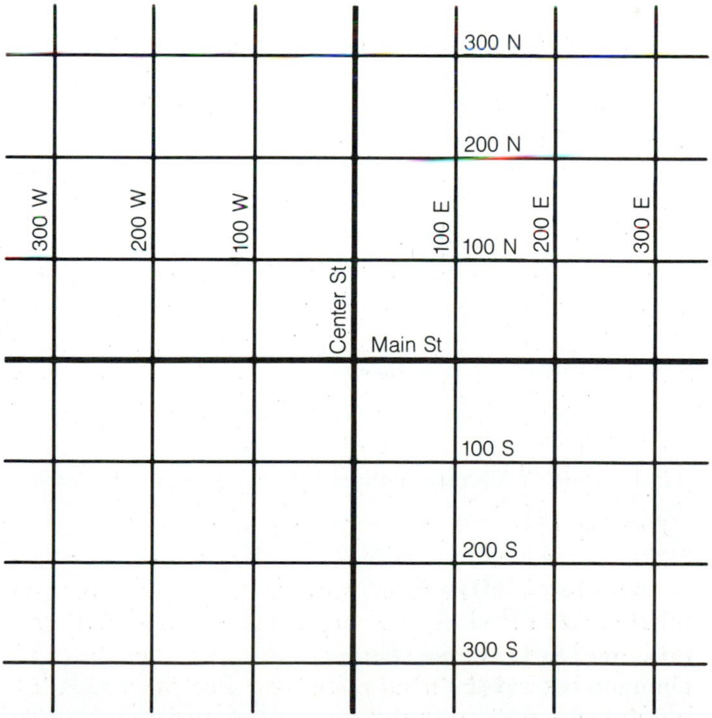

negative values to the West and South distances. For example, the following addresses would be represented by the following pairs of numbers:

Address	Pair Representation
250 East Main	250, 0
525 West 300 North	− 525, 300
100 West 100 South	− 100, − 100

We now have a way of converting a real street address into a pair of numbers that the computer can easily use.

Moving on, the output we want to generate is

Output from the Program
   Cargo Weight
   Distance for Leg 1 (blocks and miles), Cost of Leg 1
   Distance for Leg 2 (blocks and miles), Cost of Leg 2
   Distance for Leg 3 (blocks and miles), Cost of Leg 3
   Total Distance, Total Cost of Delivery

Following previous examples, let us generate a mock-up of the output to help us:

Summary of Charges for ACE TRUCKING COMPANY

Cargo Weight:	5.0 tons
From ATC to Customer:	36 blocks (6.0 miles) $ 9.00
Customer to Destination:	60 blocks (10.0 miles) $50.00
Destination to ATC:	12 blocks (2.0 miles) $ 3.00
Total Trip:	108 blocks (18.0 miles) $62.00

STEP 2: PLAN THE SOLUTION

We can quickly write the most general algorithm as

Read Customer Address, Delivery Destination, Cargo Weight

Compute Leg 1 Distance
Compute Leg 1 Cost

Compute Leg 2 Distance
Compute Leg 2 Cost

Compute Leg 3 Distance
Compute Leg 3 Cost

Compute Total Distance

Compute Total Cost

Output the Weight and all the Distances and Costs

Having written this general algorithm, we can fill in the details, following our general-to-specific approach:

Prompt 'Customer Address'
Read CustomerEW, CustomerNS

Prompt 'Delivery Destination'
Read DestinationEW, DestinationNS

Prompt 'Cargo Weight'
Read CargoWeight

However, at this point, we discover that things get extremely complicated. We need to figure out *how* we calculate distances. We also note that we must do essentially the same calculation three times! Therefore, this is a good time to use *functions*. First, this computation must be carried out more than once (three times, in fact), and it returns but a single value (the actual distance traveled). By using functions, we can defer consideration of exactly how to carry out the calculation until later! Following this approach we therefore continue by indicating a procedure call, but we ignore a consideration of the details:

Leg1 ← Distance (ATC, Customer)
Cost1 ← Leg1 × BaseRate

Leg2 ← Distance (Customer, Destination)
Cost2 ← Leg2 × (BaseRate + CargoWeight × UnitRateWt)

Leg3 ← Distance (Destination, ATC)
Cost3 ← Leg3 × BaseRate

Note that we have decided to name the function `Distance` and write it pretty much like any mathematical function. Further, in this case there are *two* arguments to the function: the first location and the second location. Again, we do not need *at this time* to consider exactly how we are going to implement this function.

We continue on with the main algorithm:

TotalLength ← Leg1 + Leg2 + Leg3
TotalCost ← Cost1 + Cost2 + Cost3

Output everything as per mock-up generated above

To come up with our final algorithm, we note that the actual arguments to the function consist of an ordered pair of integers that correspond to addresses in the city. Adding these details gives us our final algorithm:

Prompt 'Customer Address'
Read CustomerEW, CustomerNS

Prompt 'Deliver Destination'
Read DestinationEW, DestinationNS

Prompt 'Cargo Weight'
Read CargoWeight

Leg1 ← Distance (ATCEW, ATCNS, CustomerEW, CustomerNS)
Cost1 ← Leg1 × BaseRate

Leg2 ← Distance (CustomerEW, CustomerNS, DestinationEW, DestinationNS)
Cost2 ← Leg2 × (BaseRate + CargoWeight × UnitRateWt)

Leg3 ← Distance (DestinationEW, DestinationNS, ATCEW, ATCNS)
Cost3 ← Leg3 × BaseRate

TotalLength ← Leg1 + Leg2 + Leg3
TotalCost ← Cost1 + Cost2 + Cost3

Output everything as per mock-up generated above

It is important to realize that at this point we *could* generate the actual Pascal code for the main program. In fact, it is sometimes desirable to do so, since we could then test the main program to ensure that it works properly. We *still* do not need to concern ourselves with the function and how it is to be done; we can continue to keep the main program and the function separate. The Pascal program segment for the main program is shown in Figure 6-7. Note that this is NOT a compiler output; in order to generate that, we need to complete the function and include it as a part of the entire solution. However, it is nonetheless important to realize that we can in fact limit our attention and efforts to the main program part of the solution. However, we will not at this time carry out the actual coding and testing.

Note also in Figure 6-7 the use of an expression (as discussed in Chapter 4) as an item of the output lists. In order to print out the distance traveled in miles, the number of blocks needs to be divided by six (recall we are in a city that has six blocks per mile). Since this is only needed in one place, rather than generating a variable for it, we merely do the calculation immediately preceding the printout. Also, actual constants for the address of the Ace Trucking Company and the rates that the company charges have been included.

We are now ready to attack the subtask, namely, that of computing the distance between any two given addresses in Cart City. At this point, we can pretty much forget about the things we did in the main program and concentrate only on the function we need. Essentially, we begin the program development process anew, this time with the distance problem as the subject.

Figure 6-7

Main Program Segment (Excluding Distance Calculation) for the Ace Trucking Problem

```
Program ACE (Input, Output);

(*
    This program computes the charges made by the Ace Trucking Company
    for moving goods from one place in Cart City to another. The charges
    are based on the total mileage, which is calculated from the addresses
    of the end points for the move. Addresses in Cart City are given by
    specifying an east-west component and a north-south component.
*)

Const   BaseRate   = 0.25; (* Cost for truck per block moved *)
        UnitRateWt = 0.15; (* Unit wt per ton of cargo *)

        ATCEW      = 750;   (* ATC address is *)
        ATCNS      = -400;  (* 750 East 400 South *)

Var     CustomerEW, CustomerNS,                     (* Customer address *)
        DestinationEW, DestinationNS : Integer;     (* Destination address *)

        CargoWeight,

        Leg1,           (* Distance from ATC to customer *)
        Leg2,           (* Distance from customer to destination *)
        Leg3,           (* Distance from destination back to ATC *)

        Cost1, Cost2, Cost3, (* Associated costs for above distances *)

        TotalLength, TotalCost : Real;

BEGIN

  (* Input the required addresses *)

  Write ('Customer Address?    '); Readln (CustomerEW, CustomerNS);
  Write ('Destination Address? '); Readln (DestinationEW, DestinationNS);
  Write ('Weight of Cargo?     '); Readln (CargoWeight);
  Writeln;

  (* Compute distances and associated costs *)

  Leg1 := Distance (ATCEW,ATCNS,CustomerEW,CustomerNS);
  Cost1 := Leg1 * BaseRate;

  Leg2 := Distance (CustomerEW,CustomerNS,DestinationEW,DestinationNS);
  Cost2 := Leg2 *  (BaseRate + CargoWeight * UnitRateWt);

  Leg3 := Distance (DestinationEW,DestinationNS,ATCEW,ATCNS);
  Cost3 := Leg3 * BaseRate;

  TotalLength := Leg1 + Leg2 + Leg3;
  TotalCost := Cost1 + Cost2 + Cost3;

(* Write out the complete statement *)
```

Figure 6-7 continued

```
Writeln('Summary of Charges for ACE TRUCKING COMPANY');
Writeln;
Writeln('Cargo Weight :              ',CargoWeight:4:1,' tons);
Writeln;
Writeln('From ATC to Customer :      ',Leg1:4:0,' blocks (',
                                      Leg1/6:4:1,' miles ) $',Cost1:6:2);
Writeln('Customer to Destination : ',Leg2:4:0,' blocks (',
                                      Leg2/6:4:1,' miles ) $',Cost2:6:2);
Writeln('Destination to ATC :        ',Leg3:4:0,' blocks (',
                                      Leg3/6:4:1,' miles ) $',Cost3:6:2);
Writeln;
Writeln('Total Trip :                ',TotalLength:4:0,' blocks (',
Writeln                               TotalLength/6:4:1,' miles ) $',TotalCost:6:2);

END.
```

Subtask Distance: Step I—Understand the Problem. We wish to compute the distance between any two addresses in Cart City. As always, let us begin by examining the input and the output.

Input

The East-West part of the originating address

The North-South part of the originating address

The East-West part of the destination address

The North-South part of the destination address

These items, already correct, are handed over by the main program, so we need concern ourselves no further with them.

Output

The total distance, in blocks, covered by the truck

We need some way to compute this distance. Assuming that one can only travel either due North, due South, due East, or due West in Cart City, the distances between any two addresses are actually easy to calculate. You simply add up the number of blocks that must be traveled East to West and the number of blocks to be traveled North to South and you have the shortest possible distance between the two points (see Figure 6-8). Since we are using a positive/negative system to describe

Figure 6-8

The Shortest Distance Between the Points A and B Is Equal to the Total Number of East-West Blocks Spanned Plus the Total Number of North-South Blocks Spanned, Regardless of the Actual Route Taken

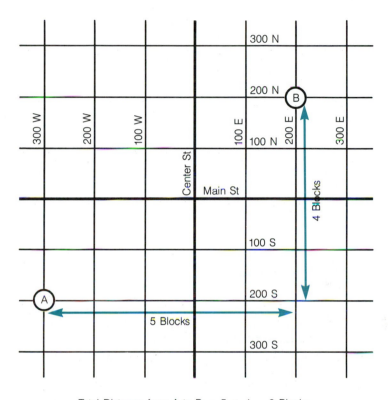

Total Distance from A to B = 5 + 4 = 9 Blocks

the two primary directions, the number of blocks between any of these is given by

| FirstEW − SecondEW |

for the East-West direction, and

| FirstNS − SecondNS |

Subtask Distance: **Step 2—Plan the Solution.** While generating the algorithm, the only thing we must keep in mind is that the addresses are multiples of 100 of the actual number of blocks. Therefore, our final distance is what we get from the addresses divided by 100. Also note that, even though the blocks we calculate are of type `Integer`, the function itself must return a real value. Taking this all into account, we may now write the algorithm. However, we want to indicate that this is a *function algorithm;* consequently, we write it as

Function Distance (FirstEW, FirstNS, SecondEW, SecondNS)
   BlocksEW ← | FirstEW − SecondEW |
   BlocksNS ← | FirstNS − SecondNS |
   Distance ← (BlocksEW + BlocksNS) /100

Subtask `Distance`**: Step 3—Code the Solution.** We now need to code the function.

Except for a few minor differences, *coding a subprogram is identical with coding a main program.* Everything that we have discussed in Chapter 4 relating to Pascal programs carries over into coding subtasks. Since we are looking at functions right now, we will examine those specifically.

The unit of organization called a function can be defined as follows:

function → f-heading-section
        f-declaration-section
        f-executable-section

Note the similarity of this definition (here the initial f in each term stands for function) with the definition of program offered in Chapter 4. As we did in that chapter, we will explain each of the terms until we have all the information necessary to write a function.

The heading section consists only of a single statement, which contains the name of the function and the parameters that will be used in the definition of the function. The definition is

f-heading-section → **function** identifier (parameter-def-list) : type;

The word "function" (in boldface type) is required. *Identifier* is the name you choose for the function, and *type* is most often one of the types discussed in Chapter 4, such as `real`, `integer`, `Boolean`, or `char`. It specifies what the result type of the function is to be. For example, if you are using a function to compute social security tax, you would expect to return a *real* value. On the other hand, if you were to calculate the sum of the squares of the first n integers, you would likely want to return an integer result.

The parameter-def list is a list of the parameters, and their associated types, used in the function definition. Each parameter definition in the list can be given by parameter-definition → parameter-list : type

The parameter list is a list of identifiers, separated by commas if there is more than one. If there are two or more definitions, they are separated by semicolons.

Let us now look at some examples of f-heading sections. We begin by taking our old friend, the Square function. Recall that it has but one parameter, which is the number to be multiplied by itself. A typical heading for this function would be

```
Function Square (Original:Real) : Real;
```

This would state that the function is called Square, that it is to be defined in terms of a single, real parameter called Original, and that the final result to be returned is also real.

As another example, let us consider a function that computes state income tax, based on gross salary and number of exemptions. The f-heading section might look like

```
Function StateTax (TotalSalary : Real; Exemp : Integer)
    : Real;
```

Let's now move on to the declaration section.

The declaration section of a function *is identical in every respect to the corresponding section found in a main program.* You may define any constants and variables you like and use any identifiers as names, as long as these do not conflict with any of the parameters. There is, however, an important difference in how these constants and variables can be used: any constants or variables defined in a function *have meaning only within the function.* As such they are said to be **local.** They can be used at will within the function, but any attempt to reference a local variable outside of the function (for example, in the main program) will cause an error to occur.

On the other hand, if you reference, within a function, a variable or constant that has been defined in the main program, everything will be all right. This is because all of the variables and constants that are defined in the main section are said to be **global,** and every subprogram knows about them. You can, if you like, even use global variables in your subprograms: such usage is termed **side effects.** Although the use of global variables in subprograms can be worthwhile and even necessary, it can also be the source of hard-to-find errors. Use global variables carefully and with discretion.

One final thought: What happens if you define a local variable that just happens to have the same identifier (name) as a global variable? In such a case, the reference will *always* mean the local variable. Consequently, there is never any confusion (at least on the part of the computer) about which variable is meant.

This brings us to the last part of the function definition, the executable section.

The executable section of a function is also exactly the same as the executable section in a main program with one difference: rather than concluding the section with a period as you do in the main program, you must conclude it with a semicolon. Other than that, there are no restrictions on what you can do. You may reference predefined functions or procedures and do anything within the function that you are permitted to do within the main program's executable section.

We are left with one final concern, namely, how do we return the value computed by the function? To do this, we must include within the function an assignment statement of the form

function-name := value

The value assigned to the function name here corresponds exactly to the value that will be returned by the function.

We may now complete the coding of the subtask, given the previously generated algorithm and our new knowledge of Pascal function syntax. The completely coded subtask can be written as shown in Figure 6-9.

Note that, just as in the case of the main program, this function may be worked with separately from any other modules. Again, this is one of the major advantages of modularity. We could even, in fact, test out this function separately. We will defer an exploration of this option until later.

STEP 3: CODE THE SOLUTION

We are now ready to combine the coding of the main program and the coding of the function. Function definitions, when used, are placed within the declaration section of the main program, immediately following the Var section. We therefore amend the definition of declaration section presented in Chapter 4 to read

declaration-section → constants
                      variables
                      functions

The completed coding of the ATC problem is shown in Figure 6-10. Take special notice of the fact that the main program calls the function

Figure 6-9

Definition of the Function Distance *for Use in the Ace Trucking Problem*

```
Function Distance (FirstEW, FirstNS, SecondEW, SecondNS : Integer) : Real;

(* This function computes the distance
   between any two points in Cart City.
*)

Var BlocksEW,             (* Number of E/W blocks between the addresses *)
    BlocksNS : Integer; (* Number of N/S blocks between the addresses *)

Begin
  BlocksEW := ABS (FirstEW - SecondEW);
  BlocksNS := ABS (FirstNS - SecondNS);
  Distance := (BlocksEW + BlocksNS) / 100.0
End (* Distance *);
```

Distance on three separate occasions, yet the function is defined only one time. The *parameters* in the definition remain the same, but each time the function is referenced, a different set of *arguments* is used in place of the parameters. This is one of the real beauties of using subprograms: the language takes care of the mechanics necessary to ensure that the correlation between the parameters of the definition and the arguments used for any given call is correct. Sometimes the term **formal parameter** is used for what we have been simply calling parameter and the term **actual parameter** is used for what we have been referring to as arguments. It is important to remember the difference between these terms.

STEP 4: CHECK OUT THE PROGRAM

We may now examine the workings of the combined main program and function. A sample run with output is shown along with the coded program of Figure 6-10. Note that the output is correct.

STEP 5: DOCUMENT

The program is well documented and easy to understand. Note especially how the presentation of the function makes it stand out.

This concludes our examination of functions, and we now move on to procedures.

Figure 6-10

Complete Trucking Program, Including the Function Definition and a
Sample Run

ACE.PAS

```
 1   Program ACE (Input, Output);
 2
 3   (*
 4       This program computes the charges made by the Ace Trucking Company
 5       for moving goods from one place in Cart City to another. The charges
 6       are based on the total mileage, which is calculated from the addresses
 7       of the end points for the move. Addresses in Cart City are given by
 8       specifying an east-west component and a north-south component.
 9   *)
10
11   Const  BaseRate   = 0.25; (* Cost for truck per block moved *)
12          UnitRateWt = 0.15; (* Unit weight per ton of cargo *)
13
14          ATCEW      = 750;  (* ATC address is *)
15          ATCNS      =-400;  (* 750 East 400 South *)
16
17   Var    CustomerEW, CustomerNS,                 (* Customer address *)
18          DestinationEW, DestinationNS : Integer; (* Destination address *)
19
20          CargoWeight,
21
22          Leg1,     (* Distance from ATC to customer *)
23          Leg2,     (* Distance from customer to destination *)
24          Leg3,     (* Distance from destination back to ATC *)
25
26          Cost1, Cost2, Cost3, (* Associated costs for above distances *)
27
28          TotalLength, TotalCost : Real;
29
30
31 Function Distance (FirstEW, FirstNS, SecondEW, SecondNS : Integer) : Real;
32
33 (* This function computes the distance
34    between any two points in Cart City.
35 *)
36
37   Var BlocksEW,             (* Number of E/W blocks between the addresses *)
38       BlocksNS : Integer; (* Number of N/S blocks between the addresses *)
39
40   Begin
41       BlocksEW := ABS (FirstEW - SecondEW);
42       BlocksNS := ABS (FirstNS - SecondNS);
43       Distance := (BlocksEW + BlocksNS) / 100.0
44   End (* Distance *);
45
46
47 BEGIN
48
49   (* Input the required addresses *)
50
51   Write ('Customer Address?    '); Readln (CustomerEW, CustomerNS);
52   Write ('Destination Address? '); Readln (DestinationEW, DestinationNS);
53   Write ('Weight of Cargo?     '); Readln (CargoWeight);
54   Writeln;
```

Figure 6-10 continued

```
55
56    (* Compute distances and associated costs *)
57
58    Leg1 := Distance (ATCEW,ATCNS,CustomerEW,CustomerNS);
59    Cost1 := Leg1 * BaseRate;
60
61    Leg2 := Distance (CustomerEW,CustomerNS,DestinationEW,DestinationNS);
62    Cost2 := Leg2 *  (BaseRate + CargoWeight * UnitRateWt);
63
64    Leg3 := Distance(DestinationEW,DestinationNS,ATCEW,ATCNS);
65    Cost3 := Leg3 * BaseRate;
66
67    TotalLength := Leg1 + Leg2 + Leg3;
68    TotalCost := Cost1 + Cost2 + Cost3;
69
70  (* Write out the complete statement *)
71
72    Writeln ('Summary of Charges for ACE TRUCKING COMPANY');
73    Writeln;
74    Writeln ('Cargo Weight :                  ',CargoWeight:4:1,' tons');
75    Writeln;
76    Writeln ('From ATC to Customer :    ',Leg1:4:0,' blocks (',
77                                         Leg1/6:4:1,' miles ) $',Cost1:6:2);
78    Writeln ('Customer to Destination : ',Leg2:4:0,' blocks (',
79                                         Leg2/6:4:1,' miles ) $',Cost2:6:2);
80    Writeln ('Destination to ATC :      ',Leg3:4:0,' blocks (',
81                                         Leg3/6:4:1,' miles ) $',Cost3:6:2);
82    Writeln;
83    Writeln ('Total Trip :              ',TotalLength:4:0,' blocks (',
84                                         TotalLength/6:4:1,' miles) $',TotalCost:6:2);
85    Writeln
86
87 END.
```

```
$ run ace

Customer Address?    700 -100
Destination Address? -1000 -900
Weight of Cargo?     8.5

Summary of Charges for ACE TRUCKING COMPANY

Cargo Weight :             8.5 tons

From ATC to Customer :      4 blocks ( 0.6 miles ) $   0.88
Customer to Destination :  25 blocks ( 4.2 miles ) $ 38.12
Destination to ATC :       23 blocks ( 3.8 miles ) $  5.63

Total Trip :               51 blocks ( 8.5 miles ) $ 44.62
```

6-4   *Procedures*

Procedures, as we explained earlier, are less rigid than functions and can be used to compute and return more than a single value. On the other hand, **procedures** tend not to be mathematical in nature and cannot be used in an expression. However, as in the case with functions, procedures are defined in terms of parameters, and any call to a procedure must supply appropriate arguments. Also, procedures are of two kinds: predefined and programmer-defined. We will examine both.

PREDEFINED PROCEDURES

As is the case for functions, there are a number of **predefined procedures** in Pascal. In fact, we have been using four of them already: `Read`, `Readln`, `Write`, and `Writeln`. Notice that these meet all the requirements of a subprogram: they carry out a specific task, they can be called from anywhere within the program, and arguments may be used as required. However, they are different from functions in that they do not return a single result and they may NOT be used within an expression. For example, it is illegal to write

```
Result := 4 * Writeln (a,b,c);  ← This is an invalid expression
```

Additional predefined procedures will be introduced as appropriate in future chapters.

We move on, then, to one of the most important aspects of computer programming, **programmer-defined procedures.** A very large part of the flexibility, modularity, and power of Pascal resides in these.

PROGRAMMER-DEFINED PROCEDURES

In a manner similar to that used for programmer-defined functions, we may define our own procedures. Procedures have different characteristics from functions, and this difference makes procedures more useful in certain applications. The primary differences are that procedures are not limited to returning a single value, and procedures may not be referenced from within an expression. The concepts of parameter and argument, as explained for functions, remain the same. We will, however, be able to extend these ideas even further in order to increase their power and utility.

As we did with functions, an example will introduce the discussion of programmer-defined procedures.

Supply and Demand

Because of your successful endeavors at the Ace Trucking Company, you have been recruited by Guided Home Operating Systems Techniques (GHOST) to help them market their product. They produce an electronic device that can be used to monitor and alter events in the average home, for example, changing thermostat settings for day and night, turning lights and heaters on and off, and setting up motion detectors to apprehend intruders. GHOST wants you to write a computer program that uses economic theory (that is, the law of supply and demand) to determine the optimum price they should charge for their product.

Let us briefly review the law of supply and demand. Basically, it says that the number of units of a given product that people are willing to buy is related to the selling price in such a way that, as the price rises, the number of units people are willing to buy (the demand) will drop. On the other hand, the number of units a manufacturer will be willing to produce (the supply) is affected by the price in exactly the opposite way: the higher the price, the more manufacturers will be willing to produce. Further, the theory states that the intersection of the two curves of supply and demand reflects the equilibrium selling price and the equilibrium number of units. That is, at the price indicated, the number of units manufactured will exactly equal the number of units bought. This is shown in Figure 6-11. Theory holds that, sooner or later, the equilibrium price (and units sold) will be reached.

Figure 6-11

Typical Supply and Demand Curves (Supply Represents the Number of Units a Manufacturer Would Be Willing to Make at a Given Price, and Demand Is the Number of Units That Would Be Bought at a Given Price)

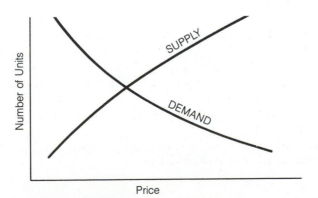

STEP 1: UNDERSTAND THE PROBLEM

GHOST would like to get a jump on the market in order to initially determine the equilibrium selling price and thereby maximize profit and minimize wasted effort. Therefore, GHOST needs to estimate each of the curves and find their intersection. The approximation of the curves can be made in a number of ways, but the simplest way is to assume the curves are straight lines that can therefore be written in the following form:

$$Demand: D = md \times P + bd$$
$$Supply: S = ms \times P + bs$$

In these equations the following symbols are used:

P—The price under consideration

D—The demand, or the number of units consumers are willing to buy at price P

S—The supply, or the number of units a manufacturer is willing to produce if they can be sold at price P

md—The slope of the demand curve

bd—The intercept of the demand curve

ms—The slope of the supply curve

bs—The intercept of the supply curve.

The process to be carried out here is threefold:

1. Estimate md and bd

2. Estimate ms and bs

3. Determine the point of intersection

The problem, then, has already been subdivided! How do we go about getting the above estimates?

For the first, estimating the demand curve, GHOST carries out a market analysis in which they determine approximately how many people will buy their product at a given price. Since the assumption is that the demand curve is a straight line, two such estimates will serve to determine the equation of the line, that is, md and bd. This is because any two points on a single line are sufficient to determine exactly the line itself.

The second estimate is a little more difficult. The number of units to be produced at a given price is a complex function of the costs associated with production and distribution and the number actually sold.

The basic idea is to maximize the profit. Although the analysis is fairly involved, it nonetheless leads to the following conclusion: the number of units to be produced is a linear function of the price, where the slope and intercept are themselves complex functions of the costs of production and the number sold. Let us assume that the administrators of GHOST have the necessary expertise and can generate for us the optimum number of units to be produced at a given price. With that information, we can generate *ms* and *bs* for the supply curve, using the techniques stated above for defining a straight line.

Given that we have the equations for the supply and demand curves, we can easily compute the intersection of the two curves: we must merely solve the two equations simultaneously (more on that later).

We can now delineate the input and output. The input would consist of the following:

*P*1 and *P*2—Two reasonable prices for the product
*D*1—The demand at price *P*1
*D*2—The demand at price *P*2
*S*1—The optimal supply at price *P*1
*S*2—The optimal supply at price *P*2

Management would like the following output:

The values for *md, bd, ms*, and *bs*
The equilibrium number of units to be manufactured, *U*
The equilibrium price of these units, *PE*

We can generate a mock-up of the output as follows:

GHOST Price Analysis Program

Estimation of Demand Curve: $D = -2.365 \times P + 364.8$
Estimation of Supply Curve: $S = 3.076 \times P - 125.5$
Optimal Price to Charge: $1200.00
Optimal Units to Make: 375

Note that, at this point, we really have no idea what the numbers themselves are going to look like, so we just do the best we can. The actual output may have to be altered a little later to make sure everything fits nicely.

STEP 2: PLAN THE SOLUTION

Now that we have a full supply (so to speak) of information, we can create an algorithm. We will, as usual, start our algorithm quite generally:

Input Demand, Supply Estimates
Compute Demand Curve
Compute Supply Curve
Determine the Intersection of Demand/Supply Curves
Output Necessary Items

We note a number of things here: first of all, we are going to be doing the same thing twice (aha!), namely, determining a curve from a set of points. Also, this particular task is not one that can be done easily with a function since *two* values are returned—the slope and the intercept. A *procedure* is indicated here. We also note that we must determine the intersection of two lines. We can, if we want, defer solving that problem by making it a procedure as well. We don't really have to, but we can if we decide it would be better to defer consideration of that particular subtask until a later time.

Assuming that we will, therefore, use two procedures, let us move on to the next, more detailed algorithm. At those places in the algorithm wherein we plan to invoke the procedures, we indicate the call by writing the name of the procedure followed by the arguments that it takes, enclosed in parentheses. In this regard, they are like the predefined procedures such as Writeln, which are called merely by using the name, along with the arguments they require inside parentheses, for example, Writeln (a,b,c). We can, therefore, generate the following:

Prompt for, Read P1, P2
Prompt for, Read D1, D2
Prompt for, Read S1, S2

ComputeCurve (P1, D1, P2, D2, md, bd)
ComputeCurve (P1, S1, P2, S2, ms, bs)

Intersection (md, bd, ms, bs, U, PE)

Output as per required

There are a few things to be aware of here. First, we plan to use two procedures. (There is nothing that limits the number we can use.) Second, we have arranged the arguments in *both* calls to ComputeCurve so that they parallel each other. Third, and this is very important, *the results of the procedures, namely the slope and intersect in Compute-Curve and the equilibrium number of units and equilibrium price in Intersection, are among the arguments sent off.* In other words, *the results to be returned* as well as the data to be used in the computations are in the argument lists. Fourth, since we are going to be calling two procedures, *these need not be detailed any further.* In fact, this is really all we need (as we did with our function before) in order to generate the code for the main program! Using the mock-up of the output that we put together earlier, we can go directly to the Pascal version of this algorithm, which is shown in Figure 6-12.

Having dispatched the main program, we may now turn our attention to the requisite procedures. Part of the beauty of this system is that we can now devote all of our attention to one small problem to be solved that is pretty much independent of the rest of the program. Therefore, let's do it.

Subtask CompuTeCurve**: Step 1—Understand the Problem.** Here we wish to determine the equation for a straight line, given two points on the line. This is actually a completely general problem in algebra, and we need the technique merely to complete the primary problem that we are solving. Again, let's begin by looking at the input and output:

Input
  Two ordered pairs of points $(X1,Y1)$ and $(X2,Y2)$

Output
  The slope and intercept of the line, M and B

Elementary algebra shows us that this can be done as follows:

$$M = \text{slope} = \frac{(Y2 - Y1)}{(X2 - X1)}$$
$$B = \text{intercept} = Y2 - M \times X2$$

Subtask CompuTeCurve**: Step 2—Plan the Solution.** No problem! This can be written directly from the equation shown above (remember to indicate that this is a procedure, however):

Procedure COMPUTECURVE (X1, Y1, X2, Y2, M, B)
    $M \leftarrow (Y2 - Y1) / (X2 - X1)$
    $B \leftarrow Y2 - M * X2$

Subtask CompuTeCurve**: Step 3—Code the Solution.** We now find ourselves in the position of having to code this subprogram. As is the case with functions, coding a procedure is identical to coding a main program. The unit of organization is termed a "procedure" and can be defined as follows:

Figure 6-12

Main Program Segment (Excluding the Procedures) for the GHOST
Problem

```
Program GHOST (Input, Output);

(*
   This program uses the economic theory of supply and demand
   to compute the equilibrium price and equilibrium number of
   units that should be manufactured by the GHOST company.
*)

Var  P1, P2,    (* Sample prices to be used for estimating *)
                (* the supply and demand curves *)

     D1, D2,    (* Estimated demand at the above two prices *)

     S1, S2,    (* Estimated supply at these prices *)

     md, bd,    (* Slope and intercept of the demand curve *)
     ms, bs,    (* Slope and intercept of the supply curve *)
     U,PE       (* Equilibrium units and price *)
          : Real;


BEGIN

   Write ('First price at which estimates have been made: ');
   Readln (P1);
   Write ('Second price at which estimates have been made:');
   Readln (P2);
   Writeln;

   Write ('Estimated demand at the price of $',P1:7:2,':   ');
   Readln (D1);
   Write ('Estimated demand at the price of $',P2:7:2,':   ');
   Readln (D2);
   Writeln;

   Write ('Estimated supply at the price of $',P1:7:2,':   ');
   Readln (S1);
   Write ('Estimated supply at the price of $',P2:7:2,':   ');
   Readln (S2);
   Writeln;
   Writeln;
   Writeln;


   ComputeCurve (P1, D1, P2, D2, md, bd); (* Compute the demand curve *)
   ComputeCurve (P1, S1, P2, S2, ms, bs); (* Compute the supply curve *)

   Intersection (md, bd, ms, bs, U, PE);  (* Determine the intersection *)
                                          (* of the two curves     *)
   (* OUTPUT THE RESULTS *)

   Writeln ('GHOST Price Analysis Program');
   Writeln;
   Writeln ('Estimation of Demand Curve: D = ',md,' x P + ',bd);
   Writeln ('Estimation of Supply Curve: S = ',ms,' x P + ',bs);
```

Figure 6-12 continued

```
Writeln;
Writeln ('Optimal Price to Charge:   $',PE:7:2);
Writeln;
Writeln ('Optimal Units to Make:     ',U:7:0);
Writeln

END.
```

procedure → p-heading-section
       p-declaration-section
       p-executable-section

The *p* prefix in each of the three elements stands for procedure. Notice how similar they are to a main program or function.

Let us examine each part of the above procedure definition. The heading section is where almost all of the differences that do exist among the three types of program units (main, procedure, function) can be found. The definition for a procedure is as follows:

p-heading-section → **procedure** identifier (parameter-def-list);

Note that, in contrast with a function, a *type* does NOT need to be, and in fact MAY NOT be, specified with a procedure. This is because a procedure does not return a single, specific result to be used in an expression. A procedure may, in fact, produce several different results, all of different types!

The identifier is, of course, the name of the procedure. The parameter-def-list, to repeat, is a list of parameters whose definition may be given by

parameter-definition → parameter-list : type

Again, the parameter list may consist of no parameters, one parameter, or several parameters separated by commas.

Here, however, we must begin to diverge somewhat. Parameters defined in accordance with the above specifications *may be used by, but not changed by, the procedure.* Such a parameter is termed a **value parameter,** or is said to be **passed by value.** It may be used in any fashion by the procedure, but if an attempt is made to change its value, *the corresponding argument from the calling program will NOT be altered in the slightest.* Almost always, in the case of functions and frequently in the case of procedures, this is exactly what we want.

However, sometimes, as in `ComputeCurve`, we wish to change one of the arguments in the calling program. In fact, this is how we wish to return *M* (the slope) and *B* (the intercept), the results of this procedure, back to the calling program.

Pascal has a mechanism that allows us to do just that. If a procedure (or function, for that matter) has to change the value of an argument from the calling program, it is called a **variable parameter** and is said to be **passed by reference.** If an argument is passed by reference, then the corresponding parameter in the procedure *is absolutely identical to the original argument:* whatever is done to the parameter in the procedure is also done to the corresponding argument from the calling program. If the parameter is set to zero, then the argument is also set to zero; if the parameter is multiplied by 4.6, then the corresponding argument is multiplied by 4.6. This is the primary mechanism used to return results from procedures.

So, how is call by reference set up in a procedure? Actually, it's incredibly simple! A parameter definition that uses call by reference is exactly the same as one that uses call by value, except that an additional `Var` is inserted. The complete definition of parameter definition becomes, therefore,

parameter-definition → parameter-list : type
    | **var** parameter-list : type

There can be as many of either type of definition (reference or value) as you want in a procedure. (Also, it is legal to use call by reference in a function if you like.)

Let's look at a couple of examples. Suppose we wish to write a procedure that finds the square *and* the square root of a number. The number to be used in the computation need not be changed, but the square and the square root MUST be changed in order for the calling program to use them. Consequently, the former must be *call by value* and the latter two must be *call by reference.* These three parameters can be defined in the heading section of the procedure as follows:

```
Procedure SSR (n : Real; Var Square, Sqroot : Real);
```

Let's take a somewhat more involved procedure. Suppose we want a procedure that carries out arithmetic operations on complex numbers. The following parameters are used in the definition:

`RealPart1`—The real part of the first incoming number

`ImagPart1`—The imaginary part of the first incoming number

`RealPart2`—The real part of the second incoming number

ImagPart2—The imaginary part of the second incoming number

RealResult—The real part of the computed result

ImagResult—The imaginary part of the computed result

Operation—A character representing the operation (i.e., addition, subtraction, or whatever) to be carried out

ResultType—A Boolean variable set to True if the result is real and False if it is complex

In this case RealPart1, ImagPart1, RealPart2, ImagPart2, and Operation are only used as input to the procedure: that is, they are not altered by the procedure as it carries out its chores. On the other hand, RealResult, ImagResult, and ResultType have values that *do* relate to what the procedure is doing. Therefore, the former must be value parameters and the latter variable parameters. The heading section of this parameter would look like this:

```
Procedure ComplexMath(RealPart1, ImagPart1 : Real;
                      RealPart2, ImagPart2 : Real;
                  Var RealResult, ImagResult : Real;
                      Operation : Char;
                  Var ResultType : Boolean);
```

The declaration section of a procedure is identical in every respect to that of a function. You may define constants and variables and the concepts of local variables; global variables and side effects remain the same.

The executable section is also identical to the one for functions. However, a statement of the form

```
procedure-name := value ← Never do this!
```

MAY NOT be included in the program. This is because procedures return values via their parameters.

This gives us the information we require to complete work on this first subtask, ComputeCurve. The resulting algorithm, as coded in Pascal, is shown in Figure 6-13.

We are now ready to move on to the second subtask, the procedure Intersection. Note again that we may proceed to do this without regard for the main program *or* ComputeCurve.

Subtask Intersection: Step 1—Understand the Problem. The second procedure we wish to generate is one that takes the equations for two

Figure 6-13

Definition of the Procedure ComputeCurve *for Use in the* GHOST *Problem*

```
Procedure ComputeCurve (X1, Y1, X2, Y2 : Real; Var M, B : Real);
(*
   This procedure calculates the slope (M) and intercept (B) of the
   straight line determined by the two points (X1,Y1) and (X2,Y2).
*)
  Begin
    M := (Y2 - Y1) / (X2 - X1);
    B := Y2 - M * X2
  End (* ComputeCurve *);
```

straight lines (in essence, their respective slopes and intercepts) and determines the coordinates of their intersection. We may write

Input

$M1, B1$—slope and intercept of the first line

$M2, B2$—slope and intercept of the second line

Output

XI, YI—The coordinate of the intersection

Algebra again comes to the rescue here. The *X*-coordinate of the intersection can be computed from

$$XI = \frac{(B2 - B1)}{(M1 - M2)}$$

and the *Y*-coordinate from

$$YI = M1 \times XI + B1$$

Subtask Intersection**: Step 2—Plan the Solution.** We can directly write down the algorithm for this subtask as

Procedure Intersection (M1, B1, M2, B2, YI, XI)
   XI ← (B2 − B1) / (M1 − M2)
   YI ← M1 × XI + B1

Subtask Intersection**: Step 3—Code the Solution.** We already know how to code procedures in Pascal, and all that remains is to determine which variables are to be set up as call by value and which as call by reference. Since only *XI* and *YI* are to be returned, those will be call by reference, and the others will be call by value. We may, therefore, generate the coded procedure immediately, and it is shown in Figure 6-14.

Figure 6-14

Definition of the Procedure Intersection *for Use in the* GHOST
Problem

```
Procedure Intersection (M1, B1, M2, B2 : Real; Var YI, XI : Real);
(*
   This procedure computes the point of intersection for the lines
   whose slopes and intercepts are M1, B1, and M2, B2, respectively.
*)
  Begin
    XI := (B2 - B1) / (M1 - M2);
    YI := M1 * XI + B1
  End (* Intersection *);
```

STEP 3: CODE THE SOLUTION

Last, but not least, we are ready to combine the coded sections of the main program and procedures into one uniform program. As is true for functions, any programmer-defined procedures are placed within the declaration section of the main program, immediately before the primary Begin. The complete declaration section of a Pascal program becomes, therefore,

declaration-section → constants
                        variables
                        functions
                        procedures

Placing ComputeCurve and Intersection in the main program completes the solution to the GHOST problem, and the final result is shown in Figure 6-15. Notice that a change was made in the main program, namely, adding better format specifications to the slope and intercept output. One must retain one's sense of aesthetics!

STEP 4: CHECK OUT THE PROGRAM

A sample run of the program is shown in Figure 6-15 as well. Note that the output is both correct and pleasing.

STEP 5: DOCUMENT

Documentation of the program is complete at this stage. The procedures stand out against the program as a whole, and the main program is much simpler because of their use.

Heeding the old saw that "too much of a good thing can be bad," you should not overdo using procedures and functions. When used in excess, they can actually confuse rather than enhance understandability. They can also eat up a lot of computer time and memory. This is not to discourage your use of them, only to caution you to use them appro-

Figure 6-15

Complete GHOST *Program, Including Procedures, and a Sample Run*

GHOST.PAS

```
  1    Program GHOST (Input, Output);
  2
  3    (*
  4       This program uses the economic theory of supply and demand
  5       to compute the equilibrium price and equilibrium number of
  6       units that should be manufactured by the GHOST company.
  7    *)
  8
  9    Var  P1, P2,      (* Sample prices to be used for estimating *)
 10                      (* the supply and demand curves *)
 11
 12         D1, D2,      (* Estimated demand at the above two prices *)
 13
 14         S1, S2,      (* Estimated supply at these prices *)
 15
 16         md, bd,      (* Slope and intercept of the demand curve *)
 17         ms, bs,      (* Slope and intercept of the supply curve *)
 18         U,PE         (* Equilibrium units and price *)
 19                 : Real;
 20
 21
 22    Procedure ComputeCurve (X1, Y1, X2, Y2 : Real; Var M, B : Real);
 23    (*
 24       This procedure calculates the slope (M) and intercept (B) of the
 25       straight line determined by the two points (X1,Y1) and (X2,Y2).
 26    *)
 27      Begin
 28        M := (Y2 - Y1) / (X2 - X1);
 29        B := Y2 - M * X2
 30      End (* ComputeCurve *);
 31
 32
 33    Procedure Intersection (M1, B1, M2, B2 : Real; Var YI, XI : Real);
 34    (*
 35       This procedure computes the point of intersection for the lines
 36       whose slopes and intercepts are M1, B1 and M2, B2, respectively.
 37    *)
 38      Begin
 39        XI := (B2 - B1) / (M1 - M2);
 40        YI := M1 * XI + B1
 41      End (* Intersection *);
 42
 43
 44    BEGIN
 45
 46      Write ('First price at which estimates have been made:  ');
 47      Readln (P1);
 48      Write ('Second price at which estimates have been made: ');
 49      Readln (P2);
 50      Writeln;
 51
 52      Write ('Estimated demand at the price of $',P1:7:2,':   ');
 53      Readln (D1);
 54      Write ('Estimated demand at the price of $',P2:7:2,':   ');
```

Figure 6-15 continued

```
55      Readln (D2);
56      Writeln;
57
58      Write ('Estimated supply at the price of $',P1:7:2,':   ');
59      Readln (S1);
60      Write ('Estimated supply at the price of $',P2:7:2,':   ');
61      Readln (S2);
62      Writeln;
63      Writeln;
64      Writeln;
65
66
67      ComputeCurve (P1, D1, P2, D2, md, bd); (* Compute the demand curve *)
68      ComputeCurve (P1, S1, P2, S2, ms, bs); (* Compute the supply curve *)
69
70      Intersection (md, bd, ms, bs, U, PE);  (* Determine the intersection *)
71                                             (* of the two curves)
72
73      (* OUTPUT THE RESULTS *)
74
75      Writeln ('GHOST Price Analysis Program');
76      Writeln;
77      Writeln ('Estimation of demand curve: D = ',md:7:3,' x P + ',bd:7:3);
78      Writeln ('Estimation of supply curve: S = ',ms:7:3,' x P + ',bs:7:3);
79      Writeln;
80      Writeln ('Optimal Price to Charge:    $',PE:7:2);
81      Writeln;
82      Writeln ('Optimal Units to Make:       ',U:7:0);
83      Writeln
84
85  END.


$ run ghost


First price at which estimates have been made: 800
Second price at which estimates have been made: 1200

Estimated demand at the price of $ 800.00:    533
Estimated demand at the price of $1200.00:    329

Estimated supply at the price of $ 800.00:    302
Estimated supply at the price of $1200.00:    425




GHOST Price Analysis Program

Estimation of Demand Curve: D =   -0.510 x P + 941.000
Estimation of Supply Curve: S =    0.307 x P +  56.000

Optimal Price to Charge:    $1082.57

Optimal Units to Make:          389
```

priately. In the remaining chapters of this book, we will strike a balance in their use; you will see that sometimes they are used extensively and sometimes they are not used at all! A little practice will help you to discern what is proper.

SUMMARY

In this chapter we examined physical modularity as a way to extend the advantages of modularity. Physical modularity was demonstrated using subprograms. The two kinds of subprograms we specifically looked at were functions and procedures. The former can return only one value and may be used in expressions, whereas the latter can return any number of values but may *not* be used in expressions. Predefined functions and procedures exist that may be used "as is," and it is also possible to define your own (programmer-defined) for increased flexibility. Both predefined and programmer-defined functions and procedures can be used to enhance modularity and the advantages of top-down programming.

EXERCISES

CONCEPTS

1. Define or explain the following terms:

Actual parameter	Physical modularity
Argument	Predefined function
Formal parameter	Predefined procedure
Function	Procedure
Global variable	Programmer-defined function
Local variable	Programmer-defined procedure
Main program	Side effect
Modularity	Subprogram
Parameter	Value parameter
Pass by reference	Variable parameter
Pass by value	

2. Briefly explain how control moves about between a main program and its subprograms.

3. List some of the advantages that can be enhanced by making modularity more explicit.

4. Describe the various properties of functions and procedures that can be used to differentiate between them.

TOOLS

5. Generate valid Pascal headings for the following functions:

   a. NthRoot, which calculates the *n*th root of a number. Parameters consist of the root that is to be taken (an integer) and the number whose root is to be computed (real).

   b. Sine, which computes the sine of a number. Parameters are the angle whose sine is to be taken, and a Boolean value that is True if the angle is in radians and False if it is in degrees.

   c. Random, a function of no parameters that generates a real random number.

   d. Biggest, which returns the largest of three real numbers presented as arguments.

6. Generate valid Pascal headings for the following procedures:

   a. Order, which takes three real numbers and puts them in order from largest to smallest.

   b. Retire, which computes retirement figures for a payroll system. Parameters include a Boolean variable, which indicates whether the retirement program is a reduction or deduction, a letter code specifying which program the person is in, and the person's gross salary. This last one may be changed by the program. The amount of retirement taken out is returned in a variable as well.

   c. ErrOut, which prints out an appropriate error message. (It has but a single parameter, which is the error number.)

   d. GetStuff, which inputs values for a program. It inputs an integer, three reals, two characters, and a Boolean value.

7. Generate complete, valid Pascal functions from the following algorithms:

   a. Tan (*x*)
   $$\text{Tan} \leftarrow \frac{\sin(x)}{\cos(x)}$$

   b. zscore (*x*, mu, sigma)
   $$\text{zscore} \leftarrow \frac{x - \text{mu}}{\text{sigma}}$$

   c. VolE (*r*)
   $$pi = 3.14159 \text{ (a constant)}$$
   $$vs \leftarrow \frac{4}{3} \times pi \times r^3$$
   $$vc \leftarrow pi \times r^2 \times 2 \times r$$
   $$\text{VolE} \leftarrow vc - vs$$

   d. Determ (a,b,c)
   $$\text{Determ} \leftarrow b^2 - 4\,ac$$

8. Generate complete, valid Pascal procedures from the following algorithms:

   a. Switch (a,b)
       temp ← a
       a ← b
       b ← temp

   b. Fib (new, old)
       wait ← new
       new ← new + old
       old ← wait

   c. Taxation (Wages, Exemptions, State, Federal)
       Erate = 22.75 (a constant)
       FedTaxable ← Wages − Erate × Exemptions
       StateTaxable ← Wages − 1.5 × Erate × Exemptions
       Count ← round (FedTaxable / 100.0)
       Rate ← sqrt (Count)
       Federal ← Rate / 10 × FedTaxable
       State ← Count / 100 × StateTaxable

   d. Trace (Place, Count, BeenThere)
       Write 'From place ', Place, 'at Trace'
       Count ← Count + 1
       BeenThere ← True

   e. GetCoefficients (a0,a1,a2)
       Prompt for, Read a0
       Prompt for, Read a1
       Prompt for, Read a2

PROBLEMS

9. Write Pascal program that computes time intervals. The input should consist of two times, each of which should be in the format of day of the month, hours (twenty-four-hour time), and minutes. Compute the elapsed time in hours, expressed as a decimal number. For example, if the following two times were read in,

5   15   23

7   1   05

the total elapsed time would be calculated as 33.7.

   Helpful Hints: Since two times will be input, write a procedure to fetch them. Also, since two times will need to be converted to a decimal number of hours, write a function to accomplish this.

   Extension: Alter your input procedures so it can read the times in the format:

5-08:45

10. Write a program that will input five weights, expressed as pounds

and ounces (integer values), and add them up. The output should look like

#1	4 lb	10 oz
#2	2 lb	14 oz
#3	0 lb	8 oz
#4	12 lb	12 oz
#5	1 lb	0 oz
	21 lb	12 oz

Helpful Hints: Write a procedure that will add up a pair of weights. Read in two weights, add them, then read in the remaining weights one at a time and add each to the total as they are read in. Also, write a procedure to input the weights, since it must be done five times.

11. Many phenomena conform to the Gaussian probability distribution, commonly called the normal curve (the so-called bell-shaped curve). For example, college entrance exam scores and people's heights and weights are all distributed normally. Using the normal curve, one can calculate probabilities. For example, if someone takes a standardized exam and gets a score x, it is possible to calculate the probability that the score will be less than or equal to a particular score z. This function is called $P(z)$, and it is used to calculate the probability that the score x in question will be less than or equal to z. It is also possible to calculate the probability that the score in question is between any two values, say a and b. This would be given by

$$P[\, a \leqslant x \leqslant b \,] = P(b) - P(a)$$

where x is a standard score (average of zero, standard deviation of one). The form of $P(z)$ is given by

$$P(z) = 1 - \tfrac{1}{2}(1 + c_1 z + c_2 z^2 + c_3 z^3 + c_4 z^4)^{-4}$$
$$\text{where } c_1 = 0.196854$$
$$c_2 = 0.115194$$
$$c_3 = 0.000344$$
$$c_4 = 0.019527$$

Write a program that will read in two values a and b and compute the probability that a given score will fall between them.

Helpful Hints: When writing the function $P(z)$, it is necessary to compute a rather ugly expression and then take it to the minus fourth power. Pascal does not have exponentiation, but since this is a known power, you can multiply it by itself four times, use the SqR function twice, or go through the Log/Exp process.

Caution: In order for this to work correctly, both a and b must be positive; hence, assume this will always be the case for this problem.

12. In the GHOST problem presented earlier in this chapter, we said that the administration would furnish points on the supply curve, that is, they would generate a figure for the best number of units to be manufactured for a given selling price. However, we would like to know where that comes from. We said that the main idea was to maximize profits. A model for profits holds that

$$\text{Profit} = (P - C)\,S$$

where P is the selling price, C is the cost (per unit) of manufacture, and S is the number of units. However, C is not a constant but another function. Again, this simple model would yield

$$C = kS + F$$

where k is the variable cost of manufacturing an item and F is the fixed cost associated with the operation. Note that *the variable cost is proportional to the number of units*. This is important because it implies that the cost per item of manufacture goes up as the number of items manufactured goes up.

In any event, the complete function for profit can be given by

$$\text{Profit} = (P + F - kS)\,S = PS + FS - kS^2$$

The idea, again, is to maximize profits; it can be shown using calculus that the maximum profit obtains under the following conditions:

$$S = \frac{(P + F)}{2k}$$

Therefore, for a given price P and known fixed costs F and variable cost rate k, the optimum number of items to make, S, can be computed!

Write a program that inputs k, F, and two values for P, computes the corresponding values for S, and prints it all out. Make use of a function in calculating S.

13. A determination of the exact location of an object, given two vantage points, can be done by a process known as *triangulation*. The process can be carried out either visually or via radio or other electromagnetic rays. The three locations, corresponding to the object under investigation and the two observation points, form a triangle. This situation is shown below:

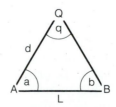

A and B are the observation points and Q is the object under scrutiny. Since the locations (coordinates) of A and B are known, then L is also known. The observations consist of the angles a and b (in degrees) and a knowledge of the coordinates of A (XA, YA) and B (XB, YB). Given this information, the following can be computed:

$$L = \sqrt{(XA - XB)^2 + (YA - YB)^2}$$
$$q = 180 - (a + b)$$
$$d = L\,\frac{\sin b}{\sin q}$$
$$XQ = XA + d \cos a$$
$$YQ = YA + d \sin a$$

Write a program that will read in the coordinates and observation angle, in degrees, for each vantage point and compute the coordinates of the object Q. Use a procedure to read in the data and write a function that will convert an angle from degrees to radians. The conversion is 2 pi radians per 360 degrees.

14. Blockhead Concrete fabricates pieces of any size and shape. In order to make their operations run smoothly, they rank all waiting jobs and choose to initiate the ones with the lowest rankings first. The major dimensions of an object to be fabricated are taken (L, W, H) and an estimate of the volume made. A time estimate for completion is computed as

$$T = 0.025\ V^2 + (L/W)^3 + W/H$$

A cost estimate is computed as

$$C = 4.75\ T + 0.35\ V$$

The ranking is then computed as

$$R = 10\ T + C$$

Before the rank is computed, the time is rounded to the nearest 10 hours, and the cost is rounded to the nearest 100 dollars. Write a program that will input the major dimensions and produce a rank.

Helpful Hints: In order to do the rounding, write a procedure that takes a real number and rounds it to the position indicated by an associated integer. For example, if V were 14,366.95, then

```
RoundItOff (V, 100)
```

would produce a value of 14,400 for V.

7

Files:

Additional Pathways for Input and Output

*B*efore going on to examine more complex problems (and methods that can be employed to solve them), we will briefly expand the concepts of input and output. Each problem we've seen in the preceding chapters has been interactive in nature, which means that the computer program generated to solve it is restricted to getting its input from the keyboard and sending its output to the CRT. Although this process is sufficient for many applications, it can sometimes be a real nuisance. Among other things, it is difficult to enter large quantities of data correctly in interactive mode (should that be required), and it is certainly inconvenient if many repetitions of the program must be run in order to properly test it. (Consider, for example, the spectroscopy problem in Chapter 5.) Further, it is frequently the case that output from one program becomes input for another. If all of the output is directed toward the CRT, processing the output becomes an impossible task. Finally, if several programs use the same data, this data must be entered over and over, once for each program. This duplication can lead to significant, difficult-to-trace errors.

In order to get around these limitations, we will extend the concept of input and output so that programs can access data and information that is kept in auxiliary storage devices. Recall from Chapter 2 that auxiliary storage almost always involves a disk unit of some kind. Of prime importance here is that a program can read data *from* a disk or write information *to* a disk in exactly the same fashion as it gets input from the keyboard and sends output to the CRT. To be sure (and consistent), Pascal treats the keyboard and CRT as if they were ordinary files. The main difference between these two manual devices and the disk unit is that any data used by or generated from the program remains on the disk after the program finishes executing. Consequently, such data and information can be used again if desired.

As always, there is a price to be paid. To realize the advantages of file usage, additional time and effort must be expended by the programmer. If you wish to use a disk file (rather than the keyboard) for input, you must go through the additional process of creating a file for your data, placing the data into the file, and then modifying your program so that it reads the data from the file rather than the keyboard. Essentially, you place the data your program is going to use into a file rather than entering it directly into the program as it executes.

A similar situation applies to output. When using a disk file for output, you must include the additional step of printing or listing the file *after* the program finishes writing it if you want to see what's in the file. Again, you must do a little more work to get the advantages you seek.

We will begin by examining the concept of a file as a way to organize and store data on auxiliary devices. We will then look at files from a Pascal point of view, and finally, a complete example will be given to demonstrate the practical use of files in a typical programming situation.

7-1 *Auxiliary Storage*

Traditionally, a **file** is a collection of similar items organized externally. At one time, the only kinds of files available were card files (consisting of punched cards), but as computer equipment grew more sophisticated, files were moved first to magnetic tape and finally to magnetic disk. A file can be defined in terms of its components, namely,

A file is a collection of similar records.

We now need to define **record** in order to understand the definition of a file. (In Pascal the term "record" has a different, although related, meaning from that in which we will use it here; consult Chapter 13 on data structures for further elaboration.) Thus,

A record is a collection of related fields.

Now we need to see what a **field** is, and so

A field is an individual data item.

An individual data item might be a name, social security number, time differential, or whatever. The basic idea is that data items be organized hierarchically according to the definitions for file, record, and field.

An example is appropriate here. A typical file is shown in Figure 7-1. In this case, we have the quintessential file example, a payroll file. Note that the file is broken up into records and the records into fields.

This structure for files essentially came into existence due to the use of punched cards. Our payroll file is shown as just such a punched card file in Figure 7-2. As technology advanced, files were moved to tape and disk (as we already mentioned), but the concepts and terminology carried over even though the devices are very different physically.

It is interesting to realize that we have been working with files all along; we have just not been calling them files. When you enter a source program into the computer, it becomes a **source file** on the disk and is used as input data to the Pascal compiler (which, as we said earlier, is nothing more than a computer program). This source file consists of records (each program line) and is made up of fields (in this case the individual characters). The compiler then goes through this file and produces, as output, an **object file,** whose records consist of the individual machine instructions to be executed.

The data in a file can be of any type. However, for our needs and purposes here, we will restrict the discussion to **text files.** These are files

Figure 7-1

Record and Field Structure of a Payroll File

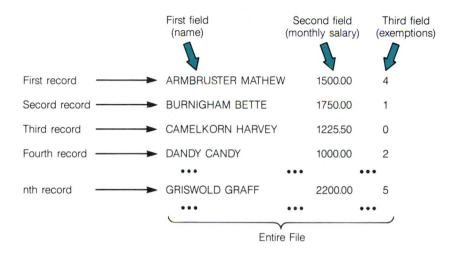

Figure 7-2

Payroll File as a Punched Card File

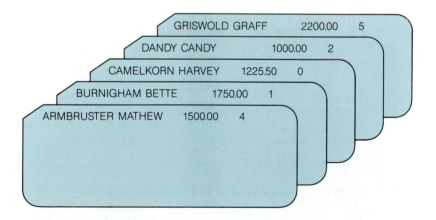

made up of characters (at the lowest level). Text files are the most frequently encountered files in any event and can be used to demonstrate all of the principles of file usage.

We are now ready to see how Pascal deals with files.

7-2 *Pascal Definition of Files*

You may be surprised to discover that you have actually been using Pascal files already. Recall from Chapter 4 the definition of the Pascal heading section:

heading-section → **program** identifier (input, output);

We said there that the words "input" and "output" are required and correspond to fetching input from the keyboard and sending output to the CRT. Strictly speaking, this is not so. You are required to include these names *only* if you actually intend to use the keyboard and CRT for input and output. In fact, *input* and *output* are predefined *files* (aha!) that are used as the default if other files are not specified. To be exact and proper, the heading section should be defined thus:

heading-section → **program** identifier (file-list);

Here, we can define file list as a list of file names that may or may not include the predefined files of "input" or "output." In other words, you can select and name any files you want here. The standard input and output files may be the most common and most useful, but they are certainly not the only ones.

Strictly speaking, the **standard files** "input" and "output" don't have to refer to the keyboard and CRT either, but they almost always do. The computer installation and organization determine just *what* these two files refer to. Standard files are merely intended to be an easy way to get input and output, whatever the physical devices they are attached to.

Let's consider some brief examples of files in the heading section. Suppose we wanted to write a program that uses neither the keyboard nor the CRT (which correspond to the Pascal files `Input` and `Output`), but instead obtains information from a file of book titles and sends results to a file of inventory amounts. The heading section, in a case like this, might look like

```
Program BookCosts (Titles, Amounts);
```

The identifiers `Titles` and `Amounts` refer to external disk files, where the former is intended to provide input values to the program and the latter is meant to collect the output generated by the program.

However, there is no way you can tell which files are intended to be used for input and which are slated for output merely by looking at the file names in the heading. In addition, you must declare the identifiers used in the heading *as* files and further indicate whether they are to be used as input or output files. The former is accomplished by declaring them in the declarations section of the program, and the latter is done by using the predefined procedures `Reset` and `Rewrite` in the executable section of the program.

Let's look at file declarations first. Since we are interested here only in text files, the files themselves must be declared to be of type *text*. In the above example, the heading and a portion of the declaration sections might look like this:

```
Program BookCosts (Titles, Amounts);
Var Titles, Amounts : Text;
```

In this context the identifier `Text` is just another data type, much like `Real` or `Integer`.

With regard to specifying which files are to be used for input and which are to be used for output, the procedures `Reset` and `Rewrite` must be used somewhere within the executable section of a program. `Reset` is used to ready an input file, and `Rewrite` is used to prepare a file for output.

Let's demonstrate with an example. Suppose we have an input file called `Grades`, which contains a series of records consisting of letter grades and credit hours. Further suppose that the final numeric averages are to be sent to an output file called `Finals`. In order to set this up properly, we must include the following Pascal statements in the program:

```
Program COMPUTEGRADES (Grades, Finals);

Var Grades, Finals : Text;
    LetterGrade : Char;
    CreditHours : Integer;
BEGIN
  Reset (Grades);
  Rewrite (Finals);

  ...
```

Note that the predefined files `Input` and `Output` MAY NOT be defined, reset, or rewritten; it is an error to even attempt to do so.

There is one additional consideration: since it is now possible to read from or write to any number of files (rather than just `Input` and `Output`), how do we let Pascal know which file we are referencing in any given I/O operation? When all we had was `Input` and `Output`, there was no confusion; we simply called the appropriate procedure. Now, however, there may be confusion, since additional files can be referenced.

This situation can be handled as follows: whenever an input operation is specified via a `Read` or `Readln` or an output operation is specified by a `Write` or `Writeln`, then the first argument in the procedure call must specify *which* file is to be utilized. (If no file is named in the procedure, then the default files of `Input` and `Output` are assumed.)

Consider another example. Suppose we have a program that gets some information from the keyboard and some from a file called `Help`, and sends some output to the CRT and the rest to `Gotcha`. These can be defined and used as follows:

```
Program ZOWIE (Input, Help, Output, Gotcha);
Var Help, Gotcha : Text;
...
BEGIN
  Reset (Help);
  Rewrite (Gotcha);

  ...

  Readln (First, Second); (* Data from Keyboard *)

  ...

  Readln (Help, Next, Last); (* Data from Help *)

  ...
  ...

  Writeln ('The result is ',Finish:5); (* Output to CRT *)

  ...

  Writeln (Gotcha, A, B, C); (* Output to Gotcha *)
```

Another warning is in order at this point: the manner in which files referenced by a Pascal program are attached to actual disk files on the computer *is very implementation dependent*. Somehow, some way, a correspondence between each Pascal file reference and the corresponding disk file must be made. Many techniques to accomplish this correspondence are available. You will need to research how things are done at your own computer installation.

We are now ready to consider an example that makes use of disk files in solving a problem.

F-Mart Financial Report

Suppose you work for F-Mart, which has two branch stores. At the end of every month, each branch supplies you with financial data concerning income and expenses for that month. Your job is to generate a statement that details the financial status of each store individually and for the chain as a whole. Let us follow our program development process to generate a solution.

STEP 1: UNDERSTAND THE PROBLEM

We begin by detailing the input that is to be used by the program. At the end of the month each store provides the following data for analysis:

Gross Sales—actual dollar amount of merchandise sold
Costs—wholesale value of merchandise sold
Returns—total value of refunds made
Salaries—amount paid to employees as salaries
Utilities—utility expenses
Rent—rent paid for premises

We next determine what the output should consist of. In this case, it is to be a report that includes the following information for each store individually and for the chain as a whole:

Net Sales—actual sales, less refunds
Gross Profit—net sales, less costs
Expenses—total outlays to stay in business
Net Profit—gross profit, less expenses
Percent Profit—percent of net sales that is profit

Let us further detail the output requirements by making a mock-up:

FINANCIAL REPORT FOR F-MART STORES 1 AND 2

	Store #1	Store #2	Combined
Gross Sales	xxxx.xx	xxxx.xx	xxxx.xx
Returns	xxxx.xx	xxxx.xx	xxxx.xx
Net Sales	xxxx.xx	xxxx.xx	xxxx.xx

Costs	xxxx.xx	xxxx.xx	xxxx.xx
GROSS PROFIT	xxxx.xx	xxxx.xx	xxxx.xx
Salaries	xxxx.xx	xxxx.xx	xxxx.xx
Utilities	xxxx.xx	xxxx.xx	xxxx.xx
Rent	xxxx.xx	xxxx.xx	xxxx.xx
EXPENSES	xxxx.xx	xxxx.xx	xxxx.xx
NET PROFIT	xxxx.xx	xxxx.xx	xxxx.xx
Pct Profit	xxxx.xx%	xxxx.xx%	xxxx.xx%

Now that we know where we have to start and where we must go, we are ready to develop an algorithm to do it.

STEP 2: PLAN THE SOLUTION

What we need to do, at least initially, is to find formulas that will relate input values to required output values. Considering only the financial categories themselves for right now, we can write

```
NetSales       ← GrossSales − Returns
GrossProfit    ← NetSales − Costs
Expenses       ← Salaries + Utilities + Rent
NetProfit      ← GrossProfit − Expenses
PercentProfit  ← NetProfit / NetSales × 100%
```

This appears simple enough. In fact, if we had only one store to deal with, we could immediately write this as an appropriate algorithm:

```
Fetch Input Values
    Read GrossSales, Costs, Returns, Salaries, Utilities, Rent
Compute Quantities
    NetSales       ← GrossSales − Returns
    GrossProfit    ← NetSales − Costs
    Expenses       ← Salaries + Utilities + Rent
    NetProfit      ← GrossProfit − Expenses
    PercentProfit  ← NetProfit / NetSales × 100%
Output the Results
    Print GrossSales, Returns, NetSales,
        Costs, GrossProfit,
        Salaries, Utilities, Rent, Expenses,
        NetProfit,
        PercentProfit
```

The problem we have been given to solve, however, involves more than a single store; the computations must be carried out for *two* stores and then for the chain as a whole. Even so, the *complete* solution merely requires that we apply this *simple* solution three times over, once for each store and then for both stores taken together.

One way to proceed would be to go through this algorithm three times, once for each store and then once for the chain. That, however, is somewhat unsatisfying, especially since only two (not three) sets of input data are required and just one output report is needed. Let's look at some alternatives.

Let's consider first what the input is. For each item (such as gross sales) we must get a value from the first store, a value from the second store, and then add these two together to get a value for the chain. As an example, for the gross sales we can express this as

Read GrossSales from Store 1
Read GrossSales from Store 2
Total GrossSales ← GrossSales from Store 1 + GrossSales from Store 2

We would have to repeat this process for each of the remaining five input categories (namely, costs, returns, salaries, utilities, and rent).

So how can we go about doing this? We could, as we have done so far for every example in this text, write the program in such a way that the twelve required values (six for each store) are prompted for and entered via the keyboard and then added properly to get the necessary totals. This approach, however, would be tedious and error prone, and the data (all twelve values) would have to be entered anew for each test run of the program. We need a better method.

As you have undoubtedly figured out by now, we can reduce the required amount of work considerably by using files. We can place the data for each store into a separate file and then just have the program read the financial data from the files as needed. The program could then do the appropriate computations and generate the required output without any additional effort on our part! The program can be run as many times as desired (or necessary) with no possibility of data entry errors, and the data itself can be verified as it is entered into the file. This is the best of all possible worlds.

There is one other thing to consider at this point: we will be doing *exactly* the same operations (namely, input from the first store, input from the second store, and the sum of both) on all six primary data categories. As we just saw in Chapter 6, this suggests the use of a procedure. In fact, we may use this concept to generate the algorithm for fetching the input values, as follows:

Fetch all input values
    Collect (GrossSales1, GrossSales2, GrossSales)
    Collect (Costs1, Costs2, Costs)
    Collect (Returns1, Returns2, Returns)
    Collect (Salaries1, Salaries2, Salaries)
    Collect (Utilities1, Utilities2, Utilities)
    Collect (Rent1, Rent2, Rent)

Here, the numbers 1 and 2 on the end of the variables indicate from which store the values come, and the variables without a suffix number represent the totals. Further, we need not worry about exactly *how* the procedure will do its work at this point, deferring consideration of the details until later.

Having simplified the input process, we may also be tempted to try a similar approach with the calculations part. However, the calculations are not nearly as uniform (sometimes we add, sometimes we subtract, and sometimes we divide), and it is easier just to specify them directly in the main algorithm.

The same holds true for the output. Since we want to generate a single report, we can place the details in the main algorithm. The complete algorithm can thus be written as

Fetch Input Values
    Collect (GrossSales1, GrossSales2, GrossSales)
    Collect (Costs1, Costs2, Costs)
    Collect (Returns1, Returns2, Returns)
    Collect (Salaries1, Salaries2, Salaries)
    Collect (Utilities1, Utilities2, Utilities)
    Collect (Rent1, Rent2, Rent)

Compute Quantities

$$NetSales1 \leftarrow GrossSales1 - Returns1$$
$$NetSales2 \leftarrow GrossSales2 - Returns2$$
$$NetSales \leftarrow NetSales1 + NetSales2$$

$$GrossProfit1 \leftarrow NetSales1 - Costs1$$
$$GrossProfit2 \leftarrow NetSales2 - Costs2$$
$$GrossProfit \leftarrow GrossProfit1 + GrossProfit2$$

$$Expenses1 \leftarrow Salaries1 + Utilities1 + Rent1$$
$$Expenses2 \leftarrow Salaries2 + Utilities2 + Rent2$$
$$Expenses \leftarrow Expenses1 + Expenses2$$

$$NetProfit1 \leftarrow GrossProfit1 - Expenses1$$
$$NetProfit2 \leftarrow GrossProfit2 - Expenses2$$
$$NetProfit \leftarrow NetProfit1 + NetProfit2$$

$$PercentProfit1 \leftarrow NetProfit1 / NetSales1 \times 100\%$$
$$PercentProfit2 \leftarrow NetProfit2 / NetSales2 \times 100\%$$
$$PercentProfit \leftarrow NetProfit / NetSales \times 100\%$$

Output the Results as per mock-up
   Print GrossSales, Returns, NetSales,
        Costs, GrossProfit,
        Salaries, Utilities, Rent, Expenses,
        NetProfit,
        PercentProfit

This is everything we need for the main algorithm, and we can work on the procedure `Collect`.

Subtask `Collect`: Step 1—Understand the Problem. We have, for all practical purposes, already done this step. When we identified the process necessary for collecting the input data, we wrote (for the gross sales) the following algorithm:

Read GrossSales from Store 1
Read GrossSales from Store 2
Total GrossSales ← GrossSales from Store 1 + GrossSales from Store 2

    We then said a similar process could be used for each of the remaining input categories. In order to convert this to a procedure, we need only generalize it.

Subtask `Collect`: Step 2—Plan the Solution. We already have the plan, too. Converting the above algorithm to a generalized sequence of steps yields

Procedure Collect (InfoStore1, InfoStore2, Total)
   Read (Store1, InfoStore1)
   Read (Store2, InfoStore2)
   Total ← InfoStore1 + InfoStore2

`Store1` indicates that the data is to be read from the file for the first store, and `Store2` indicates that the data should come from the file for the second store.

    Now that we have the algorithms for the main program and the procedure, we may combine them and convert to Pascal.

STEP 3: CODE THE SOLUTION

We are now in a position to code the complete solution. In addition to the elements we are familiar with, we must include those items necessary for the proper use of files. In this case we need data files for the first and second stores (which we will call `Store1` and `Store2`) and an output file for the results (which we shall call `Summary`). In addition, we choose to include the standard file `Output` so that the user can monitor the program as it executes. The complete, coded version is shown in Figure 7-3. Let's look at some of the salient features:

Line 1—The four files used by the program are introduced here.

Lines 9–11—The three external files are defined as text files.

Lines 55–57—The two input files are made ready via Reset, and the output file is prepared using Rewrite.

Lines 61, 71, 94, 129—Output which monitors the progress of the program is written to the standard file Output.

Lines 96–127—The actual report is written to the file Summary.

Line 47—The data for store 1 is read from the file Store1.

Line 48—The data for store 2 is read from the file Store2.

Figure 7-3

Complete REPORT *Program, Including the Input Procedure and Necessary File Specifications*

REPORT.PAS

```
  1    Program REPORT (Store1, Store2, Output, Summary);
  2
  3    (*
  4        This program takes sales and expense information for two
  5        branch stores of F-Mart and generates a financial report.
  6        The data for each store is kept in a different file.
  7    *)
  8
  9    Var Store1,            (* Data for the first store *)
 10        Store2,            (* Data for the second store *)
 11        Summary : Text;    (* File for the report *)
 12
 13        (* The following variables represent quantities for each
 14           store individually and combined *)
 15
 16        GrossSales1, GrossSales2,
 17        GrossSales,              (* Gross sales *)
 18        Costs1, Costs2,
 19        Costs,                   (* Wholesale cost of items sold *)
 20        Returns1, Returns2,
 21        Returns,                 (* Returned items *)
 22        Salaries1, Salaries2,
 23        Salaries,                (* Employee salaries *)
 24        Utilities1, Utilities2,
 25        Utilities,               (* Utility expenses *)
 26        Rent1, Rent2,
 27        Rent,                    (* Rent expense *)
 28        NetSales1, NetSales2,
 29        NetSales,                (* Net sales *)
 30        GrossProfit1, GrossProfit2,
 31        GrossProfit,             (* Gross profits *)
 32        Expenses1, Expenses2,
 33        Expenses,                (* Total of expenses *)
```

Figure 7-3 continued

```
34        NetProfit1, NetProfit2,
35        NetProfit,                    (* Net profit--the bottom line! *)
36        PctProfit1, PctProfit2,
37        PctProfit                     (* Percent profit based on net sales *)
38                   : Real;
39
40
41    Procedure Collect (Var InforStore1, InforStore2, Total : Real);
42    (*
43       This procedure reads one set of data for each of the two
44       stores and totals it up.
45    *)
46      Begin
47        Readln (Store1, InforStore1);
48        Readln (Store2, InforStore2);
49        Total := InforStore1 + InforStore2
50      End;
51
52
53    BEGIN
54
55      Reset   (Store1);
56      Reset   (Store2);
57      Rewrite (Summary);
58
59      (* Get the data from each store and total it all up *)
60
61      Writeln ('Reading Data Files');
62      Collect (GrossSales1, GrossSales2, GrossSales);
63      Collect (Costs1, Costs2, Costs);
64      Collect (Returns1, Returns2, Returns);
65      Collect (Salaries1, Salaries2, Salaries);
66      Collect (Utilities1, Utilities2, Utilities);
67      Collect (Rent1, Rent2, Rent);
68
69      (* Compute the necessary totals and subtotals *)
70
71      Writeln ('Computing Totals');
72      NetSales1 := GrossSales1 - Returns1;
73      NetSales2 := GrossSales1 - Returns2;
74      NetSales  := NetSales1 + NetSales2;
75
76      GrossProfit1 := NetSales1 - Costs1;
77      GrossProfit2 := NetSales2 - Costs2;
78      GrossProfit  := GrossProfit1 + GrossProfit2;
79
80      Expenses1 := Salaries1 + Utilities1 + Rent1;
81      Expenses2 := Salaries2 + Utilities2 + Rent2;
82      Expenses  := Expenses1 + Expenses2;
83
84      NetProfit1 := GrossProfit1 - Expenses1;
85      NetProfit2 := GrossProfit2 - Expenses2;
86      NetProfit  := NetProfit1 + NetProfit2;
87
88      PctProfit1 := NetProfit1 / NetSales1 * 100.0;
89      PctProfit2 := NetProfit2 / NetSales2 * 100.0;
90      PctProfit  := NetProfit / NetSales * 100.0;
91
92      (* Print out the report *)
```

Figure 7-3 continued

```
93
94      Writeln ('Generating Final Report');
95
96      Writeln (Summary,'        FINANCIAL REPORT FOR F-MART STORES 1 AND 2');
97      Writeln (Summary);
98      Writeln (Summary,'                    Store #1     Store #2     Combined');
99      Writeln (Summary);
100     Writeln (Summary,'Gross Sales ',GrossSales1:13:2,GrossSales2:13:2,
101                             GrossSales:13:2);
102     Writeln (Summary,'Returns     ',Returns1:13:2,Returns2:13:2,
103                             Returns:13:2);
104     Writeln (Summary,'Net Sales   ',NetSales1:13:2,NetSales2:13:2,
105                             NetSales:13:2);
106     Writeln (Summary);
107     Writeln (Summary,'Costs       ',Costs1:13:2,Costs2:13:2,
108                             Costs:13:2);
109     Writeln (Summary,'GROSS PROFIT',GrossProfit1:13:2,GrossProfit2:13:2,
110                             GrossProfit:13:2);
111     Writeln (Summary;
112     Writeln (Summary,'Salaries    ',Salaries1:13:2,Salaries2:13:2,
113                             Salaries:13:2);
114     Writeln (Summary,'Utilities   ',Utilities1:13:2,Utilities2:13:2,
115                             Utilities:13:2);
116     Writeln (Summary,'Rent        ',Rent1:13:2,Rent2:13:2,
117                             Rent:13:2);
118     Writeln (Summary,'EXPENSES    ',Expenses1:13:2,Expenses2:13:2,
119                             Expenses:13:2);
120     Writeln (Summary);
121     Writeln (Summary,'NET PROFIT  ',NetProfit1:13:2,NetProfit2:13:2,
122                             NetProfit:13:2);
123     Writeln (Summary);
124     Writeln (Summary,'Percent');
125     Writeln (Summary,'Profit' );
126     Writeln (Summary,'on Sales....',PctProfit1:13:2,' %',PctProfit2:11:2,' %',
127                             PctProfit:11:2,' %');
128
129     Writeln ('Program Complete.')
130
131     END.
```

STEP 4: CHECK OUT THE PROGRAM

Since this program does make use of external files, it will be necessary to create them *before* the program can be run and tested. This normally presents no problem, however, since the process of creating a data file is identical to the process of creating a program file. The only difference between the two is that, rather than entering program statements, you must enter data statements. The contents of the input files Store1 and Store2 are displayed at the top of Figure 7-4. Once the files have been created and checked, we may run the program itself.

A sample run of the report program is shown following the input file display in Figure 7-4. Note that the monitoring messages are dis-

Figure 7-4

Test Run of the Financial Report Program, Including a Listing of the Two Input Files and the Output File

```
$ type store1.dat

23538.54
17058.33
  675.12
 3653.51
  375.09
  750.00

$ type store2.dat

19834.17
14081.54
  822.39
 3520.27
  415.55
  900.00

$ run report

Reading Data Files
Computing Totals
Generating Final Report
Program Complete.

$ type summary.dat

          FINANCIAL REPORT FOR F-MART STORES 1 AND 2

              Store #1  Store #2  Combined

Gross Sales   23538.54  19834.17  43372.71
Returns         675.12    822.39   1497.51
Net Sales     22863.42  22716.15  45579.57

Costs         17058.33  14081.54  31139.87
GROSS PROFIT   5805.09   8634.61  14439.70

Salaries       3653.51   3520.27   7173.78
Utilities       375.09    415.55    790.64
Rent            750.00    900.00   1650.00
EXPENSES       4778.60   4835.82   9614.42

NET PROFIT     1026.49   3798.79   4825.28

Percent
Profit
on Sales....    4.49 %   16.72 %   10.59 %
```

played as they occur during execution. After execution is complete, the output file Summary is displayed. The results are correct, and everything seems to have worked properly.

STEP 5: DOCUMENT

The program itself contains rather a lot of comments, primarily because there are so many variables. In any event, the program is well written and understandable.

SUMMARY

In this chapter we saw that it is possible to read from and write to auxiliary storage devices. This requires the use of files, which greatly expand the flexibility of Pascal.

EXERCISES

CONCEPTS

1. Define or explain the following terms:

   External file
   Field
   File
   Program file
   Record
   Standard files
   Text file

2. Discuss some of the advantages of using external files.

3. Describe how a typical file is organized.

TOOLS

4. Generate all Pascal statements (headings, declarations, executable statements) that would be necessary for a program to make use of any files described in each of the following:

   a. A program is to input the exam scores for each student in a particular class and compute the averages. The results are to be collected into a file.

b. The results of three experimental runs are to be compared and the output sent to the CRT.

c. A payroll application must print checks and vouchers for all employees and keep a summary in a file of the checks written.

d. A program is to plot a graph based on 100 x,y pairs.

5. Generate valid input or output statements that will carry out the indicated tasks:

   a. Read the three integer values `A, B, C` from the file `Numbers`.

   b. Cause the value of `AmtDue` to be written to the file `Stuff` in the form `The Amount Due is $123.45`.

   c. Input a value for `x` from the keyboard, a value for `y` from the file `Addn`, and then multiply them together as `z`. Write the values of `y` and `z` to the CRT and the values of `x, y,` and `z` to the file `Answers`.

   d. Read values of `a, b, c,` and `d` from the file `Data`. It is not known how the values are arranged in the file, that is, they may be all on one line or they may be on separate lines.

PROBLEMS

6. Alter the Hal's Hamburger program of Chapter 4 as follows:

   Input an order from the keyboard (as always).

   Compute the various totals.

   Write the full bill to the file `Bill`.

   Write the amount due to the CRT.

   Read the amount tendered from the keyboard.

   Write the amount tendered to `Bill`.

   Compute the change.

   Write the amount of change to both the CRT and to `Bill`.

7. Alter the atomic spectroscopy program of Chapter 5 so that both the input and output are files rather than the keyboard and CRT.

8. Alter the `Radar` program of Chapter 6 so that the input comes from a file `RadarIn` but the output still goes to the CRT.

9. Alter the ACE Trucking Company program of Chapter 6 so that a bill is written to the file `Stmt` as well as to the CRT.

10. Write a payroll program with the following characteristics:

    a. Input should come from a file called `Employee` and should contain, for the employee, the hours worked, the rate of pay, and the number of exemptions.

b. Compute the pay information as

Gross ← Hours × Rate
FedTax ← 25% (Gross − Exemptions × 22.50)
StateTax ← 5% (Gross − Exemptions × 3.75)
FICA ← 7.2% Gross
Net ← Gross − FedTax − StateTax − FICA

c. Write a summary of the results to the CRT.
d. Write a check and voucher to a file called Pay.

8

Overview II:

Control Structures

Up to this point, the programs and algorithms we have worked with have been very simple in concept and execution. For the most part, each solution has consisted of three segments: (1) reading in data values, (2) computing the results based on the data, and (3) printing out the results. This may be fine for starters, but unfortunately life is rarely this simple. Consider, for example, Hal's Hamburgers—the first in-depth problem we solved. We wrote a program to input a food order and calculate the total bill. However, our program will only take care of one order; if we have several customers, we must reload and rerun the program for each one!

Although having to reload and rerun a program is really little more than a nuisance, attempts to write computer programs that solve more difficult problems will reveal some rather serious limitations inherent in the simple input-calculate-output approach we have been using up to now. Consider, for example, the functioning of a POS (point of sale) terminal. A POS terminal is a computer terminal that also functions as a cash register. These terminals are becoming more and more common, especially in grocery stores. The checker passes a wand over a can of beans (or, conversely, the can of beans over a mirror), and the name of the item and its price appear on the check-out tape. The prices are then added up to yield a subtotal, and the tax is computed and added to yield the total cost for all purchases. If we were writing a program for a store that uses POS terminals, how would we enter data for the items as they pass through the check-out station?

We could apply the method used in the Hal's Hamburgers problem, namely, prompt for each possible item and request the number to be purchased. However, doing so would be very time consuming, since a prompt would have to be issued for every possible food item. For example, if prompts were used in the program, the cashier would see something like the following:

Asparagus, fresh?
Asparagus, canned, small, Del Monte?
Asparagus, canned, large, Del Monte?
Asparagus, canned, small, Western Family?
Asparagus, canned, large, Western Family?
Asparagus, frozen, small, Saver Choice?
Asparagus, frozen, medium, Saver Choice?
Asparagus, frozen, large, Saver Choice?

.
.
.

Zucchini, frozen, medium, Peters?
Zucchini, frozen, large, Peters?

Can you see the problem? And that's not all. In order for the program to work, the customer's groceries would first have to be sorted alphabetically! This is obviously absurd, and a better solution is needed.

We can also encounter other categories of programming difficulties. Consider again the payroll program. In this program we simply assumed that the gross was equal to the rate times the hours. But what would happen if the company paid overtime based on the following system?

If a person works forty hours or fewer, the gross is straight time (calculated as rate times hours). However, if the person works over forty hours, the first forty hours are paid at straight time and the hours over forty are paid at time-and-a-half (that is, the rate becomes one-and-a-half times the normal rate).

The supermarket example above can be solved, albeit laboriously, by brute force, but this overtime payroll problem cannot. Does this mean it is not solvable?

Since people do get computer-generated checks that include overtime, this problem obviously can be solved. In fact, **control structures** can be used to solve all of the problems above. Control structures provide a mechanism by which sections of code can be repeated and decisions made. As their name implies, control structures are the embodiment of structure—they are building blocks for program construction. As far as Pascal syntax is concerned, control structures are merely additional statement types that can be used in the executable portion of a program. Consequently, control structures can be used in basically the same way as the three statement types (assignment, input, and output) already introduced, although control structures are somewhat more complex and require a little more effort to understand. This chapter will introduce the concept and use of control structures.

8-1   *Fundamental Control Structures*

There are many possible control structures, but three of them are fundamental in the sense that any problem that *can* be solved using a computer (and there are some, believe it or not, that cannot be) can be solved by using a program that contains only these three control structures. It is necessary to have at least these three structures; the many other control structures available are merely conveniences. The three **fundamental control structures** are

1. Sequence (or process)

2. Binary decision (or If-Then-Else)

3. Iteration (or looping)

We will first introduce these structures and show what they are and how they work. As we discussed in Chapter 3, there are two primary ways to represent instructions to a computer: flowcharting and pseudocode. These techniques can also be used to describe control structures, which are nothing more than a different type of instruction. We will represent these structures by both flowcharting (because it is a very effective way to introduce the structures) and pseudocode (because it is the method we shall use to represent problem solutions in the remainder of the book).

SEQUENCE

Sequence is the first type of fundamental control structure. It is sometimes called *process* and amounts to executing instructions sequentially one at a time, one after the other. This is exactly what we have been doing up to this point (with the exception of procedure and function calls). The sequence structure can be represented using flowcharting as

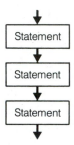

A pseudocode representation would be

Statement
Statement
Statement

Consider an example: suppose we wanted to calculate the volume of a cylinder with height h and radius r given by the geometry formula

$$v = \pi\, r^2\, h$$

An algorithm to carry out this computation requires only the sequence control structure and can be written as

Prompt 'What is the height?'
Read h

Prompt 'What is the radius?'
Read r

$v \leftarrow pi \times r^2 \times h$

Print 'The volume is ', v

Since we have been using sequence all along, there is no need to consider it further.

BINARY DECISION

Binary decision is sometimes called If-Then-Else and is the control structure that gives the computer its decision-making ability. You test a condition, and based on the results of the test, one of two possible courses of action is taken. This is important: you must always choose *exactly one* of the alternatives. You may NOT choose both and you may NOT choose neither. The flowchart representation of this structure is

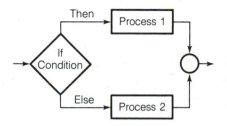

Remember that we are using a flowchart representation here as a means of explanation only. We are not really interested in the exact flow of control in this structure, since the Pascal language takes care of it for us automatically. The diagram does, however, help make clear how this particular structure works.

The pseudocode representation of binary decision would be

If condition then
    Process 1
Else
    Process 2

If the condition is true, then Process 1 is executed; if, on the other hand, the condition is not true (that is, if the condition is false), then Process 2 is carried out. Note that one and only one process is executed. Another very important point: after one of the alternatives is chosen, control resumes at the same point at the end of the structure *regardless of which process was carried out*. The binary decision structure has a *single entry point* and a *single exit point* and must be regarded as a single, indivisible unit. Take special note of the indentations in the notation. These are used to signify which process belongs to the If and which belongs to the Else.

For a more concrete example, let's look at an overtime payroll calculation. The algorithm for it can be expressed as

If the hours worked are less than or equal to 40 then
    Gross ← Hours × Rate
Else
    Gross ← Rate × 40 + (Hours over 40) × 1.5 × Rate

Putting this in a more concise mathematical way, we have

If Hours ≤ 40 then
   Gross ← Hours × Rate
Else
   Gross ← Rate × 40 + (Hours − 40) × 1.5 × Rate

Here a decision is based on the total number of hours worked. If it is less than or equal to 40, the gross is calculated (as we have always done) by multiplying the rate by the hours. If, on the other hand, overtime is a factor (the number of hours is greater than 40), then a different computation is used. In this latter case, the regular rate is paid for the first 40 hours, and one-and-a-half times the rate (time-and-a-half) is paid on the excess hours over 40. It is impossible to do this calculation correctly *without* the decision-making ability provided by the control structure.

More than any other reason, the lack of a formal binary decision structure in earlier programming languages was responsible for the writing of poor programs. Most of the early programming languages had an If statement of sorts, which could be used to transfer control from the current statement to some other statement based on the results of a condition evaluation. Although a true binary decision structure can be made from this, it takes some work and was rarely so used. What normally happened was that the programmer made a test, and the program was thenceforth divided into two main pathways, each of which was further subdivided at many points. The resultant program was nearly impossible to decipher because there were so many possible jumps. Consequently, these programs were intelligible only to the programmers who wrote the programs and then for only a couple of weeks. Correcting and testing the programs were difficult, and modification was nearly impossible.

With current languages such as Pascal, such cumbersome maneuvers are no longer necessary. Making good use of the available control structures will allow you to write easily understandable and modifiable programs. Let's move on to the last fundamental control structure.

ITERATION

This is the third fundamental control structure. **Iteration** allows a given section of the program to be repeated any number of times, from zero to infinity. (Although executing a section of the program zero times can be useful, trying to repeat it an infinite number of times will obviously cause problems.) Iteration is also called looping, since the process goes round in a loop, repeating some step or steps a number of times. There are many varieties of loops, but at this time we will introduce only two: the pretest While loop and the pretest Counted Loop.

While. This structure is used in situations where the computer must repeat a set of instructions as long as (that is, *while*) a condition or set of conditions holds true. The **While loop** will carry out the same set of instructions over and over again, never getting tired, as long as the While condition persists. The number of times the loop instructions are carried out is indeterminate; that is, the computer does not know beforehand how many times the loop will be repeated. Whether or not the loop instructions are carried out again depends on the conditions at the *beginning* of each cycle. For example, most people continue to eat as long as they are hungry or to scratch as long as they itch. Your mother even demonstrated the While structure for you when she told you, as a child, that she wanted you to behave like a little lady or gentleman as long as Grandma was there. The same is true even in computer science: as long as a given condition is true, the computer must continue to carry out a specific set of instructions.

The flowchart representation for the While statement can be written as

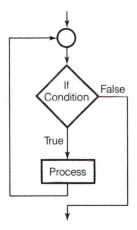

Closely examine the way in which the control moves through this flowchart. First, the condition is tested; if it is true, the process is carried out. After completing the designated process, control moves back to the top, where the condition is checked again. If the condition is still true, control reenters the loop. If, however, the condition is false, then control leaves the loop and picks up at the statement immediately following the last loop statement. Note that the test is made only *once* per cycle, after the process has been completed but before the loop is reentered. The test is *never* made in the middle of the loop. Especially note that, as with binary decision, this structure has but a *single entry point* and a *single exit point* and should be regarded as an indivisible entity.

An important feature of the While loop is that it is a **pretest loop.** This means that the condition is evaluated *before* the body of the loop (the process) is executed. This allows for the possibility that the loop *may not be executed at all*. Although this at first seems strange, it can in fact have very important consequences. Let's look at a simple example. Suppose you own a real estate business, and at the end of each day, you run your accounting program, a part of which adds up the sales made that day. Occasionally, you will have days on which nothing gets sold. What happens when the program gets run on these days? Hopefully, you would have written the tally section with a pretest loop. When the control in the program discovers that there are no sales, it simply skips the loop entirely!

Here is another example. Suppose you run a business that requires you to pay your employees daily, based on available (and intermittent) work, and that on a particular day there was nobody who was to get paid. If the payroll program (available perhaps as a part of the daily financial accounting operations) was run anyway, a pretest structure in the loop that searched employee records would keep any checks from being written. If in fact the condition was *not* tested at first (that is, a pretest loop was not utilized), an invalid check would incorrectly be written.

There are many situations in which a loop should be carried out zero times. Perhaps somebody stops at a convenience store checkout not to buy anything but just to get change; perhaps loan activity at a bank is zero. These situations can be handled nicely by using pretest loop structures. It would also be possible to handle these situations by making a special test for the condition before the loop was entered, but there is no point in taking time and trouble to do this when the loop itself can automatically handle the possibility.

The pseudocode representation for the While structure is

While Condition Do
    Process

This means that the process should be repeated *each time* the condition tests True. The flow of control is implicit in the pseudocode representation above. The first time the condition is found to be False when tested, the program skips over the process and continues on at the first statement after the end of the loop. Process is indented in the pseudocode representation to indicate that it belongs entirely to the While loop and that anything else following that is not indented does not.

Let's use our payroll program to demonstrate a While loop. Suppose we want the program to run for not just one employee but for many. We can place our original payroll program into a loop, and the algorithm will look like this:

While there are still persons to be paid Do
  Get the Inputs
    Read Hours
    Read Rate
  Do the Calculations
    Compute the Gross Wages
      Gross ← Hours × Rate
    Compute any Deductions
      FICA ← Gross × SSRate
      Federal Tax ← Gross × FedTaxRate
    Compute the Net Pay
      Net ← Gross − FICA − Federal Tax
  Do the Output
    Print Hours, Rate, Gross, FICA, Federal Tax, Net

Although we haven't indicated how to determine whether or not there are still persons to be paid, nonetheless the code corresponding to the actual payroll program will be *repeated* as long as there are more checks to be written. This is the essence of the While loop. With regard to presentation, notice that indentation is used effectively to show that *all* the instructions underneath the While statement are to be repeated. Note that the structure of the actual payroll work (as generated previously) remains undisturbed and intact and that the overall structure of the entire program still stands out clearly.

We can also use this While structure to solve our POS check-out problem. We simply direct the computer to continue accepting purchases *while* there are still items left to be checked! This can be written algorithmically as follows:

Total ← 0

While there are still items to be checked Do
  Read Product Code of item
  Fetch Price and Name of item using Product Code
  Total ← Total + Price of item
  Print Name and Price on tape

Tax ← Total × TaxRate
Grand ← Total + Tax

Print Total, Tax, Grand

Again, there are some instructions that eventually will need more detail, especially the Fetch Price and Name statement, but this is not necessary to an understanding of the loop structure at this point. Notice that a running total is kept. As long as there are items to be purchased, the prices are retrieved and added to that running total.

Of special importance is the structure. Note how the While is separated as an individual entity, with a number of substatements associated with it. In fact the While is merely another statement, albeit more complex than the ones we have studied thus far. A complete boxed structure for the POS solution is shown in Figure 8-1.

Counted loop. The second commonly encountered type of iterative structure is the **counted loop,** so called because the computer knows *before it enters the loop* how many times the loop is to be repeated. This is in contrast to the While loop, where the computer never knows exactly how many times it will repeat a set of instructions and in fact doesn't even know if it will go through the loop another time (or even the first time) until it checks the condition at the start of the loop (as in, for example, the algorithm for the POS terminal). The While loop continues until there are no more items to be processed, whenever that may be. This structure is very useful in that there is no limit to the number of items that can be processed—it can vary from zero to infinity (which, as noted before, is not normally an acceptable number).

However, for the counted loop, the actual number of times the loop instructions are to be repeated can be determined *before* the loop is

Figure 8-1

POS Check-out Algorithm Emphasizing Block Structure

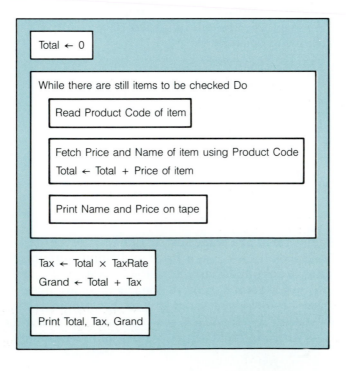

entered. Not only that, but this number remains fixed; that is, it cannot be changed once the iteration process has begun.

Let's start by looking at the pseudocode representation of the counted loop, since it's a little easier to comprehend:

For Counter ← StartValue to EndValue Do
   Process

Note that this structure requires a counter, that is, something that keeps track of how many times the loop is carried out. The counter is given an initial value, and the computer carries out the loop process while it counts from the StartValue to the EndValue, one execution of Process per count. For example, if the loop were written as

For Counter ← 1 to 10 Do
   Process

the Process would be carried out ten times, one for each value of the counter going from 1 to 10, inclusive. In Pascal, the computer *always* counts by ones.

For the sake of completeness, let's now present the flowchart version of this structure:

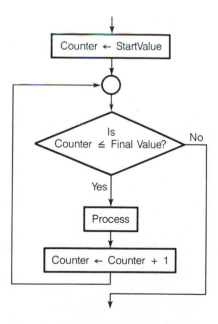

Notice two things here. First, as with *all* control structures, there is but a single entry and a single exit. Second, the structure is quite complex. However, Pascal takes care of all the details, so once you understand them you needn't be concerned with the flowchart representation again.

It turns out that the counted loop is actually just a special case of the While loop, and any counted loop can be replaced with a While loop (although the converse is NOT true). In fact, the counted loop may be represented algorithmically by, and is equivalent to, the following While loop:

Counter ← StartValue
While Counter is less than or equal to EndValue Do
    Process
    Counter ← Counter + 1

As a simple example, suppose you wanted to print out the numbers 10 through 20, inclusive. This is a job for counted loops! It can easily be written as

For Number ← 10 to 20 Do
    Output Number

This loop begins by assigning the value 10 (StartValue) to Number. The loop is then entered and the process carried out (in this case, print the current value of Number). After the value 10 is printed out, Number is incremented *automatically* to the value of 11; the value 11 is then printed out, and the process continues. Eventually, Number gets the value 20, and after this is printed out, the loop is finished, since 20 is indicated as the final value.

Also be aware that, in many applications, either a counted loop or a While loop can be used. By way of demonstration, suppose we wish to rework the POS problem so that a counted loop is used rather than the While loop. This can be written thus:

Total ← 0

Prompt 'How many items to be purchased?'
Read N

For Count ← 1 to N Do
    Read Produce Code for item
    Fetch Price and Name of item using Product Code
    Total ← Total + Price of item
    Print Name and Price on tape

Notice that, although this works well enough, it requires the entry person (cashier) to count how many items are to be purchased. Obviously, this can present serious problems in a check-out line. There are many such situations where it is at best a nuisance to have to count the number of input items. Even our simple payroll program would be considerably more difficult to run if we had to count the number of checks to be written each time. In such cases it is obviously better to use the While loop and leave it to the computer to determine how many times to repeat the task.

Nevertheless, there are applications in computing, especially scientific and mathematical, in which counted loops are superior to the While structure. An easy example (which will be expounded on later) is that of factorials. Factorials are defined for any positive integer n as follows:

$$n! = n \times (n - 1) \times (n - 2) \times \ldots \times 3 \times 2 \times 1$$

This says that $n!$ (read "n factorial") is the product of the number itself times all digits less than itself. For example,

$$5! = 5 \times 4 \times 3 \times 2 \times 1 = 120$$

This process involves counting, and a counted loop would be applicable here. The algorithm for this is simply presented as

Prompt 'Enter an integer number'
Read n

Factorial ← 1

For Digit ← 1 to n Do
       Factorial ← Factorial × Digit

Output Factorial

What happens here is that the factorial calculation is repeated n times, once for every digit between 1 and n. It is important to note that we could have, had we wanted, used a While loop to construct factorials, but in this case the counted loop is easier to understand and actually superior.

8-2 *Nonfundamental Control Structures*

There are several other commonly encountered control structures in addition to the three fundamental ones discussed above; however, they are *not* fundamental, in the sense that they can be replaced in any situation by one of the three fundamental structures (again, the converse is not true). We will very briefly introduce two of these: the Case statement, because it can be very convenient, and the GoTo, because it is ubiquitous (and dangerous!).

Case. The Case statement is also called a selection or **multiple decision** statement. Instead of having only two possible choices, as in binary decision, there are any number of choices. As an example, consider the situation in which different actions are to be taken with students depending on which of the five letter grades A through F they are awarded in a class. A different process must be carried out for each of the five letter grades. The Case statement is ideal for this: there are five possible situations or cases corresponding to the five letters, and the appropriate action can be taken for each. This can be represented with pseudocode (flowcharts don't work well here) as

```
    Case Letter of
A : Process1
B : Process2
C : Process3
D : Process4
F : Flunk 'em
```

This algorithm can be written using the binary decision structure (which is why the case structure is not fundamental), but in a situation like this, the Case structure is much more convenient and appropriate.

GoTo. This small word, a very common control structure in most older programming languages, has been blamed for 99 percent of the world's programming problems. Actually it's getting bad press: it's not the GoTo statement per se that's the problem but rather the poor use of it. In many languages, such as standard FORTRAN 77 and BASIC, it *must* be used to write structured programs! Some enhanced versions don't need it, but it is something that should be understood and avoided rather than ignored. It's like the case of Sleeping Beauty: if you are aware of the pitfalls, you can avoid them. The GoTo simply allows an unconditional transfer to a different program statement. It is even available in Pascal, although prudence requires it not be used except in very, very special circumstances. We will, therefore, not make use of it in this text.

SUMMARY

In this chapter we introduced the fundamental control structures: sequence, binary decision, and iteration. Sequence is the only one we have used prior to this chapter, and it permits instructions to be executed one after the other. The binary decision structure allows the computer to choose between alternatives. The iteration structure allows a process to be repeated over and over. We also mentioned two nonfundamental control structures: the Case statement and the GoTo—the former is a convenience, and the latter is something to be avoided.

We will proceed, in the next two chapters, to detail the use and application of binary decision and iteration (because we have been using sequence all along there is no need to cover it further). Notice, however, that although we introduced binary decision *before* iteration in this chapter, we will reverse that order and first cover iteration in Chapter 9 and *then* binary decision in Chapter 10. They were introduced in the first order because binary decision is a little easier to understand than is iteration. However, we reverse the order when covering them in detail, because iteration is the more general structure. It is more general for two reasons: first, properties common to both iteration and binary decision can be better detailed with iteration. Second, iteration (without the help of binary decision) can be used to solve a wider range of realistic problems than can binary decision (without iteration).

EXERCISES

CONCEPTS

1. Define or explain the following terms:

Binary decision   Iteration

Control structure   Multiple decision

Counted loop   Pretest loop

Fundamental control structure   While loop

2. Name and explain, using flowcharts and pseudocode, the functions of the three fundamental control structures.

3. Explain why each of the control structures should be considered an indivisible unit.

TOOLS

4. Find an example of a While process that *can also* be expressed as a counted loop.

5. Find an example of a While process that *cannot* be expressed as a counted loop.

9

Iteration:

For, While, and Repeat

We now turn our attention to a detailed examination of iteration (or looping). Iteration is a very powerful tool that permits a whole new range of problems to be solved. It can be used in situations where the same task must be repeated over and over again and could thus be used to expand the Hal's Hamburgers application for more than one person or to handle the grocery check-out problem described in the previous chapter. However, iteration also permits solutions of other classes of problems that may not, at first glance, seem to need looping. One such problem would be the calculation of square roots and another would be the generation of tax liabilities. The loop control structure also permits the computer to carry out tedious and time-consuming procedures that humans can do but don't much like to do. There was a time, for instance, when graduate students in math and statistics would help pay their way through college by hiring themselves out to various research groups for the purpose of inverting matrices by hand, a dull and tedious process fraught with opportunities for error. However, with the advent of computers (which can do loops), such human effort became unnecessary, and grad students can now do more interesting things with their time.

In this chapter we will look at two categories of loops—counted loops and conditional loops. We will also examine variations within each of these categories. Since the former is a little easier to understand, we will begin there.

9-1 *Counted Loops*

This is the most straightforward of the loop types. A counted loop is, of course, one kind of control structure, but its implementation in Pascal is such that it is actually (and merely) another kind of statement. As such it is an executable statement and is used in the executable section of a program. We may, therefore, expand our list of executable statements to

```
executable-statement → assignment statement
                     | input-statement
                     | output-statement
                     | counted-loop
```

There are actually two kinds of counted loops, so we may expand this category to read

```
counted-loop → count-up-loop
            | count-down-loop
```

As the names suggest, the **count-up loop** counts up (as you would normally count, for example, 1, 2, 3, 4, 5, etc.) and the **count-down loop** does just the reverse (for example, 10, 9, 8, 7, 6, etc.). We will look at both kinds of loops.

COUNT-UP LOOPS

The form of the count-up loop is

```
count-up-loop→for counter := start-expr to end-expr do
                  statement
```

(For simplicity and convenience we will refer to count-up loops as counted loops for the rest of this section.)

The form of this definition should look very familiar, since it is similar to the algorithmic representation of the counted loop shown in the previous chapter. The loop itself (which is merely a Pascal statement) contains *embedded within it another statement*. Note especially (this is important) that the statement inside a counted loop may be any valid Pascal statement, *including another counted loop*. When so constructed together, the loops are said to be nested. **Nested loops,** although more complex, are also more powerful. (Their properties are discussed later on in this chapter.)

Let's look at the various parts of the counted loop definition. Following our established convention, the items in boldface (for, := , to, do) are required. The counter may be any variable that is not of type Real (most often, this will be an integer variable, but it need not be; variables of type Char may be used, for example). Assuming an integer counter, the start expression and end expression may be any valid integer expression (which can include, of course, either integer constants or integer variables as well as more complex expressions).

As we go through this section on count-up loops we will look at the following: simple loops, compound statement loops (those loops that contain more than one statement), and nested loops (one loop inside another).

Simple loops. Let's begin with a demonstration of a simple loop using an example.

Simple Summation

Suppose your name was Isaac Newton, and your teacher asked you to add up the numbers from 1 to 100 as busy work to keep you quiet. Being clever, you would avoid using brute force to solve this problem (that is, you would not add the numbers up longhand). Instead, you might notice something interesting: if you count *forward* from 1 and *backward* from 99 simultaneously, each pair of numbers adds up to 100! For example,

$$1 + 99 = 100$$
$$2 + 98 = 100$$
$$3 + 97 = 100$$

You can do this for the numbers from 1 to 49, which will yield a sum of 4,900. This leaves only the numbers 50 and 100, which, when added in, yield a total of 5,050. This method is both simple and elegant. However, in this day and age you would probably write a computer program to solve the problem. Let us, therefore, develop such a program.

STEP 1: UNDERSTAND THE PROBLEM

There's really not much to understand: we want to add up all of the numbers from 1 to 100, inclusive. Note, however, that we cannot easily use Newton's elegant solution but must instead rely on brute force.

STEP 2: PLAN THE SOLUTION

We can generate a solution using the same idea that worked so well in the grocery store check-out problem, namely, we can build a loop involving a tally variable to accumulate a sum. The algorithm can be written as

1.   Sum ← 0
2.   For n ← 1 to 100 Do
3.   Sum ← Sum + n
4.   Print Sum

The lines of the algorithm are numbered for reference. Notice what we are doing here: we start off by initializing a sum to zero and then go through (in a loop) and add to that sum each of the integers from 1 to 100. It is instructive, at this point, to laboriously go through and trace this algorithm. As a part of the trace we will keep track of the values of all the variables as we would expect to see them in the computer's memory.

In line 1 we set the value of Sum to zero. After the statement on this first line has been executed, our variable memory locations (of which there are but two, namely, Sum and n) would contain

```
Sum : 0        n : x
```

where the x, indicated as the value for variable n, means that it is undefined (that is, we have not yet given it any value). A word of caution: some versions of Pascal will initialize variables to zero, but it is poor practice to get into the habit of assuming this to be the case. *Always* initialize variables yourself. (The variable n does in fact get initialized in line 2.)

Next we come to line 2, where we set up our loop. We initialize n to 1 (as predicted), and the values of our variables become

```
Sum : 0        n : 1
```

Notice that n is no longer undefined. In Pascal, counted loops are pre-test loops. Therefore, the first thing that would occur would be a comparison of the value of n with the indicated ending value, which is in this case 100. Since n is presently less than or equal to 100, the condition is True and the loop is entered.

Now that we are in the loop, we can carry out the loop statements. There is only one in this case, namely, the rather curious expression Sum ← Sum + n in line 3. However, we do just exactly what it says to do: take the contents of Sum, add to that the contents of n, and place the result (back) into Sum. The fact that the variable Sum is both the result *and* one of the operands makes no difference; the operation still works just fine. So what would we get? Sum starts out with a value of zero, and n has a value of 1; adding them together gives a value of 1. This, then, is to be stored back in Sum. Our variable storage, therefore, becomes

```
Sum : 1        n : 1
```

We have now completed the body of the loop for the first time, and we are ready to continue. At this point in the loop execution, that is, immediately following the body of the loop and just before the loop test is reapplied, the loop counter is automatically incremented by 1; consequently our memory locations will appear as

```
Sum : 1        n : 2
```

We have completed the entire loop process once and now need to go back to the beginning of the loop and check to see whether we are done looping or whether we will need to go through the loop again. To do so we apply the loop test (as we did on initially entering the loop): Is the current value of n less than or equal to the ending value? The answer is Yes; n has a current value of 2, and that is certainly less than or equal to the indicated final value of 100. We therefore reenter the loop and find ourselves once again at line 3.

Carrying out the body of the loop (that is, step 3) once again, we are told to add the variable n to Sum and place the result in Sum. This time Sum has the value of 1 and n has the value of 2; adding them up yields 3, which goes back into Sum. Therefore, we end up with

```
Sum : 3        n : 2
```

Having completed this addition, we must again increment n by 1 (to 3 this time) and check to see whether or not we are done looping. Is *n* less than or equal to 100? Yes it is, so we again enter the loop body, where we carry out step 3 by adding *n* (whose value is 3) to Sum (also at 3) to give the new values

```
Sum : 6        n : 3
```

Continuing in this manner, over and over again, we will eventually get to the point at which, on completion of the loop body at line 3, the following is in memory:

```
Sum : 4851     n : 98
```

The value of *n* is incremented (up to 99) and the test made. Since *n* is *still* less than or equal to 100, the loop is once again entered. Carrying out the instructions for line 3 yields

```
Sum : 4950     n : 99
```

The value of *n* is incremented to 100, and the test is made yet one more time. Since *n* is still less than or equal to 100, we go through the loop another time (note how boring this is to humans). The body of the loop (step 3) is executed again, adding *n* to Sum to yield 5050. As we have done many times before, we increment *n* (to 101) and go back up to the start of the loop. This time, however, n *is no longer less than or equal to the final value: it is now greater.* Consequently, we are at long last finished with the loop! Having successfully completed the entire loop, we continue on at the next statement (namely line 4), which outputs the Sum (the value 5050) for us.

This looping business, in which we are constantly looking for the end, seems really tedious. However, remember that the checking and incrementing are done *automatically* by the computer. You *never* have to explicitly increment or make the comparisons yourself in order to determine whether or not the loop is finished. That is part of the beauty of control structures!

STEP 3: CODE THE SOLUTION

Let us now convert this algorithm to a Pascal program. As always, this should be the easiest part. Using everything we know up to this point, we can immediately write down the complete program, which is shown in Figure 9-1.

Figure 9-1

Program to Add Inclusive Numbers from 1 to 100, with a Test Run and Results

```
SUMITUP.PAS

 1    Program SUMITUP (Input, Output);
 2
 3    (*
 4        This program adds up the integers from 1 to 100, inclusive.
 5    *)
 6
 7    Var Sum, n : Integer;
 8
 9    BEGIN
10
11      Sum := 0;
12
13      For n := 1 to 100 Do
14          Sum := Sum + n;
15
16      Writeln ('The sum of the numbers 1 to 100 is ',Sum:1)
17
18    END.


$ run sumitup

The sum of the numbers 1 to 100 is 5050
```

See how the structure of the algorithm is preserved. Note also that we have exactly three executable statements in the program: the counted loop is considered to be just one statement, even though it covers two lines and has another statement (an assignment statement) within it. The three executable statements are separated by semicolons. However, there is no semicolon between the `Writeln` statement and the `END`, since the `END` marks the final bit of the program.

STEP 4: CHECK OUT THE PROGRAM

A test run of the program is also shown in Figure 9-1; the expected result, 5050, is produced.

STEP 5: DOCUMENT

The program is written (and includes comments) to make it easily understandable.

General Summation

Now, a program to add up the numbers 1 to 100 is really pretty silly, so let's make things more general. Instead of going specifically from 1 to 100, let's alter the program so that we can add up the integers from any low number to any high number.

STEP 1: UNDERSTAND THE PROBLEM

Again, there's not much to understand—we'd like to add up all the numbers between any two arbitrary limits.

STEP 2: PLAN THE SOLUTION

How can we accomplish this task? Essentially, instead of using constant limits on the loop, we would use variable limits. This can be accomplished via prompts and reads, and we can write the algorithm as

Prompt 'What is the low number?'
Input Low

Prompt 'What is the high number?'
Input High

Sum ← 0

For n ← Low to High Do
    Sum ← Sum + n

Print Sum

Note that, for all practical purposes, this is the same algorithm as the first. However, instead of specifying the start value and end value with constants, we use variables. In this way we can get the sum of *any* series of numbers!

STEP 3: CODE THE SOLUTION

Converting this to Pascal gives us the program shown in Figure 9-2.

STEP 4: CHECK OUT THE PROGRAM

Along with the program in Figure 9-2, we show a test run in which the limits 3 to 17 are used and the correct sum is produced.

Program to Add All the Numbers Between Any Two Arbitrary Limits,
Along with a Sample Run

```
GENERALS.PAS

1    Program GENERALSUM (Input, Output);
2
3    (*
4        This program sums any arbitrary sequence of integers.
5    *)
6
7    Var Low, High, Sum, n : Integer;
8
9    BEGIN
10
11     Writeln('This program adds up all the integers between any');
12     Writeln('given low number and high number, inclusive.');
13     Writeln;
14     Write ('What is the low number? ');  Readln (Low);
15     Write ('What is the high number? '); Read (High);
16
17     Sum := 0;
18
19     For n := Low to High Do
20         Sum := Sum + n;
21
22     Writeln;
23     Writeln ('The sum is ', Sum:1)
24
25   END.
```

```
$ run generals


This program adds all the integers between any
given low number and high number, inclusive.

What is the low number? 3
What is the high number? 17

The sum is 150
```

STEP 5: DOCUMENT

Again, the program structure, variable names, and comments are sufficient to make the program easily understandable.

Let's look at one more example of a simple counted loop.

Factorials

Consider further the factorial problem introduced in the previous chapter.

STEP 1: UNDERSTAND THE PROBLEM

This was discussed at length in Chapter 8.

STEP 2: PLAN THE SOLUTION

As you recall from that chapter, an algorithm was developed, and it is reproduced here:

Prompt 'Enter an integer number'
Read n

Factorial ← 1

For Digit ← 1 to n Do
    Factorial ← Factorial × Digit

Print Factorial

Let's trace through this algorithm to make sure we understand it completely. Initially, we are prompted to supply a value whose factorial we want to compute. Suppose we enter, in response to the prompt, a value of 3 for n. The factorial of 3 can be calculated from the definition of factorial as

$$3! = 3 \times 2 \times 1 = 6$$

Thus, we would expect an answer of 6 from our algorithm. Let's see if that is in fact what happens. First we input the value of n, which we have said will be 3. Continuing to follow our algorithm we set Factorial equal to 1. Next we enter the loop, where we begin by assigning an initial value of 1 to Digit. This gives us, in memory,

```
n : 3    Factorial : 1    Digit : 1
```

We next test to see whether we should enter the loop at all; in this case we check to see whether Digit is less than or equal to n. Since Digit is currently 1 and n is currently 3, the condition is met and we can enter the loop. Going through the body of the loop, we find we are instructed to take the value stored in Factorial, multiply it by the value stored in Digit, and place the result (back) into Factorial. This means we multiply 1 (Factorial) times 1 (Digit) to yield a result of 1 (how boring). After this has happened, our memory still looks the same. Having completed the loop, we are now ready to increment the counter and test the loop condition again. Digit goes from 1 to 2, and we check to see whether it has reached the final value (3 in this case). Digit is still less than or equal to 3, so we must go through the loop again. We proceed to the body of the loop, where we multiply Factorial (still 1) by Digit (now 2) to produce a value of 2. Our memory thus becomes

```
n : 3     Factorial : 2     Digit : 2
```

Again we increment and then check to see if we are through. Since 3 (Digit's new value) is less than or equal to 3 (*n*), we are not finished and hence must reenter the loop. This time we have 2 (Factorial) times 3 (Digit) to give 6. This is placed in Factorial, and memory becomes

```
n : 3     Factorial : 6     Digit : 3
```

Incrementing and then going back to the beginning of the loop and checking the condition, we find that we are now done looping, since the counter (Digit, with a value of 4) is no longer less than or equal to the final value (*n*, with a value of 3). Hence, we exit the loop and print out the final result of 6, which is what we expected (or at least hoped) it would be.

It is instructive to consider what would happen if we entered a value of 0 (zero) for *n* in this particular algorithm. Assuming we did so, we would continue on by setting Factorial to 1 (as before) and initializing the loop counter (Digit) to 1. Memory would look like this:

```
n : 0     Factorial : 1     Digit : 1
```

We then come to the loop test: Is the current value of Digit (now at 1) less than or equal to the end value of *n* (currently 0)? The answer is *no*. Consequently, since this is a pretest loop and the loop test is False, *we do not enter the loop even once!* Note, however, that we still get the correct value for Factorial, which remains at 1.

STEP 3: CODE THE SOLUTION

Converting the factorial algorithm to a program gives us the complete solution shown in Figure 9-3. Note that the program conforms quite well to the algorithm.

STEP 4: CHECK OUT THE PROGRAM

A test run is made using *n* = 6 and the results are displayed in Figure 9-3. The correct result of 720 is produced.

Figure 9-3

Program to Calculate Factorials, along with a Sample Run

```
FACT.PAS

    1    Program FACT (Input, Output);
    2
    3    (*
    4           This program computes factorials.
    5    *)
    6
    7    Var n, Digit, Factorial : Integer;
    8
    9    BEGIN
   10
   11      Writeln('FACTORIAL CALCULATION PROGRAM');
   12      Writeln;
   13      Write ('Enter an integer number '); Readln (n);
   14
   15      Factorial := 1;
   16
   17      For Digit := 1 to n Do
   18          Factorial := Factorial * Digit;
   19
   20      Writeln;
   21      Writeln ('The factorial of ', n:1, ' is ', Factorial:1)
   22
   23    END.
```

```
$ run fact

FACTORIAL CALCULATION PROGRAM

Enter an integer number 6

The factorial of 6 is 720
```

STEP 5: DOCUMENT

Done.

These are elementary examples, so let's now move on to a more complex problem whose solution requires the use of loops.

Amortized Loan Payments

Suppose you are working at the loan department of a bank, and you need to calculate amortization payments. An amortized loan is one in which you figure all the interest and principal payments over the life of the loan such that payback is made in equal monthly installments. Let's explore how this may be done.

STEP 1: UNDERSTAND THE PROBLEM

We wish to write a program that amortizes loan payments. To this end, we ask: What inputs and outputs are required? The input data may be listed as follows:

Principal: the amount of the loan

Interest rate: the *annual* rate

Term: how long the loan is to be taken out (in years)

With this as input, what outputs would we like to produce? Obviously, our primary goal is to determine the

Monthly payment: the amount to be paid each month for the life of the loan

So we know what we have and what we need. Let us therefore go on to the next step.

STEP 2: PLAN THE SOLUTION

At first it appears that in order to calculate the monthly payment we must figure the total interest due (which changes from month to month as the principal drops) and somehow spread it out over the entire term of the loan. However, we really needn't work that hard. A little research shows that there is a formula that will make this calculation directly, namely,

$$\text{Payment} = a \frac{i \, (1 \, + \, i)^n}{(1 \, + \, i)^n \, - \, 1}$$

where a = the amount of the loan

i = the rate of interest per compounding period

n = the number of compounding periods

Before we can go any further, we must reconcile this formula with the definition of the problem as given above. For example, what is a compounding period? It's how much time goes by before interest is compounded again. In our case the compounding period would be one month. Therefore, combining our "Understanding" phase definitions with this formula we have

$a =$ Principal

$n =$ Term $\times$ 12

$i =$ Interest Rate / 12

Given these relationships, we can write our algorithm directly:

Prompt 'Amount of Loan'
Read Principal

Prompt 'Annual Interest Rate'
Read AnnualRate

Prompt 'Term of Loan'
Read Term

NoPeriods $\leftarrow$ Term $\times$ 12

IntRate $\leftarrow$ AnnualRate / 12

Payment $\leftarrow$ Principal $\dfrac{\text{IntRate } (1 + \text{IntRate})^{\text{NoPeriods}}}{(1 + \text{IntRate})^{\text{NoPeriods}} - 1}$

Print 'The amortized monthly payment on this loan is',
    Payment

Unfortunately, we have a problem here: Pascal does not have an exponentiation operator. What to do? Well, the obvious solution is to define exponentiation in terms of a function and defer consideration until later. Adding this function reference to our algorithm and restating it in terms that are closer to Pascal gives us

Prompt 'Amount of Loan'
Read Principal

Prompt 'Annual Interest Rate'
Read AnnualRate

Prompt 'Term of Loan'
Read Term

NoPeriods $\leftarrow$ Term $\times$ 12

IntRate $\leftarrow$ AnnualRate / 12

Compounding $\leftarrow$ PWR (1 + IntRate, NoPeriods)

Payment $\leftarrow$ Principal $\times$ IntRate $\times$ Compounding / (Compounding $-$ 1)

Print 'The amortized monthly payment on this loan is',
    Payment

Here we call the exponentiation function PWR, where a to the power b would be expressed as PWR (a, b). Also, since we have to compute the same exponential twice, we have chosen to use the auxiliary variable Compounding to store the result of the exponentiation and then use *it* twice. In fact, this variable has a real-world counterpart in that it represents the total amount of compounding on the loan.

According to our top-down methodology, we need to design the function PWR next, so let's turn our attention to that.

Subtask PWR: Step 1—Understand the Problem. We want to compute exponents. Let's see exactly what that entails. We begin by looking at the following algebraic definition of exponentiation:

$$b^0 = 1$$
$$b^1 = b$$
$$b^2 = b \times b$$
$$b^3 = b \times b \times b$$
$$b^m = b \times b \times \ldots \times b, m \text{ times}$$

Essentially, this definition says that if we raise b (base) to some power m, it is the same as multiplying b by itself m times. Such a process, of course, suggests a loop. There are a couple of caveats to observe here, though. First, the power MUST be an integer, and second, if the power is zero, the result is 1. We take all these items into account and proceed to the next phase.

Subtask PWR: Step 2—Plan the Solution. This is going to be a loop very similar to the one we used for factorials. We may write it as

Result ← 1
For i ← 1 to m Do
    Result ← Result × b

We would, of course, like to express this in the form of a function, so let us rewrite it as

Function PWR (b, m)
    Result ← 1
    For i ← 1 to m Do
        Result ← Result × b
    PWR ← Result

Note that this will work for any power m greater than or equal to zero. We may now return to the main problem.

STEP 3: CODE THE SOLUTION

We have an algorithm for the main routine and for the function; therefore, we may combine them, using the methods demonstrated in Chapter 6, into a single, coherent program. The final results are shown in Figure 9-4.

STEP 4: CHECK OUT THE PROGRAM

As always, a sample run is included with the finished program of Figure 9-4. Note that the correct results are obtained.

STEP 5: DOCUMENT

The program and function are presented in such a way that their relationships are obvious. Also, both are easy to follow and understand.

Compound statement loops. Up to this point, our loops have been simple (literally). Since our definition of a loop requires that it have only *one* statement in it, we would like to know how we can get *more* than one statement inside a loop. We can solve this problem by making use of a new kind of statement called the **compound statement** and expand our list of statement types as follows to include such a statement:

```
executable-statement → assignment-statement
                     |  input-statement
                     |  output-statement
                     |  counted-loop
                     |  compound-statement
```

A compound statement has this format:

```
compound-statement → begin
                        executable-statement-list
                     end
```

This format should look familiar, since it is exactly the same as a Pascal program executable section except for the ending period! In fact a Pascal program can be considered to be just a compound statement.

An executable statement list, as we said in Chapter 4, is one or more executable statements separated by semicolons. Of course, these other statements may also be compound statements—structure is ubiquitous!

Figure 9-4

Program and Sample Output for the Amortization Problem

```
AMORTIZE.PAS

1     Program AMORTIZE (Input, Output);
2
3     (*
4          This program computes amortized loan payments.
5     *)
6
7     Var Principle, AnnualRate, IntRate, Compounding : Real;
8          Payment : Real;
9
10         Term, NoPeriods : Integer;
11
12
13         Function PWR (b:Real; m:Integer) : Real;
14           Var Result : Real;
15                i : Integer;
16           Begin
17             Result := 1;
18             For i := 1 to m Do
19                   Result := Result * b;
20                   PWR := Result
21           End;
22
23
24    BEGIN
25
26       Writeln('AMORTIZED LOAN PAYMENTS');
27       Writeln;
28       Write ('Enter Amount of Loan : ');        Readln (Principal);
29       Write ('Enter Annual Interest Rate : '); Readln (AnnualRate);
30       Write ('Enter Term of Loan : ');          Readln (Term);
31
32       NoPeriods := Term * 12;
33       IntRate := AnnualRate / 12.0;
34
35       Compounding := PWR (1 + IntRate, NoPeriods);
36
37       Payment := Principal * IntRate * Compounding / (Compounding - 1.0);
38
39       Writeln;
40       Writeln ('The amortized monthly payment is $', Payment:4:2)
41
42    END.


$ run amortize

AMORTIZED LOAN PAYMENTS

Enter Amount of Loan : 9500.00
Enter Annual Interest Rate : 0.155
Enter Term of Loan : 6

The amortized monthly payment is $203.47
```

Table of Squares and Cubes

Let's develop an example to demonstrate the use of compound statements within a loop. Suppose we would like to generate a table of squares and cubes for the numbers 1 through n. Let's attack this problem using our step-by-step development process.

STEP 1: UNDERSTAND THE PROBLEM

We would like to generate a table with the following form:

n	square	cube
1	1	1
2	4	8
3	9	27
4	16	64

Generating such a table requires a loop in which the table elements are counted off one at a time and the corresponding squares and cubes computed.

STEP 2: PLAN THE SOLUTION

The algorithm for this can be easily written as

Prompt 'Enter n'

Read n

For k ← 1 to n Do
    Square ← k × k
    Cube ← Square × k
    Print k, Square, Cube

The indentation is used to indicate that there are three things to be done *within* the body of the loop. The concept is the same as that used when only a single action was to be carried out; there're just more actions now.

STEP 3: CODE THE SOLUTION

The only new item we need to consider here is how we should express multiple statement loops in the Pascal language. Using our newly acquired knowledge of compound statements, this can be done readily, as

Figure 9-5

Program That Generates a Table of Squares and Cubes

```
TABLE.PAS

 1    Program TABLE (Input, Output);
 2
 3    (*
 4        This program generates a table of squares and cubes
 5        for all numbers between 1 and n, inclusive.
 6    *)
 7
 8    Var n, k, Square, Cube : Integer;
 9
10    BEGIN
11
12      Writeln('TABLE OF SQUARES AND CUBES');
13      Writeln;
14      Write('Maximum Table Value : '); Readln (n);
15      Writeln;
16      Writeln('    n      Square        Cube ');
17
18      For k := 1 to n Do
19        Begin
20          Square := k * k;
21          Cube := Square * k;
22          WriteLn (k:4, Square:8, Cube:12)
23        End
24
25    END.
```

```
$ run table

TABLE OF SQUARES AND CUBES

Maximum Table Value : 12

    n      Square        Cube
    1         1           1
    2         4           8
    3         9          27
    4        16          64
    5        25         125
    6        36         216
    7        49         343
    8        64         512
    9        81         729
   10       100        1000
   11       121        1331
   12       144        1728
```

shown in Figure 9-5. Note that the structure and presentation of the original algorithm are preserved and that indentations are used to express that structure.

A couple of other observations: pay attention to the locations of the semicolons. Remember that *the loop is considered to be a single state-*

ment. However, in this case, the loop contains a compound statement; therefore it has its own `Begin` and `End`. Within this, there are *three* statements, which are separated by *two* semicolons. There is no semicolon after the `Writeln` because `end` is used to conclude the compound statement. Likewise, there is no semicolon before the final `END`. of the program.

Caution: It is crucial to understand the usage of semicolons, `Begins`, and `Ends`; misunderstanding can cause innumerable difficulties for beginning students. However, if you keep in mind the block structuring techniques of Pascal and the definition of compound statement, you should have little trouble in time.

STEP 4: CHECK OUT THE SOLUTION

A sample run of the program is shown in Figure 9-5. The table produced is neat and clean, and the computed squares and cubes are all correct.

STEP 5: DOCUMENT

The program is written, using good variable names, indentations, and pertinent comments, to make it understandable.

Nested loops. This brings us to the next question on the topic of counted loops: How can we combine several loops? Recall from the definition of a counted loop that the statement found inside a loop may in fact be another loop; these are called **nested loops.** There are many, many applications for which nested loops are useful. Let's take a sample problem to demonstrate this concept.

Decimal Multiplication Table

Suppose we wish to generate the base 10 multiplication table (yes, the very same multiplication table you learned years ago in grade school). The method for doing this is very similar to the method used to solve the squares and cubes problem, except in one regard: the multiplication table is *two dimensional*. Consequently, we must use values along the top *and* side of the table in computing the body of the table. This makes the problem fundamentally different from that of the squares and cubes problem, for which we needed to use only the values along the left-hand column to generate the body of the table.

Let's develop the program.

STEP 1: UNDERSTAND THE PROBLEM

We would like to generate the decimal multiplication table. If we begin, as usual, by specifying what input is needed, we see that, for this particular problem, *no* input is required. The limits of the problem are set by the decimal digits 0 through 9.

We do need output, however, and it is to consist of a table, with the numbers that are to be multiplied together listed along the top and the left side, such as

	0	1	2	. . .	9
0	0	0	0	. . .	0
1	0	1	2	. . .	9
2	0	2	4	. . .	18

Let's see *how* we can do this.

STEP 2: PLAN THE SOLUTION

This is the tricky part. How do we get all possible digits multiplied by all the other digits? That is, how do we get all possible combinations? We can take our cue from the table itself: first we multiply 0 successively by 0, 1, 2, and so on. Next, we multiply 1 successively by 0, 1, 2, and so on. Then we do the same thing with 3, 4, and so on. This suggests looping; in fact, we have a double loop here. We first go from 0 to 9, and then for each of these digits, we also go from 0 to 9. Hence, we repeat a loop many times, which is the same as having one loop inside another.

This may be easier to see if we look at the algorithm:

```
For Row ← 0 to 9 Do
   For Col ← 0 to 9 Do
      Product ← Row × Col
      Print Product
```

This kind of *nesting* situation occurs frequently in programming; therefore, let's examine this algorithm closely in order to understand it completely. We have only three variables here: Row (which would be the numbers along the left-hand side of the final table), Col (which would be the numbers along the top of the table), and Product (which is the result of multiplying the sets of numbers). Row would start off with the value 0 and would remain 0 during the entire time the next loop was in progress (that is, as Col went from 0 to 9). Hence, the numbers that would be multiplied together would be $0 \times 0, 0 \times 1, 0 \times 2, 0 \times 3$, and so on. Then, Row would be incremented to 1, and the Col process repeated, generating $1 \times 0, 1 \times 1, 1 \times 2$, and so forth. Row would then move to 3, and the process would continue until all combinations had been multiplied.

This takes care of actually getting the results. However, there is one aesthetic detail that needs attention. The algorithm, as written, will not produce a nice, neat table. In fact, all the results will end up in a single huge column. How do we format the output into a table? Formatting the output requires that we do a little more work on the algorithm. We must first print out the top row of digits, and then, row by row, the results of multiplying them by each column. In order to make sure everything fits nicely, it is useful to draw a sample section of the table with exact spacing. Let's do that:

		0	1	2	3
0		0	0	0	0
1		0	1	2	3

(5 spaces)   (4 spaces per result)

We allocate a total of five spaces for the left-hand column and four spaces for each result (the actual number of spaces is a matter of taste). We must also be able to get all the output for one row actually on one row and do the same for the remaining rows. This requires us to manipulate the `Write` and `Writeln` statements in such a way as to accommodate the situation (recall that `Write` does not cause a line feed but `Writeln` does). With this in mind, we can write an algorithm (albeit more detailed than usual) that takes all this into account:

```
1.    Write '     '
2.    For Col ← 0 to 9 Do
3.         Write Col:4
4.    Writeln

5.    Write '     '
6.    For Col ← 1 to 41 Do
7.         Write '-'
8.    Writeln

9.    For Row ← 0 to 9 Do
10.        Writeln '    |'
11.        Write Row:3, '    |'
12.        For Col ← 0 to 9 Do
13.             Product ← Row × Col
14.             Write Product:4
15.        Writeln
```

What exactly does this algorithm do? In order to answer that, let's trace through it. Lines 1 through 4 generate the top row (headings) of the graph and print out the numbers 0 through 9 correctly spaced. The instructions accomplish this as follows:

Line 1. Prints five blanks. Since this was done with a `Write`, anything printed out subsequently follows immediately behind the last blank.

Lines 2, 3. This is the loop whereby the top row of numbers 0 through 9 is actually printed out. Note that these are all done with a `Write` so that they all appear on the same line. Also, they are given widths of four places, so they will all be spaced correctly.

Line 4. This marks the end of the current line, so that anything else printed out will begin on a *new* line.

Looking next at lines 5 through 8, we find a clever way of placing a horizontal line (a border) to separate the top row from the actual body of the table, as we see below:

Line 5. Prints out five blanks, just as line 1 does.

Lines 6, 7. This is a loop that prints out exactly forty-one dashes and is the actual border for the table.

Line 8. Ends the border line.

Next we come to the heart of the algorithm, lines 9 through 15, where we actually generate the table. We first go through the rows numbered 0 through 9. Each of these generates a new and distinct row. Each row will consist of the number of the row, the border character, and the table values. Note the use of the `Writeln` in line 10 to doublespace the output.

Within each row is another loop, which generates the column values and the products to be placed within that column. As before, when we get to the end of a particular row, we execute a `Writeln` to terminate that row.

Now that we have generated and understood the algorithm, we may proceed to the next step of the development process.

STEP 3: CODE THE SOLUTION

We are now ready to transform our algorithm into a program, and this requires only that we be careful about proper nesting (keeping in mind the definitions of counted loop and compound statement). The indentations in the algorithm should, however, make the nesting clear. The complete program is shown in Figure 9-6. Pay particular attention to the visual presentation, `Begins`, `Ends`, and semicolons. Figure 9-7 shows the same program with the block structure emphasized.

STEP 4: CHECK OUT THE PROGRAM

The output is shown, along with the program, in Figure 9-6 and speaks for itself.

Figure 9-6

Program and Output for Generating the Decimal Multiplication Table

```
DECTABLE.PAS
    1     Program DECTABLE (Output);
    2
    3     (*
    4        This program generates the decimal multiplication table
    5        and prints it out in table form.
    6     *)
    7
    8     Var Row, Col, Product : Integer;
    9
   10     BEGIN
   11
   12       Writeln ('              DECIMAL MULTIPLICATION TABLE');
   13       Writeln;
   14
   15          (* Write the Top Row of the Table *)
   16
   17       Write ('      ');
   18       For Col := 0 to 9 Do
   19           Write (Col:4);
   20       Writeln;
   21
   22          (* Write the Border *)
   23
   24       Write ('       ');
   25       For Col := 1 to 41 Do
   26           Write ('-');
   27       Writeln;
   28
   29          (* Now Generate the Body of the Table *)
   30
   31       For Row := 0 to 9 Do
   32           Begin
   33              Writeln ('     !');
   34              Write (Row:3, '  !');
   35
   36              For Col := 0 to 9 Do
   37                  Begin
   38                     Product := Row * Col;
   39                     Write (Product:4)
   40                  End;
   41
   42              Writeln
   43           End
   44
   45     END.


$ run dectable
```

Figure 9-6 continued

```
DECIMAL MULTIPLICATION TABLE

    0  1  2  3  4  5  6  7  8  9
   ------------------------------------
0 ¦ 0  0  0  0  0  0  0  0  0  0
1 ¦ 0  1  2  3  4  5  6  7  8  9
2 ¦ 0  2  4  6  8 10 12 14 16 18
3 ¦ 0  3  6  9 12 15 18 21 24 27
4 ¦ 0  4  8 12 16 20 24 28 32 36
5 ¦ 0  5 10 15 20 25 30 35 40 45
6 ¦ 0  6 12 18 24 30 36 42 48 54
7 ¦ 0  7 14 21 28 35 42 49 56 63
8 ¦ 0  8 16 24 32 40 48 56 64 72
9 ¦ 0  9 18 27 36 45 54 63 72 81
```

STEP 5: DOCUMENT

The program is documented and understandable.

This, then, concludes our presentation of count-up loops. We next examine count-down loops.

COUNT-DOWN LOOPS

Recall that we defined counted loops as

counted-loop → count-up-loop
         | count-down-loop

Count-down loops are identical in every respect to count-up loops except that the counting goes backward. The definition of a count-down loop can be expressed as

count-down-loop → **for** counter **:=** start-expr **downto** end-expr **do**
              statement

Note that the only difference between the count-up loop and the count-down loop is that the word *to* in the former is replaced with the words *down to* in the latter. The count must still change by one, only in this case it decrements rather than increments.

Rather than go through an extensive example for this type of counted loop (since it is so similar to the count-up loop), we will simply present a small application to demonstrate.

Figure 9-7

Table Program Emphasizing the Block Structure

Program DECTABLE (Output) ;

Var   Row, Col, Product : Integer;

```
BEGIN

  Write ('              ');
  For Col :=  0 to 9 Do
      Write (Col:4);
  Writeln;

  Write ('             ');
  For Col :=  1 to 41 Do
      Write ('–');
  Writeln;

  For Row := 0 to 9 Do
  Begin
    Writeln ('            |');
    Write (Row:3, ' |');

      For Col := 0 to 9 Do
        Begin
          Product := Row * Col;
          Write (Product:4)
        End;

  Writeln
    End

END.
```

Gravitational Acceleration

Suppose we drop an object from a given height. As it falls, it accelerates, and the velocity at any subsequent point on the way down can be determined. Let us write a program that inputs a height in feet and prints out the velocity of the object as it falls.

STEP 1: UNDERSTAND THE PROBLEM

This is a problem in classical physics. The velocity of an object as it falls is given by

$$v = \sqrt{2\,g\,(h_0 - h)}$$

where v = the velocity

g = the acceleration due to gravity (32 ft/sec/sec)

h_0 = the height from which the object is dropped

h = any height after the object has been dropped

Note that g is a constant here, h_0 is the initial height, and h is what we want to change as the object drops.

STEP 2: PLAN THE SOLUTION

We will need a loop here in which the height is changed from the initial (maximum) height to the final (minimum) height. Just the thing for a count-down loop! We can write the algorithm as

Read h_0

For $h \leftarrow h_0$ down to 0 Do

$\quad v \leftarrow \sqrt{2 \times g \times (h_0 - h)}$

$\quad$ Write h, v

This algorithm inputs an initial height and then uses a loop to go through all the distances between that height and zero, printing out the heights and velocities as it goes.

STEP 3: CODE THE SOLUTION

We have already seen square roots, and we were just introduced to the count-down loop. The process is straightforward, and the result is shown in Figure 9-8.

Figure 9-8

Program That Computes Velocity as a Function of Distance
for a Falling Object

GRAVITY.PAS

```
1    Program GRAVITY (Input, Output);
2
3    (*
4       This program computes the velocity of a free falling
5       object at one foot intervals as it falls.
6    *)
7
8    Const g = 32 (* ft/sec/sec, acceleration due to gravity *);
9
10   Var   h,              (* height of the object as it falls, in feet *)
11         h0 : Integer;   (* initial height, in feet *)
12          v : Real;      (* velocity, ft/sec *)
13
14   BEGIN
15     Writeln('     FREE FALL SIMULATION');
16     Writeln;
17     Write ('Height to drop from (in feet) ? '); Readln (h0);
18     Writeln;
19     Writeln(' h,ft   v,ft/sec');
20
21     For h := h0 DownTo 0 Do
22         Begin
23           v := sqrt (2 * g * (h0 - h));
24           Writeln (h:4, v:7:0)
25         End
26
27   END.
```

```
$ run gravity

     FREE FALL SIMULATION

Height to drop from (in feet) ? 15

 h,ft v,ft/sec
  15      0
  14      8
  13     11
  12     14
  11     16
  10     18
   9     20
   8     21
   7     23
   6     24
   5     25
   4     27
   3     28
   2     29
   1     30
   0     31
```

STEP 4: CHECK OUT THE SOLUTION

A sample run of 15 feet is also shown in the figure. Note that the loop really *does* count backward!

STEP 5: DOCUMENT

Although this is a small program, documentation in the form of comments and good variable names is still included.

This, then, concludes the discussion on counted loops of all kinds. We are ready to proceed to the next category of loops, namely, conditional loops.

9-2 *Conditional Loops*

We turn our attention now to the second category of available loops, the **conditional loop.** These loops are actually a more general type of iterative control structure; counted loops can be written in terms of conditional loops. However, since a distinction between the two is useful in programming and their implementations are different, we will consider them as separate loop options. As with counted loops, conditional loops are also actually (and merely) another kind of Pascal statement. Expanding our list of executable statements to include these loops yields

executable-statement → assignment-statement
       | input-statement
       | output-statement
       | counted-loop
       | compound-statement
       | conditional-loop

In a parallel fashion to counted loops, there are also two kinds of conditional loops, namely,

conditional-loop → while-do
      | repeat-until

The **While loop** is the very same pretest loop that we discussed in the previous chapter. We will discuss it first, in greater detail. The **Repeat Until loop** is a variation on conditional loops that is sometimes useful, and we will briefly look at it following the While loops.

WHILE LOOPS

The syntax of the While loop can be expressed as follows:

while-do → **while** logical-expression **do**
         statement

As is the case with counted loops, the statement part of the While loop can be any valid statement, including a compound statement, a counted loop, or another While loop. The primary difference between the counted loop and the While loop lies in the *logical expression* part of the While loop. A logical expression is one that evaluates to a Boolean value, that is, either True or False. In carrying out a While loop, the logical expression is evaluated: if it is True, the loop body is executed and the test is made again. If, on the other hand, the logical expression is False, the body of the loop is *skipped entirely* and the program continues at the first statement after the loop. Recall from the previous chapter that this is a pretest loop, which means that the logical expression is always evaluated first, and that it is therefore possible to have a situation in which the loop is never entered at all. Also remember that, in general, there is no way of determining beforehand how many times the loop will be carried out.

Before we can do much with the While loop, it is necessary to better understand what a logical expression is. Therefore, we will take a detour to explore this concept.

Logical Expressions. Such expressions are similar to mathematical expressions except that they generate Boolean values (True, False) instead of algebraic (that is, numeric) values. A subset of logical expressions that can be used to introduce the topic is called *relational expressions*. We will look at these first, with examples, and then expand the concept to full logical expressions.

Relational expressions. As with algebraic expressions, **relational expressions** involve operators and operands, which are combined in known ways to provide a single result. For relational expressions, we would naturally have **relational operators.** There are six of these, as follows:

Relationship	Mathematical Representation	Pascal Relational Operator
Less than	$<$	$<$
Less than or equal to	$\leq$	$<=$
Equal to	$=$	$=$
Not equal to	$\neq$	$<>$
Greater than or equal	$\geq$	$>=$
Greater than	$>$	$>$

As their name implies, relational operators provide information on relationships: that is, they are used in comparisons. The relational expression (and hence the logical expression) is True if the relationship between the operands is the one expressed and otherwise is False. A simple relational expression would be

```
34.6 > 197.75
```

This expression tests the relationship between 34.6 and 197.75; that is, these numbers are compared to see if the former is greater than the latter. In this case (obviously) this is not so; therefore, the expression has a value of False.

This may seem like a pretty dumb example, since anyone (including a computer) can tell that 34.6 is not greater than 197.75. In fact, constants are never compared to other constants. Normally, comparisons involve variables. It may be something as simple as this:

```
Count < 100
```

But it may be as complex as this:

```
Angle + Delta <= Pi/4.0 - CurrentDev
```

The idea is still that two quantities are to be compared and a True or False value determined.

Nonnumeric data can also be compared. For example, one could test to see whether an exam grade (in the form of the character variable ExamGrade) was the letter 'A' by using the following:

```
ExamGrade = 'A'
```

One could also test for such things as

```
Letter <= 'K'
```

Letter in this case would have to be a character variable. But, you ask, how do you compare letters? Can one letter actually be less than another? If so, how?

For letters, comparisons are made on the basis of something called the **collating sequence.** For letters of the alphabet, this is exactly the same as alphabetical order. Hence, 'A' would be less than 'B', 'B' would be less than 'C', and so on. In the expression Letter<='K', any letter of the alphabet from 'A' to 'K' would satisfy the relationship. For example, one could test for a passing grade in a course using

```
CourseGrade <= 'D'
```

Since relational operators are operators in every sense that mathematical operators are, the question is how relational operators fit into the operator precedence scheme presented in Chapter 4. In Pascal the relational operators all have the same precedence, which is below that of mathematical operators. Consequently, the list of operators we have encountered so far, in order of precedence, is given by

```
      *  /  DIV  MOD
            +  -
   <  <=  =  <>  >=  >
```

Therefore, in any relational expression, all arithmetic expressions are evaluated first and the comparison made last.

For example, suppose we wanted to evaluate the relational expression

```
Angle + Delta <= Pi/4.0 - CurrentDev
```

How would we proceed? We would first need to know the values associated with the identifiers. Assume these are given by

```
Angle      :  0.68894
Delta      :  0.00087
Pi         :  3.14159
CurrentDev :  0.09341
```

Evaluating as before,

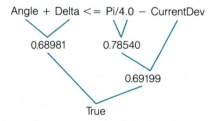

Note that the evaluation proceeds in the usual manner until we evaluate the relational operator, at which point a value of True (rather than a numeric value) is computed.

While Loop SUMITUP

Let's apply what we have learned about relational expressions to While loops. For the first example, let's reconsider Isaac Newton's add-up-the-numbers-from-1-to-100 problem.

STEP 1: UNDERSTAND THE PROBLEM

We already did this once; no need to do it again.

STEP 2: PLAN THE SOLUTION

If we choose to solve this with a While loop this time, we must take care of two things that the counted loop does automatically: we must check to see whether the loop has ended, and we must increment the counter. The algorithm can be written as

1.   Sum ← 0
2.   n ← 1
3.   While n ≤ 100 Do
4.   Sum ← Sum + n
5.   n ← n + 1
6.   Print Sum

Note, especially, two things: First, this is a more complex algorithm than the one given for the counted loop. Second, the value of *n* must be changed *explicitly within the loop* to avoid generating an infinite loop, that is, a loop that never ends if left to itself. (Of course, it would eventually end; sooner or later someone would notice something funny and interrupt.)

Let's trace this algorithm as we did for the counted loop version. Line 1, as in the case of the counted loop counterpart, initializes the Sum to 0. The second line initializes the counter to 1 (this initialization is done automatically in the counted loop). At this point, variables in memory have these values:

```
Sum : 0        n : 1
```

We now come to line 3, the beginning of the loop. First, *n* is compared with 100 in order to determine the value of the conditional expression. In this case, *n* is 1, which is less than or equal to 100, and the conditional expression is True. Since the expression is True, the body of the loop is executed. In line 4, Sum is given the value Sum + *n* (here, 0 + 1, which is 1), and in line 5, *n* is incremented, that is, given the value *n* + 1 (which in this case would be 2). At this point, memory contains

```
Sum : 1        n : 2
```

Since line 5 is the last statement in the loop, control is returned to line 3, where the test is carried out yet another time.

This sequence of events (test, enter the loop) will be repeated until the following values are in memory (at the completion of the loop):

```
Sum : 4950     n : 100
```

Since *n* (value 100) is in fact less than or equal to 100, the loop will be entered again. Sum would receive the value 5050 (by adding 100 to 4950), and *n* would get the new value 101 (by adding one to the current value of 100). At this point, control goes back to line 3. The test is made again; however, the variable *n* contains the value 101, which is no longer less than or equal to the limit of 100. Therefore, the loop is skipped and the processing continues at line 6, where the final result is output.

As you can see, this is a more difficult way to solve the problem; however, it demonstrates the use of a While loop.

STEP 3: CODE THE SOLUTION

To convert this to a Pascal program, we need only follow the Pascal syntax rules given to date. The finished program can be seen in Figure 9-9. Note the need for compound statements!

STEP 4: CHECK OUT THE PROGRAM

The results of running this program are also included in Figure 9-9. Note that the correct results are obtained.

STEP 5: DOCUMENT

All that is needed is here.

Let's now look at a more complex problem that requires While loops with relational expressions.

Figure 9-9

Program That Uses a While Loop to Add Inclusive Numbers from 1 to 100, with Test Run and Results

```
WHILEITU.PAS

  1    Program WHILEITUP (Input, Output);
  2
  3    (*
  4       This program adds up the integers from 1 to 100,
  5       inclusive, by means of a While loop.
  6    *)
  7
  8    Var Sum, n : Integer;
  9
 10    BEGIN
 11
 12      Sum := 0;
 13      n := 1;
 14
 15      While n <= 100 Do
 16        Begin
 17          Sum := Sum + n;
 18          n := n + 1
 19        End;
 20
 21      Writeln ('The (while) sum of the numbers 1 to 100 is ', Sum:1)
 22
 23    END.


$ run whileitup

The (while) sum of the numbers 1 to 100 is 5050
```

Payroll and Withholding

Suppose we need to write a payroll program in which the tax withheld is not simply a fixed percent but rather is calculated using a progressive rate based on the amount earned according to the following schedule:

Table of Tax Withheld

5% of the 1st $100

10% of the 2nd $100

15% of the 3rd $100

20% of the 4th $100

and so forth

Let's develop a payroll program that computes taxes in this fashion.

STEP 1: UNDERSTAND THE PROBLEM

We have done payroll before, so we don't need to go into it in depth again. We will need to come up with some way of computing the withholding tax, but this isn't crucial just yet. We will get to it as we move "down from the top."

STEP 2: PLAN THE SOLUTION

Since we have done payroll before, we can immediately write our preliminary algorithm as follows:

Read Hours
Read Rate

Gross ← Hours × Rate

FICA ← Gross × SSRate
Tax ← WithHold (Gross)

Net ← Gross − FICA − Tax

Print Hours, Rate, Gross, FICA, Tax, Net

Note that we have indicated the function WithHold as the means of computing the withholding tax. Next we will develop it.

Subtask WithHold: **Step 1—Understand the Problem.** In order to better see how this function works, let's use as an example an employee whose gross pay is $375.26. The withholding tax would be calculated as

$$\text{Tax} = 5\% \times 100 + 10\% \times 100 + 15\% \times 100 + 20\% \times 75.26$$

The result of this calculation would be $45.05. (This may seem like a bizarre way to calculate taxes, but some states actually do it this way.)

Let's derive an algorithm for this method. We need to find some way of peeling off incremental units of $100 from the gross wages and then multiplying those increments by appropriate percentages. The percentages can be found easily enough: they start at 5 percent and increase by 5 percent thereafter. Such a process can easily be made into a loop. The difficulty is how to figure out how many times we need to go through the loop.

One possible approach is to decrement the gross pay each time the loop is carried out. Thus, if the gross is greater than or equal to $100, we know we can go through the loop again. If it isn't, then we have arrived at the end. Let's write this down, remembering that we are generating a function here:

```
Function WithHold (Gross)
    Tax Rate ← 5%
    Tax ← 0

    While Gross ≥ $100 Do
        Tax ← Tax + TaxRate × $100
        TaxRate ← TaxRate + 5%
        Gross ← Gross − $100

    WithHold ← Tax
```

This will work well, provided the gross is an exact multiple of $100. However, if it is not, we will have some amount left over in Gross when we exit the loop. But you will notice that this leftover amount must also have tax taken out. The rate for this last little bit is equal to the final rate computed within the loop! Consequently, the correct solution can be derived by merely adding one more line to the algorithm, to wit,

```
Function WithHold (Gross)
    TaxRate ← 5%
    Tax ← 0

    While Gross ≥ $100 Do
        Tax ← Tax + TaxRate × $100
        TaxRate ← TaxRate + 5%
        Gross ← Gross − $100

    WithHold ← Tax + TaxRate × Gross
```

Strictly speaking, this algorithm *destroys* the contents of Gross as it goes through the computation. However, this is not a problem since the Gross referenced in this function is actually a parameter that has been called by value from the main program. Consequently, the value used by the function is nothing but a *copy* of the real thing, the value of which is beyond our ability to change from inside the function. (Recall from Chapter 6 that arguments to functions are normally call-by-value; consequently, the original value passed *to* the function cannot be altered.)

We now have a main algorithm and a function algorithm, which we can combine into a complete program.

STEP 3: CODE THE SOLUTION

The finished product, including the procedure, is shown in Figure 9-10. Note that the function that computes the withholding has its own set of constants and variables. Also, the payroll program proper is really no more complex than the simple version presented in Chapter 2; the function itself takes care of the additional complexity.

Figure 9-10

Payroll Program That Uses an Iterative Function to Compute Withholding Tax, with Sample Output

PAYROLL.PAS

```
1    Program PAYROLL (Input, Output);
2
3    (*
4      This program is a simple payroll application. It computes
5      payroll figures for one person.
6    *)
7
8    Const SSRate = 0.071;  (* Social security tax rate *)
9
10   Var   Hours, Rate, Gross, FICA, Tax, Net : Real;
11
12
13   Function WithHold (Gross : Real) : Real;
14   (*
15       This function computes withholding tax using an iterative
16       method in which the first $100 of income is taxed at the
17       basic rate, the second $100 at 2x the basic rate, the third
18       $100 at 3x the basic rate and so on.
19   *)
20     Const BasicTaxRate = 0.05;
21           TaxInc = 100.00;
22
23     Var   TaxRate, Tax : Real;
24
25     Begin
26       Tax := 0;
27       TaxRate := BasicTaxRate;
28
29       While Gross >= TaxInc Do
30         Begin
31           Tax := Tax + TaxRate * TaxInc;
32           TaxRate := TaxRate + BasicTaxRate;
33           Gross := Gross - TaxInc
34         End;
35
36       WithHold := Tax + TaxRate * Gross
37     End;
38
39
40   BEGIN
41
42     Write ('Number of hours worked? '); Readln (Hours);
43     Write ('Rate of pay?            '); Readln (Rate);
44
45     Gross := Hours * Rate;
46
47     FICA := Gross * SSRate;
48     Tax := WithHold ( Gross );
49
50     Net := Gross - FICA - Tax;
51
52     Writeln; Writeln;
53     Writeln ('Hours worked......$', Hours:8:2);
54     Writeln ('Rate of pay.......$', Rate:8:2);
```

Figure 9-10 continued

```
55      Writeln ('Gross Pay.........$', Gross:8:2);
56      Writeln ('SS Tax...........$', FICA:8:2);
57      Writeln ('Income Tax.......$', Tax:8:2);
58      Writeln ('Net Pay..........$', Net:8:2);
59      Writeln
60
61   END.


$ run payroll

Number of hours worked? 30.0
Rate of pay?              12.51

Hours worked.....$    30.00
Rate of pay......$    12.51
Gross Pay........$   375.30
SS Tax...........$    26.65
Income Tax.......$    45.06
Net Pay..........$   303.59
```

STEP 4: CHECK OUT THE PROGRAM

A test run is shown in Figure 9-10; note that the output is correct.

STEP 5: DOCUMENT

Done.

We are beginning to build an appreciation for the While structure. This control structure can also be used to help us get a program to run more than once without having to reload it. For example, in the last problem, we had a program that computed payroll figures with an increasing degree of sophistication, yet it could still be run only for a single person. If we required payroll computations for several people, the program would have to be loaded and executed separately each time. However, now that we have While loops at our disposal, we can avoid this repetitive effort by inserting the *entire program* into one giant While loop. There are three approaches that can accomplish this: the operator response, sentinel value, and end-of-file methods. We will look at the first two now but consider the third after we have covered full logical expressions, since these are necessary to an understanding of end-of-file loops.

Operator response. The **operator response** method is straightforward and direct. The program *asks* the person who is running it whether or not he or she would like to continue. This approach can be expressed algorithmically as

Result ← Affirmative

While Result = Affirmative Do
   Whatever needs doing
   Prompt Operator for Result, Read Result

What is Result and what is Affirmative? They can be whatever you like. Normally a question that can be answered as either yes or no is put to the operator. More likely, a code is used, for example, "Y" for yes and "N" for no. The result is usually a variable whose name suggests what the loop is for. As a simple example, consider an algorithm in which some arbitrary number of integers is squared (we will suspend the program development process here since the purpose is to demonstrate the fundamentals of operator response). The algorithm might look like this:

MoreNumbers ← Yes

While MoreNumbers = Yes Do
   Prompt, Read N
   S ← N × N
   Print S
   Prompt 'Are there more numbers?'
   Read MoreNumbers

Here, the variable MoreNumbers is set initially to Yes, the affirmative answer, so that the loop is entered at least once. As soon as the body of the loop is begun, the computer prompts for a number, reads it, squares it, and prints out the results. Then the "big loop" takes over. The person is asked whether there are more numbers. If the response is yes, then the loop is repeated. If not, the loop is exited. Note that the *input to the program controls what happens in the loop.* Therefore this is an example of what is called an **input controlled loop.**

How can this loop be implemented? A good way to start is to define the result variable to be of type Char, and let the operator answer with either the letter "Y" or the letter "N". Using the above algorithm, we could get the following Pascal program:

```
Program SQUARES (Input, Output);

Const Yes = 'Y';

Var MoreNumbers : Char;
    N, S : Integer;

BEGIN

  MoreNumbers := Yes;

  While MoreNumbers = Yes Do
    Begin
      Write ('Enter an integer:'); Readln (N);
```

```
     S := N * N;
     Writeln ('The square is ', S:10);
     Write ('Are there any more numbers? (Y or N) ');
     Readln (MoreNumbers)
   End
END.
```

(The use of the symbolic constant Yes in this program allows a more readable program to be developed.)

Sentinel value. This is an alternate method to that of requesting a yes or no answer from the operator. This approach is somewhat less cumbersome but is also less human oriented. It involves the use of a **sentinel value,** which is a predetermined value for one of the input variables that the program recognizes as signalling a termination condition. For example, in the above program, rather than asking if more numbers are to be processed, we could enter numbers with the understanding that zero means termination and anything else means continuation. Implementing this system (and again skipping the step-by-step development process for the present) results in the following program:

```
Program SQUARES (Input, Output);

Var N, S : Integer;

BEGIN
  Write ('Enter an integer, zero to end...');
  Readln (N);

  While N <> 0 Do
    Begin
      S := N * N;
      Writeln ('The square is ', S:10);
      Write ('Enter an integer: '); Readln (N)
    End
END.
```

This program is, in fact, simpler, even though it has the same basic structure as the previous loop. Information regarding the sentinel (or terminal) value is presented, and the loop inputs numbers and computes their squares. When a zero is entered, the While condition will no longer be met; therefore the loop will NOT be entered again. *Note that the variable* N *must be read in prior to entering the loop and again at the end of the loop body.*

Looped Payroll

To demonstrate the concept of complete program looping, let us incorporate the payroll program we just did into an input controlled loop.

STEP 1: UNDERSTAND THE PROBLEM

We want to design a payroll program that works for an arbitrary number of people rather than for just one person. This will require the use of an input controlled loop.

STEP 2: PLAN THE SOLUTION

The entire program, as developed earlier, must be placed within the boundaries of an input controlled loop. An algorithm to do just that can be expressed as

Answer ← Yes
While Answer = Yes Do

   Read Hours
   Read Rate

   Gross ← Hours × Rate
   FICA ← Gross × SSRate
   Tax ← WithHold (Gross)

   Net ← Gross − FICA − Tax

   Print Hours, Rate, Gross, FICA, Tax, Net

   Prompt 'Another Person?'
   Read Answer

Again, note the structure of the algorithm; you can recognize each of the individual components, from the tax computation (which is still a function) to the overall program loop, with no difficulty.

STEP 3: CODE THE SOLUTION

Converting this algorithm to a program requires very little additional work. The completed program is shown in Figure 9-11.

STEP 4: CHECK OUT THE PROGRAM

A sample run, which includes four different people, is shown in Figure 9-12. Note that the loop works perfectly, is easy to use for the operator, and produces the correct results.

Figure 9-11

PAYROLL *Program Inserted into a Loop to Permit It to Be Run for*
More Than One Person

```
PAYLOOP.PAS

  1    Program PAYROLL (Input, Output);
  2
  3    (*
  4        This program is a simple payroll application. It computes
  5        payroll figures for an arbitrary number of persons by way
  6        of an operator response loop.
  7    *)
  8
  9    Const SSRate = 0.071; (* Social security tax rate *)
 10          Yes = 'Y';       (* Affirmative operator response *)
 11
 12    Var Hours, Rate, Gross, FICA, Tax, Net : Real;
 13
 14        Answer : Char;    (*Actual operator response *)
 15
 16
 17    Function WithHold (Gross: Real) : Real;
 18    (*
 19        This function computes withholding tax using an iterative
 20        method in which the first $100 of income is taxed at the
 21        basic rate, the second $100 at 2x the basic rate, the third
 22        $100 at 3x the basic rate, and so on.
 23    *)
 24      Const BasicTaxRate = 0.05;
 25            TaxInc = 100.00;
 26
 27      Var   TaxRate, Tax : Real;
 28
 29      Begin
 30        Tax := 0;
 31        TaxRate := BasicTaxRate;
 32
 33        While Gross >= TaxInc Do
 34          Begin
 35            Tax := Tax + TaxRate * TaxInc;
 36            TaxRate := TaxRate + BasicTaxRate;
 37            Gross := Gross - TaxInc
 38          End;
 39
 40        WithHold := Tax + TaxRate * Gross
 41      End;
 42
 43
 44    BEGIN
 45
 46      Writeln('PAYROLL PROGRAM');
 47      Writeln;
 48
 49      Answer := Yes;
 50      While Answer = Yes Do
 51        Begin
 52          Write ('Number of hours worked? '); Readln (Hours);
 53          Write ('Rate of pay?            '); Readln (Rate);
 54
```

Figure 9-11 continued

```
55              Gross := Hours * Rate;
56
57              FICA := Gross * SSRate;
58              Tax := WithHold (Gross);
59
60              Net := Gross - FICA - Tax;
61
62              Writeln; Writeln;
63              Writeln ('Hours worked.....$', Hours:8:2);
64              Writeln ('Rate of Pay......$', Rate:8:2);
65              Writeln ('Gross Pay........$', Gross:8:2);
66              Writeln ('SS Tax...........$', FICA:8:2);
67              Writeln ('Income Tax.......$', Tax:8:2);
68              Writeln ('Net Pay..........$', Net:8:2);
69              Writeln;
70
71              Write ('Is there another Person? (Y/N) ');
72              Readln (Answer)
73           End; (* Calculation Loop *)
74
75        Writeln ('End Payroll Program.')
76
77   END.
```

Figure 9-12

Test Run and Output from the Looped PAYROLL *Program*

```
PAYROLL PROGRAM

Number of hours worked? 30.0
Rate of Pay?            12.51


Hours worked.....$   30.00
Rate of Pay......$   12.51
Gross Pay........$  375.30
SS Tax...........$   26.65
Income Tax.......$   45.06
Net Pay..........$  303.59

Is there another Person? (Y/N) Y
Number of hours worked? 40.0
Rate of Pay?             5.50


Hours worked.....$   40.00
Rate of Pay......$    5.50
Gross Pay........$  220.00
SS Tax...........$   15.62
Income Tax.......$   18.00
Net Pay..........$  186.38

Is there another Person? (Y/N) Y
Number of hours worked? 37.5
Rate of Pay?            18.75
```

Figure 9-12 continued

```
Hours worked.....$   37.50
Rate of pay......$   18.75
Gross pay........$  703.13
SS Tax...........$   49.92
Income Tax.......$  141.25
Net pay..........$  511.95

Is there another person? (Y/N) Y
Number of hours worked? 20.0
Rate of pay?              3.50


Hours worked.....$   20.00
Rate of pay......$    3.50
Gross pay........$   70.00
SS Tax...........$    4.97
Income Tax.......$    3.50
Net pay..........$   61.53

Is there another person? (Y/N) N
End Payroll Program.
```

STEP 5: DOCUMENT

This is essentially the same program we had before, so documentation is already taken care of.

Now that we have an understanding of While loops that use relational expressions, let's expand this concept to include full logical expressions, as we earlier promised to do.

Full logical expressions. The main difference between these and relational expressions is that full logical expressions may also contain **logical operators** and **logical variables** (termed Boolean variables in Pascal).

There are many possible logical operators, but the three most commonly encountered (and the only ones available in Pascal) are AND, OR, and NOT. These are used to combine logical values (that is, True or False, or expressions that evaluate to True or False) into new values. In this respect they are similar to arithmetic operators (for example, +), which can combine numbers (such as 3 and 5) into new values (in this case 8). Let's look at each of these three logical operators in detail.

AND. This is used to combine *two* logical values; the result is True *if and only if* both of the values being combined are True. The AND operator can be used to control a loop when you have two separate conditions that must be satisfied simultaneously. For example, suppose you are going through a loop, and you wish to continue on in the loop as long as the difference between two numbers is greater than some minimum, provided you have not already gone through the loop more than 100 times. How could you state this? Algorithmically, we could write

While NewX − OldX > Minimum and Iterations ≤ 100 Do
   Whatever

Note that there are two relational expressions here, namely, NewX − OldX > Minimum, and Iterations ≤ 100. Since these are relational expressions, they evaluate to values of either True or False and hence are logical values. These two logical expressions are combined with the logical operator AND so that they form a logical expression, which also evaluates to a logical value of True or False.

OR. This operator is also used to combine two logical values; in this case the result is True if *either or both* of the values being combined are True, and is False otherwise (that is, it is False if and only if both of the values to be combined are False). Logical expressions containing OR can be used to control loops in which only one of two possible conditions must be satisfied. For example, suppose you are going through a loop and you wish to continue as long as the value of one number is equal to zero or as long as a second number is less than some maximum value. This could be expressed as

While Flag=0 or HighVal < Biggest Do
   Whatever

Note again that there are two relational expressions here, each of which can evaluate to True or False. These two logical values are then combined with the OR operator in such a way that if either or both of them are true, the whole logical expression becomes True.

NOT. This operator is unique among those presented thus far in that it does not combine two logical values but rather works on a single value. It takes a single logical value and inverts it, which is to say, if the value starts out as True it ends up as False and vice versa. An example of this is

While not Angle > Pi Do
   Whatever

In this case the relational expression is evaluated and then changed to the opposite value. This expression can, of course, be alternately written as

```
While Angle ≤ Pi Do
  Whatever
```

However, using the NOT alternative can be useful in other situations, especially more complex logical expressions.

We might also mention logical (Boolean, in Pascal) variables at this point. These variables can assume values of True or False and can be assigned in one of several ways, as demonstrated below. (For the purposes of explanation, assume that the variables AllDone, SufficientCount, and NotPreempted are Boolean.)

1. Direct assignment, for example,
```
AllDone := True;
```

2. Assigned via a relational expression, for example,
```
AllDone := Inner <= Outer;
```

3. Assigned by way of a full logical expression, for example,
```
AllDone := SufficientCount AND NotPreempted
```

Note that logical variables can be used to derive other logical variables.

Since the logical operators are, in fact, operators, how do they fit in with the precedence scheme of the arithmetic and relational operators so far defined? The total picture is

```
             NOT
    *  /  DIV  MOD  AND
         +  -  OR
   <  <=  =  <>  >=  >
```

The logical operators are mixed in with the arithmetic operators, and therefore the programmer should exercise some caution when using them. For example, if we were to convert our algorithm for the AND example above into the following Pascal statement, we would get

```
While NewX - OldX > Minimum AND Iterations <= 100 Do
```

Following the operator precedence in the above table would yield an evaluation order of

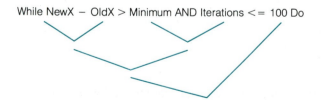

In other words, Pascal would attempt to first combine the variables `Minimum` and `Iterations` using the logical AND operator. Since these are arithmetic variables *and are not Boolean*, they could NOT be so combined and an error would result. In general, whenever a relational expression is used in a logical expression, parentheses MUST be used to delimit the relational expression. The correct Pascal statement for the above would actually be

```
While (NewX - OldX > Minimum) AND (Iterations <= 100) Do
```

Assuming values of

```
NewX        :  2.56309
OldX        :  2.54008
Minimum     :  0.01000
Iterations  :  52
```

the evaluation would yield

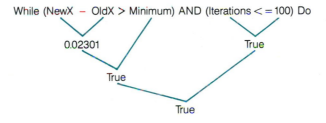

The evaluation order can now be seen to be correct. For the sake of further enlightenment, let's take a very complex logical expression and evaluate it:

```
(Time < Limit) OR (Size > Need) AND NOT (ErrorCond or ReStart)
```

Assuming values of

```
Time     :  122.3
Limit    :  120.0
Size     :  83
Need     :  50
ErrCond  :  FALSE
ReStart  :  FALSE
```

then this expression would be evaluated as follows:

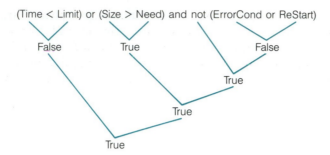

(Time < Limit) or (Size > Need) and not (ErrorCond or ReStart)

False   True   False

                                           True

                              True

        True

A word of caution about the evaluation of logical expressions. We have heretofore been assuming that whenever a logical expression appears, it is completely evaluated. However, sometimes it is possible to determine the value of a logical expression *without completely evaluating it*. This is termed, naturally enough, partial evaluation.

How can this be, you ask? Let us examine once again the logical expression shown above, namely,

```
(Time < Limit) OR (Size > Need) AND NOT (ErrorCond or ReStart)
```

If, on evaluation, we first examine the relational expression `Time < Limit` and determine that it is `TRUE`, we need not examine anything else in the entire logical expression, because no matter what values the other parts of the expression have, the resulting expression *will still be true!* The reason for this is that when two expressions are connected by `OR`, if either of them is true, the whole expression is true. The above expression is just such a one; hence, if the first relation is `True`, the whole expression is `True`. If, on the other hand, the first relation is `False`, then more of the logical expression must be examined to determine its truth value.

The question then becomes: Does Pascal always do full evaluations, or is it "smart" enough to get away with partial evaluations? The answer is: it depends on the system. However, unless you know for a fact that your system does partial evaluations of logical expressions, *always assume it does full evaluations*. This will save you much grief in the long run. (The full implication of partial versus full evaluation is explored in Chapter 10.)

End-of-file loops. Now that we have looked at full logical expressions, we can examine the third and final kind of input controlled loop, the **end-of-file loop.** End-of-file loops are used most often in conjunction with external files, that is, when the input to a program is obtained from external files (see Chapter 7) rather than from the keyboard. The essential feature of this method is that the computer looks ahead into the file being read to determine whether there is more data or whether the end of the file (hence the name) has been reached. Normally, an end-of-file loop is set up in such a way that the loop continues to execute as long as the end of the file has *not* been reached. A typical end-of-file (EOF) loop takes the following form:

```
While not EOF (file) Do
    Read (file)
    Process
```

EOF is a special, predefined Pascal Boolean function that returns True if the end of the indicated file has been reached and False if the file end has not been reached. File, in this algorithm, is the file currently being read to provide data values for the program. When defined this way, an end-of-file loop will continue to execute as long as there is still data to be processed. The loop terminates *only* when everything in the file has been processed.

Note how much simpler this method is than either of the input controlled loops discussed previously. No prompts are necessary and no special values need be included in the data stream (and looked for by the program) to determine when the end has been reached.

Since this method of looping is so elegant, you might be tempted to use an EOF loop with an interactive program that utilizes a terminal. PLEASE DON'T! All manner of bizarre things tend to occur in such a situation. Prompts come out in the wrong places, and the end of the file must be signalled by the operator anyway, thus effectively making it an operator response loop. However, for typical external data file applications, the end-of-file loop is without equal.

Looped Payroll Using EOF

For the sake of demonstration, let's convert the looped payroll program of Figure 9-11 to a looped payroll program that uses EOF instead of operator response. Since this new program is essentially identical to the operator response version, we will dispense with the program development process and just present the final result, which is shown in Figure 9-13. A sample run, including a listing of the input and output files, is shown in Figure 9-14.

Figure 9-13

Complete PAYROLL *Program, Using External Files and an* EOF *Loop*

PAYEOF.PAS

```
 1    Program PAYROLL (Output, PayData, PayResults);
 2
 3    (*
 4        This program is a simple payroll application. It computes
 5        payroll figures for an arbitrary number of persons by way of
 6        an EOF loop on the input file PayData. Results are written
 7        to the file PayResults.
 8    *)
 9
10    Const SSRate = 0.071; (* Social security tax rate *)
11
12    Var   Hours, Rate, Gross, FICA, Tax, Net : Real;
13
14          Person : Integer; (* Index to keep track of the number
15                               of people being paid *)
16          PayData, PayResults : Text;
17
18    Function WithHold (Gross : Real) : Real;
19    (*
20        This function computes withholding tax using an iterative
21        method in which the first $100 of income is taxed at the
22        basic rate, the second $100 at 2x the basic rate, the third
23        $100 at 3x the basic rate and so on.
24    *)
25      Const BasicTaxRate = 0.05;
26            TaxInc = 100.00;
27
28      Var   TaxRate, Tax : Real;
29
30      Begin
31        Tax := 0;
32        TaxRate := BasicTaxRate;
33
34        While Gross >= TaxInc Do
35          Begin
36            Tax := Tax + TaxRate * TaxInc;
37            TaxRate := TaxRate + BasicTaxRate;
38            Gross := Gross - TaxInc
39          End;
40
41        WithHold := Tax + TaxRate * Gross
42      End;
43
44
45    BEGIN
46
47      Reset (PayData);
48      Rewrite (PayResults);
49
50      Writeln ('PAYROLL PROGRAM');
51      Writeln ('  Processing...');
52      Person := 1;
53
54      While not EOF (PayData) Do
```

Figure 9-13 continued

```
55        Begin
56          Writeln ('  Person #',Person:1);
57
58          Readln (PayData, Hours, Rate);
59
60          Gross := Hours * Rate;
61
62          FICA := Gross * SSRate;
63          Tax := WithHold (Gross);
64
65          Net := Gross - FICA - Tax;
66
67          Writeln (PayResults,'Hours worked.....$', Hours:8:2);
68          Writeln (PayResults,'Rate of pay......$', Rate:8:2);
69          Writeln (PayResults,'Gross pay........$', Gross:8:2);
70          Writeln (PayResults,'SS Tax...........$', FICA:8:2);
71          Writeln (PayResults,'Income Tax.......$', Tax:8:2);
72          Writeln (PayResults,'Net pay..........$', Net:8:2);
73          Writeln (PayResults);
74
75          Person := Person + 1
76
77        End (* Calculation Loop *)
78
79   END.
```

Figure 9-14

Test Run of the PAYROLL *Program That Uses an* EOF *Loop, with a Listing of the Input Data File and the Resulting Output File*

```
$ type paydata.dat

30.0   12.51
40.0    5.50
37.5   18.75
20.0    3.50
12.5    2.25

$ run payeof

PAYROLL PROGRAM
  Processing...
    Person #1
    Person #2
    Person #3
    Person #4
    Person #5

$ type payresul.dat

Hours worked.....$  30.00
Rate of pay......$  12.51
Gross pay........$ 375.30
```

Figure 9-14 continued

```
SS Tax............$  26.65
Income Tax.......$  45.06
Net Pay..........$ 303.59

Hours worked.....$  40.00
Rate of Pay......$   5.50
Gross Pay........$ 220.00
SS Tax............$  15.62
Income Tax.......$  18.00
Net Pay..........$ 186.38

Hours worked.....$  37.50
Rate of Pay......$  18.75
Gross Pay........$ 703.13
SS Tax............$  49.92
Income Tax.......$ 141.25
Net Pay..........$ 511.95

Hours worked.....$  20.00
Rate of Pay......$   3.50
Gross Pay........$  70.00
SS Tax............$   4.97
Income Tax.......$   3.50
Net Pay..........$  61.53

Hours worked.....$  12.50
Rate of Pay......$   2.25
Gross Pay........$  28.13
SS Tax............$   2.00
Income Tax.......$   1.41
Net Pay..........$  24.72
```

Let's now move on to the second kind of conditional loop, the Repeat Until loop. We will also take the opportunity to use full logical expressions in an example generated for the purpose of demonstrating such loops.

REPEAT UNTIL LOOPS

Recall that conditional loops come in two types, namely,

conditional-loop → while-do
       | repeat-until

The Repeat Until loop is different from all of the other loops we have presented so far in that it is *not* a pretest loop but is an example of a posttest loop. The implication is that the test is applied at the end rather than at the beginning of the loop. Therefore, you must always go through a Repeat Until loop *at least once* because you don't get to the test until you reach the end of the loop. Such a loop can be useful, provided you are certain that the loop must be entered at least once. In fact, it is always possible to reframe a problem in terms of a While loop instead of a Repeat Until. However, we present a Repeat Until loop here for the sake of completeness.

The Repeat Until loop takes the following form:

repeat-until → **repeat**
              executable-statement-list
              until logical-expression

Note another oddity with respect to this kind of loop: if multiple statements are used within the structure, *they need not be written as a compound statement*. The structure begins with Repeat and is then followed by an executable statement list *without* the need for Begin/End delimiters: the words Repeat and Until double for that purpose.

Let's look at an example that utilizes a Repeat Until loop (and a full logical expression).

Wind Resistance

Objects that undergo an acceleration within the earth's atmosphere tend to be slowed down by wind resistance. For example, if a person falls out of an airplane, he will drop and accelerate up to a certain point but no further. Sooner or later, he will reach a constant speed called terminal velocity. At this point, his acceleration due to gravity is just balanced by the deceleration due to wind resistance. A similar situation affects bicyclists, who normally cannot pedal at speeds in excess of 30 miles per hour because of wind resistance. (As an interesting aside, on a pedalled vehicle that is designed to reduce wind resistance substantially, it is possible to attain speeds of about 60 miles per hour.) Let us design a program to simulate the effects of wind resistance.

STEP 1: UNDERSTAND THE PROBLEM

As we said, we are dealing here with two opposing forces. The positive velocity (whether due to gravity or a car engine) is proportional to the acceleration and time. The negative component is due to wind resistance, which is proportional to the velocity cubed. These may be written algebraically as follows:

$$v = v_0 + a\,t$$
$$r = k\,v^3$$

The first formula describes the final velocity v as a function of the initial velocity v_0, the acceleration a, and the elapsed time t. The second formula describes the wind resistance r as proportional to the velocity v cubed. The actual value of the proportionality constant k depends on the shape of the moving object.

We may combine these relationships into a single formula as follows:

$$v = v_0 + a\,t - k\,v^3$$

Note, however, that we have here a situation in which the velocity is described in terms of the velocity! This may cause a problem, but it can be overcome by using iteration. Rather than using the *elapsed* time, we will divide up the total time into many small intervals and compute the velocity at the end of each. We start with a velocity of zero and then compute the velocity after a certain constant time interval. We then use these newly calculated values to compute the values for the *next* interval. This process, of course, requires iteration. Let's see how to do it.

STEP 2: PLAN THE SOLUTION

We need an algorithm that computes velocity values repeatedly, one time interval after another. Given an initial velocity, we can do that as follows:

```
Repeat
   t ← t + inc
   v1 ← v2

   v2 ← v1 + a × inc − kv³
   Write t, v2
Until we reach terminal velocity
```

Notice what we are doing within the loop: we first increment the time, then make the old velocity equal the new velocity, and finally calculate a *new* new velocity. The acceleration and time serve to *increase* the velocity, and the wind resistance serves to *decrease* it. We go through and update the values at each iteration.

The next question is, of course, how can we tell when (or if) we've reached terminal velocity? Terminal velocity would be indicated by any two consecutive velocities being the same. However, trying to equate real (computer) values is chancy, because the computer looks for true equality all the way down to the last bit. A better method is to continue until the difference between any two consecutive velocities is less than an arbitrarily small value. Hence, we may rewrite the algorithm as

```
Repeat
   t ← t + inc
   v1 ← v2
```

$$v2 \leftarrow v1 + a \times inc - kv^3$$
Write t, v2
Until abs(v1 − v2) < 0.1

Here, we choose to call the velocities equal if they differ by no more than 0.1; the actual value used is quite arbitrary and is normally chosen on the basis of how accurate you want the results to be. The use of the absolute value function ensures that the difference will be positive.

There is one other thing to consider here: if the constant of proportionality is small enough, terminal velocity may never be reached! In that case, we would still like to somehow terminate the loop. We can therefore add a second condition that will cause the loop to quit after a certain time period has expired if terminal velocity has not been reached; for our purposes here let's just use fifteen seconds. The loop can be expressed, therefore, as

Repeat
   t ← t + inc
   v1 ← v2
   $v2 \leftarrow v1 + a\ inc - kv^3$
   Write t, v2
Until abs (v1 − v2) < 0.1 or t > 15

The only other things we need to do are to input *a* and *k* and initialize the time and velocity. Adding these yields the final algorithm of

Read (a)
Read (k)
t ← 0
v2 ← 0
Repeat
   t ← t + inc
   v1 ← v2
   $v2 \leftarrow v1 + a\ inc - kv^3$
   Write t, v2
Until abs (v1 − v2) < 0.1 or t > 15

We may now move on to the next step.

STEP 3: CODE THE SOLUTION

The coded version of this algorithm is shown in Figure 9-15. As required by Pascal, each of the relational expressions in the logical expression that terminates the loop must be enclosed in parentheses. Also, we have added, at the end, an output statement that gives the terminal velocity and the time at which it was reached.

Figure 9-15

Program That Computes Velocity as a Function of Acceleration and Wind Resistance (Drag)

DRAG.PAS

```
1     Program DRAG (Input, Output);
2
3     (*
4         This program simulates an object being accelerated in
5         the atmosphere. Wind resistance is taken into account
6         and terminal velocity computed. This is done by breaking
7         up the whole time into small time increments and computing
8         appropriate values at the end of each interval.
9     *)
10
11    Const TimeInc = 1.0; (* Size of time interval for repeated calculations *)
12
13    Var t,   (* Elapsed time *)
14        v1,  (* Velocity at beginning of time interval *)
15        v2,  (* Velocity at end of time interval *)
16        a,   (* Acceleration of object under consideration *)
17        k    (* Wind resistance proportionality constant *)
18          : Real;
19
20    BEGIN
21
22      Writeln('TERMINAL VELOCITY SIMULATION');
23      Writeln;
24
25      Write ('Enter value for acceleration : '); Readln (a);
26      Write ('Enter wind resistance factor : '); Readln (k);
27
28      Writeln;
29      Writeln('Time   Velocity');
30
31      t  := 0;
32      v2 := 0;
33
34      Repeat
35        t  := t + TimeInc;
36        v1 := v2;
37        v2 := v1 + a * TimeInc - k * v1 * v1 * v1;
38        Writeln (t:4:1,'  ',v2:5:1)
39      Until (abs(v1 - v2) < 0.1) or (t >= 15);
40
41        Writeln ('Terminal velocity of ',v1:3:1,' reached in ',t:3:1,' seconds.')
42
43    END.
```

STEP 4: CHECK OUT THE PROGRAM

Figure 9-16 shows two test runs for this program. The first checks to make sure that terminal velocity really is recognized by the program when it occurs; this is correct. The second tests to ensure that, if terminal velocity is *not* reached, then the time limit will kick it out; this one works properly also.

Figure 9-16

Two Trial Runs of the Velocity/Drag Problem, Each of Which Terminates According to Different Criteria

```
$ run drag

TERMINAL VELOCITY SIMULATION

Enter value for acceleration : 25.0
Enter wind resistance factor : 0.0001

Time   Velocity
 1.0    25.0
 2.0    48.4
 3.0    62.1
 4.0    63.2
 5.0    63.0
 6.0    63.0
Terminal velocity of 63.0 reached in 6.0 seconds.

$ run drag

TERMINAL VELOCITY SIMULATION

Enter value for acceleration : 25.0
Enter wind resistance factor : 0.0000001

Time   Velocity
 1.0    25.0
 2.0    50.0
 3.0    75.0
 4.0    99.9
 5.0   124.8
 6.0   149.6
 7.0   174.3
 8.0   198.8
 9.0   223.0
10.0   246.9
11.0   270.4
12.0   293.4
13.0   315.9
14.0   337.7
15.0   358.9
Terminal velocity of 337.7 reached in 15.0 seconds.
```

False

STEP 5: DOCUMENT

No problem, especially since this is a pretty small program.

SUMMARY

In this chapter we examined loop, or iteration, structures in detail. We saw that such structures can be categorized as either counted loops or conditional loops and that there are two kinds of each. Counted loops include count-up loops and count-down loops; conditional loops include the pretest While loop and the posttest Repeat Until loop. While exploring conditional loops, we learned about logical expressions as well.

One final question at this point: How do we decide which of these loops is the best to use in a given situation? We can determine this by asking the following questions:

1. Is it easy to determine precisely the number of times we must execute the loop? (For example, in the factorial problem it was.) When this is the case, we would use a counted loop. If it is easier to count forward, we would use a count-up loop; otherwise, we would use a count-down loop.

2. If we cannot determine precisely (or easily) how many iterations are required (as, for example, in a grocery check out), a conditional loop would be best. Unless we know for certain that the loop *must* be entered at least once, we would choose the While loop; otherwise we may choose the Repeat Until loop.

EXERCISES

CONCEPTS

1. Define or explain the following terms:

Compound statement	Logical operator
Conditional loop	Nested loops
Count-down loop	Relational expression
Count-up loop	Relational operator
Input controlled loop	Repeat Until loop
Logical expression	Sentinel value

2. Explain how the logical operators AND, OR, and NOT combine truth values.

3. Describe the two kinds of input controlled loops.

TOOLS

4. Evaluate each of the following relational expressions, assuming the following values in memory:

```
Pi      : 3.14159      Epsilon : 1E-6
Angle   : 0.39458      NewX    : -14.226
Delta   : 0.00185      OldX    : -12.995
```

(handwritten:) $((\text{Jean}=\text{boy or Jean}=\text{girl) and Jean}<12)$ or $(\quad " \quad)$ or $(J=dead)$ or (outer space)

```
Count     : 1745        MaxSize  : 1200
Good      : 'A'         Bad      : 'F'
```

(handwritten F) **a.** Angle > Pi/4
(handwritten F) **b.** Good > Bad
(handwritten F) **c.** NewX > OldX
(handwritten F) **d.** OldX - NewX <= Epsilon
(handwritten F) **e.** MaxSize DIV Count > 0
(handwritten T) **f.** Angle + Delta <= 2*Pi/3
(handwritten F) **g.** Good <> 'A'

5. Evaluate each of the following logical expressions, assuming the following values in memory:

```
Hours     : 45         PayRate  : 7.50
Credits   : 18         MaxDue   : 210.00
AllDone   : True       Pretty   : False
Great     : 15870      Unit     : 1
Cost      : 1258.35    X        : -1.56
Y         : 2.03       Z        : 4.98
```

a. not Pretty *(T)*
b. (Hours > 40) or (PayRate >= 5.00) *(T)*
c. ((Cost > 2000.0) or (MaxDue <= 250.0)) and not *(F)*
AllDone
d. (4 * X + Y/2 <> Z) *(T)* and (Unit >= 0) and (Great
= Hours * Credits) *(F)* →F
(handwritten X) **e.** not ((Pretty and AllDone) or *(T)* not (Cost <=
MaxDue))   *(✱ F)*
f. (X=Y) or (X=Z) or (Y=Z) *(F)*
g. not ((X=Y) and (X=Z) and (Y=Z)) *(T)*

6. Write relational or logical expressions that express the following notions:
   (handwritten: UCOST * NOPROD <> UPRICE * NOSOLD *)*
   a. The unit cost times the number produced does not equal unit price times the number sold.
   b. John is twice as old as Mary.   *(handwritten:* JohnAge = 2 * MaryAge *)*
   (handwritten: $((T_{max} - T_{min}) > 25)$ and $(\text{Time} < 15.25)$ *)*
   c. The difference between the maximum temperature and the minimum temperature is greater than 25 degrees, and the total elapsed time is less than 15.25 seconds.
   d. Jean is a boy or a girl and is less than 12 years old, is a man or a woman and less than 100 years old, is dead, or is a creature from outer space.
   e. The difference between the new value of *x* and the old value of *x* is greater than or equal to the standard and the total number of iterations is less than 150, or an error has occurred.

(handwritten: $((\text{NewX} - \text{OldX}) >= \text{standard})$ and $(\text{iter} < 150)$ or error *)*

7. Mary works in an office where she must frequently add up large (and arbitrary) numbers of cashed checks to get the grand total. Write a program that will allow her to do this using

    a. an operator response loop
    b. a sentinel value loop

8. Write a program that will add all odd numbers between 1 and *n*, and which is implemented using

    a. a While loop
    b. a counted loop

Which is the easier to implement?

PROBLEMS

9. Population growth (human or otherwise) tends to grow exponentially, which means that the rate of growth is proportional to the current population. Consequently, as the population itself increases in size, the rate of increase also goes up. In mathematical terms, this can be stated as

$$\text{NewPop} = \text{OldPop} \times (1 + \text{BirthRate} - \text{DeathRate})^{\text{Time}}$$

where

NewPop	=	the predicted population at some time in the future
OldPop	=	the current population at time zero
BirthRate	=	the annual rate of birth, expressed as a fraction
DeathRate	=	the annual death rate, expressed as a fraction
Time	=	the total time (in years) for which the prediction is made

    a. Write a program that inputs the current population, the birthrate, the deathrate, and the number of years and predicts the future population.
    b. Augment the above program so that it lists the population year by year.

10. Write a program that simulates a simple cash register. The program should handle an arbitrary number of customers, each of whom may have an arbitrary number of purchases. For each person, the prices of individual items bought should be entered one at a time until all purchases have been entered. The end of each individual shopping list should be marked by entering a zero for a purchase amount. At that time the subtotal, tax, and total should be printed out.

    Extension: Incorporate into the program the ability to keep track of total purchases for all customers. At the end of the day (that is, after the last customer has left), the total of all receipts for the day should be printed out. Indicate the end of the day by entering a negative purchase value after the last customer has left.

11. Write a program that will calculate the arithmetic mean (average) and variance for an arbitrary number of data points. Have the program count the number of data points as they are entered. Use a negative value for the data to indicate the end of the list. (This requires, of course, that the data points be positive or zero. How can you get around this problem?) The formulas for this are

$$\text{Mean} = \frac{\Sigma x}{n}$$

where $\Sigma x = x_1 + x_2 + \ldots + x_{n-1} + x_n$

and

$$\text{Variance} = \frac{\Sigma x^2 - \dfrac{(\Sigma x)^2}{n}}{n - 1}$$

where $\Sigma x^2 = x_1^2 + x_2^2 + \ldots + x_{n-1}^2 + x_n^2$

12. Write a program (using loops) to solve the following puzzle: Freddie Frog is trapped inside a deep (fifty-foot), dark well. Each day Freddie works and works and manages to climb three feet. However, while he sleeps at night, he slides back down two feet. How many days will it take Freddie to get out of the well?

13. A number of mathematical functions, such as sine, cosine, and natural logarithms, can be computed using infinite series. For example, the sine of x can be calculated using the following formula:

$$\sin x = x - \frac{x^3}{3!} + \frac{x^5}{5!} - \frac{x^7}{7!} + \ldots$$

The formula for the cosine of x is similar, namely,

$$\cos x = 1 - \frac{x^2}{2!} + \frac{x^4}{4!} - \frac{x^6}{6!} + \ldots$$

Once the sine and cosine of x have been calculated, it is an easy matter to determine the tangent as follows:

$$\tan x = \sin x / \cos x$$

Write a program that will generate a table of sines, cosines, and tangents for values of x from 0 to 1.6 in increments of 0.1.

Quandry: In determining the sine for any specific value of x, how do you know how far to go in the series? One good method is to progressively calculate the sine in a loop, each time computing one more term and adding it in until the difference between any two successive values is less than some predetermined amount, say, 0.00001. This would require a loop something like

```
While Difference > 0.00001 Do
```

Of course, other loops will be necessary to calculate powers and factorials and to generate the table as a whole.

14. Write a program to reconcile a bank statement with a checkbook register. First of all, input the statement balance and the checkbook balance. Next, enter any transactions in the checkbook that have not as yet cleared the bank, indicating checks as being negative and deposits as being positive. As each transaction is entered, *subtract* it from the checkbook balance. (This will ensure that the checkbook balance is increased by outstanding checks and decreased by outstanding deposits, while at the same time preserving the natural idea that checks should be negative and deposits positive.) Indicate the end of the transactions with a zero amount. Print out and label the initial checkbook balance, the total transaction amounts (a running total of these will have to be kept), and the new checkbook balance. Finally, print the difference between the new checkbook balance and the statement balance. (It should be zero if all goes well.)

15. Consider a computer science class in which four exams were given to determine the final grade. Write a program that will input, for each student, the four exam grades and calculate the average. Also have the program compute the average for the entire class. Assume an arbitrary number of students for the class.

16. A console controlling pressure in a reaction vessel has three switches on it. The first is a safety valve and can be in positions 0 or 1; the second controls the amount of reactant that enters the chamber and can be in positions 1, 2, or 3; the third regulates the compression and has positions 1, 2, 3, and 4. The total pressure in the vessel is given by

$$P\,(s_1, s_2, s_3) = s_1 \times (7.35 \times s_2) \times 2s_3 - 1$$

Write a program that will generate a table of pressures for all possible switch combinations.

   Hint: This will require three nested loops plus one loop for doing powers.

17. Take the RADAR program that was developed in Chapter 6 and place it into a loop so that it will cycle as follows:

Input Range, Angle, Time
Output Distance, Altitude, GroundSpeed, Velocity, Rise

It should continue to do this over and over. Note that it should *not* have to read two sets of input data to generate one set of output information, but rather it should use the most recent input values and the input values read just prior to them to do the calculations.

10

Decision:

If/Else and Case

*I*n this chapter we will look at the last of the three fundamental control structures, binary decision. Recall from Chapter 8 that this structure allows a choice to be made between two alternatives: you *must* choose exactly one and you cannot choose both or neither. With the addition of this final control structure to our repertoire, we will be able to solve *any* problem that *can* be solved on a computer. Although binary decision itself only allows a choice to be made between one of two alternatives, it can be extended to allow selection from more than two.

As in the case of looping structures, the binary decision structure is defined in Pascal as just another executable statement. Our list of available excutable statements in Pascal, therefore, becomes

executable-statement → assignment-statement
        | input-statement
        | output-statement
        | counted-loop
        | compound-statement
        | conditional-loop
        | binary-decision

The syntax of this new statement is given by

binary-decision → **if**   logical-expression **then**
              statement
       else
              statement

      | **if**   logical-expression **then**
              statement

As we have come to expect, the actual Pascal statement is very similar to the pseudocode version presented in Chapter 8. The logical expressions referred to in this definition are exactly the same as those discussed in the previous chapter on loops: they may be relational expressions or logical expressions of any complexity. And, of course, the statements referred to in the definition can be any valid Pascal statement, including loops, compound statements, or other binary decision statements.

Note especially that the `Else` part of this structure is optional, that is, you may have a `Then` without an `Else` if it suits your purpose. Using a binary decision structure without an explicit `Else` is equivalent, of course, to having the `Else` alternative be nothing. For example, we may have a situation in which a correction needs to be applied if a number exceeds a certain value but nothing needs to be done otherwise. In this case there is no `Else` needed, and the structure need not explicitly include one.

We will begin by considering simple binary decision, in which we have only two alternatives. We will then expand the concepts to *nested* decision structures, in which we may choose between more than two alternatives. We will then finish up the chapter by examining the `Case` statement, which can, in certain situations, be a very concise alternative to using nested binary decision.

10-1 *Simple Binary Decision*

Consider as the first example the situation of overtime pay in our pay-roll calculation. Recall that the algorithm for overtime payroll was first presented in Chapter 8 as

If Hours ≤ 40 then
    Gross ← Hours × Rate
Else
    Gross ← Rate × 40 + (Hours − 40) × 1.5 × Rate

This algorithm can be converted to Pascal very directly and very easily as follows:

```
If Hours <= 40.0 then
  Gross := Hours * Rate
Else
  Gross := Rate * 40.0 + (Hours - 40.0) * 1.5 * Rate
```

Note that this is a single statement (even though it is spread out over four lines); consequently, no internal semicolons are used. Any attempt to insert semicolons within this structure in order to separate the parts will cause an error to occur.

At the risk of overstating the case, remember that only one of the gross pay calculations will actually be carried out. The computer takes care of the details of how to get from the beginning of the structure to the correct alternative inside the structure and then out of the structure.

In the overtime payroll example, each decision alternative contains only one statement; however, it is frequently necessary to execute more than one statement per alternative. Compound statements can be used to do this. To demonstrate such a situation, let's suppose you work for a bank and need to write a program that prepares customer statements. The bank has the following rules regarding service charges and interest to be paid on checking accounts:

> If the balance at the end of the month is less than $100, then no interest is paid but a service charge of $2 is taken out. On the other hand, if the balance at the end of the month is greater than or equal to $100, then no service charge is taken out and interest is paid at the current monthly rate.

How can this be written algorithmically? Simply, as follows:

If Balance < $100 then
    ServiceCharge ← $2
    Interest ← 0

Else
   ServiceCharge ← 0
   Interest ← Balance × MonthlyRate

Note that each of the alternatives requires two statements.

    Converting this to Pascal is fairly straightforward. We simply follow the definition for a binary decision statement that contains compound statements, and we get

```
If Balance < 100.00 then
  Begin
    ServiceCharge := 2.00;
    Interest := 0
  End
Else
  Begin
    ServiceCharge := 0;
    Interest := Balance * MonthlyRate
  End;
```

Note that this statement contains only two semicolons, which separate the statements that make up each of the two compound statements.

    Now let's look at a situation in which we do *not* have an explicit Else clause. Suppose we need to count up the number of times a given value occurs in a list of values. We can write an algorithm to accomplish this as follows:

Read Datum

If Datum = CriticalValue then
   Count ← Count + 1

    Converting this to a Pascal program segment is easy:

```
Read (Datum);

If Datum = CriticalValue then
    Count := Count + 1;
```

    As with the complete If-Then-Else, the action taken may be a compound statement; that is, you may do more than one thing inside the If. In the above example, we may wish to print a message indicating that a particular value has indeed been found. The algorithm could be altered to read

Read Datum

If Datum = CriticalValue then
   Count ← Count + 1
   Write 'Value seen ', Count, 'times.'

This, of course, could be written in Pascal as

```
Read (Datum);
If Datum = CriticalValue then
  Begin
    Count := Count + 1;
    Writeln ('Value seen ', Count:4, ' times.')
  End;
```

Take note of the location and number of semicolons. (You should be seeing a pattern to this now.)

Let's now look at a problem whose solution requires that we use binary decision structures.

Tuition Statements

Suppose we are to generate tuition statements for students at the University of Quaville at Toledo (UQT). Tuition is charged at the rate of $20 per credit hour, with a maximum of $300, and students who live on campus are charged $475 for room and board. In addition, any students who are registered for nine hours or more are charged a $25 activity fee. We want to write a program that will use registration and housing data for a given student to print out an itemized statement. This should be done for as many students as necessary.

STEP 1: UNDERSTAND THE PROBLEM

There are three charges to be dealt with. The first concerns tuition. The maximum amount of tuition that can be charged is $300. This means that the rate of $20 per hour is paid on the first fifteen hours only, and if anyone registers for more than fifteen hours, he or she is essentially charged a flat fee of $300. As for room and board, a student is either charged nothing or is charged exactly $475. Finally, any students who are registered for nine or more hours pay a fee of $25, and any others pay nothing. This billing process is to be done for an arbitrary number of students.

What should the inputs be?

Input: Number of hours
       Whether student is on campus or not

And what about the outputs?

Output: Tuition
        Room and Board
        Fee
        Total Owed

Let's use this information to make a mock-up of the output, that is, a sample of exactly what we want the completed statements to look like:

**University of Quaville, Toledo
Tuition Statement**

Credits Registered : 16

On Campus Student: Yes

Tuition .... $ 300.00

Room and Board.. $ 475.00

Activity Fee........ $ 25.00

Total Due .... $ 800.00

Next, let's generate the algorithm.

STEP 2: PLAN THE SOLUTION

We begin, as always, with a very general solution:

For all Students Do the following
   Get the Inputs
   Do the Calculations
   Write the Outputs

We can expand this algorithm, relatively quickly, into the following:

While there still are students Do

   Input CreditHours
   Input StudentOnCampus

   If CreditHours > 15 then
      Tuition ← $300
   Else
      Tuition ← $20 × CreditHours

   If StudentOnCampus then
      RoomBoard ← $475
   Else
      RoomBoard ← 0

   If CreditHours ≥ 9 then
      Fee ← $25

```
Else
   Fee ← 0
```

Total ← Tuition + RoomBoard + Fee

Print CreditHours, StudentOnCampus, Tuition, RoomBoard, Fee,
      Total

This algorithm essentially solves the problem, although a little more detail is required. First, we must decide how to control the loop. Let's use a query on the operator, which can be answered as 'Y' or 'N' (an input controlled loop). Second, we must decide how to indicate whether or not the student is on campus. Let's practice using Boolean variables here; we will simply ask the operator. If he answers 'Y', then we will set the appropriate variable equal to `True`; otherwise it will be set to `False`. Incorporating these new details yields our complete algorithm:

```
MoreStudents ← Yes
While MoreStudents = Yes do

   Prompt, Input CreditHours
   Prompt 'Student on Campus', Input Answer
   StudentOnCampus ← Answer = Yes

   If CreditHours > 15 then
      Tuition ← $300
   Else
      Tuition ← $20 × CreditHours

   If StudentOnCampus then
      RoomBoard ← $475
   Else
      RoomBoard ← 0

   If CreditHours ≥ 9 then
      Fee ← $25
   Else
      Fee ← 0

   Total ← Tuition + RoomBoard + Fee

   Print CreditHours, StudentOnCampus, Tuition, RoomBoard, Fee,
         Total

   Prompt 'Are there any more students', Input MoreStudents
```

All that remains to be done is to format the final printed statement, which we can do easily in the next step.

STEP 3: CODE THE SOLUTION

The solution can be coded directly from the algorithm; the result is shown in Figure 10-1. There are two things to be aware of here: First,

Figure 10-1

Program to Produce Tuition Statements for Students at UQT

```
UQT.PAS

1     Program UQT (Input, Output);
2
3     (*
4          This program figures up and prints out tuition statements
5          for students at UQT.
6     *)
7
8     Const CurrentRate =     20.00; (* Charge per credit hour *)
9           CurrentMax  =    300.00; (* Maximum tuition charge (15 hours) *)
10          CurrentRB   =    475.00; (* On-campus housing room and board charge *)
11          CurrentFee  =     25.00; (* Activity fee for persons registered
12                                        9 hours and over *)
13
14          Yes = 'Y';                (* Affirmative operator response *)
15
16    Var   CreditHours, Tuition, RoomBoard, Fee, Total : Real;
17
18          StudentOnCampus : Boolean;
19
20          MoreStudents, Answer : Char;
21
22    BEGIN
23
24      Writeln ('UQT TUITION STATEMENTS');
25      Writeln ('   Interactive Version');
26      Writeln;
27
28      MoreStudents := Yes;
29
30      While MoreStudents = Yes Do
31         Begin
32            Write ('Number of hours registered : ');
33            Readln (CreditHours) ;
34            Write ('Is the student on campus (Y,N) : ');
35            Readln (Answer);
36
37            StudentOnCampus := Answer = Yes;
38
39            If CreditHours > 15 then
40               Tuition := CurrentMax
41            Else
42               Tuition := CurrentRate * CreditHours;
43
44            If StudentOnCampus then
45               RoomBoard := CurrentRB
46            Else
47               RoomBoard := 0;
48
49            If CreditHours >= 9 then
50               Fee := CurrentFee
51            Else
52               Fee := 0;
53
54            Total := Tuition + RoomBoard + Fee;
55
```

Figure 10-1 continued

```
56          Writeln ; Writeln ;
57          Writeln ('University of Quaville, Toledo');
58          Writeln ('   Tuition Statement');
59          Writeln ;
60          Writeln ('   Credits Registered : ', CreditHours:3:0);
61          Write   ('   On Campus Student   : ');
62          If StudentOnCampus then
63              Writeln ('Yes')
64          Else
65              Writeln ('No');
66          Writeln;
67          Writeln ('   Tuition.........$', Tuition:7:2);
68          Writeln ('   Room and Board..$', RoomBoard:7:2);
69          Writeln ('   Activity Fee....$', Fee:7:2);
70          Writeln;
71          Writeln ('   Total Due.......$', Total:7:2);
72          Writeln;
73
74          Write ('Are there any more students? (Y,N) ');
75          Readln (MoreStudents)
76      End (* While *)
77
78   END.
```

symbolic constants have been supplied in lieu of the actual rates and amounts (so they can be more easily changed when they go up). Second, an additional binary decision has been incorporated into the output section in order to print out the words 'Yes' or 'No' with regard to whether the student is on campus. Also note the use of a logical assignment statement in line 37.

STEP 4: CHECK OUT THE PROGRAM

Shown in Figure 10-2 are the results of a test run. All possibilities—more than fifteen hours, less than fifteen hours, less than nine hours, on-campus and off-campus students—are tested and generate the correct results.

STEP 5: DOCUMENT

The program is quite readable and understandable and includes comments to identify the various constants.

Now that we can use simple binary decision to make a choice between two alternatives, let's extend the concept so that we can make a choice among any number of alternatives.

Figure 10-2

Test Run and Sample Output of the UQT Tuition Statement Program

```
$ run uqt

UQT TUITION STATEMENTS
   Interactive Version

Number of hours registered : 12
Is the student on campus (Y,N) : Y


University of Quaville, Toledo
   Tuition Statement

   Credits Registered : 12
   On Campus Student  : Yes

   Tuition..........$ 240.00
   Room and Board..$ 475.00
   Activity Fee....$  25.00

   Total Due.......$ 740.00

Are there any more students? (Y,N) Y
Number of hours registered : 18
Is the student on campus (Y,N) : N


University of Quaville, Toledo
   Tuition Statement

   Credits Registered : 18
   On Campus Student  : No

   Tuition..........$ 300.00
   Room and Board..$   0.00
   Activity Fee....$  25.00

   Total Due.......$ 325.00

Are there any more students? (Y,N) Y
Number of hours registered: 4
Is the student on campus (Y,N) : N


University of Quaville, Toledo
   Tuition Statement

   Credits Registered : 4
   On Campus Student  : No

   Tuition..........$  80.00
   Room and Board..$   0.00
   Activity Fee....$   0.00

   Total Due.......$  80.00

Are there any more students? (Y,N) N
```

10-2 *Nested Binary Decision*

An important aspect of the binary decision structure is its ability to be nested, which gives it a very powerful decision-making capability. We may nest full If-Then-Else statements, If-Then (without the Else) statements, or combine the nesting of If-Then-Else statements with If-Then statements. We will look at each of these three possibilities in turn.

NESTED IF-THEN-ELSE

To demonstrate the use of this type of nesting, let's reconsider our payroll program. Suppose that, in computing the gross wages, overtime is paid at not one but *two* levels, as follows:

> If employees work forty hours per week or less, they get straight pay. If they work between forty and sixty hours per week, they get straight pay for the first forty hours and time-and-a-half for all hours between forty and sixty; however, if they work over sixty hours, they get double time for those hours over sixty as well as time-and-a-half for all hours between forty and sixty.

Sounds pretty tough, doesn't it? Actually, it can be done rather easily using binary decision *if* the structures are nested, that is, placed one inside the other. The algorithm for this, although somewhat more complicated, is fairly easy to write:

```
If Hours ≤ 40 then
    Gross ← Hours × Rate
Else
    If Hours ≤ 60 then
        Gross ← 40 × Rate + 1.5 × Rate × (Hours − 40)
    Else
        Gross ← 40 × Rate + 1.5 × Rate × 20 + 2 × Rate × (Hours − 60)
```

There are a number of things to notice in this algorithm. First, look at the structure. We have a primary If-Then-Else that divides the gross calculation into two parts: no overtime (Then) and overtime (Else). For the no overtime situation, we do what we have always been doing, namely, calculate the gross by multiplying the rate by the hours.

The Else part of this outermost structure consists of a single If-Then-Else, which divides the *overtime* into two parts, namely, overtime between 40 and 60 hours and overtime beyond 60 hours. It is important to note how the conditional is expressed. It is written as

Hours ≤ 60

rather than the more complete

Hours $>$ 40 and Hours $\leq$ 60

Why is this? When considering this first level of overtime, do we not mean that the hours must be between 40 and 60 (that is, greater than 40 but less than or equal to 60)? Yes, we do. So how can we merely say Hours $\leq$ 60? We can do this because the condition that the hours are greater than 40 is implicit in the structure. *We could not have arrived at the point of this test unless the hours were in fact greater than 40!* In the same way, in order to get to the overtime calculation for time over 60 hours, we merely need an Else, and *not* another If such as

Hours $>$ 60

because it is implicit in the structure; we could not have arrived at this particular Else unless the hours were in fact greater than 60.

Also important are the numbers in the calculation. We can use the number 40 in the second and third alternatives because that is *exactly* how many hours are paid at straight time. Also, we can use 20 hours for the intermediate overtime, because that is exactly how much is paid at that rate for maximum overtime.

A second, more sophisticated point is that in constructing this overtime payroll scheme, we are actually differentiating among *three alternatives*. The algorithm can be physically rearranged in order to visually accentuate this. We may, for example, rewrite our algorithm as

If Hours $\leq$ 40 then
   Gross $\leftarrow$ Hours $\times$ Rate
Else if Hours $\leq$ 60 then
   Gross $\leftarrow$ 40 $\times$ Rate + 1.5 $\times$ Rate $\times$ (Hours $-$ 40)
Else
   Gross $\leftarrow$ 40 $\times$ Rate + 1.5 $\times$ Rate $\times$ 20 + 2 $\times$ Rate $\times$ (Hours $-$ 60)

It is important to understand that this algorithm and the first one are *absolutely identical*. The only difference is the way in which they are broken up into lines. And, as we well know, such visual arrangements do not matter at all in Pascal. The two different arrangements are strictly for the convenience of the programmer. You can think about them logically however you wish. In the first arrangement, we think in terms of two Ifs nested one inside the other. In the second, we consider the situation to consist of three possible alternatives.

If we view the structure in this latter way, we can state it thus: we check to see whether the number of hours worked is 40 or less. If it is, we calculate the gross by multiplying the hours by the rate. If it is not, we then check to see whether the hours are less than or equal to 60; if they are, we use the second method. If the second condition is not true either, we must take the third alternative.

Finally, let's see how these things look when coded in Pascal. The first algorithm becomes

```
If Hours <= 40.0 then
  Gross := Hours * Rate
Else
  If Hours <= 60.0 then
    Gross := 40.0 * Rate + 1.5 * Rate * (Hours - 40.0)
  Else
    Gross := 40.0 * Rate + 1.5 * Rate * 20.0 + 2.0 * Rate
          * (Hours - 60.0)
```

And the second algorithm becomes

```
If Hours <= 40.0 then
  Gross := Hours * Rate
Else if Hours <= 60.0 then
  Gross := 40.0 * Rate + 1.5 * Rate * (Hours - 40.0)
Else
  Gross := 40.0 * Rate + 1.5 * Rate * 20.0 + 2 * Rate
          * (Hours - 60.0)
```

Note that there are NO semicolons inside this structure anywhere! We have simply nested two binary decision statements, and hence we need no semicolon separators.

Calculator Simulation

Let's next develop a complete example that uses nested binary decision. Suppose we want to write a program that simulates a calculator. We wish to input two numbers and an operator, compute the result obtained by combining the numbers according to the specified operator, and then print out the result.

STEP I: UNDERSTAND THE PROBLEM

We first ask ourselves what operations we want to consider. Suppose these are addition, subtraction, multiplication, division, and exponentiation. We will present those operations by using the operators +,

−, *, /, ^. We would like the program to work by first prompting for the two numbers and the operation and then printing out the result. A sample run might look like this:

```
Enter Operator   : +
Enter 1st number : 3.5
Enter 2nd number : 7.6

Result : 11.1
```

Now let's come up with an algorithm.

STEP 2: PLAN THE SOLUTION

Following our top-down approach, we begin with

Prompt, Read Op
Prompt, Read N1
Prompt, Read N2

Calculate Res of N1 Op N2

Output Res

That was easy, but it doesn't give us nearly enough detail. We obviously must examine the operator in order to decide what to do. That, of course, will require decisions on our part. Actually, the algorithm can be written fairly easily as follows:

Prompt, Read Op
Prompt, Read N1
Prompt, Read N2

If Op = '+' then
    Res ← N1 + N2
Else if Op = '−' then
    Res ← N1 − N2
Else if Op = '*' then
    Res ← N1 * N2
Else if Op = '/' then
    Res ← N1 / N2
Else if Op = '^' then
    Res ← PWR (N1, N2)
Else
    Write 'Invalid Operator'
    Res ← 0

Output Res

See how easy the nested binary decision structure is to understand when it is presented in this fashion! Also, in order to implement the exponentiation, we will have to utilize the PWR function developed in the previous chapter. Note that we have included a catch-all Else just in case an invalid operator has been entered (we make the result equal to zero in such a case).

The final thing we want to do with this algorithm is to place it within a loop so that it can run continuously until stopped by the operator. We could use any of the input controlled loop methods discussed in Chapter 9. In order to make the program run quickly and easily, let's use a sentinel value: we choose ` x ` (as in exit) to be the sentinel value. In other words, if the operator ` x ` is entered, we assume it's time to quit. Adding this feature gives us our final algorithm:

Prompt, Read Op
While Op ≠ 'x' Do

   Prompt, Read N1
   Prompt, Read N2

   If Op = ' + ' then
     Res ← N1 + N2
   Else if Op = ' − ' then
     Res ← N1 − N2
   Else if Op = '*' then
     Res ← N1 * N2
   Else if Op = '/' then
     Res ← N1 / N2
   Else if Op = '^' then
     Res ← PWR (N1, N2)
   Else
     Write 'Invalid Operator'
     Res ← 0

   Output Res

   Prompt, Read Op

We must still define PWR. You may think that since we used just such a function in the last chapter, we need do nothing but copy it for use here. However, there is an important difference between the PWR function we used last time and the one we need here. In the initial version, the exponent to which we raised the base was an integer; in this example it is a real number. Consequently, we must adapt the function generated in the last chapter for use in this problem.

Subtask PWR: Step 1—Understand the Problem. The problem is that the loop that computes the powers must have an integer counter. This can be taken care of easily enough by converting the real exponent to an integer as a part of the function. We already have a function that does this (from Chapter 6) called Trunc.

Subtask PWR: **Step 2—Plan the Solution.** The solution is identical, with the exception of the integer/real conversion. Making this alteration gives us

Function PWR (b, e)
   m ← Trunc (e)
   r ← 1.0
   For i ← 1 to m Do
      r ← r × b
   PWR ← r

With this algorithm, then, we are ready to code the solution.

STEP 3: CODE THE SOLUTION

The actual program written from this algorithm is shown in Figure 10-3. Note how well the program follows the structure and presentation of the algorithm itself.

Figure 10-3

Calculator Simulation Program That Utilizes Nested Binary Decision

```
CALCSIM.PAS

  1    Program CALCSIM (Input, Output);
  2
  3    (*
  4       This program simulates a calculator. It inputs two numbers and
  5       an operator, carries out the indicated operation on the numbers,
  6       then prints out the results.
  7    *)
  8
  9    Var  N1, N2, Res : Real; (* Operands and result *)
 10
 11        Op : Char;          (* Operator: + addition
 12                                         - subtraction
 13                                         * multiplication
 14                                         / division
 15                                         ^ exponentiation
 16
 17                                         x to exit               *)
 18
 19    Function PWR (b, e : Real) : Real;
 20    (*
 21
 22       This function computes exponentiation of a real base (b)
 23       to a real power (e); the power is converted to an integer (m)
 24       before use.
 25    *)
 26      Var m,i : Integer; (* i is just the loop counter *)
 27          r   : Real;     (* result of the exponentiation *)
```

Figure 10-3 continued

```
28     Begin
29       m := Trunc (e);
30       r := 1.0;
31       For i := 1 to m Do
32           r := r * b;
33       PWR := r
34     End;
35
36
37
38   BEGIN
39
40     Writeln('Calculator Simulation');
41     Writeln;
42     Write ('Enter operator or ''x'' to end : '); Readln
43
44     While Op <> 'x' Do
45         Begin
46           Write ('Enter 1st number : '); Readln (N1);
47           Write ('Enter 2nd number : '); Readln (N2);
48
49           If Op = '+' then
50             Res := N1 + N2
51           Else if Op = '-' then
52             Res := N1 - N2
53           Else if Op = '*' then
54             Res := N1 * N2
55           Else if Op = '/' then
56             Res := N1 / N2
57           Else if Op = '^' then
58             Res := PWR (N1, N2)
59           Else
60             Begin
61               Writeln ('Invalid Operator: Must be + - * / ^');
62               Res := 0
63             End;
64
65           Writeln ('Result : ', Res:5:3);
66           Writeln;
67           Write ('Enter Operator : '); Readln (Op)
68
69         End (* While *) ;
70
71     Writeln;
72     Writeln ('Exit Calculator.')
73
74   END.
```

STEP 4: CHECK OUT THE PROGRAM

A test run of this program is shown in Figure 10-4. All possible operators (including an invalid one) are tried; they all work properly.

STEP 5: DOCUMENT

The program is documented and easy to understand.

Figure 10-4

Output from the Calculator Simulation Program

```
$ run calcsim

Calculator Simulation

Enter operator or 'x' to end : +
Enter 1st number : 4
Enter 2nd number : 25
Result : 29.000

Enter Operator   : -
Enter 1st number : 4
Enter 2nd number : 25
Result : -21.000

Enter Operator   : *
Enter 1st number : 4
Enter 2nd number : 25
Result : 100.000

Enter Operator   : /
Enter 1st number : 4
Enter 2nd number : 25
Result : 0.160

Enter Operator   : ^
Enter 1st number : 2
Enter 2nd number : 10
Result : 1024.000

Enter Operator   : !
Enter 1st number : 3
Enter 2nd number : 4
Invalid Operator: Must be + - * / ^
Result: 0.000

Enter Operator   : x

Exit Calculator.
```

NESTED IF-THEN

We may also nest If-Then (without the Else) structures. In general, though, if you are nesting several If-Thens (with no other statements), these can always be rewritten into a single If-Then statement. For example, suppose we need to reset some important variable under the conditions that (1) the variable exceeds some maximum value and (2) a key character variable is equal to a certain value. We could write this as

If ImportantValue > SomeMaximumValue then
   If KeyCharacter = CertainValue then
     ImportantVariable ← ResetValue

This algorithm would, in fact, do the right thing. First, the important variable is tested; if it exceeds the maximum, then the key value is tested. If this is equal to a certain value, then the variable is reset. If either of the tests fails, nothing is done. The Pascal equivalent of this would be

```
If ImportantVariable > SomeMaximumValue then
  If KeyCharacter = CertainValue then
    ImportantVariable := ResetValue;
```

However, this can be written algorithmically using only a single If as follows:

```
If ImportantVariable > SomeMaximumValue and
   KeyCharacter = CertainValue then
      ImportantVariable ← ResetValue
```

This algorithm will do *exactly the same thing*, and both versions are equally efficient. Translating this second version into Pascal, we have

```
If (ImportantVariable > SomeMaximumValue) and
   (KeyCharacter = CertainValue) then
      ImportantVariable := ResetValue ;
```

Note the use of parentheses to keep the operator priorities straight.

Unfortunately there can be a glitch here; these two variations are *always* equivalent *only* if the version of Pascal being used takes advantage of partial evaluation of logical expressions (recall the introduction of full versus partial evaluation in Chapter 9). If full evaluation is done, more often than not the two forms will be identical, *but not always*. As an example, consider the following algorithm:

```
If NumFound ≠ 0 and NumOut/NumFound < 2 then
   Do An Important Task
```

The only purpose of the first condition (NumFound $\neq$ 0) is to ensure that division by zero is not attempted in the second conditional (NumOut/NumFound < 2). The two conditionals are connected by logical And; therefore, if the first test fails (that is, NumFound *does* equal zero), then the entire logical expression is false and there is no need to test the second condition.

However, the algorithm will work this way *only if partial evaluation of logical expressions is used*. If full evaluation is the norm, then the second test will be made regardless of the outcome of the first test, and then division by zero becomes a real possibility.

In situations like this where the correct evaluation of one part of a logical expression depends on the results of evaluating another part of the same expression and when full evaluation is used, it is necessary to express the algorithm as nested If-Then statements. For example, we may rewrite the above algorithm as

```
If NumFound ≠ 0 then
  If NumOut/NumFound < 2 then
    Do An Important Task
```

You must be careful when deciding how to structure the solution based on the specifics of the problem. (We will see many additional examples of how to structure solutions in later chapters.)

NESTED IF-THEN-ELSE WITH IF-THEN

It is also possible to nest If-Then-Elses with simple If-Thens, *but you must be exceedingly careful!* It is very easy to write an ambiguous structure under these circumstances, and the computer may *not* interpret your instructions as you intend.

Let's first look at an example of a situation where this nesting *does* work properly. Suppose we have to write a program to handle the following situation:

> If the clocked time is greater than or equal to the interval size, then we need to test the count size. If the count size is greater than the previous maximum, we set the maximum to this count and print it out. Otherwise we print out a sequence number and the count.

The algorithm for this could be written as

```
If Clock ≥ Interval then
  If Count > Max then
    Maximum ← Count
    Write 'New maximum is', Count
  Else
    Write Sequence, Count
    Sequence ← Sequence + 1
```

Note that we have an If-Then-Else inside an If-Then. In this case there is no problem with interpretation, because the computer will understand the structure in the same way we do. Written in Pascal, this algorithm would become

```
If Clock >= Interval then
```

```
If Count > Max then
    Begin
      Maximum := Count;
      Writeln ('New maximum is ', Count:5)
    End
Else
    Begin
      Writeln (Sequence:5, Count:5);
      Sequence := Sequence + 1
    End;
```

Next, let's look at an example of the horrible things that can happen if you do not watch your step while nesting If-Thens with If-Then-Elses. Suppose that instead of checking Count if the Clock interval is too big to determine what to do, we *check Clock, and if the interval is too big we check Count, but otherwise we merely write the sequence.* This would correspond to the following algorithm:

If Clock ≥ Interval then
  If Count > Max then
    Maximum ← Count
    Write 'New maximum is', Count
Else
  Write Sequence, Count
  Sequence ← Sequence + 1

Note that we have the same statements but that the structure is a little different. Namely, the Else is associated with the *first* rather than the *second* If. We would probably write the Pascal equivalent of this new algorithm as follows:

```
If Clock >= Interval then
  If Count > Max then
    Begin
      Maximum := Count;
      Writeln ('New maximum is', Count:5)
    End
Else
  Begin
    Writeln (Sequence:5, Count:5);
    Sequence :=Sequence + 1
  End;
```

However, note that, except for the indentations, *this program section is identical to that of the first example.* Since Pascal does *not* use indentations to convey information, the computer will interpret this section exactly as it would interpret the first section; that is, it will associate the Else with the *second*, not the *first*, If. Therefore, if you use this Pascal segment to stand for the second algorithm, you will get the wrong results.

This situation is called the **dangling Else** problem. It is similar to the dangling (or misplaced) modifier sometimes found in English usage, for example, "The handsome young man sat under the tree with his woman, a huge green one." The reason this sentence is funny is because it has two possible antecedents to the final modifying clause. According to English syntax, this clause is to be associated with the most recent antecedent (woman), whereas the author intends that it be associated with the first antecedent (tree). In our Pascal example, the same thing is true: the computer associates the Else clause with the most recent If, but the logic of the second program segment requires that the Else clause be associated with the first If. In the English language example, the result is funny. Such a problem in programming is not humorous, and you may end up spending a lot of time trying to find out what is wrong. Whenever you utilize the simple If-Then, be aware of the potential dangers.

So, how can we correct this error? The If-Then part of the algorithm must be constructed so that it is truly a single If-Then statement with no Else clause. The best way to do this is by using a compound statement, that is, by adding an extra set of Begin-Ends. The correct Pascal program is

```
If Clock >= Interval then
    Begin
      If Count > Max then
          Begin
             Maximum := Count;
             Writeln ('New maximum is ', Count:5)
          End
    End
Else
    Begin
      Writeln (Sequence:5, Count:5);
      Sequence := Sequence + 1
    End;
```

Here we have an obvious Then section, consisting of a single If statement, and an obvious Else section, consisting of a write and an assignment statement.

We next look at another method for choosing among many alternatives—the Case statement. Although not as general as nested binary decision, it is, given an appropriate situation, much more convenient and efficient.

10-3 *The Case Statement*

Binary decision allows a choice to be made between *two* alternatives. The nesting of binary decision structures allows a choice to be made among several alternatives. This nesting technique was used in the simple calculator simulation above. This is termed **multiple decision** or **multiple selection**. Under certain restricted conditions, a special, non-fundamental control structure can be used that implements multiple selection more efficiently (and clearly) than does nesting binary decision. This structure (introduced in Chapter 8) is called the **Case statement,** and we can add this type of executable statement to our list, as follows:

```
executable-statement → assignment-statement
                     | input-statement
                     | output-statement
                     | counted-loop
                     | compound-statement
                     | conditional-loop
                     | binary-decision
                     | case-statement
```

The Case statement can be used instead of the nested binary decision whenever the various Ifs and Else Ifs of the structure involve testing integers or characters for specific values. In other words, the conversion can be made provided that the logical expressions of all the nested If-Then-Elses are of this form:

variable = constant

(The calculator simulation presented previously does in fact satisfy this criterion.)

We can define the Case statement as follows:

```
case-statement → case selector of
                    selector-list
                 end
```

For the first time in our experience, we have a situation in which there is an End *that does not have an associated* Begin. The End here is used to mark the end of the Case statement. You may, of course, have additional Begins and Ends throughout the Case structure to mark off compound statements.

Now, onward. The selector is either an integer or character variable (actually, other data types may be used, but these are not discussed until Appendix A). The selector list, which consists of the possible alternatives, contains one or more selection definitions of the form

selection-definition → value-list : statement;

Here, a value list is either a single value or a list of values separated by commas, and any individual value is *one* of the possible values that the selector may take on. The statement is any valid statement that we have encountered so far, including compound statements or other Case statements.

The simplest way to demonstrate the Case statement is by example. Let's use the Case statement rather than the nested If-Then-Else to solve the calculator simulation problem of Figure 10-3.

Case Calculator Simulation

We want to rewrite this program using Case statements rather than nested binary decision. Everything else we have done will be exactly the same.

STEP 1: UNDERSTAND THE PROBLEM

We already went through this once; no need to do it again.

STEP 2: PLAN THE SOLUTION

Here is where the change comes in. The algorithm we used for the selection part was

```
If Op = '+' then
   Res ← N1 + N2
Else if Op = '−' then
   Res ← N1 − N2
Else if Op = '*' then
   Res ← N1 * N2
Else if Op = '/' then
   Res ← N1 / N2
Else if Op = '^' then
   Res ← PWR (N1, N2)
Else
   Write 'Invalid Operator'
   Res ← 0
```

Let's convert this to an algorithm using the Case statement. The above algorithm would become

```
        Case Op of
'+' : Res ← N1 + N2
'−' : Res ← N1 − N2
'*' : Res ← N1 * N2
'/' : Res ← N1 / N2
'^' : Res ← PWR (N1, N2)
```

Observe how much more compact and understandable this version is! You simply go down the list of possible alternatives until you find the one you want.

There is a rather messy problem here, namely, how do we catch the possibility that an incorrect operator has been specified? There are a number of ways to deal with this problem, all of them inelegant, to say the least. We will merely ignore the problem at this point and retain the above algorithm as it stands. (However, almost every version of Pascal does in fact provide an easy way out of this problem; check your version.) The Pascal for the Case section of the algorithm can be written as

```
        Case Op of
'+' : Res := N1 + N2;
'-' : Res := N1 - N2;
'*' : Res := N1 * N2;
'/' : Res := N1 / N2;
'^' : Res := PWR (N1, N2);
        End (* Case *);
```

Note that we have placed a comment, (* Case *), after the actual end of the case structure. Although not required, this does help with the documentation and presentation of the structure, since this End does not have a corresponding Begin.

STEP 3: CODE THE SOLUTION

The program is identical, except for the substitution of the Case statement for the nested binary decision. Incorporating this new structure into the calculator simulation program produces the results shown in Figure 10-5.

STEP 4: CHECK OUT THE PROGRAM

We may use the same test data as we did with the nested version (with the exception of the invalid operator) and obtain the same results, as seen in Figure 10-6.

Figure 10-5

Calculator Simulation Program That Utilizes the Case *Statement*

CALCCASE.PAS

```
 1    Program CALCCASE (Input, Output);
 2
 3    (*
 4        This program simulates a calculator. It inputs two numbers and
 5        an operator, carries out the indicated operation on the numbers,
 6        then prints out the results. It makes use of the Case statement
 7        to choose among operators.
 8    *)
 9
10    Var  N1, N2, Res : Real;  (* Operands and result *)
11
12        Op : Char;             (* Operator: + addition
13                                             - subtraction
14                                             * multiplication
15                                             / division
16                                             ^ exponentiation
17
18                                             x to exit          *)
19
20
21    Function PWR (b, e : Real) : Real;
22    (*
23        This function computes exponentiation of a real base (b)
24        to a real power (e); the power is converted to an integer (m)
25        before use.
26    *)
27      Var m,i : Integer; (* i is just the loop counter *)
28          r   : Real;    (* result of the exponentiation *)
29      Begin
30        m := Trunc (e);
31        r := 1.0;
32        For i := 1 to m Do
33            r := r * b;
34        PWR := r
35      End;
36
37
38
39    BEGIN
40
41      Writeln('Calculator Simulation');
42      Writeln;
43      Write ('Enter operator or ''x'' to end : '); Readln)Op);
44
45      While Op <> 'x' Do
46          Begin
47            Write ('Enter 1st number : '); Readln (N1);
48            Write ('Enter 2nd number : '); Readln (N2);
49
50                Case Op of
51            '+' : Res := N1 + N2;
52            '-' : Res := N1 - N2;
53            '*' : Res := N1 * N2;
54            '/' : Res := N1 / N2;
55            '^' : Res := PWR (N1, N2);
56                End (* Case *);
```

Figure 10-5 continued

```
57
58            Writeln ('Result : ', Res:5:3);
59            Writeln;
60            Write ('Enter Operator : '); Readln (Op)
61
62         End (* While *);
63
64      Writeln;
65      Writeln ('Exit Calculator.')
66
67   END.
```

Figure 10-6

Output from the Case *Calculator Simulation Program.*

```
$ run calccase

Calculator Simulation

Enter operator or 'x' to end : +
Enter 1st number : 4
Enter 2nd number : 25
Result : 29.000

Enter Operator   : -
Enter 1st number : 4
Enter 2nd number : 25
Result : -21.000

Enter Operator   : *
Enter 1st number : 4
Enter 2nd number : 26
Result : 97.837

Enter Operator   : /
Enter 1st number : -17
Enter 2nd number : 15
Result : -1.126

Enter Operator   : ^
Enter 1st number : 2
Enter 2nd number : 15
Result : 32768.000

Enter Operator   : x

Exit Calculator.
```

STEP 5: DOCUMENT

Done.

As we stated earlier, it is also possible to use an integer variable as the selector in a Case statement. An example of this might be appropriate and enlightening. Let's say that you are interested in law and order and are hired by the local sheriff to write a program that indicates what action should be taken when someone is stopped for a traffic violation. The action should be based on the number of traffic violations the person has had in the previous calendar year, as follows:

> If offenders have no violations, then only a warning should be issued. If offenders have one, two, or three violations, they must appear in court and pay a fine of $25. If four or five violations are outstanding, they must appear in court and pay a fine of $50. If six violations are outstanding, they must go to court and pay $90. If seven are extant, they are to be arrested and the vehicle impounded.

This could be easily handled by the Case structure. An algorithm to carry this part out could be written as follows:

```
        Case NumViolations of
0     : Write 'Issue warning'
1,2,3 : Write 'Appear in court, fine of $25'
4,5   : Write 'Appear in court, fine of $50'
6     : Write 'Appear in court, fine of $90'
7     : Write 'Arrest driver, impound vehicle'
```

Note how easily this can be put together. It also demonstrates that multiple values are permitted for each action.

Converting the algorithm to Pascal is direct and straightforward:

```
        Case NumViolations of
0     : Writeln ('Issue warning');
1,2,3 : Writeln ('Appear in court, fine of $25');
4,5   : Writeln ('Appear in court, fine of $50');
6     : Writeln ('Appear in court, fine of $90');
7     : Writeln ('Arrest driver, impound vehicle');
        End (* Case *)
```

A point to keep in mind here is that the Case structure is usually much more efficient in execution than the nested binary decision. With nested If-Then-Elses, the computer goes through the alternatives one at a time until it finds the correct one. With the Case statement, the computer calculates the correct alternative *and goes directly to the right place*. This can be an important factor when you are deciding which method to use.

Now that we have examined all of the fundamental control structures and their variations, let's take this opportunity to bring them all together in a single demonstration program.

10-4 *Synthesis*

The problem that we will consider is one that to many people may sound trivial. On closer examination, however, the problem is really rather challenging. It makes use of all the control structures, exemplifies structured programming, and is actually useful as well as interesting.

Change for a Dollar

Consider the following situation: you go into a store, make a purchase that costs you $3.17, and pay for it with a five dollar bill. How does the cashier calculate your change? Specifically, how many of each kind of coin or bill should be returned to you?

Let's simplify the problem by assuming that the total purchases will be less than a dollar and that they will be paid for with a one dollar bill. The change to be returned, therefore, will also be less than a dollar. The problem then reduces to one of determining the number of each kind of coin to be returned. To simplify the problem even further, the only allowed coins will be pennies, nickels, dimes, and quarters (no half dollars).

STEP 1: UNDERSTAND THE PROBLEM

How can we approach this? One (trivial) solution is simply to return the change using all pennies. Doing so, however, will return the *maximum* number of coins. What we would really like to do is return the *least* number of coins.

Let's start by looking at the problem heuristically (that is, by determining the steps used by a human being in solving the problem) and see whether its solution can be easily adapted to a computer. Generally, there are two methods that can be used by a cashier to come up with the correct change. Let's look at both.

Method 1: Count to Tendered Total. This was the method most often used before the advent of "fancy" cash registers. Once you knew the total of all purchases and the amount tendered, you simply counted *from* the purchase total *to* the amount tendered, and the change would be correct. For example, if you purchased seventeen cents worth of items and paid for them with a dollar bill, the cashier would say something like the following (The coins you would be handed are indicated in square brackets.):

> Eighteen, nineteen, twenty [three pennies], twenty-five [one nickel], fifty, seventy-five, a dollar [three quarters].

This method has the advantage of producing the correct change *without* first having to subtract the purchases from the amount tendered, and it also produces the change with the least total number of coins. The problem is that this method requires a little more intelligence, because you have to know when to shift to the next coin as a function of multiples of the values of each coin. For example, suppose you were providing change for a thirty-nine-cent purchase. You would begin by returning one penny (which makes the total forty cents), but then what would you do? You could next return a nickel, but that would not result in the least number of coins. The next coin you ought to return is a dime, because that *immediately* makes the total fifty cents, which is a multiple of the quarter (that is, twenty-five cents). This is not as easy for a machine to do.

Method 2: Count the Change. When the purchase total (say, seventeen cents again) is subtracted from the total amount tendered (a dollar), the cash register shows the amount of change (in this case eighty-three cents). The cashier then counts the change, saying something like

> Twenty-five, fifty, seventy-five [three quarters], eighty [one nickel], eighty-one, eighty-two, eighty-three [three pennies].

This method has a disadvantage: you must first subtract the cost of the purchases from the amount tendered to get the amount of the change. This drawback is balanced by the fact that choosing the correct coins is a lot easier. In general, if returning the largest coin available will result in too much change, then you don't use that coin but rather go to the next smallest denomination coin. This method permits an easy way to determine which coin to return next. Consider a thirty-nine cent purchase, where the change would be sixty-one cents. In making the change, it would be fine to start with a quarter, since a quarter would *not* take you over the change amount of sixty-one cents. If you used another quarter, you would have fifty cents, still not over sixty-one cents. However, if you were to hand out a third quarter, the total would be seventy-five cents—too much. You would therefore try the next biggest coin, namely a dime. This would give you sixty cents—*not* over and therefore OK. If you try returning a second dime, you would have given out seventy cents—too much. Therefore, you return a nickel. However, even one nickel is too much, since your total will be sixty-five cents. Consequently, you use pennies and return one penny.

People do not actually make change this way, but they unconsciously follow this decision-making process. This second method starts with the coin of largest worth and gradually works its way down to the lowest-value coin. Hence, it is easier to produce change using the least number of coins. We will, therefore, concentrate on this second method when generating our algorithm.

STEP 2: PLAN THE SOLUTION

How can we incorporate the ideas just discussed into an algorithm? Well, we know we must start with quarters and see whether or not returning a quarter would exceed the total change. One way to do this is to have a running total of all the change given out so far and compare that total with the total change. However, there is a somewhat easier alternative: as you return the change, you can subtract, one at a time, the value of the coins you return from the amount of change. Then, you just need to compare the *remaining* amount of change with the value of the current denomination of coin to see if you can take out another coin. Let's illustrate with an example. Assume that we are still dealing with a seventeen-cent purchase, where the change from a dollar would be eighty-three cents. To get the correct number of coins for the change, we would proceed as follows: First we would ask: Can we hand back a quarter as change? The answer is yes, since the total amount of change yet to be returned is still eighty-three cents, and a quarter would not cause this amount to be exceeded. Having done this, the change so far would consist of one quarter, and the remaining change would be eighty-three minus twenty-five, or fifty-eight cents. We would ask again: Can we take out a quarter? The answer would again be yes, since the change remaining is fifty-eight cents. If we hand back another quarter, we would have given two quarters in change, and there would remain an amount of fifty-eight minus twenty-five, or thirty-three cents. We could give back one more quarter, whereupon we would have returned three quarters as change, leaving a remaining amount of thirty-three minus twenty-five, or eight cents.

At this point, we compare the remaining amount to a quarter, and we see that we *cannot* take out another quarter, since there isn't that much money left. We then go to the next smaller denomination, namely a dime. However, we cannot take out a dime either. Hence, no dimes are used. We try a nickel, and that works. Our remaining total is eight minus five, or three cents. We cannot take out another nickel, so we return the rest of the change in pennies. We have therefore determined that the change should be three quarters, one nickel, and three pennies. Voilà!

Let's begin to formalize this. What general algorithm can we use to determine the change? Being careful not to do too much at once, we can write

```
For as many persons as we have
    Input Purchases
    Calculate Change
    Determine number of Quarters
    Determine number of Dimes
    Determine number of Nickels
    Determine number of Pennies
    Output the results
```

We can expand this a little already, to

```
For as many persons as we have
    Input Purchases
    Change ← $1 − Purchases
    Determine number of Quarters
    Determine number of Dimes
    Determine number of Nickels
    Determine number of Pennies
    Output Quarters, Dimes, Nickels, Pennies
```

This, however, brings up a problem: how shall we represent one dollar? We could simply use 1.00, a floating point number. However, since we are dealing here with purchases that are all less than a dollar, let's use pennies instead. This way, a dollar will be 100 cents, a quarter 25 cents, and so forth. Making this alteration yields

```
For as many persons as we have
    Input Purchases
    Change ← 100 − Purchases
    Determine number of Quarters
    Determine number of Dimes
    Determine number of Nickels
    Determine number of Pennies
    Output Quarters, Dimes, Nickels, Pennies
```

Now we can get down to the problem of determining the number of each type of coin.

Quarters. We would like to distill the description of the process needed to find quarters into a neat algorithm. We know the test, namely,

If the remaining change is greater than or equal to twenty-five cents, then hand out a quarter and subtract twenty-five cents from the remaining change.

How long do we do this? As long as the remaining change is greater than or equal to twenty-five cents. This suggests a While loop. In fact, this can easily be written as follows:

```
While Change ≥ 25 Do
    Add a quarter to the coins given back
    Change ← Change − 25
```

We need, at this point, a method to keep track of the coins returned. Let's use running totals for each denomination; in the case of quarters we will use a variable called Quarter, which retains the total number of such coins returned (we must remember to initialize it!). Doing this gives us the following algorithm:

```
Quarters ← 0
While Change ≥ 25 Do
    Quarters ← Quarters + 1
    Change ← Change − 25
```

We may now use the algorithm for quarters as a model for the other coins.

Dimes. We need to do exactly the same thing for dimes as for quarters, thus

```
Dimes ← 0
While Change ≥ 10 Do
    Dimes ← Dimes + 1
    Change ← Change − 10
```

Note that the only differences are the substitution of Dimes for Quarters and the amount 10 (the value of a dime) for 25 (the value of a quarter).

Nickels. We might be tempted to handle nickels in the same way. However, there is an interesting limitation here: if we ever gave out more than one nickel, we would have given out at least one dime. Consequently, we know that we can never give out more than one nickel. In fact, we will give out either *one* nickel or *no* nickels. Sound familiar? It's a simple binary decision mechanism!

```
If Change ≥ 5 then
    Nickels ← 1
    Change ← Change − 5
```

Else
   Nickels ← 0

Pennies. **This** is the easiest, because the number of pennies is equal to whatever is left. This algorithm is trivial:

Pennies ← Change

One more thing: the algorithm as written destroys our initial change amount. Therefore, we must print out the value of the change amount *before* it gets destroyed. Modifying the algorithm for that purpose yields

```
For as many persons as we have
    Input Purchases
    Change ← 100 − Purchases
    Output Change
    Determine number of Quarters
        Quarters ← 0
        While Change ≥ 25 Do
            Quarters ← Quarters + 1
            Change ← Change − 25
    Determine number of Dimes
        Dimes ← 0
        While Change ≥ 10 Do
            Dimes ← Dimes + 1
            Change ← Change − 10
    Determine number of Nickels
        If Change ≥ 5 then
            Nickels ← 1
            Change ← Change − 5
        Else
            Nickels ← 0
    Determine number of Pennies
        Pennies ← Change
    Output Quarters, Dimes, Nickels, Pennies
```

The only thing left is to determine exactly how to terminate the outermost loop. Let's implement this by way of a sentinel value: whenever the input is negative or zero, we quit. Making this last modification gives us our final algorithm:

```
1.    Input Purchases
2.    While Purchases > 0 Do
3.        Change ← 100 − Purchases
4.        Output Change
          Determine number of Quarters
5.            Quarters ← 0
```

6.   While Change ≥ 25 Do
7.   Quarters ← Quarters + 1
8.   Change ← Change − 25
            Determine number of Dimes
9.   Dimes ← 0
10.   While Change ≥ 10 Do
11.   Dimes ← Dimes + 1
12.   Change ← Change − 10
            Determine number of Nickels
13.   If Change ≥ 5 then
14.   Nickels ← 1
15.   Change ← Change − 5
16.   Else
17.   Nickels ← 0
            Determine number of Pennies
18.   Pennies ← Change
19.   Output Quarters, Dimes, Nickels, Pennies
20.   Input Purchases

Just to make sure that this algorithm works as planned, let's trace through it. We'll abbreviate the trace by just writing down the contents of the various memory locations *after* each step has been executed. We will write the steps in the order of execution, taking into account the control structures. Make sure you can follow the program and convince yourself that the contents of the memory locations are correct. We will trace a purchase of 17 cents to be consistent with previous examples.

Step 1   Purchases: 17   Change   : x   Quarters : x
          Dimes   : x   Nickels : x   Pennies : x
Step 2   The purchases are greater than zero; therefore we enter the main
          loop.
Step 3   Purchases: 17   Change   : 83   Quarters : x
          Dimes   : x   Nickels : x   Pennies : x
Step 4   Output Change : 83
Step 5   Purchases: 17   Change   : 83   Quarters : 0
          Dimes   : x   Nickels : x   Pennies : x
Step 6   Change is greater than 25, so we enter this loop.
Step 7   Purchases: 17   Change   : 83   Quarters : 1
          Dimes   : x   Nickels : x   Pennies : x
Step 8   Purchases: 17   Change   : 58   Quarters : 1
          Dimes   : x   Nickels : x   Pennies : x
          We have completed this loop, so we go back to step 6.
Step 6   Change is still greater than or equal to 25, so we once again enter
          the loop.
Step 7   Purchases: 17   Change   : 58   Quarters : 2
          Dimes   : x   Nickels : x   Pennies : x
Step 8   Purchases: 17   Change   : 33   Quarters : 2
          Dimes   : x   Nickels : x   Pennies : x

We have again completed the loop, so we go back again to step 6.

Step 6   Change is once again greater than or equal to 25, so we enter the loop a third time.

Step 7
```
Purchases: 17      Change  : 33     Quarters : 3
Dimes     : x      Nickels : x      Pennies  : x
```

Step 8
```
Purchases: 17      Change  : 8      Quarters : 3
Dimes     : x      Nickels : x      Pennies  : x
```

Yet again we have finished the loop, so we go back to step 6.

Step 6   Change is no longer greater than or equal to 25, so we skip the loop and proceed to step 9.

Step 9
```
Purchases: 17      Change  : 8      Quarters : 3
Dimes     : 0      Nickels : x      Pennies  : x
```

Step 10   Change is *not* greater than or equal to 10; therefore we skip this loop and go immediately to step 13.

Step 13   Change is, in fact, greater than or equal to 5, so we take the Then clause of the binary decision rather than the Else. Therefore, we go to step 14.

Step 14
```
Purchases: 17      Change  : 8      Quarters : 3
Dimes     : 0      Nickels : 1      Pennies  : x
```

Step 15
```
Purchases: 17      Change  : 3      Quarters : 3
Dimes     : 0      Nickels : 1      Pennies  : x
```

Step 18
```
Purchases: 17      Change  : 3      Quarters : 3
Dimes     : 0      Nickels : 1      Pennies  : 3
```

Step 19   Output Quarters, Dimes, Nickels, Pennies
                   3   0   1   3

Step 20   Etc.

Note that we do in fact get the right answers. This suggests that the algorithm is correct. Let us, therefore, code it.

STEP 3: CODE THE SOLUTION

The coded Pascal solution is shown in Figure 10-7. Note that the output section (lines 62 through 69) has been implemented in such a way that the number of each kind of coin returned is printed out *only* if it is greater than zero. This has been done via If-Then (without Else) statements.

STEP 4: CHECK OUT THE PROGRAM

A test run is also shown in Figure 10-8. The correct change, with the smallest number of coins, is returned each time.

STEP 5: DOCUMENT

The program is written in such a way as to be completely understandable. Note especially the presentation, which visually divides up the solution, and the judicious use of comments to enhance comprehension.

Figure 10-7

Program to Compute Change from a Dollar

CHANGER.PAS

```
 1    Program CHANGER (Input, Output);
 2
 3    (*
 4       This program computes the change for purchases totaling $1.00 or
 5       less and paid for with a $1.00 bill. It returns the change using
 6       the fewest coins possible. Permissible coins are quarters, dimes,
 7       nickels, and pennies.
 8    *)
 9
10    Var Purchases,                        (* Amount of purchase (in cents) *)
11        Change,                           (* Amount of change (also in cents) *)
12        Quarters, Dimes,
13        Nickels, Pennies : Integer;
                                            (* Number of each type of coin
14                                               to be returned as change  *)
15
16    BEGIN
17
18      Writeln ('PROGRAM TO COMPUTE CHANGE FOR A DOLLAR');
19      Writeln;
20      '
21      Write ('Enter purchase amount between 1-99 cents, or 0 to exit : ');
22      Readln (Purchases);
23      While Purchases > 0 Do
24         Begin
25            Change := 100 - Purchases;
26            Writeln ('Your change is ', Change:2); Writeln;
27
28            (* Determine number of quarters *)
29
30            Quarters := 0;
31            While Change >= 25 Do
32               Begin
33                  Quarters := Quarters + 1;
34                  Change := Change - 25
35               End (* Quarters *);
36
37            (* Determine number of dimes *)
38
39            Dimes := 0;
40            While Change >= 10 Do
41               Begin
42                  Dimes := Dimes + 1;
43                  Change := Change - 10
44               End (* Dimes *);
45
46            (* Determine number of nickels *)
47
48            If Change >= 5 then
49               Begin
50                  Nickels := 1;
51                  Change := Change - 5
52               End
```

Figure 10-7 continued

```
53              Else
54                 Nickels := 0;
55
56              (* Determine number of pennies *)
57
58              Pennies := Change;
59
60              (* Output the results *)
61
62              If Quarters > 0 then
63                 Writeln ('Quarters = ', Quarters:1);
64              If Dimes > 0 then
65                 Writeln ('Dimes    = ', Dimes:1);
66              If Nickels > 0 then
67                 Writeln ('Nickels  = ', Nickels:1);
68              If Pennies > 0 then
69                 Writeln ('Pennies  = ', Pennies:1);
70
71              (* Repeat the loop *)
72
73              Writeln;
74              Write ('Enter purchase amount : '); Readln (Purchases)
75
76           End (* Customer Loop *)
77
78    END.
```

Figure 10-8

Test Run of the Change for a Dollar Program

```
$ run changer

PROGRAM TO COMPUTE CHANGE FOR A DOLLAR

Enter purchase amount between 1-99 cents, or 0 to exit : 17
Your change is 83

Quarters = 3
Nickels  = 1
Pennies  = 3

Enter purchase amount : 39
Your change is 61

Quarters = 2
Dimes    = 1
Pennies  = 1

Enter purchase amount : 99
Your change is 1

Pennies  = 1
```

Figure 10-8 continued

```
Enter purchase amount : 1
Your change is 99

Quarters = 3
Dimes    = 2
Pennies  = 4

Enter purchase amount : 58
Your change is 42

Quarters = 1
Dimes    = 1
Nickels  = 1
Pennies  = 2

Enter purchase amount : 0
```

SUMMARY

In this chapter we have examined the third of the fundamental control structures, binary decision. We saw its usefulness in allowing the computer to make decisions between two alternatives. We then went on to extend binary decision by the concept of nesting, which makes it possible to choose between any arbitrary number of alternatives. We also demonstrated the Case statement, which can, under certain conditions, be used as an alternative to nesting.

Finally we have shown with the CHANGER program how a complex program can be solved using the three fundamental control structures. At this point you know all you need to write a solution (that is, a sequence of instructions) for any computer-solvable problem. There is still much to learn, including a few interesting things about data. Nonetheless, this understanding of control structures provides the fundamental basis for all that is to come.

EXERCISES

CONCEPTS

1. Define or explain the following terms:

Case statement

Dangling Else

Multiple selection

Nested binary decision

2. Explain what restrictions must be met in order to use the Case statement instead of binary decision.

3. Discuss the interchangeability of complex conditional expressions versus nested binary decision.

TOOLS

4. Minimize the conditional expressions used in the following algorithm and convert to Pascal:

If property value > 100,000 then
   Tax Rate ← 12.5%
Else if 50,000 < Property Value ≤ 100,000 then
   Tax Rate ← 10.0%
Else if 25,000 < Property Value ≤ 50,000 then
   Tax Rate ← 8.5%
Else if 10,000 < Property Value ≤ 25,000 then
   Tax Rate ← 6.0%
Else if 0 < Property Value ≤ 10,000 then
   Tax Rate ← 4.25%

5. Develop algorithms to accomplish the following selections:

   a. Long distance telephone company ACTH offers service for which a substantial up-front connection fee is charged. Long distance telephone company SPRINKLE charges no connection fee. However, SPRINKLE calling charges are based on distance and time, whereas ACTH charges a flat monthly rate for any number of calls up to a certain maximum, and then a flat fee per call regardless of distance or time. Based on the average number, distance, and times of calls made by Whah Co., determine which long distance carrier should be contracted.

   b. Cities are to be categorized economically according to their respective unemployment rates as follows:

   > 0 − 4 %: Outward bound
   > 4 − 6 %: Healthy
   > 6 − 10 %: Normal

   Greater than 10 %: Depressed

   c. If any two of width, length, and height are greater than zero, calculate the area of the figure. If all three are greater than zero, calculate a volume. Otherwise, print an error message.

6. Consider each of the following and write algorithms for them using both complex conditionals and nested binary decision. Determine which are equivalent and which are not (assuming full evaluation).

   a. If the temperature of a chemical mixture is greater than 125 degrees and the pressure is greater than 2.226 atmospheres, sound the alarm.

   b. If NOUT is greater than NIN, and Time is greater than zero, calculate Throughput ← Time / (NOUT − NIN).

   c. If F is greater than −42, and G is less than or equal to 25, and H/((F + 42) × (G − 25)) is more than 0.01, then proceed with the benefit evaluation.

7. A numeric code of 0 to 7 is used to categorize employee productivity. Raises are based on this code as follows:

0 or 1	− No increase
2	− 2% increase
3, 4, or 5	− 3% increase
6	− 5% increase
7	− 10% increase

   Write an algorithm to determine new salaries based on old salaries and the productivity code. Solve this using both nested binary decision and the Case statement. Which approach is better?

PROBLEMS

8. Exponentiation, as defined in the calculator simulation programs of Figures 10-3 and 10-5, works only if the exponent is positive or zero. Extend the program (that is, the function PWR) so that it will also work for negative exponents.

9. Extend the CHANGER program above to permit it to accept any purchase amount whatever. Have the program determine the change to be given using the coins pennies, nickels, dimes, and quarters, and the paper currency of one, five, ten, twenty, and fifty dollar bills.

10. In general, any problem can be solved in more than one way. The change problem above, for example, may be solved by substituting a little more mathematical sophistication for all the control structures. If you divide (using *integer* arithmetic) the amount of change remaining by the value of a particular coin, the quotient will be the number of such coins to be returned and the remainder will be the new remaining change. For example, if the total amount of change was to be 83 cents, we could determine the number of quarters as follows:

$$\begin{array}{r} 3 \\ 25\overline{)83} \\ 75 \\ \hline 8 \end{array}$$

Note that, as we expect, three quarters are to be given for change, and eight cents is left over. Rework the solution to the change problem using this method. Recall the Pascal operators DIV and MOD in solving this problem.

11. Write a program to generate checking account statements for the First National Federal State Savings and Loan. Inputs should consist of the account number (an integer), the beginning balance, and all transactions. For the transactions, use positive numbers to identify credits (that is, deposits) and negative numbers to identify debits (checks). The following rules apply:

ALL accounts are paid monthly interest on an annual rate of 5.5 percent on the final balance at the end of the month.

If, AT ANY TIME, the current balance drops below $100, a service charge of $7.50 is taken out. (This means that you must check the balance after each transaction is processed.)

The output should look something like the following:

FIRST NATIONAL FEDERAL STATE SAVINGS AND LOAN

Account Number : 20566

Beginning Balance : $ 135.25

Transactions (− indicates debit):

   $ − 10.00
   $ 50.00
   $ − 25.00
   $ − 18.00
   $ − 30.00
   $ −   5.00
   $ 20.00

Service Charge : $ 7.50

Interest   : $ 0.54

Ending Balance : $ 110.04

12. Write a program to determine whether a given number is *prime*. A prime number is one that has no even divisors other than 1 and itself. Some examples are 2, 3, 19, and 97.

   Hints: You must try to divide the candidate number by many, but not all numbers, between 2 and the number. For example, there is no use trying anything larger than one-half of the candidate, since there could not possibly be anything that would work above that size (in fact, the upper limit is the square root of the number). As soon as a number divides evenly, the number has been determined *not* to be prime. Recall the Pascal operator MOD in doing this.

13. The AceyDeucy Used Car Lot pays its salespersons according to the following schedule:

Total Sales	Salary	Commission (percent)
$0	$0	0
Between $1 and $100	$0	5
Between $101 and $1000	$0	10
Between $1000 and $5000	$100	12
Over $5000	$250	18

Write a program that will calculate gross pay for the sales force.

14. The FlyByNight Parcel Service guarantees overnight delivery of any package within the continental United States. Its charges are based on the following:

Weight (lbs.)	Cost
1	$20.00
2	$35.00
3	$42.50
4	$47.50
5 or more	$50.00 plus $2.25 per pound over 5 pounds

Write a program that will determine the appropriate cost, given the weight of the parcel.

15. Derive a table of function values (from -10 to $+10$ in steps of one-half) for the mathematical function described by

$$f(x) = -5 - x \quad \text{for } x < -5$$
$$= -x^2 + 25 \text{ for } -5 \leqslant x \leqslant 5$$
$$= 5 - x \quad \text{for } x > 5$$

16. The University of Remington at Quince Terrace (URAQT) needs a program to calculate grade point averages. Write one to carry this out. The input should consist of an arbitrary number of pairs of letter grades (A, B, C, D, F) and credit hours. In the scheme of things, the point values for the letter grades are as follows:

A   4.00

B   3.00

C   2.00

D   1.00

F   0.00

The grade-point average is computed by dividing the grade points by the total number of credits. The grade points are computed by adding up the products obtained by multiplying the numerical equivalents of each grade by the number of corresponding credit hours. For example, a student whose grades are

A   4

B   5

A   3

C   3

B   3

D   2

would get a grade point calculated as follows:

GradePoints $= (4 \times 4) + (3 \times 5) + (4 \times 3) + (2 \times 3) + (3 \times 3) + (1 \times 2)$
$\qquad\qquad = 60$
TotalCredit $= 4 + 5 + 3 + 3 + 3 + 2 = 20$
GPA $= 60 / 20 = 3.00$

Extension: Assume $+$ and $-$ are allowed in the letter grades; that is, one may get a B$+$ or a C$-$, for example. Use the following point values:

A   4.00

A$-$ 3.66

B$+$ 3.33

B   3.00

B$-$ 2.66

C$+$ 2.33

C   2.00

C$-$ 1.66

D$+$ 1.33

D   1.00

D$-$ 0.66

F   0.00

Hint: You must read in two characters for the grade, the letter grade itself and its augmend (that is, a $+$, $-$, or blank).

17. Dr. Whoa (who teaches at URAQT) gives an exam and would like to have the computer determine letter grades based on numerical results. The grading scale is as follows:

Percent	Letter Grade
100–94	A
91–82	B
81–70	C
69–50	D
49–0	F

Write a program to carry this out.

18. Write an improved calculator simulation in which you can *chain* operations, that is, you may continue to enter sequences of numbers and operators. For example, you might enter

```
5 * 6 + 4 =
```

and the calculator would present the result of 34. You will need to add the operator ' = ' to this and keep track of intermediate results.

    Warning: Do not try to implement operator precedence; just take the operators as they come. For example, the sequence

```
5 + 7 * 2 =
```

should result in a value of 24, *not* a value of 70.

19. A survey is taken to determine population percentages of various blood types, which are A, B, AB, and O. Further, the rH factor may be positive (+) or negative (−). Write a program that uses as input a series of blood types such as

A+

AB −

B+

O −

A −

and so forth and generates the following percentages:

a. Percent of each blood type, regardless of rH factor
b. Percent of each rH factor, regardless of blood type
c. Percent of each blood type and rH factor considered together

    Hint: This will require reading in several characters and checking each as it is received.

11

A Case Study:

The Complete Development of a Dice Game Simulation

*I*n the previous nine chapters, we have discussed the elements necessary to writing good programs. At the highest level, these elements are the concepts of top-down design (the general-to-specific approach to solution generation) and modularity, both logical (via program presentation) and physical (by way of programmer-defined functions and procedures). At the next level, we have examined the fundamental programming tools available to generate a computer solution to a problem, namely the control structures of sequence, iteration, and decision. Finally, we have studied the specific language elements of Pascal that enable us to implement our solutions on a computer.

In covering a complex subject such as computer programming, however, it is necessary to break the subject down into smaller units and focus on only one thing at a time. This is exactly what we did in the last nine chapters. (In fact, the presentation of these chapters is an example of top-down design and modularity.) In these chapters we focused on the subject and relegated everything else more or less to the background. For example, when we explored selection, we purposely avoided any extensive discussion of iteration or subprograms. When dealing with a completely general problem, however, we cannot assume that our focus will be so limited. There are many more possible courses of action that can be used to solve a complex problem, and it thus becomes correspondingly more difficult to find a proper solution.

Although there is a certain amount of art involved in finding proper solutions to complex problems, this art nonetheless is something that can be developed with experience. To this end it is helpful to observe how actual problems are solved. The purpose of this chapter is to present in entirety the solution to a significantly complex problem. All phases of the program development process, including error recovery and testing, will be explicitly described as they are carried out for this problem. This will involve a lot of detail, but remember that the goal in this chapter is to study the *process as a whole* and not the individual aspects that make up the process.

Owing to the nature of the problem being solved in this chapter, some additional information concerning procedures and functions will be presented. However, this material fits in naturally and complements the goal of the chapter.

Craps

We begin by taking a preliminary look at the problem we wish to solve. We wish to write a program that allows a person to play a game of dice (commonly known as craps) interactively with the computer. There are many variations on how the game is played, but a common thread runs through them all. We will implement here a somewhat simplified version of craps in order to keep the problem within manageable limits. We are about to write a program that is only an *approximation* of the game of craps. However (and this is true with regard to any computer programming project), the program can be made to represent reality as closely as you want, provided only that you are willing to expend sufficient time and energy to do so.

Let us now begin the formal program development process.

STEP 1: UNDERSTAND THE PROBLEM

An exposition of the rules is a good place to start. The game of craps, as you might know, makes use of two dice. Each die (the singular of *dice*) is a cube with six faces. Each of these faces has from one to six dots engraved on it and represents a number from one to six. Further, the dots (numbers) are arranged on the cube in such a way that the sum of the dots appearing on opposite faces is equal to seven (see Figure 11-1).

Craps is played as follows: a person makes a bet (usually within specified limits) and then throws the dice. After they come to rest, the dots on the two uppermost faces of the dice are added together. Depending on what the sum is, one of three different actions is taken:

If the sum is 7 or 11, the player wins.
If the sum is 2 or 12, the player loses.

Figure 11-1

Typical Dice Used in Playing Craps. (a) The Sum of These Dice Would Be Five; (b) Exploded View of a Single Die.

If the sum is anything else, it is termed a *point*, and the player continues to roll the dice until one of the following happens:

1. The player makes the point (that is, rolls the same sum again) and wins.
2. The player rolls 2, 7, or 12 and loses.

If the player wins, he or she gets back double the bet. If the player loses, the bet is lost. Play continues until the player either runs out of money or voluntarily quits.

It may appear that there is not much more to understand, but before we can begin designing algorithms, we must decide exactly what we want to implement. For example, what are the limits on the bets? What are the termination conditions? For that matter, what are the inputs and outputs? These questions require some thought.

Let's start with an easy question. What limits, if any, do we want to impose on the bets? We can choose anything we like, as long as it doesn't conflict with the original problem statement. Let us, therefore, choose a lower limit of $1 and an upper limit of $10, for no other reason than these are nice round numbers.

Let's look next at termination conditions. When should we stop? Well, we should certainly stop when the player decides to. Also, we should stop if the player loses everything or wins too much.

We then ask ourselves: how can we tell if the player has lost all of his or her money or won too much? One way to do this is to start the player off with a certain amount of money and keep a running tally as the player wins and loses. If the money goes negative or zero, then the player has lost it all and will have to quit. If the player doubles the initial amount of money, then we'll consider this winning too much and likewise the player will have to quit. What should the initial amount be? Again, this decision is totally arbitrary. Let us, therefore, choose an amount of $100, another nice round number.

Now we know the financial limits and how to stop the game. We now consider specifically what the inputs and outputs should be. This is not as straightforward as it appears, because the program will be reading and writing all the time. But we can come up with a summary of sorts as follows:

Inputs

Whether the player wants to continue

The amount of the bet, if the game does continue

Outputs

The roll(s) of the dice

The outcome, win or lose

How much money the player has

We now have a pretty good idea of how the game is to be played. We may, therefore, move on to the next phase.

STEP 2: PLAN THE SOLUTION

We begin, of course, by writing a very general algorithm for a single game, using the rules of the game as described above:

Main Algorithm I

1. Make a bet
2. Roll the dice
3. Sum ← first die + second die
4. If the Sum is 7 or 11 then
5.   You win
6. Else if the Sum is 2 or 12 then
7.   You lose
8. Else
9.   Point ← Sum
10.   Continue to do the following
11.   Roll the dice
12.   Sum ← first die + second die
13.   If Sum = point then
14.   You win
15.   Else if Sum is 2, 7 or 12 then
16.   You lose
17.   Until you win or lose
18. If You win Then
19.   Bankroll ← Bankroll + Bet
20. Else
21.   Bankroll ← Bankroll − Bet
22. State the condition of the Bankroll

There are a number of things to note about this algorithm:

1. First, it isn't much like Pascal yet, but the underlying *structure* is nonetheless very evident.

2. We have not considered how to do such things as "Make a bet" or "Roll the dice." These items are obviously candidates for procedures.

3. The structure of the Else statements in lines 10 through 17 is somehow not very satisfying. But, as an initial approximation, we have the rudiments of a loop, so that at least the structure is one that can eventually be implemented in Pascal.

4. The betting business at the end *is* correct. At first glance it appears rather strange looking because we said that a win corresponded to getting back *twice* your bet, but the bet is only added in once on line 18. However, the original bet wasn't subtracted out at first; hence the algorithm as written is equivalent to taking the bet out initially and

then putting back twice the bet. In similar fashion, the losing bet in line 20 is subtracted once instead of not at all.

The next thing we need to do is envelop the above algorithm for a single game into another loop so that it can be repeated as long as the termination conditions remain unmet. We can also include at this point the initialization conditions; that is, we can start off the bankroll. Making these amendments yields

Main Algorithm II

InitialBankroll = $100

Bankroll ← InitialBankroll
As long as the player wants to continue
  and Bankroll > 0
  and Bankroll < 2 × InitialBankroll Do
 Make a bet
 Roll the dice
 Sum ← first die + second die
 If the Sum is 7 or 11 then
  You win
 Else if the Sum is 2 or 12 then
  You lose
 Else
  Point ← Sum
  Continue to do the following
   Roll the dice
   Sum ← first die + second die
   If Sum = point then
    You win
   Else if Sum is 2, 7 or 12 then
    You lose
  Until you win or lose
 If You win then
  Bankroll ← Bankroll + Bet
 Else
  Bankroll ← Bankroll − Bet
 State the condition of the bankroll
 Ask if the player wants to continue
Make any concluding comments

The things to notice here are

1. We have a run-of-the-mill, input-controlled While structure here: the input condition (whether the player wants to continue) is determined at the very end of the loop. We will still have to figure out just how to set this up.

2. We haven't yet decided what our concluding comments are, but we can leave consideration of that until later.

We still need to work out a few details with regard to loop conditions and the dice; that is, we need to detail the variables a little better. We also need to make the procedures look a little more like procedures. Doing so yields the following:

Main Algorithm III

InitialBankroll = $100

```
Bankroll ← InitialBankroll
PlayerWantsToContinue ← True
While PlayerWantsToContinue
        and Bankroll > 0
        and Bankroll < 2 × InitialBankroll Do
    Make (Bet)
    YouWin ← False
    YouLose ← False
    Roll (Die1, Die2)
    Sum ← Die1 + Die2
    If the Sum is 7 or 11 then
       YouWin ← True
    Else if the sum is 2 or 12 then
       YouLose ← True
    Else
       Point ← Sum
       Repeat
         Roll (Die1, Die2)
         Sum ← Die1 + Die2
         If Sum = Point then
             YouWin ← True
         Else if sum is 2, 7 or 12 then
             YouLose ← True
       Until YouWin or YouLose
    If YouWin then
       Bankroll ← Bankroll + Bet
    Else
       Bankroll ← Bankroll − Bet
    Describe (Bankroll)
    AskIf (PlayerWantsToContinue)
MakeConcludingCommentsAbout (Bankroll)
```

Things to be aware of:

1. We have used a lot of Boolean variables here, but see how they improve the readability! It's almost like reading a story.

2. The procedure names, along with their associated arguments, make sense when read. Some of the names are rather lengthy, but, in this case, they provide a dramatic improvement in readability.

3. The algorithm is now in a very Pascal-like form, where all of the control structures are evident and look almost like the final form.

4. Even though most of the variables used as arguments could be global, we choose to use arguments/parameters anyway. This improves the readability of the algorithm, enhances the structure of the whole, and makes the procedures more independent.

5. We have implemented the *point* loop using a Repeat rather than a While. Although we could have made it a While loop as well, notice how much more natural it is as written.

At this point we have the complete algorithm for the main process. However, before we go any further we need to consider some things.

11-1 Top-Down Testing

We have everything for the main program, but nothing at all for the procedures. We may be tempted to continue by developing algorithms for the procedures, but this would be a mistake. The difficulty is that we will eventually end up with an extremely complex set of programs consisting of a main program and its associated subprograms, all of which must be tested simultaneously for actual functioning and the relationships between them. This approach is very error-prone and inefficient.

However, we may take a cue from the program development process itself in which we use the top-down approach to break up one large task into several smaller tasks. We can do a similar thing with our program sections, namely, work with them independently, one at a time. Doing so means that we code and test the main program section *before* going on to develop any of the procedures: this is referred to as **top-down testing**, and it has the same advantages for testing as top-down design does for algorithms.

However, we now seem to find ourselves between a rock and a hard place: we don't want to write the procedures yet, but we can't test the main program until we do! How can we get around this?

11-2 Stub Programs

What we do is write procedures that really don't do anything and include these in the program so that it can be compiled and tested. These are referred to as **dummy procedures** (or **dummy functions**), and their only purpose is to allow us to test the main program. Although they are defined in terms of appropriate parameters, they do not carry out their assigned tasks but merely provide the minimum substance necessary to allow the main program to be compiled and tested. Such a (main) program section is called a **stub program** (or simply "stub") and permits top-down testing to be implemented.

Using these concepts we can code and test the main program.

Subtask CRAPS: **Step 3—Code the Solution.** Our algorithm can be readily converted into Pascal. The result of this, including appropriate dummy procedures, is shown in Figure 11-2. Note that these procedures are very unsophisticated and that little, if any, work is expended on them. For the most part, rather than actually generating data, they merely request it from the terminal. Also, the compiler readily accepts the whole thing without protest.

Subtask CRAPS: **Step 4—Check Out the Program.** We now have the main program written in the form of a program stub. At this point, we want to test the main program and ensure that it works correctly. We will formalize this process next.

11-3   *Test Sets*

In order to test the program properly, we must decide exactly what we want to test and how to test it. A little thought reveals that the following items, at this point, are the ones we want to test:

1. Make sure the outer loop will "go" if player wants to continue.

2. Recognize a win or lose on the first roll.

3. Recognize a win or lose in the point loop.

4. Carry out the bookkeeping (amount of money in bankroll) properly.

5. Make sure termination will occur if bankroll goes out of bounds.

In order to carry out the testing, we must next generate a **test set**. The test set consists of data that we can enter as the program is running and which will either confirm proper operation of various phases of the program or generate an error that we can track down. At this point it is our (almost sacred) duty to do everything we can *to make the program fail*. It is better to have it fail now with us than later with somebody else.

It is worth emphasizing again that since we have used top-down development to generate this program, it will be much less work to test it and fewer errors will exist. Top-down development has allowed us to proceed in an orderly fashion, one step at a time, and to concentrate on each individual aspect of the solution in turn.

Now, on to testing the program. We will need one run to test each of the first four items and two runs to test the last item (one for each ter-

Figure 11-2

Stub Program CRAPS1 *That Utilizes Dummy Procedures for Testing Purposes*

CRAPS1.PAS

```
1       Program CRAPS1 (Input, Output);
2
3       (*
4           This is the initial version of program intended to play
5           craps interactively. It is a stub program (including
6           dummy procedures) written for the express purpose of
7           testing the main program for proper operation.
8       *)
9
10      Const InitialBankroll = 100.00;  (* Total amount of money a
11                                           player starts with  *)
12
13
14      Var Bankroll,                    (* Current amount of money
15                                           the player has *)
16          Bet          : Real;
17
18          Die1, Die2, Sum, Point : Integer;
19
20          PlayerWantsToContinue,
21          YouWin, YouLose       : Boolean;
22
23
24      (* DUMMY PROCEDURES *)
25
26      Procedure Make (Var Bet:Real);
27      (* Lets the player make a bet *)
28        Begin
29          Write ('Enter bet - '); Readln (Bet)
30        End;
31
32      Procedure Roll (Var D1, D2 : Integer);
33      (* Rolls the dice for the player *)
34        Begin
35          Write ('Enter roll of dice (2 numbers) - '); Readln (D1, D2)
36        End;
37
38      Procedure Describe (Money:Real);
39      (* Lets the player see how much money he's got left *)
40        Begin
41          Writeln ('Current amount in bankroll is ', Money:5:0)
42        End;
43
44      Procedure AskIf (Var KeepGoing:Boolean);
45      (* Lets the player decide whether he wants
46         to continue or to stop playing *)
47      Var Answer : Char;
48        Begin
49          Write ('Continue? Enter Y,N - '); Readln (Answer);
50          KeepGoing := Answer = 'Y'
51        End;
52
53      Procedure MakeConcludingCommentsAbout (Money:Real);
54      (* Comments that conclude the game and summarize the results *)
```

Figure 11-2 continued

```
55      Begin
56        Writeln ('Ending balance is - ', Money:5:0)
57      End;
58
59    (*END OF DUMMY PROCEDURES *)
60
61
62    BEGIN (* to play the game! *)
63
64      Bankroll := InitialBankroll;
65      PlayerWantsToContinue := True;
66      While PlayerWantsToContinue
67              and (Bankroll > 0)
68              and (Bankroll < 2.0 * InitialBankroll) Do
69        Begin (* this round of play *)
70          Make (Bet);
71          YouWin := False;   (* When the game first starts player *)
72          YouLose := False;  (* has neither won nor lost...       *)
73          Roll (Die1, Die2);
74          Sum := Die1 + Die2;
75          If (Sum = 7) or (Sum = 11) then
76              YouWin := True
77          Else if (Sum = 2) or (Sum = 12) then
78              YouLose := True
79          Else
80            Begin (* rolling for a point *)
81              Point := Sum;
82              Repeat
83                  Roll ( Die1, Die2 );
84                  Sum := Die1 + Die2;
85                  If Sum = Point then
86                      YouWin := True
87                  Else if (Sum = 2) or (Sum = 7) or (Sum = 12) then
88                      YouLose := True
89              Until YouWin or YouLose
90            End (* trying for the point *);
91          If YouWin then
92              Bankroll := Bankroll + Bet
93          Else
94              Bankroll := Bankroll - Bet;
95          Describe (Bankroll);
96          AskIf ( PlayerWantsToContinue )
97        End (* this round of play *);
98
99      MakeConcludingCommentsAbout (Bankroll)
100
101   END (* of CRAPS *).
```

mination condition of too much money or too little money). Let's write down the data we need to use:

Run 1

Test for win on first roll
   Bet: 5
   Roll: 7
Test for win on first roll
   Bet: 10
   Roll: 11
Test for loss on first roll
   Bet: 15
   Roll: 2
Test for loss on first roll
   Bet: 20
   Roll: 12
Test for loss on point
   Bet: 5
   Roll: 6
   Roll: 2
Test for loss on point
   Bet: 5
   Roll: 8
   Roll: 7
Test for loss on point
   Bet: 5
   Roll: 10
   Roll: 12
Test for win on point
   Bet: 12
   Roll: 4
   Roll: 4
Test for win on point
   Bet: 12
   Roll: 8
   Roll: 3
   Roll: 10
   Roll: 5
   Roll: 8
Quit

This set of data tests not only the win/lose conditions but also the functioning of all the loops. On the point loop, we make sure that the program can determine a win on either the first roll or any subsequent roll. On the continue loop, the program continues or terminates, depending on the player's response.

Now that we have this data, let us try it out on the program. Running the program and entering the test set data yield the output shown in Figure 11-3. We are struck by two things: first, the correct answers

Figure 11-3

Test Run of the Stub Program CRAPS1

```
$ run craps1

Enter bet - 5
Enter roll of dice (2 numbers) - 5 2
Current amount in bankroll is    105
Continue? Enter Y,N - Y
Enter bet - 10
Enter roll of dice (2 numbers) - 6 5
Current amount in bankroll is    115
Continue? Enter Y,N - Y
Enter bet - 15
Enter roll of dice (2 numbers) - 1 1
Current amount in bankroll is    100
Continue? Enter Y,N - Y
Enter bet - 20
Enter roll of dice (2 numbers) - 6 6
Current amount in bankroll is     80
Continue? Enter Y,N - Y
Enter bet - 5
Enter roll of dice (2 numbers) - 4 2
Enter roll of dice (2 numbers) - 1 1
Current amount in bankroll is     75
Continue? Enter Y,N - Y
Enter bet - 5
Enter roll of dice (2 numbers) - 4 4
Enter roll of dice (2 numbers) - 3 4
Current amount in bankroll is     70
Continue? Enter Y,N - Y
Enter bet - 5
Enter roll of dice (2 numbers) - 6 4
Enter roll of dice (2 numbers) - 6 6
Current amount in bankroll is     65
Continue? Enter Y,N - Y
Enter bet - 12
Enter roll of dice (2 numbers) - 3 1
Enter roll of dice (2 numbers) - 2 2
Current amount in bankroll is     77
Continue? Enter Y,N - Y
Enter bet - 12
Enter roll of dice (2 numbers) - 3 5
Enter roll of dice (2 numbers) - 2 1
Enter roll of dice (2 numbers) - 6 4
Enter roll of dice (2 numbers) - 2 3
Enter roll of dice (2 numbers) - 4 4
Current amount in bankroll is     89
Continue? Enter Y,N - N
Ending balance is -      89
```

are all there. Hurray! Second, there is no indication anywhere in the output that the player has ever won or lost after a round! This is an oversight in the original design (that is, we have discovered an error). Let us, therefore, correct it by altering the procedure Describe so that it tells not only the current amount in the bankroll but also whether the round was won or lost. To do this we need to include a second argument to the procedure, a Boolean variable `YouWin`, which indicates whether the round was won (if it is `True`) or lost (if it is `False`). This involves altering the call to the procedure to read

```
Describe (YouWin, Bankroll);
```

Making these changes gives the corrected program shown in Figure 11-4. A test run of this corrected version is displayed in Figure 11-5, and the results indicate that the alteration does what we want.

We are now ready to proceed with the remainder of the testing for the main program, namely, to make sure that termination will occur if the player's account drops to zero or below or if it doubles. To test this we need to lower (or raise) the balance in order to force the limits to be exceeded. Two test sets will be required, as follows:

Run 2

Test for termination on losing all money

Bet: 105

Roll: 6 6

Run 3

Test for termination on winning too much

Bet: 105

Roll: 5 2

Note that the bets are out of range, but what we're doing is testing the *termination* of the program, and the easiest way to do this is to set up appropriate conditions immediately. The runs incorporating this test data are shown in Figure 11-6. Although the program does in fact terminate correctly both times, it still asks whether the player wants to continue before it forces him or her to quit. How inelegant! (This is another problem that needs to be fixed.) There are, as we well know, several ways to get around this. Probably the most straightforward is just to put a condition on whether or not the player is asked to quit, for example, by adding

```
If (Bankroll > 0) and (Bankroll < 2.0 * InitialBankroll)
  then AskIf ( PlayerWantsToContinue );
```

This, however, is not very satisfying, because we find ourselves testing two of the same three conditions that will be tested in the very next step when the program loops back to the While conditional. We can clean this up by changing the While statement to read

```
While PlayerWantsToContinue Do
```

Figure 11-4

Corrected Stub Program CRAPS2

CRAPS2.PAS

```
 1    Program CRAPS2 (Input, Output);
 2
 3    (*
 4        This is the second version of the CRAPS program, which
 5        corrects a deficiency found in the first version. In this one
 6        an indication of whether a roll was won or lost has been
 7        added to the procedure Describe.
 8    *)
 9
10    Const InitialBankroll = 100.00;  (* Total amount of money a
11                                         player starts with    *)
12
13
14    Var Bankroll,                    (* Current amount of money
15                                         the player has *)
16        Bet            : Real;
17
18        Die1, Die2, Sum, Point : Integer;
19
20        PlayerWantsToContinue,
21        YouWin, YouLose        : Boolean;
22
23
24    (* DUMMY PROCEDURES *)
25
26    Procedure Make (Var Bet:Real);
27    (* Lets the player make a bet *)
28      Begin
29        Write ('Enter bet - '); Readln (Bet)
30      End;
31
32    Procedure Roll (Var D1, D2 : Integer);
33    (* Rolls the dice for the player *)
34      Begin
35        Write ('Enter roll of dice (2 numbers) - '); Readln (D1,D2)
36      End;
37
38    Procedure Describe (Won:Boolean; Money:Real);
39    (* Tells the player whether he won or lost the roll,
40      and how much money he's got left *)
41      Begin
42        If Won then
43            Writeln ('You won.')
44        Else
45            Writeln ('You lost.');
46        Writeln ('Current amount in bankroll is ', Money:5:0)
47      End;
48
49    Procedure AskIf (Var KeepGoing:Boolean);
50    (* Lets the player decide whether he wants
51      to continue or to stop playing *)
52    Var Answer:Char;
53      Begin
54        Write ('Continue? Enter Y,N - '); Readln (Answer);
55        KeepGoing := Answer = 'Y'
56      End;
```

Figure 11-4 continued

```
57
58    Procedure MakeConcludingCommentsAbout (Money:Real);
59    (* Comments that conclude the game and summarize the results *)
60      Begin
61        Writeln ('Ending balance is - ', Money:5:0)
62      End;
63
64    (* END OF DUMMY PROCEDURES *)
65
66
67    BEGIN (* to play the game! *)
68
69      Bankroll := InitialBankroll;
70      PlayerWantsToContinue := True;
71      While PlayerWantsToContinue
72              and (Bankroll > 0)
73              and (Bankroll < 2.0 * InitialBankroll) Do
74        Begin (* this round of play *)
75          Make (Bet);
76          YouWin := False;    (* When the game first starts player *)
77          YouLose := False;   (* has neither won nor lost...        *)
78          Roll (Die1, Die2);
79          Sum := Die1 + Die2;
80          If (Sum = 7) or (Sum =11) then
81             YouWin := True
82          Else if (Sum = 2) or (Sum or = 12) then
83             YouLose := True
84          Else
85            Begin (* rolling for a point *)
86              Point := Sum;
87              Repeat
88                Roll (Die1, Die2);
89                Sum := Die1 + Die2;
90                If Sum = Point then
91                   YouWin := True
92                Else if (Sum = 2) or (Sum = 7) or (Sum =12) then
93                   YouLose := True
94              Until YouWin or YouLose
95            End (* trying for the point *);
96          If YouWin then
97             Bankroll := Bankroll + Bet
98          Else
99             Bankroll := Bankroll - Bet;
100         Describe (YouWin, Bankroll);
101         AskIf (PlayerWantsToContinue)
102       End (* this round of play *);
103
104     MakeConcludingCommentsAbout (Bankroll)
105
106   END (* of CRAPS *).
```

Figure 11-5

Test Run of the Corrected Stub Program CRAPS2

```
$ run craps2

Enter bet - 5
Enter roll of dice (2 numbers) - 3 4
You won.
Current amount in bankroll is 105
Continue? Enter Y,N - Y
Enter bet - 10
Enter roll of dice (2 numbers) - 2 1
Enter roll of dice (2 numbers) - 1 1
You lost.
Current amount in bankroll is  95
Continue? Enter Y,N - Y
Enter bet - ?5
Enter roll of dice (2 numbers) - 3 5
Enter roll of dice (2 numbers) - 1 5
Enter roll of dice (2 numbers) - 2 2
Enter roll of dice (2 numbers) - 5 6
Enter roll of dice (2 numbers) - 5 2
You lost.
Current amount in bankroll is  70
Continue? Enter Y,N - N
Ending balance is -  70
```

Figure 11-6

Remaining Two Test Runs of the Stub Program CRAPS2, *Which
Check for Proper Termination*

```
$ run craps2

Enter bet - 105
Enter roll of dice (2 numbers) - 6 6
You lost.
Current amount in bankroll is     -5
Continue? Enter Y,N - Y
Ending balance is -    -5

$ run craps2

Enter bet - 105
Enter roll of dice (2 numbers) - 5 2
You won.
Current amount in bankroll is 205
Continue? Enter Y,N - Y
Ending balance is -   205
```

We can then force the variable PlayerWantsToContinue to False if the players limits are exceeded:

```
If (Bankroll > 0) and (Bankroll < 2.0 * InitialBankroll)
  then AskIf (PlayerWantsToContinue)
Else (* Player has exceeded the limits, make Player stop *)
  PlayerWantsToContinue := False
```

These changes are incorporated into the program shown in Figure 11-7. The results of the sample run shown in Figure 11-8 now indicate that the program does in fact do exactly what we want it to do. The testing phase for the main program, therefore, is complete.

Recognize the fact that although the original version was close to being correct, there were a few (relatively minor) changes that had to be made. The process involves a certain amount of trial and error, but it is nonetheless directed by an overall scheme.

Subtask CRAPS: Step 5—Document. The documentation for the main CRAPS stub is also complete at this point.

We have already done a fair amount of work and we haven't yet dealt with the procedures at all. The main program is written, debugged, and documented, and we need not concern ourselves with it further, unless testing in conjunction with the procedures shows further errors in the main program. We are therefore ready to direct all our attention to the procedures.

Let's now go through the associated procedures one at a time in the order they appear, using the program development process.

Subtask Make: Step 1—Understand the Problem. The first procedure we come to is the one named Make. It is here that we allow the person to make a bet. Recall that the bet must be between $1 and $10. Further, let's stipulate that the bet must be a round number of dollars (that is, no cents). We must take into account the possibility that the bet will not be entered correctly, and we must continue to ask until it is. This, of course, suggests a loop. Let's see what we can do with this.

Subtask Make: Step 2—Plan the Solution. How can we implement the above requirements? We'll need to read the bet and check it for consistency. Since we want to continue requesting the bet until it's correct, a loop whose termination condition is a *correct* bet suggests itself; something on the order of the following is a good place to start:

```
Repeat
  Read (Bet)
  If Bet < 1 then
    Write 'The bet is too small'
```

Figure 11-7

Third Version of the Stub Program CRAPS3, *Which Does Terminate Properly*

CRAPS3.PAS

```
1     Program CRAPS3 (Input, Output);
2
3     (*
4         This is the third version of the CRAPS stub program, which corrects
5         yet another problem found in the second version. This program
6         now terminates as soon as the player exceeds either money limit
7         rather than waiting until asked.
8     *)
9
10    Const InitialBankroll = 100.00;  (* Total amount of money a
11                                          player starts with     *)
12
13
14    Var Bankroll,                    (* Current amount of money
15                                          the player has *)
16        Bet            : Real;
17
18        Die1, Die2, Sum, Point : Integer;
19
20        PlayerWantsToContinue,
21        YouWin, YouLose        : Boolean;
22
23
24    (* DUMMY PROCEDURES *)
25
26    Procedure Make (Var Bet:Real);
27    (* Lets the player make a bet *)
28      Begin
29        Write ('Enter bet - '); Readln (Bet)
30      End;
31
32    Procedure Roll (Var D1, D2 : Integer);
33    (* Rolls the dice for the player *)
34      Begin
35        Write ('Enter roll of dice (2 numbers) - '); Readln (D1,D2)
36      End;
37
38    Procedure Describe (Won:Boolean; Money:Real);
39    (* Tells the player whether he won or lost the roll,
40       and how much money he's got left *)
41      Begin
42        If Won then
43            Writeln ('You won.')
44        Else
45            Writeln ('You lost.');
46        Writeln ('Current amount in bankroll is ', Money:5:0)
47      End;
48
49    Procedure AskIf (Var KeepGoing:Boolean);
50    (* Lets the player decide whether he wants
51       to continue or to stop playing *)
52    Var Answer:Char;
```

Figure 11-7 continued

```
53      Begin
54        Write ('Continue? Enter Y,N - '); Readln (Answer);
55        KeepGoing := Answer = 'Y'
56      End;
57
58   Procedure MakeConcludingCommentsAbout (Money:Real);
59   (* Comments that conclude the game and summarize the results *)
60      Begin
61        Writeln ('Ending balance is - ', Money:5:0)
62      End;
63
64   (* END OF DUMMY PROCEDURES *)
65
66
67   BEGIN (* to play the game! *)
68
69      Bankroll := InitialBankroll;
70      PlayerWantsToContinue := True;
71      While PlayerWantsToContinue Do
72         Begin (* this round of play *)
73            Make (Bet);
74            YouWin := False;   (* When the game first starts player *)
75            YouLose := False;  (* has neither won nor lost...        *)
76            Roll (Die1, Die2);
77            Sum := Die1 + Die2;
78            If (Sum = 7) or (Sum = 11) then
79               YouWin := True
80            Else if (Sum = 2) or (Sum = 12) then
81               YouLose := True
82            Else
83               Begin (* rolling for a point *)
84                 Point := Sum;
85                 Repeat
86                    Roll (Die1, Die2);
87                    Sum := Die1 + Die2;
88                    If Sum = Point then
89                       YouWin := True
90                    Else if (Sum = 2) or (Sum = 7) or (Sum = 12) then
91                       YouLose := True
92                 Until YouWin or YouLose
93               End (* trying for the point *);
94            If YouWin then
95               Bankroll := Bankroll + Bet
96            Else
97               Bankroll := (Bankroll - Bet;
98            Describe (YouWin, Bankroll);
99            If (Bankroll > 0) and (Bankroll < 2.0 * InitialBankroll) then
100              AskIf (PlayerWantsToContinue)
101           Else
102              PlayerWantsToContinue := False
103
104        End (* this round of play *);
105
106     MakeConcludingCommentsAbout (Bankroll)
107
108   END (* of CRAPS *).
```

Figure 11-8

Two Test Runs of the Newest Version of the Stub, CRAPS3, Which Terminate Properly

```
$ run craps3

Enter bet - 55
Enter roll of dice (2 numbers) - 3 7
Enter roll of dice (2 numbers) - 5 5
You won.
Current amount in bankroll is    155
Continue? Enter Y,N - Y
Enter bet - 55
Enter roll of dice (2 numbers) - 3 4
You won.
Current amount in bankroll is    210
Ending balance is -    210

$ run craps3

Enter bet - 55
Enter roll of dice (2 numbers) - 6 6
You lost.
Current amount in bankroll is     45
Continue? Enter Y,N - Y
Enter bet - 55
Enter roll of dice (2 numbers) - 3 2
Enter roll of dice (2 numbers) - 1 1
You lost.
Current amount in bankroll is    -10
Ending balance is -     -10
```

> Else if Bet > 10 then
>   Write 'The bet is too large'
> Else if Bet is not even dollars then
>   Write 'No pennies, please'
> Else
>   Bet is Right
> Until the Bet is Right

In order to do it this way, we must figure out how to determine whether or not the bet is an integral number of dollars. The easiest way is to use the standard Pascal function Trunc. If the truncated bet is the same as the bet, then the bet is in dollars only. Making this change gives us

> Repeat
>   Read (Bet)
>   If Bet < 1 then
>   Write 'The bet is too small'
>   Else if Bet > 10 then
>   Write 'The bet is too large'

```
      Else if Bet <> Trunc (Bet) then
          Write 'No pennies, please'
      Else
          Bet is Right
Until the Bet is Right
```

This is sufficiently detailed to permit us to move on to the next step.

Subtask Make: **Step 3—Code the Solution.** The Pascal implementation of the loop can be taken care of easily by way of a Boolean variable. Remembering that the procedure takes a single parameter (which must be returned to the main program), we can convert the above algorithm to Pascal directly. This is shown in Figure 11-9. Note that quality prompts and messages have been added.

Subtask Make: **Step 4—Check Out the Program.** We are now ready to test this procedure. We could make it a part of the main program to test it, but that would introduce other variables (in the experimental sense). It would be better if we could test it independently, ensure that it is correct, and *then* include it in the main program. The ability to do this is one of the advantages of modularity, so let us explore just how we might proceed.

Figure 11-9

Pascal-Coded Version of the Procedure Make (Bet)

```
Procedure Make (Var TheBet:Real);
(*
    This procedure permits the player to make a bet. Rules are:
          Minimum bet is $ 1.00
          Maximum bet is $10.00
          Bet must be an even number of dollars
*)
Var TheBetIsRight : Boolean;
Begin
  TheBetIsRight := False;
  Repeat
      Write ('How much would you like to bet? '); Readln (TheBet);
      If TheBet < 1.00 then
          Writeln ('Your bet is too small. Minimum bet is $1.00')
      Else if TheBet > 10.00 then
          Writeln ('Your bet is too big. Maximum bet is $10.00')
      Else if TheBet <> Trunc (TheBet) then
          Writeln ('No pennies, please. Bets must be in dollars only.')
      Else (* He finally got it right! *)
          TheBetIsRight := True
  Until TheBetIsRight
End (* of the procedure MAKE *);
```

11-4 *Drivers*

Our current situation is similar to the one in which we found ourselves when we wanted to test the main program but did not yet have the procedures. In that case we used simple-minded procedures in the main program so we could test it. In the current case, we're dealing with the *actual* procedures, and so we merely generate a simple-minded *main* program that does nothing but call the procedure! Such a temporary main program is termed a **driver program**. We can place the procedure that we wish to test (in this case Make) into such a driver program. Doing so yields the program shown in Figure 11-10. Note that the driver essentially consists of a loop, which calls Make as many times as the programmer wants.

Now that we have a complete driver and procedure, we need to come up with a test set. In this case it's quite simple. We need to test for values that are too large, too small, and fractional. Three different tests are required, and the results of trying them all out are shown in Figure 11-11. The procedure appears to be doing what we want.

Subtask Make: **Step 5—Document.** The program is documented well enough. We don't want to expend too much time and effort on it, since the driver is essentially just a throw-away program.

We have now introduced all of the techniques necessary to carry out a top-down design and top-down test of a complex program. At this point we have only to do exactly the same thing with the remaining procedures and then put all of the subprograms together into a unified whole. When this is done, we will need to test the total package as a coherent program, looking primarily at the relationships between the sections rather than at the functioning of the individual processes. Let's finish this up.

Subtask Roll: **Step 1—Understand the Problem.** The next procedure that we come to is Roll. Its purpose is to generate integer values ranging from 1 to 6 for each of two dice in a way that approximates what would happen if real dice were rolled. Let's see what can be done with it.

Subtask Roll: **Step 2—Plan the Solution.** This is obviously not going to be a trivial pursuit, but let us continue the top-down development and see where it leads us. We need to do the same thing with both dice, so let's express that directly. We may generate an algorithm easily enough:

```
Procedure ROLL (Die1, Die2)
    Toss (Die1)
    Toss (Die2)
```

Figure 11-10

Procedure Make (Bet) *Inserted in a Driver Program for Test*
Purposes

```
DRIVER.PAS

1    Program DRIVER (Input, Output);
2
3    (* This is a driver program to test the procedure MAKE. It
4       simply loops around calling the procedure so that we can
5       be sure it accepts correct bets and refuses incorrect bets. *)
6
7    Var Bet : Real;
8        AnotherTest : Char;
9
10   Procedure Make (Var TheBet:Real);
11   (*
12      This procedure permits the player to make a bet. Rules are:
13           Minimum bet is $ 1.00
14           Maximum bet is $10.00
15           Bet must be an even number of dollars
16   *)
17   Var TheBetIsRight : Boolean;
18   Begin
19     TheBetIsRight := False;
20     Repeat
21        Write ('How much would you like to bet? '); Readln (TheBet);
22        If TheBet < 1.00 then
23           Writeln ('Your bet is too small. Minimum bet is $1.00')
24        Else if TheBet > 10.00 then
25           Writeln ('Your bet is too big. Maximum bet is $10.00')
26        Else if TheBet <> Trunc (TheBet) then
27           Writeln ('No pennies, please. Bets must be in dollars only.')
28        Else (* He finally got it right! *)
29           TheBetIsRight := True
30     Until TheBetIsRight
31   End (* of the procedure MAKE *);
32
33
34
35   BEGIN (* Driver *)
36     AnotherTest := 'Y';
37     While AnotherTest = 'Y' Do
38       Begin
39         Make (Bet);
40         Writeln;
41         Writeln ('*** A correct bet of ', Bet:4:2,' was entered.' );
42         Writeln;
43         Write ('Another test? '); Readln (AnotherTest)
44       End
45   END.
```

Figure 11-11

Test Run of Make (Bet) *Using a Driver*

```
$ run driver

How much would you like to bet? 375.00
Your bet is too big. Maximum bet is $10.00
How much would you like to bet? 25.00
Your bet is too big. Maximum bet is $10.00
How much would you like to bet? 10.01
Your bet is too big. Maximum bet is $10.00
How much would you like to bet? 10.00

*** A correct bet of 10.00 was entered.

Another test? Y
How much would you like to bet? 0.25
Your bet is too small. Minimum bet is $1.00
How much would you like to bet? 0.99
Your bet is too small. Minimum bet is $1.00
How much would you like to bet? 1.00

*** A correct bet of 1.00 was entered.

Another test? Y
How much would you like to bet? 5.75
No pennies, please. Bets must be in dollars only.
How much would you like to bet? 5.00

*** A correct bet of 5.00 was entered.

Another test? N
```

Here, "tossing" a die means generating a number from 1 to 6 for it. Note that we really haven't gotten very far, but we have reduced the overall task by half, that is, we need now only uncover something to generate a number for a single die.

Subtask Roll: **Step 3—Code the Solution.** We can write down the Pascal-coded procedure immediately:

```
Procedure ROLL (Var FirstDie, SecondDie : Integer);
  Begin
    Toss (FirstDie);
    Toss (SecondDie)
  End;
```

We have now replaced (and reduced) the problem of generating the procedure Roll with the problem of generating the procedure Toss. But a question arises: what do we do with Toss after we get it? Is it another procedure that we will have to include in the definition section of the main program, CRAPS?

We could do that, but if we did, some of the elegance and structure we have been seeking would be lost. Since we are now happy with the main program, we certainly don't want to mess with it in order to solve a subtask. Not only that, but the CRAPS program as we've written it has no need to be aware of Toss directly; it only must be aware of Roll.

The answer to our apparent dilemma lies in the fact that Pascal allows procedure and function definitions to be included not only within the definition section of a main program *but also within the definition section of other procedures and functions*. What this means is that if Procedure A needs Procedure B in order to carry out its assigned task, it is perfectly legitimate to include Procedure B as a definition within Procedure A! In this regard, procedure and function definitions are completely analogous to main programs. This is called *nesting* and is similar to the nesting discussed with regard to control structures. The nesting of procedures and functions can be carried out to any extent (or depth, actually). As is the case with control structures, nesting shouldn't be overdone, because it then becomes cumbersome and confusing.

Let us now consider how we shall write the procedure Toss.

Sub-Subtask Toss: *Step 1—Understand the Problem.* Here we begin to get to the meat of the dice problem. When we take a real die and roll it, we get a number between 1 and 6 *in a random fashion*, which means that there is no way to predict in advance what number will show up on any given roll of the dice. If we want Toss to simulate the actual rolling of a die, then somehow we are going to have to simulate a random process. Let's next explore how to do that.

Sub-Subtask Toss: *Step 2—Plan the Solution.* Random processes can be simulated, of course, but the method requires that we be able to generate random numbers (that is, numbers that have no apparent relationship to one another). A little research shows that there are methods for doing this. However, the available techniques for doing so are usually designed to produce random numbers that are in the range of 0 to 1 (for example, 0.256, 0.999, 0.004). Assuming that (eventually) we'll be able to generate such numbers, how can we convert real numbers between 0 and 1 to integers between 1 and 6?

The first thing that comes to mind is that we might try multiplying the original real (as opposed to integer) random number by 6; this would, however, generate real (as opposed to integer) random numbers between 0 and 6. Furthermore, the *only* way we would ever get a six is if the random number itself were exactly 1.0, a very rare occurrence. We could take care of the real/integer problem by using the Trunc function, which would generate integer numbers between 0 and 6, with 6 being a once-in-a-blue-moon occurrence. The formula could be expressed simply as

DieNumber ← Trunc (6.0 × RandomNumber)

A few examples will convince us that this works:

RandomNumber	DieNumber
0.2533	1
0.0000	0
0.9733	5
0.6031	3
0.9999	5
1.0000	6

This method generates zeros every now and again. However, we can eliminate this problem by adding 1 to the result. This way we eliminate the possibility of 0, and a nice range of numbers between 1 and 6 will be generated. We still have a slight problem, however, in that we will occasionally (albeit very rarely) generate a 7. The solution to this problem is to test for a 7 result, and if we have a 7, change it to a 6. Again, this occurrence will be extremely rare and will not affect the results (some methods of generating random numbers can be written so that the actual value of 1 never turns up, thus eliminating the possibility of a 7 ever occurring).

Taking all this into account, we may write out the algorithm for the procedure Toss as

Procedure TOSS (DieNumber)
   DieNumber ← Trunc (6.0 × RandomNumber) + 1
  If DieNumber > 6 then
    DieNumber ← 6

Sub-Subtask Toss: *Step 3—Code the Solution.* We can now write out the Pascal for this procedure:

```
Procedure TOSS (Var DieNumber : Integer);
  Begin
    DieNumber := Trunc (6.0 * RandomNumber) + 1;
    If DieNumber > 6 then
      DieNumber := 6
  End;
```

We now have a way of generating random numbers between 1 and 6 that simulates what happens when dice are actually tossed. The only thing we have left to do now is to figure out how to generate random numbers between 0.00 and 1.00. Note that, with the procedure Toss, we are in the same situation as we originally were with Roll; namely, we are referencing another subprogram (this time RandomNumber) that needs to be solved before Toss is functional.

However, before we get involved with that, we need to make sure that Toss works properly. Let's test it in conjunction with Roll. In order to do this, we need two things: a dummy for RandomNumber and a driver for Roll. Putting these all together with our coded procedures of Roll and Toss gives us the program listed in Figure 11-12. Note that Toss is nested inside Roll just as Roll will be nested inside CRAPS and that RandomNumber (the dummy function that we have so far) is nested inside Toss. All of this, of course, is nested inside the driver program.

Figure 11-12

Procedures Roll *and* Toss *Inside a Driver Program for Test Purposes, Along with a Test Run*

```
DRIVER.PAS

    1    Program DRIVER (Input, Output);
    2
    3    (* This is a driver program to test Roll and Toss *)
    4
    5    Var Die1, Die2 : Integer;
    6        K : Integer;
    7
    8
    9    Procedure Roll (Var FirstDie, SecondDie : Integer);
   10    (*
   11        This procedure simulates the rolling of two dice.
   12    *)
   13
   14
   15        Procedure Toss (Var DieNumber : Integer);
   16        (*
   17            This procedure simulates the rolling of a single die.
   18            It generates random integers between 1 and 6 based on
   19            pseudo-random real numbers between 0.00 and 1.00.
   20        *)
   21
   22            Function RANDOMNUMBER : Real;
   23            (* DUMMY DUMMY DUMMY
   24                that provides real numbers between 0.00 and 1.00 *)
   25            Var RN : Real;
   26            Begin
   27                Write ('RN : '); Readln(RN);
   28                RANDOMNUMBER := RN
   29            End;
   30
   31        Begin (* TOSS *)
   32            DieNumber := Trunc (6.0 * RandomNumber) + 1;
   33            If DieNumber > 6 then
   34                DieNumber := 6
   35        End (* TOSS *);
   36
   37
```

Figure 11-12 continued

```
38    Begin (* ROLL *)
39       Toss (FirstDie);
40       Toss (SecondDie)
41    End (* ROLL *);
42
43
44    BEGIN (* Driver Program *)
45      For K:=1 to 5 Do
46           Begin
47              Roll (Die1, Die2);
48              Writeln ('The dice values are ', Die1:1,' and ', Die2:1)
49           End
50    END.


$ run driver

RN : 0.0
RN : 0.1
The dice values are 1 and 1
RN : 0.2
RN : 0.3
The dice values are 2 and 2
RN : 0.4
RN : 0.5
The dice values are 3 and 4
RN : 0.6
RN : 0.7
The dice values are 4 and 5
RN : 0.8
RN : 1.0
The dice values are 5 and 6
```

Subtask Roll: **Step 4—Check Out the Program.** The test set for this data would include samples of all possible numbers that could be generated by RandomNumber, including the end points of 0 and 1. A sample run is shown along with the listing in Figure 11-12. Note that both Roll and Toss work correctly (assuming that RandomNumber works correctly).

Subtask Roll: **Step 5—Document.** Both Roll and Toss are easy to read and understand.

We are now ready to generate the function that actually computes the random numbers, RandomNumber. Since this is nested inside Toss (which is nested inside roll) it becomes a sub-sub-subtask. Let's work on it next.

Sub-Sub-Subtask RandomNumber: *Step 1—Understand the Problem.* There are in fact many ways that a computer can be programmed to generate random numbers, but the results of all methods have two important properties in common:

1. The numbers are not really random.

2. They are all based upon an algorithm that generates a new random number from an old, existing random number.

The numbers are not really random because a computer must use an algorithm to generate them. Hence, they are in fact not random but deterministic. If you know one random number and the algorithm used to generate random numbers, you can predict what every other random number will be. This is not the case with tossing real dice, where it is impossible to predict the next roll based on the results of the present roll. The computer numbers generated are random in the sense that they follow a typical distribution and they "look" random. This latter characteristic is important because, for example, the sequence 1 2 3 4 5 6 1 2 3 4 5 6 1 2 3 4 5 6 is statistically random with respect to distribution (there are as many of one number as any other), but it doesn't "look" random. Also, random numbers generated by a computer will sooner or later begin to repeat themselves—the epitome of nonrandomness. Consequently, random numbers generated by computer are referred to as **pseudo-random numbers.**

The second characteristic listed above has import for how we can write the algorithm. If each random number is based on a previous random number, where does the first number come from? Further, the second property implies that the computer must remember each random number in order to generate the subsequent random number. This complicates our function, since a function and its associated variables don't even *exist* between calls. However, let's see what can be done.

Sub-Sub-Subtask `RandomNumber`*: Step 2—Plan the Solution.* At this point we will merely present an algorithm that generates random numbers. As mentioned earlier, there are several methods for doing this, and we will simply choose one for use in this problem. Please be aware that the algorithm we are about to present is *not* the sort of thing you would be expected to come up with on your own. Generating this particular algorithm is really just a matter of researching the particulars on how it works and adapting it to the specific constraints of the problem at hand.

For our project, we will use a trigonometric method based on the sine function. In this case, the following simple formula can be used:

$$\text{New} = \text{Old} + A \times \sin(\text{Old})$$

In other words, if we have an existing random number (in this case, Old) we can compute a new random number (New) based on (that is, as a function of) the old number. Using a more common terminology, the above formula can be expressed as

Seed = Seed + A × Sin (Seed)

where Seed represents the random number. Once an initial value for Seed is chosen, a complete series of random numbers can be generated by repeatedly using the formula.

In order to make this trigonometric method work, a judicious choice of the values for A and the initial Seed must be made. Since we are dealing with a trigonometric function Sin here, Seed should be initialized somewhere between 0 and 2π. A is then chosen to ensure that the value of the function will never exceed 2π. When this is done, the function will always generate future values for the seed that are also between 0 and 2π, so the function remains consistent. A value that works well for A is 4.4, and the initial seed can be set at about 4.

Of course, we want the random numbers that we generate to be between 0 and 1, *not* between 0 and 2π. However, this is easy to fix: we need merely to divide Seed by 2π, and we've got it.

The next question is: how do we write a procedure to generate random numbers? At first this seems rather easy; we can write an algorithm as follows:

If this is the first time through then
   Seed ← 4.0

Seed ← Seed + 4.4 × Sin (Seed)

$$\text{Random Number} \leftarrow \frac{\text{Seed}}{2\pi}$$

The last line is used to convert Seed from a number between 0 and 2π to a number between 0 and 1. There are, however, two problems with this. First, how can we tell whether or not this is the first time through the function? Second, and even worse (as we mentioned previously), if Seed belongs to the function, it will cease to exist after we leave the function. Therefore, the function cannot "remember" the values of Seed that are produced.

The solution to this dilemma requires that we do something embarrassing: we have to make Seed a global variable! We said in Chapter 6 that changing global variables in a procedure or function constitutes a side effect and is something to be avoided. However, in some cases we have no choice, and this is such a case.

Having accepted the necessity of using a global variable, we generate an algorithm for the function, namely,

Seed ← Seed + 4.4 × Sin (Seed)

$$\text{Random Number} \leftarrow \frac{\text{Seed}}{2\pi}$$

We need no longer worry about where Seed comes from, at least not in the function.

Sub-Sub-Subtask RandomNumber: *Step 3—Code the Solution.* **From this** description, we may now write the complete function as

```
Function RandomNumber : Real;
  Const TwoPi = 6.2831852 (* 2 Pi *)
  Begin
    Seed := Seed + 4.4 * Sin (Seed);
    RandomNumber := Seed / TwoPi
  End;
```

Note that there are no parameters for the function.

Sub-Sub-Subtask RandomNumber: *Step 4—Check Out the Program.* **Next,** of course, we would like to test the function. In order to do this, we will enclose it within a driver program. In this case, however, not only will the driver have to call the procedure, but it will also have to define Seed as a global variable and initialize it. Doing all this gives us the program shown in Figure 11-13. Also shown in this figure are the results of a test run that displays a list of generated random numbers. We note, with some satisfaction, that the function apparently works. We have generated numbers that are, in fact, between 0 and 1, and there is no apparent relationship among them (that is, they do not seem to be in any kind of order).

Sub-Sub-Subtask RandomNumber: *Step 5—Document.* **As always, this is** taken care of as a matter of course.

The next step in the testing process is to ensure that Roll, Toss, and RandomNumber all work together when they are nested properly. Figure 11-14 shows this completely nested set of subprograms within an appropriate driver program. Figure 11-15 shows the output from a test run. We again see (not without some satisfaction) that it all works fine.

There is, however, one fly in the ointment: Seed is initialized in the main program with a constant. This means, unfortunately, that every time the program is run, it will produce the same set of random numbers. The implication for CRAPS is that it will play the same game each and every time it is run! Can we do anything about this?

Well, we can, but the solution is not trivial: we need to randomize the initial Seed. Essentially, then, we want to be able to randomly choose an initial value for Seed; however, we cannot get a random value until we have chosen a seed! (Caught again between a rock and a hard place!) The solution is to in some way get a value for Seed that does not

Figure 11-13

*Random Number Generator Function in a Test Driver, Including a
Sample Run*

DRIVER.PAS

```
1     Program DRIVER (Input, Output);
2
3     Var k : Integer;
4         Seed : Real;  (* Global variable for use in the *)
5                       (* Random Number Generator        *)
6
7
8         Function RandomNumber : Real;
9         (* This function generates random numbers between 0 and 1
10            using a trigonometric formula. Seed is a global
11            variable and must be initialized by the main program
12            to a value between 0 and 2 Pi. This function requires
13            no parameters in the definition. *)
14
15         Const TwoPi = 6.2831852; (* 2 Pi *)
16
17         Begin (* RANDOM NUMBER *)
18           Seed := Seed + 4.4 * Sin (Seed);
19           RandomNumber := Seed / TwoPi
20         End (* RANDOM NUMBER *);
21
22    BEGIN (* Driver Program *)
23      Seed := 4.0;
24      For k:=1 to 20 Do
25        Writeln (k:2, RandomNumber:8:4)
26    END.
```

```
$ run driver

 1 0.1066
 2 0.5415
 3 0.3608
 4 0.8981
 5 0.4798
 6 0.5684
 7 0.2766
 8 0.9671
 9 0.8235
10 0.1967
11 0.8580
12 0.3128
13 0.9593
14 0.7821
15 0.0961
16 0.4936
17 0.5219
18 0.4259
19 0.7403
20 0.0413
```

Figure 11-14

Completely Assembled Procedure Roll, *with Nested Procedure* Toss
and Function RandomNumber, *within a Driver for Test Purposes*

DRIVER.PAS

```
1     Program DRIVER (Input, Output);
2
3     (* This is a driver program to test Roll, Toss, and
4        RandomNumber all together *)
5
6     Var Die1, Die2 : Integer;
7         Seed : Real;              (* Global seed for random number generator *)
8
9         K : Integer;
10
11
12    Procedure Roll (Var FirstDie, SecondDie : Integer);
13    (*
14        This procedure simulates the rolling of two dice.
15    *)
16
17
18        Procedure Toss (Var DieNumber : Integer);
19        (*
20           This procedure simulates the rolling of a single die.
21           It generates random integers between 1 and 6 based on
22           pseudo-random real numbers between 0.00 and 1.00.
23        *)
24
25            Function RandomNumber : Real;
26            (* This function generates random numbers between 0 and 1
27               using a trigonometric formula. Seed is a global
28               variable and must be initialized by the main program
29               to a value between 0 and 2 Pi. This function requires
30               no parameters in the definition. *)
31
32            Const TwoPi = 6.2831852; (* 2 Pi *)
33
34            Begin (* RANDOM NUMBER *)
35               Seed := Seed + 4.4 * Sin (Seed);
36               RandomNumber := Seed / TwoPi
37            End (* RANDOM NUMBER *);
38
39        Begin (* TOSS *)
40           DieNumber := Trunc (6.0 * RandomNumber) + 1;
41           If DieNumber > 6 then
42              DieNumber := 6
43        End (* TOSS *);
44
```

Figure 11-14 continued

```
45
46    Begin (* ROLL *)
47       Toss (FirstDie);
48       Toss (SecondDie)
49    End (* ROLL *);
50
51
52    BEGIN (* Driver Program *)
53      Seed := 4.0;
54      For k:=1 to 20 Do
55            Begin
56              Roll (Die1, Die2);
57              Writeln ('The dice values are ', Die1:1,' and ', Die2:1)
58            End
59    END.
```

Figure 11-15

Test Run of the Completed and Assembled Roll *and* Toss *Procedures and* RandomNumber *Function*

```
$ run driver

The dice values are 1 and 4
The dice values are 3 and 6
The dice values are 3 and 4
The dice values are 2 and 6
The dice values are 5 and 2
The dice values are 6 and 2
The dice values are 6 and 5
The dice values are 1 and 3
The dice values are 4 and 3
The dice values are 5 and 1
The dice values are 2 and 6
The dice values are 4 and 3
The dice values are 6 and 2
The dice values are 6 and 5
The dice values are 1 and 2
The dice values are 6 and 4
The dice values are 2 and 6
The dice values are 5 and 1
The dice values are 2 and 6
The dice values are 5 and 1
```

depend on the program itself. We must somehow venture outside the confines of the program. Frequently, the time of day is used as a basis for randomizing, but in standard Pascal there is no way to get the time from within a program. Another way of randomizing is to request a number from the player and use it somehow to come up with a seed. Such a method is totally gauche, but it will serve for now. Let us, therefore, write a new procedure called Randomize to carry out the task. For want of something better, let's simply prompt the player for a number between 1 and 1,000. Of course, if the player enters the same number each time, and then rolls the dice that many times, he or she will get the same game, but nothing is perfect. A procedure that will accomplish the process is given in Figure 11-16. Randomize is simple enough so that we can dispense with the full development process. Note in the figure that we have placed the procedure within a driver and tested it and that it works correctly.

Let's make a few observations about Randomize. Recall that the main program must be in charge of initializing Seed to the value 4.0, since Seed must be global. The procedure Randomize simply takes it from there. That way, at least, this particular procedure does not violate our dictum about side effects. Also, since Randomize is a procedure that calls another procedure (it references Roll), we must be sure that Roll is defined *before* we define Randomize. Notice that the driver in which this is enclosed has a dummy procedure Roll defined prior to the Randomize definition. (We use a dummy procedure rather than the real Roll procedure just to keep testing simple.) Of course, since we've decided to include the procedure Randomize in the CRAPS game program, we'll have to go back and alter the main program by adding a call to Randomize—something we didn't want to do. What a lot of trouble!

Now that we have completed everything needed to simulate the rolling of dice, let's return to the remaining procedures.

Subtask Describe: **Step 1—Understand the Problem.** The next procedure we come upon is Describe. This procedure indicates whether the current game has been won or lost and the amount of money remaining in the bankroll.

Subtask Describe: **Step 2—Plan the Solution.** The outline for this procedure is quite straightforward, namely,

If Won then
    Indicate a win
Else
    Indicate a loss
Write 'Current balance is', Money

Figure 11-16

Procedure Randomize *in a Driver, with Test Results*

```
DRIVER.PAS

    1    Program DRIVER (Input, Output);
    2
    3    (* This one tests Randomize *)
    4
    5    Var Seed : Real;
    6
    7
    8    Procedure Roll (Var One, Two : Integer);
    9    (* This is a DUMMY DUMMY DUMMY for testing Randomize *)
   10    Begin
   11      One := 1;
   12      Two := 6
   13    End;
   14
   15    Procedure Randomize ;
   16    (* This procedure randomizes the random number generator so
   17       that the same sequence of dice is not produced every time
   18       the program is run. It counts on the good nature of the
   19       player by requesting a number between 1 and 1000, and the
   20       dice are rolled that many times before the game begins. *)
   21    Var Times : Integer;
   22        K, OneDie, TwoDie : Integer;
   23    Begin (* to Randomize *)
   24      Writeln('PASCAL PLAYS DICE');
   25      Writeln;
   26      Write ('Pick a number between 1 and 1000 : '); Readln (Times);
   27      While (Times < 1) or (Times > 1000) Do
   28          Begin
   29            Write ('That"s not between 1 and 1000...try again : ');
   30            Readln (Times)
   31          End;
   32      Writeln;
   33      Writeln ('Ok, good choice. Let''s play dice!');
   34      Writeln;
   35      For K:=1 to Times Do
   36          Roll (OneDie, TwoDie)
   37    End (* of Randomize *);
   38
   39    BEGIN (* Driver *)
   40      Seed := 4.0;
   41      Randomize
   42    END.
```

```
$ run driver

PASCAL PLAYS DICE

Pick a number between 1 and 1000 : 2001
That's not between 1 and 1000...try again : 1001
That's not between 1 and 1000...try again : 0
That's not between 1 and 1000...try again : -5
That's not between 1 and 1000...try again : 5

Ok, good choice. Let's play dice!
```

Subtask Describe: **Step 3—Code the Solution.** The procedure itself is shown in Figure 11-17, within a driver. Note that we have indulged ourselves with respect to the "conversation" of the computer.

Subtask Describe: **Step 4—Check Out the Program.** A test run, showing that all is well, is included in Figure 11-17.

Figure 11-17

Procedure Describe *in a Driver, with Test Results*

DRIVER.PAS

```
1    Program DRIVER (Input, Output);
2
3    (* This one does Describe *)
4
5    Var Balance : Real;
6        YouWin  : Boolean;
7
8
9    Procedure Describe (ThePlayerWon : Boolean; Money : Real) ;
10   (* This procedure merely indicates whether the player won
11      or lost the current round and his financial situation *)
12   Begin (* Describe *)
13     If ThePlayerWon then
14       Begin
15         Writeln ('You won that time!');
16         Write ('Your bankroll is up to $')
17       End
18     Else (* The Player Lost *)
19       Begin
20         Writeln ('Sorry, but you lost that one!');
21         Write ('You are now down to $')
22       End;
23     Writeln (Money:3:0)
24   End (* Describe *);
25
26
27   BEGIN (* Driver *)
28     Balance := 135.00;
29     YouWin := True;
30     Describe (YouWin, Balance);
31     Writeln;
32     YouWin := False;
33     Describe (YouWin, Balance)
34   END.
```

```
$ run driver

You won that time!
Your bankroll is up to $135

Sorry, but you lost that one!
You are now down to $135
```

Subtask Describe: **Step 5—Document.** Done.

The remaining two procedures, namely AskIf and Make-ConcludingCommentsAbout, are very simple, so we just present the finished products. Our sense of the aesthetic has been stretched somewhat in the conversations, but they are nonetheless appropriate and entertaining. The resulting procedures, along with their respective drivers and tests, are given in Figure 11-18 and Figure 11-19.

At this point we have written, compiled, and tested all parts of the project. The main program and all of the subprograms are correct, and all that remains is to put them all together. We proceed to that task next.

Figure 11-18

Procedure AskIf *in a Driver, with a Test Run*

DRIVER.PAS

```
    1     Program DRIVER (Input, Output);
    2
    3     (* Tests out AskIf *)
    4
    5     Var GoForIt : Boolean;
    6
    7
    8     Procedure AskIf (Var KeepGoing : Boolean);
    9     (* This procedure queries the player after each round to see
   10        if he wants to keep going *)
   11       Var Answer : Char;
   12       Begin (* AskIf *)
   13         Writeln('Would you like to play another round?');
   14         Write ('Answer with a Y or an N --> ');
   15         Readln (Answer);
   16         KeepGoing := (Answer = 'Y') or (Answer = 'y')
   17       End (* AskIf *);
   18
   19
   20     BEGIN (* Driver *)
   21       GoForIt := True;
   22       While GoForIt Do
   23           AskIf (GoForIt);
   24       Writeln('All Done.')
   25     END.
```

```
$ run driver

Would you like to play another round?
Answer with a Y or an N → Y
Would you like to play another round?
Answer with a Y or an N → Y
Would you like to play another round?
Answer with a Y or an N → N
All Done.
```

Figure 11-19

Procedure `MakeConcludingCommentsAbout` *in a Driver, with a*
Test Run

DRIVER.PAS

```
 1    Program DRIVER (Input, Output);
 2
 3    (* Test out final procedure *)
 4
 5    Var Bankroll : Real;
 6
 7
 8    Procedure MakeConcludingCommentsAbout (Money : Real);
 9    (* This procedure just makes some wisecracks about the amount of
10       money the player ends up with and displays a final balance.
11       This is strictly for laughs. *)
12      Begin (* The comments *)
13        If Money >= 200.00 then
14           Begin
15              Writeln ('Looks like you did pretty good for yourself.');
16              Writeln ('Sorry I have to make you quit, but you''re');
17              Writeln ('breaking the bank. You end up with $', Money:4:0)
18           End
19        Else if Money > 100 then
20           Begin
21              Writeln ('Not bad for a beginner. Looks like you even');
22              Writeln ('picked up a few bucks. Your final total is $', Money:4:0)
23           End
24        Else if Money > 0 then
25           Begin
26              Writeln ('Didn''t do so well, did you? You lost some, but at');
27              Writeln ('least you still have something left, a grand total of $',
28                      Money:4:0)
29           End
30        Else if Money = 0 then
31           Begin
32              Writeln ('I guess you don''t play this game very well. You');
33              Writeln ('lost all you had and are left with zip.')
34           End
35        Else (* the player has gone in the hole *)
36           Begin
37              Writeln ('I have seen few people who do this so poorly. You now');
38              Writeln ('owe ME $', -Money:4:0,'!')
39           End;
40        Writeln;
41        Writeln ('See you again soon!')
42      End (* Comments section *);
43
44
45    BEGIN (* Driver *)
46      Bankroll := 205.00;
47      MakeConcludingCommentsAbout (Bankroll);
48      Bankroll := 175.00;
49      MakeConcludingCommentsAbout (Bankroll);
50      Bankroll := 95.00;
51      MakeConcludingCommentsAbout (Bankroll);
52      Bankroll := 0;
53      MakeConcludingCommentsAbout (Bankroll);
54      Bankroll := -2.00;
55      MakeConcludingCommentsAbout (Bankroll)
56    END.
```

Figure 11-19 continued

```
$ run driver

Looks like you did pretty good for yourself.
Sorry I have to make you quit, but you're
breaking the bank. You end up with $ 205

See you again soon!
Not bad for a beginner. Looks like you even
picked up a few bucks. Your final total is $ 175

See you again soon!
Didn't do so well, did you? You lost some, but at
least you still have something left, a grand total of $ 95

See you again soon!
I guess you don't play this game very well. You
lost all you had and are left with zip.

See you again soon!
I have seen few people who do this so poorly. You now
owe ME $ 2!

See you again soon!
```

11-5 *Assemble the Subprograms*

This is now a very straightforward task, precisely because we took the trouble to work on each piece individually. We must, however, remember to alter the main program by defining and initializing the global variable Seed within it and by adding the procedure and references for Randomize. When we put all these pieces together, we get the complete program.

STEP 3: CODE THE SOLUTION

We are not so much coding the solution as assembling the pieces. Essentially, we bring all the individually written and tested programs together (we defer displaying the final result for the moment).

STEP 4: CHECK OUT THE PROGRAM

Figure 11-20 displays the initial test run of our newly completed program. Although everything seems to be working correctly, we have overlooked a few aesthetic details. First and foremost, the program never displays the results of any dice rolls! This can be corrected quite simply by adding appropriate Writeln statements. Also, it would be nice if the program displayed the point, when there is one, and whether the

Figure 11-20

Initial Test Run of the Completely Assembled CRAPS *Program*

```
$ run craps

PASCAL PLAYS DICE

Pick a number between 1 and 1000 : 2001
That's not between 1 and 1000...try again : 50

Ok, good choice. Let's play dice!

How much would you like to bet? 25
Your bet is too big. Maximum bet is $10.00
How much would you like to bet? 5
You won that time!
Your bankroll is up to $105
Would you like to play another round?
Answer with a Y or an N --> N
Not bad for a beginner. Looks like you even
picked up a few bucks. Your final total is $ 105

See you again soon!
```

point is subsequently made or not. Adding these *very* minor details produces the complete program as shown in Figure 11-21.

Finally, a comprehensive test run using the completed program is shown in Figure 11-22. Note that everything does work as designed, and in fact playing the game is quite entertaining (at least for a little while!).

11-6 *Observations and Conclusions*

Let us now make some observations about the completed project:

1. Although each of the bits and pieces was relatively simple, the entire project is quite extensive.

2. Trying to work on the project as a single entity would have been difficult; however, there was never a great deal of effort expended at one time on any subprogram.

3. If we had waited until the point of completion to test this project, we would have an exceedingly difficult task ahead of us. Isolating problems would be a chore of giant proportions, given the number of units we need to deal with.

4. The program, when it was finally put together, required little in the way of testing, and those problems that appeared were of a very minor nature.

Figure 11-21

Complete Listing of the Finished CRAPS *Project*

CRAPS.PAS

```
1    Program CRAPS (Input, Output);
2
3    (*
4        This program plays the dice game craps interactively.
5    *)
6
7    Const InitialBankroll = 100.00;  (* Total amount of money a
8                                        player starts with  *)
9
10
11   Var Bankroll,                    (* Current amount of money
12                                        the player has *)
13       Bet           : Real;
14
15       Die1, Die2, Sum, Point : Integer;
16
17       PlayerWantsToContinue,
18       YouWin, YouLose         : Boolean;
19
20       Seed : Real;  (* This is the seed for the random number
21                        generator. It must be global even though
22                        it is used only within nested functions *)
23
24
25   (* PROCEDURE DEFINITIONS *)
26
27
28   Procedure Make (Var TheBet : Real);
29   (*
30      This procedure permits the player to make a bet. Rules are:
31           Minimum bet is $ 1.00
32           Maximum bet is $10.00
33           Bet must be an even number of dollars
34   *)
35   Var TheBetIsRight : Boolean;
36   Begin
37     TheBetIsRight := False;
38     Repeat
39        Write ('How much would you like to bet? '); Readln (TheBet);
40        If TheBet < 1.00 then
41           Writeln ('Your bet is too small. Minimum bet is $1.00')
42        Else if TheBet > 10.00 then
43           Writeln ('Your bet is too big. Maximum bet is $10.00')
44        Else if TheBet <> Trunc (TheBet) then
45           Writeln ('No pennies, please. Bets must be in dollars only.')
46        Else (* He finally got it right! *)
47           TheBetIsRight := True
48     Until TheBetIsRight
49   End (* of the procedure MAKE *);
50
51
52   Procedure Roll (Var FirstDie, SecondDie : Integer);
53   (*
54      This procedure simulates the rolling of two dice.
55   *)
56
```

Figure 11-21 continued

```
57          Procedure Toss (Var DieNumber : Integer);
58          (*
59             This Procedure simulates the rolling of a single die.
60             It generates random integers between 1 and 6 based on
61             Pseudo-random real numbers between 0.00 and 1.00.
62          *)
63
64              Function RandomNumber : Real;
65              (* This function generates random numbers between 0 and 1
66                 using a trigonometric formula. Seed is a global
67                 variable and must be initialized by the main program
68                 to a value between 0 and 2 Pi. This function requires
69                 no parameters in the definition. *)
70
71              Const TwoPi = 6.2831852; (* 2 Pi *)
72
73              Begin (* RANDOM NUMBER *)
74              Seed := Seed + 4.4 * Sin (Seed);
75              RandomNumber := Seed / TwoPi
76              End (* RANDOM NUMBER *);
77
78          Begin (* TOSS *)
79              DieNumber := Trunc (6.0 * RandomNumber) + 1;
80              If DieNumber > 6 then
81                  DieNumber := 6
82          End  (* TOSS *);
83
84
85      Begin (* ROLL *)
86          Toss (FirstDie);
87          Toss (SecondDie)
88      End (* ROLL *);
89
90
91   Procedure Randomize ;
92   (*
93      This Procedure randomizes the random number generator so
94      that the same sequence of dice is not produced every time
95      the program is run. It counts on the good nature of the
96      Player by requesting a number between 1 and 1000, and the
97      dice are rolled that many times before the game begins.
98   *)
99      Var Times : Integer;
100         k, OneDie, TwoDie : Integer;
101     Begin (* to Randomize *)
102        Writeln ('PASCAL PLAYS DICE');
103        Writeln;
104        Write ('Pick a number between 1 and 1000 : '); Readln (Times);
105        While (Times < 1) or (Times > 1000) Do
106           Begin
107              Write ('That"s not between 1 and 1000...try again : ');
108              Readln (Times)
109           End;
110        Writeln;
111        Writeln ('Ok, good choice. Let''s play dice!');
112        Writeln;
113        For K:=1 to Times Do
114           Roll (OneDie, TwoDie)
115     End (* of Randomize *);
```

Figure 11-21 continued

```
116
117
118   Procedure Describe (ThePlayerWon : Boolean; Money : Real);
119   (*
120      This procedure merely indicates whether the player won
121      or lost the current round and his financial situation
122   *)
123     Begin (* Describe *)
124       If ThePlayerWon then
125           Begin
126             Writeln ('You won that time!');
127             Write ('Your bankroll is up to $')
128           End
129       Else (* The Player Lost *)
130           Begin
131             Writeln ('Sorry, but you lost that one!');
132             Write ('You are now down to $')
133           End;
134       Writeln (Money:3:0)
135     End (* Describe *);
136
137
138   Procedure AskIf (Var KeepGoing : Boolean);
139   (*
140      This procedure queries the player after each round to see
141      if he wants to keep going
142   *)
143     Var Answer : Char;
144     Begin (* AskIf *)
145       Writeln ('Would you like to play another round?');
146       Write ('Answer with a Y or an N -->');
147       Readln (Answer);
148       KeepGoing := (Answer = 'Y') or (Answer = 'y')
149     End (* AskIf *);
150
151
152   Procedure MakeConcludingCommentsAbout (Money : Real);
153   (*
154      This procedure just makes some wisecracks about the amount of
155      money the player ends up with and displays a final balance.
156      This is strictly for laughs.
157   *)
158     Begin (* The comments *)
159       If Money >= 200.00 then
160           Begin
161             Writeln ('Looks like you did pretty good for yourself.');
162             Writeln ('Sorry I have to make you quit, but you''re');
163             Writeln ('breaking the bank. You end up with $', Money:4:0)
164           End
165       Else if Money > 100 then
166           Begin
167             Writeln ('Not bad for a beginner. Looks like you even');
168             Writeln ('picked up a few bucks. Your final total is $', Money:4:0)
169           End
170       Else if Money > 0 then
171           Begin
172             Writeln ('Didn''t do so well, did you? You lost some, but at');
173             Writeln ('least you still have something left, a grand total of $',
174                       Money:4:0)
175           End
```

Figure 11-21 continued

```
176          Else if Money = 0 then
177             Begin
178                Writeln ('I guess you don''t play this game very well. You');
179                Writeln ('lost all you had and are left with zip.')
180             End
181          Else (* the player has gone in the hole *)
182             Begin
183                Writeln ('I have seen few people who do this so poorly. You now');
184                Writeln ('owe ME $', -Money:4:0,'!')
185             End;
186          Writeln;
187          Writeln ('See you again soon!')
188       End (* Comments section *);
189
190
191    (* END OF PROCEDURE DEFINITIONS *)
192
193
194    BEGIN (* to play the game! *)
195
196       Seed := 4.0; (* Initialize the seed for the random number  *)
197       Randomize;   (* generator and then randomize the generator *)
198                    (* itself with the aid of the player.          *)
199
200       Bankroll := InitialBankroll;
201       PlayerWantsToContinue := True;
202       While PlayerWantsToContinue Do
203          Begin (* this round of play *)
204             Make (Bet);
205             YouWin := False;  (* When the game first starts player *)
206             YouLose := False; (* has neither won nor lost...       *)
207             Roll (Die1, Die2);
208             Sum := Die1 + Die2;
209             Writeln ('You rolled a ',Die1:1,' and a ',Die2:1,'.');
210             If (Sum = 7) or (Sum = 11) then
211                YouWin := True
212             Else if (Sum = 2) or (Sum = 12) then
213                YouLose := True
214             Else
215                Begin (* rolling for a point *)
216                   Point := Sum;
217                   Writeln ('Your point is ', Point:1,'.');
218                   Repeat
219                      Roll (Die1, Die2);
220                      Sum := Die1 + Die2;
221                      Writeln ('You rolled a ',Die1:1,' and a ', Die2:1,'.');
222                      If Sum = Point then
223                         Begin
224                            YouWin := True;
225                            Writeln ('You made your point!')
226                         End
227                      Else if (Sum = 2) or (Sum = 7) or (Sum = 12) then
228                         Begin
229                            YouLose := True;
230                            Writeln ('You rolled CRAPS!')
231                         End
232                   Until YouWin or YouLose
233                End (* trying for the point *);
234             If YouWin then
235                Bankroll := Bankroll + Bet
```

Figure 11-21 continued

```
236           Else
237               Bankroll := Bankroll - Bet;
238           Describe (YouWin, Bankroll);
239           If (Bankroll > 0) and (Bankroll < 2.0 * InitialBankroll) then
240               AskIf (PlayerWantsToContinue)
241           Else
242               PlayerWantsToContinue := False

244       End (* this round of play *);

246    MakeConcludingCommentsAbout (Bankroll)

248  END (* of CRAPS *).
```

Figure 11-22

Sample Run of the Completed CRAPS Program

```
$ run craps

PASCAL PLAYS DICE

Pick a number between 1 and 1000 : 22

OK, good choice. Let's play dice!

How much would you like to bet? 5
You rolled a 5 and a 2.
You won that time!
Your bankroll is up to $105
Would you like to play another round?
Answer with a Y or an N --> Y
How much would you like to bet? 12
Your bet is too big. Maximum bet is $10.00
How much would you like to bet? 8
You rolled a 6 and a 3.
Your point is 9.
You rolled a 5 and a 1.
You rolled a 2 and a 6.
You rolled a 2 and a 6.
You rolled a 4 and a 1.
You rolled a 3 and a 6.
You made your point!
You won that time!
Your bankroll is up to $113
Would you like to play another round?
Answer with a Y or an N --> Y
How much would you like to bet? 5
You rolled a 4 and a 3.
You won that time!
Your bankroll is up to $118
Would you like to play another round?
Answer with a Y or an N --> Y
How much would you like to bet? 10
You rolled a 6 and a 3.
Your point is 9.
```

Figure 11-22 continued

```
You rolled a 4 and a 2.
You rolled a 5 and a 1.
You rolled a 4 and a 2.
You rolled a 6 and a 5.
You rolled a 1 and a 5.
You rolled a 1 and a 2.
You rolled a 5 and a 1.
You rolled a 5 and a 1.
You rolled a 2 and a 5.
You rolled CRAPS!
Sorry, but you lost that one!
You are now down to $108
Would you like to play another round?
Answer with a Y or an N --> Y
How much would you like to bet? 7.50
No pennies, please. Bets must be in dollars only.
How much would you like to bet? 7
You rolled a 1 and a 5.
Your point is 6.
You rolled a 1 and a 2.
You rolled a 5 and a 1.
You made your point!
You won that time!
Your bankroll is up to $115
Would you like to play another round?
Answer with a Y or an N --> Y
How much would you like to bet? 10
You rolled a 4 and a 1.
Your point is 5.
You rolled a 4 and a 2.
You rolled a 6 and a 3.
You rolled a 6 and a 5.
You rolled a 1 and a 2.
You rolled a 6 and a 5.
You rolled a 2 and a 6.
You rolled a 3 and a 5.
You rolled a 1 and a 2.
You rolled a 5 and a 1.
You rolled a 4 and a 2.
You rolled a 6 and a 5.
You rolled a 1 and a 2.
You rolled a 6 and a 2.
You rolled a 6 and a 5.
You rolled a 1 and a 2.
You rolled a 5 and a 1.
You rolled a 5 and a 1.
You rolled a 2 and a 5.
You rolled CRAPS!
Sorry, but you lost that one!
You are now down to $105
Would you like to play another round?
Answer with a Y or an N --> Y
How much would you like to bet? 10
You rolled a 1 and a 4.
Your point is 5.
You rolled a 2 and a 6.
You rolled a 5 and a 1.
You rolled a 4 and a 1.
```

Figure 11-22 continued

```
You made your point!
You won that time!
Your bankroll is up to $115
Would you like to play another round?
Answer with a Y or an N --> N
Not bad for a beginner. Looks like you even
picked up a few bucks. Your final total is $ 115

See you again soon!
```

In conclusion, we want to again emphasize the usefulness of the top-down approach to design and testing. The steps of this approach can be summarized as follows:

1. Write the main program first. Whenever an apparently complex sub-task presents itself, indicate a subprogram rather than continuing with the solution of the subtask.

2. After the main program is complete, code and test it with the help of dummy subprograms.

3. Work on each of the subprograms, using the same techniques as for the main program described in steps 1 and 2 above.

4. After all of the subsections are complete and functional, place them into the main program at their respective places.

5. Test the project as a whole, making any necessary alterations.

It takes some practice to be able to use this system easily, but the payoff is more than worth the effort.

EXERCISES

CONCEPTS

1. Define or explain the following terms:

Driver	Simulation
Nested subprograms	Stub
Pseudo-random numbers	Test set
Random numbers	Top-down testing

2. Explain how stubs and drivers can be used to enhance the advantages of top-down development.

3. A main program M calls the procedures A, B, and C. Should the definitions of A, B, and C be nested? Why or why not?

4. A main program M calls the procedure A, which calls the procedure B, which in turn calls the procedure C. Should the definitions of A, B, and C be nested? Why or why not?

TOOLS

5. A procedure is needed to do complex math. The call is of the form

```
ComplexMath (Oper, R1, I1, R2, I2, R, I);
```

where `Oper` is a character that expresses the operation to be carried out, namely, +, - or *; `R1`, `I1` are the real and imaginary parts of the first operand; `R2`, `I2` are the real and imaginary parts of the second operand; and `R`, `I` are the real and imaginary parts of the result.

The mathematical results can be expressed as follows:

+ R = R1 + R2,	I = I1 + I2
− R = R1 − R2,	I = I1 − I2
* R = R1 × R2 − I1 × I2,	I = R1 × I2 + I1 × R2

Write this using nested functions within the procedure `ComplexMath`.

PROBLEMS

Note: The following problems are more extensive than those presented in previous chapters. They are intended to give you practice in all phases of problem solving using the top-down approach. Extensive use of subprograms and control structures is required to solve them.

6. Write a function that generates integer random numbers between 0 and 9. Then write a program that uses this function to generate random numbers and determines whether the distribution is *uniform*. A uniform distribution means that after a large quantity of these numbers has been generated, the total numbers of each digit produced should be about the same. For example, if 1,000 such numbers were produced, one would expect to find approximately 100 each of the digits 0, 1, . . . , 9.

7. Write a program that simulates a Las Vegas slot machine. In such a device, three wheels are made to spin by pulling a lever. Each of the wheels has a number of pictures (or symbols) on it, and each stops randomly to present one of its pictures (symbols). If the right com-

bination of symbols shows up, then the person pulling the handle wins according to a predetermined formula!

In our case, let us assume that the player may feed the machine one, two, three, or four quarters before pulling the lever. Further, let us assume that each wheel contains the following symbols:

? ? ? * * $

that is, each contains three question marks, two asterisks, and one dollar sign. Winners are determined as follows:

If the three symbols appearing are	Then the machine returns
$ $ $	35 × bet
$ $ —	5 × bet
* * *	4 × bet
* * —	2 × bet
? ? ?	1 × bet

The — (dash) means that the third symbol may be anything. If any other combination of symbols shows up, the player loses the money he or she put into the machine. Include in the program a way of inputting the number of quarters, pulling the lever, determining the ending position of the wheels, and then making the payoff (if any).

8. Write an enhanced solution to problem 5 in Chapter 6, which deals with the use of triangulation to compute the location of an object. Change the problem to the more general case in which (1) the observation posts may have any position, and that position is described by a latitude and longitude; (2) the angle of observation is described in degrees clockwise from due north; and (3) the position of the observed object is to be given in latitude and longitude. We will assume that plane geometry can be used here. In such a case, the latitude, longitude, and direction (angle) are given in degrees, minutes, and seconds, where the following is true:

360 degrees in a circle

60 minutes per degree

60 seconds per minute

In addition, assume the following holds true for distances:

68 miles per degree of latitude
59 miles per degree of longitude

The general situation is shown in the figure below:

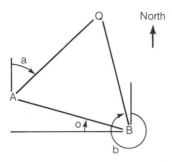

The angle o is given by

$$o = \arctan \frac{(Y_A - Y_B)}{(X_B - X_A)}$$

9. Write an extension of problem 3 in Chapter 6. In that problem, probabilities of a given score falling between two standard scores were computed. However, the solution suffered from two limitations, namely: (1) the limits (a and b) had to already be standard scores, and (2) the limits (a and b) both had to be greater than zero (actually, they had to be greater than the mean). Let us remove these restrictions. We can remove the first restriction easily. Given any score or limit (call it x) and given that the mean (m) and standard deviation (s) are known, then the corresponding standard score (call it z) can be computed from

$$z = \frac{x - m}{s}$$

Given appropriate standard scores, the second restriction can be removed as follows:

$$P\,[a \leq z \leq b] = R(b) - R(a)$$

where

$$R(n) = \frac{1}{2} + \mathrm{SIGN}(n) \times Q(\,|n|\,)$$

and where, further,

$$\mathrm{SIGN}(n) = \quad 1 \text{ if } n \geq 0$$
$$= -1 \text{ if } n < 0$$

$$Q(\,|n|\,) = P\,(\,|n|\,) - \frac{1}{2}$$

and, finally, P is the function described in problem 3 of Chapter 6. Therefore, write a program that will

   a. Read in the mean and standard deviation of the scores in question.
   b. Read in the limits.
   c. Compute the probability that any given score will fall between the two limits.

10. Write a program that will do arithmetic on fractions that are expressed as fractions. Input $n1, d1$ (numerator 1 and denominator 1), $n2, d2,$ and the operation to be performed (+ - */) and generate rn and rd (result numerator and result denominator). The operations of multiplication and division can be defined as follows:

$$* \quad rn = n1*n2, rd = d1*d2$$
$$/ \quad rn = n1*d2, rd = d1*n2$$

   However, addition and subtraction are much more complex in that the operations can be carried out ONLY if the denominators are the same. Therefore, the LCD must be determined and appropriate changes made in the numerators.

   For all operations, reduce to the lowest terms before presenting the answer. For example, given the following fractions, the return value should be

$$\frac{3}{4} \times \frac{6}{9} = \frac{18}{36} = \frac{1}{2}$$

Use only integer numbers in this program.

12

Recursion:

An Elegant Control Structure

We have been making considerable use of subprograms in the form of procedures and functions as a way of helping us write good structured programs that are easy to read and understand. Not only do subprograms make the finished program better but they also greatly assist in the development process itself by allowing us to break up a complex task into distinct (and easier to work with) subproblems.

In the course of studying subprograms, we have discovered many of their characteristics, as follows:

1. A main program can call any number of procedures and functions.

2. Procedures and functions must be defined before they can be called.

3. Procedures and functions can also call other procedures and functions.

4. Procedures and functions can be nested.

5. The constants and variables that have been defined by a procedure or function exist *only* during the time that the procedure or function is active (that is, while it is actually carrying out its task).

However, there is an interesting question concerning subprograms that might have occurred to you as we discussed procedures and functions, namely: Can a procedure or function call itself? The answer to this question, at least as far as Pascal is concerned, is yes. In fact, this process is so special that it is given a name:

> Recursion is a situation in which a subprogram (procedure or function) calls itself.

Recursion is not a new concept at all but has been used in mathematics for a long time. In mathematics the term "recursion" normally describes a function that is defined partly in terms of itself. This view of recursion is equivalent to recursion as used in programming, as we shall explain shortly.

Given that a subprogram can call itself, however, another question arises: Why in the world would you ever want a procedure or function to call itself? The answer to this question is that recursion allows you to simply and elegantly solve certain problems that may, at first glance, appear intractable.

It is important to realize that *any problem that can be solved with recursion can also be solved without recursion*. This is due to the fact that, strictly speaking, recursion is just another control structure, and as we have shown, only the three fundamental control structures of sequence, decision, and iteration are needed to solve any computer-solvable problem. However, similar to the (nonfundamental) Case statement, recursion is a powerful technique that can simplify many programming tasks. Many problems that appear difficult or impossible to solve using standard control structures can become almost trivial when recursion is used.

As always, however, there is a price to be paid. In the case of recursion, the price involves the amount of time and memory the computer must use when solving a problem recursively. Recursive solutions almost always require significantly greater amounts of time and memory than nonrecursive alternatives. Part of learning how to use recursion involves learning how to recognize those problems for which the price of a recursive solution is commensurate with the level of simplification it provides for the solution.

We will begin our study of recursion by examining how processes can be defined recursively and then look at some simple problems that can be solved using recursion. Then we will look at two problems that are very, very difficult to solve nonrecursively but are rather easy to solve recursively. Finally, we will introduce the topic of mutual recursion, a situation in which more than one procedure or function is involved in the recursion.

12-1 Recursive Definitions

Let us begin by looking at a problem that lends itself to a recursive definition and solution.

Recursive Factorials

We looked at factorials already in Chapters 8 and 9, where they were used to demonstrate loops. Recall that factorials were defined as

$$n! = n \times (n - 1) \times (n - 2) \times \ldots \times 3 \times 2 \times 1$$

The algorithm for the solution to factorials was given as

```
Factorial ← 1
For Digit ← 1 to n Do
   Factorial ← Factorial × Digit
```

We can rewrite this algorithm as a function, as follows:

```
Function Factorial (n:Integer) : Integer;
  Var F, Digit : Integer;
  Begin
    F := 1;
    For Digit := 1 to n Do
        F := F * Digit;
```

```
      Factorial := F
   End;
```

Defining factorial as a function then permits us to call it from some other program unit, perhaps as shown below:

```
• • •

Read (K);
m := Factorial (K);
• • •
```

Although this approach works well enough, it's not very elegant. The factorial definition contains ellipses (which is kind of tacky), and the definition of factorial and its algorithmic expression do not appear very similar. However, if we want, we can work this problem recursively rather than iteratively. Let's do just that.

STEP 1: UNDERSTAND THE PROBLEM

We may feel that we already understand factorials, but remember that we are interested in recursion. Let us begin, therefore, by presenting the *recursive* definition of factorial:

$$n! = 1 \qquad \text{if } n \le 1$$
$$n! = n \times (n - 1)! \qquad \text{if } n > 1$$

Note the simple beauty of this definition. Also note that it is defined partly *in terms of itself*. In this case the factorial of one number (namely, n) is defined in terms of the factorial of another number (namely, $n - 1$). It is exceedingly important to recognize that only *part* of the definition is done this way. Another part of it (specifically, $n! = 1$ for $n \le 1$) is not. If, in fact, the function were defined only in terms of itself, we would have not a recursive definition but a *circular* definition. An example of a circular definition in English would be to say that a tree is a collection of connected branches and to then say that branches are collections of things that make up trees. You could go on forever in this manner and never figure out what either branches or trees were. A similar thing happens with respect to math and computers. Circular definitions are improper and incorrect and can lead to infinite (never-ending) recursion.

To see the difference between recursive and circular definitions, suppose we defined factorial (incorrectly) as

$$n! = n \times (n - 1)!$$

This is a circular definition. Why? Because if we tried to take the factorial of 5 the following sequence would get started:

> 5! is defined in terms of 4!
> 4! is defined in terms of 3!
> 3! is defined in terms of 2!
> 2! is defined in terms of 1!
> 1! is defined in terms of 0!
> 0! is defined in terms of —1!
> −1! is defined in terms of −2!

This would go on forever and ever and is why, in a recursive definition, part of the definition must NOT involve itself. That part that does not involve itself is important because it *terminates the definition*. In our factorial example, the definition of 1! as 1 would cause the sequence of steps defining 5! to cease. Using our correct recursive definition of factorial, we would find the following:

> 5! is defined in terms of 4!
> 4! is defined in terms of 3!
> 3! is defined in terms of 2!
> 2! is defined in terms of 1!
> **1! IS DEFINED TO BE 1**

Hence, using our recursive definition, the "buck" eventually stops. In a circular definition, it goes on forever.

So how do we compute factorials with this recursive definition? The process would be as follows for 5!:

$$5! = 5 \times 4!$$

We therefore need to define 4! But that is given in the definition also, so we may "evaluate" it as follows:

$$5! = 5 \times 4!$$
$$4! = 4 \times 3!$$

We cannot as yet evaluate 5! until we have evaluated 4!. But now we cannot evaluate 4! until we evaluate 3!, which we proceed to do:

$$5! = 5 \times 4!$$
$$4! = 4 \times 3!$$
$$3! = 3 \times 2!$$

We must do it again! Will this go on forever? *No, because sooner or later we will get to the termination condition.* Continuing on, we have

$$5! = 5 \times 4!$$
$$4! = 4 \times 3!$$
$$3! = 3 \times 2!$$
$$2! = 2 \times 1!$$

Aha! Remember that we have a definition for 1! that is not based on another factorial. In this case, 1! is defined to be 1; therefore, this sequence becomes

$$5! = 5 \times 4!$$
$$4! = 4 \times 3!$$
$$3! = 3 \times 2!$$
$$2! = 2 \times 1!$$
$$1! = 1$$

At this point we have bottomed out and gone as far as we can go. However, and this is also important, we have yet to actually do any calculating. We have a number of computations to do, but these are all on hold.

Having reached this point, we can now start doing some computations. We have an actual value for 1! (namely, it equals 1) that we can use in further computations. Our pyramid now looks like this:

$$5! = 5 \times 4!$$
$$4! = 4 \times 3!$$
$$3! = 3 \times 2!$$
$$2! = 2 \times 1$$

Since 1! has a definite value, we can substitute it in at the next higher level. We are now in a position to evaluate 2!, because we know what makes it up. Making this evaluation yields a value for 2! of 2, which we may now substitute at the next higher level as follows:

$$5! = 5 \times 4!$$
$$4! = 4 \times 3!$$
$$3! = 3 \times 2$$

We can now evaluate 3! as 3 times 2, or 6, and substitute it farther up:

$$5! = 5 \times 4!$$
$$4! = 4 \times 6$$

Next comes $4! = 4 \times 6 = 24$, which when substituted gives

$$5! = 5 \times 24$$

We are now, finally, in a position to solve the original problem, namely,

$$5! = 5 \times 24 = 120$$

To summarize this process: we work our way *down* the solution by successively applying the recursive definition until we reach a place where the terminating definition (rather than the recursive definition) holds. At this point we do the indicated computations and work our way back *up* through the definitions we have established until the original problem is solved.

Pay particular attention to the similarity of the process described above to that found in normal subroutine execution. We have an originating process (in this case the multiplication of 5 by 4!, which is analogous to the main program) that must be temporarily suspended while we begin another task (multiplying 4 by 3!, which is analogous to the subprogram). This series of events repeats itself for several more levels—the equivalent of several additional subprogram calls. The difference between a normal subroutine call and a recursive call is that in the latter the subprogram being called is the same every time.

You can also begin to see some disadvantages of recursion. Although the recursive definition looks elegant, the actual execution is a lot of work! Essentially, the high-level representation (the definition) is natural and simple, but the low-level representation (the work that must actually be done) is very extensive and tedious. However, computers are rather good at carrying out such tedious tasks, and when we invoke recursion, we are basically choosing to allow the computer to do more of the work necessary to solve the problem.

Let's now look at the computer aspects of the recursive factorial problem.

12-2   *Simple Recursion*

STEP 2: PLAN THE SOLUTION

Using the recursive definition of factorial, we can write an algorithm as follows:

```
If n ≤ 1 then
    Factorial ← 1
Else
    Factorial ← n × Factorial (n − 1)
```

This definition is quite elegant: no muss, no fuss, no loops. Also, recursion here is used as it was originally defined: a subprogram (in this case a function) that calls itself.

The next question is: How do we convert this algorithm to Pascal?

STEP 3: CODE THE SOLUTION

Actually there is nothing to it. We write the conversion as we always have, since in Pascal there's no problem with having a function refer to itself. Factorial could, therefore, be defined recursively in Pascal as

```
Function Factorial (n : Integer) : Integer;
  Begin
    If n <= 1 then
        Factorial := 1
    Else
        Factorial := n * Factorial (n - 1)
  End;
```

STEP 4: CHECK OUT THE PROGRAM

To convince ourselves that this function actually works, we enclose it in a driver program and run it, as shown in Figure 12-1. Let us trace the program for some of the values of Number to see exactly what's happening.

Let's start with the case in which the value read in for Number is 1 (third trial). After the input operation at line 25 is completed, the memory for the main program TESTFACT would look as follows:

```
TESTFACT    Number : 1    Result    : x
```

The x, of course, means that Result hasn't yet been defined. In line 26 we indicate that a value is to be assigned to Result, but in order to complete the assignment process we must first carry out the function entitled Factorial, the argument to which is Number. Therefore, we mark the return location (which is line 26) and transfer to the beginning of the function Factorial in line 11. The value of the argument (Number, which is currently 1) is given to the function parameter (n in this case), and memory becomes

```
TESTFACT    Number : 1    Result    : x
Factorial   n      : 1    Factorial : x    return to: line 26
```

Note that we now have memory locations associated both with the main program TESTFACT and with the function Factorial. Also note that the memory from the function includes a variable whose name is the same as the function, namely, Factorial. Recall from Chapter 6 that this is the mechanism by which the function value is returned to the calling program. Recall further that the memory associated with the function Factorial comes into existence only *after* the function is actually referenced. The memory from Factorial also

Figure 12-1

Recursive Implementation of the Factorial Function in a Driver, with a Test Run

```
TESTFACT.PAS

    1    Program TESTFACT (Input, Output);
    2
    3    (*
    4         Driver for testing recursive factorial function.
    5    *)
    6
    7    Var Number, Result : Integer;
    8        Answer : Char;
    9
   10
   11    Function Factorial (n : Integer) : Integer;
   12    (* This function computes factorials recursively *)
   13      Begin
   14        If n <= 1 then
   15           Factorial := 1
   16        Else
   17           Factorial := n * Factorial (n - 1)
   18      End;
   19
   20
   21    BEGIN
   22      Answer := 'Y';
   23      While Answer = 'Y' Do
   24        Begin
   25          Write ('Enter n : '); Readln (Number);
   26          Result := Factorial (Number);
   27          Writeln ('The factorial is ', Result:1);
   28          Writeln;
   29          Write ('Another? (Y/N) '); Readln (Answer)
   30        End
   31    END.


$ run testfact

Enter n : 5
The factorial is 120

Another? (Y/N) Y
Enter n : 2
The factorial is 2

Another? (Y/N) Y
Enter n : 1
The factorial is 1

Another? (Y/N) Y
Enter n : 0
The factorial is 1

Another? (Y/N) N
```

contains the location to which control should return upon completion of the function.

We may now proceed to line 14, where we test the value of n. Since the value of n is, in fact, less than or equal to 1, we proceed to line 15. The instruction here says to give Factorial a value of 1. Doing so gives us a memory picture of

```
TESTFACT    Number  : 1   Result    : x
FACTORIAL   n       : 1   Factorial : 1    return to : line 26
```

Having done this we find ourselves at line 18, which is the end of the function. The value computed by the function is 1 (the value stored in Factorial). We therefore return to the line from which the function was originally called and which the subprogram "remembers" (line 26 in this case), and we place the value computed by Factorial into Result. Therefore, memory becomes

```
TESTFACT    Number  : 1   Result    : 1
```

Note that, having completed the function call, the memory for Factorial *no longer exists*. We may next proceed to line 27, where we output the results.

That wasn't too bad at all, and in fact it is exactly what we would expect from a procedure call. Let's try a more interesting example, however, by tracing through what happens if a value of 5 for Number is input. Doing so (from line 25) results in the following memory picture:

```
TESTFACT    Number  : 5   Result    : x
```

Again, Result is undefined. We next move on to line 26, where we are told to assign a value to Result. As in the previous example, however, we must first call the procedure Factorial. The argument is again Number. We consequently transfer to line 11 (in the function Factorial), where the parameter n is given a value of 5 (the value of the argument). Memory now looks like this:

```
TESTFACT    Number  : 5   Result    : x
Factorial   n       : 5   Factorial : x    return to : line 26
```

Memory is again associated both with the main program *and* with the function, the latter having come into existence when the function was called. The function also stores the location we must return to when the function is all finished.

We now proceed to line 14, where n is tested. In this case, n is NOT less than or equal to 1, and consequently we must go to line 17. This is where things begin to get interesting. Line 17 tells us to multiply n by the value of the factorial of n - 1 and place the result into Factorial. What do we do now? We are already *in* Factorial. Well, we do just what we always do. We evaluate the argument and go to the function. The fact that the function we want just happens to be the function we are in *doesn't matter in the slightest*. We carry on exactly as if nothing was out of the ordinary.

So let's do it. The argument to the function call is n - 1, and since n is 5 right now, that makes the value of the argument 4. Therefore, we transfer to line 11, where the parameter n is given a value of 4 (the value of the argument used in the call). Memory *now* looks like

```
TESTFACT    Number  : 5    Result    : x
Factorial   n       : 5    Factorial : x    return to : line 26
Factorial   n       : 4    Factorial : x    return to : line 17
```

All right, what is going on here? We have two occurrences of Factorial, Factorial, and return to. What does this all mean?

Recall that every time a procedure or function is called, new memory is assigned to it. Consequently, the memory for the second invocation of the function Factorial *is completely separate and distinct* from the memory for the first invocation of the function Factorial. Also, each n, each Factorial, and each return to is associated with a different function call. There is no conflict or confusion whatever because completely different sections of memory are assigned to each call. We have what are termed two "activations" of the function, and the computer never confuses them. When we refer to n, or Factorial, or whatever, we always assume we are using the most recently created local variables.

We now find ourselves at line 14. We check the (most recent) value of n, find it is NOT less than or equal to 1, and move to line 17. From here the entire sequence is repeated. In order to compute a value for the most recent activation of the function Factorial, we must multiply n (4) by the factorial of n - 1 (3). To do this we must call the function Factorial one more time. The argument has a value of 3, and we transfer to line 11, where memory looks like

```
TESTFACT    Number  : 5    Result    : x
Factorial   n       : 5    Factorial : x    return to : line 26
Factorial   n       : 4    Factorial : x    return to : line 17
Factorial   n       : 3    Factorial : x    return to : line 17
```

Can you see what's happening? Once back inside the function, this entire process would occur again, this time yielding

```
TESTFACT    Number  : 5   Result     : X
Factorial   n       : 5   Factorial  : X   return to : line 26
Factorial   n       : 4   Factorial  : X   return to : line 17
Factorial   n       : 3   Factorial  : X   return to : line 17
Factorial   n       : 2   Factorial  : X   return to : line 17
```

As this process continues, that is, as more activations of the function Factorial are called, more and more memory is required. If it goes on long enough, it is entirely possible that we would run out of memory! (An event that wouldn't happen if we used an iterative solution.)

Entering the function one more time, we find ourselves at line 11 with memory looking like

```
TESTFACT    Number  : 5   Result     : X
Factorial   n       : 5   Factorial  : X   return to : line 26
Factorial   n       : 4   Factorial  : X   return to : line 17
Factorial   n       : 3   Factorial  : X   return to : line 17
Factorial   n       : 2   Factorial  : X   return to : line 17
Factorial   n       : 1   Factorial  : X   return to : line 17
```

Continuing on to line 14, we see that n is (finally!) less than or equal to 1. Consequently, the most recently encountered Factorial is given a value of 1, and memory becomes

```
TESTFACT    Number  : 5   Result     : X
Factorial   n       : 5   Factorial  : X   return to : line 26
Factorial   n       : 4   Factorial  : X   return to : line 17
Factorial   n       : 3   Factorial  : X   return to : line 17
Factorial   n       : 2   Factorial  : X   return to : line 17
Factorial   n       : 1   Factorial  : 1   return to : line 17
```

The most recently defined value of Factorial now has a value! We next move to line 18 of the function Factorial, where the function ends. At this point, we have a value (namely, 1) to be returned by the function, and we know where to return to (line 17). We therefore execute the return, and when we do so, the memory allocated to this particular activation is released (that is, it ceases to exist). We therefore find ourselves at line 17 (of the previous activation) with a returned value of 1 and a memory map of the following:

```
TESTFACT    Number  : 5   Result     : X
Factorial   n       : 5   Factorial  : X   return to : line 26
Factorial   n       : 4   Factorial  : X   return to : line 17
Factorial   n       : 3   Factorial  : X   return to : line 17
Factorial   n       : 2   Factorial  : X   return to : line 17
```

We may now complete the instruction at line 17, which says to give `Factorial` the value obtained by multiplying n (which is 2 for this most recent activation) by the value returned from the function call (which is 1, from above). The product, therefore, is 2. Memory now looks like

```
TESTFACT    Number  : 5   Result      : x
Factorial   n       : 5   Factorial : x   return to : line 26
Factorial   n       : 4   Factorial : x   return to : line 17
Factorial   n       : 3   Factorial : x   return to : line 17
Factorial   n       : 2   Factorial : 2   return to : line 17
```

We now return from *this* activation of the function, which returns a value of 2, to line 17 of the next activation back up. As before, when we execute the return, the memory allocated for the current activation is gone. We thence find ourselves at line 17, with a returned value of 2 and memory of

```
TESTFACT    Number  : 5   Result      : x
Factorial   n       : 5   Factorial : x   return to : line 26
Factorial   n       : 4   Factorial : x   return to : line 17
Factorial   n       : 3   Factorial : x   return to : line 17
```

We again complete the computation by multiplying n (3) by the returned value (2) to get 6. Memory therefore becomes

```
TESTFACT    Number  : 5   Result      : x
Factorial   n       : 5   Factorial : x   return to : line 26
Factorial   n       : 4   Factorial : x   return to : line 17
Factorial   n       : 3   Factorial : 6   return to : line 17
```

If we go through this whole *return* process again, we will end up with

```
TESTFACT    Number  : 5   Result      : x
Factorial   n       : 5   Factorial : x    return to : line 26
Factorial   n       : 4   Factorial : 24   return to : line 17
```

Going through the process once more, we will find ourselves at line 17 with a returned value of 24 and memory of

```
TESTFACT    Number  : 5   Result      : x
Factorial   n       : 5   Factorial : x   return to : line 26
```

Continuing on, we must multiply n (5 this time) by the returned value of 24 to yield 120. This, of course, is then stored in `Factorial`. The memory becomes

```
TESTFACT    Number : 5   Result    : x
Factorial   n      : 5   Factorial : 120    return to : line 26
```

Having completed the calculations of line 17, we find ourselves one more time at line 18, the end of the function. We therefore return to line 26 (the return location as saved by the function), with a value to be returned of 120. We are then at line 26 (of the main program), where we may assign the value returned by the function to Result, as instructed. Memory consequently becomes

```
TESTFACT    Number : 5   Result    : 120
```

We can finally proceed to line 27, where the result is output.

This trace was fairly complicated, but it reveals the essentials of recursive programming. Recursive subprogram calls require large amounts of computer memory (to contain all the values in all the activations) and time (to move all this memory around). When choosing whether or not to solve a problem recursively, we need to consider whether the added ease and elegance of solving the problem recursively is worth the added computer resources necessary to actually carry out the solution. For simple programs, such as factorials, we would probably not bother with recursion. However, some problems (such as the two we will look at later in this chapter) are so much easier to solve with recursion that it is worth the price.

STEP 5: DOCUMENT

The factorial function itself, shown in Figure 12-1, is easy to read and follow. The driver in which it is placed is, of course, not nearly as extensive, since (as we said in the previous chapter) it is meant to be discarded eventually.

Let's do another example using simple recursion.

Recursive Exponentiation

Consider the problem of exponentiation in Pascal. We solved that problem once already in Chapter 9 by using iteration. Let's solve it again, this time using recursion.

STEP 1: UNDERSTAND THE PROBLEM

Let us first, as always, delimit the problem. We want to be able to compute

$$b^p$$

where b = the base

p = the exponent

We will use only integer values for the exponent, but to keep the problem interesting, let's permit any real value for the base and further allow the exponent p to be negative, zero, or positive.

STEP 2: PLAN THE SOLUTION

Since we are going to do this recursively, we must develop a recursive definition for exponentiation. How can we do this? The first step involves finding the limiting situation, which in this case would be raising the base b to the power of 0. We can therefore immediately write down this first part of the definition as

$$b^p = 1 \quad \text{if } p = 0$$

Now let's turn our attention to the case in which p is greater than zero. A recursive definition is actually quite simple here, as follows:

$$b^p = b \times b^{p-1} \quad \text{if } p > 0$$

Will this work? Let's try a simple example. Given values of $b = 2$ and $p = 4$, what would happen? Working down through the recursive definition would yield

$$2^4 = 2 \times 2^3$$
$$2^3 = 2 \times 2^2$$
$$2^2 = 2 \times 2^1$$
$$2^1 = 2 \times 2^0$$

At this point we reach the terminus of our definition, since 2 to the power 0 is defined as 1. We can then work our way back out of the definition as follows:

$$2^1 = 2 \times 1 = 2$$
$$2^2 = 2 \times 2 = 4$$
$$2^3 = 2 \times 4 = 8$$
$$2^4 = 2 \times 8 = 16$$

Bingo! Our definition now consists of

$$b^p = 1 \qquad\quad \text{if } p = 0$$
$$b^p = b \times b^{p-1} \quad \text{if } p > 0$$

We need now only figure out what to do with negative exponents. Using the rules of algebra, we obtain

$$b^{-p} = \frac{1}{b^p} = \frac{1}{b} \times \frac{1}{b} \times \cdots \frac{1}{b}$$

We may, therefore, use a definition similar to the one for p greater than zero:

$$b^{-p} = \frac{1}{b} \times b^{p+1} \quad \text{if } p < 0$$

In this case, we must *add* one to the exponent rather than *subtract* one. Defining negative exponentiation this way also has the convenient effect of requiring the same termination condition as the case for p > 0. Let's run through an example just to make sure it works properly. Assume values of $b = 3$ and $p = -2$:

$$3^{-2} = \tfrac{1}{3} \times 3^{-1}$$
$$3^{-1} = (\tfrac{1}{3}) \times 3^0$$
$$3^{-1} = (\tfrac{1}{3}) \times 1 = \tfrac{1}{3}$$
$$3^{-2} = \tfrac{1}{3} \times \tfrac{1}{3} = \tfrac{1}{9}$$

We may now put the entire definition together as

$$b^p = 1 \qquad\qquad \text{if } p = 0$$
$$b^p = b \times b^{p-1} \qquad \text{if } p > 0$$
$$b^p = \frac{1}{b} \times b^{p+1} \qquad \text{if } p < 0$$

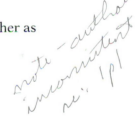

Once we have a recursive definition, we may write an algorithm forthwith:

```
If p = 0 then
    Power ← 1
Else if p > 0 then
    Power ← b × Power (b, p − 1)
Else
    Power ← 1 / b × Power (b, p + 1)
```

STEP 3: CODE THE SOLUTION

At this point the Pascal function may be written directly. The completed function (along with a driver) is shown in Figure 12-2. Note the simplicity and elegance with which the procedure can be written. (At the same time, bear in mind the extensive amount of work the computer must carry out during execution.)

Figure 12-2

Recursive Implementation of Exponentiation in a Driver, with a Test Run

TESTPWR.PAS

```
 1    Program TESTPWR (Input, Output);
 2
 3    (*
 4        Driver for testing recursive exponentiation function.
 5    *)
 6
 7    Var Base   : Real;
 8        Expn   : Integer;
 9        Result : Real;
10        Answer : Char;
11
12
13        Function Power (Base : Real; Pwr : Integer) : Real;
14        (*
15            This function computes positive, negative, and zero
16            (integer) exponentiation of real numbers recursively.
17        *)
18          Begin
19            If Pwr = 0 then
20                Power := 1.0
21            Else if Pwr > 0 then
22                Power := Base * Power (Base, Pwr - 1)
23            Else
24                Power := (1.0/Base) * Power (Base, Pwr + 1)
25          End;
26
27
28    BEGIN
29      Answer := `Y`;
30      While Answer = `Y` Do
31        Begin
32          Write (`Enter real base : `); Readln (Base);
33          Write (`Enter integer exponent : `); Readln (Expn);
34          Result := Power (Base, Expn);
35          Writeln (`The result is `, Result:6:4);
36          Writeln;
37          Write (`Another? (Y/N) `); Readln (Answer)
38        End
39    END.
```

```
$ run testpwr

Enter real base : 2.5
Enter integer exponent : 0
The result is 1.0000

Another? (Y/N) Y
Enter real base : 2.5
Enter integer exponent : 1
The result is 2.5000

Another? (Y/N) Y
Enter real base : 2.5
Enter integer exponent : 4
The result is 39.0625
```

Figure 12-2 continued

```
Another? (Y/N) Y
Enter real base : 2.5
Enter integer exponent : -3
The result is 0.0640

Another? (Y/N) Y
Enter real base : -0.125
Enter integer exponent : 0
The result is 1.0000

Another? (Y/N) Y
Enter real base : -0.125
Enter integer exponent : 2
The result is 0.0156

Another? (Y/N) Y
Enter real base : -0.125
Enter integer exponent : -3
The result is -512.0000

Another? (Y/N) N
```

STEP 4: CHECK OUT THE PROGRAM

The test output is also shown in Figure 12-2. All of the results check out properly.

STEP 5: DOCUMENT

The recursive nature of the function definition is well presented, and the function can be read and understood easily.

An important property of recursion is that it can be used to solve *any* problem that can be solved with iteration. In order to better demonstrate this property, let's look at one more example of simple recursion.

Recursive General Sum

To show the complete generality of recursion in solving iterative problems, let's consider the General Sum problem solved in Chapter 9.

STEP 1: UNDERSTAND THE PROBLEM

Recall that in Chapter 9 we wrote a program that would add up any sequence of numbers. The algorithm was expressed as

```
Input Low, High
Sum ← 0
For n ← Low to High Do
   Sum ← Sum + n
Print Sum
```

Let's show how this problem can be solved recursively.

STEP 2: PLAN THE SOLUTION

As before, we must first come up with a recursive definition. Let's start with one of the easy parts of it. If High is less than or equal to Low, the sum will be Low all by itself; therefore, we can write

$$Sum = Low \quad \text{if High} \le \text{Low}$$

So what would the remainder of the definition be? Well, it would be the low number plus the sum of all the other digits! Therefore, we could write the rest of the definition as

$$Sum = Low + GeneralSum (Low + 1, High) \quad \text{if High} > \text{Low}$$

It's pretty easy once you get the hang of it. Our complete definition, therefore, would be

$$Sum = Low \qquad\qquad\qquad \text{if High} \le \text{Low}$$
$$Sum = Low + GeneralSum (Low + 1, High) \quad \text{if High} > \text{Low}$$

An algorithm based on this definition can be expressed as

```
If High ≤ Low then
   Sum ← Low
Else
   Sum ← Low + GeneralSum (Low + 1, High)
```

STEP 3: CODE THE SOLUTION

This algorithm can be converted to Pascal directly. The code for this function, along with a driver program, is shown in Figure 12-3. Again notice how elegant the function is.

STEP 4: CHECK OUT THE PROGRAM

A test run is included with the program of Figure 12-3. We get all the right answers for any limits, positive or negative.

STEP 5: DOCUMENT

The function is easy to understand, in large part because of the elegance provided by the recursion.

Figure 12-3

Recursive Implementation of Arithmetic Summation, with a Test Run

TESTSUM.PAS

```
1    Program TESTSUM (Input, Output);
2
3    Var L, H, Sum : Integer;
4        Answer : Char;
5
6
7    Function GeneralSum (Low, High : Integer) : Integer;
8    (* This function adds up a sequence of numbers recursively *)
9      Begin
10       If High <= Low then
11           GeneralSum := Low
12       Else
13           GeneralSum := Low + GeneralSum (Low + 1, High)
14     End;
15
16
17   BEGIN
18     Answer := 'Y';
19     While Answer = 'Y' Do
20       Begin
21         Write ('Enter low value : '); Readln (L);
22         Write ('Enter high value : '); Readln (H);
23         Sum := GeneralSum (L, H);
24         Writeln('The sum is ', Sum:1);
25         Writeln;
26         Write ('Another? (Y/N) '); Readln (Answer)
27       End
28   END.
```

```
$ run testsum

Enter low value : 1
Enter high value : 5
The sum is 15

Another? (Y/N) Y
Enter low value : 1
Enter high value : 100
The sum is 5050

Another? (Y/N) Y
Enter low value : -7
Enter high value : -4
The sum is -22

Another? (Y/N) Y
Enter low value : 3
Enter high value : 3
The sum is 3

Another? (Y/N) Y
Enter low value : 20
Enter high value : 15
The sum is 20

Another? (Y/N) N
```

12-3 *More Complex Recursion*

Up to this point, we have considered only recursive solutions to simple problems, and recursion has been used essentially as a control structure in place of iteration. (Recall that we said any iterative process can be expressed recursively and vice versa.) We will now examine two problems for which nonrecursive solutions would be extremely complex but for which recursive solutions would be simple and elegant. Our first example is a game called the Towers of Hanoi, and our second is the parsing problem, which involves determining whether a sentence in a language is grammatically correct.

Towers of Hanoi

We would like to write a computer program that can play Towers of Hanoi. Although usually referred to as a game, Towers of Hanoi is said to have originated as a religious ritual performed by certain Eastern monks (in Hanoi, naturally) to determine the "end of time." When the "game" ends, the monks' belief is that time, the universe, and mankind will also come to an end.

The game (if we can call it that) is played with three pegs and a collection of disks of varying sizes. Initially, all the disks are placed on one of the pegs in order of decreasing size from bottom to top. A typical starting configuration is shown in Figure 12-4. (The exact number of disks used is not significant to the way the game is played.) The object of the game is to move all of the disks from the starting peg to one of the other pegs. However, the following rules must be observed:

1. Only one disk may be moved at a time.

2. A larger disk may never be placed on a smaller disk.

It turns out that the minimum number of moves required to transfer all of the disks from one peg to another is 2^{n-1}, where n is the number of disks. This actually bodes well for the universe, since the original Eastern religious game required the use of sixty-four disks. Moving sixty-four disks from one peg to another, therefore, requires 2^{64-1}, or approximately 2×10^{19}, moves. If the moves could be made at the rate of one per second, the game would require some 580 billion years to complete!

Figure 12-4

Initial Configuration for the Four-Disk Towers of Hanoi Game

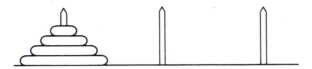

Let's use the program development process to generate a program that will play this game.

STEP 1: UNDERSTAND THE PROBLEM

We would like to write a computer program that generates the correct (that it, the minimum) sequence of moves necessary to transfer an arbitrary number of disks from one peg to another. As usual, let's consider what we would like the input and output to be before going further. In order to make the game general, let's write it in such a way that it will solve Towers of Hanoi for any number of disks that are to be moved from any one peg to any other peg. For simplicity, let's refer to the pegs as L, M, and R, for left, middle, and right. Therefore, the input to the program would consist of

1. The number of disks to be moved

2. The start peg (L, M, R)

3. The destination peg (L, M, R)

As far as output goes, we would like the computer to print out a sequence of instructions that will solve the problem. A typical output instruction might be of the form

```
1. Move a disk from the left peg to the right peg
```

Now that we know the input and output, let's see if we can figure out how the game is actually played. First, let's learn to play the game by hand. We begin with the trivial case of moving one disk from the left-most peg to the right-most peg. The solution to that task is

1. Move a disk from the left peg to the right peg

That really was easy. Let's now try moving *two* disks from the left peg to the right peg. This is almost as easy, and the solution is

1. Move a disk from the left peg to the middle peg

2. Move a disk from the left peg to the right peg

3. Move a disk from the middle peg to the right peg

The two-disk solution is shown in Figure 12-5. So far, there is still not much to this game! However, when we try it with three pegs, things get a little more interesting, as follows:

1. Move a disk from the left peg to the right peg

2. Move a disk from the left peg to the middle peg

3. Move a disk from the right peg to the middle peg

4. Move a disk from the left peg to the right peg

5. Move a disk from the middle peg to the left peg

6. Move a disk from the middle peg to the right peg

7. Move a disk from the left peg to the right peg

Figure 12-5

Solution to the Two-Disk Towers of Hanoi Problem

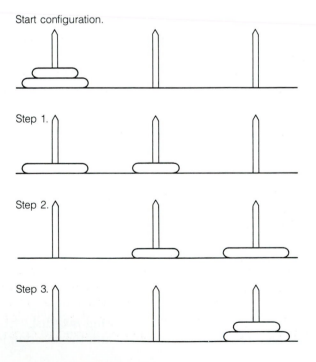

Start configuration.

Step 1.

Step 2.

Step 3.

This solution to the three-disk game is shown in Figure 12-6. (There is really nothing significant about which peg the disks start on and which they end up on; they are all equivalent as far as the game is concerned, and any of the pegs can be used as the start and finish pegs.)

A similar process is invoked for more disks. With a little practice, you can get the feel of the game and move as many disks as you like from one peg to another. (Build a game out of nails and cardboard and see for yourself.)

We are now ready to try to plan a solution for this game.

STEP 2: PLAN THE SOLUTION

Towers of Hanoi, as we are choosing to solve it, can be played with any number of disks, and the disks can be moved from any of the three available pegs to any of the other remaining pegs. Obviously, we are going to need a procedure to carry this process out. Let us begin, however, by writing an initial algorithm that simply sets up the game to be played (that is, determines the number of disks to be used and the start and destination pegs) and then calls a *procedure* to solve the problem. We can write this initial algorithm as

```
Read #Disks
Read Start Peg
Read Destination Peg
Move (#Disks, Start Peg, Destination Peg)
Write 'That's all there is to it.'
```

We indicate the actual solution to the problem as the procedure `Move`. Before we examine the procedure itself, however, let's incorporate this first algorithm into a loop so that several games can be played. If we do this via an operator response loop, the new algorithm can be written as

```
Another One ← Yes
While Another One = Yes Do
    Read #Disks
    Read Start Peg
    Read Destination Peg
    Move (#Disks, Start Peg, Destination Peg)
    Write 'That's all there is to it.'
    Prompt 'Do it again?'
    Read Another One
```

Now that we have this algorithm out of the way, we are ready to work on the tough part, namely, the procedure `Move`. However, when we begin to think about what this procedure must be, it seems difficult to figure out. The game requires strategy. The particular disk that must be moved and exactly where it must be moved to depend on what you

Figure 12-6

Solution to the Three-Disk Towers of Hanoi Problem

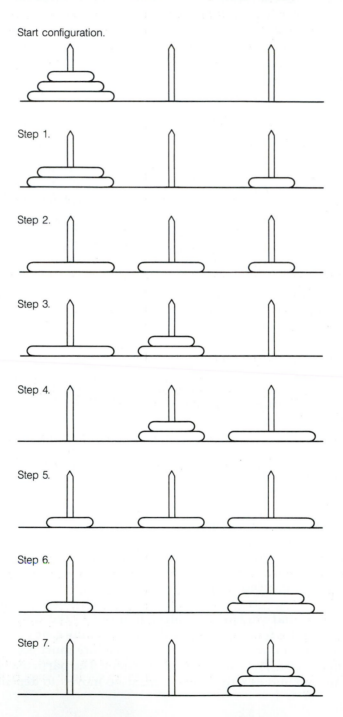

Start configuration.

Step 1.

Step 2.

Step 3.

Step 4.

Step 5.

Step 6.

Step 7.

have done before and what you plan to do next. Furthermore, at any point in the game, there are usually two possible moves. How can the correct one be chosen?

This is where recursion comes in. As we know, recursive definitions have two parts: a limiting situation (usually the trivial case) and a general situation that is defined recursively (that is, in terms of itself). Let's try this technique with the Towers of Hanoi game and see where it leads.

We begin by expressing the limiting part of the solution. For Towers of Hanoi, the limiting case is the one in which we have to move only a single disk. We need only know which is the start peg and which is the destination peg. Given this, we can write the solution as

If there is one disk to be moved then
   Move the disk from the start peg to the destination peg

That part really *is* trivial. We next consider the more difficult part: If we have *more* than one disk, how can we proceed? We need to think recursively. Since we already know how to move one disk (the limiting case), we must find some way to frame the rest of the moves in terms of the limiting case. Since the limiting case involves moving a single disk from the start to the destination peg, how can we incorporate that simple process into the solution as a whole? We can do it as follows:

If there is more than one disk to be moved then

1. Move all but the bottom disk from the start peg to the auxiliary peg (that is, the peg that is neither the start nor the destination peg)

2. Move the bottom disk from the start peg to the destination peg

3. Move the remaining disks that were placed on the auxiliary peg to the destination peg

This simple three-step process is shown schematically in Figure 12-7. Note the following:

1. Step 1 amounts to a (recursive) call to the procedure in which we move all but one of the disks from the start peg to the *auxiliary peg*. (That is, the auxiliary peg now becomes the destination peg.) The task being called recursively is simpler than the original problem, because the number of disks to be moved is fewer by one. Sooner or later, therefore, we will reach the limiting case.

2. Step 3 is also a recursive call that moves the remaining disks from the auxiliary peg to the destination peg where they belong.

Figure 12-7

Schematic Representation of the Recursive Solution to the Towers of Hanoi Problem

Start configuration.

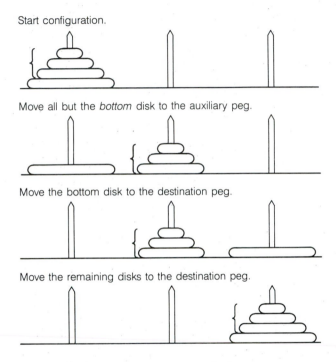

Move all but the *bottom* disk to the auxiliary peg.

Move the bottom disk to the destination peg.

Move the remaining disks to the destination peg.

Let's combine the two parts of this recursive definition into an algorithm and then rewrite it so it looks more like a procedure:

Procedure Move (#Disks, Start Peg, Destination Peg)
  If #Disks = 1 then
    Write 'Move from Start Peg to DestinationPeg'
  Else
    Move (#Disks − 1, Start Peg, Auxiliary Peg)
    Write 'Move from Start Peg to Destination Peg'
    Move (#Disks − 1, Auxiliary Peg, Destination Peg)

Believe it or not, this is all there is to it! The solution is simple, straightforward, and elegant. Note that we're not really moving anything but merely recording the instructions necessary to solve the problem.

We really do need one other item. Since the parameters of the procedure involve the number of disks, the start peg (which can be any of the pegs L, M, or R), and the destination peg (which can be any of the remaining two pegs but not the start peg), we must have some way of determining which peg is left over and (consequently) is the auxiliary peg. Let's just reference a function for that purpose. Our final algorithm, therefore, becomes

Procedure Move (#Disks, Start Peg, Destination Peg)
　Auxiliary Peg ← Third Peg (Start Peg, Destination Peg)
　If #Disks = 1 then
　　Write 'Move disk from Start Peg to Destination Peg'
　Else
　　Move (#Disks − 1, Start Peg, Auxiliary Peg)
　　Write 'Move disk from Start Peg to Destination Peg'
　　Move (#Disks − 1, Auxiliary Peg, Destination Peg)

How can we determine which peg is the auxiliary peg, that is, which peg is neither the start peg nor the destination peg? We will answer this question next.

Subtask ThirdPeg: **Step 1—Understand the Problem.** We want to write a function that returns the name of the third peg, given the names of any other two pegs. This sounds like it ought to be trivial, but in fact the solution is rather complex. The reason is that there are six ways the three pegs can be distributed among the start, destination, or auxiliary positions, namely,

Start	Destination	Auxiliary
L	M	R
L	R	M
M	L	R
M	R	L
R	L	M
R	M	R

There really is no easy way to determine the missing peg except by brute force, which requires that we test for all possible combinations.

Subtask ThirdPeg: **Step 2—Plan the Solution.** So we will now simply test all possibilities, as follows:

Function ThirdPeg (First, Second)
If First = L then
　If Second = M then
　　ThirdPeg ← R
　Else
　　Thirdpeg ← M
Else if First = M then
　If Second = L then

```
      ThirdPeg ← R
  Else
      ThirdPeg ← L
Else (* First must be R *)
  If Second = L then
      ThirdPeg ← M
  Else
      ThirdPeg ← L
```

Now that we have algorithms for the main program, the procedure Move, and the function ThirdPeg, we can go on to the next step of the program development process.

STEP 3: CODE THE SOLUTION

The coded Pascal program is shown in Figure 12-8 and is a direct combination and translation of the algorithms. One enhancement has been added: a global variable Level is included so that the steps to the solution can be numbered. Level starts out at zero, and every time the procedure MoveThem writes out an instruction, Level is incremented by one and printed out along with the instruction.

STEP 4: CHECK OUT THE PROGRAM

A test run is shown in Figure 12-9. The first game played involves moving a single disk from the left peg to the right peg; the program generates the correct instruction. The second game requires that two disks be moved from the left peg to the right peg. (This game is the same game shown in Figure 12-5.) Note that the correct sequence of instructions is generated. The third test in the series uses three disks, which are to be moved from the left peg to the right peg (the game shown in Figure 12-6). Again, the correct sequence of instructions is displayed.

The fourth and final test involves moving *four* disks from the *middle* peg to the *left* peg. We do this just to make sure there is nothing special about any of the pegs. Again, the correct solution is generated. (Work through it and prove to yourself that it is correct.)

STEP 5: DOCUMENT

The program itself follows the algorithms designed to solve the problem, and the comments are sufficient to make the program easy to understand and follow.

Again, take note of the ease with which the heart of the program (in the form of the procedure MoveThem) has been generated and the elegance with which the solution has been expressed.

We now move on to a second problem whose solution can benefit greatly from the use of recursion. We wish to examine sentences of a

Figure 12-8

Solution to Towers of Hanoi Problem, Using a Recursive Procedure

HANOI.PAS

```
1    Program HANOI (Input, Output);
2
3    (*
4        This program determines and prints out the (minimum) sequence
5        of moves necessary to play Towers of Hanoi for an arbitrary
6        number of disks. The three pegs of the game are referenced
7        as L (for left), M (for middle), and R (for right).
8    *)
9
10   Const Yes = 'Y';                    (* Affirmative operator response *)
11
12   Var StartFrom, MoveTo : Char;       (* Start peg and destination peg *)
13       N : Integer;                    (* Number of disks *)
14       Level : Integer;                (* Global variable that counts the number
15                                          of moves as they are played out *)
16       AnotherOne : Char;              (* Whether player wants to do another one *)
17
18
19   Function ThirdPeg (First, Second : Char) : Char;
20   (*
21        This function determines which peg is being used as
22        the auxiliary peg (as opposed to the start peg and
23        destination peg) when the disks are being moved.
24   *)
25     Begin
26       If First = 'L' then
27          If Second = 'M' then
28             ThirdPeg := 'R'
29          Else
30             ThirdPeg := 'M'
31       Else if First = 'M' then
32          If Second = 'L' then
33             ThirdPeg := 'R'
34          Else
35             ThirdPeg := 'L'
36       Else (* First = 'R' *)
37          If Second = 'L' then
38             ThirdPeg := 'M'
39          Else
40             ThirdPeg := 'L'
41     End;
42
43
44   Procedure MoveThem (NumDisks : Integer; FromPeg, ToPeg : Char);
45   (*
46        This recursive procedure actually plays Towers of Hanoi.
47   *)
48   Var ExtraPeg : Char;
49     Begin
50       ExtraPeg := ThirdPeg (FromPeg, ToPeg); (*Determine the auxiliary peg *)
51       If NumDisks = 1 then
52          Begin
53             Level := Level + 1;
54             Writeln (Level:3,'. Move a disk from ', FromPeg:1,' to ', ToPeg:1)
55          End
```

Figure 12-8 continued

```
56        Else
57           Begin
58              MoveThem (NumDisks - 1, FromPeg, ExtraPeg);
59              Level := Level + 1;
60              Writeln (Level:3,`. Move a disk from `, FromPeg:1,` to `, ToPeg:1)
61              MoveThem (NumDisks - 1, ExtraPeg, ToPeg)
62           End
63     End;
64
65
66    BEGIN
67       Writeln(`TOWERS OF HANOI`);
68       Writeln;
69       Writeln(`This program will print out the solution to the Towers`);
70       Writeln(`of Hanoi problem for any number of disks. The three peg`);
71       Writeln(`are called L (for left), M (for middle) and R (for right).`);
72       Writeln;
73
74       AnotherOne := Yes;
75       While AnotherOne = Yes Do
76          Begin
77             Write (`How many disks? `); Readln (N);
78             Write (`Start from peg (L,M,R)? `); Readln (StartFrom);
79             Write (`Move to peg (L,M,R)? `); Readln (MoveTo);
80
81             Writeln;
82             Level := 0;
83             Writeln (`Proceed as follows:`);
84             MoveThem (N, StartFrom, MoveTo);
85             Writeln (`And that``s all there is to it.`);
86             Writeln;
87
88             Write (`Would you like to see another? (Y/N) `);
89             Readln (AnotherOne)
90          End;
91
92       Writeln (`All done.`)
93
94    END.
```

Figure 12-9

A Test Run of the Towers of Hanoi Program

```
$ run hanoi

TOWERS OF HANOI

This program will print out the solution to the Towers
of Hanoi problem for any number of disks. The three pegs
are called L (for left), M (for middle) and R (for right).

How many disks? 1
Start from peg (L,M,R)? L
Move to peg (L,M,R)? R
```

Figure 12-9 continued

```
Proceed as follows:
  1. Move a disk from L to R
And that's all there is to it.

Would you like to see another? (Y/N) Y
How many disks? 2
Start from peg (L,M,R)? L
Move to peg (L,M,R)? R

Proceed as follows:
  1. Move a disk from L to M
  2. Move a disk from L to R
  3. Move a disk from M to R
And that's all there is to it.

Would you like to see another? (Y/N) Y
How many disks? 3
Start from peg (L,M,R)? L
Move to peg (L,M,R)? R

Proceed as follows:
  1. Move a disk from L to R
  2. Move a disk from L to M
  3. Move a disk from R to M
  4. Move a disk from L to R
  5. Move a disk from M to L
  6. Move a disk from M to R
  7. Move a disk from L to R
And that's all there is to it.

Would you like to see another? (Y/N) Y
How many disks? 4
Start from peg (L,M,R)? M
Move to peg (L,M,R)? L

Proceed as follows:
  1. Move a disk from M to R
  2. Move a disk from M to L
  3. Move a disk from R to L
  4. Move a disk from M to R
  5. Move a disk from L to M
  6. Move a disk from L to R
  7. Move a disk from M to R
  8. Move a disk from M to L
  9. Move a disk from R to L
 10. Move a disk from R to M
 11. Move a disk from L to M
 12. Move a disk from R to L
 13. Move a disk from M to R
 14. Move a disk from M to L
 15. Move a disk from R to L
And that's all there is to it.

Would you like to see another? (Y/N) N
All done.
```

language (in this case, a computer language) and determine whether or not the sentences are syntactically correct. This process is called **parsing** and is one of the primary tasks performed by a compiler.

Arithmetic Parsing

Recall from Chapter 4 our discussion of languages and syntax. We said that the *syntax* of a language defines the permissible ways in which language elements (words and punctuation, for example) may be combined. This is true for both natural languages and computer languages. Given a description of the syntax of a language, it is possible to construct correct and (syntactically) meaningful statements (actually, sentences) in the language. Beginning with Chapter 5, we have been presenting, a little at a time, the syntax of the Pascal language. The description of specific syntax elements has allowed us to build programs that express algorithms in Pascal. For example, we said that the heading section of a Pascal program can be described as

heading-section → **program** identifier (**input, output**);

By following this description, you can always generate proper headings for your programs.

We will now consider the reverse process. Given a sequence (normally termed a *string*) of language elements (called *symbols* or *tokens*), how does one determine whether or not it is a correct *sentence* of the language? In other words, is the string correct according to the syntax rules of the language under consideration? This is *not* a trivial problem. When dealing with humans and natural languages, the process appears to be automatic, and people who speak English, for example, can recognize proper English sentences immediately. But how do you get a computer to "recognize" a correct Pascal statement and reject an incorrect one?

The computer makes this determination by parsing, which is one of the fundamental processes carried out by a compiler. Essentially, a string of language symbols is sent to the compiler, which then returns a value of `True` if the string is correct Pascal and `False` (hopefully with specific error messages as well) if it is not. For example, if the following heading were submitted to a Pascal compiler

`Program (Input, Output);`

we would expect the parser to return a value of `False` (it is NOT a correct Pascal heading) with an indication of what is wrong, namely, that the program name is missing.

STEP 1: UNDERSTAND THE PROBLEM

It is beyond the scope of this chapter to present a parser for the entire Pascal language, but we can certainly develop a parser for a limited subset. Let us therefore consider a parser that will recognize proper arithmetic expressions. We know that expressions of the form

```
a + b * (c - d)
```

are correct in Pascal, whereas expressions of the form

```
(a + * - b c)) d
```

are not. In order to be able to even recognize the correct from the incorrect, however, we must first know what the syntax rules are. The collection of syntax rules for a language is called its grammar. English grammar is quite complex, and even Pascal grammar is not exactly trivial. (We have yet to see it in its entirety.) Since we are only interested in parsing arithmetic expressions, we will begin by defining a grammar for such expressions as follows:

1. $E \rightarrow E + E$
2. $\rightarrow E - E$
3. $\rightarrow E * E$
4. $\rightarrow E / E$
5. $\rightarrow (E)$
6. $\rightarrow v$

Here E stands for expression and v stands for variable. The grammar shows ways in which expressions can be formed. According to rule 6, for example, an expression may be a variable, and according to rule 1, it may be the sum of two other expressions. Note that this grammar is recursive in that expressions are defined in terms of other expressions. Also, this grammar does *not* worry about what is meant by addition (that is, what process should be carried out to accomplish it) *or* about such things as operator precedence. It is merely interested in determining whether or not a given string is correct according to the grammar.

Let's look at a couple of examples. Suppose we have this string:

v * (v + v)

Would this be correct according to the grammar? Yes, it would. We can tell that intuitively, but how would a computer do it? The computer would essentially start at the left of the expression, examine each symbol one at a time, and see whether or not each corresponded to an expression as defined by the grammar. Let's trace this process.

The computer would first see a v and ask: is this a valid expression? In fact it is, according to rule 6. Therefore, the computer would interpret the string as

E * (v + v)

The next symbol the computer would come across is the *, and the computer would ask whether or not this is an expression. Although the symbol per se is not, the string E* *could very well be* the beginning of an expression according to rule 3. Therefore, the computer would explore this possibility further.

The next symbol, of course, is (. This is not an expression either, but according to rule 5 *it could very well be*. Therefore, the computer puts this on hold (sound like a subroutine?) and goes for the *next* symbol, which *is* a v. This is an expression, and the computer would interpret what it has seen so far as

E * (E

Moving on, a + is seen next. Since the computer is currently looking at E, it is entirely appropriate for a + to follow, because this may also very well be the start of an expression.

The next symbol is another v, which can be converted to an expression. The computer now has seen

E * (E + E

Continuing, the computer comes to a right parenthesis,), and has

E * (E + E)

According to rule 1, however, E + E is an expression; hence, the string can be reduced to

E * (E)

But then, according to rule 5, (E) is an expression; therefore, we can reduce further to

E * E

Finally, according to rule 3, E * E is an expression, and the whole thing turns into

E

Since this is, in fact, an expression, the parser concludes that the original string was correct.

Contrast this result with what happens when the following string is entered:

v + * v

The computer would first see the v and replace it with an E, giving

E

The next symbol encountered is a +, which according to rule 1 *may* be an expression. The next symbol, however, is the *. *There is no grammar rule that says that the sequence + * may be the start of an expression.* Therefore, the parser would conclude that this string is invalid.

STEP 2: PLAN THE SOLUTION

How do we program something like this? The essential feature is that, given the symbols you have already "seen" and a knowledge of what's next, you can tell whether or not it all fits together. For example, suppose the computer has seen the following string:

v +

The action to be taken by the parser depends on exactly what the next input symbol is. These actions can be summarized in tabular form as follows:

If the next symbol is	Then
v	This is an expression
(	May lead to an expression, keep looking
)	Error—you may not start a new expression with the symbol)
+	Error—a + may not appear after a +
−	Error—a − may not appear after a +
*	Error—ditto
/	Error—ditto

The trick, then, is to write a procedure that will get the next symbol and, based on that symbol and a knowledge of what came before, determine whether or not an error has occurred. Here is where recursion comes in. We need to solve the problem *only* for the limiting cases, and recursion takes care of everything else. (This is the true beauty of recursion.) Remember that when we solved the factorial problem, the only thing we really needed to solve was the limiting case (for $n \leq 1$), and recursion took care of the general case in which the solution was expressed as a single product of the number times another factorial. We will do something similar in the parsing problem.

Let us, as always, use the top-down approach. We will define a procedure called Parse, designed by considering what needs to be done when the first symbol of a string is parsed. This means we must decide what actions should be taken for each symbol we may encounter. The action taken depends not only on the current symbol being considered, *but on the next symbol as well*. For example, if the first thing we run across is a left parenthesis, it may be the start of an expression if the *next* symbol is a variable. But it will definitely be an error if the very next symbol is a plus sign. The derivation of the algorithm then reduces to a matter of stating an appropriate course of action for each possible input symbol.

Let's next see what kind of input we can expect. We can define several categories of input as follows:

Variable	a,b,c, , , , x,y,z
Left parenthesis	(
Right parenthesis	)
Operators	+-*/
End of expression	;

In other words, we will allow variables to be individual lowercase letters; operators can be addition, subtraction, multiplication, and division; left and right parentheses may be used; and (just to keep things Pascal-like) a semicolon will mark the end of an expression.

We can now generate our preliminary algorithm by considering appropriate actions to be taken for each possible input symbol:

1. Get the next symbol

2. If the next symbol is a variable then
   It is an expression (rule 6)

If the first thing we come across *is* a variable, we need do nothing else, because we have found an expression according to one of the syntax rules!

3. If the next symbol is a '(' then
   Parse what comes next
   Get the next symbol
   If this symbol is a ')' then

> This is an expression (rule 5)
> Else
> > Error—right parenthesis is missing

Recursion is showing up already. Let's examine this situation in a little more detail. If we come across a left parenthesis first thing, we *may* have the start of an expression. In order to determine for sure whether or not we have a parenthesized expression, we must first parse what comes next to see if *it* is an expression. Note that this is recursion. We must parse a second expression before we can complete the parse of the first expression. Once we have completed the second parse, we check for a closing right parenthesis. If it's there, we have an expression, but if it's not, we have an error! Since we are using recursion, we needn't worry about *how* to parse this intermediate expression; it just takes care of itself.

4. If the next symbol is anything else then
> Error—missing operand

In other words, if we first come across anything other than a variable or left parenthesis, we have found an error because nothing else may be used to start an expression.

At this point in the parse, we have found either an expression according to rules 5 and 6 or an error. However, we still have not found an expression according to rules 1 through 4. To do so, we must determine whether or not we have an operator followed by another expression, and we proceed with that task:

5. Get the next symbol

6. If the next symbol is an operator then
> Parse what comes next (We apparently have an expression
> > according to rules 1–4.)

If we next come across an operator, we know that we have the beginnings of an expression according to rules 1 through 4, and we need to parse the remainder of the string to determine that it is also a proper expression.

7. If the next symbol is the end of the string then
> We have come to the end of the expression

We can stop now because there is nothing else to do. We are at the end of the string, and we have determined that we do have a valid expression.

8. If the next symbol is a ')' then
> Continue

This may seem a bit strange at first. How can it be permissible to end an expression with a right parenthesis? Bear in mind that this is a *recursive* procedure, and recall that in line 3 we searched for an expression of the form (E). It is allowable for a right parenthesis to follow an expression, provided that a left parenthesis opened the expression. At this point in the process, we cannot judge whether or not a left parenthesis has been used to start the expression. Therefore, we must let this go until such a time when we can make a proper determination.

One other fine point: the procedure should do the same thing in the case of *either* a closing right parenthesis *or* the end of the string, since both mark the termination of an expression. We may, if we like, combine rules 7 and 8 into a single test, as follows:

7, 8. If the next symbol is the end of the string or ')' then
         We have come to the end of the expression, continue

Moving right along:

9. If the symbol is anything else then
        Error—missing operator
        Continue the parse

We expect an operator (or the end of the string) at this point, so if we do not find either, we must have an error. However, even if we *do* have an error, we must continue the parse to see whether or not the string contains any additional errors.

We have now shown what must be done with an expression in terms of terminating conditions (finding a variable, for example) and recursive subprogram calls. Let us consolidate what we have and make it look a little more like Pascal. The resulting algorithm is

1.   Get the next symbol

2.   If the next symbol is a variable then
3.   It is an expression (rule 6)
4.   Else if the next symbol is a '(' then
5.   Parse what comes next
6.   Get the next symbol
7.   If this symbol is a ')' then
8.   This is an expression (rule 5)
9.   Else
10.   Error—right parenthesis is missing
11.   Else
12.   Error—missing operand

13.   Get the next symbol

14.   If the next symbol is an operator then
15.   Parse what comes next (We apparently have an expression
                                according to rules 1–4.)

16.   Else if the next symbol is the end of the string or ')' then
17.   We have found an end; continue
18.   Else
19.   Error—missing operator
20.   Continue the parse

This is the essence of the procedure `Parse`. Appreciate what has happened here. We have constructed this procedure to parse generalized arithmetic expressions, and we have done so by considering in detail only what we'd have to do with the *first* symbol of a string. Recursion takes care of everything else for us!

To continue developing the solution, we must consider four more items:

1. How do we recognize a variable?

2. How do we recognize an operator?

3. What does it mean to "get" the next symbol?

4. How do we determine, when we come across a right parenthesis, whether or not it closes a previous left parenthesis or whether it is an error?

We can dispatch items 1 and 2 quite easily by using Boolean functions. We merely send off the symbol under consideration and see whether (for item 1) it is a lowercase letter between a and z or whether (for item 2) the symbol is a +, -, *, or /. The algorithms for these functions can be written directly as

Function Variable (Symbol)
If Character is between 'a' and 'z' then
    Variable ← True
Else
    Variable ← False

Function Operator (Symbol)
If Character is + − * or / then
    Operator ← True
Else
    Operator ← False

Item 3 in our list asks what it means to "get" the next symbol. At first the meaning appears to be intuitively obvious: we execute a `Read` in order to input the next symbol to be used by the program. More often than not, this is the correct interpretation. However, the process is complicated by the fact that sometimes the parser uses the newly fetched symbol immediately and sometimes it does not. For example, when the symbol (is found in line 1 of the algorithm, it points the way to line 4, but after that the (is no longer needed and may be disposed of. Contrast this with what happens, for example, if a variable is fetched as the symbol in line 13. In this case we would end up at line 18, since the symbol is neither an operator nor the end of the string. We would know that we have a missing operator (as indicated in line 19). However, we must not dispose of the symbol at this point *since we need it to continue the parse in line 20*.

There are a number of ways we can deal with this complication. The easiest is to make use of two new procedures, one of which fetches the next *unused* symbol and the second of which indicates that the current symbol is no longer needed (effectively disposing of it). Let's call the former procedure GetNext and the latter Accept.

We can incorporate these two new procedures into the algorithm. While we're about it, let's name the symbol we are fetching a Token (actually the proper term for it). The algorithm now is

```
 1.   GetNext (Token)

 2.   If Variable (Token) then
 3.      Accept (Token)              E → v
 4.   Else if Token = '(' then
 5.      Accept (Token)
 6.      Parse
 7.      GetNext (Token)
 8.      If Token = ')' then
 9.         Accept (Token)           E → (E)
10.      Else
11.         Error—right parenthesis is missing
12.   Else
13.      Error—missing operand

14.   GetNext (Token)

15.   If Operator (Token) then
16.      Accept (Token)              E → E + E (or whatever operator)
17.      Parse
18.   Else if Token = ';' or ')' then
19.      We have found an end; continue
20.   Else
21.      Error—missing operator
22.      Parse
```

Let's take just a moment to explain our use of the procedure Accept in lines 3, 5, 9, and 16:

Line 3. A variable is *always* a correct expression. Consequently, when we come across one, we don't ever need to consider it further.

Line 5. When we find a left parenthesis, it indicates the beginning of a new expression. Once we start the new expression, we don't need the opening parenthesis anymore.

Line   9. Once we come across a right parenthesis that closes an expression, we don't need to consider the closing parenthesis any further.

Line 16. Once we find an operator, we know it begins a new expression and we can dispense with it.

What will these functions look like? Actually, they are rather simple. The `Accept` procedure merely scratches or blanks out `Token`. This procedure can be expressed as

Procedure Accept (Token)
    Token ← ' '

The procedure `GetNext` simply reads a new token if there isn't one; otherwise, it just keeps what it has. Writing this procedure yields

Procedure GetNext (Token)
    If Token = ' ' Then
        Read (Token)

Moving on to item 4 in our list of additional considerations, we must consider how, when we come across a right parenthesis, we can tell whether it is the closing right parenthesis of a previous opening left parenthesis or whether it is an error. This is not easy, because a right parenthesis can indicate that the end of an expression has been reached during parsing, whether or not it is matched with a left parenthesis. When we are deep into the recursion, we have no way of knowing whether the parentheses match up. Therefore, we cannot mark the occurrence of a right parenthesis as an error *unless* it occurs during a first-time entry into `Parse`. Unfortunately, there is no way that a procedure activation can, unassisted, determine whether or not this parenthesis is the first of many. What are we to do?

There are a number of ways we can handle this situation. One way is to use a global variable (let's call it `Depth`) that counts the number of times the procedure is entered. Whenever the procedure `Parse` is entered, `Depth` is incremented by one, and when the procedure is exited, `Depth` is decremented by one. Therefore, the variable `Depth` will always contain a number that corresponds to the number of times the procedure has been entered. In order to determine whether or not we have a right parenthesis error, we must check at the end of the procedure to see whether or not we are looking at the token) , while simultaneously being at the outermost depth of recursion (depth of zero). If we are, then there is an error. In order to permit the parse to continue, we must remove the right parenthesis and replace it with a variable. The reason we do this is so spurious errors will not result. A right parenthesis generally means that an expression has been found. Replacing the offending right parenthesis with a v just makes the assumption explicit. Modifying the algorithm accordingly gives us

Depth ← Depth + 1

GetNext (Token)

If Variable (Token) then
    Accept (Token)   E → v
Else if Token = '(' then
    Accept (Token)
    Parse
    GetNext (Token)
    If Token = ')' then
        Accept (Token)   E → (E)
    Else
        Error—right parenthesis is missing
Else
    Error—missing operand

GetNext (Token)

If Operator (Token) then
    Accept (Token)   E → E + E (or whatever operator)
    Parse
Else if Token = ';' or ')' then
    We have found an end; continue
Else
    Error—missing operator
    Parse

Depth ← Depth − 1
If Depth = 0 and Token = ')' then
    Error—no matching left parenthesis
    Token ← 'v'
    Parse

The only thing we need now is a main program to drive the `Parse` procedure. This program would consist of a loop (so that any number of strings could be parsed) that contains initializations and a call to `Parse`. We may write the main program as

Repeat
    Token ← ' '   (* Initialize token to blank *)
    Depth ← 0   (* Initialize recursive depth to zero *)
    Parse
    Prompt 'Do it again?'
    Read Answer
Until Answer = No

We now have all we need to carry out a parse of arithmetic expressions, and we may collect, combine, and convert these algorithms to Pascal.

STEP 3: CODE THE SOLUTION

Conversion to Pascal yields the program shown in Figure 12-10. Very little additional work is required to code the solution. Also, we have written a parser for arithmetic expressions that is every bit as good as Pascal's. Our parser can find and report any error that Pascal can. And, last but not least, we have written this program in a compact and even elegant manner, especially considering the work we put into it. This

Figure 12-10

Recursive Implementation of a Parser for Arithmetic Expressions

PARSER.PAS

```
1     Program PARSER (Input, Output);
2
3     (*
4         This program parses arithmetic expressions that contain the
5         following components:
6             Variables : letters 'a' through 'z'
7             Operators : + - * /
8             Parens    : ( )
9             End       : ;
10    *)
11
12    Const No = 'n';          (* Negative operator response *)
13
14    Var   Token : Char;      (* Current input token (global) *)
15          Depth : Integer;   (* Global variable that keeps track of the
16                                 depth of recursion in the parse *)
17
18          Answer : Char;     (* Operator response *)
19
20    Procedure Parse;
21    (*
22        This procedure does the actual parsing.
23    *)
24
25        Procedure GetNext (Var Token : Char);
26        (* This procedure gets the next input token to be processed;
27           if the previous token has been accepted by the program, the
28           procedure gets the next token in the input stream, otherwise
29           it returns the same token as previously fetched. *)
30        Begin
31          If Token = ' ' then
32             Read (Token)
33        End;
34
35        Procedure Accept (Var Token : Char);
36        (* This procedure marks a token as having been
37           accepted by the parser so that a new token can
38           be fetched next time around. *)
39        Begin
40          Token := ' '
41        End;
42
```

Figure 12-10 continued

```
43      Function Variable (Token : Char) : Boolean;
44      (* This function determines whether an input token
45         is a variable *)
46        Begin
47          Variable := (Token >= `a`) and (Token <= `z`)
48        End;
49
50      Function Operator (Token : Char) : Boolean;
51      (* This function determines whether an input token
52         is an operator *)
53        Begin
54          Operator := (Token=`+`) or (Token=`-`) or
55                      (Token=`*`) or (Token=`/`)
56        End;
57
58    Begin (* Parse *)
59      Depth := Depth + 1;    (* Increment the depth of the parse every
60                                 time we reenter the procedure *)
61      GetNext (Token);
62      If Variable (Token) then
63          Accept (Token)              (*    E --> v    *)
64      Else if Token = `(` then
65          Begin
66            Accept (Token);
67            Parse;
68            GetNext (Token);
69            If Token = `)` then
70                Accept (Token)          (*    E --> ( E )   *)
71            Else
72                Writeln (` <Error 1 - missing right paren`)
73          End
74      Else
75          Writeln (` <Error 2 - missing operand`);
76
77      GetNext (Token);
78
79      If Operator (Token) then
80          Begin
81            Accept (Token);
82            Parse                     (*    E --> E + E   *)
83          End
84      Else if (Token = `;`) or (Token = `)` ) then
85          (* Return, we've got it *)
86      Else
87          Begin
88            Writeln (` <Error 3 - missing operator`);
89            Parse
90          End;
91
92      Depth := Depth - 1;    (* Decrement the depth of the parse every time
93                                 we're ready to leave the procedure *)
94
95      If (Depth = 0) and (Token = `)` ) then
96          Begin
97            Writeln (` <Error 4 - no matching left paren`);
98            Token := `v`;
99            Parse
100          End
101
102    End;
```

Figure 12-10 continued

```
103
104    BEGIN
105      Writeln (`ARITHMETIC EXPRESSION PARSING PROGRAM`);
106      Writeln;
107      Repeat
108        Write (`Enter string --> `);
109        Token := ` `;                    (* Initialize the input token stream *)
110        Depth := 0;                       (* Initialize the depth of the recursion *)
111        Parse;
112        Writeln;
113        Writeln (` ** Parse complete **`);
114        Writeln;
115        Write (`Parse another expression? `);
116        Readln (Answer)
117      Until Answer = No;
118      Writeln;
119      Writeln (`End parser.`)
120
121    END.
```

program is even less extensive than our CRAPS program of the previous chapter, and recursion is the reason.

STEP 4: CHECK OUT THE PROGRAM

We now run the program and see if it actually does what it's supposed to do. We see in Figure 12-11 that correct expressions are accepted and that errors are pointed out in appropriate places of incorrect expressions. Not bad for only 121 lines of code!

STEP 5: DOCUMENT

The program itself is readable and understandable, in no small part because it is recursive.

Up to this point, our use of recursive techniques has involved only individual subprograms. However, the concept of recursion may be extended to include any number of procedures and functions that can call each other back and forth. This is termed **mutual recursion** and is the topic of the next section.

12-4   *Mutual Recursion*

Let's consider an example to motivate our discussion of mutual recursion. In fact, let's consider an extension of the above parsing problem. Suppose we wanted to parse control structures as well as arithmetic

Figure 12-11

Test Run of the Recursive Parser, Using Both Correct and Incorrect
Expressions

```
$ run parser

ARITHMETIC EXPRESSION PARSING PROGRAM

Enter string --> a;
 ** Parse complete **

Parse another expression? y
Enter string --> (b);
 ** Parse complete **

Parse another expression? y
Enter string --> (a+b)/(c-d);
 ** Parse complete **

Parse another expression? y
Enter string --> (a-b*(c*c-f*a*c))/(t*a);
 ** Parse complete **

Parse another expression? y
Enter string --> x+* <Error 2 - missing operand
y;
 ** Parse complete **

Parse another expression? y
Enter string --> x+yz <Error 3 - missing operator
;
 ** Parse complete **

Parse another expression? y
Enter string --> ((a+b)/g; <Error 1 - missing right paren

 ** Parse complete **

Parse another expression? y
Enter string --> a-b) <Error 4 - no matching left paren
;
 ** Parse complete **

Parse another expression? y
Enter string --> () <Error 2 - missing operand
+* <Error 2 - missing operand
cd <Error 3 - missing operator
) <Error 4 - no matching left paren
) <Error 4 - no matching left paren
( <Error 3 - missing operator
t( <Error 3 - missing operator
- <Error 2 - missing operand
; <Error 2 - missing operand
 <Error 1 - missing right paren
 <Error 1 - missing right paren

 ** Parse complete **

Parse another expression? n

End parser.
```

expressions. A logical division of the task would be to write one procedure for expressions and one procedure for each type of control structure. For example, we might have

Procedure `BeginEnd`—Parse compound statements

Procedure `IfThenElse`—Parse binary decision

Procedure `WhileLoop`—Parse While loops

Since these structures may all be nested, it is possible that when parsing an `IfThenElse` statement, we may come upon a While loop. Therefore, `IfThenElse` would have to call `WhileLoop` (to parse the loop) so that `IfThenElse` can finish *its* parse. But as we are carrying out a parse within `WhileLoop`, it is also possible that we would encounter a decision statement (as a part of the While loop) and therefore have to call `IfThenElse`. Consequently, we would have a situation where `IfThenElse` calls `WhileLoop`, which then calls `IfThenElse`! This is termed "mutual recursion," because we have subprograms that are calling themselves and each other. It's the same concept as in regular recursion; it just takes a little longer for the recursion to manifest itself.

The concept is easy enough to see, but how can this be done in Pascal? Remember that in Pascal you are *required* to define a subprogram *before* you reference it. Given that the above procedures are all calling each other (and themselves) back and forth, it is impossible to have each procedure defined before it is used. (Try it, and you'll see.) Talk about cognitive dissonance!

Fortunately, Pascal provides an "escape clause" in the form of the **forward declaration**. By using this device, you can inform Pascal of the existence of a subprogram *without having to define it*. The form of the forward declaration is

forward-declaration → f-heading-section; **forward**;
                      p-heading-section; **forward**;

In other words, a forward declaration is merely the subprogram heading followed by the word "forward" rather than by an actual definition. This gives Pascal the information it needs to properly link up the given subprogram with the rest of the program units and is all that is required to implement mutual recursion.

One other question then arises: What must be done differently when the subprogram finally does get explicitly written out? The subprogram definitions are written exactly as we have been writing them all along, except that *parameter lists are omitted*. Having been already specified in the forward declarations, these parameters need not be specified again. Therefore, if we were to use the two procedures `IfThenElse` and

WhileLoop, which are mutually recursive, we could define them this way:

```
Procedure IfThenElse (Var a, b, c : Char); Forward
Procedure WhileLoop (Var d, e, f : Char);
   (* Actual Definition of WhileLoop *)
Procedure IfThenElse;
   (* Actual Definition of IfThenElse *)
```

This method can be extended to any number of procedures.

SUMMARY

In this chapter we examined the concept of recursion, which means that a procedure or function can call itself. Conversely, recursion can mean that the procedure or function is partially defined in terms of itself. Recursion allows very elegant procedure and function definitions to be written, although the price paid is in the computer time and memory necessary to implement the recursion.

Recursion is not absolutely necessary to writing programs, since any recursive solution can, theoretically at least, be replaced by an iterative solution. Consequently, the programmer must determine when recursion is preferable to iteration. Normally, considering the nature of the problem will help you make the decision. For example, you would probably choose iteration over recursion for the factorial or summation programs presented earlier in the chapter, since nothing but a little elegance is gained by using recursive solutions. However, in the case of the Towers of Hanoi problem, where an iterative solution is not even easy to envision, recursion would be the method of choice. In parsing arithmetic expressions, nonrecursive solutions are available but are not nearly as easy to understand or implement; so again, recursion is the method to use. In this chapter we have implemented a rather complicated program, namely, a parser for arithmetic expressions, and we have done so with little mental effort! We can thank two concepts for this: modularity and recursion. Although recursion is not necessary in a fundamental sense, its use can nonetheless reduce the problem-solving effort immensely. And, of course, modularity should *always* be used.

EXERCISES

CONCEPTS

1. Define or explain the following terms:

   Activation   Recursion

   Forward declaration   Termination condition

   Mutual recursion

2. Explain the difference between a recursive definition and a circular definition.

3. What are the two parts of a recursive definition?

4. Briefly describe what happens when a subprogram calls itself. Include a discussion of constants, variables, and parameters.

TOOLS

5. Trace the function `Power` when it is called with a value of 3 for the base and 4 for the exponent.

6. Trace the function `GeneralSum` when it is called with a value of -5 for low and -1 for high.

7. Trace the procedure `Parse` for the following strings:

   a. `(a*(b+c)-d)/e;`
   b. `((a+*bcd/;`

8. Write a recursive definition for 2^n where n is greater than or equal to zero. Convert this definition to a valid Pascal function.

9. Write a recursive definition for the sum of the squares of the first m integers. Convert this definition to a valid Pascal function.

10. Write a recursive definition for the multiplication of two positive integers. Convert this definition to a valid Pascal function.

11. Write a recursive definition for the division of two positive integers. Convert this definition to a valid Pascal function.

12. Write a recursive definition for a procedure that counts the number of letters in a word. Convert this to a valid Pascal procedure.

PROBLEMS

13. The population dynamics of certain organisms can be described by a sequence of numbers discovered by Fibonacci. (These Fibonacci numbers also occur frequently in freshman computer science texts.)

The series itself is essentially a function that can be written explicitly as

n 0 1 2 3 4 5 6 7 8 9 10 11   12 . . .
Fibonacci(n) 0 1 1 2 3 5 8 13 21 34 55 89 144 . . .

For example, Fibonacci(6) is 8 and Fibonacci(10) is 55. Any number in the sequence is given by the sum of the previous two numbers in the sequence. Fibonacci numbers can be defined recursively as follows:

Fib (0) = 0
Fib (1) = 1
Fib (n) = Fib (n − 1) + Fib (n − 2)

Write a valid Pascal function that computes Fibonacci numbers recursively. The function should have a single parameter n. Place this function in a driver program that accepts values for n, computes Fib(n), and prints out the results.

14. A Fibonacci sequence is actually quite general and need not start with zero and one. Any integer can be used to define a unique sequence. For example, we can have

n 0 1 2 3   4   5   6   7   8 . . .
Fibonacci(n) 20 21 41 62 103 165 268 433 701 . . .

Write a recursive definition for general Fibonacci numbers, where L is the value of element zero in the series. Convert this definition into a valid Pascal function of two parameters, L and n.

15. Recursive functions play a significant role in mathematics. One example can be found in integral calculus, where many functions can be integrated by means of a recursive definition. For example, the integral

$$\int_0^x \sin^n t \, dt$$

can be evaluated by the function $J(n, x)$ as follows:

If $n = 0$ then $J(n,x) = 0$
If $n = 1$ then $J(n,x) = -\cos x$
If $n > 1$ then $J(n,x) = \dfrac{(n-1)\, J(n - 2, x) - \sin^{n-1} x \times \cos x}{n}$

Write a valid Pascal function that computes $J(n,x)$.

16. A sequence of characters can be examined recursively in order to find a specific character. For example, it may be necessary to find the location of the first occurrence of the character * in a sequence of characters. If we were to search the sequence

```
delimit * expression *
```

for an asterisk, we would expect to return the value nine, since the first asterisk is in the ninth position. Write a valid Pascal procedure, which would be called as

```
Find (Character, Position);
```

where `Character` is the character to be found and `Position` is the value returned by the procedure. Enclose your procedure in a driver to test it.

17. You can do some other interesting things with recursion. It is possible, for example, to completely reverse an input sequence of characters. Write a recursive procedure to do just that. For example, if the following were entered

```
this is a sentence
```

the procedure would write out

```
ecnetnes a si siht
```

18. You work in the switching yard of the BOUP train company. Each of the trains arriving at the yard has a priority associated with its cargo. Your job is to examine the priorities of the trains that arrive and hold the train with the lowest priority while sending off the train with the highest priority immediately. Write a recursive procedure that will read the train number and priority of the incoming trains and write out the train number of the lowest and highest priority. Assume no duplication in priority numbers.

19. Consider the following grammar:

S→ BSE
  → ISLS
  → WS
  → m

This essentially means that a statement (S) can be Begin Statement End, If Statement Else Statement, While Statement, or a simple math statement m. Write a recursive parser for the language described by this grammar.

13

Overview III:

Data Structures

*A*t this point we have all the tools necessary to generate a computer solution to any problem that can be solved with a computer. Our tools are (1) the fundamental control structures of sequence, iteration, and binary decision (which permit a solution to be formulated); (2) the enhancements of procedures and functions (which increase the modularity and reduce the effort needed to generate a correct solution); and (3) the elegance of recursion (which allows the solution to some difficult problems to be expressed with ease). However, with all this we are still not in a position to solve every theoretically soluble problem with anything approaching practicality, much less grace.

Consider the following situation. You are asked to write a program that will input a series of exam scores (in no particular order) and then calculate the mean, standard deviation, and median (the score that is exactly in the middle, such that half the scores are better than it and half the scores are worse). Computation of the mean and standard deviation presents no problem, since appropriate running totals for the calculations can be maintained as the individual scores are entered. However, finding the median of the scores requires that they be arranged sequentially from smallest to largest so that the middle score (the median) can be pulled out. This presents a new kind of problem: How can we rearrange the scores so that they are in order from smallest to largest? Doing so would require that each score be *compared* to every other score so that the scores can be ordered. This means that all scores must reside simultaneously in memory.

Theoretically, we *could* do this as follows. Assuming for the moment that there are five scores, we could designate five separate variables for these scores, perhaps named S1, S2, S3, S4, and S5. We could then generate an algorithm that would place the value of the smallest score in S1 and the other values, in increasing size, in the variables S2 through S5 (with S5 being the largest):

```
If S2 < S1 then
    Exchange S2, S1        (* Smallest of S2, S1 now in S1 *)
If S3 < S1 then
    Exchange S3, S1        (* Smallest of S3, S2, S1 in S1 *)
If S4 < S1 then
    Exchange S4, S1        (* Smallest of S4, S3, S2, S1 in S1 *)
If S5 < S1 then
    Exchange S5, S1        (* Smallest of all now in S1 *)

If S3 < S2 then
    Exchange S3, S2
If S4 < S2 then
    Exchange S4, S2
If S5 < S2 then
    Exchange S5, S2        (* Next to smallest now in S2 *)

If S4 < S3 then
    Exchange S4, S3
If S5 < S3 then
    Exchange S5, S3        (* Third smallest now in S3 *)

If S5 < S4 then
    Exchange S5, S4        (* S4 and S5 now also in order *)
```

Now the five scores are in ascending order, where S1 contains the smallest, S5 contains the largest, and S3 is the sought-after median. (There are two scores smaller than S3 and two scores larger than it.) There are, unfortunately, a number of serious drawbacks to this approach:

1. This method works for five and *only* five elements. If we wanted to sort more or fewer items, the entire program would have to be rewritten.

2. It's very awkward and cumbersome. We must deal with five distinct scores, all of which have identical properties.

3. Finally, it is very repetitive. Similar operations are carried out over and over again. Whenever we see this, we expect a loop of some kind to be applicable.

Even recursion is of no help here, since we must deal with all of the scores simultaneously.

We consequently find ourselves in the situation where, despite our knowledge of all the necessary computer programming techniques, we are unable to easily formulate a general solution to this problem. Why is this? We will try to answer this question in the next section.

13-1   *Collections of Data*

Our dilemma stems from our understandable attempt to use the same kinds of data we have been using. Up to this point, we have considered only elementary data types that consist of simple individual variables and constants. For example, we might use the constants pi and e, a real variable here, an integer variable there, and a character elsewhere. These data types are sufficient for many applications but certainly not all. Such types are called **primitives** because they are data elements that a typical computer is designed to manipulate, using its basic hardware. For example, a computer can easily multiply two integers to generate a third; hence, an integer would be a primitive data type.

However, some problems (such as finding the median) require a higher level of data organization to make practical solutions possible. We are again in a situation analogous to the one we were in prior to Chapter 8, when we discovered that we couldn't compute something as simple as overtime payroll. There the problem had to do with flow of control through the program, and here it has to do with the kinds of data we use. Our difficulties in the current problem are due to the fact that certain properties accrue only when objects are brought together. That is, there are things you can say about a group of objects that you cannot say about the individual elements that make up the group. These properties are termed global properties, because they exist only with respect to the collection as a whole. For example, you might say that 35 percent of college students study computer science. That is a global property of the group. You cannot make such a statement about one student, since, in general, a single student will not spend 35 percent of his or her time studying computers. For another example, consider the median problem again. The median cannot be determined simply by examining each of the scores individually but *only* by looking at the collection as a whole. Global properties of collections include such things as number of elements, maximum value, average value, median value, rank, and so on. Some of these properties (such as median and rank) further require that some kind of overall order be imposed on the elements.

To take advantage of the properties of collections of objects, we must know how data can be brought together and organized. There are many, many ways this can be done, and such collections of data are called **data structures**. The definition of a data structure is as follows:

> A data structure is an organized collection of data elements that can be treated as a unit.

The remainder of this chapter presents brief descriptions of some commonly encountered data structures, followed by an introduction to the kinds of operations that can be carried out on these structures. Such operations are inextricably tied to the structures themselves. In a sense, the characteristics of an individual data structure are motivated by the operations that must be carried out on the collection as a whole. Thus, we will take a preliminary look at both structures and operations in this chapter.

Let's begin with the structures themselves: arrays, linked lists, queues, stacks, trees, records, sets, and files.

13-2 Arrays

Arrays can be defined as data structures that have the following characteristics:

1. **Homogeneous.** All data elements in an array must be of the same type.

2. **Fixed size.** Although an array can be of any arbitrary size (that is, it can contain any number of elements), once the size is chosen, it cannot be changed. Thus, an array is said to be a *static* structure.

3. **Contiguous elements.** The elements of an array always follow one right after the other in the computer's memory. The second element is always immediately behind the first, and the forty-fifth element is immediately behind the forty-fourth.

4. **Random access.** An individual array element can be accessed at any time by specifying only the name of the array and its relative position (first, second, three hundred and eighty-fourth) within the array.

Since array elements in a computer are located in contiguous memory cells, the size of an array must be fixed to allow efficient use of the computer's memory. Consequently, the location of any individual data element can be calculated relative to the location of the first element. For example, if an array starts at location 340, then the first array element would be at location 340, the second at location 341, and the nth element at location $340 + n - 1$ (assuming, of course, that the elements of the array each require one memory location).

Let's see how this actually works by looking at some arrays. We will examine one-dimensional arrays, strings, two-dimensional arrays, and finally higher-dimensioned arrays.

ONE-DIMENSIONAL ARRAYS

The **one-dimensional (1-D) array,** sometimes referred to as a **vector,** consists of elements that can be arranged in a single column. (This would be the appropriate structure to use, for example, in the find-the-median problem discussed earlier.) A typical one-dimensional array can be represented as follows:

	SCORE
1	87.0
2	35.8
3	90.5
4	75.2
5	61.6

The above is a contiguous collection of objects (exam grades) placed in a single column, where each element can be referenced independently of all the others. To reference a particular score in the array, you must specify (1) the name of the array (Score) and (2) the relative position of the element in the array (1 through 5). Note that you cannot say that Score has a value of 35.8, because it doesn't; rather, you can only say that the second element of Score has a value of 35.8.

The positional reference to an element in an array is termed its **index** or its **subscript.** This terminology comes from mathematics as in, for example, the following equations:

$$\text{Sum} = x_1 + x_2 + x_3 + x_4$$

$$y = a_0 + a_1 x + a_2 x^2 + a_3 x^3$$

Using this mathematical terminology, we can make the following statement about our array:

$$\text{Score}_1 = 87.0$$

This means that the first element of Score (or, conversely, Score sub 1) is equal to 87.0. For ease of writing, Pascal places the subscript within square brackets next to the array name. Using this Pascal notation, we can write the above mathematical statement as

```
Score[1] = 87.0
```

The following terms apply:

Score: the array name

1: the subscript or index

Score[1]: an **array element**, or **subscripted variable**

It is important to not confuse the *value of the subscript* with the *value of the array element itself.* In the above case, the subscript has a value of 1, but the corresponding array element has a value of 87.0. However (and this is important), *the subscript used to reference a particular array element need not be a constant; it can be any valid expression.* More often than not, it is an integer expression, but it is not necessary that it be so. (For now, however, we will deal only with integer subscripts.)

The fact that a subscript can be a variable expression makes all the difference in the world. For example, suppose we wanted to print out all five exam scores. We no longer need to write (algorithmically) the process as

Write S1
Write S2
Write S3
Write S4
Write S5

Instead we can write it as

For Person ← 1 to 5 Do
    Write Score[Person]

Observe how this second algorithm works. The first time through the loop, Person (which is both the loop counter *and* the variable used to denote the subscript) will have a value of 1. When the Write statement is carried out, the information being referenced will be Score[1], which is the first element of the array Score. The second time through the loop, however, the variable `Person` will have a value of 2. Consequently, when the `Write` statement is executed this time, `Score[2]`, the second element of the array, will be referenced. This process will continue until all five array elements have been printed out.

A comparison of the two algorithms yields some important information. For starters, the latter algorithm can be expanded to write out *any number of elements* by merely changing the final value of the loop counter. The former algorithm requires that each element you want printed out be listed explicitly. We can conclude that the latter version is more general, more compact, more efficient (with regard to computer memory), and easier to alter. Therein is the advantage of arrays in particular and data structures in general.

What kinds of data can you put into arrays? There are no restrictions; you can have arrays of any valid data type. The array of exam scores we just looked at is an array of real data, but arrays of any type are possible. For example,

Count		Truth		Grade	
1	1024	1	True	0	`F`
2	978	2	True	1	`D`
3	−101	3	False	2	`C`
4	0	4	True	3	`B`
5	1662			4	`A`
6	1				
7	2				
8	20				

The first array, `Count`, is an array of integers. The second, `Truth`, is an array of Boolean values. The third, `Grade`, is an array of characters. This array demonstrates yet another principle: *the subscripts of an array do not have to begin with 1*. In this case they begin with 0.

One final point: an array element can be used in any way that an ordinary variable can be used.

STRINGS

We next look at what, in Pascal, is called a **packed array of char**. This is frequently referred to as a **string** and is usually considered a distinct data structure in its own right (although not in standard Pascal).

To begin our discussion of strings, consider a problem we have encountered before. When developing the payroll application, we were unable to input a name for each employee whose pay we were computing, because we had no way to do so! To use names, we need strings, which we define as an ordered sequence of characters. Hence, the name "Harold Wright" is a string, since it is a sequence of characters wherein the order matters. And order is important! Rearranging the name to "WHgt arldori" for example makes the string lose much of its meaning.

The packed array of character data structure allows us to input and process words, names, or whatever. In general, strings are required to have a fixed length (as does any array in Pascal). The important thing to remember about strings is that even though they are a type of array, *they can be treated as a unit* under certain conditions. As an example, if we defined a string named Word to contain up to ten characters, we could write the following:

Word ← 'NotVeryBig'
Write 'The word you entered is', Word

Even though Word is really an array containing ten elements (characters), we could still treat it as a unit and refer to it as a complete entity. Be aware, however, that since Word is in fact an array, we may, if we choose, refer to each individual letter. (Again, this is the beauty of arrays.)

An interesting property of strings is that you may construct an array of them (which would be an array of arrays!). This makes it possible to create, for an example, an array of people's names. For such an array, you could refer to the fifth name in the list, for instance, and not have to consider the name letter by letter. In this way we can treat *words* exactly as we have been treating numbers.

TWO-DIMENSIONAL ARRAYS

So far we have discussed arrays that are one dimensional, which means that they are composed of a single column of elements. However, it is possible to take arrays to higher dimensions. We begin by introducing the **matrix,** or **two-dimensional (2-D) array.** A typical example of a two-dimensional array is

	Exam Score		
	1	2	3
Student			
1	90	95	100
2	45	30	0
3	80	82	83
4	89	85	90
5	63	64	63
6	70	69	72

In this case we have three columns of data instead of just one. The data elements themselves range over two dimensions, length and width. In order to reference a specific array element in a two-dimensional array, you must specify, in addition to the array name, both the *row* and the *column* of the element. In other words, you must now specify *two subscripts*, one for each dimension. For example, if we wanted to work with the exam score of the fourth student on the second exam, we would need to specify the element as being in row 4 and column 2 (for the data element at the intersection of the fourth row and the second column). Mathematically, we could write this as

$$Score_{4,2} = 85$$

In Pascal, it would be

```
Score[4,2] = 85
```

Note that `Score[4,2]` (which equals 85) is NOT the same as `Score[2,4]` (which doesn't even exist in this case). As is true for one-dimensional arrays, variable expressions are permitted as subscripts, and the data in the array can be of any type.

HIGHER-DIMENSIONED ARRAYS

Higher-dimensioned arrays may also exist, although they are not used very often. All that's required to add dimensions is an additional subscript for each new dimension desired. This makes referencing data rather easy, but the cost in terms of computer memory used is phenomenal. Suppose, for example, we wanted to reference college students by name, class, and exam score. If we enrolled 1,000 students, offered 500 classes, and gave 3 exams, we would need $1,000 \times 500 \times 3$ array elements, or one-and-a-half million memory cells—and that's just for the data! However, we could immediately pull out *any* score for any student in any class. A typical reference to an element would look like this:

```
Grade[Student, Class, Exam]
```

With this brief description of higher-dimensioned arrays, we complete our survey of arrays and are ready to move on to new and different data structures.

13-3 *Linked Lists*

The properties of **linked lists** are, for the most part, quite different from those of arrays. In general, a list (by which we mean a linked list) has the following characteristics:

1. **Heterogeneous.** The data elements of a list are not required to be the same type.

2. **Variable size.** A list is said to be *dynamic* because its size is *not* fixed but can shrink or grow as the need arises.

3. **Noncontiguous.** The elements of a list, in general, do *not* follow one another in the computer's memory but rather are scattered about depending on where there is available space.

4. **Limited access.** Normally, one cannot go directly to a list element but rather must follow a trail of elements to get to the desired location.

A necessary component of any list structure is the **pointer,** which is a variable that gives the exact memory location (usually as an address) of the list element being considered. For example, a typical list would be referenced by giving a pointer to the first element in the list. The first element would then contain a pointer to the second element, the second would have a pointer to the third, and so forth. List elements are strung together much as a train, which accounts for their properties as described above. Any kind of element may be placed in the list (property 1); elements may be added or removed at will—therefore the size of the list containing them can change (property 2); and their respective locations needn't be implied by having them in contiguous memory (property 3). Finally, direct access is impossible, since the elements lead one to the other via their pointers. You must always start at the beginning of a list to get anywhere (property 4).

Linked lists are sequential, which means that you can get to any element in a list you want, but in order to do so, you must start at the very beginning and work through the list one element at a time until you find what you are looking for. Again, the concept of the linked list is inextricably bound to the idea of pointers. We can represent a linked list as follows:

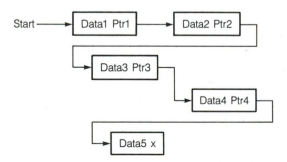

To get around in a list, you start with the first element and follow the pointers. In the above example, you begin with a special pointer (in this case Start), which indicates where the list originates. Going to the location pointed to by Start, you can access your first data element, which, in this case, is Data1. Attached to Data1 is another pointer, which shows you where the *next* data element is. You continue to follow pointers, one element after another, in the sequence described. You cannot skip around; the only way you can get where you are going is by following the trail of pointers. Eventually, you get to a pointer (indicated by an x here) that doesn't point to anything. This means you have reached the end of the list.

Although this method may seem laborious, it is really no different from following a road map from one place to another. In addition (and this is a great advantage of the linked list), you can easily order, insert, and delete list elements as you desire. (Such operations are much more difficult to do using an array.) For example, if you were keeping track of the names and phone numbers of the people in your bridge club, a list would be ideal. You could keep it in alphabetical order, and any time a new member joined, his or her name could be inserted so that the entire list remained in order. If someone left, the name could be deleted. At all times the length of the list would correspond exactly to the number of persons in it, thus wasting no space or effort.

13-4 Queues

The next data structure we will look at is the **queue,** often referred to as a line (like standing in line). In this data structure, elements are added at one end and taken off at the other end. The quintessential example of a queue can be found in a theater ticket line. Elements (in this case people) are added at the back (the queue forms in the rear) and taken off in the front (when tickets are bought). Thus, a queue is said to be a FIFO structure, which means First In, First Out. (The first person in line is the first to get a ticket, and the last person in line is the last to get one.)

As with linked lists, queues can shrink and grow. However, they can only grow from the back and shrink from the front. A typical queue can be represented as

Queue Forms

Queue Elements Removed

Data3 — Data2 — Data1

13-5 *Stacks*

The **stack** is a data structure characterized by the fact that the only element that can be accessed is the one at the very top. A common example of a stack is the cafeteria plate dispenser, where you can only take (access) the very top plate. As with linked lists and queues, the size of a stack is dynamic and may shrink (plates can be removed) or grow (the dishwasher can add more plates).

The only way that an element inside a stack can be accessed is by first removing all of the elements above it. A stack has one very interesting property: things come *off* the stack in exactly the opposite order that they are placed *on* it. For example, consider the cafeteria plate dispenser mentioned above. Let's assume that we have four plates of different colors, as follows:

Red Blue Green Yellow

Further, suppose that they are placed on the stack in this order. The resulting stack of dishes would look like this:

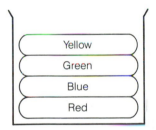

As the plates are removed, the first one off is the Yellow plate, which was the *last* one on. The next plate removed would be the Green one, followed by the Blue, and then the Red plate. The order in which they were removed would be

Yellow Green Blue Red

This order is exactly *opposite* from the way the plates were placed on the stack in the first place! Because of this property, a stack is said to be a LIFO structure (Last In, First Out). Stacks can be useful particularly in implementing procedure and function calls (recursive and otherwise). Recall that you must return from subprogram calls in exactly the opposite order that you entered them, so a stack is the mechanism by which you can accomplish this.

13-6 *Trees*

As was true for arrays, linked lists may also exist in higher dimensions. The only higher-dimensional linked list typically encountered, however, is the two-dimensional list structure called a **tree.** One example of a tree is the family tree, wherein the complex relationships across generations can be visually expressed, as in the following:

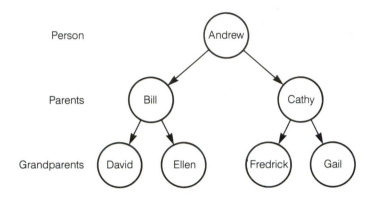

Even here, pointers are used to connect the various elements.

13-7 *Records*

In our introduction to linked lists, we said that each element of a given list contains data and a pointer to the next element of the list. Apparently, each list element is itself a composite of at least two separate items: the actual data and the pointer to the next node. In order to construct a linked list, therefore, we must be able to somehow combine a pointer and data into a list element. How can we do this?

A typical list element is an example of yet another data structure: the **record.** A record is a collection of related fields, where a **field** is an individual data item. The fields of a given record *need not* all be (and in fact rarely would be) of the same type. Suppose, for example, that we wanted to construct a linked list of payroll records. We could define a payroll record as follows:

Payroll Record

Name	Field 1 (String)
Salary	Field 2 (Real)
Exemptions	Field 3 (Integer)
Next	Field 4 (Pointer)

This record is made up of many kinds of data: string, real, integer, and pointer. (Field 4 points to the next element in the list.) A typical linked list of such records would look like this:

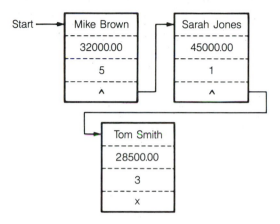

Each record can be accessed as a unit, or any of the fields within a given record can be accessed individually.

There is a marked similarity between the *record* data structure presented here and the conceptual components we discussed concerning files in Chapter 7. Don't be confused. The *record* structure is a way of storing data in the computer's main memory, whereas the concepts discussed in Chapter 7 deal with auxiliary storage.

13-8 *Files*

This is actually a good place to reintroduce files, this time in a new context. In Pascal a file is actually a type of data structure. In Chapter 7 we examined text files, which are most often used in conjunction with external storage devices. Strictly speaking, however, in Pascal files may be of any type and may make use of internal memory or external storage. The primary characteristic of a file is that its size is not fixed and that it may grow indefinitely. (Of course, sooner or later, a physical limit will be reached, but the Pascal language does not limit the size of a file.)

Recall also from Chapter 7 that we conceptualized a text file as being made up of records. However, since a record usually means the record data structure in Pascal, text files in this language are said to be composed of **lines.** The concepts, however, remain valid, and the term *record* is sometimes used to refer to a line in a Pascal text file. The context in which the terms are used invariably makes the meaning clear.

13-9   *Sets*

A **set** is an unordered collection of objects. The primary function of a set is to collect objects and to then determine whether various items are in the set. This technique can simplify a number of tasks, for example, how you determine whether an input symbol is a letter of the alphabet or a digit. You can define one set that contains letters of the alphabet and another that contains digits. Then when you input a character, you may ask whether or not it is in one or the other of these sets and in this simple way make the determination. A discussion of sets is presented in Appendix B.

13-10   *Operations*

Having examined a number of data structures, let's next look at the kinds of operations frequently carried out on these structures. Not all operations are appropriate to every structure, and some structures make certain operations much easier than others. However, the study of data structures is related to the operations on these structures, which are as follows:

1. Traversal

2. Insertion

3. Deletion

4. Searching

5. Sorting

Traversal. This operation means going through the entire collection of elements that make up the data structure and, sooner or later, doing something with each one. For example, if a data structure consists of a list of patients in a hospital, their room numbers, and their diagnoses, then a simple traversal could be used to print out the information for each patient.

Insertion. The insertion operation involves adding a new element to the collection. In the hospital example, if a new person were to be admitted, that person's name (and corresponding data) would be inserted into the list of hospital patient names.

Deletion. As you might expect, deletion is the opposite of insertion and permits elements to be removed from a list. In the hospital example, we would delete a patient's name from the list if that patient was discharged from the hospital.

Searching. Trying to find a specific element in the collection is what constitutes a search. For example, we may want information on one of the patients in our hospital. To locate a specific element, we need a **key,** which is a data item (such as a name or social security number) that can be compared to corresponding data items in the collection. In this case the patient's name would be an appropriate key. We would go through the list of names until (1) we found a patient name that matched the key, at which point we would know we've got the right patient; or (2) we could determine that the patient's name was not in the list. Searching *can* be done via traversal, but usually a somewhat more sophisticated method is used.

Sorting. As we mentioned in Chapter 6, sorting means to rearrange a collection of items into some kind of order. We could arrange the names of our hospital patients into alphabetical order, for example.

In general, these operations work together. Searching can be greatly simplified by having the data elements already in order. But then, sorting usually involves a great deal of searching! However, some data structures are self-organizing in the sense that they are ordered as soon as they are constructed. Also, deleting an object from a collection often requires finding it first, which of course involves searching.

As another example, reconsider the problem of finding the median in a group of scores. We could input the scores individually, *insert* them into an appropriate data structure, *sort* them, and finally *search* for the median.

SUMMARY

We introduced in this chapter the concept of data structures as organized collections of data elements and then went on to discuss specific data structures. We pointed out an analogy between this chapter and Chapter 8 on control structures. We may extend the analogy further by noting that data structures have other characteristics in common with structured programs. They may be hierarchical (that is, nested), and there may be relationships among the various levels and elements.

We are now ready to move on to a detailed study of data structures and their uses. In Chapter 14 we discuss arrays and go on in Chapter 15 to examine how the operations of searching and sorting are carried out with arrays. In Chapter 16 we look at list-type structures (linked lists, queues, and stacks), and then finally in Chapter 17 we discuss trees, the two-dimensional list structure.

EXERCISES

CONCEPTS

1. Define or explain the following terms:

Array	Random access
Array element	Record structure
Array name	Searching
Data structure	Set
Deletion	Sorting
Dynamic structure	Stack
Field	Static structure
File	String
Global property	Subscript
Index	Subscripted variable
Insertion	Traversal
Linked list	Tree
Matrix	Vector
Primitive	
Queue	

2. Explain the differences between array structures and list structures.

3. Explain how the concept of structure applies to data as well as to programs.

TOOLS

4. Indicate what type of data structure would be appropriate for each of the following:

a. A department store wants to keep sales figures for each of its ten departments.

b. A collection of five fifth-degree polynomials is to be stored by way of their respective coefficients.

c. Multiple-choice exams are to be graded.

d. The salesmen whose total sales for the month are the largest are to be listed.

e. Two matrices are to be multiplied.

f. Form letters must be typed up.

g. The frequency of words used in a text are to be counted.

h. Titles in a library are to be managed.

i. Railroad cars are to be attached to the correct trains.

j. Multiple terminals are to be attached to a single processor.

k. Recursive subroutine calls are to be kept track of.

l. Information concerning the date and time documents are to be created and distributed is needed.

m. Class lists are to be maintained.

14

Arrays:

A Fundamental Data Structure

We begin our detailed examination of data structures by looking at the most versatile and widely used of all data structures, the array. As we indicated in the last chapter, an array is a collection of data items in which each individual element can be accessed by relative location. Thus, we can obtain any element at any time provided only that we know its relative position. This capability allows us a great deal of ease and flexibility when working with large amounts of data.

There is so much that can be done with arrays that we are going to dedicate two chapters to them. This first chapter will begin with an explanation of how to set up arrays in one dimension and will demonstrate their use with some very common and typical applications. We will then look at the very special case of one-dimensional packed arrays of character (strings), so that text and word processing can become a part of our repertoire. Next, we will study parallel arrays, where several arrays containing different kinds of data work together in concert. After we look at parallel arrays, we will use arrays of records to present an equivalent but alternative representation. We will finally end this chapter by looking at arrays of two dimensions.

We will continue in Chapter 15 by examining the operations of searching and sorting in conjunction with arrays. These operations are widely used in computer science, so we will look at the large number of standard algorithms that exist for searching and sorting arrays.

For now, however, let's consider problems that make use of simple one-dimensional arrays.

14-1   *One-Dimensional Arrays*

Let's start with a problem that is fairly easy to solve using arrays but is quite difficult to solve without them. We will carry out a complete program development process for this example.

The Percent Problem

The organization Help Our Wonderful Legislators (HOWL) retains figures on the total contributions it makes to its favorite politicians, whose number can vary between zero and twenty-five. The organization would like to convert, at any given time, the actual contribution dollar amounts for each candidate to a percent of total contributions.

STEP I: UNDERSTAND THE PROBLEM

We want to take a list consisting of the total dollar value of contributions made to each candidate and convert each contribution to an equivalent percent of the total contribution amount. Input is to consist of the list of contributions, and the output should consist of a similar list expressed as percents. Essentially, the program must convert the actual dollar amounts to percents.

However, there is a slight complication. Since we want a percent, we need to divide each of the actual amounts by the sum of all the amounts. We cannot compute the total, however, until we have added up all the amounts! This leaves us with two choices: either we retain the original amounts for use in the percent computation or we read the original amounts a second time after they have been totaled. Obviously, we don't want to have to read in the same data twice, so we need some way to retain the original dollar amounts after they have been read in the first time. Arrays make it possible to do just that.

STEP 2: PLAN THE SOLUTION

We begin our top-down development process by writing a very general solution, namely,

```
Input the original amounts
Total them up
Compute the percent of the total for each amount
```

Since we are going to be working with a large number of contributions, we obviously need a loop. And we can use the old familiar method of the running total to get the sum of all the contributions easily. Changing our algorithm accordingly yields

```
Input the original amounts and total them up
    Total ← 0
    For as many amounts as we have Do
        Read Amount
        Total ← Total + Amount
Compute the percent of the total for each amount
```

Although this gives us our total, it does not permit us to retain the values for later conversion to percents. To do so, we must make use of an array. This technique involves reading each contribution into an *array element* as the loop progresses. The process is similar to that introduced in the last chapter, where we printed out an array of exam scores. We simply use a variable index that changes by one at each loop iteration. Thus, each time a `Read` is carried out, the data will go into a different array element. This can be expressed as follows:

```
Input the original amounts and total them up
    Total ← 0
    Index ← 0
    While there are amounts remaining to be read Do
        Index ← Index + 1
        Read Amount[Index]
        Total ← Total + Amount[Index]
Compute the percent of the total for each amount
```

Note that we must manually increment the array index each time through; other than that, this is a straightforward input loop. The only other thing we need to consider is how to recognize the end of the incoming values. Since the input consists of contribution amounts, it would be logical to store them in a file and have the program access the file. Consequently, it's appropriate to use an EOF loop here. Incorporating this into the algorithm gives us

Input the original amounts and total them up
    Total ← 0
    Index ← 0
    While not EOF (Contributions) Do
        Index ← Index + 1
        Read Amount[Index] from Contributions
        Total ← Total + Amount[Index]
Compute the percent of the total for each amount

This loop counts the number of contributions in the file as it reads them into the array and adds them up. We thus have the added benefit of knowing exactly how many data values we will be working with for the duration of the program! We can make this explicit by adding one more line to the algorithm:

    Input the original amounts and total them up
1.   Total ← 0
2.   Index ← 0
3.   While not EOF (Contributions) Do
4.   Index ← Index + 1
5.   Read Amount[Index] from Contributions
6.   Total ← Total + Amount[Index]
7.   NumItems ← Index
    Compute the percent of the total for each amount

Before we go any further, let's trace through the first seven lines of this algorithm to make sure we understand what's happening. This is also an opportune time to look a little more closely at external files. Let's assume that the contributions file has the following data in it:

Contributions File
→   38.00
    100.00
    25.00
    ⟨eof⟩

The symbol → marks the position of the *next* data item waiting to be read by the program and in Pascal is called the **file window.** The symbol ⟨eof⟩ represents a special character that marks the end of the file and is called, naturally enough, the **end-of-file marker.** At this point the contributions file is ready to be used for input.

When we begin carrying out the instructions of the algorithm, all memory locations are undefined:

```
Total  :  x       Index  :  x       Amount            NumItems  :  x
                                       1  :  x
                                       2  :  x
                                       3  :  x
                                       4  :  x
```

For the sake of this trace, we show only four array elements in Amount, all of which are undefined at this point. After we execute line 1 and line 2, both Total and Index will have values, and memory will look like this:

```
Total  :  0       Index  :  0       Amount            NumItems  :  x
                                       1  :  x
                                       2  :  x
                                       3  :  x
                                       4  :  x
```

When we get to line 3, things become a little more interesting. We must determine whether or not we are at the end of the file. Since the file window is pointing to a data element (rather than pointing to ⟨eof⟩), we *do* have some data. This means that we have *not* reached the end of the file, the logical expression of the While loop is true, and we enter the loop. The first instruction inside the loop (line 4) says to increment Index. Doing so yields memory values of

```
Total  :  0       Index  :  1       Amount            NumItems  :  x
                                       1  :  x
                                       2  :  x
                                       3  :  x
                                       4  :  x
```

Next, line 5 says to read a data item from the file and place the value so obtained into location Amount[Index]. To which location does that correspond? Index has a value of 1; therefore, we mean the *first* element of Amount. Placing the input value in the correct location results in the following memory picture:

```
Total  :  0       Index  :  1       Amount            NumItems  :  x
                                       1  :  38.00
                                       2  :  x
                                       3  :  x
                                       4  :  x
```

Notice that on completion of the Read instruction at line 5, *the data file itself has changed* and now can be represented as

Contributions File
```
      38.00
→    100.00
      25.00
    <eof>
```

We are now at line 6, which says to tally `Amount[Index]` into `Total`. Carrying this out, we get

```
Total   : 38.00    Index : 1    Amount           NumItems   :   x
                                 1   :   38.00
                                 2   :   x
                                 3   :   x
                                 4   :   x
```

We have now completed the last loop instruction; therefore, we return to line 3 to test the loop condition again. As we just saw, another data item is being pointed to in the file, and therefore we will enter the loop a second time. `Index` is incremented at line 4, giving us

```
Total   : 38.00    Index : 2    Amount           NumItems   :   x
                                 1   :   38.00
                                 2   :   x
                                 3   :   x
                                 4   :   x
```

At line 5 again, we are instructed to read `Amount[Index]`. However, since `Index` now has a value of 2, the input data is stored at the *second* element of `Amount`. Even though the element to be read in line 5 is always indicated as `Amount[Index]`, *it corresponds to an entirely different storage location each time through the loop.* After completing the `Read` instruction at line 5, memory looks like this:

```
Total   : 38.00    Index : 2    Amount           NumItems   :   x
                                 1   :   38.00
                                 2   :   100.00
                                 3   :   x
                                 4   :   x
```

And the file looks like this:

Contributions File
```
      38.00
     100.00
→     25.00
    <eof>
```

The newly read-in value is then tallied in line 6, and memory becomes

```
Total   : 138.00   Index : 2    Amount              NumItems   :   x
                                 1  :   38.00
                                 2  :  100.00
                                 3  :    x
                                 4  :    x
```

Having completed the second iteration, we return to line 3 to make the test another time. Again, since the file has additional data, we pass the test and reenter the loop at line 4. Completing the instruction in that line, we have in memory

```
Total   : 138.00   Index : 3    Amount              NumItems   :   x
                                 1  :   38.00
                                 2  :  100.00
                                 3  :    x
                                 4  :    x
```

We are once again at line 5, where we do another Read, this time to Amount[Index], which is the *third* element in the array. Completing the Read, memory becomes

```
Total   : 138.00   Index : 3    Amount              NumItems   :   x
                                 1  :   38.00
                                 2  :  100.00
                                 3  :   25.00
                                 4  :    x
```

And the file looks like this:

Contributions File
```
     38.00
    100.00
     25.00
→    <eof>
```

We then move on to line 6, where the tallying process continues:

```
Total   : 163.00   Index : 3    Amount              NumItems   :   x
                                 1  :   38.00
                                 2  :  100.00
                                 3  :   25.00
                                 4  :    x
```

This completes the loop for the third time, and we return once again to the test at the beginning of the While loop. This time, however, when we check for EOF, we find that the file window is indeed pointing to the end-of-file marker <eof>. Therefore, the While test fails, and we continue on with the algorithm at line 7. Note that the fourth element of the array *remains undefined*. Since the end-of-file condition was detected, another `Read` is *not* carried out, and memory remains unchanged from the most recent configuration.

We are instructed, at line 7, to compute `NumItems`. The final memory picture then becomes

```
Total  : 163.00   Index : 3    Amount          NumItems  :  3
                                1  :  38.00
                                2  : 100.00
                                3  :  25.00
                                4  :   x
```

At this point in the algorithm, we have read in all the values from the file, computed their sums, recorded their values, and counted them as well. Not bad for only seven lines! And this algorithm will work for *any* number of items, not just the three used here.

We are now ready to continue developing the algorithm. Actually, there's really not much left to do. We just need to go through the entire array and convert each contribution amount to a percent. We can even use a counted loop, since we now know exactly how many elements there are. Making this adjustment yields the following complete algorithm:

Input the original amounts and total them up
    Total ← 0
    Index ← 0
    While not EOF (Contributions) Do
        Index ← Index + 1
        Read Amount[Index] from Contributions
        Total ← Total + Amount[Index]
    NumItems ← Index
Compute the percent of the total for each amount
    For Index ← 1 to NumItems Do
        Percent ← Amount[Index] / Total × 100
        Write 'Percent for politician' Index 'is' Percent

The second part of this algorithm simply divides each contribution by the total contribution (to generate the correct fraction) and then multiplies by 100 to make it a percent.

STEP 3: CODE THE SOLUTION

We now have everything we need to code the final solution except the knowledge of how to declare an array. It turns out, however, that there is no such type as *array* in Pascal; every array declaration is considered a distinct data type. Therefore, we need some way of defining array types. In essence, we must expand the data types available for our use. If the standard types of `Real`, `Integer`, `Char`, and `Boolean` are not sufficient for our needs, then in Pascal we may define new types. This flexibility is one of the things that makes Pascal so useful. We will next find out how to define and declare array types.

To define new array types, we must augment the declarations section of our program as follows:

```
declaration-section → constants
                      types
                      variables
```

Prior to this chapter, we utilized only constants and variables, but now we see that it is also possible to define new data types in the declaration section of a program. Such definitions must come between the constant and variable declarations. Type declaration is done as follows:

```
types → type type-definition-list
      | nil
```

A type definition list, as we have come to expect of all such syntax lists, is a collection of type definitions. A type definition may be expressed as

```
type-definition → array-type-definition
```

where

```
array-type-definition → identifier = array[lower..upper] of type;
```

At this point, we will discuss the method used to define array types only. There are in fact many other types that can be defined, and we will see more of these further on in this chapter and in Appendix A.

The identifier mentioned in the array type definition corresponds to the name you wish to give to the array type. The word "array" is required. The words "lower" and "upper" correspond to the lowest allowed index to the array (frequently, but not always, 1) and the highest allowed index to the array (which corresponds to its size if the lower bound is 1). The "type" in the definition means the type of data that the array is intended to hold. If we want, for example, we can define an array type of integers to hold 100 student identification numbers as follows:

```
Type StudentIDs = Array [1..100] of Integer;
```

This statement only *defines* the appropriate array type. We have not as yet actually *declared* any variables to be of this type. However, once a new type has been defined it can be used in the declaration section of the program to declare variables exactly as the standard Pascal types of Real, Integer, Char, and Boolean can be used. If we actually want an array of this type, it must subsequently be declared in the Var section of the program as, for example,

```
Var ID : StudentIDs;
```

The above declares an array with the name ID, which can contain 100 student identification numbers.

Let's look at a couple more examples of array definition and declaration before going on with the HOWL example. Suppose we have a program that requires us to shuffle around 12 letter codes, 100 integer IDs, and two real arrays of 250 elements each. Appropriate arrays for this could be generated as follows:

```
Type LetterCodes = Array [1..12] of Char;
     Idents = Array [1..100] of Integer;
     Measurements = Array [1..250] of Real;
Var  Code : LetterCodes;
     ID : Idents;
     Length, Mass : Measurements;
```

Now let's return to the HOWL problem. We can define the necessary array type as

```
Type DollarAmounts = Array [1..25] of Real;
```

Then we can declare an actual array of this type as

```
Var Amount : DollarAmounts;
```

Given this, it is a simple task to convert our algorithm to a valid Pascal program. The final result is shown in Figure 14-1. Observe that we have included all the statements necessary for the program to read the contribution amounts from an external file.

STEP 4: CHECK OUT THE PROGRAM

A sample run, with a listing of the input file, is shown in Figure 14-2. Note that the conversions work properly.

STEP 5: DOCUMENT

The program is quite well documented.

Figure 14-1

Program That Converts Contributed Dollar Amounts to Percents

```
HOWL.PAS

1    Program HOWL (Contributions, Output);
2
3    (*
4       This program reads in actual dollar amount contributions for
5       political candidates and converts them to a percent of the
6       total of all contributions.
7    *)
8
9    Type DollarAmounts = Array [1..25] of Real;
10
11   Var  Total,                    (* Total amount of ALL contributions *)
12        Percent                   (* Percent equivalent of one contribution *)
13               : Real;
14        Index,                    (* Index to array elements *)
15        NumItems                  (* Total number of contributions *)
16               : Integer;
17        Amount  : DollarAmounts;  (* The array of contribution amounts *)
18
19        Contributions : Text;     (* File containing the contributions *)
20
21   BEGIN
22
23   (* Ready the input file *)
24
25       Reset (Contributions);
26
27   (* Get the individual values and compute the total *)
28
29       Total := 0;
30       Index := 0;
31       While not EOF (Contributions) Do
32         Begin
33           Index := Index + 1;
34           Readln (Contributions, Amount[Index]);
35           Total := Total + Amount[Index]
36         End;
37       NumItems := Index;
38
39   (* Compute the percent of the total for each amount *)
40
41       Writeln;
42       Writeln ('Summary of Percent Contributions to HOWL Candidates');
43       Writeln;
44
45       For Index := 1 to NumItems Do
46         Begin
47           Percent := Amount[Index] / Total * 100.0;
48           Writeln ('The percent contributed to politician ', Index:1,
49                    ' is ', Percent:5:1, '%.')
50         End
51
52   END.
```

Figure 14-2

Input File Data for and Sample Output from the HOWL Program

```
$ type contribu.dat

100.00
250.00
 25.00
500.00
  7.50
 10.00
 50.00


$ run howl

Summary of Percent Contributions to HOWL Candidates

The percent contributed to politician 1 is 10.6%.
The percent contributed to politician 2 is 26.5%.
The percent contributed to politician 3 is  2.7%.
The percent contributed to politician 4 is 53.1%.
The percent contributed to politician 5 is  0.8%.
The percent contributed to politician 6 is  1.1%.
The percent contributed to politician 7 is  5.3%.
```

Multiple-Choice Exam Grading

To reinforce our understanding of arrays, let's consider another example. Suppose we work in an academic setting and want to automate the grading of multiple-choice exams. The input will consist of (1) the number of questions on the exam, (2) the number of choices per question, (3) the correct answers to the exam (the key), and (4) the answer sheets for all the students who take the exam. The output for each student is to consist of (1) the score adjusted for guessing (computed as Number Right − Number Wrong / (Number of Choices − 1)), (2) the score computed as a percent, and (3) a copy of the actual student answers, along with the corrected answers to the missed questions. We would also like to compute the average score for the class as a whole.

STEP 1: UNDERSTAND THE PROBLEM

Let's start by defining precisely what we want the input and output to look like. Typical input data should consist of

```
10                      (* The number of questions on the exam *)
 4                      (* The number of choices per question; in this
                           case there would be 4 labeled A,B,C,D *)
BCADABDACB              (* The answer key *)
1234 BCAABBDBCB         (* The first student's ID and answers *)
5678 ACADABBACB         (* The second student's ID and answers, etc. *)
```

We must consider, also, *how* we wish to supply the input data to the program. Since, as in the contribution problem we just solved, we are dealing with potentially large quantities of data, it is again a good idea to place this data into a file.

As far as output goes, we want something like the following:

```
Student ID = 1234
Responses : B B   D E A B C D E
Corrections A   C
Number Right = 8
Number Wrong = 1
Raw Score = 7.75
Final Score = 77.50 %
```

Corrected answers are marked directly below any incorrect (or blank) answers. The reason for permitting a blank response is so if a student really doesn't know the answer to a question, he or she can just leave it blank and avoid the penalty for guessing. (A blank response is not counted either right or wrong.)

STEP 2: PLAN THE SOLUTION

We can write our first algorithm as follows:

Read the number of questions
Read the number of choices
Read the Key
For each student Do
   Count this student
   Read (and echo) ID number
   Read (and echo) answer sheet
   Compare each answer to the correct answer
   Tally up the number of right and wrong answers
      and make appropriate corrections
   Compute raw score
   Compute percent score
   Do the output for the student
   Add score to a running total for the class
Compute the average for everybody

Note that we "echo" the student's ID and answer sheet. This simply means that we print out this data while it is being read in. This is useful, since the data is *not* coming from the keyboard, and we will therefore never see it unless we do echo it.

The complete solution to this problem is going to involve, naturally, arrays and loops. Adding these (and attendant details) to our algorithm gives

```
Read NumQuestions
Read NumChoices
Read the Key
   For q ← 1 to NumQuestions Do
      Read Key[q]
TotalOfExams ← 0
Student ← 0
While not EOF Do
   Student ← Student + 1
   Read ID
   Write ID
   Read answer sheet
      For q ← 1 to NumQuestions Do
         Read Answer[q]
         Write Answer[q]
   Correct answers
      NumRight ← 0
      NumWrong ← 0
      For q ← 1 to NumQuestions Do
         If Answer[q] = Key[q] then
            NumRight← NumRight + 1
         Else if Answer[q] = Blank then
            (* Don't count this one either way *)
            Write Key[q] (* Print out a correction *)
         Else
            NumWrong ← NumWrong + 1
            Write Key[q] (* Correction, again *)
   Compute raw score
      RawScore ← NumRight − NumWrong / (NumChoices − 1)
   Compute percent score
      Percent ← RawScore/NumQuestions × 100
   Do the output for the student
      Write ID, NumRight, NumWrong, RawScore, Percent
   Add score to the running total
      TotalOfExams ← TotalOfExams + Percent
Compute the average for everybody
   Average ← TotalOfExams / Student
   Writeln Average
```

We have included explicitly in this algorithm the necessary initializations and running totals. Also, we have used an EOF loop here, since we are planning to read the input data from a file. We have not made this explicit in the algorithm because we already know that all of the input will be read from a file and thus adding file references to the algorithm will just clutter things up. For the sake of consistency, let's also use a file to collect the output, so that we can print it out at our leisure. With these additional considerations in mind, we can proceed to the next step of the development process.

STEP 3: CODE THE SOLUTION

This algorithm is sufficiently detailed to permit us to convert it to Pascal. The solution requires the use of two arrays, one for the key and one for the student answers. Other than that, it is straightforward, and the result is shown in Figure 14-3. Note the details by which the corrected answers are printed out underneath the student answers in lines 103, 106, and 110. If a student response is blank or wrong, the correct answer is printed out in line 106 and 110. If the student answer is right, blanks are printed out (line 103) so that the corrected answers line up with the incorrect answers. Also notice that we print to the standard file *output* in lines 52, 53, and 80 so that whoever is running the program can monitor its progress.

One other item concerns the character variable Skip, which is defined in line 31 and used in line 83. Since, in the data file, we have a blank space between the student ID and the list of answers, we must remove this blank before we begin to read the actual answers. This is accomplished by Skip; the blank is simply read into Skip and then discarded.

Figure 14-3

Program That Grades Multiple-Choice Exams

MC.PAS

```
 1    Program MC (Exams, Results, Output);
 2
 3    (*
 4        This program grades multiple-choice exams. It will grade an
 5        arbitrary number of exams containing an arbitrary number
 6        of questions having an arbitrary number of choices.
 7        A correction for guessing is made. The program also
 8        computes the class average for the exam.
 9    *)
10
11    Const Blank = ' ';    (* Blank student response (guessing) *)
12
13    Type Answers = Array [1..100] of Char; (* Array definition for the
14                                              answer key and student
15                                              answers *)
16
17    Var  NumQuestions, NumChoices, NumRight, NumWrong : Integer;
18         RawScore, Percent : Real;
19
```

Figure 14-3 continued

```
20        SumOfScores : Real;     (* Sum of the scores for the whole class *)
21        Student : Integer;      (* Counts up the number of students as
22                                   their exams are read in and graded *)
23
24        Average : Real;         (* Class average *)
25
26        Key, Answer : Answers;(* The answer key and student answer arrays *)
27        q : Integer;            (* Index to the answers and key as grading
28                                   of an individual exam proceeds *)
29
30        ID : Integer;           (* Student ID number *)
31        Skip : Char;            (* So we can place a blank between the
32                                   student ID and his answers *)
33
34        Exams : Text;           (* File containing the exams to be graded.
35                                   It must be constructed as follows:
36                                     Record 1 : Number of questions on exam
37                                     Record 2 : Number of choices per question
38                                     Record 3 : Answer key
39                                   The remaining records consist of the
40                                   student answers, one record per student.
41                                   They should contain the student ID followed
42                                   by a space followed by the student's answer.
43                                   (NOTE - a blank response to a question
44                                   indicates a decision on the part of a
45                                   student not to choose an answer and
46                                   thus not be penalized for guessing *)
47
48        Results : Text;         (* File to which the graded results are sent *)
49
50   BEGIN
51
52      Writeln ('MULTIPLE CHOICE EXAM GRADING PROGRAM');
53      Writeln;
54
55   (* Ready the files *)
56      Reset (Exams);
57      Rewrite (Results);
58
59   (* Get the info on the exam and report what we're doing *)
60      Readln (Exams, NumQuestions);
61      Readln (Exams, NumChoices);
62
63      Writeln (Results, 'MULTIPLE CHOICE EXAM RESULTS');
64      Writeln (Results);
65      Writeln (Results, 'The exam contains ', NumQuestions:1,' questions.');
66      Writeln (Results, 'Each question has ', NumChoices:1,' possible choices.');
67      Writeln (Results);
68
69   (* Read in the key *)
70      For q := 1 to NumQuestions Do
71          Read (Exams, Key[q]);
72      Readln (Exams);
73
74   (* Now go through all the exams *)
75      SumOfScores := 0;
76      Student := 0;
77      While not EOF (Exams) Do
```

Figure 14-3 continued

```
78          Begin
79            Student := Student + 1;
80            Writeln ('Grading #', Student:1);
81
82          (* Read in the answers for this student and echo them to Results *)
83            Read (Exams, ID, Skip);
84            Writeln (Results, 'Student ID = ',ID:1);
85            Write (Results, 'Responses : ');
86            For q := 1 to NumQuestions Do
87              Begin
88                Read (Exams, Answer[q]);
89                Write (Results, Answer[q]:2)
90              End;
91            Readln (Exams);
92            Writeln (Results);
93
94          (* Grade the answers and print any corrections to Results *)
95            Write (Results, 'Corrections ');
96            NumRight := 0;
97            NumWrong := 0;
98            For q := 1 to NumQuestions Do
99              Begin
100               If Answer[q] = Key[q] then          (* Got this one right *)
101                 Begin
102                   NumRight := NumRight + 1;
103                   Write (Results, ' ')             (* Print a blank if his answer is OK *)
104                 End
105               Else if Answer[q] = Blank then       (* No penalty for guessing *)
106                   Write (Results, Key[q]:2)        (* Print out the correct answer *)
107               Else
108                 Begin
109                   NumWrong := NumWrong + 1;        (* He missed this one *)
110                   Write (Results,Key[q]:2)         (* Print out the correct answer *)
111                 End
112             End; (* Grading this student *)
113           Writeln (Results);
114
115         (* Compute raw score *)
116           RawScore := NumRight - NumWrong / (NumChoices - 1);
117
118         (* Compute percent score *)
119           Percent := RawScore / NumQuestions * 100.0;
120
121         (* Write this to Results *)
122           Writeln (Results, 'Number Right = ', NumRight:1);
123           Writeln (Results, 'Number Wrong = ', NumWrong:1);
124           Writeln (Results, 'Raw Score    = ', RawScore:4:2);
125           Writeln (Results, 'Final Score  = ', Percent:4:2,' %');
126           Writeln (Results);
127
128         (* Accumulate totals for the class *)
129           SumOfScores := SumOfScores + Percent
130
131       End; (* Of the exams loop *)
```

Figure 14-3 continued

```
132
133   (* Compute and print out the results for the class as a whole *)
134      Writeln (Results, 'There were ',Student:1,' students who took the exam.');
135      Average := SumOfScores / Student;
136      Writeln (Results, 'The class average is ', Average:4:2,'.');
137      Writeln (Results)
138
139   END.
```

STEP 4: CHECK OUT THE PROGRAM

A copy of the test (input) file, along with the output produced when the program is run, is shown in Figure 14-4. The output is correct and neat.

STEP 5: DOCUMENT

The program is well written and well documented.

Figure 14-4

Test Run and Output from the Program that Grades Multiple-Choice Exams

```
$ type exams.dat

14
 5
ABCDEABCDEABCD
1024 ABCDEABCDEABCD
9077 BBCDEABCDEABCD
1122  BCDEABCDEABCD
3214 BADCEBBDEACBEA
6666  BCDEA CDEABCD
1234 ABCC ABBDD   CD

$ run mc

MULTIPLE CHOICE EXAM GRADING PROGRAM

Grading #1
Grading #2
Grading #3
Grading #4
Grading #5
Grading #6

$ type results.dat

MULTIPLE CHOICE EXAM RESULTS
```

Figure 14-4 continued

```
The exam contains 14 questions.
Each question has 5 possible choices.

Student ID = 1024
Responses :  A B C D E A B C D E A B C D
Corrections
Number Right = 14
Number Wrong = 0
Raw Score    = 14.00
Final Score  = 100.00 %

Student ID = 9077
Responses :  B B C D E A B C D E A B C D
Corrections  A
Number Right = 13
Number Wrong = 1
Raw Score    = 12.75
Final Score  = 91.07 %

Student ID = 1122
Responses :    B C D E A B C D E A B C D
Corrections  A
Number Right = 13
Number Wrong = 0
Raw Score    = 13.00
Final Score  = 92.86 %

Student ID = 3214
Responses :  B A D C E B B D E A C B E A
Corrections  A B C D   A   C D E A   C D
Number Right = 3
Number Wrong = 11
Raw Score    = 0.25
Final Score  = 1.79 %

Student ID = 6666
Responses :    B C D E A   C D E A B C D
Corrections  A           B
Number Right = 12
Number Wrong = 0
Raw Score    = 12.00
Final Score  = 85.71 %

Student ID = 1234
Responses :  A B C C   A B B D D     C D
Corrections        D E     C   E A B
Number Right = 8
Number Wrong = 3
Raw Score    = 7.25
Final Score  = 51.79 %

There were 6 students who took the exam.
The class average is 70.54.
```

Let's now examine another use of arrays. One of the most important properties of arrays is that their individual elements may be accessed *directly*. In other words, if you know the subscript for an array element, it is possible to get and use the element as a matter of course without having to worry in the slightest about *how* to pull it out. For example, if you want to use array element three, you need only reference it and you've got it! In order to demonstrate this, let's generate an example.

Grade Distribution

Consider the problem of computing final letter grades and a grade distribution from a list of the final numerical scores earned by each student in a class. We would like to take each student's score, convert it to a letter grade, and then tally up the number of students receiving each possible letter grade (in this case, A, B, C, D, and F).

STEP 1: UNDERSTAND THE PROBLEM

We are to input a sequence of student averages for a whole semester and determine from this (1) the letter grade for each person, (2) the total number of each letter grade given out (the grade distribution), and (3) the class average based on a 4.00 grading system. We will assume that we have a generous instructor who assigns grades as follows:

Range	Letter Grade	Grade Points
100–88	A	4
87–75	B	3
74–62	C	2
61–49	D	1
48–0	F	0

STEP 2: PLAN THE SOLUTION

How can we solve this? One method would be to use nested If/Else structures to determine the grade and then keep a running tally for each grade. For example, we might do it this way:

Read Ave
Total ← Total + 1
If Ave ≥ 88 then

```
    Write 'Grade is A'
    nA ← nA + 1
Else if Ave ≥ 75 then
    Write 'Grade is B'
    nB ← nB + 1
Else if Ave ≥ 62 then
    Write 'Grade is C'
    nC ← nC + 1
Else if Ave ≥ 49 then
    Write 'Grade is D'
    nD ← nD + 1
Else
    Write 'Grade is F'
    nF ← nF + 1
```

We would at this point have the complete grade distribution and could then compute the final grade point of the class from

ClassGPA ← (nA × 4 + nB × 3 + nC × 2 + nD × 1) / Total

This solution really doesn't seem too unreasonable. However, consider a similar problem: What if we wanted to categorize salaries in brackets from a low of five thousand to a high of one hundred thousand in increments of five thousand? This would involve twenty separate categories! Writing the solution using the nested If/Else would require a great deal of repetitive code.

The fact that we are keeping large amounts of similar data suggests that we might somehow use arrays (surprised?). So let us define an array for the grading problem as

```
  nGrade
0
1
2
3
4
```

In this case the array (called nGrade) will have five elements, with the subscripts ranging from 0 to 4, corresponding to the letter grades of F through A. If we want to tally a B, for example, we will use nGrade[3]. Interestingly, the subscript to the array just happens to correspond to the point value for that grade!

Our next problem is, How do we determine the subscript, given a semester average? We could use the nested If/Else structure, but we want to explore other alternatives. In fact it is possible to *compute* the correct array subscript from the semester average. (These subscripts are called, not surprisingly, **computed subscripts**.) A certain amount of trial and error is the best way to determine a formula that works. A good place to start is to list the grades and their corresponding indexes, for example,

If the Average is	Then we want this subscript
100	4
99	4
. . .	
89	4
88	4
87	3
86	3
. . .	
75	3
74	2
. . .	
62	2
61	1
. . .	
49	1
anything else	0

As you can see, we want the various possible grades to be converted to equivalent grade points that just happen to be the correct index to the tally array! After a little work, we discover that the following formula correctly computes the index:

$$\text{GradePoint} \leftarrow \text{Trunc } \frac{\text{Semester Average} - 36}{13}$$

Trunc is the truncation function, 13 is the number of units difference between any adjacent grade categories, and 36 would normally be the bottom of the F range. (Since zero is actually the bottom, we will need to adjust the final algorithm to take this into account.) One other consideration: if all of the numbers are integers and we use integer division, we won't need to use the Trunc function, since integer arithmetic takes care of that automatically. (Recall from Chapter 4 that dividing integers produces a quotient with no fractional part.)

We can, therefore, write the main part of the algorithm as follows:

```
Read Ave
Total ← Total + 1
GradePoint ← (Ave − 36) / 13
If GradePoint < 0 then
    Grade Point ← 0
Write 'Grade is', LetterGrade[GradePoint]
nGrade[GradePoint] ← nGrade[GradePoint] + 1
```

In six lines we have done what our previous nested If/Else algorithm did in seventeen lines! And if we were solving this type of problem with, say, the twenty categories mentioned in the salary problem, we would *still* need only six lines!

We have added a second array here called LetterGrade. This array is intended to be an array of Char (not packed!), which contains the letter equivalent of each grade, specifically,

```
    LetterGrade
0     'F'
1     'D'
2     'C'
3     'B'
4     'A'
```

Once we have input all the data, the grade distribution will automatically reside in the array. A simple loop is all that is needed to print out the entire distribution. We can write this all out thus:

```
For GradePoint ← 4 downto 0 Do
    Write LetterGrade[GradePoint], nGrade[GradePoint]
```

Again, note the simple elegance with which we can output this information. Larger distributions will require no more effort to output.

What about the last part of the problem, namely, computing the overall average? This is even simpler and consists of the following statements:

```
ClassGPA ← 0
For GradePoint ← 0 to 4 Do
    ClassGPA ← ClassGPA + GradePoint × nGrade[GradePoint]
ClassGPA ← ClassGPA / Total
```

This is simple and elegant; also, it will work just as well with our salary problem!

Let's finish this example by filling in the remaining details and putting all of our algorithm sections together. Again, since we are dealing with large amounts of data that take some time to enter, it is appropriate to use a file for the input data. Consequently, we can use an EOF loop. We must also initialize totals and the letter-grade array. Including these steps gives us the following complete algorithm:

```
LetterGrade[0] ← 'F'
LetterGrade[1] ← 'D'
LetterGrade[2] ← 'C'
LetterGrade[3] ← 'B'
LetterGrade[4] ← 'A'
Total ← 0
For GradePoint ← 0 to 4 Do
    nGrade[GradePoint] ← 0
While not EOF Do
    Read Ave
    Total ← Total + 1
    GradePoint ← (Ave − 36) / 13
    If GradePoint < 0 then
        GradePoint ← 0
    Write Total, Ave, LetterGrade[GradePoint]
    nGrade[GradePoint] ← nGrade[GradePoint] + 1

For GradePoint ← 4 downto 0 Do
    Write LetterGrade[GradePoint], nGrade[GradePoint]

Class GPA ← 0
For GradePoint ← 0 to 4
    Class GPA ← ClassGPA + GradePoint × nGrade[GradePoint]
ClassGPA ← ClassGPA / Total
Write ClassGPA
```

STEP 3: CODE THE SOLUTION

In order to correctly code this algorithm, we need to deal with two arrays, one of which (LetterGrade) essentially contains constants. However, the coding is quite direct, and the solution can be written easily. The results are shown in Figure 14-5.

STEP 4: CHECK OUT THE PROGRAM

A sample data file and output are shown in Figure 14-6. The letter grades and distribution are all computed properly.

STEP 5: DOCUMENT

The program is easily read and understood.

Figure 14-5

Program to Convert Exam Scores to Letter Grades and Generate the
Grade Distribution, Using Computed Subscripts and Direct Array
Access

GPA.PAS

```
1    Program GPA (GradeBook, Output);
2
3    (*
4       This program determines the letter grade corresponding to the
5       average for each student processed. It also generates the
6       grade distribution and class average.
7    *)
8
9    Type Grades = Array [ 0..4 ] of Char;
10        Totals = Array [ 0..4 ] of Integer;
11
12   Var  Ave,                     (* Current student's average *)
13        GradePoint,              (* Point equivalent of the letter grade for
14                                    the current student's average *)
15        Total                    (* Counter of students processed *)
16              : Integer;
17        LetterGrade : Grades;    (* Letter grades A,B,C,D,F *)
18        nGrade : Totals;         (* Running totals for each letter grade *)
19        ClassGPA : Real;
20
21        GradeBook : Text;        (* Input file containing the student averages *)
22
23   BEGIN
24     (* Get the input file ready *)
25     Reset (GradeBook);
26
27     (* Set up the LetterGrade array *)
28     LetterGrade[0]:='F'; LetterGrade[1]:='D'; LetterGrade[2]:='C';
29     LetterGrade[3]:='B'; LetterGrade[4]:='A';
30
31     (* Generate headings for the output *)
32     Writeln ('Student  Average  Grade');
33     Writeln;
34
35     (* Compute the grades and tally them up *)
36     Total := 0;
37     For GradePoint := 0 to 4 Do
38         nGrade[GradePoint] := 0;
39     While not EOF (GradeBook) Do
40       Begin
41         Readln (GradeBook, Ave);
42         Total := Total + 1;
43         GradePoint := (Ave - 36) DIV 13;
44         If GradePoint < 0 then
45             GradePoint := 0;
46         Writeln (Total:4, Ave:8, LetterGrade[GradePoint]:9);
47         nGrade[GradePoint] := nGrade[GradePoint] + 1
48       End;
49
50     (* Output the grade distribution *)
51     Writeln;
52     Writeln('Grade distribution is as follows:');
53     For GradePoint := 4 downto 0 do
54         Writeln('    ',LetterGrade[GradePoint],nGrade[GradePoint]:5);
```

Figure 14-5 continued

```
55
56        (* Compute the class average *)
57        ClassGPA := 0;
58        For GradePoint := 0 to 4 Do
59            ClassGPA := ClassGPA + GradePoint * nGrade[GradePoint];
60
61        ClassGPA := ClassGPA / Total;
62        Writeln;
63        Writeln ('The GPA for the class is ',ClassGPA:5:2)
64
65    END.
```

Figure 14-6

Test Data and Sample Run of the GPA Program

```
$ type gradeboo.dat

65
50
99
88
87
75
74
62
61
20
49
100
91
85
75
63
86
87
80

$ run gpa

Student Average Grade

    1       65      C
    2       50      D
    3       99      A
    4       88      A
    5       87      B
    6       75      B
    7       74      C
    8       62      C
    9       61      D
   10       20      F
   11       49      D
   12      100      A
```

Figure 14-6 continued

```
13      91      A
14      85      B
15      75      B
16      63      C
17      86      B
18      87      B
19      80      B


Grade distribution is as follows:
    A       4
    B       7
    C       4
    D       3
    F       1

The GPA for the class is 2.53
```

14-2 *Strings*

We now turn our attention to a very special category of one-dimensional array, the packed array of Char, commonly referred to as the string. As we mentioned in Chapter 13, the properties of strings are different enough from ordinary arrays that strings are usually considered separate data structures. However, in Pascal there is a strong overlap such that strings can be used to do some "string" things (such as print the strings out as a unit) and some "array" things (such as work with the individual characters that make the strings up). Strings are the fundamental data structures concerned with character manipulation and word processing. Up to this point, for example, we have been unable even to input words, names, or text of any kind. This will now change.

Since strings can be considered a data type in their own right and since individual data structures can also, in Pascal, be considered data types, we may view strings as being another data type. In fact, for many applications it is quite useful to consider strings as separate data types. Let us examine strings from this perspective.

We have defined the term "string" (Chapter 13) as an ordered sequence of characters. A string may in fact be an individual character or several characters. These are some examples of strings:

```
'This is a string.'
'and so is this a string'
'25.67'
```

```
`  `

`$%^&*`

`Michael M. Morgen`
```

A string is represented as a sequence of characters enclosed between single quotes. These are called **string constants,** and, in fact, we have been using them in our output all along. Especially note the constant `25.67`, which looks a lot like a numeric real constant. You cannot, however, do arithmetic operations of any kind with such a constant. It is a *string constant*, and can only be used in such a way as to work with the individual characters that make up the string.

Now let's introduce the **string variable,** which allows us to input, manipulate, and output strings in a way similar to how we have been reading and writing numeric, Boolean, and character data. Like any other values, strings can also be assigned and compared. Even so, it is still possible to access an individual character of a string just as if it was a regular array. Therefore, you have the advantages of strings (unit access) with the advantages of arrays (element access)—and all in the same structure!

Let's look at an example.

Mail Order Refunds

Suppose you work in the accounting department of a mail-order firm. Part of your job is to generate refund checks for dissatisfied customers. The input consists of the customer's name, the catalog number of the item being refunded, a brief description of the item, and the amount of the refund. The output should consist of a check for the correct amount and a voucher explaining what the refund is for.

STEP 1: UNDERSTAND THE PROBLEM

This problem consists of merely getting the input and generating an appropriate check and voucher. Let's begin by designing the output. We want it to be aesthetic, so let's make the check and voucher look like this:

MAILBOX USA   No 1664

                               Nov 3, 1985

PAY TO THE ORDER OF Harold P. Sloane

THE AMOUNT $12.75

Refund for APPLE CORE PEELER

Catalog No. 154-302B

That's really all we need. Let's go on to the next step.

STEP 2: PLAN THE SOLUTION

We know the input and we know the output, so we're ready to generate the algorithm. A look at the output, however, shows that we need to consider dates and check numbers in addition to the data we have already considered. (In this case we are gaining a little more understanding at a later stage.) Taking dates and check numbers into account, we can write the following algorithm:

Read Date
Read Check Number
For as many customers as need refunds Do
    Read Customer Name
    Read Catalog Number
    Read Item Description
    Read Refund Amount

    Write Out the Check
       Write Check Number, Date, Customer Name,
          Refund Amount,
          Item Description, Catalog Number

    Increment the Check Number

Notice that, although we must provide the very first check number, the program takes care of numbering after that.

    The next thing we have to do is decide on a looping mechanism. Let's use an input controlled loop. If we enter the word STOP in place of the customer name, we will terminate the loop. Restructuring in this fashion and adding a few more details, we get the following algorithm:

Read Date
Read Check Number
Read Customer Name
While Customer Name ≠ 'STOP' Do
    Read Catalog Number
    Read Item Description
    Read Refund Amount

    Write Out the Check
       Write Check Number, Data, Customer Name,

Refund Amount,
Item Description, Catalog Number
Check Number ← Check Number + 1
Read Customer Name

That's all there is to it.

STEP 3: CODE THE SOLUTION

We are now ready to code, but of course we need to see how strings are defined and declared in Pascal. In order to do this, we expand our type definition category in the following manner:

type-definition → array-type-definition
| string-type-definition

string-type-definition →
identifier = **packed array[1..upper] of char;**

This is very similar to a standard array definition, except that the word "packed" must be used, the lower limit must be 1, and the type must be Char. The upper limit essentially determines the length of the string, that is, the number of characters it may contain. As with regular arrays, the type must first be defined and *then* a variable of that type declared.

A simple example is in order. Suppose we have a program that needs to read words of five and twenty-five characters. Appropriate strings may be declared as follows:

```
Type LongWord = Packed Array [1..25] of Char;
     ShortWord = Packed Array [1..5] of Char;

Var  Fancy : LongWord;
     Plain : ShortWord;
```

We would then be able to use Fancy and Plain as variables in the very same way we use numeric variables.

Let's now return to the refund example. In order to carry out its solution, we will need several strings corresponding to the date, the catalog number, the catalog description, and the customer name. For the sake of simplicity, we will only define strings of one length, as follows:

```
Type String = Packed Array [1..20] of Char
Var Date, CatalogNo, CustomerName, Item Description : String;
```

As we said, strings may be treated just like any other standard data type. Unfortunately, there is one bizarre twist on all this. Even though it is possible to write, assign, and compare strings as a unit, in standard Pascal *you cannot read a string as a unit:* it must be input *one character at a time.* Not only that but you are not even permitted to input a string element, such as

```
Readln (String[k]);  ← This is not allowed!
```

In order to read a string, you must input a single character and then assign it to the correct packed array element.

That's the bad news. The good news is that it's just about impossible to find a version of Pascal that's mean enough to really make you input strings this way. At the very least, most current Pascal compilers *will* let you input a string element, and often they will also permit you to input an entire string as a unit. Find out what you can get away with on your system. As a compromise, in this text we will input strings via a procedure that reads in string elements character by character. In fact, we will use the following procedure:

Procedure ReadString (String)
  For k ← 1 to length Do
    Read (String[k])
  Readln

This would be equivalent to the (nonstandard) Pascal

```
Readln (String);
```

Another very unfortunate result of all this is that such a procedure will work only on strings of a single length. If you have several strings of *different* lengths, you will need a different procedure to input each kind of string. We will live with this limitation in this text, but see what you can do at your own installation.

In any event, we are now in a position to complete programming for this example. The final result is shown in Figure 14-7 and includes the ReadString procedure. One important point: notice in line 26 that the most recently input name is compared with the constant string 'STOP'. In Pascal, strings must be of the same length to be compared or assigned. Consequently, the actual string constant must have the correct number of blanks appended to it so that it will be the same size as the string variable.

STEP 4: CHECK OUT THE PROGRAM

A sample run, using typical data, is shown in Figure 14-8. The output actually looks quite nice, and the program works properly.

Figure 14-7

Program That Uses Strings to Write Refund Checks

REFUNDS.PAS

```
1    Program REFUNDS (Input, Output);
2
3    (*
4        This program generates refund checks.
5    *)
6
7    Type String = Packed Array [1..20] of Char;
8
9    Var CheckNo : Integer;
10       RefundAmount : Real;
11       Date, CatalogNo, CustomerName, ItemDescription : String;
12
13   Procedure ReadString (Var S:String);
14     Var k : Integer;
15     Begin
16       For k:=1 to 20 Do
17           Read (S[k]);
18       Readln
19     End;
20
21
22   BEGIN (* Doing Refunds *)
23     Write('Enter today''s date :                 '); ReadString (Date);
24     Write('Enter beginning check number :       '); Readln (CheckNo);
25     Write('Enter customer name, ''STOP'' to end : '); ReadString (CustomerName);
26     While CustomerName <> 'STOP                ' Do
27       Begin
28           Write('Enter catalog number :   '); ReadString (CatalogNo);
29           Write('Enter item description : '); ReadString (ItemDescription);
30           Write('Enter refund amount :    '); Readln (RefundAmount);
31
32           (* Write Out the Check *)
33           Writeln;
34           Writeln('MAILBOX USA                            No ',CheckNo:4);
35           Writeln('                                      ',Date);
36           Writeln;
37           Writeln('PAY TO THE ORDER OF ',CustomerName);
38           Writeln('THE AMOUNT            $',RefundAmount:7:2);
39           Writeln;
40           Writeln('Refund for  ',ItemDescription);
41           Writeln('Catalog No. ',CatalogNo);
42           Writeln;
43           Writeln('***');
44           Writeln;
45
46           CheckNo := CheckNo + 1;
47           Write('Enter customer name :   '); ReadString (CustomerName)
48       End (* Refund Loop *)
49
50   END.
```

Figure 14-8

Test Run of the REFUNDS *Program*

```
$ run refunds

Enter today's date :                    May 1, 1986
Enter beginning check number :          1024
Enter customer name, 'STOP' to end : Harold P. Brown
Enter catalog number :   541-774B
Enter item description : Apple Core Peeler
Enter refund amount :    12.75

MAILBOX USA                             No 1024
                                        May 1, 1986

PAY TO THE ORDER OF Harold P. Brown
THE AMOUNT            $   12.75

Refund for  Apple Core Peeler
Catalog No. 541-774B

***

Enter customer name :    Linda Lowery
Enter catalog number :   A34-119C
Enter item description : Bell Shaped Lampshad
Enter refund amount :    36.95

MAILBOX USA                             No 1025
                                        May 1, 1986

PAY TO THE ORDER OF Linda Lowery
THE AMOUNT            $   36.95

Refund for  Bell Shaped Lampshad
Catalog No. A34-119C

***

Enter customer name :    Thomas Jones
Enter catalog number :   MPL3-5576
Enter item description : Polka Dot Phone
Enter refund amount :    29.99

MAILBOX USA                             No 1026
                                        May 1, 1986

PAY TO THE ORDER OF Thomas Jones
THE AMOUNT            $   29.99

Refund for  Polka Dot Phone
Catalog No. MPL3-5576

***

Enter customer name :    Jaine Dowe
Enter catalog number :   PPQ456-009N1
Enter item description : Self-Propelled Refri
Enter refund amount :    239.95
```

Figure 14-8 continued

```
MAILBOX USA                       No 1027
                                  May 1, 1986

PAY TO THE ORDER OF Jaine Dowe
THE AMOUNT             $ 239.95

Refund for  Self-Propelled Refri
Catalog No. PPQ456-009N1

***

Enter customer name :  STOP
```

STEP 5: DOCUMENT

Done, for all practical purposes.

14-3 *Parallel Arrays*

For many applications, a single array is insufficient to hold all the data needed to solve a problem. Consider, for example, the grocery store check-out problem introduced in Chapter 8, where we wanted to process items brought to the check-out counters. For each shopper this involved getting the name and price of all the items bought and then computing the subtotal, tax, and total amount due. To carry out this task, we needed to access the name and price of each item purchased. The concept of arrays can be used as part of the solution for this problem, because if we store the name and price information for each item in appropriate arrays, we can then randomly access this information for any product. In fact, this is how the problem is handled in many grocery stores. Each item for sale in the store is marked with a unique UPC (universal product code), which is read by the cash register and used as an index to the required information. For example, the information could be stored as

UPC	Item	Cost
1	ASPARAGUS SMALL	0.57
2	ASPARAGUS LARGE	0.85
3	BROCCOLI SMALL	0.55
4	BROCCOLI LARGE	0.82
. . .		

35	MILK QT	0.75
36	MILK HALF GAL	1.45
37	MILK GAL	1.85

We could read in the UPC for each item purchased (either by entering it manually or using a laser reader) and then go directly to the information for that item. We would know (from the first array) the name of the item and (from the second array) its cost. The subtotal could be computed with ease.

The two arrays used here, namely `Item` and `Cost`, are called **parallel** or **related arrays,** because corresponding elements in each array have known relationships with each other. Item 35 above, for example, consists of a quart of milk, and the price of that very same item is $0.75. There is an obvious parallel relationship between the arrays; that is, each UPC is used to reference a unique (and corresponding) name and price.

Grocery Check Out

Let us pursue this by writing a program that simulates the functioning of a grocery check-out counter.

STEP 1: UNDERSTAND THE PROBLEM

We will use arrays to store information on items for sale at our store and use direct access to pull out the names and prices as we check out a customer's purchases.

STEP 2: PLAN THE SOLUTION

A general algorithm can be written as follows:

Set up the arrays
   Read all the products and their prices into arrays

While there are customers Do
   While there are items to be checked for this customer Do
      Read UPC of item
      Fetch the name and cost of the item
      Keep a running total of the customer's items
      Output the name and cost of the item
   Calculate the Tax
   Calculate the Total

    Output the SubTotal
    Output the Tax
    Output the Total
    Keep a running total of the day's receipts
Output the day's total receipts

To carry out this process, we will need two arrays: one for the item name (let us call it Item) and one for the item cost (we'll call that Cost). The first statement of our general algorithm merely puts the arrays all together. A reasonable way to do this is to read the names and associated costs of all items for sale at our store from an external file. Moving the name and cost information from the file to the arrays can be done easily and efficiently by way of an end-of-file (EOF) loop. Since the number of items sold by the store can change from one day to the next, let's count the number of items as we read them in from the external file. Adding these details to the algorithm gives us

Set up the arrays
    UPC $\leftarrow$ 0
    While not EOF (StockFile)
        UPC $\leftarrow$ UPC + 1
        Read Item[UPC], Cost[UPC]
    StockSize $\leftarrow$ UPC
While there are customers Do
    While there are items to be checked for this customer Do
        Read UPC of item
        Fetch the name and cost of the item
        Keep a running total of the customer's items
        Output the name and cost of the item
    Calculate the Tax
    Calculate the Total
    Output the SubTotal
    Output the Tax
    Output the Total
    Keep a running total of the day's receipts
Output the day's total receipts

The next (outer) loop for the customers is also relatively easy. Let's use an input controlled loop to handle this. We will define a code such that the letter "C" means to process another customer and the letter "E" means to quit for the day and print out the total sales.

We can do something similar for the sales (inner) loop. We will use a sentinel value loop that will continue to read UPCs for the customer's purchases until a 0 is entered as the UPC by the checker.

The only other thing left to do is to fill in the calculation details. Remember that we are using direct access to get the information we need for the purchases. Adding these and the two loop details gives us the following complete algorithm:

```
Set up the arrays
    UPC ← 0
    While not EOF (StockFile) Do
        UPC ← UPC + 1
        Read Item[UPC], Cost[UPC]
    StockSize ← UPC

GrandTotal ← 0
Read FunctionCode
While FunctionCode = 'C' Do
    SubTotal ← 0
    Read UPC
    While UPC > 0 Do
        SubTotal ← SubTotal + Cost[UPC]
        Write Item[UPC], Cost [UPC]
        Read UPC
    Tax ← SubTotal × TaxRate
    Total ← SubTotal + Tax
    Write SubTotal
    Write Tax
    Write Total
    GrandTotal ← GrandTotal + Total
    Read FunctionCode
Write GrandTotal
```

We have included here all the initializations necessary to keep the running totals.

STEP 3: CODE THE SOLUTION

We now have a sufficiently detailed algorithm to permit coding the solution. We next must decide the maximum number of items our store will sell in order to define our arrays, but that's really all there is left. The complete solution is shown in Figure 14-9. Note that we have used an array of strings to formulate the Item array. Since strings can be considered a valid data type, there is nothing unusual or exciting about defining a whole array of them. In line 18 we have defined the data type Names to be string and then declared an array called Products, which is an array of strings. This is a perfectly valid way to structure data.

There are two other items of note about this program. First, look at the procedure ReadString, which begins at line 40. This procedure reads strings from a file. Consequently, the name of the file being read must be explicitly passed as a parameter to the procedure.

The second point concerns lines 77 through 84, where we have decided to check for a valid UPC. Since the store carries only a limited number of items, which we count when we read the names and costs from the file, we can easily make sure that the UPC does not exceed the number of items for sale.

Figure 14-9

Simulation, Using Direct Array Access, of an Automated Grocery
Check Out System

GROCER.PAS

```
 1    Program GROCER (StockFile, Input, Output);
 2
 3    (*
 4        This program simulates a POS terminal at a grocery store. All
 5        items stocked by the store have a UPC code associated with them.
 6        As customers go through the check out, the UPC code for each
 7        purchase is entered, and the program uses direct array access to get
 8        the name and price of each item. The names and prices of the items
 9        sold in the store are kept in a file called StockFile, and these
10        are read in at the beginning of the program.
11    *)
12
13    Const TaxRate  = 0.0525;
14          MaxStock = 100;            (* Maximum number of items that the store
15                                        can sell *)
16          Tab = `        `;          (* Tab: move output over 6 spaces *)
17
18    Type  Names  = Packed Array[ 1..10 ] of Char;    (* Definition of string *)
19
20          Products = Array[ 1..MaxStock ] of Names;   (* Array definitions *)
21          Prices   = Array[ 1..MaxStock ] of Real;
22
23    Var   Item : Products;           (* Array of item names *)
24          Cost : Prices;             (* Array of item prices *)
25          UPC  : Integer;            (* UPC code, used as the index to the
26                                        Item and Cost arrays *)
27          StockSize : Integer;       (* Current number of items being sold
28                                        by the store *)
29
30          GrandTotal, Total, SubTotal, Tax : Real;
31
32          FunctionCode : Char;       (* Code that determines whether we
33                                        are to process another customer or
34                                        end for the day. The codes are C
35                                        and E, respectively *)
36
37          StockFile : Text;          (* External file containing names and
38                                        prices of items sold in the store *)
39
40    Procedure ReadString ( Var TheFile : Text;
41                           Var S : Names);
42       Var K : Integer;
43       Begin
44         For K := 1 to 10 Do
45             Read (TheFile, S[K])
46       End;
47
48
49    BEGIN
50
51    (* Read all the products and their prices *)
52
53       Reset (StockFile);
54       Writeln (`Reading Names and Prices`);
```

Figure 14-9 continued

```
55      UPC := 0;
56      While not EOF (StockFile) Do
57        Begin
58          UPC := UPC + 1;
59          ReadString (StockFile, Item[UPC]);
60          Readln      (StockFile, Cost[UPC])
61        End;
62      StockSize := UPC;
63      Writeln (UPC:1, ' Products Read In');
64      Writeln;
65
66    (* Initialize and Go for Today! *)
67      GrandTotal := 0;
68      Write ('C/E > '); Readln (FunctionCode);
69      Writeln;
70      While FunctionCode = 'C' Do
71        Begin
72
73          SubTotal := 0;
74          Write ('> '); Readln (UPC);
75          While UPC > 0 Do
76            Begin
77              If UPC <= StockSize then
78                  Begin
79                    SubTotal := SubTotal + Cost[UPC];
80                    Writeln (Tab, Item[UPC],' ',Cost[UPC]:5:2)
81                  End
82                Else
83                    Writeln ( Tab, '** Invalid UPC **');
84              Write ('> '); Readln (UPC)
85            End; (* Purchases Loop *)
86
87          Tax := SubTotal * TaxRate;
88          Total := SubTotal + Tax;
89          Writeln (Tab, 'Subtotal   ',SubTotal:5:2);
90          Writeln (Tab, 'Tax        ',Tax:5:2);
91          Writeln (Tab, 'Total      ',Total:5:2);
92          Writeln;
93          Writeln (Tab, 'Thank You!');
94          Writeln;
95          Writeln;
96
97          GrandTotal := GrandTotal + Total;
98          Write ('C/E > '); Readln (FunctionCode);
99          Writeln
100
101       End; (* Customer Loop *)
102
103     Writeln;
104     Writeln ('Grand Total of Today''s Receipts is $', GrandTotal:8:2)
105
106   END.
```

STEP 4: CHECK OUT THE PROGRAM

An extended test run is shown in Figure 14-10. After the name and price information is read in at the beginning of the program, it's a simple matter to go through and check out customers just as in real life!

STEP 5: DOCUMENT

Done.

Figure 14-10

Test Run of the Grocery Check Out Program, Including a Listing of the File Containing the Names and Prices of the Items Sold

```
$ type stockfil.dat

MILK QT    0.82
MILK GAL   1.93
MILK CHOC  1.01
CHEDDAR    2.43
SWISS CHS  2.75
CRACKERS   3.09
COOKIES    2.17
CAN SODA   0.48
CANDY      0.35
HAM        0.67
TURKEY     0.65
CHICKEN    0.63
WHITE BRD  1.12
WHEAT BRD  1.20
RYE BREAD  1.25
CHIPS      1.09
PRETZELS   1.11
DOUGHNUT   0.36
FRITTER    0.54
MUSTARD    1.37
KETCHUP    1.50
SALT       0.33
PEPPER     0.45
APPLE      0.12
ORANGE     0.15


$ run grocer

Reading Names and Prices
25 Products Read In

C/E > C

> 1
      MILK QT         0.82
> 0
      Subtotal        0.82
      Tax             0.04
      Total           0.86

      Thank You!
```

Figure 14-10 continued

```
C/E > C

> 8
        CAN SODA        0.48
> 8
        CAN SODA        0.48
> 9
        CANDY           0.35
> 7
        COOKIES         2.17
> 0
        Subtotal        3.48
        Tax             0.18
        Total           3.66

        Thank You!


C/E > C

> 14
        WHEAT BRD       1.20
> 10
        HAM             0.67
> 11
        TURKEY          0.65
> 21
        KETCHUP         1.50
> 23
        PEPPER          0.45
> 24
        APPLE           0.12
> 25
        ORANGE          0.15
> 0
        Subtotal        4.74
        Tax             0.25
        Total           4.99

        Thank You!


C/E > C

> 4
        CHEDDAR         2.43
> 5
        SWISS CHS       2.75
> 6
        CRACKERS        3.09
> 3
        MILK CHOC       1.01
> 0
        Subtotal        9.28
        Tax             0.49
        Total           9.77

        Thank You!
```

Figure 14-10 continued

```
C/E > C

> 17
      PRETZELS       1.11
> 30
      ** Invalid UPC **
> 19
      FRITTER        0.54
> 8
      CAN SODA       0.48
> 0
      Subtotal       2.13
      Tax            0.11
      Total          2.24

      Thank You!


C/E > E

Grand Total of Today's Receipts is $   21.52
```

14-4 *Arrays of Records*

The use of parallel arrays as a way to hold extensive data together is but one possible technique we can use. Pascal allows us an alternate method: the **array of record.** Rather than keeping the related elements in separate arrays, only one array is used, but each element of the array is a record, so that the individual items become fields of the record. (Recall the discussion of records and fields from Chapter 13.) Let's explore this new method.

RECORDS AND FIELDS

Suppose we want to use the array of record technique to solve the grocery check-out example. Rather than defining a separate cost and item array, we could instead define a single array (called Item) made of records, each of which has a name field and a cost field. A schematic representation of such an array would be as follows:

	Item (an array)	
	Name	**Cost**
	(the first field)	**(the second field)**
Element 1	CAN SOUP	0.57
Element 2	CAN FRUIT	0.66

Element 3	MILK QT	0.82
Element 4	MILK GAL	1.93
. . .	. . .	. . .

A reference to the array element itself would still be the same, for example, `Item[UPC]`. However, in order to reference a specific field, its name must also be mentioned. In Pascal this is done by appending a field name to the record reference. If, for instance, we wanted to reference the cost field of the fourth record, we could do it this way:

```
Item[4].Cost
```

This would provide us with the cost of item 4. If we wanted the name of the fourth item, we could write

```
Item[4].Name
```

We get the same information and can access it just as easily as we can with parallel arrays. However, the use of record structures is a little more elegant.

Let us examine how to define record structures in Pascal. Essentially, we are generating a new data type; hence, we can expand our type definitions once again:

type-definition → array-type-definition
       | string-type-definition
       | record-type-definition

We can then define the record type as

record-type-definition → identifier = **record**
                       field-definitions
                end;

Here is a second example of the use of the `End` without a corresponding `Begin`. (The first instance was in the `Case` statement described in Chapter 10.) A field definition is simply

field-definition → identifier : type;

If we wanted to use an array of records with the grocery example (rather than parallel arrays), we could define the necessary data structure as follows:

```
Type String   = Packed Array[1..10] of Char;
     Product  = Record
                    Name : String;
                    Cost : Real
                End;
     ProductList = Array[ 1..20] of Product;
Var  Item : ProductList;
```

Note the use of nesting in these definitions. First, we define a String, then a Record that contains a string, then an Array that contains records containing strings.

Let's look at another example of record definitions. Suppose we want to represent objects in three-space (that is, the regular three-dimensional universe) by storing the coordinates of their vertices. For example, a cube might be represented by the coordinates as shown in Figure 14-11. An appropriate data structure could be defined thus:

```
Type Space3 = Record
                    X : Real;
                    Y : Real;
                    Z : Real
                End;
     Coordinates = Array [1..8] of Space3;
Var  Block1, Block2 : Coordinates;
```

Figure 14-11

Three-dimensional Block, Showing the Coordinates of Its Vertices,
with Each Vertex Numbered for Reference

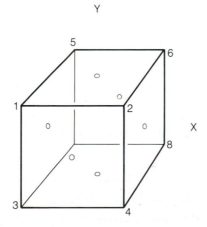

The coordinates of the fifth vertex of Block2 could then be referenced as

Block2[5]

The Z coordinate of the third vertex of Block1 would be referenced as

Block1[3].Z

Next, let's consider a problem where we can make good use of arrays of records.

Inventory Control

Suppose we are asked to develop an inventory control program. Inventory control involves keeping track of the quantity of items a company has on hand for sale at any given time. In order to keep the inventory information current, we must be able to access and alter the various items maintained in the store.

STEP 1: UNDERSTAND THE PROBLEM

Typical inventory control requires that the following operations be carried out:

1. Add items to the inventory
2. Remove items from the inventory
3. Display information about a particular item in the inventory
4. Compute the value of the entire inventory
5. Display the entire inventory

We begin by assuming that the information to be kept on each item is as follows:

Index number. An integer between 100 and 200
Catalog number. A five-character string
Description. A ten-character string
Retail cost. A real number (dollars and cents)

Wholesale cost. Another real number

Number in stock. An integer

This information can be neatly arranged within a record that contains six fields. The list of fields immediately above is, for all practical purposes, a full description of the record to be used. In fact we may at this point define the primary data structure as

```
Type ShortString = packed Array[1..5] of Char;
     LongString  = packed Array[1..10] of Char;
     Items = Record
                 CatalogNo : ShortString;
                 Description : LongString;
                 RetailCost : Real;
                 WholeSaleCost : Real;
                 NumInStock : Integer
             End;
     Inventory = Array [100..200] of Items;
Var  Stock : Inventory;
```

The type Inventory is an array of records, where the index may range from 100 to 200.

STEP 2: PLAN THE SOLUTION

Now that we understand what we're about to do and have defined the appropriate data structures, let's move on to writing an algorithm. Essentially, the inventory control process involves requesting a specific inventory function to be carried out and then carrying it out. We will begin with the most general algorithm, namely,

For as long as we want Do
  Input which function to be carried out
  Carry out that function

We can increase the detail by outlining the functions to be carried out:

Function Code	Function
A	Add item to inventory
R	Remove item from inventory
D	Display information about item
C	Compute the value of the inventory
T	Display entire inventory
X	Exit from the program

What we have here is an example of a **menu,** which is a list of the functions that the program can carry out. The person running the program chooses one of the functions, and it is then carried out. Filling in the loop details and explicitly referencing the menu, we can write

Display the menu
Input Function Code
While FunctionCode ≠ 'X' Do
    Case Function Code of
  A Add Item
  R Remove Item
  D Display Item
  C Compute Value
  T Display All

  Display the menu
  Input Function Code

There is one other thing to consider: How do we get the initial inventory into the program so that we will have something to process? Let's read the initial inventory from an external file. Adding this to the algorithm gives us

Read the initial inventory from an external file
Display the menu
Input Function Code
While FunctionCode ≠ 'X' Do
    Case Function Code of
  A Add Item
  R Remove Item
  D Display Item
  C Compute Value
  T Display All

  Display the menu
  Input Function Code

This is perhaps the epitome of modularity! We can work on each function, including the main program, individually. Let's do just that and go through the procedures one at a time, developing their respective algorithms. To be absolutely correct procedurally, we should first code the main algorithm and test it and then design, code, and test each procedure. However, for the sake of simplicity, we will dispense with a detailed presentation and merely develop the subalgorithms and present the solution as a whole. (Don't worry; this example *was* in fact developed by using the full program development process.) Let's go ahead and look at each of the procedure algorithms in turn.

`DisplayMenu.` This produces "pretty" output. We simply need to display the possible choices and input whatever option was selected by the operator. The algorithm can be written as

```
Procedure DisplayMenu
    Write
        Select one of the following options
            A : Add an item
            R : Remove an item
            D : Display an item
            C : Compute value
            T : Display complete inventory
            X : Exit
    Write 'Enter option'
    Read Option
```

`AddItem.` Here we wish to add quantities of an item to the inventory. To do this we must request the index number of the item to be added, confirm the item, and then read the quantity added to the inventory and update the records. We also ought to check for the possibility that the index number that was entered might not correspond to an item, since it is likely that at least some of the index numbers from 100 to 200 will be undefined. (Let's assume that an item is undefined if it has a blank `CatalogNo`.) Taking all this into account, the procedure algorithm can be written as

```
Procedure AddItem
    Read the Index Number of Item
    For this Index Number Do
        If CatalogNo ≠ Blank then
            Write CatalogNo, Description
            Read Number to be Added
            NumInStock ← NumInStock + Number to be Added
            Write 'Addition confirmed'
        Else
            Write 'Invalid index'
```

Of special concern here is the use of the line "For this Index Number Do" in the procedure. What we mean by this is that for any associated and indented code, any reference to a record field implies that it is a field from the array element associated with the subscript `Index`. For example, when we say `Read CatalogNo`, what we *really* mean is that we want to read `Item[Index].CatalogNo`. This is a shorthand method of expressing the reference, and, in fact, Pascal has a method by which this can be done easily. (This will be discussed after a presentation of the subalgorithms.)

RemoveItem. This procedure takes items *out* of inventory (hopefully, items to be sold). However, we must not take out more items than we have on hand. An algorithm for this procedure can be written as

```
Procedure RemoveItem
    Read Index
    For this Index Do
        If CatalogNo ≠ Blank then
            Write CatalogNo, Description
            Read Number to be Removed
            If Number to be Removed ≤ NumInStock then
                NumInStock ← NumInStock − Number to be Removed
                Write 'Removal confirmed'
            Else
                Write 'Insufficient quantity on hand; not removed'
        Else
            Write 'Invalid index'
```

Note that, as in the previous procedure, we ensure that the item actually exists.

DisplayItem. Again, this can be written as a fairly straightforward algorithm:

```
Procedure DisplayItem
    Read Index
    For this Index Do
        If CatalogNo ≠ Blank then
            Write CatalogNo, Description,
                    RetailCost, WholesaleCost,
                    NumInStock
        Else
            Write 'Invalid index'
```

Again, we must ensure that an item exists before we try to print out any information about it.

ComputeValue. This procedure computes both the wholesale and retail values of the entire inventory. A simple loop will suffice:

```
Procedure ComputeValue
    TotalRetail ← 0
    TotalWholeSale ← 0
    For Index ← 100 to 200 Do
        For this Index Do
            TotalRetail ← TotalRetail + NumInStock × RetailCost
            TotalWholeSale ← TotalWholeSale + NumInStock × WholeSaleCost
    Write TotalRetail, TotalWholeSale
```

This requires any value of `NumInStock` other than those belonging to items already entered *to have an initial value of zero.* Since Pascal does not initialize values, we will have to include such an initialization routine in the main program.

`DisplayAll.` This procedure lists the entire inventory. Again, a simple counted loop will suffice:

```
Procedure DisplayAll
    For Index ← 100 to 200 Do
        For this Index Do
            If NumInStock > 0 then
                Write Index, CatalogNo, Description,
                    RetailCost, WholeSaleCost,
                    NumInStock
```

We do *not* print out the entire array, only those items that have some stock in inventory. This one, as the procedure above, requires that the `NumInStock` field be initialized to zero.

We have workable algorithms for each of the procedures and are therefore ready to move on to the next step.

STEP 3: CODE THE SOLUTION

We are almost ready to code the solution. We have algorithms for all of the procedures as well as for the main program, but there are two things we must do before we proceed. The first concerns the nature of the inventory array, and the second, a shortcut we can use in referencing the various fields of the individual array elements. (Recall the discussion just above.)

Let's look at the inventory array first. We have *not* indicated in any of the procedures that the actual inventory (the array `Stock`) is passed as a parameter to the various functions. Rather, we choose to reference the inventory array as global data, because each individual function of the inventory accesses exactly this same data. It would be much less efficient and even confusing to pass the same data to every procedure as an argument. In a sense, the array can be considered a **data base,** which means that it is a constant source of information that can be accessed by any part of the program. (We have here a second case in which it is appropriate to use global data; the first case was in the `CRAPS` program of Chapter 11; where the random number seed had to be global.)

THE WITH CONSTRUCT

Our second concern is with the elegance (or lack thereof) of the field references made in each of the procedures. For example, in the procedure `ComputeValue` we have written

For Index ← 100 to 200 Do
 For this Index Do
  TotalRetail ← TotalRetail + NumInStock × RetailCost
  TotalWholeSale ← TotalWholeSale + NumInStock × WholeSaleCost

Strictly speaking, what we mean is the following:

For Index ← 100 to 200 Do
 TotalRetail ← TotalRetail + Stock[Index].NumInStock ×
           Stock[Index].RetailCost
 TotalWholeSale ← TotalWholeSale + Stock[Index].NumInStock ×
           Stock[Index].WholeSaleCost

See how cumbersome this is?

However, we can remedy this by using a new Pascal construct, the With structure. This structure permits us to reference the fields of a record *without* having to explicitly state the record of interest. The syntax of the With structure is as follows:

with-structure → **with** record-identifier **do**
       statement

Within the scope of the With structure, you may reference any field of a record without mentioning which record it comes from. For example, we could rework our above algorithm as follows:

For Index ← 100 to 200 Do
 With Stock[Index] Do
  TotalRetail ← TotalRetail + NumInStock × RetailCost
  TotalWholeSale ← TotalWholeSale + NumInStock × WholeSaleCost

Notice how much easier this is to read and understand! Writing this in Pascal would look like

```
For Index := 100 to 200 Do
  With Stock[Index] Do
    Begin
      TotalRetail := TotalRetail + NumInStock * RetailCost;
      TotalWholeSale := TotalWholeSale +
                            NumInStock * WholeSaleCost
    End;
```

This is much better.

We are now ready to assemble the algorithm sections into a coherent whole and complete the conversion to Pascal. We include the With construct everywhere it can be usefully employed (as indicated in each algorithm section by the statement "For this Index Do"). The final result is shown in Figure 14-12. Although the program is rather extensive, its

Figure 14-12

*Completed Version of the Inventory Control Program, Including
Finished Procedures*

STOCKS.PAS

```
 1    Program STOCKS (InvList, Input, Output);
 2
 3    (*
 4        This program carries out inventory control. New items may be
 5        added to the inventory, and quantities of any existing items
 6        may be added to or subtracted from the inventory. The wholesale
 7        and retail value of the inventory may also be computed. The initial
 8        inventory is read from the file InvList.
 9    *)
10
11    Const First = 100;        (* Smallest permissible index number *)
12          Last  = 200;        (* Largest permissible index number *)
13
14          Blank = '     ';    (* Permits comparison of catalog number to
15                                   blank entry *)
16
17    Type ShortString = Packed Array[1..5] of Char;
18         LongString  = Packed Array[1..10] of Char;
19
20         Items = Record                      (* Information kept on each *)
21                    CatalogNo : ShortString;  (* item stocked in the inventory *)
22                    Description : LongString;
23                    RetailCost : Real;
24                    WholeSaleCost : Real;
25                    NumInStock : Integer
26                 End;
27         Inventory = Array [First..Last] of Items;
28
29    Var  Stock : Inventory;
30         FunctionCode : Char;
31         Index : Integer;
32
33         Skip : Char;         (* This permits skipping over a blank character
34                                  while reading the original inventory file *)
35
36         InvList : Text;      (* Inventory file *)
37
38
39    Procedure ReadString5  (Var FromFile:Text;
40                            Var S:ShortString);
41    (* This procedure reads a 5 character string from the inventory file *)
42    Var k : Integer;
43      Begin
44        For k := 1 to 5 Do
45            Read (FromFile, S[k])
46      End;
47
48    Procedure ReadString10 (Var FromFile:Text;
49                            Var S:LongString);
50    (* Same as above, except it reads 10 character strings *)
51    Var k : Integer;
52      Begin
53        For k:=1 to 10 Do
54            Read (FromFile, S[k])
55      End;
56
```

Figure 14-12 continued

```
57
58     Procedure DisplayMenu;
59     (* This procedure displays the menu options available to the user *)
60        Begin
61          Writeln;
62          Writeln ('Select one of the following options:');
63          Writeln ('   A   :   Add an item to the inventory');
64          Writeln ('   R   :   Remove an item from the inventory');
65          Writeln ('   D   :   Display an item');
66          Writeln ('   C   :   Compute retail and wholesale value of inventory');
67          Writeln ('   T   :   Display complete inventory');
68          Writeln ('   X   :   Exit');
69          Write   (' Enter your choice --> ')
70        End;
71
72
73     (* These next are the functions carried out by the inventory program *)
74
75     Procedure AddItem;
76     (* This procedure adds items to the inventory *)
77     Var Index, PlaceIn : Integer;
78
79        Begin (* AddItem *)
80          Writeln;
81          Write ('Enter index number : '); Readln (Index);
82          With Stock[Index] Do
83            If CatalogNo <> Blank then
84                Begin
85                  Writeln ('Catalog number : ',CatalogNo);
86                  Writeln ('Description    : ',Description);
87                  Writeln;
88                  Write   ('How many items to add? '); Readln (PlaceIn);
89                  Writeln;
90                  NumInStock := NumInStock + PlaceIn;
91                  Writeln ('Addition of ', PlaceIn,' items confirmed')
92                End
93            Else
94                Writeln('Invalid index number: please try again')
95        End; (* Add Item *)
96
97     Procedure RemoveItem;
98     Var Index, TakeOut : Integer;
99        Begin
100         Writeln;
101         Write('Enter index number : '); Readln (Index);
102         With Stock[Index] Do
103           If CatalogNo <> Blank then
104               Begin
105                 Writeln('Catalog Number : ',CatalogNo);
106                 Writeln('Description    : ',Description);
107                 Writeln;
108                 Write  ('How many items to remove? '); Readln (TakeOut);
109                 Writeln;
110                 If TakeOut <= NumInStock then
111                     Begin
112                       NumInStock := NumInStock - TakeOut;
113                       Writeln('Removal of ',TakeOut:1,' items confirmed')
114                     End
```

Figure 14-12 continued

```
115              Else
116                  Writeln('Insufficient quantity in stock: not removed')
117              End
118          Else
119              Writeln('Invalid index number: please try again')
120      End (* Remove Item *);
121
122  Procedure DisplayItem;
123  Var Index:Integer;
124      Begin
125          Writeln;
126          Write('Enter index number : '); Readln (Index);
127          With Stock[Index] Do
128              If CatalogNo <> Blank then
129                  Begin
130                      Writeln('Catalog Number    : ',CatalogNo);
131                      Writeln('Description       : ',Description);
132                      Writeln('Retail Cost        $',RetailCost:8:2);
133                      Writeln('Wholesale Cost     $',WholeSaleCost:8:2);
134                      Writeln('Quantity in Stock : ',NumInStock)
135                  End
136              Else
137                  Writeln('Invalid index number: please try again')
138      End (* Display Item *);
139
140  Procedure ComputeValue;
141  Var Index : Integer;
142      TotalRetail, TotalWholesale : Real;
143      Begin
144          Writeln;
145          TotalRetail := 0;
146          TotalWholesale := 0;
147          For Index := First to Last Do
148              With Stock[Index] Do
149                  Begin
150                      TotalRetail := TotalRetail + NumInStock * RetailCost;
151                      TotalWholesale := TotalWholesale + NumInStock * WholeSaleCost
152                  End;
153          Writeln('Total retail value is    $',TotalRetail:8:2);
154          Writeln('Total wholesale value is $',TotalWholesale:8:2)
155      End (* Compute Value *);
156
157  Procedure DisplayAll;
158  Var Index : Integer;
159      Begin
160          Writeln;
161          Writeln('Index Catalog Description  Retail  Wholesale Quantity');
162          For Index := First to Last Do
163              With Stock[Index] Do
164                  If NumInStock > 0 then
165                      Writeln (Index:4,'   ',CatalogNo,'  ',Description,'  ',
166                              RetailCost:8:2,'   ',WholeSaleCost:8:2,
167                              '   ',NumInStock:5)
168      End; (*DisplayAll *)
169
170
171  (* End of Procedures *)
172
173
```

Figure 14-12 continued

```
174    BEGIN
175
176       Writeln ('INVENTORY CONTROL PROGRAM');
177       Writeln;
178
179       (* Initialize NumInStock throughout the entire array *)
180
181       For Index := First to Last Do
182          With Stock[Index] Do
183             Begin
184                NumInStock := 0;
185                CatalogNo := Blank
186             End;
187
188       (* Read the complete inventory *)
189       Writeln ('Reading Inventory...');
190       Writeln;
191       Reset (InvList);
192       While not EOF (InvList) Do
193          Begin
194             Read (InvList, Index);
195             Read ( InvList, Skip );
196             With Stock[Index] Do
197                Begin
198                   ReadString5(InvList, CatalogNo);
199                   Read(InvList, Skip);
200                   ReadString10(InvList, Description);
201                   Readln(InvList, RetailCost, WholeSaleCost, NumInStock)
202                End (* with *)
203          End; (* Reading the file *)
204
205       DisplayMenu;
206       Readln (FunctionCode);
207       While FunctionCode <> 'X' Do
208          Begin
209                   Case FunctionCode of
210             'A' : AddItem;
211             'R' : RemoveItem;
212             'D' : DisplayItem;
213             'C' : ComputeValue;
214             'T' : DisplayAll;
215                   End; (* Case *)
216
217          DisplayMenu;
218          Readln (FunctionCode)
219          End (* While *);
220
221       Writeln ('End of Inventory Control Program' )
222
223    END.
```

natural modularity makes it very easy to put together. The differences that exist between the algorithms and the final code are primarily changes that make the output aesthetically pleasing. We have also used constants for the array sizes and limits. This program demonstrates quite well the use of arrays of records for direct access of information.

STEP 4: CHECK OUT THE PROGRAM

An extensive test run is shown in Figure 14-13. Note a couple of things. First, the external file from which the initial inventory is read does *not*

Figure 14-13

Test Run of the Completed Inventory Control Program

```
$ type invlist.dat

199 GU411 AM/FM RADI   95.95   75.00    4
101 R56YX SPARK PLUG    1.25    0.95   87
112 XX112 OIL FILTER    6.75    4.00   32
200 GBV01 TAPE PLAYR  119.99  100.00    7
133 R457W TIRE         57.00   40.00   60
102 MV030 QT 30W OIL    1.10    0.55  142
103 MV104 QT 40W OIL    1.24    0.62  139


$ run stocks

INVENTORY CONTROL PROGRAM

Reading Inventory...


Select one of the following options:
   A  :  Add an item to the inventory
   R  :  Remove an item from the inventory
   D  :  Display an item
   C  :  Compute retail and wholesale value of inventory
   T  :  Display complete inventory
   X  :  Exit
Enter your choice --> T

Index Catalog Description Retail Wholesale Quantity
  101    R56YX   SPARK PLUG    1.25    0.95     87
  102    MV030   QT 30W OIL    1.10    0.55    142
  103    MV104   QT 40W OIL    1.24    0.62    139
  112    XX112   OIL FILTER    6.75    4.00     32
  133    R457W   TIRE         57.00   40.00     60
  199    GU411   AM/FM RADI   95.95   75.00      4
  200    GBV01   TAPE PLAYR  119.99  100.00      7

Select one of the following options:
   A  :  Add an item to the inventory
   R  :  Remove an item from the inventory
   D  :  Display an item
   C  :  Compute retail and wholesale value of inventory
```

Figure 14-13 continued

```
      T   :  Display complete inventory
      X   :  Exit
Enter your choice --> C

Total retail value is      $ 5297.04
Total wholesale value is $ 3774.93

Select one of the following options:
      A   :  Add an item to the inventory
      R   :  Remove an item from the inventory
      D   :  Display an item
      C   :  Compute retail and wholesale value of inventory
      T   :  Display complete inventory
      X   :  Exit
Enter your choice --> D


Enter index number : 195
Invalid index number: please try again

Select one of the following options:
      A   :  Add an item to the inventory
      R   :  Remove an item from the inventory
      D   :  Display an item
      C   :  Compute retail and wholesale value of inventory
      T   :  Display complete inventory
      X   :  Exit
Enter your choice --> D


Enter index number : 199

Catalog Number      :  GU411
Description         :  AM/FM RADI
Retail Cost         :  $    95.95
Wholesale Cost      :  $    75.00
Quantity in Stock   :  4

Select one of the following options:
      A   :  Add an item to the inventory
      R   :  Remove an item from the inventory
      D   :  Display an item
      C   :  Compute retail and wholesale value of inventory
      T   :  Display complete inventory
      X   :  Exit
Enter your choice --> R


Enter index number : 195
Invalid index number:  please try again

Select one of the following options:
      A   :  Add an item to the inventory
      R   :  Remove an item from the inventory
      D   :  Display an item
      C   :  Compute retail and wholesale value of inventory
      T   :  Display complete inventory
      X   :  Exit
Enter your choice --> R


Enter index number : 199
```

Figure 14-13 continued

```
Catalog Number : GU411
Description    : AM/FM RADI

How many items to remove? 3

Removal of 3 items confirmed

Select one of the following options:
    A   :   Add an item to the inventory
    R   :   Remove an item from the inventory
    D   :   Display an item
    C   :   Compute retail and wholesale value of inventory
    T   :   Display complete inventory
    X   :   Exit
Enter your choice --> D

Enter index number : 199

Catalog Number    : GU411
Description        : AM/FM RADI
Retail Cost        : $    95.95
Wholesale Cost     : $    75.00
Quantity in Stock  : 1

Select one of the following options:
    A   :   Add an item to the inventory
    R   :   Remove an item from the inventory
    D   :   Display an item
    C   :   Compute retail and wholesale value of inventory
    T   :   Display complete inventory
    X   :   Exit
Enter your choice --> R

Enter index number : 199

Catalog Number : GU411
Description    : AM/FM RADI

How many items to remove? 2

Insufficient quantity in stock: not removed

Select one of the following options:
    A   :   Add an item to the inventory
    R   :   Remove an item from the inventory
    D   :   Display an item
    C   :   Compute retail and wholesale value of inventory
    T   :   Display complete inventory
    X   :   Exit
Enter your choice --> A

Enter index number : 107
Invalid index number: please try again

Select one of the following options:
    A   :   Add an item to the inventory
    R   :   Remove an item from the inventory
    D   :   Display an item
    C   :   Compute retail and wholesale value of inventory
```

Figure 14-13 continued

```
     T   :   Display complete inventory
     X   :   Exit
Enter your choice --> A

Enter index number : 199

Catalog number : GU411
Description    : AM/FM RADI

How many items to add? 12

Addition of 12 items confirmed

Select one of the following options:
     A   :   Add an item to the inventory
     R   :   Remove an item from the inventory
     D   :   Display an item
     C   :   Compute retail and wholesale value of inventory
     T   :   Display complete inventory
     X   :   Exit
Enter your choice --> D

Enter index number : 199

Catalog Number    : GU411
Description       : AM/FM RADI
Retail Cost       $    95.95
Wholesale Cost    $    75.00
Quantity in Stock : 13

Select one of the following options:
     A   :   Add an item to the inventory
     R   :   Remove an item from the inventory
     D   :   Display an item
     C   :   Compute retail and wholesale value of inventory
     T   :   Display complete inventory
     X   :   Exit
Enter your choice --> R

Enter index number : 103

Catalog Number : MV104
Description    : QT 40W OIL

How many items to remove? 10

Removal of 10 items confirmed

Select one of the following options:
     A   :   Add an item to the inventory
     R   :   Remove an item from the inventory
     D   :   Display an item
     C   :   Compute retail and wholesale value of inventory
     T   :   Display complete inventory
     X   :   Exit
Enter your choice --> D

Enter index number : 103

Catalog Number    : MV104
Description       : QT 40W OIL
```

Figure 14-13 continued

```
Retail Cost        $      1.24
Wholesale Cost     $      0.62
Quantity in Stock  : 129

Select one of the following options:
    A   :   Add an item to the inventory
    R   :   Remove an item from the inventory
    D   :   Display an item
    C   :   Compute retail and wholesale value of inventory
    T   :   Display complete inventory
    X   :   Exit
Enter your choice --> T

Index Catalog Description Retail Wholesale Quantity
  101  R56YX  SPARK PLUG    1.25     0.95       87
  102  MV030  QT 30W OIL    1.10     0.55      142
  103  MV104  QT 40W OIL    1.24     0.62      129
  112  XX112  OIL FILTER    6.75     4.00       32
  133  R457W  TIRE         57.00    40.00       60
  199  GU411  AM/FM RADI   95.95    75.00       13
  200  GBV01  TAPE PLAYR  119.99   100.00        7

Select one of the following options:
    A   :   Add an item to the inventory
    R   :   Remove an item from the inventory
    D   :   Display an item
    C   :   Compute retail and wholesale value of inventory
    T   :   Display complete inventory
    X   :   Exit
Enter your choice --> C

Total retail value is    $ 6148.19
Total wholesale value is $ 4443.73

Select one of the following options:
    A   :   Add an item to the inventory
    R   :   Remove an item from the inventory
    D   :   Display an item
    C   :   Compute retail and wholesale value of inventory
    T   :   Display complete inventory
    X   :   Exit
Enter your choice --> X
End of Inventory Control Program
```

have the items in order of index number. This is allowable because the arrays are being filled by way of direct access, and the index number itself will tell the program where to place the associated data. Second, testing is done methodically by working through the menu items one option at a time to test both correct and incorrect index numbers. Everything seems to work fine.

STEP 5: DOCUMENT

Again, the natural modularity and good presentation techniques make this program quite easy to read and understand.

We have now completed our introduction to one-dimensional arrays and their variations. Let us, therefore, move on to higher levels of arrays and explore two-dimensional arrays.

14-5 *Two-Dimensional Arrays*

As we saw in the preceding chapter, it is possible to extend the idea of arrays to two or more dimensions. In this section we will look only at two-dimensional arrays, but remember that it is possible to have as many dimensions as we want.

Recall from the last chapter that a two-dimensional array is configured in two dimensions, rows and columns, and each array element requires two subscripts to represent it. We can show a typical 2-D (two-dimensional) array as follows:

$$\text{Time}$$
$$\begin{bmatrix} 34 & 16 & 91 & 22 \\ 1 & 4 & 20 & 100 \\ 19 & 900 & 7 & 3 \end{bmatrix}$$

The array name is Time, and it is a 3 × 4 (three by four) array. The first number (3) is the number of rows, and the second number (4) is the number of columns. The individual array elements are referenced by specifying the array name and the row and the column the element is in. For example, the element in the upper right-hand corner can be written in Pascal as `Time[1,4]`, and it has a value of 22. The value 4 in the second row can be referenced as `Time[2,2]`, and the last value in the array is `Time[3,4]`.

We may represent a generalized two-dimensional array as follows:

$$\begin{bmatrix} a_{11} & a_{12} & a_{13} & a_{14} & \cdots & a_{1n} \\ a_{21} & a_{22} & a_{23} & a_{24} & \cdots & a_{2n} \\ & \cdots & & \cdots & & \cdots \\ a_{m1} & a_{m2} & a_{m3} & a_{m4} & \cdots & a_{mn} \end{bmatrix}$$

This would be an $m \times n$ array (the index of each element is shown explicitly). For example, a_{24} is the element in the second row and fourth column. A 2-D array can have an arbitrary number of rows and columns.

Let's now go on to develop an example and see some specific 2-D arrays.

Matrix Addition

Since a two-dimensional array is often referred to as a matrix, let us do a problem that literally uses matrices. Matrix operations are important in math and science and are frequently implemented using computers. For this example let's look at the relatively simple matrix operation of addition.

STEP 1: UNDERSTAND THE PROBLEM

We would like to add any two arbitrary matrices. Matrix addition requires that the matrices to be added both have the same dimensions. The result (sum) matrix is computed simply by adding the corresponding elements of each operand matrix. For example, if we want to add the matrix

$$\begin{bmatrix} 1 & 4 & 8 & 3 \\ 2 & 0 & -1 & 7 \\ 3 & 3 & 2 & -5 \end{bmatrix}$$

to the matrix

$$\begin{bmatrix} 4 & 6 & 1 & 1 \\ -2 & 10 & 3 & -7 \\ 4 & -9 & 22 & 1 \end{bmatrix}$$

we can do so, since they have the same dimensions (in this case, 3 by 4). We simply add the corresponding elements of each matrix to yield

$$\begin{bmatrix} 5 & 10 & 9 & 4 \\ 0 & 10 & 2 & 0 \\ 7 & -6 & 24 & -4 \end{bmatrix}$$

STEP 2: PLAN THE SOLUTION

The algorithm for this can be written as

Input the First Matrix
Input the Second Matrix
Add the First and Second Matrices, producing the Result Matrix
Print out the Result Matrix

A logical (and easy) way to implement the operations required would be via procedures. Let's make our algorithm include these:

Read Rows, Columns of matrices

ReadMatrix (First, Rows, Cols)
ReadMatrix (Second, Rows, Cols)

AddMatrix (First, Second, Result, Rows, Cols)

WriteMatrix (Result, Rows, Cols)

We must input the matrix dimensions in the form of rows and columns before we can do anything else. These quantities are necessary for correct operation of the procedures and must be included as arguments to them.

As we did with the previous example, let's define the necessary procedures individually first.

ReadMatrix. The values must be entered into a matrix, but we encounter two problems with this. First, how can we adjust the size of the matrix to fit the rows and columns being passed? Second, how can we make it so that the input is aesthetically pleasing? In other words, when we input the matrix values, we'd like them to be entered so they are arranged in the form of a matrix (that is, one row at a time) rather than as a list of numbers.

With regard to the size of the matrix, we must define and declare the matrix to be as big as the largest matrix we ever expect to see and then just use as much of it as we need. With regard to aesthetics, Pascal allows us to use Read or Readln. Thus, we can Read the data one line at a time and then issue a Readln to terminate the line.

So, how to write the algorithm? Since we will be reading our matrices in two dimensions, we will need two loops to carry out the process: one for the rows and one for the columns. The technique is quite predictable and can be written as

```
Procedure ReadMatrix (A, Rows, Cols)
For r ← 1 to Rows Do
  For c ← 1 to Cols Do
    Read (A[r,c])
  Readln
```

Here, Rows and Cols represent the size of the matrix to be read in, A is the matrix itself, and r and c are variables local to the procedure that allow us to build the loop. We have included a Readln to terminate each row of the matrix as it is read in.

WriteMatrix. While we're about it, let's take care of the inverse process. The algorithm for writing a matrix is just about the same as the algorithm for reading a matrix, namely,

```
Procedure WriteMatrix (A, Rows, Cols)
For r ← 1 to Rows Do
  For c ← 1 to Cols Do
    Write (A[r,c])
  Writeln
```

Using the `Writeln` as the last step of the inner loop is necessary so that each row of the matrix is placed on a separate line of output. If we did nothing but `Write`, the whole matrix would appear on a single line. (Recall the decimal table problem of Chapter 9.)

`AddMatrix.` We are now ready to add the matrices. The computation requires that we go through all of the rows and columns of both matrices and add up the corresponding elements in each. It would be nice if we could make this a function, but we can't, so we must write a procedure:

```
Procedure AddMatrix (A, B, S, Rows, Cols)
For r ← 1 to Rows Do
  For c ← 1 to Cols Do
    S[r,c] ← A[r,c] + B[r,c]
```

STEP 3: CODE THE SOLUTION

Now that we have algorithms for the main routine and all the procedures, we can write a Pascal program. The only thing we lack is the knowledge of how to define 2-D arrays in Pascal. Therefore, we need a new array-type definition for 2-D arrays, which is

array-type-definition → identifier = **array**[lower..upper] **of** type
　　　　　　　　　　 | identifier = **array**[lower1..upper1 ,
　　　　　　　　　　　　　　　　　　　　　lower2..upper2] **of** type

This new array-type definition is the same as the old one, with the exception that we must specify *two* sets of lower and upper bounds, one for each dimension (subscript). By way of example, suppose we have a program that needs two kinds of 2-D arrays: a square matrix that is 5 by 5 and another matrix that is 8 by 10. Appropriate types could be defined as follows:

```
Type Square = Array [1..5, 1..5] of Real;
     BigPicture = Array [1..8, 1..10] of Real;
```

Of course, we are then required to declare variables of this type, for example,

```
Var A, B, C : Square;
    Scene, Bounty : BigPicture;
```

Returning to our matrix addition example, we must decide how large to make the largest matrix we ever expect the program to use before we define the arrays. For the sake of argument, let's go with a 10 by 10 matrix. Our definition and declaration, therefore, would be

```
Type Matrix = Array [1..10, 1..10] of Real;
Var  First, Second, Result : Matrix;
```

The remainder of the coding is straightforward. The results of our efforts are displayed in Figure 14-14.

Figure 14-14

Program That Inputs, Adds, and Outputs Matrices, Including a Test Run

ADDMAT.PAS

```
1    Program ADDMAT (Input, Output);
2
3    (*
4        This program adds two compatible matrices.
5    *)
6
7    Type Matrix = Array [1..10, 1..10] of Real;
8
9    Var First, Second, Result : Matrix;
10       Rows, Cols : Integer;
11
12
13   Procedure ReadMatrix (Var A : Matrix; nr, nc : Integer);
14   (* This procedure reads a matrix of arbitrary size from the
15      keyboard, one row at a time *)
16     Var r,c : Integer;
17     Begin
18       For r := 1 to nr Do
19            Begin
20              For c := 1 to nc Do
21                   Read (A[r,c]);
22              Readln
23            End
24      End;
25
26
27   Procedure AddMatrix (Var A,B,S : Matrix; nr,nc :Integer);
28   (* This procedure adds two compatible matrices *)
29     Var r,c : Integer;
30     Begin
31       For r := 1 to nr Do
32            For c := 1 to nc Do
33                 S[r,c] := A[r,c] + B[r,c]
34      End;
35
```

Figure 14-14 continued

```
36
37     Procedure WriteMatrix (A : Matrix; nr, nc : Integer);
38     (* This procedure writes a matrix to the CRT in row/column order *)
39       Var r,c : Integer;
40       Begin
41        For r := 1 to nr Do
42            Begin
43              For c := 1 to nc Do
44                    Write ( A[r,c]:4:1,' ');
45              Writeln
46            End
47       End;
48
49
50     BEGIN
51
52        Writeln ('MATRIX ADDITION PROGRAM');
53        Writeln;
54
55        Write ('Enter #rows, #columns of the matrices : ');
56        Readln (Rows, Cols);
57
58        Writeln;
59        Writeln ('Enter the first matrix');
60        ReadMatrix (First, Rows, Cols);
61
62        Writeln;
63        Writeln ('Enter the second matrix');
64        ReadMatrix (Second, Rows, Cols);
65
66        AddMatrix (First, Second, Result, Rows, Cols);
67
68        Writeln;
69        Writeln ('The result matrix is');
70        WriteMatrix (Result, Rows, Cols)
71
72     END.
```

```
$ run addmat

MATRIX ADDITION PROGRAM

Enter #rows, #columns of the matrices : 3 4

Enter the first matrix
  4  7  22    1
  1  2  -1    5
 11  9   2    4

Enter the second matrix
 -1 -5    3   13
  0  6   -3  -22
 22 -6    3    7

The result matrix is
  3.0   2.0  25.0   14.0
  1.0   8.0  -4.0  -17.0
 33.0   3.0   5.0   11.0
```

STEP 4: CHECK OUT THE PROGRAM

A sample run is also shown in Figure 14-14, and the matrix addition works correctly.

STEP 5: DOCUMENT

We've got all the documentation we need.

Before concluding this chapter, let's work through an example of a different kind of 2-D array application.

Grade Book

Let's use a two-dimensional array as a means of keeping track of student class grades. (We briefly presented this example in Chapter 13.) The grades are recorded vertically by student (rows) and horizontally by exam (columns). Typically the data would look like this:

Student	Exam 1	Exam 2	Exam 3	. . .
1	97	87	92	
2	56	63	75	
3	79	81	80	
. . .				

The grades can be placed into a 2-D array, where the first subscript corresponds to the student and the second to the exam. For example, the grade for student 3 on exam 1 would be 79, referenced as `Score[3,1]`.

Rather than just placing this information in an array, we would, of course, like to do something useful with it. Typically, we want to compute the average grade for each student, the average grade for each exam, and an overall average for the whole class.

Rather than going through this example in detail, we will merely present the final result and make a few comments about it. The completed program is shown in Figure 14-15, and a sample run (including a listing of the input) is shown in Figure 14-16.

Data Structure Definitions. We have defined the primary 2-D array type `Book` itself in line 12 and declared an array of that type, `Grade`, in line 17. We have assumed here that we will need a maximum of 50 students

Figure 14-15

Program That Reads Student Names and Scores from a File and Computes Appropriate Final Averages

GRADER.PAS

```
 1    Program GRADER (GradeBook, Output);
 2
 3    (*
 4        This program reads in a set of grades for an entire class and
 5        computes the average for each student, the average on each exam,
 6        and the average for the entire class. The grades and averages
 7        are then printed out.
 8    *)
 9
10    Type Strings = Packed Array [1..10] of Char;
11
12         Book = Array [1..50,1..10] of Real;
13         NameList = Array [1..50] of Strings;
14
15         PlainArray = Array [1..50] of Real;
16
17    Var  Grade : Book;         (* Two-dimensional array that stores the
18                                  grades as read from the external file.
19                                  The first dimension corresponds to the
20                                  student number and the second dimension
21                                  to the exam number *)
22
23         Name  : NameList;     (* One-dimensional array of strings that stores
24                                     the students` names as read from the file *)
25         TheName : Strings;    (* Current name being read in *)
26
27         Student, Exam : Integer;  (* Indexes to the Grade array *)
28
29         NumStudents, NumExams : Integer;
30
31         StudentAve,           (* Array that stores the averages
32                                   for each student *)
33         ExamAve               (* Array that stores the averages
34                                   for each exam  *)
35                 : PlainArray;
36
37
38         Total,                (* Used to sum up scores *)
39
40         ClassTotal, ClassAve(* Class-wide total and average *)
41                           : Real;
42
43         GradeBook : Text;     (* External file that stores the
44                                  students` names and grades. It is
45                                  constructed as follows:
46                                      1st record : Number of exams
47                                      Subsequent : Student name, exam scores *)
48
49    Procedure ReadString (Var TheFile : Text;
50                          Var S : Strings);
51       Var K : Integer;
52       Begin
53         For K := 1 to 10 Do
54             Read (TheFile, S[K])
55       End;
56
```

Figure 14-15 continued

```
57
58   BEGIN
59
60      (* Input the Grade Book *)
61      Reset (GradeBook);
62
63      Writeln ('Reading GradeBook...');
64      Writeln;
65
66      Readln (GradeBook, NumExams);
67      Student := 0;
68      While not EOF (GradeBook) Do
69         Begin
70            Student := Student + 1;
71            ReadString (GradeBook, TheName);
72            Name[Student] := TheName;
73            For Exam := 1 to NumExams Do
74                 Read (GradeBook, Grade[Student,Exam]);
75            Readln (GradeBook)
76         End;
77      NumStudents := Student;
78
79      (* Compute the average for each student *)
80      For Student := 1 to NumStudents Do
81            Begin
82               Total := 0;
83               For Exam := 1 to NumExams Do
84                    Total := Total + Grade[Student,Exam];
85               StudentAve[Student] := Total / NumExams
86            End;
87
88      (* Compute the average for each exam and the class as a whole *)
89      ClassTotal := 0;
90      For Exam := 1 to NumExams Do
91            Begin
92               Total := 0;
93               For Student := 1 to NumStudents Do
94                    Total := Total + Grade[Student, Exam];
95               ClassTotal := ClassTotal + Total;
96               ExamAve[Exam] := Total / NumStudents
97            End;
98      ClassAve := ClassTotal / (NumStudents * NumExams);
99
100     (* Print out the complete set of grades *)
101     Writeln; Writeln ('Final Class Grades'); Writeln;
102     For Student := 1 to NumStudents Do
103           Begin
104              Write (Name[Student]);
105              For Exam := 1 to NumExams Do
106                   Write (Grade[Student,Exam]:6:1);
107              Writeln(' - ', StudentAve[Student]:6:1)
108           End;
109
110     Writeln;
111     Write ('Exam Ave ');
```

Figure 14-15 continued

```
112      For Exam := 1 to NumExams Do
113          Write (ExamAve[Exam]:6:1);
114      Writeln;
115
116      Writeln;
117      Writeln ('Class Average is ',ClassAve:6:1)
118
119   END.
```

Figure 14-16

Test Run of the GRADER *Program, Including a Listing of the File Containing the Input Data*

```
$ type gradeboo.dat

            4 exams
Anne        92   85   77   80
Bill        75   69   80   72
Carl        45   60   76   50
Dennis     100   95   97   87
Ellen       95   90   88   90
Glenn       34    0   56   60
Ingred      87   87   90   95
Karen       75   69   77   77
Laurie      82   88   78   79
Michael     68   70   62   65


$ run grader

Reading GradeBook...


Final Class Grades

Anne        92.0    85.0   77.0   80.0 -   83.5
Bill        75.0    69.0   80.0   72.0 -   74.0
Carl        45.0    60.0   76.0   50.0 -   57.7
Dennis     100.0    95.0   97.0   87.0 -   94.7
Ellen       95.0    90.0   88.0   90.0 -   90.7
Glenn       34.0     0.0   56.0   60.0 -   37.5
Ingred      87.0    87.0   90.0   95.0 -   89.7
Karen       75.0    69.0   77.0   77.0 -   74.5
Laurie      82.0    88.0   78.0   79.0 -   81.7
Michael     68.0    70.0   62.0   65.0 -   66.2


Exam Ave    75.3    71.3   78.1   75.5

Class Average is     75.0
```

and 10 exams. We have also defined an array of strings for keeping the students' names (line 23) and two 1-D arrays for the computed averages (lines 31 and 33).

Input. The entire input, including names and scores, is read from an external file, between lines 66 and 77. Note that the number of students is counted as the data is read, and an inner loop is used to obtain the actual scores for each student.

Student Averages. This calculation is carried out between lines 79 and 86. There really isn't much code here, but it's important to understand what's happening. An outer loop, based on the student index, goes through the entire list of students. For each student a second, inner loop adds up all the scores on all the exams for that student. We use nested loops that will eventually work through each exam for each student. The special 1-D array StudentAve contains the computed averages for each student.

Exam Averages. Occupying lines 88 through 98, this section is very similar to that of the average computations, except that we are calculating the average for each *exam* rather than the average for each *student*. To accomplish this, we merely *reverse* the two loops. Here, the outer loop goes through the exams, and the inner loop goes through the students.

Results. The final results are written out at lines 100 through 117, and the method used is similar to that used for the matrix addition problem. We use nested loops to print out each row and each element within the row.

Spend a little time examining this program in detail so you can understand the workings of the various loops.

SUMMARY

This concludes our introduction to arrays. We have seen one- and two-dimensional arrays and examples of how they can be used in typical settings. Further, we looked at the special case of strings, and we are now able to input and process words and text. We also examined ways of working with large amounts of varying data by using parallel arrays and arrays of records. All in all, we've covered a considerable amount of material!

We are now ready to examine some very specific operations for which arrays are quite useful, namely searching (finding things) and sorting (putting things in order). The two operations work together and are the topics of the next chapter.

EXERCISES

CONCEPTS

1. Define or explain the following terms:

Army of records   String constant

Computed subscripts   String variable

Direct array access   Parallel arrays

Matrix   Related arrays

Menu   With construct

2. Discuss whether or not it is possible to write a general Pascal procedure `ReadString` that can be used for strings of any length.

TOOLS

3. Define, in correct Pascal, appropriate array types that would be useful for declaring the following arrays:

a. Time: the durations of up to 50 telephone calls

b. X,Y: 100 x and y values for a given algebraic function

c. Outcome: the outcome of 1,000 coin tosses

d. Name: a person's name (up to 25 characters)

e. Die1, Die2: the results of rolling two dice up to 500 times

f. Success: whether or not a person correctly identifies a hidden card using ESP (100 tests)

g. Device: a five-letter word designating an output device

h. Yield: the per-acre yield on an experimental plot (10 plots)
   Fert: the rate of fertilizer applications on the plots
   Water: the rate of watering on the plots
   Light: the number of days of sunlight reaching the plots
   Code: code letter for the plots

i. XWord: an array to contain a crossword puzzle

j. Board: a chess board

k. XO: a tic-tac-toe game

4. Generate appropriate type definitions, in correct Pascal, for the following records:

    a. Common name (20 letters)
       Order (15 letters)
       Genus (15 letters)
       Species (15 letters)
    b. Altitude (in feet)
       Velocity (in miles per hour)
       Direction (in degrees)
    c. Account number (integer)
       Balance
       Activity (whether or not it has been accessed in the last six
            months)
    d. Month
       Day
       Year
       Time
    e. User name (8 characters)
       Password (8 characters)
       Memory (maximum page allotment)
       CPU time (maximum time, in seconds, per session)

5. Generate appropriate type definitions, in correct Pascal, for the following structures:

    a. A list of 15 book titles, each 30 characters long
    b. A list of 50 computers, including:
       Brand (15 letters)
       List Price
       Bytes of Memory
       Processor (10 characters)
       Length (inches)
       Width (inches)
       Height (inches)
    c. A sentence (one word at a time) of up to 25 words (words can be up to 10 letters each)
    d. 75 locations in spherical coordinates:
       R (a distance)
       Theta (an angle)
       Phi (an angle)
    e. 500 students:
       Name (25 letters)
       GPA
       Class (1–4)
       Hours (0–200)

6. Generate an expression to calculate the proper index for the following categories of tomato size distribution:

Index	Category (in ounces)
1	0–2
2	2–4
3	4–6
4	6–8
5	8–10
6	10–12
7	over 12

7. Generate an expression to calculate the proper index for the following categories of performance times:

Index	Category (in seconds)
0	0–10.00
1	10.01–12.50
2	12.51–15.00
3	15.01–17.50
4	17.51–20.00
5	20.01–22.50
6	22.51–25.00

PROBLEMS

8. Write a program that will correct true/false exams. True is expressed as a + and False is expressed as a −. Each test can have a maximum of 25 problems. For each exam the key is followed by an arbitrary number of marked exams. The raw score is computed using the formula

Score = Number Right − Number Wrong

Output the score for each student as originally computed and also as a percent of the total. At the conclusion of the program, output the average score for the class.

9. Write a program that will convert a decimal number to an equivalent number in any other base, where this new base is less than 10. For example, if the decimal number 29 was entered, the equivalent binary number (base 2) would be 11101 and the equivalent octal number (base 8) would be 35. Input the decimal number and the new base, convert the number to the new radix (that is, base), and

output it. The conversion can be carried out easily by successive division. Consider the conversion of 29 (base 10) to binary:

Number	Base	Quotient	Remainder
29	2	14	1
14	2	7	0
7	2	3	1
3	2	1	1
1	2	0	1

The original number is successively divided by the base until a quotient of 0 is obtained. The converted number is obtained by reading the remainder column *from bottom to top*. (This is where arrays come in.) The conversion to octal would be

Number	Base	Quotient	Remainder
29	8	3	5
3	8	0	3

10. Extend problem 9 above so that *any* base less than 20 can be used. The process is similar, except that the digits produced in the conversion of bases greater than 10 extend beyond 9. It is customary to use letters of the alphabet for these. For example, in the base 20 number system, the following digits are used:

Base 20	0 1 2 3 4 5 6 7 8 9 A B C D E F G H I J
Equivalent Base 10	0 1 2 3 4 5 6 7 8 9 10 11 12 13 14 15 16 17 18 19

For example, converting the decimal number 227 to hexadecimal (base 16) would entail the following:

Number	Base	Quotient	Remainder	Equivalent Hex Digit
227	16	14	3	3
14	16	0	14	E

Therefore, the decimal number 227 has a hexadecimal equivalent of E3. More arrays must be used in this problem to generate digits beyond 9.

11. Write a program that will generate statements for customers of the First Federal State Savings Bank of Binghamton. Input will consist of the following items:

Customer Name
Account Number
Beginning Balance
List of Checks

Check Number

Amount of Check

List of Deposits

Amount of Deposit

From this, compute the interest earned, the service charge, and the ending balance. The interest and service charge should be computed as follows:

If the ending balance is under $300 then
  Service charge is $7.50
  No interest is earned
Otherwise
  There is no service charge
  Interest is computed on the ending balance at the rate of
    5.25% annually adjusted to a monthly basis

Finally, output everything in the following format:

First Federal State Savings Bank of Binghamton
Statement of Account

JOHN PAUL JONES	**Account Number 548226**
Balance Last Statement	483.22
CHECKS	
Number	5
Amount	217.48
DEPOSITS	
Number	2
Amount	261.05
Service Charge	0.00
Interest	2.30
Balance This Statement	529.09

***   ***

Account Transactions
CHECKS

Number	Amount
225	13.75
226	47.12
227	3.45
229	143.16
232	10.00

DEPOSITS

Number	Amount
1	236.05
2	25.00

The deposits do not have numbers associated with them (as the checks do) but are simply numbered consecutively. The check numbers *do not* need to be in order.

12. Write a program that will generate a relative histogram. A sequence of percents will be input and categorized as follows:

Category	Range (percent)	Category	Range (percent)
1	0–9	6	50–59
2	10–19	7	60–69
3	20–29	8	70–79
4	30–39	9	80–89
5	40–49	10	90–99

Once all the input has been entered, the categories are converted to percents based on the relative size of each category to the total. Finally, each category is output as a line of asterisks, with the number of asterisks corresponding to the (percent) relative size of the category. For example, if the following percents were entered

12 25 36 79 56 90 1 45 67 98 23 55 64 35 55 62 73 99 49 50

then the ten categories would accumulate the following counts:

1 1 2 2 2 4 3 2 0 3

These would then be converted to percents (based on a total of 20) as follows:

5 5 10 10 10 20 15 10 0 15

Note that the total adds up to 100. Finally, the histogram would be generated using these percents as the number of asterisks. This example would generate

```
*****
*****
**********
**********
**********
********************
***************
**********

**************
```

13. Write a program that will print out a plot of an arbitrary algebraic function. Use a two-dimensional array of Char (not packed!) to store the ordered pairs that would result. For example, if the function were

$$y = x^2 + 3x - 5$$

a series of $x - y$ pairs would be produced as follows:

x	y
-5	25
-4	16
-3	9

   Use these values as a key to the 2-D character array and insert into the array the character '*' at each place where a point for the plot would be generated. Then print out the array. The results should look something like this:

```
*                       *
   *                   *
      *             *
         *  *  *
```

14. Augment the above problem so that the results are scaled and the coordinate axes are also shown on the plot.

15. Write a program that will input an integer number and convert it to English. The following are some examples:

0	zero
5	five
17	seventeen
128	one hundred twenty-eight
1985	one thousand nine hundred eighty-five

16. Write a program that will multiply two matrices. Two matrices can be multiplied if and only if they are compatible, which means that the number of columns of the first must equal the number of rows of the second. For example, the following two matrices would be compatible, since the first is 3 by 2 and the second is 2 by 4:

$$\begin{bmatrix} 2 & 4 \\ 7 & 1 \\ 6 & 3 \end{bmatrix} \qquad \begin{bmatrix} 7 & 3 & 9 & 1 \\ 4 & 1 & 0 & 8 \end{bmatrix}$$

   The operation of matrix multiplication is defined as

$$C\,[i, j] = \sum_{k} A\,[i, k] \times B\,[k, j]$$

where C = result matrix

A, B = operand matrices

If an m by n matrix is multiplied by an n by p matrix, the resulting matrix will be m by p. In the above case, the result of multiplying the 3 by 2 and the 2 by 4 matrices would be

$$\begin{bmatrix} 30 & 7 & 18 & 34 \\ 53 & 22 & 62 & 15 \\ 54 & 21 & 54 & 30 \end{bmatrix}$$

17. The response of a photometer is given by the following function:

Volts = $ke^{aI/t}$

where   Volts = the output voltage

k = a constant based on the material

a = a constant based on the wavelength of light

I = the light intensity

t = the temperature

Write a program that will generate a table of voltages based on intensities of light that may range from 0 to 10 and temperatures that may range from 10 to 30 degrees. Then input combinations of I and t and use the table to look up and write out the voltages that correspond to these. Use the following constants:

k = 2.528

a = 1.375

15

More About Arrays:

Searching and Sorting

We continued our study of arrays by examining two activities very pertinent to arrays, namely, searching and sorting. People generally (and computer scientists particularly) spend a great deal of time looking for things (searching) and putting things in order (sorting). Searching and sorting are fairly complex tasks, but they are so commonly encountered that well-developed techniques exist for these processes. In this chapter we will present some algorithms for searching and sorting.

After we complete our discussion of algorithms for searching and sorting, we will look at algorithm analysis, which is the art of scrutinizing different solutions (algorithms) to the same problem in order to see if one is better than another. Searching and sorting algorithms, being both varied and complex, readily lend themselves to this kind of analysis. The principles of algorithm analysis, however, are completely general and can be applied to *any* algorithms, not just those for searching and sorting.

15-1 *Searching*

We will begin by considering searching with regard to arrays. **Searching,** as the term implies, involves trying to find something. However, the make-up of the array to be searched and exactly what is being searched for are significant factors in determining how best to carry out the search. Say, for example, that we have an array consisting of the total monthly sales (in no particular order) of salesmen for the company By-Rite and we want to determine who has sold the most (the maximum sales) and who has sold the least (the minimum sales). Finding these numbers requires that we go through the entire array, one element at a time, and compare each element to all the others. When we have gone through the whole array in this fashion, we will then know both the largest and smallest sales figures.

Let's take a different kind of example. Suppose we want to pull out the first word of a sentence that has been entered into the computer as a string. How can this be done? One method is to input the sentence as an array (packed or otherwise) of character and carry out an appropriate search. But what exactly do we search for? Words in a sentence are delimited by blanks, so what we want to look for is the first non-blank character we come to in the sentence (which will signify the beginning of the first word) and then the first blank we come to after that (which will signify the end of the first word). One difference between this example and the sales problem above is that for this example there is no need to go all the way through the string array. We can stop whenever we find the appropriate delimiter (that is, a blank).

Also, the way an array is organized affects the methods used to carry out the search. In our first example, if the sales figures contained in the array are in no particular order, we must go all the way through the array one element at a time to find the maximum and minimum sales figures. Only then can we be sure that we have the largest and smallest values. On the other hand, if the array is arranged in order from smallest to largest, we can pull out the largest value from the top of the array and the smallest value from the bottom; this requires (for all practical purposes) no searching at all!

Consider yet another situation. Suppose we want to look up a word in the dictionary. We would not, in general, start with *A* and continue reading page after page until the desired word was found. We would instead take advantage of the fact that a dictionary lists its entries (words) in alphabetical order. Such listing permits us to locate the word relatively quickly. This search is fundamentally different from the kinds of searching we have been discussing. We do not go in sequence from beginning to end, but rather we skip around in a manner that substantially reduces the total amount of work required.

The above discussion reveals a number of features of searches. First, arrays to be searched can be either unordered or ordered. If unordered, searches must be carried out from beginning to end (or from end to beginning), one element at a time. This search mechanism is termed a **linear search.** If a linear search is called for, two different situations may arise:

1. You must go through the entire array to find what you are looking for (as in the case of finding the largest sales figure).

2. You will be able to find what you want before you get to the end of the array (as in looking for the beginning and end of the first word in a sentence).

On the other hand, an array may be ordered. If so, it is still possible to do a linear search. In this case, the ordering will save time and effort, because it generally will be possible to determine whether or not the item is even in the array well before reaching the end. However, as demonstrated by the process of finding a word in the dictionary, a completely different search strategy can be employed. This strategy is called a **binary** (or logarithmic) **search.** Although more complex to implement than linear searching, it can result in an astounding saving of time.

One final comment before we examine searching and sorting in depth. Since the techniques of searching and sorting are well developed, we will depart from our usual method of presentation, where we use a typical problem to motivate a solution. Instead, for each technique, we will present a generalized (abstract) algorithm followed by a demonstration of how it can be used in a specific problem setting.

LINEAR SEARCHES

There are two kinds of linear searches: those that search an unordered array and those that search an ordered array. The algorithms in each case are somewhat different, and we will look at each in turn.

Linear search of unordered arrays. There are two situations that can arise with regard to searching unordered arrays. In one case, a search of the entire array is required (such as in the sales problem); in the other case, it is possible to find the item before the search has progressed through the entire array (such as the word extraction problem). The two types differ only in that the terminating conditions (the conditions that stop the search) are not the same.

We will consider first the case in which the entire array must be searched. During such a search we must examine each array element in turn, all the way through the array. The algorithm for such a search is quite simple. We use a counted loop to go from the beginning of the array to the end, and as we go we compare each element to the selection criteria. The algorithm can be expressed as

For Index ← First to Last Do
  If ArrayElement[Index] meets selection criteria then
    IndexOfInterest ← Index

Notice that we retain the index to the value of interest, rather than the value itself. That's because it is always possible to get the value once we know its index. Also, what we actually do with the value of interest is not specified but is determined by the nature of the problem in which we use the search.

Salesman Problem

To demonstrate the use of this kind of linear search, let's work through the salesman problem. We will assign each salesman in the company an ID, and these IDs will range from 1 to the number of salesmen employed. Further, suppose that individual sales are tallied and credited to each salesman's account as the sales occur. At the end of the month after all the sales have been entered, we would like to print out a list of the sales totals for each salesman and indicate who has made the highest and the lowest sales.

STEP 1: UNDERSTAND THE PROBLEM

Our task is to keep track of the sales totals for each of the salesmen and then search for the highest and lowest sales figures. The best way to do this is through direct access of arrays, where we tally the individual sales into the array element corresponding to each salesman. We can then search the finished array for the largest and smallest values, and when we print out the final list, we can indicate to whom the values belong.

STEP 2: PLAN THE SOLUTION

Given all the above information, we can write our initial algorithm as

Initialize Accounts to 0

For the duration of the month Do
    Read Salesman Number, Sale Amount
    Account[Salesman Number] ← Account[Salesman Number] + Sale Amount

Find the index to the largest sales
Find the index to the smallest sales

For all the salesmen Do
    Write Account[Salesman Number]
    If Salesman Number = Index to the largest then
        Write 'MOST SALES'
    Else if Salesman Number = Index to the smallest then
        Write 'LEAST SALES'

We next need to fill in more details. We first consider how to write the loop that reads and tallies the individual sales. Let's use the sentinel value approach, where we enter a salesman number of 0 to indicate the end of sales inputs. Modifying the loop in this fashion and also adding a little more detail to the rest of the algorithm, we can write

For Salesman Number ← 1 to 10 Do
    Account[Salesman Number] ← 0

Read Salesman Number
While Salesman Number > 0 Do
    Read Sale Amount
    Account[Salesman Number] ← Account[Salesman Number] + Sale Amount
    Read Salesman Number

Index of Largest ← Max (Account)
Index of Smallest ← Min (Account)

For Salesman Number ← 1 to 10 Do
    Write Account[Salesman Number]
    If Salesman Number = Index of Largest then
        Write 'MOST SALES'
    Else if Salesman Number = Index of Smallest then
        Write 'LEAST SALES'

The functions Max and Min are to be used to find the largest and smallest values. Now we approach the subtask of generating these functions. Since we have already presented the general algorithm for a linear search, we need only to adapt it to this particular application. The selection criteria for Max are that the current element be bigger than the biggest element found so far. The selection criteria for Min are that the element be smaller than the smallest found so far. Formalizing these ideas into an algorithm yields

Function Max (Total)
Biggest ← 1

```
For k ← 2 to 10 Do
   If Total[k] > Total[Biggest] then
      Biggest ← k
Max ← Biggest

Function Min (Total)
Smallest ← 1
For k ← 2 to 10 Do
   If Total[k] < Total[Smallest] then
      Smallest ← k
Min ← Smallest
```

Pay particular attention to how these functions work. We start by assuming that the largest element (or smallest, as the case may be) is the first array element. We then go through the *remainder* of the array one element at a time. Whenever we find an element that is bigger (or smaller), we set the search index to the index of that element. Notice that we do *not* actually store the value of the biggest or smallest element, just its index. When we get out of the loop, we set the function name (as required by Pascal syntax) to the index.

STEP 3: CODE THE SOLUTION

We now have a sufficiently detailed algorithm to properly code the solution. We do not need anything new in the way of syntax for this problem. The results are shown in Figure 15-1. A couple of things to note. First, we have passed an array to the functions `Max` and `Min`. That's no problem. Notice, though, that we've passed it by value, which is fine. We have no intention of actually changing anything in the array; we are merely looking through it. Second, we have added whatever `Write` statements are necessary to make the output and prompting look good.

STEP 4: CHECK OUT THE PROGRAM

A test run of this program is shown in Figure 15-2, and everything works properly.

STEP 5: DOCUMENT

Documentation, as always, has been built into the program. Note that a constant has been used to represent the number of salesmen. This allows us to change this number easily if more or fewer salesmen are employed.

Next, let's consider linear searches through unordered arrays, where it is possible to find the element of interest *without* necessarily having to go through the entire array. One example of such a search, as we said earlier, is the problem of how to pull the first word out of a sentence. Suppose that the sentence is

Figure 15-1

Sales Program, Including Functions to Search an Array for the Largest and Smallest Values

SALES.PAS

```
 1    Program SALES (Input, Output);
 2
 3    (*
 4        This program inputs and tallies sales figures, as they occur,
 5        for an arbitrary number of salesmen in the By-Rite company.
 6        An array is used to keep track of the total sales for each
 7        person. After all sales have been entered and tallied, the
 8        total sales for each salesman are printed out, along with an
 9        indication of who has the most sales and who has the least sales.
10    *)
11
12    Const NumSalesmen = 10;              (* Number of salesmen employed *)
13
14    Type Sales = Array [1..NumSalesmen] of Real;
15
16    Var  Account : Sales;                (* Array of sales *)
17         SalesmanNumber : Integer;       (* Salesman ID *)
18         SaleAmount : Real;              (* Current sale amount being entered *)
19
20         IndexLargest, IndexSmallest   (* Index to the person with the most *)
21                        : Integer;      (* and least sales, respectively  *)
22
23    (* SEARCH PROCEDURES *)
24
25    Function Max (Total : Sales): Integer;
26    Var k, Biggest : Integer;
27    (* This function finds the largest element in an array *)
28      Begin
29        Biggest := 1;
30        For k := 2 to NumSalesmen Do
31            If Total[k] > Total[Biggest] then
32                Biggest := k;
33        Max := Biggest
34      End;
35
36
37    Function Min (Total : Sales): Integer;
38    (* This function finds the smallest element in an array *)
39    Var k, Smallest : Integer;
40      Begin
41        Smallest := 1;
42        For k := 2 to NumSalesmen Do
43            If Total[k] < Total[Smallest] then
44                Smallest := k;
45        Min := Smallest
46      End;
47
48
49    BEGIN
50
51      (* Initialize all the accounts to zero *)
52      For SalesmanNumber := 1 to NumSalesmen Do
53          Account[SalesmanNumber] := 0;
54
```

Figure 15-1 continued

```
55      (* Read in the figures, one sale at a time *)
56      Writeln ('BY-RITE SALES FOR THE MONTH');
57      Writeln;
58      Writeln ('Enter Salesman Number and Sale Amount,');
59      Writeln ('or zero to end...');
60      Writeln;
61      Write('Salesman Number : '); Readln (SalesmanNumber);
62      While SalesmanNumber > 0 Do
63        Begin
64          Write('Sale Amount     : '); Readln (SaleAmount);
65          Account[SalesmanNumber] := Account[SalesmanNumber] + SaleAmount;
66          Writeln;
67          Write('Salesman Number : '); Readln (SalesmanNumber)
68        End;
69
70      (* Find the largest and smallest sales totals *)
71      IndexLargest  := Max (Account);
72      IndexSmallest := Min (Account);
73
74      (* Output the total sales, flagging the best and the worst *)
75      Writeln;
76      Writeln ('    ***   ***   ***');
77      Writeln;
78      Writeln ('Monthly Sales Totals');
79      Writeln;
80      Writeln('Salesman Number  Total Sales');
81      For SalesmanNumber := 1 to NumSalesmen Do
82          Begin
83              Write(SalesmanNumber:8, Account[SalesmanNumber]:18:2);
84              If SalesmanNumber = IndexLargest then
85                  Writeln(' <--  MOST SALES!!!')
86              Else if SalesmanNumber = IndexSmallest then
87                  Writeln(' <--  least sales')
88              Else
89                  Writeln
90          End
91
92   END.
```

Figure 15-2

Test Run of the SALES *Program*

```
$ run sales

BY-RITE SALES FOR THE MONTH

Enter Salesman Number and Sale Amount,
or zero to end...

Salesman Number : 1
Sale Amount     : 75.00

Salesman Number : 2
Sale Amount     : 85.00
```

Figure 15-2 continued

```
Salesman Number : 3
Sale Amount     : 100.00

Salesman Number : 4
Sale Amount     : 25.00

Salesman Number : 5
Sale Amount     : 36.00

Salesman Number : 6
Sale Amount     : 12.00

Salesman Number : 7
Sale Amount     : 10.00

Salesman Number : 8
Sale Amount     : 5.00

Salesman Number : 9
Sale Amount     : 17.00

Salesman Number : 10
Sale Amount     : 45.00

Salesman Number : 8
Sale Amount     : 33.50

Salesman Number : 2
Sale Amount     : 25.50

Salesman Number : 10
Sale Amount     : 1.50

Salesman Number : 3
Sale Amount     : 95.50

Salesman Number : 6
Sale Amount     : 55.50

Salesman Number : 1
Sale Amount     : 22.50

Salesman Number : 7
Sale Amount     : 18.50

Salesman Number : 5
Sale Amount     : 33.50

Salesman Number : 4
Sale Amount     : 16.50

Salesman Number : 9
Sale Amount     : 42.50

Salesman Number : 4
Sale Amount     : 77.75

Salesman Number : 1
Sale Amount     : 13.75
```

Figure 15-2 continued

```
Salesman Number : 9
Sale Amount     : 7.75

Salesman Number : 0

   ***    ***    ***

Monthly Sales Totals

Salesman Number   Total Sales
       1             111.25
       2             110.50
       3             195.50  <-- MOST SALES!!!
       4             119.25
       5              69.50
       6              67.50
       7              28.50  <-- least sales
       8              38.50
       9              67.25
      10              46.50
```

- - - - - Herein-we-have-a-sentence.

(The hyphens here represent blanks.) If we want to pull out the first word, we must search through the sentence from the beginning until we find a character that is *not* a blank. This occurs in position 6, counting from the left, where we find the beginning of the word. We then continue searching through the array until we find a character that *is* a blank, which occurs in position 12. This blank *must be one position beyond the end of the first word*. Therefore, we know that the first word begins in position 6 and ends in position 11 (one less than the position of the first blank).

Although the word extraction process requires that we search for a nonblank character at first and then go on to search for a blank character, each part of the search is still the same. That is, we go through the array one element at a time until we find what we are looking for or until we reach the end of the array. This search process differs from the first type of linear array search in that this time we will quite likely *not* have to go all the way through the array before we find what we are looking for.

The algorithm for such a search is fairly easy to write, and we can use a While loop as follows:

Index ← 1
While ArrayElement[Index] does NOT meet the selection criteria
                     AND Index ≠ Last Do
     Index ← Index + 1

Here, the While loop takes care of all the conditions that may terminate the search, and the actual loop body does nothing but increment the index.

Address Labels

Let's write a program that makes use of such conditional array searches. Consider the problem of printing out address labels. Normally, each address is stored alphabetically by last name, with its associated information. A typical address might be

DOE JOHN   344 CANTOR   WONTON   WV 20754

In this example, the name is allotted fifteen characters, the street and number are allotted twelve, the city, ten, the state, two, and the zip code, five. We would like to rearrange this format and output an address label as follows:

JOHN DOE

344 CANTOR

WONTON, WV 20754

The salient features involved here are that (1) the name has been reversed from last name-first name to first name-last name and (2) the name of the city is followed by a comma, a single space, the state, another space, and finally the zip code.

STEP 1: UNDERSTAND THE PROBLEM

To begin with, we need to know exactly how the input addresses are arranged. Assume they are as follows:

	Starts in Col	Ends in Col	Length
Name	1	20	20
Street	21	35	15
City	36	50	15
State	51	52	2
Zip	53	57	5

The algorithm will need to work with the name, in order to reverse the first and last names, and the city, in order to find exactly where it ends so that the state and zip code can be easily appended.

STEP 2: PLAN THE SOLUTION

Our initial algorithm can be expressed thus:

For as many addresses as we have Do
   Read Name, Street, City, State, Zip
   Reverse First and Last Names
   Find the end of the City name
   Write the Reversed Name
   Write the (unchanged) Street
   Write the City name, a comma, State, and Zip

We have two subtasks that must be considered here, namely, how do we reverse the person's first and last names and how do we find the last character of the city name (so that we can append the state and zip)? Both subtasks require that we search arrays of character. Let us begin with the name reversal problem by examining a typical case in point:

```
SAMUELS ROBERT T.
--------------------
```

The dotted line again represents spaces. Since there is a total of twenty characters allotted to the name, this name has three trailing blanks. To reverse the last and first names, we must determine where the first name begins and ends and where the last name begins and ends. In this case, the begin and end points are:

```
SAMUELS ROBERT T.
--------------------
↑        ↑ ↑        ↑
1        7 9        17
   Last     First
   Name     Name
```

Included in the first name is anything that is not a part of the last name, such as middle initials or titles. Once we have properly delimited the first and last names, it is an easy matter to print them out in the desired order. Thus, in the above case we would print out elements 9 through 17 (the first name), a space, and then elements 1 through 7 (the last name).

    Let's assume that the last name always starts in the first column, so that all we have to do is find the end of the last name. To do so we need only search through the name from beginning to end until we come across a blank. In the above case this happens at position 8. We then know that the end of the last name is in column 7!

In a similar fashion, we can find the start of the first name. We continue the search where we left off previously (in this case at position 8) and proceed until we find something that is *not* a blank. This occurs at position 9, and we therefore know that the first name begins there.

However, to find the end of the first name we would *not* continue through the array until we found the next blank. To do so would falsely lead us to believe that the first name ended at position 14. Although this is actually so, as we said earlier, anything that is not the last name is considered a part of the first name, including middle names, initials, or titles. To accommodate this situation, we must conduct the search a little differently. We must begin at the *end* of the array and work our way *backward*. In this case we would start at position 20 and go backward until we came to an element that was *not* a blank. This occurs at position 17, which corresponds to the sought-after end of the "first" name.

We can now formalize this process and include it in our former algorithm. Doing so yields

```
While not EOF Do
    Read Name, Street, City, State, Zip
    Reverse First and Last Names
        StartLastName ← 1
        EndLastName ← Position of next blank − 1
        StartFirstName ← Position of next nonblank
        EndFirstName ← Position of first nonblank from right end
    Find the end of the City name
    Write the Reversed Name
        Write Name[StartFirstName to EndFirstName],
            Blank,
            Name[StartLastName to EndLastName]
    Write the (unchanged) Street
    Write the City name, a comma, State, and Zip
```

We have specified the outer loop as an end-of-file loop (so that we may store the addresses in an external file).

Next, we need to find the end of the city name so that we can append the state and zip code properly. This task requires a process similar to (but easier than) reversing the person's name. For example, suppose the city name is

```
SALT LAKE CITY
---------------
```

To find the start and end of the city name, we assume, as we did with the person's name, that the city name begins in the first column. We can then find the end of the city name in exactly the same fashion as we found the end of the person's first name, by searching *backward* from the right-most end of the array for the first occurrence of a nonblank character. (If we were to search forward for a blank from the left-most end, we would conclude, incorrectly, that the name of the city is Salt.)

Adding this process to the previous algorithm yields

```
While not EOF Do
   Read Name, Street, City, State, Zip
   Reverse First and Last Names
      StartLastName ← 1
      EndLastName ← Position of next blank − 1
      StartFirstName ← Position of next nonblank
      EndFirstName ← Position of first nonblank from right end
   Find the end of the City name
      EndCityName ← Position of first nonblank from right end
   Write the Reversed Name
      Write Name [StartFirstName to EndFirstName],
            Blank,
            Name[StartLastName to EndLastName]
   Write the (unchanged) Street
   Write the City name, a comma, State, and Zip
      Write City[1 to EndCityName], Comma, State, Space, Zip
```

We need now only fill in the details of the various searches. We might be tempted to use functions here, but unfortunately Pascal will not allow us to pass (transmit) strings of different lengths as arguments. Therefore, since we would need a different procedure for each search anyway, we will just include the searches as part of the main program. Doing this gives us our next algorithm:

```
While not EOF Do
   Read Name, Street, City, State, Zip
   Reverse First and Last Names
      StartLastName ← 1
      EndLast Name ← 1
      While Name[EndLastName] ≠ Blank Do
         EndLastName ← EndLastName + 1
      EndLastName ← EndLastName − 1
      StartFirstName ← EndLastName + 2
      While Name[StartFirstName] = Blank Do
         StartFirstName ← StartFirstName + 1
      EndFirstName ← 20
      While Name[EndFirstName] = Blank Do
         EndFirstName ← EndFirstName − 1
   Find the end of the City name
      EndCityName ← 15
      While City[EndCityName] = Blank Do
```

EndCityName ← EndCityName − 1
Write the Reversed Name
   Write Name[StartFirstName to EndFirstName],
      Blank,
      Name[StartLastName to EndLastName]
Write the (unchanged) Street
Write the City name, a comma, State, and Zip
   Write City[1 to EndCityName], Comma, State, Space, Zip

For all practical purposes, searching backward is the same as searching forward; the only difference is that in the former case, you subtract one from the index each time; in the latter case, you add one to the index each time.

The only other item of interest is the manner in which we shall actually print out the labels. We need to print out the various arrays in bits and pieces. Let's do this with counted loops. Making this addition gives us our final algorithm:

```
While not EOF Do
  Read Name, Street, City, State, Zip
  Reverse First and Last Names
    StartLastName ← 1
    EndLastName ← 1
    While Name[EndLastName] ≠ Blank Do
       EndLastName ← EndLastName + 1
    EndLastName ← EndLastName − 1
    StartFirstName ← EndLastName + 2
    While Name[StartFirstName] = Blank Do
       StartFirstName ← StartFirstName + 1
    EndFirstName ← 20
    While Name[EndFirstName] = Blank Do
       EndFirstName ← EndFirstName − 1
  Find the end of the City name
    EndCityName ← 15
    While City[EndCityName] = Blank Do
       EndCityName ← EndCityName − 1
  Write the Reversed Name
    For Index ← StartFirstName to EndFirstName Do
       Write Name[Index]
    Write Blank
    For Index ← StartLastName to EndLastName Do
       Write Name[Index]
  Write the (unchanged) Street
  Write the City, State, and Zip
    For Index ← 1 to EndCityName
       Write City[Index]
    Write Comma
    Write State
    Write Zip
```

STEP 3: CODE THE SOLUTION

The properly coded solution is shown in Figure 15-3. We have added appropriate constants and comments as necessary.

STEP 4: CHECK OUT THE PROGRAM

A sample run, using a variety of personal names and cities, is shown in Figure 15-4, with a listing of the input file. Features of the addresses include a city name, made up of three separate words, and persons' names, which contain all manner of middle initials and titles. All are converted to address labels correctly.

Figure 15-3

Program That Generates Address Labels

LABELS.PAS

```
1    Program LABELS (AddressFile, Output);
2
3    (*
4        This program generates address labels from a file that contains
5        names and addresses.
6    *)
7
8    Const NameLength = 20;
9          CityLength = 15;
10
11         Blank = ' ';
12         Comma = ',';
13
14   Type  LongString = Packed Array [1..NameLength] of Char;
15         MidString = Packed Array [1..CityLength] of Char;
16         ShortString = Packed Array [1..5] of Char;
17         TinyString = Packed Array [1..2] of Char;
18
19   Var   Name    : LongString;
20         Street  : MidString;
21         City    : MidString;
22         State   : TinyString;
23         Zip     : ShortString;
24
25         StartLastName, EndLastName, StartFirstName, EndFirstName : Integer;
26         EndCityName : Integer;
27         Index : Integer;
28
29         AddressFile : Text; (* File containing the names and addresses *)
30
31
32   BEGIN
33
34     (* Ready the input file *)
35     Reset (AddressFile);
36
37     (* Go for it... *)
38     While not EOF (AddressFile) Do
```

Figure 15-3 continued

```
39        Begin
40
41            (* Input the person's name *)
42            For Index := 1 to NameLength Do
43                Read (AddressFile, Name[Index]);
44
45            (* Input the street address *)
46            For Index := 1 to CityLength Do
47                Read (AddressFile, Street[Index]);
48
49            (* Input the city, state, and zip *)
50            For Index := 1 to CityLength Do
51                Read (AddressFile, City[Index]);
52            For Index := 1 to 2 Do
53                Read (AddressFile, State[Index]);
54            For Index := 1 to 5 Do
55                Read (AddressFile, Zip[Index]);
56
57            Readln (AddressFile);
58
59            (* Reverse the first and last name *)
60
61                (* Delimit the last name *)
62                StartLastName := 1;
63                EndLastName := 1;
64                While Name[EndLastName] <> Blank Do
65                    EndLastName := EndLastName + 1;
66                EndLastName := EndLastName - 1;
67
68                (* Delimit the first name *)
69                StartFirstName := EndLastName + 2;
70                While Name[StartFirstName] = Blank Do
71                    StartFirstName := StartFirstName + 1;
72                EndFirstName := NameLength;
73                While Name[EndFirstName] = Blank Do
74                    EndFirstName := EndFirstName - 1;
75
76            (* Find the end of the city name *)
77            EndCityName := CityLength;
78            While City[EndCityName] = Blank Do
79                EndCityName := EndCityName - 1;
80
81            (* Write out the address *)
82
83                (* NAME *)
84                Writeln;
85                For Index := StartFirstName to EndFirstName Do
86                    Write (Name[Index]);
87                Write (Blank);
88                For Index := StartLastName to EndLastName Do
89                    Write (Name[Index]);
90                Writeln;
91
92                (* STREET *)
93                Writeln (Street);
94
95                (* CITY, STATE, ZIP *)
96                For Index := 1 to EndCityName Do
97                    Write (City[Index]);
98                Write (Comma);
```

Figure 15-3 continued

```
99              Write (Blank);
100             Write (State);
101             Write (Blank);
102             Write (Zip);
103             Writeln;
104             Writeln
105
106        End (* Address Loop *)
107
108    END.
```

Figure 15-4

Test Run of the Address Labels Program, Including a Listing of the Input File

```
$ type addressf.dat

HARRIS CHARLES T     2254 MAPLE AVE MORNINGDALE      CA97243
LYLE DR ANTHONY P    PO BOX 77      CLINTON          MA03612
POTTS,JR M B A       851 W 3300 S   SALT LAKE CITY   UT84381
SMITH HARRY          3543 ANGLIS ST PITTSBURGH       PA15223
TORR MR ED           PO BOX 1433    VERNIER          KY47099
XENO XAVIER          23 HIGHLAND #45MURIEL           MO66921


$ run labels

CHARLES T HARRIS
2254 MAPLE AVE
MORNINGDALE, CA 97243


DR ANTHONY P LYLE
PO BOX 77
CLINTON, MA 03612


M B A POTTS,JR
851 W 3300 S
SALT LAKE CITY, UT 84381


HARRY SMITH
3543 ANGLIS ST
PITTSBURGH, PA 15223


MR ED TORR
PO BOX 1433
VERNIER, KY 47099


XAVIER XENO
23 HIGHLAND #45
MURIEL, MO 66921
```

STEP 5: DOCUMENT

With regard to documentation, note the use of comments and appropriate indentations to set off the various sections of the program. Also, constants have been used for the string sizes, and the character constants Blank and Comma are added to improve readability and ease of maintenance.

Up to this point, we have been concerned only with searching single *unordered* arrays. We will extend our discussion by examining techniques available for searching arrays whose elements are in order.

Linear search of ordered arrays. When searching ordered arrays, two situations may arise. In the first, we are interested in finding an exact match, and so we go through the array to determine whether or not a particular element is in the array and if so where it is. In the second situation, we are interested in *categorizing* the search element; that is, we want to find out which two array elements the search element falls between (if it does not match one of them exactly). The algorithms are similar, but the applications are different.

Also, ordered arrays are rarely if ever encountered singly, and the existence of one ordered array invariably means that others exist (such as parallel arrays or an equivalent array of records). Usually only one of the arrays is searched, but the actual target of the search is the corresponding element of a *different* array. This is similar to looking up a phone number in a phone book. You look up a person's name in the left-hand column, but your real interest is in the associated phone number in the right-hand column. Another example is when you determine the value of log 5.8 by consulting a table of common logarithms. Such a search is termed a *table look-up* and is characterized by a *key*, which is the item you actually search for, or look up, in the table. Once the key is located, the index of the key leads you to the actual target data, which is located in another array.

A linear search can be appropriate in such a case. The primary advantage of a linear search in an ordered array is that it will usually be possible to determine whether or not the key is in the array *before* reaching the end of the array. For example, if you are looking up the name Aardvark Alice in the phone book, you can be sure that the name is not there as soon as you find the name Abend Phillip without first having come across Aardvark Alice. (The idea of searching parallel arrays is valid even for unordered arrays; we discuss parallel, ordered arrays in this context because they are more common.)

Let's first examine a situation in which we want to search an ordered array for an exact match. Suppose, for example, that a company keeps its payroll information in parallel arrays, one of which is an array of sequenced social security numbers. If we wish to obtain payroll information for an employee, we can execute a linear search for his or her social security number in the appropriate array. While we are searching, if we ever reach the point where the value of the array element being looked at is greater than the one for which we are searching (the key), we may conclude that the number is *not* in the table and terminate the search.

What follows is an algorithm for a linear search through an ordered array:

```
Index ← 1
While TableValue[Index] < Key AND Index ≠ Last Do
   Index ← Index + 1
If Key = TableValue[Index] then
   Eureka (which is to say, we have found it)
Else
   Key is not in the Table
```

This algorithm assumes that the array (table) values are in ascending order (that is, the values go from smallest to largest). If the table is organized the other way around (in descending order, from largest to smallest), the algorithm must be altered to take this into account and can be written as

```
Index ← 1
While TableValue[Index] > Key AND Index ≠ Last Do
   Index ← Index + 1
If Key = TableValue[Index] then
   Eureka (which is to say, we have found it)
Else
   Key is not in the Table
```

In either case a search is made until the key is found or until it can be determined that the key is not in the array.

Hospital Records

Let's consider an example that uses a linear search through an ordered array. Suppose we are to keep track of hospital patients. For each patient we want to have the following information:

Patient's Name
Social Security (SS) Number

Date Admitted

Diagnosis

Room Number

Once we have this information for all patients, we would like to look up a patient by SS number and extract the pertinent information. Hence, the program should input an SS number, look it up in a table, and then print out the information for that patient or, if the SS number is not in the table, indicate the number's absence.

STEP 1: UNDERSTAND THE PROBLEM

We will start by defining appropriate data structures. A record format would be ideal here, so we define one as follows:

Patient Record
SS Number
Name
Date Admitted
Diagnosis
Room Number

Concerning the data types of the fields, we might make SS Number an integer, Name a string, Date Admitted an integer, Diagnosis a string, and Room Number an integer. However, we ought to consider two things: First, in order to make the date more readable, it would perhaps be better to make it a string, so that we can have it in the form of something like 23 May 85. Second, social security numbers are generally nine-digit integers, and it is quite possible that the system on which you are writing your programs will not accept integers this large. To be on the safe side, let's make the data type of SS Numbers a character string rather than an integer.

Since we have the primary data structure and we understand the function we wish the program to carry out, we may now move on to the next step of the program development process.

STEP 2: PLAN THE SOLUTION

We begin by writing down a preliminary algorithm as

For as long as we want to keep this up
Read SS Number
Find Record of corresponding SS Number
If Record was found
Write out the information so obtained
Else
Write 'Record not found'

Let's first decide how we want to implement the loop. We can use a sentinel value loop, which terminates whenever zero is entered for the SS number. We also need to figure out how to *find* the patient. Let's make Find a procedure (so that we can defer the details until later) in which we will have, as arguments, the array of patients, the size of the array, the SS number for which we are searching, and the index to the array corresponding to the record of interest. Next, we must decide how to transmit the knowledge of whether or not our procedure found the patient's record. To do this let's return, from the procedure, a zero value for the index if in fact the record was not found. Incorporating all this (with some of the output details) into a new version of the algorithm gives us

```
Read SS Number
While SS Number > 0 Do
    Find (Patient, Size, SS Number, WhichOne)
    With Patient[WhichOne] Do
      If WhichOne > 0 then
          Write Name, SS Number, Date Admitted,
                  Diagnosis, Room Number
      Else
          Write 'Record not found'
    Read SS Number
```

Note the use of the With structure.

We have written this algorithm under the assumption that the array of records exists. However, this array must come from somewhere, so let's read the patient data in from an external file via an EOF loop. Adding this gives us

```
(* Read in the patient data *)
Index ← 0
While not EOF (PatientData) Do
    Index ← Index + 1
    With Patient[Index] Do
      Read Name, SS Number, Date Admitted,
              Diagnosis, Room Number
Size ← Index

(* Look patients up *)
Read SS Number
While SS Number > 0 Do
    Find (Patient, Size, SS Number, WhichOne)
    With Patient[WhichOne] Do
      If WhichOne > 0 then
          Write Name, SS Number, Date Admitted,
                  Diagnosis, Room Number
      Else
          Write 'Record not found'
    Read SS Number
```

This is the final algorithm. Patient represents the array of patient records. These records are counted as they are read from the external file, so that the correct size can be transmitted to the procedure Find.

As we did in the previous chapter, we will abbreviate the program development process here and not display the coding and testing phases of the main program. We will instead develop the algorithm for the Find procedure. Be aware, however, that the coding and testing of the main program really are the next steps and in fact this was done during actual development of this program. We are simply not *showing* that part of the process.

The Find procedure does the actual search in the array of records. Since we have already presented the fundamental algorithm for the linear search of an ordered array, we have only to adapt the algorithm to this particular use. Doing so involves little more than designating appropriate variable names. Using the general search algorithm as a starting point, we can modify it for this problem and obtain

```
Procedure Find (PatientList, Size, SSKey, Who)
Who ← 1
While PatientList[Who].SSNo < SSKey and Who ≠ Size Do
   Who ← Who + 1
If SSKey = PatientList[Who].SSNo then
   (* We have found it *)
Else
   Who ← 0 (*Not there*)
```

Note that we have used the full record description of PatientList fields. We have not used the With structure, because to work properly, the With would have to become a part of the While so the array index could get through correctly. If we nested the While inside the With, only the first array element would ever be referenced! For example, if we wrote

```
Who ← 1
With PatientList[Who] Do
   While SSNo < SSKey and Who ≠ Size Do
```

the entire loop would revolve around the first value encountered, namely, PatientList[1], since that is the value that exists when the While loop is entered. There is no easy way to get around this problem except to write out the full record description.

STEP 3: CODE THE SOLUTION

Having come up with algorithms for the main program and all the sub-tasks, we may put them together and code the complete solution. This completed solution is shown in Figure 15-5. We have included a string constant Zero = '000000000' for use in determining whether the

Figure 15-5

Completed Program, Including the Search Procedure, That Finds and Displays Patient Information

HOSPITAL.PAS

```
 1    Program HOSPITAL (PatientData, Input, Output);
 2
 3    (*
 4        This program reads hospital records into an array of records,
 5        then permits the user to search the array to get
 6        specific information on any of the patients.
 7    *)
 8
 9    Const NoPatients = 100;  (* Maximum number of patients *)
10          Zero = '000000000';(* String equivalent of the social
11                                security number 0 *)
12
13    Type  LongString = Packed Array [1..20] of Char;
14          ShortString = Packed Array [1..9] of Char;
15
16          Person = Record
17                       SSNo : ShortString;
18                       Name : LongString;
19                       DateAdmitted : ShortString;
20                       Diagnosis : LongString;
21                       Room : Integer;
22                   End;
23
24          Patients = Array [1..NoPatients] of Person;
25
26    Var   Patient : Patients;            (* Array of patient records *)
27          Size : Integer;               (* Current number of patients *)
28          KeySSNo : ShortString;        (* Search key; an SS number *)
29          WhichOne : Integer;           (* Index of the array element
30                                           found via the search  *)
31
32          Index : Integer;     (* Counter for reading the records from the
33                                   external file into the array *)
34
35          PatientData : Text;  (* External file containing original patient
36                                   information *)
37
38
39    Procedure ReadShort (Var TheFile : Text;    (*This reads a shortstring *)
40                         Var S : ShortString); (* from an external file *)
41    Var k : Integer;
42      Begin
43        For k := 1 to 9 Do
44            Read (TheFile, S[k])
45      End;
46
47    Procedure ReadLong (Var TheFile : Text;  (* This reads a longstring *)
48                        Var S : LongString); (* from an external file *)
49    Var k : Integer;
50      Begin
51        For k := 1 to 20 Do
52            Read (TheFile, S[k])
53      End;
54
```

Figure 15-5 continued

```
55   Procedure ReadKey (Var TheKey:ShortString); (* This reads a key SS number *)
56                                               (* from the keyboard *)
57   Var k : Integer;
58     Begin
59       For k:=1 to 9 Do
60            Read (TheKey[k]);
61       Readln
62     End;
63
64
65   Procedure Find (PatientList : Patients; Size : Integer;
66                   SSKey : ShortString;
67                   Var Who : Integer);
68     Begin
69       Who := 1;
70       While (PatientList[Who].SSNo < SSKey) and (Who <> Size) Do
71          Who := Who + 1;
72       If SSKey = PatientList[Who].SSNo then
73          (* Congratulate yourself, you found it *)
74       Else
75          Who := 0
76     End; (* Find *)
77
78   (* End of the procedures *)
79
80
81   BEGIN
82
83     Writeln ('HOSPITAL RECORD SEARCH');
84     Writeln;
85     Writeln ('Reading Patient Records...');
86
87     (* Get the records to be searched *)
88     Reset (PatientData);
89     Index := 0;
90     While not EOF (PatientData) Do
91       Begin
92          Index := Index + 1;
93          With Patient[Index] Do
94              Begin
95                 ReadShort (PatientData, SSNo);
96                 ReadLong  (PatientData, Name);
97                 ReadShort (PatientData, DateAdmitted);
98                 ReadLong  (PatientData, Diagnosis);
99                 Readln    (PatientData, Room)
100             End
101      End; (* Input Loop *)
102    Size := Index;
103    Writeln (Size:1,' records read.');
104    Writeln;
105
106    (* Pull out the records for whomever *)
107    Write ('Enter SS Number (all zeros to end) : ');
108    ReadKey (KeySSNo);
109    While KeySSNo > Zero Do
110      Begin
111         Find (Patient, Size, KeySSNo, WhichOne);
112         With Patient[WhichOne] Do
113            If WhichOne > 0 then
```

Figure 15-5 continued

```
114              Begin
115                 Writeln;
116                 Writeln ('Hospital records for ', Name);
117                 Writeln ('                    ID ', KeySSNo);
118                 Writeln;
119                 Writeln ('Admitted ', DateAdmitted);
120                 Writeln ('Diagnosis : ', Diagnosis);
121                 Writeln ('Room Number ', Room);
122                 Writeln
123              End
124           Else
125              Begin
126                 Writeln;
127                 Writeln ('*** Invalid ID Number : Patient not found ***');
128                 Writeln
129              End;
130           Write ('Enter SS Number (all zeros to end) : ');
131           ReadKey (KeySSNo)
132        End (* While Loop *)
133
134   END.
```

termination condition has been met. This constant can be used with the string SS numbers in exactly the same fashion that we could have used the integer 0 with integer SS numbers.

We have also included three string input procedures: ReadShort, which reads short strings from the external file; ReadLong, which reads long strings from the external file; and ReadKey, which inputs the social security key from the keyboard.

STEP 4: CHECK OUT THE PROGRAM

The results of a sample run are shown in Figure 15-6. Note that for the search to work properly, the data must first be entered in order. We could have had the computer order the array for us, but that process is treated in a later section of this chapter.

Let's take a closer look at the test run. The test is organized so that all possible accesses are attempted. Access is made to the very first element, the very last element, and one element from the middle. These all work properly. Next, the program is tested to make sure that *invalid* keys produce the expected error message. Again, numbers are entered that would fall before the first element, after the last element, and somewhere in the middle. No problems are encountered. Finally, the program terminates properly.

STEP 5: DOCUMENT

The documentation is sufficient.

Figure 15-6

Test Run for the Hospital Program, Including a Listing of the Input Data File

```
$ type patientd.dat

001552397JONES JOHN PAUL       1 APR 85RHINORRHEA         125
025130965MOORE MARY TYLER      5 APR 85APPENDICITIS       104
161378412SMITH PETER P         1 JAN 85MENTAL EXHAUSTION   222
212407133BIKLO TERRY          12 APR 85TONSILITIS         117
375128461POLO MARCO            7 APR 85HALITOSIS          010
455091734WINKLER HENRY        15 APR 85SPRAINED ANKLE     105
456091352WALTERS BARBARA      13 APR 85LARYNGITIS         131
799124576COKELY JAMES         10 APR 85NEARSIGHTEDNESS    101


$ run hospital

HOSPITAL RECORD SEARCH

Reading Patient Records...
8 records read.

Enter SS Number (all zeros to end) : 161378412

Hospital records for SMITH PETER P
               ID 161378412

Admitted  1 JAN 85
Diagnosis : MENTAL EXHAUSTION
Room Number 222

Enter SS Number (all zeros to end) : 001552397

Hospital records for JONES JOHN PAUL
               ID 001552397

Admitted  1 APR 85
Diagnosis : RHINORRHEA
Room Number 125

Enter SS Number (all zeros to end) : 799124576

Hospital records for COKELY JAMES
               ID 799124576

Admitted 10 APR 85
Diagnosis : NEARSIGHTEDNESS
Room Number 101

Enter SS Number (all zeros to end) : 000237543

*** Invalid ID Number : Patient not found ***

Enter SS Number (all zeros to end) : 901543765

*** Invalid ID Number : Patient not found ***

Enter SS Number (all zeros to end) : 412670987
```

Figure 15-6 continued

```
*** Invalid ID Number : Patient not found ***

Enter SS Number (all zeros to end) : 212407133

Hospital records for BIKLO TERRY
                    ID 212407133

Admitted 12 APR 85
Diagnosis : TONSILITIS
Room Number 117

Enter SS Number (all zeros to end): 000000000
```

This completes our examination of linear searches for a specific key in an ordered array. We will now examine a case where we search an ordered array to find a category. In this case we do not necessarily expect to find the exact key, but instead we want to determine the two array elements *between* which the key should fall. A good example of such a search is the percentage method of calculating federal withholding tax. A typical tax withholding table is shown in Figure 15-7. To demonstrate its use, suppose we want to compute the amount of tax to be withheld on gross wages of $200. According to the table, the amount of the wages is over $196 but not over $273. The tax withheld, therefore, would be

$$\text{Tax} = \$31.29 + 26\% (\$200 - \$196) = \$32.33$$

Solving this problem requires searching the table for the correct category and then using related columns to compute the final amount. This is a case of searching an ordered array that is a part of several parallel arrays.

The algorithms for such a search are quite similar to the algorithms used to find an exact match in an ordered array. The only differences involve the sense of the inequalities and the fact that we will not be testing for exactness at the conclusion of the search proper. The prototype algorithm (assuming the array is in ascending order) is

Index ← 1
While TableValue < Key AND Index ≠ Last Do
    Index ← Index + 1

This is all there is to it. The variable Index will represent the correct category at the conclusion of the loop. However, as we shall see shortly, a certain amount of caution is needed in setting up the arrays.

Figure 15-7

*Typical Table Used to Compute Federal Withholding Tax Using the
Percentage Method*

Table for Percentage Method of Withholding

Weekly Payroll Period
Married Person—Including Head of Household

If the amount of wages is:		The amount of income tax to be withheld shall be	
Not over $27 0			
Over	*But not over*		*of excess over*
$27	$63 . . . . 15%		$27
$63	$131 . . . . $5.40 plus 18%		$63
$131	$196 . . . . $17.64 plus 21%		$131
$196	$273 . . . . $31.29 plus 26%		$196
$273	$331 . . . . $51.31 plus 30%		$273
$331	$433 . . . . $68.71 plus 34%		$331
$433 . . . . $103.39 plus 39%			$433

To carry out such a search on an array that is in descending order,
the above algorithm must be changed to

Index ← 1
While TableValue[Index] ≥ Key AND Index ≠ Last Do
    Index ← Index + 1

The following example illustrates the use of this algorithm.

Withholding Tax

Let's work out the withholding tax problem. Rather than generate a
complete payroll program, however, we shall just write a procedure to
calculate the tax and put it in a driver program for test purposes.

STEP 1: UNDERSTAND THE PROBLEM

Input to the procedure will be the amount of wages to be taxed, and
output from the procedure will be the amount of tax withheld. To carry
this out, a table look-up is required. There are, according to Figure 15-

7, a number of tables that must be used. We could pass all of these to the procedure as parameters. However, since the tables contain constant information (which never changes), let us instead consider the tables as global data. This is another example of a situation in which the use of global information by a procedure is proper and appropriate.

STEP 2: PLAN THE SOLUTION

The first thing to do is decide how to represent the tax tables shown in Figure 15-7. There are five columns in the table, which suggests that we need five arrays. However, there is a lot of duplication in the table columns, and we can condense them to only three: a table of limits, a table of fixed tax amounts, and a table of percents. A set of tables that will work is shown in Figure 15-8. We can use the search algorithm given above to categorize the wage amount and then use the information in the related arrays to compute the actual tax. Note that, in order for the search and subsequent computation to work properly, we have had to add an additional category (index of 0) at the low end. Also, the last category (8) has 0 for the limit entry. If we were to get to this point in the search, the search would be terminated by the fact that the index number exceeds the table size rather than that the category searched for had been found. This means that any amount over $433 must fall into this last category.

Once the correct wage category has been determined by the search procedure, the tax can be computed as follows:

Tax = Fixed Amount[Index] + Percent[Index] × (Wages − Limit[Index − 1])

Let's do a hand trace using a $200 wage amount as the key to convince ourselves that this method works. We first set Index equal to 1. The test in the While loop checks to see if the first value of Limit (which is $27) is less than the key; in this case it is, so we increment Index to 2. We then carry out the test again and once again find that the second Limit value ($63 this time) is also less than the key. Index is then incremented to 3. Testing again, we compare Limit[3] (value of $131) to key, succeed in the test, and increment Index to 4. Limit[4] (at $196) is *still* less than the key, so we increment to 5. At this point, we see that Limit[5] is no longer greater than the key, and we stop with Index having a value of 5.

Using the value of 5 so obtained for Index results in the following tax computation:

Tax = Fixed Amount[5] + Percent[5] × (Wages − Limit[4])

Filling in the numbers yields

$$Tax = 31.29 + 0.26 \times (200 - 196) = 32.33$$

This is exactly the result we would have expected!

Figure 15-8

Tax Withholding Table (from Figure 15-7) Converted to Arrays for Use in Solving the Tax Withholding Problem

Index	Limit	Fixed Amount	Percent
0	0	0	0
1	27	0	0
2	63	0	0.15
3	131	5.40	0.18
4	196	17.64	0.21
5	273	31.29	0.26
6	331	51.31	0.30
7	433	68.71	0.30
8	0	103.39	0.34
			0.39

We now have our tables, the tax computation formula, and an algorithm for the search; hence, we may generate an algorithm for the procedure.

```
Procedure Taxation (Wages, Taxes)
Index ← 1
While Limit[Index] < Wages AND Index ≠ Last Do
    Index ← Index + 1
Taxes = Fixed Amount[Index] +
            Percent[Index] × (Wages − Limit[Index − 1])
```

Note that, although the table starts with entry 0, we nonetheless initiate the search with element 1. Having a zeroth element in the tables just allows for consistency in the computation of the taxes when we refer to the previous (Index − 1) value.

STEP 3: CODE THE SOLUTION

Coding this procedure is quite straightforward. We must for test purposes envelop it in a driver program that inputs the tables and calls the procedure. (The tax tables are read from an external file.) The final coded procedure, along with an appropriate driver, is shown in Figure 15-9.

STEP 4: CHECK OUT THE PROGRAM

The test results are shown in Figure 15-10. A number of sample wages are used to test the procedure. As always, we have included borderline situations, such as no wages, wages over $433, and wages that are exactly at the boundary of the categories. All trials work properly.

Figure 15-9

Procedure (in a Driver) to Compute Withholding Tax According to the Percentage Method

DRIVER.PAS

```
1    Program DRIVER (TaxTables, Input, Output);
2
3    (* This program drives a procedure that calculates withholding
4       tax based on the percentage method. All the driver does
5       is input the tables (for use by the procedure) and try
6       out various wages to make sure they all produce correct
7       results.
8    *)
9
10   Type Tables = Array [0..8] of Real;
11
12   Var  Limit,              (* Boundaries of the tax categories *)
13        Fixed,              (* Fixed amount of tax              *)
14        Percent : Tables;   (* Percentage amount of tax         *)
15
16        Salary, Tax : Real;
17        K : Integer;
18
19        TaxTables : Text;   (* External file containing the tax tables *)
20
21   Procedure Taxation (Wages : Real; Var Taxes : Real);
22   (* This procedure uses the percentage method for computing federal
23      withholding tax. It makes use of the global tables Limit,
24      Fixed, and Percent. *)
25   Var Index : Integer;
26     Begin
27       Index := 1;
28       While (Limit[Index] < Wages) AND (Index <> 8) (*the table size *) Do
29          Index := Index + 1;
30       Taxes := Fixed[Index] + Percent[Index] * (Wages - Limit[Index-1])
31     End (* Taxation *); (* Don't you just wish! *)
32
33
34   BEGIN (* Driver *)
35
36     (* Input the tables to be used *)
37     Writeln ('Reading tax tables...');
38     Writeln;
39     Reset (TaxTables);
40     For K := 0 to 8 Do
41        Readln (TaxTables, Limit[K], Fixed[K], Percent[K]);
42
43     (* Read in a bunch of salaries and compute the taxes for them *)
44     Write ('Enter salary --> '); Readln (Salary);
45     While Salary >= 0 Do
46       Begin
47         Taxation (Salary, Tax);
48         Writeln ('The tax due on this salary is $',Tax:6:2);
49         Writeln;
50         Write ('Enter salary --> '); Readln (Salary)
51       End
52
53   END.
```

Figure 15-10

Test Run of the Procedure to Compute Withholding Tax According to the Percentage Method

```
$ type taxtable.dat

    0       0.00    0.00
   27       0.00    0.00
   63       0.00    0.15
  131       5.40    0.18
  196      17.64    0.21
  274      31.29    0.26
  331      51.31    0.30
  433      68.71    0.34
    0     103.39    0.39


$ run driver

Reading tax tables...

Enter salary --> 200
The tax due on this salary is $ 32.33

Enter salary --> 25
The tax due on this salary is $  0.00

Enter salary --> 0
The tax due on this salary is $  0.00

Enter salary --> 500
The tax due on this salary is $129.52

Enter salary --> 27
The tax due on this salary is $  0.00

Enter salary --> 63
The tax due on this salary is $  5.40

Enter salary --> 131
The tax due on this salary is $ 17.64

Enter salary --> 433
The tax due on this salary is $103.39

Enter salary --> -1
```

STEP 5: DOCUMENT

The comments and structure make the procedure easy to read and follow.

We now have completed our examination of linear search strategies. However, especially for larger arrays, a linear search can be very time consuming. For an ordered array, there are techniques that can significantly reduce the amount of time required to search, and these methods are explored next.

BINARY SEARCHES

A binary search is carried out by successively eliminating, with each test or comparison, exactly one-half of the *remaining* array elements until the key (or nothing, if the key is not in the array) is the only thing left. Contrast this method with a linear search, which can eliminate only one element with each test or comparison.

Let's explore the difference between a binary search and a linear search. Suppose we have an array of 1,000 elements and wish to search it. In a linear search, we test the first element; if it does not equal the key, then we eliminate it from consideration and search the remaining 999 elements. However, in a binary search, we examine not the first element of the array but rather the *middle* element of the array. If this middle element is not the key, we eliminate from consideration not only that particular element but an additional 499 elements as well (one-half of the array). This means that, after only one comparison, we have reduced the number of elements to be searched to only 500 instead of the 999 that remained in the linear search!

The binary search process continues in the same fashion on whatever half of the array remains. The following table compares for these two methods the number of elements that remain to be searched after each test:

	Number of Elements Left to Be Searched	
Test Number	**Linear Search**	**Binary Search**
0	1,000	1,000
1	999	500
2	998	250
3	997	125
4	996	63
5	995	32
6	994	16
7	993	8
8	992	4
9	991	2
10	990	1
11	989	0

See how much more quickly an element can be found with a binary search? Even starting out with one thousand elements, the *largest* number of tests the binary search procedure will have to make is only eleven. For a linear search, the maximum number of tests required is one thousand. Not only that, but if we search an array of two thousand elements, a binary search will require only one additional comparison, whereas the linear search could require as many as one thousand more comparisons!

There is a twofold price to be paid for this efficiency. First, the array must be in order, and getting it in order is not a trivial task. Second, the algorithm for a logarithmic search is somewhat more complicated than the algorithm for a linear search. There is, therefore, a trade-off. Because of the increased complexity of the binary search, smaller arrays can be searched more efficiently using a linear search, while larger arrays can be searched more efficiently using a binary search.

The essence of a binary search is as follows: Compare the key to the middle element of the array; if this element is equal to the key, then we have found what we are looking for. If it is not, then check to see whether the key comes before the middle element or after it in the array. (Remember that the array is ordered.) If the key comes before the middle element in the array, then eliminate the second half of the array from consideration and continue to search in the first half of the array only. However, if the key comes after the middle element in the array, continue to search only the second half of the array (thus eliminating the first half). Proceed in this fashion either until you find the key or until all the array elements have been eliminated (which means that the key is not in the array).

As an example, consider a binary search of the twenty-five alphabetized words shown in Figure 15-11. Suppose we want to see if the word "forget" is in the list. When we first begin the search, we find the middle element and compare it with the key. Since the last word in the list is number 25, the middle word would be number 13, the word "logarithm." We compare this with our key word of "forget" and see that the two words are *not* equal. However, alphabetically, our keyword of "forget" comes before the word "logarithm." Consequently, we conclude that all of the array elements from "logarithm" to the end can be eliminated—there is no way that the word we seek can be in the array. We know that the word we seek must be somewhere in the array between elements 1 and 12. The search has been narrowed considerably!

We then repeat the process, using only the first twelve elements of the array. The middle element of this remaining portion would be number 6, the word "display." We see that this word does not equal the key and that the word "forget" comes *after* the word "display." Therefore, we conclude that the word we seek must be located somewhere between elements 7 and 12. Again, half of the remaining list elements have been eliminated.

Repeating the process yet another time, we find that the middle element of the remaining array elements is number 9. Element 9 is the word "input," which is still not the key. However, our key word "forget" falls before the word "input," so we can narrow the search range to elements 7 and 8.

Figure 15-11

A List of Words and Their Definitions for Use with the Binary Search Procedure

Index	Word	Definition
1	array	collection of like elements
2	bad	not good
3	computer	device which executes algorithms
4	control	making things happen
5	decision	choice
6	display	show off
7	forget	fail to remember
8	good	not bad
9	input	items used
10	iteration	doing something over and over
11	keyboard	board full of keys
12	list	collections of things
13	logarithm	inverse function to exponential
14	money	purchasing power
15	output	items produced
16	remember	not to forget
17	search	look for
18	sequence	one thing after another
19	sort	put in order
20	ugly	not pretty
21	wisdom	knowledge and understanding
22	wise	possessing wisdom
23	yesterday	previous day
24	xenophobe	one who fears others
25	xylophone	musical instrument

Doing this one more time, we compute the center value, which in this case turns out to be 7. Element 7 is, in fact, the word we seek!

Although, in this example, we found the word we sought, what would happen if the key was not in the list? In such a case the range would narrow to a single element. If this happens and the element is not the key, we can then conclude that the key is not in the array. The way this situation is actually manifested in a program is that the lower bound of the search will exceed the upper bound.

Let's now formalize this process with an algorithm. Because we carry out the same task over and over, we can use recursion; in fact a recursive algorithm can be quite elegant, as we can see below:

```
Procedure BinarySearch (Key, Array, LowBound, HighBound, Index)
(*Recursive *)
MiddleBound ← (LowBound + HighBound) / 2
If LowBound > HighBound then
    Index ← 0                          (* It's not here *)
Else if Array[MiddleBound] = Key then
    Index ← MiddleBound                (* We found it *)
Else                                   (* Keep looking *)
  If Key < Array[MiddleBound] then
    BinarySearch (Key, Array, LowBound, MiddleBound − 1, Index)
  Else
    BinarySearch (Key, Array, MiddleBound + 1, HighBound, Index)
```

The parameters in this case consist of the key for which we are searching, the array itself, the low bound on the search, the high bound on the search, and the index of the key if found. (This is set to zero if the key is not found.)

We can also implement a binary search nonrecursively, as follows:

```
Procedure BinarySearch (Key, Array, Size, Index)
(* Nonrecursive *)
LowBound ← 1
HighBound ← Size
Done ← False
While not Done Do
  MiddleBound ← (LowBound + HighBound) / 2
  If LowBound > HighBound then
    Index ← 0                          (* It's not here *)
    Done ← True
  Else if Array[MiddleBound] = Key then
    Index ← MiddleBound                (*We found it *)
    Done ← True
  Else                                 (* Keep looking *)
    If Key < Array[MiddleBound] then
      HighBound ← MiddleBound − 1
    Else
      LowBound ← MiddleBound + 1
```

Although this solution isn't as elegant, it requires fewer parameters to implement. The option you choose to solve a particular problem is arbitrary. Also, as in the case of ordered linear searches, parallel arrays (or arrays of records) are frequently encountered.

Dictionary Search

Let's use a binary search to implement word look-ups in a dictionary. We'll use the words and definitions in Figure 15-11 instead of a whole dictionary. We will need a main program to drive the search procedure. However, since the primary focus of this chapter is on searching and sorting, we will forego a detailed description of the development of the driver program. We only point out that the driver program has two functions: to input the dictionary (that is, the words and their associated definitions) and to call the binary search procedure. Given this, let's now proceed to the binary search procedure.

STEP 1: UNDERSTAND THE PROBLEM

Having already generated the general binary search algorithm, we need only adapt it to our specific problem. This involves little more than specifying the arrays we want to use. In this case we will use two related arrays, one of words (maximum length of 10) and one of the words' definitions (maximum length of 30).

STEP 2: PLAN THE SOLUTION

As we mentioned, the algorithms have already been presented. However, we need to decide whether we want to implement the search recursively or nonrecursively. Let's do it nonrecursively. Supplying appropriate variable names to the nonrecursive algorithm gives us

```
Procedure BinarySearch (Word, WordList, Size, Index)
(* Nonrecursive *)
LowBound ← 1
HighBound ← Size
Done ← False
While not Done Do
   MiddleBound ← (LowBound + HighBound) / 2
   If LowBound > HighBound then
      Index ← 0              (* It's not here*)
      Done ← True
   Else If WordList[MiddleBound] = Word then
      Index ← MiddleBound   (* We found it *)
      Done ← True
   Else                      (* Keep looking *)
     If Word < WordList[MiddleBound] then
        HighBound ← MiddleBound − 1
     Else
        LowBound ← MiddleBound + 1
```

STEP 3: CODE THE SOLUTION

Figure 15-12 shows the coded solution of the binary search algorithm embedded within the driver program. One point of interest is the use of Var (that is, call by reference) for the array to be searched. Since we are not going to change any of the array values, why use this method rather than call by value? We do so because it makes the execution more efficient. Had we specified call by value here, Pascal would have made a copy of the entire array for use by the procedure! This doubles the amount of storage space required for the words and their definitions. When using call by reference, the original array is used and no additional space is required. Of course, since we are using call by reference, we must be *very* careful not to alter the array within the procedure. Also note that the dictionary is read in from an external file.

STEP 4: CHECK OUT THE PROGRAM

Figure 15-13 shows the output that is obtained in a test run of the binary search routine, where the word list being searched is the one shown in Figure 15-11. Test words consist of the first word in the list, the last word in the list, and several interior words. Also note that the program correctly recognizes when a word is *not* in the list; "missing" words are chosen that would (if they were there) normally come before the first word of the list, after the final word of the list, or anywhere in between. Recall that it is a good idea to test programs in such a way that boundary conditions are all tried and shown to work properly.

STEP 5: DOCUMENT

The procedure is self-explanatory. Appropriate comments have been added to clarify the various sections.

It may be hard to appreciate the true beauty of a binary search with this example, where a dictionary of only twenty-five words is used. However, consider this: if we were to utilize this technique on a dictionary of ten thousand words, the maximum number of comparisons needed to find *any* word would be only fifteen. In other words, a binary search could deal as easily with an array of ten thousand elements as a linear search could with an array of fifteen elements.

This completes our coverage of searching. We have been using ordered arrays for a number of our examples, and the question naturally arises: How do we get them in order in the first place? They can be entered in order (as we did with our little dictionary), but more often than not it is easier to have the computer order the array for us. Methods of doing just this are explored next.

Figure 15-12

Program That Uses a Binary Search Procedure to Look Up Words in a
Dictionary

DRIVER.PAS

```
1    Program DRIVER (Dictionary, Input, Output);
2
3    (*
4        This program tests a nonrecursive binary search procedure.
5    *)
6
7    Const MaxSize = 100;  (* Maximum number of words to be searched *)
8
9    Type  ShortString = Packed Array [1..10] of Char;
10          LongString  = Packed Array [1..30] of Char;
11
12          Words = Array [1..MaxSize] of ShortString;
13          Definitions = Array [1..MaxSize] of LongString;
14
15    Var   WordList : Words;        (* Array of words *)
16          DefList  : Definitions; (* Parallel array of definitions *)
17
18          KeyWord  : ShortString; (* Word to be looked up *)
19
20          OneWord  : ShortString; (* For use in reading dictionary *)
21          OneDefn  : LongString;  (* Ditto *)
22          k        : Integer;     (* Ditto *)
23
24          Size : Integer;         (* Number of words in the array *)
25          Index : Integer;        (* Index to the looked-for word *)
26
27          Dictionary : Text;      (* External file containing the words
28                                       and their definitions *)
29
30    Procedure ReadKey (Var Key : ShortString);
31    (* This procedure reads in the Key word from the Keyboard *)
32    Var K : Integer;
33      Begin
34        For K:= 1 to 10 Do
35            Read (Key[K]);
36        Readln
37      End;
38
39
40    Procedure BinarySearch (TheWord:ShortString; Var WordArray:Words;
41                            Size : Integer; Var Index:Integer);
42
43    (* This is a nonrecursive implementation of a binary search *)
44
45    Var LowBound, MiddleBound, HighBound : Integer;
46        Done : Boolean;
47
48        Begin
49          LowBound := 1;
50          HighBound := Size;
51          Done := False;
52          While not Done Do
```

Figure 15-12 continued

```
53                 Begin
54                    MiddleBound := (LowBound + HighBound) DIV 2;
55                    If LowBound > HighBound then
56                       Begin        (* The word isn't here *)
57                          Index := 0;
58                          Done := True
59                       End
60                    Else if WordArray[MiddleBound] = TheWord then
61                       Begin  (* We have found it! *)
62                          Index := MiddleBound;
63                          Done := True
64                       End
65                    Else           (* Keep looking *)
66                       If TheWord < WordArray[MiddleBound] then
67                          HighBound := MiddleBound - 1
68                       Else
69                          LowBound := MiddleBound + 1
70                 End (* While *)
71        End (* BinarySearch *);
72
73
74    BEGIN
75
76       Writeln ('DICTIONARY LOOK-UP');
77       Writeln;
78
79       (* Read in the dictionary *)
80       Writeln ('Reading dictionary...');
81       Writeln;
82       Reset (Dictionary);
83       Index := 0;
84       While not EOF (Dictionary) Do
85          Begin
86             Index := Index + 1;
87
88             For k := 1 to 10 Do               (* Read in a word *)
89                Read (Dictionary, OneWord[k]);
90             WordList[Index] := OneWord;
91
92             For k := 1 to 30 Do               (* Read in its definition *)
93                Read (Dictionary, OneDefn[k]);
94             DefList[Index] := OneDefn;
95             Readln (Dictionary)               (* Skip to the next line *)
96          End;
97       Size := Index;
98       Writeln (Size:1, ' words read in.');
99       Writeln;
100
101      (* Input a word and look up its definition *)
102      Writeln ('Enter words to be looked up. They must be in all');
103      Writeln ('lower case letters. Enter the word ''stop'' to quit.');
104      Writeln;
105
106      Write (' -->'); ReadKey (KeyWord);
107      While KeyWord <> 'stop       ' Do
```

Figure 15-12 continued

```
108        Begin
109          BinarySearch (KeyWord, WordList, Size, Index);
110          If Index = 0 then
111            Writeln ('   ** This word is not in the dictionary.')
112          Else
113            Writeln ('   ', DefList[Index]);
114          Writeln;
115          Write '--> '); ReadKey (KeyWord)
116        End
117
118   END.
```

Figure 15-13

Test Run of the Dictionary Look-Up Program

```
$ run driver

DICTIONARY LOOK-UP

Reading dictionary...

25 words read in.

Enter words to be looked up. They must be in all
lower case letters. Enter the word 'stop' to quit.

--> array
    collection of like elements

--> xylophone
    musical instrument

--> list
    collections of things

--> good
    not bad

--> abbot
    ** This word is not in the dictionary.

--> zephyr
    ** This word is not in the dictionary.

--> nanny
    ** This word is not in the dictionary.

--> stop
```

15-2 *Sorting*

Let's next examine ways in which unordered arrays can be transformed into ordered arrays. We have already seen applications in which ordered arrays are useful, and sometimes the ordering itself is all that is needed. For example, a list of students registered for a class can be printed out in alphabetical order. The usefulness of the data is enhanced by having it in order.

There are several kinds of orderings for sorting values. The two primary orderings are

1. Ascending order (smallest to largest)

2. Descending order (largest to smallest)

For example, the list of numbers

$$-20.2 \quad -5.75 \quad -1 \quad 0 \quad 2.3 \quad 7.98$$

is in ascending order. The same list in descending order is

$$7.98 \quad 2.3 \quad 0 \quad -1 \quad -5.75 \quad -20.2$$

Related orderings also exist. For example, if we are using strings of letters, all of which are the same case (either upper or lower), then ascending order corresponds to **alphabetical order.** A more general case of such ordering is termed **lexical order,** which means that any and all characters of the computer can be ordered. The specific ordering is defined by the **collating sequence** of the computer. The collating sequence is nothing more than a list of the characters the computer can handle in some predetermined order. There are two such orderings in common usage: one is ASCII (which is an acronym for American Standard Code for Information Interchange) and the other is EBCDIC (Extended Binary Coded Decimal Interchange Code). The latter is used almost exclusively on IBM computers and the former on all other machines. A partial ordering of characters according to the ASCII sequence (the ASCII collating sequence) is

```
! " # $ % & ` ( ) * + , - . / 0 1 2 3 4 5 6 7 8 9 0
: ; < = > ? @ A B C D E F G H I J K L M N O P Q R S
T U V W X Y Z [ ] ^ a b c d e f g h i j k l m n o p
q r s t u v w x y z { | }
```

According to this sequence, the string `#456` comes before the string `187.99`, which comes before `ZEALOUS`, which comes before `arnold`. As we mentioned previously, if the strings are made up strictly of letters of the same case, lexical order is the same as alphabetical order, which is a special case of ascending order.

OVERVIEW OF COMMON SORTING TECHNIQUES

To appreciate the wide variety of sorting techniques available, we will briefly describe five sorting methods: the insertion sort, the bubble sort, the selection sort, the QuickSort, and the heap sort. We will then look at the selection sort in detail and develop an application for it.

Insertion sort. The insertion sort operates by constructing a list, one element at a time, in such a way that the list is always in order. As each element is added to the list, it is inserted into the proper position necessary to keep the whole list in order at all times. This process is similar to the way you order a stack of index cards. You start with one card, take a second, and then put it either in front of or behind the first, so that the two cards are in order. You then pick a third card and place it either in front of, behind, or between the two cards you have, so that all three cards are in order. You continue in this way until all the cards are properly ordered. This method of sorting is demonstrated in Figure 15-14. The data structure most appropriate to the insertion sort is the list, since lists can expand as needed. Consequently, this sort is explored further in Chapter 16.

Bubble sort. This is probably the most famous of all the elementary sorts and the least efficient. The bubble sort operates by going through the array from beginning to end, comparing each pair of adjacent elements and putting each pair in order. When the sort has gone through the entire array one time (that is, made one pass), the largest element will be in the last position (which is to say, it will be in order). Another pass is made through the array (again comparing adjacent elements), after which *two* elements will be in order. This is continued until the entire array is in order. The method is demonstrated in Figure 15-15. This sort derives its name from the fact that the smaller-valued array elements slowly move (bubble) up to the beginning of the array as the sort progresses.

Selection sort. This sort is a little more efficient and easier to follow than the bubble sort. The selection sort is carried out by searching the entire array and locating (selecting) the smallest element. Once this smallest element is located (the first pass is complete), it is exchanged with whatever element is currently in the first position of the array. This, of course, means that the first array element will now be in order. Another pass is then made to find the smallest element in the *remaining* elements of the array. When this element is found, it is exchanged with

Figure 15-14

Operation of the Insertion Sort

This is the initial list of words to be sorted:

```
new, old, good, bad, indifferent
```

1. The first word is taken, and the sorted list is made up of only this word:

```
new
```

2. The next word is taken and placed in the correct order relative to the first word:

```
new, old
```

3. The third word is then taken and inserted into the list in the proper order relative to the two already there:

```
good, new, old
```

4. This process is repeated for the next word:

```
bad, good, new, old
```

5. The last item is then inserted into the list properly, and the sort is complete:

```
bad, good, indifferent, new, old
```

Figure 15-15

Operation of the Bubble Sort

This is the initial array to be sorted:

```
new
old
good
bad
indifferent
```

1. The first and second array elements are compared; since they are already in order, they are not exchanged.

2. The second and third elements are compared next; since they are *not* in order they are exchanged, and the following array results:

Figure 15-15 continued

```
new
good
old
bad
indifferent
```

3. The third and fourth elements are compared next; since they are not in order they are exchanged, and the result is

```
new
good
bad
old
indifferent
```

4. Finally, the fourth and fifth elements are compared; since they are not in order either they are exchanged, with this result:

```
new
good
bad
indifferent
old
```

5. This completes the first pass. At this point the fifth element is in order. The process is then started over again by comparing the first and second elements, which are not in order and must be exchanged.

```
good
new
bad
indifferent
old
```

6. Continuing, the second and third elements are compared and then exchanged.

```
good
bad
new
indifferent
old
```

7. The third and fourth are compared and exchanged.

```
good
bad
```

Figure 15-15 continued

```
indifferent
new
old
```

8. The fourth and fifth elements are in order. Hence, no exchange is necessary. This completes the second pass, and we know for sure that the last two elements are now in order. The process is started over once again; the first and second elements are compared and then exchanged.

```
bad
good
indifferent
new
old
```

The process will continue. However, since the list is now in order, no further exchanges will take place.

whatever is in the second array position. This process is repeated until all the elements are in the right order. The selection sort is demonstrated in Figure 15-16. (We will present specific algorithms for this sort in the next section.)

QuickSort. The QuickSort is a recursive technique in which one element, called the pivot, is chosen and the remaining elements partitioned on either side of it such that only values less than the pivot are placed to the left of the pivot (in no particular order) and values greater than the pivot are placed to the right (also in no particular order). The procedure is then called recursively for the elements to the left of the pivot and then for the elements to the right of the pivot. Each of these elements is then partitioned, and the procedure is called as often as needed until the entire array is in order. The process is demonstrated in Figure 15-17. This sort can be much more efficient than the sorts already mentioned, especially for larger arrays.

Heap sort. This is one of the most efficient of all sorting techniques. However, it requires the use of a **heap**, which , as the name implies, is a two-dimensional data structure that tapers from the bottom to the top. (Heaps in general, and this sort in particular, will be discussed further in Chapter 17.) The fundamental property of a heap is that the magnitude of the values of the elements in the heap get smaller as you go from the bottom of the heap to the top. Consequently, the uppermost value

Figure 15-16

Operation of the Selection Sort

This is the initial array to be sorted:

```
new
old
good
bad
indifferent
```

1. Position 1 will be ordered first. A search is made for the smallest element in the array, which is found in position 4. Therefore, the elements at positions 1 and 4 are exchanged, and the result is

```
bad
old
good
new
indifferent
```

2. Position 1 is now correct, so we move on to position 2. A search is made for the smallest remaining element, which is found to be in position 3. Therefore positions 2 and 3 are exchanged, yielding

```
bad
good
old
new
indifferent
```

3. Positions 1 and 2 are now correct, so we move on to position 3. The smallest element remaining can be found in position 5, therefore, it is exchanged with position 3:

```
bad
good
indifferent
new
old
```

The process will continue. However, since the list is now in order, no further exchanges will take place.

Figure 15-17

Operation of the QuickSort

This is the initial array to be sorted:

```
new
old
good
bad
indifferent
```

1. We will make the center the pivot. The array is searched from the beginning toward the pivot for an element that is on the wrong side of the pivot; the word "new" is it. Then a search is made from the end for an element that is also on the wrong side; the word "bad" is it. These two are then exchanged:

```
bad
old
good
new
indifferernt
```

2. The search continues on each side until the pivot is reached by both. The words so located are "old" and "good," and these are exchanged:

```
bad
good
old
new
indifferent
```

3. The array is now divided into two parts: all those elements before the pivot "good" and all those after it. Since there is only one element in the array section before "good," it must be already in order. The sort then moves to the second half of the array and begins the process all over again.

4. The pivot for the right half of the array would become "new." A search is made both from the beginning and the end to find words in the wrong positions. Both "indifferent" and "old" are incorrect. Therefore, they are exchanged, giving

Figure 15-17 continued

```
bad
good
indifferent
new
old
```

The array is now sorted.

of the heap is the smallest of all. The heap sort essentially pulls off this top (smallest) value, then "shakes" the heap so the next smallest value rises to the top. The process is shown schematically in Figure 15-18.

DETAILS OF THE SELECTION SORT

Having looked at several sorting methods, we will examine one of them, the selection sort, in detail. Although the selection sort is only one possible way of ordering an array, it contains many subtasks common to other sorts, such as searching and exchanging array elements. In this sense the selection sort can be considered a paradigm for sorting procedures in general, and studying this sort will give us a clearer understanding of how computers sort data.

In keeping with our methods for this chapter, we will present an algorithm for the selection sort. Recall that the fundamental process in the selection sort involves finding (selecting) the lowest value in the array and then exchanging it with the first array position (provided, of course, that the smallest element is not already the one in the first position). This process is then repeated for each succeeding position until the entire array has been sorted. The algorithm is as follows:

```
 1.     For Position ← 1 to n − 1 Do
 2.         Index of Smallest ← Position
 3.         For Check ← Position + 1 to n Do
 4.             If Element[Check] < Element[Index of Smallest] then
 5.                 Index of Smallest ← Check
 6.         If Index of Smallest ≠ Position then
 7.             Exchange these two elements
 8.                 Hold ← Element[Position]
 9.                 Element[Position] ← Element[Index of Smallest]
10.                 Element[Index of Smallest] ← Hold
```

Let's dissect this algorithm to make its functioning clear. Line 1 (the start of the outer loop) indicates that the algorithm sorts the array one position at a time, starting with the first and going up through and

Figure 15-18

Operation of the Heap Sort

This is the initial list of words to be sorted:

`new, old, good, bad, indifferent`

1. The first word is taken and the heap is made up of only this word:

`new`

2. The second word is placed correctly into the heap. Since it comes after the word "NEW," it goes underneath:

```
       new
    old
```

3. The word "good" is taken. However, it should come further up the heap than the word "New" so the two are reversed, yielding

```
        good
    old      new
```

4. The next word, "bad," comes even before "good," so the heap becomes

```
         bad
      good   new
   old
```

5. The last word goes on the bottom. The complete heap, therefore, is

```
         bad
      good      new
   old     indifferent
```

6. The heap is now formed. The smallest element is on the top, and the elements get larger as you go deeper into the heap. The first word is then pulled from the top of the heap to become part of the sorted list. The remaining elements are then shuffled upward by moving the smallest ones first. The result is

```
         good
    indifferent    new
 old

 bad
```

7. The top word is again removed and placed into the sorted list. The heap is then adjusted once again to yield

Figure 15-18 continued

```
        indifferent
   old            new

 bad, good
```

8. This process is repeated once again, giving

```
           new
        old

 bad, good, indifferent
```

9. One more time:

```
        old

 bad, good, indifferent, new
```

10. Note that there is only one word left on the heap. This is also removed and placed at the end of the sorted list:

```
 bad, good, indifferent, new, old
```

including the next to the last position (position n − 1). The last position doesn't need to be sorted explicitly, because if all the other positions are correct, the last one will have to be correct also.

Lines 2 through 5 are nothing more than a linear search that finds the smallest element between the current position and the end of the array. Once the smallest element is found, line 6 tests to see whether this smallest element coincides with the current position being sorted. If they do coincide, nothing further is done; however, if they do not, then lines 7 through 10 exchange the two elements.

The exchange itself requires some comment. At first glance you might be tempted to carry out an exchange of two elements, let's call them A and B, as follows:

A ← B
B ← A

However, this will not work. When you give the variable A the value of B in the first line, *you have destroyed the value of A*. After the first line is executed, A and B will have the same value. Consequently, setting B equal to A in the next line will not complete the exchange; in fact it will not do anything at all, since both elements will already have the same value. In order to carry out an exchange of this kind, a temporary location is required as follows:

Temp ← A
  A ← B
  B ← Temp

In other words, we have to make a copy of A *before* we put the value of B into A. We can then place into B the value of the temporary location, which is an exact copy of A, and the exchange is complete.

The algorithm for a selection sort presented above provides a way to reform an array into ascending order. Should we want descending order instead, we can use the same sort, except that instead of searching for the *smallest* element at each pass we search for the *largest*.

Let's now look at a problem that requires sorting as part of the solution.

Registration Lists

Let's suppose you're still working at the University of Remington at Quince Terrace (URAQT) and that the registrar wants you to write a program that will print out registration lists. Registration information for each semester is kept in a single large file. The registrar would like this information sorted alphabetically by class and alphabetically by student within each class and then printed out.

STEP 1: UNDERSTAND THE PROBLEM

Let's begin by looking at the input and output. As we just said, the input data is kept in a single file. We will construct the file in such a way that each record consists of the name of one student and one class for which he or she is registered. Typically, the data would look like this:

SMITH PETER	CS101
JONES HARRY	MATH 105
MARTIN MARY	CS 235
JARVIS SANDY	CS 101

. . .

The records in the file are simply in the order in which they were originally entered. Our task is to sort the records so that the output becomes

CS 101
> 1. ADAMS WILLIAM
> 2. ANDREWS BOB
>
> . . .

MATH 200
> 1. JONES TIM
> 2. TEWES BOBBY
>
> . . .

The input and output having now been defined, we should next decide how to organize the data. In this case let's use parallel arrays: one for the course names and one for the student names. We are ready to move on to the next step.

STEP 2: PLAN THE SOLUTION

We know we have to do some sorting, but let's not get involved with that just yet. If we were to start with the sorting process, we would be solving the problem *bottom up* rather than top down, a process that can be very frustrating. We must, however, think about exactly what's going on here. We do *not* have just a straightforward sort, because the output is to be sorted by course, and within each course it must be sorted by name. Were we to sort either by course or student name, we would not get the desired result. We are, unfortunately, going to have to do more than one sort.

But how will we do this? As a place to start, suppose we sort the entire list by course. The result will be a list of the registration data in which all of the courses are in alphabetical order but in which the associated names (that is, the students who are in the respective courses) are *not* in order. What we can do next, however, is divide up the list by course and then sort the names *within each course*. For example, perhaps elements 1 through 7 correspond to the first course, elements 8 through 10 correspond to the second, and so forth. We could sort the elements corresponding to each course separately and thereby convert the list to the form we want! Before we go on, however, let's summarize what we have in an initial algorithm:

Read all the registration records into an array
Sort them by course name
Go through the array and delimit each course
> For each delimited course Do
> > Sort by student name
> > Output the sorted, delimited course list

The next question is: How do we delimit the individual courses in the array? The easiest way is just to go through the array one element at a time and see where the course names change. To do this we compare the name of the first course to the name of each subsequent course in the array. Whenever we come across a different course name (or reach the end of the list), we know that we have come to the end of the particular course under scrutiny. Consequently, we also know both the beginning element and the end element of the course. We then can carry out a sort on these elements only. Adding these details to our algorithm gives us

Read all the registration records into an array
Sort them by course name
Go through the array and delimit each course
   Count ← 1
   While Count ≤ Size of the array Do
     Start of course ← Count
     Finish of course ← Count + 1
     While Finish ≤ Size of the array AND
       Course Name[Finish] = Course Name[Start] Do
         Finish ← Finish + 1
     Finish ← Finish − 1

     Sort from element Start to element Finish, by student name
     Output the course from Start to Finish

     Go on to the next course
       Count ← Finish + 1

We have within this algorithm a search algorithm (looking for a change in course name). We also have an outer loop that permits us to go through the entire array and break it up into courses.

We can make good use of three procedures here: one to input the data, one to sort it, and one to output the results. We will not dwell on the input and output procedures at this time, since we have done similar operations before. The sort, however, requires some thought. First, since we will not be sorting just a single array, we will have to sort one and have the other tag along, so that the corresponding elements of each don't get mixed up. Second, sometimes we will be sorting by course, and sometimes we will be sorting by student name. Finally, we will not necessarily be sorting the entire array. Taking this all into account, we may alter the selection sort procedure given earlier so that it becomes

Sort (FirstArray, SecondArray, FirstElement, LastElement)

Here, FirstArray is the array that is actually sorted, SecondArray is the one that just tags along, FirstElement is the index to the first element to be sorted, and LastElement is the index to the last element to be sorted. This adds generality so that we don't have to write more than one sort routine.

Incorporating this procedure into our general algorithm yields

Read all the registration records into an array
  ReadIn (StudentNames, CourseNames, Size of Arrays)
Sort them by course name
  Sort (CourseNames, StudentNames, 1, Size of Array)
Go through the list and delimit each course
    Count ← 1
    While Count ≤ Size of the array Do
      Start of course ← Count
      Finish of course ← Count + 1
      While Finish ≤ Size of the array AND
        Course Name[Finish] = Course Name[Start] Do
          Finish ← Finish + 1
      Finish ← Finish − 1

      Sort from element Start to element Finish, by student name
        Sort (StudentNames, CourseNames, Start, Finish)
      Output the course from Start to Finish
        PrintList (CourseNames, StudentNames, Start, Finish)

      Go on to the next course
        Count ← Finish + 1

As we have been doing, we will omit here the actual details of coding the main program and develop the procedure algorithms. Also, we will not concern ourselves with the details of the procedures ReadIn and PrintList, so we can move on to develop the Sort routine. Since this is a significantly difficult task, we will present all of the developmental phases for it.

Subtask Sort: **Step 1—Understand the Problem.** Actually we already understand Sort. The only complications here concern the fact that (1) we sort one array but have a second array tag along, and (2) we sometimes sort only part of an array. A few modifications of our basic algorithm will take care of this for us.

Subtask Sort: **Step 2—Plan the Solution.** As we just said, a few minor alterations will suffice here. The modified algorithm is

Procedure Sort (A, B, First, Last)
For Position ← First to Last − 1 Do
   Index of Smallest ← Position
   For Check ← Position + 1 to Last Do
     If A[Check] < A[Index of Smallest] then
       Index of Smallest ← Check
   If Index of Smallest ≠ Position then
     Exchange (A[Index of Smallest], A[Check])
     Exchange (B[Index of Smallest], B[Check])

There are a couple of things to note here. First, all we need to do to keep the corresponding array elements of the two arrays from getting scrambled is to carry out exchanges on *both* arrays simultaneously. Second, the sort can be used on part of an array simply by going from First to Last rather than from 1 to *n*. Third, we have implemented the exchange as another procedure (since we have to carry it out more than once). The Exchange procedure can be written as

Procedure Exchange (A, B)
  Hold ← A
    A ← B
    B ← Hold

The only further complication concerns the arrays that are being sorted. Since they can be used interchangeably in the sort, *they must both be of exactly the same type*. This is only a minor difficulty in that the length of the course names and the student names must be the same.

STEP 3: CODE THE SOLUTION

Now that we have all of our procedure algorithms, we may proceed to code the registration problem. The Pascal solution is given in Figure 15-19. Examine carefully the data structures used and the structure of the program as a whole.

Figure 15-19

Program That Uses a Selection Sort to Order Registration Lists

REGSTRAR.PAS

```
 1    Program REGSTRAR (RegFile, Output, ClassLists);
 2
 3    (*
 4        This program takes registration data from an input file and
 5        sorts it according to class and alphabetically by name within
 6        each class. The individual class lists are then printed out.
 7    *)
 8
 9    Const MaxRecords = 100; (* Maximum number of registration records
10                                the program will work with *)
11
12    Type  String15 = Packed Array [1..15] of Char;
13          Strings  = Array [1..MaxRecords] of String15;
14
15    Var   Course,             (* Course names *)
16          Student : Strings;(* Student names *)
17          Size : Integer;    (* Number of records read in to be sorted *)
18
19          Count : Integer;   (* Counter to walk through the arrays *)
20
21          Start,             (* First record of the course to be sorted *)
22          Finish : Integer; (* Last record of the course to be sorted *)
23
24          RegFile    : Text;(* External file containing the registration data *)
25          ClassLists : Text;(* External file to contain the sorted lists *)
```

Figure 15-19 continued

```
26
27
28    Procedure ReadIn (Var TheFile : Text;
29                      Var Person, Class : Strings; Var N : Integer);
30    (* This procedure reads in the registration data from the external file *)
31    Var Item : String15;
32
33        Procedure ReadString (Var TheFile : Text;
34                              Var S : String15);
35        (* This procedure reads in one 15 character string *)
36        Var k : Integer;
37          Begin
38            For k := 1 to 15 Do
39                  Read (TheFile, S[k])
40          End;
41
42    Begin (* ReadIn *)
43      N := 0;
44      While not EOF (TheFile) Do
45        Begin
46          N := N + 1;
47          ReadString (TheFile, Item);
48          Person[N] := Item;
49          ReadString (TheFile, Item);
50          Class[N] := Item;
51          ReadIn (TheFile)    (* Go to the next record in the file *)
52        End
53    End; (* ReadIn *)
54
55
56    Procedure PrintList (Var OutFile : Text;
57                         Var Class, Person : Strings;
58                             First, Last   : Integer);
59    (* This procedure prints out one, single class list to the output file *)
60    Var k,s : Integer;
61      Begin
62        Writeln;                                        (* Monitor Progress *)
63        Writeln  (`Printing list for `, Class[First]);
64        Writeln  (OutFile);
65        Writeln  (OutFile);
66        Writeln  (OutFile, Class[First]);
67        s := 1;    (* Number the students in the class list *)
68        For k := First to Last Do
69          Begin
70            Writeln (OutFile, s:5, `, `, Person[k]);
71            s := s + 1
72          End
73      End; (* PrintList *)
74
75
76    Procedure Sort (Var A, B : Strings; First, Last : Integer);
77    (* This procedure sorts the first array into ascending order and
78       lets the second array tag along so that the corresponding
79       elements of each don't get mixed up. *)
80
81    Var Position, IndexSmallest, CheckNext : Integer;
82
83        Procedure Exchange (Var A, B : String15);
84        (* This procedure exchanges any two strings *)
85        Var Hold : String15;
```

Figure 15-19 continued

```
86              Begin
87                Hold := A;
88                  A := B;
89                  B := Hold
90              End;
91
92      Begin (* Sort *)
93        For Position := First to Last - 1 Do
94          Begin
95            IndexSmallest := Position;
96            For CheckNext := Position + 1 to Last Do
97                If A[CheckNext] < A[IndexSmallest] then
98                    IndexSmallest := CheckNext;
99            If IndexSmallest <> Position then
100             Begin
101               Exchange (A[Position], A[IndexSmallest]);
102               Exchange (B[Position], B[IndexSmallest])
103             End
104          End
105     End; (* Sort *)
106
107
108     BEGIN
109
110       Writeln ('REGISTRATION LISTS');
111       Writeln;
112       Writeln ('Reading registration data...');
113
114       (* Get the files ready *)
115       Reset (RegFile);
116       Rewrite (ClassLists);
117
118       (* Fetch the registration records *)
119       ReadIn (RegFile, Student, Course, Size);
120
121       Writeln (Size:1, ' records input.');
122       Writeln;
123
124       (* Sort alphabetically by course *)
125       Sort (Course, Student, 1, Size);
126
127       (* Go through and delimit each course *)
128       Count := 1;
129       While Count <= Size Do
130         Begin
131           Start := Count;
132           Finish := Start + 1;
133           While (Finish <= Size) and (Course[Start] = Course[Finish]) Do
134               Finish := Finish + 1;
135           Finish := Finish - 1;
136
137           (* Sort THIS course, then print it out *)
138           Sort (Student, Course, Start, Finish);
139           PrintList (ClassLists, Course, Student, Start, Finish);
140
141           (* Go on to the next course *)
142           Count := Finish + 1
143         End
144
145     END.
```

STEP 4: CHECK OUT THE PROGRAM

Sample input and output are shown in Figure 15-20. Note that the output is sorted exactly as we want it.

STEP 5: DOCUMENT

Again, we have been doing this all along, and the program structure and accompanying comments make it easy to follow and understand.

This completes our coverage of array sorting. Sorting is a very important and frequently encountered operation. This is why, as we saw, there are so many methods available. In this chapter we looked at only one sorting technique, but we shall look at other techniques shortly. For example, the selection sort (which uses linear lists) is covered in Chapter 16, and the heap sort (which uses heaps) is discussed in Chapter 17.

We will next look at algorithms in and of themselves rather than just as ways of expressing problem solutions. We want to see what properties they have in general and then categorize them accordingly.

Figure 15-20

Test Run of the Registration List Program, Including a Listing of the Input and Output Files

```
$ type regfile.dat

SMITH PETER        CS 101
JONES HARRAY       MATH 105
MARTIN MARY        CS 235
JONES TIM          MATH 200
ANDREWS BOB        CS 101
KENNEDY RALPH      MATH 105
THOMAS MIKE        CS 235
THOMAS JIM         CS 235
JARVIS SANDY       CS 101
ADAMS WILLIAM      CS 101
BANKER RICHARD     MATH 105
TEWES BOBBY        MATH 200
MANDY RAYMOND      MATH 105
MARQUART TIM       CS 101
ARBY SUZAN         MATH 105
SMITH PETER        MATH 200
JONES TIM          CS 101
ARBY SUZAN         CS 235
JARVIS SANDY       MATH 105


$ run regstrar

REGISTRATION LISTS

Reading registration data...
19 records input.
```

Figure 15-20 continued

```
Printing list for CS 101

Printing list for CS 235

Printing list for MATH 105

Printing list for MATH 200

$ type classlis.dat


CS 101
     1. ADAMS WILLIAM
     2. ANDREWS BOB
     3. JARVIS SANDY
     4. JONES TIM
     5. MARQUART TIM
     6. SMITH PETER


CS 235
     1. ARBY SUZAN
     2. MARTIN MARY
     3. THOMAS JIM
     4. THOMAS MIKE


MATH 105
     1. ARBY SUZAN
     2. BANKER RICHARD
     3. JARVIS SANDY
     4. JONES HARRAY
     5. KENNEDY RALPH
     6. MANDY RAYMOND


MATH 200
     1. JONES TIM
     2. SMITH PETER
     3. TEWES BOBBY
```

15-3 *Algorithm Analysis*

We have been using (and will continue to use) algorithms as a way of expressing problem solutions. In this regard we have been concerned with aspects of algorithms such as readability, structure, and correctness. There are, however, additional properties of algorithms that may sometimes need to be considered. We shall conclude this chapter by introducing the concept of algorithm analysis, which involves examining specific algorithms to determine how efficient they are. In other words, we want to find out how well a given algorithm can be expected to use the resources of a computer when converted to a program and then run.

To pursue this goal, we will begin by looking at the idea of algorithm comparison and then develop a notation for expressing such comparisons. We will then apply what we have learned to searching and sorting algorithms.

RELATIVE COMPARISONS

A computer has two primary resources at its disposal: time and memory. Up to this point in the book, we have not been too concerned with efficient use of these resources for the following reasons:

1. Our primary purpose has been to write structured, readable programs, since these are more efficient in terms of human resources.

2. Computer speeds continue to increase, computer memory continues to get cheaper, and efficiency isn't as important as it once was.

3. The programs that we have been writing have not, in any case, been very demanding of computer resources, since the programs are short and the data they use rather limited.

In this chapter, however, we encountered cases in which efficiency might be a consideration. For example, although a computer can quickly look up a word in a dictionary of twenty-five words (as we saw in Figure 15-13), even a computer might require a significant amount of time to locate a word in a dictionary of one million words. Generally, as the amount of data to be processed increases, so does the amount of time required by the computer to process the data. As the amount of data becomes very, very large, processing times become significant, and the efficiency of the process becomes more important. Therefore, we would like to have the ability to examine algorithms for efficiency so that, all else being equal, they can make the best use of computer resources. Again, since the time factor is usually insignificant for small amounts of data, our primary concern here is with how an algorithm handles large amounts of data.

However, any attempt to directly compare speeds or memory requirements between algorithms is doomed to failure, since there are so many factors involved. For example, the speed of the computer, the language used, the implementation of the language, and the actual code used for the problem solution will all affect the final outcome. However, it is nonetheless possible to make relative comparisons of different algorithm efficiencies based on the number of steps (instructions) the computer would have to carry out when using the algorithm to process a given amount of data. *The assumption is that the time required to carry out an algorithm is directly related to the number of steps that must be executed.* Consider for a moment the algorithm used in Chapter 9 to find the sum of the numbers between any two limits. This algorithm is reproduced below:

```
Prompt 'What is the low number?'
Input Low

Prompt 'What is the high number?'
Input High

Sum ← 0

For n ← Low to High Do
   Sum ← Sum + n

Print Sum
```

How many steps are involved in this algorithm? We may be tempted to say that there are eight steps, but this is naive. The number of steps carried out by the computer when executing this algorithm actually depends on the values of Low and High (that is, the amount of data involved). For example, if Low is 1 and High is 2, the number of steps is actually nine, as follows:

1 for the first prompt

1 for the first input

1 for the second prompt

1 for the second input

1 for initializing the sum

1 for initializing the loop

2 for carrying out the loop twice, once for $n = 1$ and once for $n = 2$

1 for printing the sum

Therefore, if Low is 1 and High is 100, there would actually be 107 steps required: 7 for the nonloop steps and 100 for the loop iterations. Note what happens here: as the spread between Low and High increases, the number of steps required also increases. Although we cannot say exactly how much time would be required to implement this algorithm on any computer, we can state with certainty that the number of steps required (and consequently the time required) increases as the range of numbers increases. In fact, the increase is approximately linear: if you double the range, you approximately double the execution time.

Consider an alternate algorithm for this process. We could, if we liked, compute the sum as follows:

Prompt 'What is the low number?'
Input Low

Prompt 'What is the high number?'
Input High

$$\text{Sum} \leftarrow \frac{\text{High} \times (\text{High} + 1) - \text{Low} \times (\text{Low} + 1)}{2}$$

Print Sum

This algorithm (which we shall call the computational algorithm) requires six lines. The instructions of this algorithm and the instructions of the iterative algorithm are not strictly comparable, because the computations are considerably more complex in the computational algorithm. However, since we are making relative comparisons, we can also make the following observation: the computational algorithm requires the *same* number of steps *regardless* of the range of numbers. This one is just as efficient in calculating the sum of one thousand numbers as it is in calculating the sum of two numbers.

Let's demonstrate this graphically. If we plotted the approximate execution time versus the range of numbers on a single graph for both algorithms, we would get the curves shown in Figure 15-21. Note that, although the computational algorithm runs in constant time, this constant time is a little high due to the more complex calculations required. However, since the iterative algorithm requires time proportional to the range, its execution time soon overtakes the execution time of the second algorithm as the range widens. This is true in many cases. One algorithm is more efficient for small ranges, and another is more efficient for larger ranges.

Figure 15-21

Comparison of Iterative and Computational Algorithm Times for Finding the Sum of a Series of Numbers

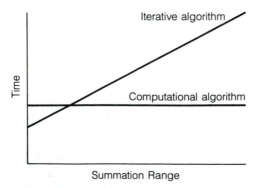

Before going further, let's mention again that when comparing algorithms, we are comparing how the amount of time needed to complete a task increases as the amount of data being processed increases. In other words, we are comparing the execution time behavior of algorithms as the amount of data gets very large.

BIG O NOTATION

We can now see how it is possible to compare algorithms, but it would be nice if there were some way to express the comparisons. A notation exists that can be used to express the way in which execution time increases as the amount of data increases. This is termed "Big O notation" (which stands for "On the Order Of"). The speed required for the iterative algorithm above increases linearly as n, the range of numbers being added together, increases. This algorithm is therefore said to be $O(n)$ (which is read "Big O of n," or "on the order of n"). However, the computational algorithm times remain constant no matter what the range. It is, consequently, said to be $O(1)$, since the time of execution does not depend on n, the range, at all. There are a number of commonly encountered types of algorithm timings, and these are summarized in Figure 15-22, along with relative speeds for varying amounts of data.

We will now use the technique of algorithm analysis with searching and sorting. Two categories of searching have been discussed in this chapter, namely, linear searches and binary searches. There were several varieties of linear searches discussed, but for the purposes of algorithm analysis, these may be considered together, since they are really just variations of one type of search. Since a linear search means exactly that the data (frequently in an array) is examined in order one element at a time, it is obvious that all linear searches will be $O(n)$. If you double the size of the array to be searched, you will also, on the average, double the time it takes to find something. This does not mean that one type of

Figure 15-22

Some Commonly Encountered Algorithm-Timing Functions

Classification		Relative Speed of Algorithm	
Big O Notation	*Name*	*n = 2*	*n = 100*
$O(1)$	constant	1	1
$O(n)$	linear	2	100
$O(\log n)$	logarithmic	1	7
$O(n \log n)$	$n \log n$	2	700
$O(n^2)$	quadratic	4	10,000
$O(n^3)$	cubic	8	1,000,000
$O(2^n)$	exponential	4	1×10^{30}

linear search is better than another. Obviously, if you are looking for a match in an ordered array, you will not have to examine as many elements as you would if you had to search an entire array for its largest element. The analysis merely shows how the time of execution changes as the number of elements changes.

Now, let's look at the binary search, which is O(log *n*). This is one of the most efficient search mechanisms available and is used to search large quantities of data. Recall, however, that there is a price to be paid: the data elements must be ordered. Further, owing to the more complex nature of the binary search algorithm, it is actually less efficient than linear searching for small arrays, as shown in Figure 15-23. (In this regard, the differences are similar to those found when comparing computational versus iterative summation algorithms.)

Finally, let's apply algorithm analysis to sorting. Sorting is one of the most widely used yet most time consuming of all computer processes. Let's consider the selection sort. The fundamental operation in the selection sort involves a linear search of the array, one search for each element to be sorted. It's true that the amount of searching decreases with every element, but that doesn't alter the fact that we have a loop (the search) inside a loop. Consequently, we find that, on the whole, we must search *n* array elements for each of the *n* elements we want to sort. This makes the selection sort O(n^2), which is unfortunately the way most sorts turn out. The bubble sort and the insertion sort are also both O(n^2). The QuickSort can do a little better: although it can be as bad as O(n^2), under favorable circumstances, it can be as good as O(*n* log *n*). The heap sort (to be discussed in Chapter 17) is one of the best sorts, being always O(*n* log *n*).

Algorithm analysis allows us to make rough estimates of resource requirements and is useful for comparing, within limits, the efficiency of different algorithms designed to carry out the same task.

Figure 15-23

Comparison of Average Search Times Required for a Linear Search Versus a Binary Search

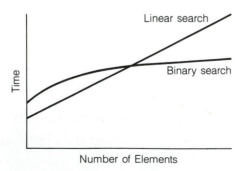

SUMMARY

In this chapter we focused on searching and sorting. We saw how it is possible to seek and find information contained in both ordered and unordered arrays. We then examined exactly *how* arrays can be ordered, or sorted, and surveyed five common sorting techniques. Finally, we discussed techniques for comparing algorithms (especially searching and sorting algorithms), namely, algorithm analysis, and presented a notation for expressing the results of such algorithms.

Although this chapter completes our study of arrays, we have not yet finished exploring data structures and will examine the list structure and its variations in the next two chapters. We will also look in detail at two sorting procedures introduced in this chapter, the insertion sort and the heap sort.

EXERCISES

CONCEPTS

1. Define or explain the following terms:

Algorithm analysis	EBCDIC
ASCII	Lexical order
Ascending order	Linear search
Big O notation	Logarithmic search
Binary search	Searching
Collating sequence	Sorting
Descending order	Table look-ups

2. Briefly discuss the differences inherent in searching an ordered versus an unordered array.

3. Briefly differentiate the following sorts:

   a. Insertion sort
   b. Bubble sort
   c. Selection sort
   d. QuickSort
   e. Heap sort

4. Briefly discuss some common relative execution orders.

5. Analyze the following algorithms and state the results using Big O notation:

    a. Iterative factorial computations (Figure 9-3)
    b. Recursive factorial computations (Figure 12-1)
    c. Iterative exponentiation (Figure 9-4)
    d. Recursive exponentiation (Figure 12-2)
    e. Multiplication table (Figure 9-6)
    f. Percent computations (Figure 14-1)

TOOLS

6. Trace the function `Max` shown in Figure 15-1.

7. Trace lines 59 through 74 in Figure 15-3, which reverse a person's first and last names.

8. Trace the procedure `BinarySearch` shown in Figure 15-12.

9. Trace the procedure `Sort` in Figure 15-19.

PROBLEMS

10. The people at HOWL (see Figure 14-1) also accept donations for their cause. They keep a list of all donors that includes the donors' names and the amount of their contributions for the year. In order to increase the efficiency of their operation, HOWL would like a list of their major donors. A major donor is anyone who contributes $1,000 or more per year. Write a program that searches through the list and prints out the names of the major donors and their respective donations. Also have the program tally the total amount given by the major donors and the total amount given by everybody else. (Do not list these minor donors.)

11. Write another program that HOWL can use (see problem 10 above) that lists all donors alphabetically.

12. Write yet another program for HOWL that will list all donors in *descending* order of their contributions.

13. Rewrite the procedure `BinarySearch` in Figure 15-12 using recursion instead of iteration.

14. Write a program that will input a list containing the total points earned by each student in a class for a given semester and the total number of points possible for the semester. Then normalize each student's score to 100 percent, find the highest and the lowest score, and compute the median and the mean. The mean is the arithmetic average, but the median is the center score in a list of scores ordered from highest to lowest. If there is an odd number of scores, then the median is the center score. If there is an even number of scores, there is no "center" score, and the median is the average of the *two* scores closest to the center.

15. Reconsider problem 11 from Chapter 14. In that problem you were asked to generate a bank statement, given an array of checks (consisting of the check number and amount) and an array of deposits. Alter the program so that a single array of transactions is input rather than separate arrays of checks and deposits. The program should separate the transaction array into two separate arrays. The two should be differentiated by the fact that checks have a number associated with them that is greater than zero, and deposits have a zero instead of a check number. Finally, sort the checks into ascending order of check number before printing them out.

16. Write a program that will input a sentence, separate the words, alphabetize them, and then print them out. For example, if the sentence

i know who you are

is entered, the output should consist of

are

i

know

who

you

17. Although we are concerned with the Pascal programming language in this text, other languages are available. One of these is FORTRAN, which has the peculiar property of totally ignoring blanks within statements. For example, the statement

```
Do while (GoForIt ,ge, Small Beans)
```

could be written as

```
dowhile(goforit,ge,smallbeans)
```

or even

```
do while ( go for it , g e , small beans )
```

The reason for this is that the very first thing FORTRAN does is remove all the blanks from a program line. Write a program that will remove all blanks from a line. Input any line and then output it without the blanks.

18. Rewrite the HOSPITAL program of Figure 15-5 so that it uses a binary search to find the patients.

19. Show, by algorithm analysis, that the Towers of Hanoi problem (Chapter 12) is $O(2^n)$.

20. Derive an iterative algorithm, using arrays, for computing Fibonacci numbers (problem 13, Chapter 12). Analyze the two algorithms. Which is the one to use?

16

Linear Linked Structures:

Lists, Queues, and Stacks

We are now ready to examine a class of data structures that is separate and distinct from arrays. The members of this class are characterized by the use of pointers, or links, and are termed, naturally enough, "linked structures." They include the linked list, the stack, and the queue. Two-dimensional linked structures also exist, and we will examine the most common of these, the tree and the heap, in Chapter 17.

Recall from Chapter 13 that the fundamental properties of linked structures are twofold, namely, they can grow or shrink as needed, and the elements of the structure cannot be accessed directly (as can be done with array elements). This limited access is not a problem; on the contrary, the fact that the structure permits only certain kinds of access makes them very useful. In general, insertions and deletions can be made with ease (especially when compared to arrays), they can be manipulated with elegant recursive algorithms, and the best sorting techniques (which are O(n log n)) make use of them.

   Without further ado, then, let us examine the most fundamental linked structure, the linked list.

16-1 *Linked Lists*

A typical **linked list** is shown in Figure 16-1. Each of the list elements is termed a **node** and must be a record structure consisting of whatever data is required (for example, a name and phone number) and a pointer to the *next* node in the series. The last node in the series has a pointer that points nowhere; this final pointer is said to be **nil.** There is also a special pointer called the head, which starts the list (and which may or may not be a node in the list). Also, recall from Chapter 13 that the nodes of a list are not necessarily located one right after another in the computer's memory but rather can be located anywhere at all. It is the *links* (pointers) that hold the nodes together.

Figure 16-1

Typical Linked List Structure, Including Nodes and Pointers

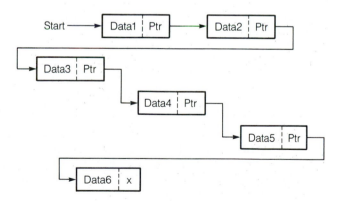

Shopping List

In order to get a handle on linked lists, let's take a simple list problem and implement its solution in Pascal. Suppose we want to generate a shopping list that consists of the names and quantities of items to be purchased. Making such a list manually is easy: as you think of items to buy, you write them down at the end of the list. When you are ready to go shopping, you take the list with you. Let's do something similar using linked lists.

STEP 1: UNDERSTAND THE PROBLEM

We would like to construct a list in such a way that we merely add items to the end of the list as we think of them and then print out the completed list when we are finished. This process will involve insertion (simple insertion at the end of the list) and traversal (going through the list in order to print it out). Note that the process of constructing a list (even a shopping list) involves nothing more than carrying out a series of insertions. At first you have no list, then you insert the first element, then the second, and so forth; and before you know it, you have a long list!

Note, however, that there is only one way to traverse a list: you have to start at the beginning and follow the pointers one node at a time, in order. Consequently, a linear search mechanism must be employed.

STEP 2: PLAN THE SOLUTION

Let's briefly examine the data structures we will use to solve this problem. We will, of course, use a linked list. Each node of the linked list will consist of a shopping list entry, which is a record containing the following information:

> Item
> Quantity
> Pointer to the next node

We can now write a preliminary algorithm as

Make the shopping list
Print out the shopping list

Not terribly profound, but it does divide up the task nicely for us. Let's now add a little more detail:

Make the shopping list
    For as many entries as we care to include Do
        Input the entry
            Read Item
            Read Quantity
        Add this entry to the end of the list

Print out the shopping list
    For each entry on the list
        Write Item
        Write Quantity

Before we get any more involved with lists, let's make the loops in the algorithm recognizable. The data input loop can be written using the sentinel value approach; the output loop can be based on the list itself: we go on printing until we get to the end. Making these loops explicit yields

Make the shopping list
    Read Item
    While Item ≠ 'exit' Do
        Read Quantity
        Combine Item and Quantity into an Entry
        Add this Entry to the end of the list
        Read Item

Print out the shopping list
    While there are Entries left in the list
        Write Item
        Write Quantity

NODE CREATION

This is about as far as we can get without considering how to put a list together. Remember that a list is a dynamic structure, which means that it doesn't exist until you create it. It is not like an array, which you can declare before the program and have waiting for you when the program begins executing. Therefore, when we start the program in our current shopping list example, there simply *is no list*. It must be created and expanded as needed.

In Pascal there is a standard procedure that will create a new node for you on request. It is called `New` (imagine that), and when invoked, it creates a node and tells you where the node is located. The function takes a single argument, which must be a pointer. For example, if we wanted a new shopping list entry we might call `New` as follows:

```
New (NewEntry);
```

NewEntry would be a pointer variable that, at the conclusion of the procedure call, points to the node just created.

As we mentioned earlier, each node is a record that contains fields (in this case the three fields of item, quantity, and pointer to the next node). The question that faces us now is, How do we reference each of these fields?

The fields of a list node are referenced in much the same way as the fields of a record array element: the specific element, followed by a period, followed by the field name, is given. For example, if we had an array Who of records containing the fields Name and Number, we could reference each as follows:

```
Who[K].Name
Who[K].Number
```

We do the same sort of thing with list nodes. In the above example, since the pointer variable NewEntry now points to a node, we can reference each of its fields as

```
NewEntry^.Item
NewEntry^.Quantity
NewEntry^.Next
```

The caret symbol ^ signifies that a node is being pointed to. Other than that, the field references are the same as for arrays.

SIMPLE LIST INSERTION

We can now create a node and reference its fields, but how do we attach the nodes to each other? This is done by making the *pointer field of the first node* point to the second node. Let's show how this is done with an example. Suppose we create two nodes FirstEntry and Second-Entry using the New procedure:

```
New (FirstEntry);
New (SecondEntry);
```

We can make a list of these two items by making the first entry point to the second entry as follows:

```
FirstEntry^.Next := SecondEntry;
```

Bear in mind that FirstEntry and SecondEntry are NOT records but merely *pointers* to the records. The left-hand side of the assignment statement references the pointer field of the first entry, and the right-hand side of the statement consists of a pointer to the second entry. After the assignment is made, the first record then points to the second! Also note that, after the assignment is completed, there are *two* pointers pointing to the second entry: the pointer variable `Second-Entry` itself (which, of course, is not changed in the statement) and the pointer field of the first record (which *is* changed).

Now that we can create and link together records, we may use this new information to add more detail to our algorithm. (We will only concentrate on the formation of the shopping list for right now.) Adding this information, we get

1. Make the shopping list
2.   New (Start)
3.   Start^.Next ← Nil
4.   LastEntry ← Start
5.   Read TheItem
6.   While TheItem ≠ 'exit' Do
7.   Read TheQuantity
8.   Combine Item and Quantity into an Entry
9.   New (NewEntry)
10.   NewEntry^.Item ← TheItem
11.   NewEntry^.Quantity ← TheQuantity
12.   NewEntry^.Next ← Nil
13.   Add this Entry to the end of the list
14.   LastEntry^.Next ← NewEntry
15.   LastEntry ← NewEntry
16.   Read Item

    Print out the shopping list
      While there are Entries left in the list
        Write Item
        Write Quantity

Let's trace through some of these lines to make sure we understand what's happening.

Line 2. We create the start node here. After this line is executed, the pointer variable `Start` points to the start node. It is important to distinguish between the `Start` node and the first node. The `Start` node will not be used to actually contain any of the data; it is merely the node from which the list originates. The reason for having this node at all is that it makes working with the list both consistent and easier.

Line 3. We make the pointer of the start node `Nil` (it points nowhere), because at this place in the algorithm, there *is* no list yet (that is, there is no first element).

Line 4. The pointer variable `LastEntry` is intended to point to the end of the list. Since there is no list yet, it should point to the `Start` node, which also happens to be the end of the list.

Line 9. We create a new entry (node) here to contain the information about the next shopping item to be attached to the list.

Lines 10–11. We attach the information just read in to the newest node created.

Line 12. Since the current node we are working with is the most recent (the last) addition to the list so far, we make its pointer field point nowhere.

Line 14. We make the pointer field of the *previous* list entry point to this newest node.

Line 15. We make this newest entry the last entry.

Carried out iteratively, this section of the algorithm will successfully build up the list by tacking on entries one at a time to the end of the list.

SIMPLE TRAVERSAL

We can now turn our attention to the second part of the algorithm, in which the completed list is printed out. To do this, we must traverse the list one node at a time and print out the appropriate information along the way. The procedure is a modification of the linear search in which we continue through the loop as long as there are any remaining nodes. How can we tell if there are remaining nodes? We simply must look at the pointer field of the current node: if it is `Nil`, we have reached the end; if it is not `Nil`, we keep on going. We begin with the `Start` node and keep moving through the list until we get to a `Nil` pointer field.

Changing the algorithm to reflect this gives us

```
Make the shopping list
   New (Start)
   Start^.Next ← Nil
   LastEntry ← Start
   Read TheItem
   While TheItem ≠ 'exit' Do
     Read TheQuantity
     Combine Item and Quantity into an Entry
        New (NewEntry)
        NewEntry^.Item ← TheItem
        NewEntry^.Quantity ← TheQuantity
        NewEntry^.Next ← Nil
     Add this Entry to the end of the list
        LastEntry^.Next ← NewEntry
        LastEntry ← NewEntry

   Read Item
```

Print out the shopping list
   TheEntry ← Start^.Next
   While TheEntry ≠ Nil Do
     Write TheEntry^.Item
     Write TheEntry^.Quantity
     TheEntry ← TheEntry^.Next

Note that if the Start node has a Nil pointer, *nothing will be printed out.* This is as it should be, since a Nil starting pointer indicates that there *is* no list. Also, the last statement in the loop makes the pointer variable TheEntry point to the location of the *next* node.

STEP 3: CODE THE SOLUTION

We now have the logic of the solution, and all we need are the particulars of the correct Pascal syntax. In fact, we have already covered just about all we need with regard to referencing nodes and fields. The only thing left is to determine how pointer types are declared.

We have to define a new data type here; consequently, we expand our type definitions as follows:

type-definition → array-type-definition
             | string-type-definition
             | record-type-definition
             | pointer-type-definition

We define the newest of these as

pointer-type-definition → identifier = ^ type

The caret (^) indicates a pointer type. A pointer can point to any data type at all, predefined or otherwise. Most often, however, it points to a record of some sort. One of the unusual features of the pointer type definition is that you can define a pointer for a type *before* you define the data type. As an example, let's define the appropriate pointers and record structure for the shopping list problem:

```
Type String = Packed Array [1..15] of Char;
     PtrEntry = ^Entry;
     Entry = Record
               Item : String;
               Quantity : Integer;
               Next : PtrEntry
             End;
```

We define the pointer type for the list *prior* to defining the record type to which it points. Also, in the definition of the record Entry, the last field (Next) is also a pointer. Be cautioned that this pointer field means that it contains a pointer to the data type `Entry`; it does NOT mean that the record points to itself.

Knowing this, then, we may proceed to code the entire solution. This is shown in Figure 16-2. Note that a number of pointers are defined: `NewEntry`, `TheEntry`, and `LastEntry`.

STEP 4: CHECK OUT THE PROGRAM

A test run is also shown in Figure 16-2. The construction and traversal processes work exactly as planned.

Figure 16-2

Program to Construct and Output a Shopping List via a Linked List, with a Test Run

SHOPPING.PAS

```
1    Program SHOPPING (Input, Output);
2
3    (*
4         This program builds and prints a shopping list by using
5         a linked list.
6    *)
7
8    Type String15 = Packed Array [1..15] of Char;
9
10        PtrEntry = ^Entry;
11
12        Entry = Record                     (* Shopping list entry *)
13                 Item : String 15;
14                 Quantity : Integer;
15                 Next : PtrEntry
16              End;
17
18   Var  Start,                (* Head of the shopping list       *)
19        NewEntry,             (* Newest list entry               *)
20        TheEntry,             (* Current list node being worked with *)
21        LastEntry : PtrEntry; (* Last list entry                 *)
22
23        TheItem : String15;
24        TheQuantity : Integer;
25
26
27   Procedure ReadString (Var S:String15);
28     Var K : Integer;
29     Begin
30       For  K := 1 to 15 Do
31            Read (S[K]);
32       Readln
33     End;
34
35
36   BEGIN
37     Writeln ('SHOPPING LIST');
38     Writeln;
39
```

Figure 16-2 continued

```
40      (* Input the shopping list *)
41      New (Start);
42      Start^.Next := Nil;
43      LastEntry := Start;
44      Write ('Enter item name (exit to stop) : ');
45      ReadString (TheItem);
46      While TheItem <> 'exit           ` Do
47        Begin
48          Write ('Enter quantity desired : ');
49          Readln (TheQuantity);
50          (* Combine the item and quantity into a new entry *)
51            New (NewEntry);
52            NewEntry^.Item := TheItem;
53            NewEntry^.Quantity := TheQuantity;
54            NewEntry^.Next := Nil;
55          (* Add this entry to the end of the list *)
56            LastEntry^.Next := NewEntry;
57            LastEntry := NewEntry;
58
59          Write ('Enter item name         : ');
60          ReadString (TheItem)
61        End;
62
63      (* Print out the shopping list *)
64      Writeln;
65      Writeln ('The completed list is :');
66      TheEntry := Start^.Next;
67      While TheEntry <> Nil Do
68        Begin
69          Writeln (TheEntry^.Item, TheEntry^.Quantity:3);
70          TheEntry := TheEntry^.Next
71        End
72
73    END.


$ run shopping

SHOPPING LIST

Enter item name (exit to stop) : Cereal
Enter quantity desired : 2
Enter item name         : Soup
Enter quantity desired : 5
Enter item name         : Soap
Enter quantity desired : 1
Enter item name         : Nuts
Enter quantity desired : 8
Enter item name         : Apples
Enter quantity desired : 12
Enter item name         : exit

The completed list is :
Cereal          2
Soup            5
Soap            1
Nuts            8
Apples         12
```

STEP 5: DOCUMENT

The program is well documented and readable.

LIST OPERATIONS

The shopping list problem introduced us to a number of simple linked list operations. We would now like to look at the more general situation in which we (1) insert nodes at *any* point within the list (not just at the end), (2) delete nodes, and (3) traverse the list to find something. Let's consider another example.

Real Estate Listings

We would like to write a program that keeps track of real estate listings for Acme Real Estate (ARE). For each house listed with their agency, ARE wants to keep the following information:

Owner's Name
Address
Price

They want to be able to add a new listing (insert) or remove an existing listing (delete), while keeping the entire list in alphabetical order by owner's name. This will allow them to print out the list alphabetically at any time. We can keep the list alphabetical by inserting new listings in such a way that the whole list always remains in order. This process is nothing less than the *insertion sort* we introduced in the previous chapter.

Let's see what we can do.

STEP 1: UNDERSTAND THE PROBLEM

This problem really boils down to list maintenance. We insert new listings (nodes) in such a way as to ensure that the list as a whole remains alphabetical, and we delete old listings in a way that will not disturb the ordering of the remaining list nodes. And, of course, we print out the list occasionally. If the list is maintained properly, a simple traversal (as described in the shopping list example) will produce an alphabetical list. Let us see exactly *how* we shall carry out these tasks.

STEP 2: PLAN THE SOLUTION

We can break down the problem into logical subtasks according to the following preliminary algorithm:

```
For as long as you want to keep this up Do
   Read Option
   If Option is Insert then
      Create a new node
      Input the data for it
      Insert it into the list
   Else if Option is Delete then
      Input the Key for the node to be deleted
      Find the node
      Delete that node
   Else if Option is Output then
      Traverse the list and print out the nodes
   Else if Option is Quit then
      Say Good-bye
   Else
      This has got to be an invalid choice
```

We can finish the loop easily enough. Let's just prompt for and input a code for the function to be performed (the option) via a menu and convert to a While loop. While we're at it, let's also introduce some error checking, such as making sure a given listing is not already in the list before inserting it and making sure a listing *is* there before deleting it. Adding these details will give us the following algorithm:

```
Option ← anything but Quit
While Option ≠ Quit Do
   Display the Menu
   Read Option
   If Option is Insert then
      Read TheOwner
      See if TheOwner is already in the list
      If TheOwner is NOT there then
         Generate a new node
         Get the listing information for the node
         Insert the node into the list
      Else
         Write 'Listing already exists'
   Else if Option is Delete then
      Read TheOwner
      See if TheOwner is already in the list
      If TheOwner is there then
         Delete that node
      Else
         Write 'Listing not found'
```

Else if Option is Output then
    Print out the alphabetized list
Else if Option is Quit then
    Say Good-bye
Else
    This has got to be an invalid choice

At this point we have pretty much organized the solution. Since printing out the complete list is exactly the simple traversal process that we used in the shopping list problem, we needn't worry about it. Most of the rest of the algorithm is also straightforward. There are, in fact, only a few things left that we must work on, the first of which is the statement "See if TheOwner is already in the list." To check for proper insertion and deletion, we must determine if and where the node of interest is located. We must also examine the particulars of insertion and deletion.

Let's begin with the "See if TheOwner is already in the list" statement. The process is, for all practical purposes, a linear search. In other words, a search is carried out on the list (via a traversal in this case), and a determination is made as to whether the key (the listing being searched for) is in the list or not. However, the search actually provides more information than that. According to what we learned about searching ordered arrays, if we do in fact find the key, then we also return with a knowledge of *where* the key is located. On the other hand, if the key is *not* in the list, then we return with a knowledge of where it *should* be (recall searching for a category in Chapter 15). This actually will simplify the insertion and deletion processes in that we can make this search a procedure that returns with an indication of whether the key was found or not and with a pointer to the correct location!

The characteristics of a linear search on an ordered, linked list are a little different from a similar search on an array. We do not return with an index to an array element but rather with a pointer to the node (if it exists) or a pointer to either the previous or subsequent node (if it does not exist). As we also learned in the last chapter, the search will terminate at the correct position whether or not the key has been found.

Let us, therefore, define a procedure that traverses a linked list while searching for a key and returns either the location of the node of interest (if it's there) or the locations of the nodes between which it should fall (if it's not there). We shall invoke our search procedure as follows:

Search (Owner, Location, Found);

Owner represents the information by which we can recognize the node we are looking for (that is, the *key*, which in this case would be the name of the owner of the house for sale). Found is a Boolean variable, which informs us whether or not the key was located. Location represents the location of the node *immediately preceding* either the node to be deleted (if we're doing a deletion) or the position into which the insertion is to be made (if that's what we're doing). The reason for choosing the *preceding* node rather than the *actual* node is that we get more pointer information in this way (as we shall see shortly). Amending our algorithm to incorporate the key acquisition and the `Search` procedure gives us

```
Option ← anything but Quit
While Option ≠ Quit Do
   Display the Menu
   Read Option
   If Option is Insert then
      Read TheOwner
      Search (TheOwner, Location, Found);
      If not Found then
         Generate a new node
         Get the listing information for the node
         Insert it after Location
      Else
         Write 'Listing already exists'
   Else if Option is Delete then
      Read TheOwner
      Search (TheOwner, Location, Found);
      If Found then
         Delete the node immediately following Location
      Else
         Write 'Listing not found'
   Else if Option is Output then
      Print out the alphabetized list via simple traversal
   Else if Option is Quit then
      Say Good-bye
   Else
      This has got to be an invalid choice
```

This algorithm requires the use of all five of the basic operations presented in Chapter 13: Insertion (which, in this case, effectively *sorts* the list as well) and deletion and searching (which in turn require traversal). Let us, therefore, proceed to an exposition of algorithms for these processes and then implement them for the real estate problem on which we are currently working.

Insertion. Let's continue by detailing insertion, the first option in our main algorithm. We will assume that the procedure `Search` works properly and that on returning from it we have a pointer `Location` that points to the node immediately *preceding* the position where the insertion is to occur. In other words, the new node must be inserted between the node pointed to by `Location` and the very next one. We assume further that the new node to be inserted has been created and

Figure 16-3

Situation Prior to Inserting a New Node but Immediately Following a Call to the Procedure SEARCH

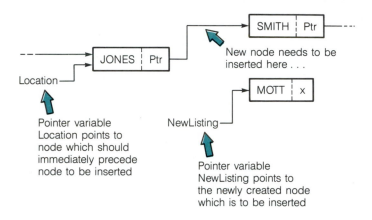

is pointed to by the pointer NewListing. The situation is shown in Figure 16-3.

Now here is where the beauty of the linked list comes in: in order to insert this element, *the data itself need not be moved.* The only thing required is that two pointers be changed (see Figure 16-4). In the ensuing discussion, we refer to the key node as the one being pointed to by Location. The process is as follows:

Make the pointer of the node to be inserted point to the same node currently being pointed to by the key node.

Make the key node point to the inserted node.

The fact that Location and NewNode still point to elements of the list is immaterial.

We may express this entire process algorithmically as

NewListing^.Next ← Location^.Next
Location^.Next ← NewListing

Now we've got it!

Deletion. The next option is that of deletion. Again, we assume that Search works properly and that Location will point to the *predecessor* of the (key) node to be deleted. The situation is shown in Figure 16-5. The process can be described as follows:

Figure 16-4

*The Actual Node Insertion Process (a) Causes the Inserted Node to
Point to Its New Successor, and (b) Makes the Predecessor to the
Inserted Node Point to the Inserted Node*

a.

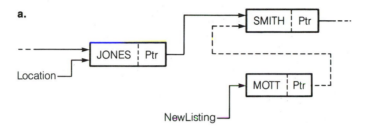

b.

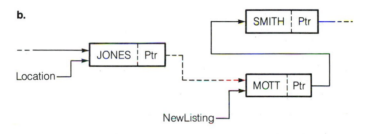

Figure 16-5

*Situation Prior to Node Deletion but Immediately Following a Call to
the Procedure SEARCH*

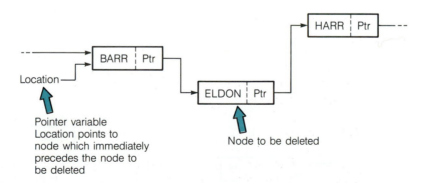

Make the pointer of the key point to the node currently being pointed to by the node to be deleted.

Get rid of the deleted node.

A problem occurs here, however: if we change the pointer of the key, the node to be deleted will become inaccessible and therefore impossible to remove. To overcome this problem, we simply generate a new pointer (essentially a copy of the key pointer) that points to the node we intend to delete. This entire process is shown in Figure 16-6 and can be written thus:

Make a copy of the key pointer.

Make the pointer of the key point to the node currently being pointed to by the node to be deleted.

Get rid of the node being pointed to by the copy.

Figure 16-6

The Actual Deletion Process (a) Generates a Pointer to the Node to Be Deleted; (b) Makes the Predecessor to the Deleted Node Point to the Successor of the Node to Be Deleted, Effectively Removing It from the List; and (c) Physically Removes the Deleted Node

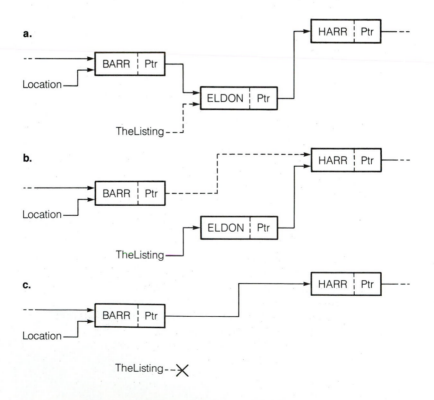

Stated algorithmically, we can write this as

TheListing ← Location^.Next
Location^.Next ← TheListing^.Next
Dispose (TheListing)

We introduce here the predefined Pascal procedure Dispose, which completely removes the node and its associated information from memory, thus freeing it for other uses (an example of dynamic memory *de*allocation). As with the case of insertion, the fact that Location continues pointing to a list element does not matter in the least.

We may now complete the main algorithm for our solution to the real estate problem. To do so we need only consider how best to read in the requisite data when we create a new list node. Since we faced (and solved) a similar subproblem in the shopping list example, we'll simply repeat the solution here. Filling in these remaining details yields our final algorithm:

Option ← anything but Quit
While Option ≠ Quit Do
   Display the Menu
   Read Option
   If Option is Insert then
      Read TheOwner
      Search (TheOwner, Location, Found)
      If not Found then
         Generate a new node
            New (NewListing)
         Get the listing information for the node
            Read TheAddress
            Read ThePrice
            NewListing^.Owner ← TheOwner
            NewListing^.Address ← TheAddress
            NewListing^.Price ← ThePrice
         Insert it after Location
            NewListing^.Next ← Location^.Next
            Location^.Next ← NewListing
      Else
         Write 'Listing already exists'
   Else if Option is Delete then
      Read TheOwner
      Search (TheOwner, Location, Found);
      If Found then
         Delete the node immediately following Location
            TheListing ← Location^.Next
            Location^.Next ← TheListing^.Next
            Dispose (TheListing)

        Else
           Write 'Listing not found'
      Else if Option is Output then
        Print out the alphabetized list via simple traversal
      Else if Option is Quit then
        Say Good-bye
      Else
        This has got to be an invalid choice

Now, at long last, we must consider the procedure `Search`. The search process we must carry out here on the linked list is very similar to the process we used to search an ordered array (Chapter 15). We must, however, use pointers (instead of subscripts) to move through the list until we have either found the element we seek or determined that the element is not in the list. As was the case with an array search, the node under examination at termination is either the element we are looking for or the element that the key would precede if it *was* there. This latter case, in other words, means that the key would have to be inserted between the element that terminated the search and its predecessor if the order of the elements is to be preserved.

Let us begin to develop the list search technique by reproducing the linear array search presented in the last chapter as follows:

Index ← 1
While TableValue[Index] < Key and Index ≠ Last Do
  Index ← Index + 1

This particular algorithm assumes that there is at least *one* element in the array to be searched. Also, a test for equality can be made after the search is complete in order to determine whether the element is actually there or whether we have merely found the correct category.

However, when we are dealing with a list, we cannot assume that the list exists. (We may, in some instances, have a null list.) Further, we would be in real trouble if we simply transform the above algorithm to this:

Node ← Start^.Next
While Node^.Data < Key and Node ≠ Nil
  Node ← Node^.Next

If the list is null or if it is *not* null and we reach the end of the list at the point where `Node` is `Nil`, we *cannot* use `Node^.Data` because *it does not exist* (the pointer `Node` is `Nil` and doesn't point to any data). Note that this would actually work just fine IF (a big if) (1) we could assume a nonnull list, (2) the order of the tests in the While loop were reversed, and (3) we could count on partial evaluation of logical expressions (see Chapter 9).

To further add to our difficulties, we do not want to return a pointer to the actual node of interest (as described previously) but rather to its *predecessor*. We must do this to facilitate insertions and deletions, but doing so is actually not as hard as it sounds. We merely need to keep track of *two* pointers, one for the node of interest and one for its predecessor.

We can't assume a nonnull list, we must be careful not to run off the end of the list, and we can't assume partial evaluation of logical expressions. Therefore, we have to break up the loop tests into a smaller While expression and associated If statements and write the algorithm like this:

```
PredecessorNode ← Start
Node ← PredecessorNode^.Next
DoneSearching ← False
While Node ≠ Nil and not DoneSearching Do
   If Node^.Data < Key then
      PredecessorNode ← Node
      Node ← Node^.Next
   Else
      DoneSearching ← True
If Node ≠ Nil then
   ExactMatch ← Node^.Data = Key
Else
   ExactMatch ← False
```

In fact, this technique can be applied to ordered array searches as well if we want to make them completely general.

We now have all of the algorithms we need to write a program, so let's do it.

STEP 3: CODE THE SOLUTION

As always, this is the simplest part, and we have all that we need to convert the above algorithm into Pascal. A few frills have been added (for example, when printing out the list the entries are numbered), but for the most part, the program is a straightforward implementation of the algorithm. Also, since real estate record keeping is interactive by nature, we have not used external files to hold the initial data. The resulting program is hown in Figure 16-7.

STEP 4: CHECK OUT THE PROGRAM

A test run for this program is shown in Figure 16-8. Everything works as planned; for example, insertions and deletions can be made anywhere in the list (first, middle, or last), and missing or duplicate entries are caught and identified.

Figure 16-7

Program That Uses Searching, Insertion, and Deletion on a Linked List to Maintain Real Estate Listings

ARE.PAS

```
1     Program ARE (Input, Output);
2
3     (*
4         This program handles listings for the Acme Real Estate company.
5         Functions available are:
6             1. Insert a new listing
7             2. Delete an old listing
8             3. Print out (alphabetically) all current listings
9         The program utilizes a linked list to carry out these functions.
10    *)
11
12    Type String20 = Packed Array [1..20] of Char;
13
14        PtrListing = ^Listing;
15
16        Listing = Record                    (* Information for a single listing *)
17                     Owner   : String20;
18                     Address : String20;
19                     Price   : Real;
20                     Next    : PtrListing
21                  End;
22
23    Var  Start, NewListing, TheListing : PtrListing;
24         TheOwner : String20;
25         TheAddress : String 20;
26         ThePrice : Real;
27
28         Option : Char;          (* Function selected by the user *)
29
30
31         Found : Boolean;        (* Whether a particular listing was located
32                                    by the search procedure *)
33         Location : PtrListing;(* The location of the PREDECESSOR to the
34                                    node being looked for *)
35
36         Count : Integer;        (* Used to number the listings when they
37                                    are all printed out *)
38
39
40    Procedure ReadString (VarS:String20);
41      Var k : Integer;
42      Begin
43        For k:= 1 to 20 Do
44            Read (S[k]);
45            Readln
46      End;
47
48
49    Procedure Search (Key : String20; Var PredecessorNode : PtrListing;
50                                      Var ExactMatch : Boolean);
51      (* This procedure searches a linked list via a traversal.
52         If the node is found, the pointer to its PREDECESSOR is
53         returned (rather than a pointer to the node itself) in
54         order to facilitate insertions and deletions. If the
55         node is NOT found, then the node returned consists of
```

Figure 16-7 continued

```
56          the predecessor to the location in which the key node
57          should be inserted
58      *)
59
60      Var Node : PtrListing;
61          DoneSearching : Boolean;
62      Begin
63          PredecessorNode := Start;
64          Node := PredecessorNode^.Next;
65          DoneSearching := False;
66          While (Node <> Nil) and not DoneSearching Do
67              If Node^.Owner < Key then
68                  Begin
69                      PredecessorNode := Node;
70                      Node := Node^.Next
71                  End
72              Else
73                  DoneSearching := True;
74          If Node <> Nil then
75              ExactMatch := Node^.Owner = Key
76          Else
77              ExactMatch := False
78      End;
79
80
81      BEGIN
82          Writeln;
83          Writeln (' ARE Listing Maintenance Program ');
84          Writeln;
85
86          (* Create an empty list *)
87          New (Start);
88          Start^.Next := Nil;
89
90          (* Begin the loop and go for it... *)
91          Option := ' ';
92          While Option <> 'Q' Do
93              Begin
94                  (* Display a Menu and get a response *)
95                  Writeln;
96                  Writeln ('    Choose one of the following:');
97                  Writeln ('I : Insert a new listing');
98                  Writeln ('D : Delete an existing listing');
99                  Writeln ('P : Print out complete set of listings');
100                 Writeln ('Q : Quit and Exit');
                    Write   ('    Enter option --> '); Readln (Option);
102                 Writeln;
103
104                 If Option = 'I' then
105                     Begin
106                         Write('Name of owner to be inserted : ');
107                         ReadString (TheOwner);
108                         Search (TheOwner, Location, Found);
109                         If not Found then
110                             Begin
111                                 (* Generate a new node *)
112                                 New (NewListing);
113                                 (* Get the listing information *)
114                                 Write ('Address of new listing   : ');
```

Figure 16-7 continued

```
115                      ReadString (TheAddress);
116                      Write ('Asking Price              : ');
117                      Readln (ThePrice);
118                      NewListing^.Owner := TheOwner;
119                      NewListing^.Address := TheAddress;
120                      NewListing^.Price := ThePrice;
121                 (* Insert it after Location *)
122                      NewListing^.Next := Location^.Next;
123                      Location^.Next := NewListing
124            End
125          Else
126            Writeln ('Listing already exists')
127       End
128
129       Else if Option = 'D' then
130          Begin
131            Write ('Name of owner to be deleted : ');
132            ReadString (TheOwner);
133            Search (TheOwner, Location, Found);
134            If Found then
135              Begin
136                (* Delete the node after Location *)
137                 TheListing := Location^.Next;
138                 Location^.Next := TheListing^.Next;
139                 Dispose (TheListing);
140                 Writeln ('Listing Deleted')
141              End
142            Else
143              Writeln ('Listing not found')
144          End
145
146       Else if Option = 'P' then
147          (* Print out the list using a simple traversal *)
148          Begin
149            Count := 1;
150            TheListing := Start^.Next;
151            If TheListing = Nil then
152              Begin
153                Writeln ('No listings currently exist.');
154                Writeln
155              End
156            Else
157              Begin
158                Writeln ('Current ARE Listings:');
159                Writeln
160              End;
161            While TheListing <> Nil Do
162              Begin
163                 Write (Count:2,'. ');
164                 With TheListing^ Do
165                   Begin
166                     Writeln (Owner);
167                     Writeln ('     ', Address);
168                     Writeln ('    $', Price:4:2);
169                     Writeln
170                   End;
171                 TheListing := TheListing^.Next;
172                 Count := Count + 1
173              End
```

Figure 16-7 continued

```
174              End
175
176          Else if Option = `Q` then
177              Writeln (`All Done ... Bye!`)
178
179          Else
180              Writeln (`Invalid Option ... Try Again`)
181
182       End (* While *)
183    END.
```

Figure 16-8

Test Run and Output from the Real Estate Maintenance Program

```
$ run are

ARE Listing Maintenance Program


        Choose one of the following:
I : Insert a new listing
D : Delete an existing listing
P : Print out complete set of listings
Q : Quit and Exit
        Enter option --> P


No listings currently exist.


        Choose one of the following:
I : Insert a new listing
D : Delete an existing listing
P : Print out complete set of listings
Q : Quit and Exit
        Enter option --> I

Name of owner to be inserted : SMITH PETER
Address of new listing       : 125 W CANTOR
Asking price                 : 48900

        Choose one of the following:
I : Insert a new listing
D : Delete an existing listing
P : Print out complete set of listings
Q : Quit and Exit
        Enter option --> P

Current ARE Listings:

  1. SMITH PETER
     125 W CANTOR
     $48900.00
```

Figure 16-8 continued

```
     Choose one of the following:
I : Insert a new listing
D : Delete an existing listing
P : Print out complete set of listings
Q : Quit and Exit
     Enter option --> I

Name of owner to be inserted : JONES HARRY
Address of new listing        : 355 E 700 S
Asking price                  : 37500

     Choose one of the following:
I : Insert a new listing
D : Delete an existing listing
P : Print out complete set of listings
Q : Quit and Exit
     Enter option --> P

Current ARE Listings:

  1. JONES HARRY
     355 E 700 S
     $37500.00

  2. SMITH PETER
     125 W CANTOR
     $48900.00


     Choose one of the following:
I : Insert a new listing
D : Delete an existing listing
P : Print out complete set of listings
Q : Quit and Exit
     Enter option -->  I

Name of owner to be inserted : REED LARRY
Address of new listing        : 125 BOULDER
Asking price                  : 75000

     Choose one of the following:
I : Insert a new listing
D : Delete an existing listing
P : Print out complete set of listings
Q : Quit and Exit
     Enter option --> P

Current ARE Listings:

  1. JONES HARRY
     355 E 700 S
     $37500.00

  2. REED LARRY
     125 BOULDER
     $75000.00

  3. SMITH PETER
     125 W CANTOR
     $48900.00
```

Figure 16-8 continued

```
     Choose one of the following:
I : Insert a new listing
D : Delete an existing listing
P : Print out complete set of listings
Q : Quit and Exit
     Enter option --> I

Name of owner to be inserted : WATERMAN PETER
Address of new listing        : 3544 GRANDE
Asking price                  : 124900

     Choose one of the following:
I : Insert a new listing
D : Delete an existing listing
P : Print out complete set of listings
Q : Quit and Exit
     Enter option --> P

Current ARE Listings:

  1. JONES HARRY
     355 E 700 S
     $37500.00

  2. REED LARRY
     125 BOULDER
     $75000.00

  3. SMITH PETER
     125 W CANTOR
     $48900.00

  4. WATERMAN PETER
     3544 GRANDE
     $124900.00


     Choose one of the following:
I : Insert a new listing
D : Delete an existing listing
P : Print out complete set of listings
Q : Quit and Exit
     Enter option --> I

Name of owner to be inserted : REED LARRY
Listing already exists


     Choose one of the following:
I : Insert a new listing
D : Delete an existing listing
P : Print out complete set of listings
Q : Quit and Exit
     Enter option --> D

Name of owner to be deleted : WATERMAN PETER
Listing Deleted
```

Figure 16-8 continued

```
     Choose one of the following:
I  : Insert a new listing
D  : Delete an existing listing
P  : Print out complete set of listings
Q  : Quit and Exit
     Enter option --> P

Current ARE Listings:

  1. JONES HARRY
     355 E 700 S
     $37500.00

  2. REED LARRY
     125 BOULDER
     $75000.00

  3. SMITH PETER
     125 W CANTOR
     $48900.00


     Choose one of the following:
I  : Insert a new listing
D  : Delete an existing listing
P  : Print out complete set of listings
Q  : Quit and Exit
     Enter option --> D

Name of owner to be deleted : REEL LARRY
Listing not found


     Choose one of the following:
I  : Insert a new listing
D  : Delete an existing listing
P  : Print out complete set of listings
Q  : Quit and Exit
     Enter option --> D

Name of owner to be deleted : REED LARRY
Listing Deleted

     Choose one of the following:
I  : Insert a new listing
D  : Delete an existing listing
P  : Print out complete set of listings
Q  : Quit and Exit
     Enter option --> P

Current ARE Listings:

  1. JONES HARRY
     355 E 700 S
     $37500.00

  2. SMITH PETER
     125 W CANTOR
     $48900.00
```

Figure 16-8 continued

```
      Choose one of the following:
I : Insert a new listing
D : Delete an existing listing
P : Print out complete set of listings
Q : Quit and Exit
      Enter option --> D

Name of owner to be deleted : JONES HARRY
Listing Deleted

      Choose one of the following:
I : Insert a new listing
D : Delete an existing listing
P : Print out complete set of listings
Q : Quit and Exit
      Enter option --> P

Current ARE Listings:

  1. SMITH PETER
     125 W CANTOR
     $48900.00


      Choose one of the following:
I : Insert a new listing
D : Delete an existing listing
P : Print out complete set of listings
Q : Quit and Exit
      Enter option --> D

Name of owner to be deleted : SMITH PETER
Listing Deleted

      Choose one of the following:
I : Insert a new listing
D : Delete an existing listing
P : Print out complete set of listings
Q : Quit and Exit
      Enter option --> P

No listings currently exist.


      Choose one of the following:
I : Insert a new listing
D : Delete an existing listing
P : Print out complete set of listings
Q : Quit and Exit
      Enter option --> X

Invalid Option ... Try Again

      Choose one of the following:
I : Insert a new listing
D : Delete an existing listing
P : Print out complete set of listings
Q : Quit and Exit
      Enter option --> Q

All Done ... Bye!
```

STEP 5: DOCUMENT

The program is well documented and easy to read.

Take a moment to appreciate how much more appropriate a list structure is to this problem than an array could ever be. First, there are no limits on the size of the list. We can never overrun our size definition because there *is* no size definition, and at no time do we ever use more space than necessary. Second, the list and its concomitant nodes *never* have to be moved around (even when the list is alphabetized), because the links (pointers) provide the connections between nodes. Finally, inserting and deleting nodes require almost no work, again because only the pointers have to be changed.

DOUBLY LINKED LISTS

At this point let's take a moment to briefly introduce a variation on the linked list, the **doubly linked list.** Our normal, garden-variety linked list can be traversed in one direction only, because the pointers always aim forward. However, there is nothing to keep the pointers from going both forward and backward. If two pointers are used in such a fashion, it is possible to traverse the list in either direction, starting from any of the nodes. Such a list is shown schematically in Figure 16-9.

Figure 16-9

Typical Doubly Linked List Structure, Including Nodes and Pointers
(Bptr is Back Pointer and Fptr is Forward Pointer)

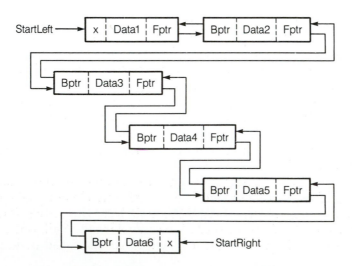

Using a doubly linked list simplifies the basic list operations considerably. The improvements in traversal are obvious and include the ability to traverse to and from any point; this avoids having to start at the beginning each time. Insertion and deletion are also made easier, since the node of interest is all that has to be located. The forward and backward pointers will automatically define the predecessor and successor to the node.

Implementing such a doubly linked list in Pascal is quite simple. Rather than having a single pointer in the record structure, two pointers are included. If we would like to use a doubly linked list in our previous problem, for example, we need only alter the record definition as follows:

```
Listing = Record
            BackPtr : PtrListing;
            Owner   : String;
            Address : String;
            Price   : Real;
            ForePtr : PtrListing
          End;
```

We would also have to include nodes marking the front and back ends of the list, such as

```
Var StartLeft, StartRight : PtrListing;
```

rather than just the Start pointer used previously.

16-2 Queues

We next move on to the data structure known as the **queue.** Recall from Chapter 13 that the main property of a queue is that it is a FIFO (First In, First Out) structure; that is, elements are inserted at one end and deleted from the other end. A linked list can be used to easily implement a queue. In addition to the typical list nodes themselves, two special pointers are used to mark the beginning of the queue (the head) and the end of the queue (the tail). Such a structure is shown schematically in Figure 16-10. Note that the two special pointers Head and Tail need not be nodes.

The most common queue operations are insertion and deletion. Normally, however, deletion of the first element in a queue involves more than simply deleting the node from the queue. Take, for example, a computer print queue, which keeps track of all jobs (files) waiting to be printed out by the computer. When the head node is deleted from

Figure 16-10

Typical Queue Structure Implemented with Links

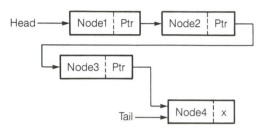

the queue, the corresponding file is printed out. Another example can be found on a (computer) job queue: when the head node is deleted, the corresponding job is loaded into memory and then run. Consider also a queue to buy theater tickets: persons are "deleted" after they purchase their tickets. In general, a queue involves items waiting to be processed in some fashion, and deletion occurs only in conjunction with the processing.

Since a queue is constantly growing and shrinking, it is entirely possible that, occasionally, one might have an *empty queue*. Such a queue has no elements. This would be indicated by the `Nil` value in the pointers `Head` and `Tail`.

The actual processes of insertion and deletion are identical to those used for a regular linked list; in fact, they are simpler because such insertions and deletions *always* occur in the same places, namely, at the tail and head, respectively. Normally, the queue is not traversed in the sense of trying to find something.

Let us now develop generalized algorithms for the insertion and deletion processes.

INSERTION AT THE TAIL

The process of inserting a node at the tail of a queue is, for all practical purposes, identical with general insertions into linked lists. In the case of a queue, however, there is only one place for the insertion to take place; thus, the algorithm can be very specific with regard to the pointers that are used. The process involves making both the (current) last queue node *and* the tail point to the (new) last queue node. We must also take into account the possibility that the queue is currently empty, in which case the head of the queue must also be made to point to the node being inserted. Specifying this algorithmically yields

```
Insert Node at the tail
  If Tail ≠ Nil then
      Tail^.Next ← Node
      Tail ← Node
  Else
      Tail ← Node
      Head ← Node
```

This algorithm assumes that the node to be inserted into the queue has been created and its fields defined, *including* assigning its pointer the value of Nil. It also assumes that Head and Tail have both been set to Nil initially so that, as expected, the queue starts off empty.

DELETION AT THE HEAD

Deletion at the head of the queue is even easier. It simply involves making Head point to the next element in the queue. If the (current) element to be deleted is the final element in the queue, then Head is automatically (and correctly) set to Nil. If this is the case, however, Tail must *also* be set to Nil for consistency. The algorithm itself can be written as

```
Head ← Head^.Next
If Head = Nil then
    Tail ← Nil
```

This particular algorithm does not actually dispose of the unwanted node; it merely removes it from the queue. If, in fact, the deleted node is to be used for something useful (such as indicating a file to be printed out), the process taking care of the desired action (in this case the print routine) may be used to properly dispose of the node. The algorithm also checks to see whether or not the element just removed was the last one in the queue, and if it is, it marks the tail appropriately.

Print Queue

We will now consider a problem that uses a queue and the above algorithms as a part of its solution. Since we have already used the idea of a print queue to demonstrate the use of queues, let's work with such a queue. Let us write a simulation of a print queue, which means that we will generate a program that does many of the same things a computer operating system would have to do to manage print requests from users. Simulating the operation of a typical print queue will allow us to learn many of the details of how such a queue works without involving us with details (such as interruptions and communication protocols) that are not directly related to the queue. Also, in general, simulations tend to be cheaper, faster, and easier to understand than the real thing.

STEP 1: UNDERSTAND THE PROBLEM

We want to simulate the functioning of a print queue in a typical operating system. This involves retaining in a queue any and all print requests that have been received, in the order in which they were received, and then printing them out in that same order as the printer or printing device becomes available. A complication arises, however, in that print requests are received not in a regular but rather in a *random* fashion. This is because print requests are made as individual users see fit, without any coordination. Further, the amount of material to be printed varies from one request to another and consequently so does the amount of time needed to print the material. We therefore have a situation in which additions and deletions to the queue follow a random pattern; this random pattern must be taken into account.

Before moving on to the planning stage, let's briefly examine what information (and data structures) is appropriate for the queue nodes. We would like to have the name of the job to be printed, its size, and of course a pointer to the next node in the queue. However, it is common to also include an identification number for easy reference to the queue jobs. Therefore, our queue node should look like this:

```
Node = Record
          Number : Integer;
          Name   : String;
          Size   : Integer;
          Next   : PtrNode
       End;
```

STEP 2: PLAN THE SOLUTION

The level of difficulty of this problem seems formidable, but let's use our top-down approach and take it one step at a time. Fundamentally, all we have to do is the following: if a print request is waiting, we must add it to the queue; and if the printer is not busy, we must remove a request from the queue and send it to the printer. To handle pending print requests, the system basically takes turns going around to all the users to see what, if anything, each user wants to do. This process is called polling. If a user wants to print something, then the information regarding the print request is obtained and added to the print queue. One of the other things the system checks on is whether or not the printer is busy. If it is, the operating system does nothing, but if the printer is not busy, then the operating system sends in the leading print request. This initial (and simple) procedure can be turned into an initial (and simple) algorithm as follows:

See if there is a job request

If there is, add it to the queue

See if the printer is busy

If it isn't, send it the next print request (if there is one)

Although the print requests and printer availability are random processes, *this algorithm is not*. The algorithm loops at regular intervals and checks to see what needs to be done. We may therefore incorporate a timing loop (where we simulate the passage of time) and schedule our work:

While Time < QuittingTime
  Poll (for print requests)
  If there is a print request then
    Create a new print job (node)
    Insert it into the queue
  If the printer is *not* busy then
    Dispose of any previous print jobs
    If the queue is not empty then
      Take the next job in the queue and send it
      to the printer
  Display the current print queue
  Increment the time

We have added considerable detail to this algorithm. We have explicitly included disposal of completed print jobs (if and when there are any). Also, we have added the ability to dynamically display the print queue so that we can watch it change as time goes by. Without this display, we wouldn't be able to tell what was going on and couldn't learn anything. We have also, of course, inserted the entire process into a timing loop.

Now that we have our fundamental algorithm, we can begin to work in more detail. The first item we come to is the procedure Poll. We would like three pieces of information from this procedure: whether there is indeed a print request and, if so, its name and size. We can summarize this as follows:

```
Poll (JobRequested, JobName, JobSize)
```

The first argument must be a Boolean variable; the second, a string; and the third, an integer. Recall from our initial discussion that we also want to have a job number associated with each request. (We will, how-ever, let the main program rather than this procedure generate the job number.)

We next need to create a new node; we have done node creation many times before, so we will not belabor the process here.

The next major item of the main algorithm concerns the insertion of the new node into the queue. Let's make a procedure of this also. One significant point here: a typical operating system works with more than one queue; therefore, our procedure should permit us to specify the queue of interest.

Making these additions to the first part of our algorithm gives us the following:

```
While Time < QuittingTime
   Poll (JobRequested, JobName, JobSize)
   If JobRequested then
      Create a new job
         JobNumber ← JobNumber + 1
         New (NewJob)
         NewJob^.Number ← JobNumber
         NewJob^.Name ← JobName
         NewJob^.Size ← JobSize
         NewJob^.Next ← Nil
      Insert it into the queue
         InsertQ (PrintQ, NewJob)
```

Note that the algorithm now generates consecutive job numbers as well.

One other item worthy of note in this algorithm is the way in which specific queues are referenced. For example, the first parameter in the call to `InsertQ` (namely, `PrintQ`) identifies the queue into which the new node should be inserted. What exactly should `PrintQ` represent? Since a queue (unlike an array) cannot be referenced by name, `PrintQ` must be a pointer, but what kind of pointer?

Well, we can do something clever here. Suppose we define a queue as

```
Queue = Record
          Head : PtrNode;
          Tail : PtrNode
        End;
```

We can then define `PrintQ` as

```
PrintQ : Queue;
```

If we use this more generalized method of queue definition, we can, if we like, define and use any number of queues and have the `InsertQ` procedure work properly for any and all of them!

Now that we're satisfied with our queue definitions and insertions, let's work with the part of the algorithm that deals with the printer proper. We reproduce that portion of the algorithm here for reference:

If the printer is *not* busy then
    Dispose of any previous print jobs
    If the queue is not empty then
        Take the next job in the queue and send it
        to the printer

First of all, we must find a way to determine whether or not the printer is busy. Let's simply define a Boolean function, perhaps called `PrinterBusy`, which returns a value of `True` if the printer is busy and `False` otherwise. In so doing, of course, we defer details of the actual determination until later.

The next step requires that we dispose of any previously completed print jobs (that is, any jobs that were sent to the printer during a previous cycle and subsequently completed). If there is such a completed job, its existence will be indicated by the fact that the pointer `NextJob` (which is what we will call the most recent job sent to the printer) will not be `Nil`. In that case we do a dispose.

Having properly disposed of any completed jobs, we may take the next job from the queue (again, if there is one) and send it to the printer. The existence of an awaiting job is indicated by a nonnil pointer `Head`. In order to send this job to the printer, we will do the following three things: First, we will make a *copy* of the information contained in the node at the head of the queue. Second, we will *remove* the node from the queue. Third, we will send the *copy* of the print request to the printer.

We finally come to the last part of the main algorithm, namely,

Display the current print queue
Increment the time

We wish to display the queue in its entirety. At this point in the algorithm, however, the queue is actually in two pieces. The first consists of the job currently being printed (which is *not* in the queue any longer), and the second is made up of pending jobs that still *are* in the queue proper. Let us carry out the display by calling a procedure that sends, as arguments, a pointer to the job currently being printed and the print queue itself. Of course, we also have to increment the time, but that's easy.

The second half of our main algorithm, therefore, becomes

```
If not PrinterBusy then
   Dispose of any previous print jobs
      If NextJob ≠ Nil then Dispose (NextJob)
      NextJob ← Nil

   See if the queue is empty
      If PrintQ.Head ≠ Nil then
         Get the next job in the queue
            NextJob ← PrintQ.Head
         Remove it from the queue
            DeleteQ (PrintQ)
         Send it to the printer
            PrintOut (NextJob)
Display (NextJob, PrintQ)
Time ← Time + 1
```

Last, but not least, we have to initialize everything. Adding this to our algorithm gives us

```
Bring up (initialize) the system
   JobNumber ← 0
   Time ← 0
   PrintQ.Head ← Nil
   PrintQ.Tail ← Nil
   NextJob ← Nil

While Time < QuittingTime
   Poll (JobRequested, JobName, JobSize)
   If JobRequested then
      Create a new job
         JobNumber ← JobNumber + 1
         New (New Job)
         NewJob^.Number ← JobNumber
         NewJob^.Name ← JobName
         NewJob^.Size ← JobSize
         NewJob^.Next ← Nil
      Insert it into the queue
         InsertQ (PrintQ, NewJob)

If not PrinterBusy then
   Dispose of any previous print jobs
      If NextJob ≠ Nil then Dispose (NextJob)
      NextJob ← Nil

See if the queue is empty
   If PrintQ.Head ≠ Nil then
      Get the next job in the queue
         NextJob ← PrintQ.Head
      Remove it from the queue
         DeleteQ (PrintQ)
      Send it to the printer
         PrintOut (NextJob)
```

Display (NextJob, PrintQ)
Time ← Time + 1

How shall we treat `QuittingTime`? We will make it a constant, so that the program will terminate after a predetermined length of time (that is, after a fixed number of cycles).

At this point the main algorithm is complete, but we have the following (as yet) undefined procedures and functions:

`ReadString` (unspoken but necessary)
`Poll`
`InsertQ`
`DeleteQ`
`DisplayQ`
`PrintOut`
`PrinterBusy`

`ReadString` we have seen many times before, so we really needn't bother with it again. `DisplayQ`, also, is little more than the simple list traversal we used in the shopping list example, and we will not work with it further either. However, the remaining subprograms are new, so we will examine each of them in turn.

`Poll`. This subprogram can be made very easy or very hard; let's make it very easy. We will simply ask the person running the program whether or not there is a print request and, if so, to input its name and size. We could generate all of the necessary information using statistics and end up with a more valid simulation, but such effort really is beyond the scope of this text. Taking the easy way out gives us

Procedure Poll (Requested, Name, Size)
   Write 'Print Request (Y/N)'
   Read Answer
   Requested ← Answer = 'Y'
   If Requested then
     Read Name
     Read Size

`InsertQ`. We have already generated an algorithm for this during our discussion of linked lists. We may, therefore, simply adapt it to our present queue application:

Procedure InsertQ (WhichQ, Job)
   If WhichQ.Tail ≠ Nil then
     WhichQ.Tail^.Next ← Job
     WhichQ.Tail ← Job
   Else

WhichQ.Tail ← Job
WhichQ.Head ← Job

Note that we have used the rather odd-looking construct `WhichQ.Tail^.Next`. This is really not as funny as it seems; the head of the queue in question is merely a field of the data type `Queue`. Hence, in this case, the pointer itself is actually `WhichQ.Tail`. We then use it just like any other pointer. We can, if we like, use `With` here to make it a little easier to see, as follows:

Procedure InsertQ (WhichQ, Job)
  With WhichQ Do
    If Tail ≠ Nil then
      Tail^.Next ← Job
      Tail ← Job
    Else
      Tail ← Job
      Head ← Job

`DeleteQ.` Again, we already have an algorithm for this and we need merely adapt it to the problem at hand, which gives us

Procedure DeleteQ (WhichQ)
  WhichQ.Head ← WhichQ.Head^.Next
  If WhichQ.Head = Nil then
    WhichQ.Tail ← Nil

As with the case of `InsertQ`, we may use `With` to make it a little easier to understand, namely,

Procedure DeleteQ (WhichQ)
  With WhichQ Do
    Head ← Head^.Next
    If Head = Nil then
      Tail ← Nil

We are now ready to tackle the final two procedures, `PrintOut` and `PrinterBusy`. These two procedures must work together in such a way as to simulate the passage of time with regard to the printer. We begin by assuming that the time required to print out any particular job is proportional to the size of the job. For the sake of simplicity, let's make the time required to print out a job exactly *equal* to the size of the job.

We will next create a variable named `PrinterTimeRemaining`, which will store the amount of time the printer still requires in order to complete printing out its current job. When a job is accepted by the printer, `PrinterTimeRemaining` will be set equal to the time needed to print out the job, and as time goes by (that is, as the program cycles), `PrinterTimeRemaining` will be decremented. Note that when the remaining time required to complete a job has reached zero, then the printer is not busy! However, in order for this to work properly, both `PrintOut` and `PrinterBusy` must have access to `PrinterTimeRemaining`, since each must be able to alter it without regard to the other. That, in turn, requires making this variable a ("dreaded") global variable. However, we have seen the need for this before, and if we are careful in how we use it, we will have no problems.

Let's now look specifically at the two remaining procedures.

`PrintOut.` When we send something to the printer (at least in our simple simulation), all we really need to do is set `PrinterTime-Remaining` equal to the time the job should take for completion:

```
Procedure PrintOut (Job)
    PrinterTimeRemaining ← Job^.Size
```

`PrinterBusy.` We need to check here only to see if `PrinterTime-Remaining` is greater than zero. If it is, the printer is busy; otherwise, it is not. We may also take the opportunity, at this point, to decrement the time remaining. Since this procedure is called each cycle, the time elements will be consistent. Remember that this is a Boolean function. The algorithm, therefore, can be expressed as

```
Function PrinterBusy : Boolean;
    If PrinterTimeRemaining > 0 then
        PrinterTimeRemaining ← PrinterTimeRemaining − 1
        PrinterBusy ← True
    Else
        PrinterBusy ← False
```

This, then, concludes our expositions of the main program and associated procedures, and we may move on to the next step in the development process.

STEP 3: CODE THE SOLUTION

The final coded solution is shown in Figure 16-11. (Note the paranoia with which we mark the one and only global variable.)

STEP 4: CHECK OUT THE PROGRAM

A sample run is shown in Figure 16-12. The program works correctly for all combinations of insertions, deletions, and empty queues, and we can watch as the queue builds up and goes back down. Success!

Figure 16-11

Print Queue Simulation Implemented via Linked Lists

```
PRQUEUE.PAS
    1    Program PrQueue (Input, Output);
    2
    3    (*
    4        This program simulates the operation of a computer print queue.
    5        Print jobs of arbitrary length may be added to the queue, and
    6        the queue is automatically emptied by sending one job at a time
    7        from the head of the queue to the printer.
    8    *)
    9
   10    Const QuittingTime = 20; (* This is the number of cycles through which
   11                                the program runs before it quits
   12                                automatically. *)
   13
   14    Type  String8 = Packed Array [1..8] of Char;
   15
   16          PtrNode = ^Node;
   17
   18          Node = Record              (* Individual print job *)
   19                   Number : Integer;  (*   Job number        *)
   20                   Name   : String8;  (*   Job name          *)
   21                   Size   : Integer;  (*   Job size          *)
   22                   Next   : PtrNode   (* Pointer to the next job in the queue *)
   23                 End;
   24
   25          Queue = Record             (* Definition of a queue *)
   26                    Head : PtrNode;
   27                    Tail : PtrNode
   28                  End;
   29
   30    Var   PrintQ : Queue;            (* This simulation uses only one queue *)
   31
   32          NewJob, NextJob : PtrNode;
   33
   34          Time : Integer;            (* Elapsed (simulation) time *)
   35
   36          JobNumber, JobSize : Integer; (* Information about the *)
   37          JobName : String8;            (* current job           *)
   38
   39          JobRequested : Boolean;       (* Whether or not a print job
   40                                            has been requested *)
   41
   42          PrinterTimeRemaining : Integer; (* GLOBAL (system) VARIABLE *)
   43
   44
   45
   46    Procedure ReadString (Var S:String8);
   47      Var K : Integer;
   48      Begin
   49        For K := 1 to 8 Do
   50            Read (S[K]);
   51        Readln
   52      End;
   53
   54
   55    Procedure Poll (Var Requested:Boolean;
   56                    Var Name:String 8;
   57                    Var Size:Integer);
```

Figure 16-11 continued

```
58      (* This procedure simulates the entry of a print request from
59          a terminal; it simply asks the operator whether or not
60          a print request is being made and, if so, reads in the
61          appropriate information *)
62
63      Var Answer : Char;
64      Begin
65        Write ('Print Request? (Y/N) : '); Readln (Answer);
66        Requested := Answer = 'Y';
67        If Requested then
68           Begin
69              Write ('File name : '); ReadString (Name);
70              Write ('File size : '); Readln (Size)
71           End
72      End;
73
74
75      Procedure InsertQ (Var WhichQ:Queue; Job:PtrNode);
76      (* This procedure inserts a node into the tail of a queue *)
77      Begin
78        With WhichQ Do
79           If Tail <> Nil then
80              Begin
81                 Tail^.Next := Job;
82                 Tail := Job
83              End
84           Else
85              Begin
86                 Tail := Job;
87                 Head := Job
88              End
89      End;
90
91
92      Procedure DeleteQ (Var WhichQ:Queue);
93      (* This procedure deletes a node from the head of a queue *)
94      Begin
95        With WhichQ Do
96           Begin
97              Head := Head^.Next;
98              If Head = Nil then
99                 Tail := Nil
100          End
101     End;
102
103
104     Function PrinterBusy : Boolean;
105     (* This function determines whether or not the printer is
106         currently active *)
107     Begin
108       If PrinterTimeRemaining > 0 then
109          Begin
110             PrinterTimeRemaining := PrinterTimeRemaining - 1;
111             PrinterBusy := True
112          End
113       Else
114          PrinterBusy := False
115     End;
116
117
```

Figure 16-11 continued

```
118    Procedure DisplayQ (Job:PtrNode; WhichQ:Queue);
119    (* This procedure displays the contents of the print queue,
120       including any jobs currently in progress at the printer. *)
121     Var ThisNode : PtrNode;
122     Begin
123       Writeln;
124       Writeln ('Printer Queue : Current Status');
125       Writeln;
126       If Job = Nil Then
127          Writeln ('* No jobs *')
128       Else
129          Begin
130            With Job^ Do
131              Writeln ('Active : ', Number:5, ' ', Name, Size:5);
132            Writeln;
133            ThisNode := WhichQ.Head;
134            While ThisNode <> Nil Do
135               Begin
136                 With ThisNode^ Do
137                   Writeln ('Pend   : ', Number:5, ' ', Name, Size:5);
138                 ThisNode := ThisNode^.Next
139               End
140          End;
141       Writeln
142     End;
143
144
145    Procedure PrintOut (Job:PtrNode);
146    (* This procedure simulates the actual printing of a job by
147       assigning a time interval in which the job is to be
148       printed. *)
149     Begin
150       PrinterTimeRemaining := Job^.Size
151     End;
152
153
154    BEGIN
155      (* Bring up (initialize) the system *)
156         PrinterTimeRemaining := 0;
157         JobNumber := 0;
158         Time := 0;
159         PrintQ.Head := Nil;
160         PrintQ.Tail := Nil;
161         NextJob      := Nil;
162
163      (* Kick it in and go *)
164
165      While Time < QuittingTime Do
166         Begin
167
168            Poll (JobRequested, JobName, JobSize);
169
170            If JobRequested then
171               Begin
172                 (* Create a new job *)
173                    JobNumber := JobNumber + 1;
174                    New (NewJob);
175                    NewJob^.Number := JobNumber;
176                    NewJob^.Name   := JobName;
```

Figure 16-11 continued

```
177                    NewJob^.Size   := JobSize;
178                    NewJob^.Next   := Nil;
179              (* Insert it into the queue *)
180                    InsertQ (PrintQ, NewJob)
181           End;
182
183        If not PrinterBusy then (* send it something to print *)
184           Begin
185              If Next Job <> Nil then Dispose (NextJob);
186              NextJob := Nil;
187              If PrintQ.Head <> Nil then (*if there is something in the queue *)
188                 Begin
189                    NextJob := PrintQ.Head;
190                    DeleteQ (PrintQ);
191                    PrintOut (NextJob)
192                 End
193           End;
194
195        DisplayQ (NextJob, PrintQ);
196
197        Time := Time + 1
198
199        End;
200
201     Writeln ('SYSTEM SHUTDOWN : Out of time')
202
203    END.
```

Figure 16-12

Test Run and Sample Output for the Print Queue Simulation

```
$ run prqueue

Print Request? (Y/N) : N

Printer Queue : Current Status

* No Jobs *

Print Request (Y/N) : Y
File name : FIRSTONE
File size : 1

Printer Queue : Current Status

Active :     1 FIRSTONE     1


Print Request? (Y/N) : N

Printer Queue : Current Status

Active :     1 FIRSTONE     1
```

Figure 16-12 continued

```
Print Request? (Y/N) : N

Printer Queue : Current Status

* No Jobs *

Print Request? (Y/N) : Y
File name : NEXTONE
File size : 3

Printer Queue : Current Status

Active :      2 NEXTONE       3

Print Request? (Y/N) : Y
File name : ANOTHER
File size : 1

Printer Queue : Current Status

Active :      2 NEXTONE       3

Pend   :      3 ANOTHER       1

Print Request? (Y/N) : Y
File name : GOFORIT
File size : 2

Printer Queue : Current Status

Active :      2 NEXTONE       3

Pend   :      3 ANOTHER       1
Pend   :      4 GOFORIT       2

Print Request? (Y/N) : Y
File name : KEEPGOIN
File size : 1

Printer Queue : Current Status

Active :      2 NEXTONE       3

Pend   :      3 ANOTHER       1
Pend   :      4 GOFORIT       2
Pend   :      5 KEEPGOIN      1

Print Request? (Y/N) : Y
File name : ONEMORE
File size : 1

Printer Queue : Current Status

Active :      3 ANOTHER       1

Pend   :      4 GOFORIT       2
Pend   :      5 KEEPGOIN      1
Pend   :      6 ONEMORE       1
```

Figure 16-12 continued

```
Print Request? (Y/N) : N

Printer Queue : Current Status

Active :      3 ANOTHER      1

Pend   :      4 GOFORIT      2
Pend   :      5 KEEPGOIN     1
Pend   :      6 ONEMORE      1

Print Request? (Y/N) : N

Printer Queue : Current Status

Active :      4 GOFORIT      2

Pend   :      5 KEEPGOIN     1
Pend   :      6 ONEMORE      1

Print Request? (Y/N) : N

Printer Queue : Current Status

Active :      4 GOFORIT      2

Pend   :      5 KEEPGOIN     1
Pend   :      6 ONEMORE      1

Print Request? (Y/N) : N

Printer Queue : Current Status

Active :      4 GOFORIT      2

Pend   :      5 KEEPGOIN     1
Pend   :      6 ONEMORE      1

Print Request? (Y/N) : N

Printer Queue : Current Status

Active :      5 KEEPGOIN     1

Pend   :      6 ONEMORE      1

Print Request? (Y/N) : Y
File name : LASTONE
File size : 1

Printer Queue : Current Status

Active :      5 KEEPGOIN     1

Pend   :      6 ONEMORE      1
Pend   :      7 LASTONE      1

Print Request? (Y/N) : N

Printer Queue : Current Status
```

Figure 16-12 continued

```
Active :       6 ONEMORE      1

Pend    :      7 LASTONE      1

Print Request? (Y/N) : N

Printer Queue : Current Status

Active :       6 ONEMORE      1

Pend    :      7 LASTONE      1

Print Request? (Y/N) : N

Printer Queue : Current Status

Active :       7 LASTONE      1

Print Request? (Y/N) : N

Printer Queue : Current Status

Active :       7 LASTONE      1

Print Request? (Y/N) : N

Printer Queue : Current Status

* No Jobs *

SYSTEM SHUTDOWN : Out of time
```

STEP 5: DOCUMENT

As with all our examples so far, the program is well documented with regard to comments and presentation.

16-3 *Stacks*

We now come to the last of the linear linked structures we intend to examine in this chapter, the **stack.** Recall from Chapter 13 that a stack is a LIFO structure (Last In, First Out) wherein ALL insertions and deletions occur at the top, or head, of the stack. Insertion onto a stack is termed a **push** and deletion from a stack is called a **pop** or pull. Stacks can be implemented easily with a linked list mechanism, as shown in Figure 16-13. A special pointer (Top, in this case) is used to mark the beginning of the stack, and each stack element points to the *next* element further down in the stack. A stack is normally visualized as a vertical structure much like the cafeteria plate dispenser mentioned in Chapter 13.

Figure 16-13

Typical Stack Structure Implemented with Links

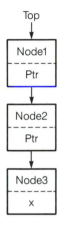

Before proceeding to a discussion of stack implementation, let's briefly examine the ways in which stacks can be used. They play a crucial role in computer science because they can record the paths of a series of processes and then return back through the processes in reverse order. Stacks are used primarily in computer programming as a way of implementing procedure and function calls and as an aid to translating (compiling) computer programs.

Let's first look at procedure calls. As we saw in Chapter 6, a main program can call a procedure (or function), the procedure itself can call another procedure, and so on. Further, we saw in Chapter 12 that a procedure may also call itself. A stack mechanism is used to make this work properly.

Let's look at a typical set of nonrecursive procedure calls, such as those shown in Figure 16-14. Main calls a procedure ProcA, which in turn calls a procedure ProcB, which in turn calls ProcC. After completion of ProcC, control returns to the instruction immediately following the procedure call in ProcB and continues to the end of ProcB. Control *then* returns to where *it* was called in ProcA. When ProcA is completed, control returns to that point in Main wherein the initial procedure call was made. In other words, we go into the calls in this order:

Main → ProcA → ProcB → ProcC

We then return from the calls in this order:

Figure 16-14

Flow of Control Through a Typical Set of Nonrecursive Procedure Calls

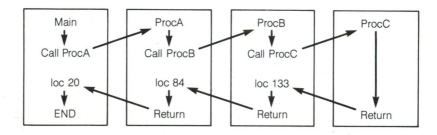

ProcC → ProcB → ProcA → Main

Note that the order is exactly reversed. *This is precisely what happens when items are placed onto and then removed from a stack* (recall the plate dispenser example from Chapter 13). Let us trace through this series of calls in order to better see what transpires on the stack as the calls and returns are carried out.

When we start out in the main program, the stack is empty. We can represent the situation as

Stack : Top → X

When we reach (in Main) the call to ProcA, the address (location) of the instruction *immediately following* the call (let's say it's 020) is pushed onto the stack. The stack, therefore, becomes

Stack : Top → 020
                X

Control is then transferred to ProcA, and the computer continues as though nothing had happened. Eventually, however, the call to ProcB (which is located inside ProcA) is encountered. At that point, the return address for ProcA is pushed onto the stack and control transferred to ProcB. Assuming the return location in ProcA is 084, the stack becomes

Stack : Top → 084
                020
                X

A similar process is carried out when ProcB calls ProcC; assuming a return address of 133 in ProcB, the stack becomes

Stack : Top → 133
             084
             020
              X

and we transfer to ProcC.

Look closely at the stack: it contains a record of *how* we got to where we are and a map of how to get back. And it all happens automatically because of the properties of stacks!

Now let's see how we get back. Since ProcC is, in fact, a procedure, the last (machine) instruction of ProcC will be a *return*. This return instruction tells us that the procedure is now complete and it is time to go back to the calling routine (whatever that may have been). The mechanism by which the return is accomplished consists of (1) popping the stack to get the return address and (2) transferring control to that address. In the present case, the return instruction will cause us to pop an address of 133 off the stack and then transfer to that location. Of course, location 133 is exactly the point at which we interrupted the execution of ProcB to jump to ProcC. The stack becomes

Stack : Top → 084
             020
              X

Control then proceeds normally to the end of ProcB, where another return is encountered. This causes, again, the stack to be popped (yielding an address of 020), and control proceeds to location 020 in ProcA. The stack now consists of

Stack : Top → 020
              X

At the termination of ProcA, yet another return will be found, and control will transfer to the location indicated at the top of the stack (in this case location 020). The stack will become empty, and execution will continue through to the end of the main program.

Please note that this process will work just as well for recursive procedures as for nonrecursive procedures. The stack operations are exactly the same in either case.

As we said earlier, the second major use of stacks involves the translation (compilation) of computer programs. When we worked on the parsing problem in Chapter 12, we were dealing with one aspect of program translation. In solving that problem, we used a recursive procedure to accomplish the feat, but in fact *we were indirectly using a stack via the technique of recursion*. We will examine yet another translation scheme in this chapter as a way of demonstrating the use of stacks.

Before we go on to a specific example, however, let's see how we can implement stacks and their attendant operations via linked lists.

PUSH

A stack push involves inserting a node at the beginning of the structure and is invariably implemented as a procedure. The procedure arguments normally consist of the name of the stack to be pushed and the data to be pushed onto it. We would like the procedure to handle all aspects of the push; therefore, let's have the procedure create the stack node to be pushed. (The argument supplies the *data*, not the actual node, to be placed onto the stack.) Since we want to implement the stack via a linked list and, further, since we have done linked list insertions before, we can immediately write in procedure form an algorithm for the push process:

```
Procedure Push (Top, Data);
    New (Node)
    Node^.Element ← Data
    Node^.Next ← Top
    Top ← Node
```

Here, Top represents a pointer to the top of the stack of interest, Data is the information to be pushed onto the stack, Node is the node created to be inserted, and Element is the data field in the node. This algorithm works even if the stack is empty, provided that Top has been initialized to Nil somewhere.

POP

A stack pop involves taking off the top node and is usually written as a function. This is because, as was the case with queues, the top node of the structure normally is intended to be used in some way. The pop function must do two things: first, it removes the top element from the stack; second, it returns the information so removed. With that in mind we can write an algorithm as

```
Function Pop (Top)
    If Top ≠ Nil then
        Pop ← Top^.Element
        Temp ← Top
        Top ← Top^.Next
        Dispose (Temp)
    Else (* We are trying to pop an empty stack *)
        Pop ← 0
        Write 'Error'
```

Again, Top is a pointer to the stack from which we want to obtain data. Since Pop is a function, we return the popped information as the value of the function. We then change the Top pointer and dispose of the note that was on top. If a pop is attempted when the stack is empty, zero is returned and an error message produced.

Occasionally, it is useful to be able to *look at* the top element of a stack without actually removing the element. We can define a function TopOf that does just this:

Function TopOf (TheStack)
   TopOf ← TheStack^.Element

Now that we know how to push, pop, and look at items on a stack, let's develop an application that makes use of them.

Calculator Simulation

We will generate a calculator simulation that functions much as a typical calculator. For example, we would like to be able to carry out long sequences of calculations of the type

$$5 + 3 \times 7 - 9 =$$

We want the calculator to display the intermediate results and the final answer. (This is essentially a more complex version of the calculator simulations generated in Chapter 10.)

In defining the function of this new calculator, we will assume that the person working the calculator can make only two kinds of errors: either two consecutive operators or two consecutive numbers could be entered. If either of these events occurs, it should be regarded by the calculator as an error, and the calculator should clear itself and start over.

STEP 1: UNDERSTAND THE PROBLEM

Let's start by deciding what keys we want our calculator to have. Suppose we permit the following:

0 1 2 3 4 5 6 7 8 9

= Complete the calculations

+ Addition

− Subtraction

∗ Multiplication

/ Division

^ Exponentiation

For the sake of convenience we will also include a c/x key that permits the operator to *c*ontinue with another computation or to e*x*it.

Since we have not provided a decimal point key, we restrict the calculator to integer arithmetic. Also, we would like to build operator precedence into the calculator, as follows:

^   Highest Precedence

* /   Next Precedence

+ -   Lowest Precedence

Now let's look at input and output. Typically, we would like entries such as those shown below to produce output as

Enter	Output
3	
+	
4	
*	
6	
−	24
	27
7	
=	20

That is to say, the intermediate results should be displayed as they are generated. (Enter this input sequence into a typical calculator and see what we mean.)

STEP 2: PLAN THE SOLUTION

The process of changing the input symbols (operators and numbers) to computations can be done relatively easily and is similar to the process used by a compiler to translate a source program to an object program. In this sense it is the logical successor to the parsing problem we solved in Chapter 12. However, in this calculator problem, parsing turns out to be a relatively minor aspect (there are, after all, only two possible errors). The bulk of the problem deals with actual translation and execution of the arithmetic sequence of instructions.

We will simply present the fundamental algorithm, since generating the algorithm from scratch is well beyond the scope of this chapter.

We begin by assigning precedence values to the operators. We may choose these arbitrarily; therefore, let us assign a value of 1 to the additive operators (+ −), 2 to the multiplicative operators (∗ /), and 3 to the exponentiation operator (^). Also in this algorithm, we use an equal sign (=) to terminate a series of computations. Bearing this all in mind we have

1.   Read the next Entry
2.   While the Entry is not ' = ' Do
3.   If the Entry is a number then
4.   Push the Entry onto the Numeric stack
5.   Else (* the Entry is an operator *)
6.   If the Entry is + or − then
7.   Precedence ← 1
8.   Else if the Entry is * or / then
9.   Precedence ← 2
10.   Else (* we must have ^ *)
11.   Precedence ← 3

12.   While the Operator stack is not empty and
               the precedence of the current operator
               is less than or equal to the precedence
               of the operator at the top of operator stack then

13.   Compute a result by popping off the top two
               elements of the Numeric stack and
               combining them according to the operator
               we get by popping the Operator stack,
               and then Push the result back onto
               the Numeric stack
14.   Push the current operator onto the Operator stack
15.   Push the current precedence onto the Precedence stack

16.   Read the next Entry

17.   While the Operator stack is not empty Do
18.   Compute (as above)

19.   Pop the final result off of the Number stack

The nesting in this algorithm is complicated, so look at it carefully. Note that we use three stacks here: the number stack (which contains the actual data), the operator stack (which is associated with two corresponding numbers), and the precedence stack (whose elements have a one-to-one correspondence with the elements on the operator stack). We choose to have three separate stacks instead of, say, having a given operator and its precedence be two fields of a record on one stack; this way we need to write only one set of push and pop procedures.

Before adapting this algorithm to our particular needs, let's trace through it and see how it works. Consider the following sequence:

5 +4 * 2 / 3 =

The result should be 7 (integer arithmetic!) as opposed to 54, because even though the addition is entered first, multiplication has priority and should be performed first. Therein lies the utility of stacks: the stack automatically saves for later any operations that must be postponed because a higher precedence operation has been encountered.

In order to properly carry out the algorithm, we need the following items in memory:

Number Stack	Operator Stack	Precedence Stack	Entry	Precedence

Let's trace through the algorithm step by step (with appropriate comments) to aid in understanding how the algorithm solves the problem.

1. Get the first input entry, which in this case is the number 5, and place it in memory.

Number Stack	Operator Stack	Precedence Stack	Entry	Precedence
			5	

2. The entry is not =, so enter the loop.

3. Entry is a number, so push it onto the number stack.

Number Stack	Operator Stack	Precedence Stack	Entry	Precedence
5			5	

16. The rest of this loop is an Else, so we skip it and go to step 16, where we read in the next Entry, in this case the operator +.

Number Stack	Operator Stack	Precedence Stack	Entry	Precedence
5			+	

2. We return to the loop test in step 2; since the Entry is not =, we reenter the loop.

3. The Entry is not a number, so we skip the If and go to the Else.

6. Since Entry is a +, we set the precedence to 1.

Number Stack	Operator Stack	Precedence Stack	Entry	Precedence
5			+	1

12. We skip the other If alternatives and go to the beginning of the While loop. Since, however, the operator stack is empty, we do not enter the loop but go instead to step 14.

14. We push the current operator onto its stack.

15. We push the current precedence onto its stack, yielding

5	+	1	+	1
Number Stack	Operator Stack	Precedence Stack	Entry	Precedence

16. We read the next Entry, in this case 4.

5	+	1	4	1
Number Stack	Operator Stack	Precedence Stack	Entry	Precedence

2. We are back to the beginning of the loop, where we again see that the Entry is NOT =, so we go back in.

3. The Entry is a number, so it gets pushed onto its stack.

4				
5	+	1	4	1
Number Stack	Operator Stack	Precedence Stack	Entry	Precedence

16. We have again completed as much of the loop as we are able, and hence go to step 16, where we input the next Entry, the operator ∗.

4				
5	+	1	∗	1
Number Stack	Operator Stack	Precedence Stack	Entry	Precedence

2. Same old story; back in again.

3. The entry is not a number, so we proceed to the Else section.

6. The operator is not + or −.

8. The operator IS ∗, so we set precedence to 2.

4				
5	+	1	∗	2
Number Stack	Operator Stack	Precedence Stack	Entry	Precedence

13. We move, therefore, to the While. The operator stack is NOT empty, but the precedence of the current operator is GREATER than the precedence at the top of the stack, so we AGAIN do not enter this loop but proceed directly to step 14.

14. Push the operator.

15. Push its precedence.

4	∗	2		
5	+	1	∗	2
Number Stack	Operator Stack	Precedence Stack	Entry	Precedence

16. Having done that, we get the next Entry, which is the number 2.

	4	*	2		
	5	+	1	2	2
	Number Stack	Operator Stack	Precedence Stack	Entry	Precedence

2. Back home again.

3. A number, so we push it.

	2				
	4	*	2		
	5	+	1	2	2
	Number Stack	Operator Stack	Precedence Stack	Entry	Precedence

16. Loop completed, get the next Entry, the operator /.

	2				
	4	*	2		
	5	+	1	/	2
	Number Stack	Operator Stack	Precedence Stack	Entry	Precedence

2. Back again, in again.

3. This is not a number, so we go to the Else.

6. Entry is not a + or − .

8. Entry IS a /, so set precedence to 2.

	2				
	4	*	2		
	5	+	1	/	2
	Number Stack	Operator Stack	Precedence Stack	Entry	Precedence

12. Move ahead to step 12, the loop. Finally, at long last, we have met the conditions for entering it. The operator stack is not empty, and the precedence of the current operator is less than or equal to the precedence at the top of the stack. Go directly to step 13!

13. This is a big step and actually must be a procedure. Be that as it may, we can carry out the instructions. If we pop the first two elements off the number stack, we get 2 and 4; if we pop the operator off the operator stack we get *. We should, therefore, multiply the 4 and the 2 together. This is our first operation, and note that it is *exactly* the operation we would have performed first had we been doing it by hand! The result is 8, which we then push back onto the number stack, giving us

	8				
	5	+	1	/	2
	Number Stack	Operator Stack	Precedence Stack	Entry	Precedence

Note that the add operation is held in abeyance.

12. We return to this loop test but fail this time because the precedence on the stack is less than the current operator precedence.

14. Put this operator back on;

15. Along with its precedence.

8	/	2		
5	+	1	/	2
Number Stack	Operator Stack	Precedence Stack	Entry	Precedence

16. Get another input, in this case the number 3.

8	/	2		
5	+	1	3	2
Number Stack	Operator Stack	Precedence Stack	Entry	Precedence

2. Back to the top.

3. It's a number, so push it.

3				
8	/	2		
5	+	1	3	2
Number Stack	Operator Stack	Precedence Stack	Entry	Precedence

16. Skip down to the read and get =.

3				
8	/	2		
5	+	1	=	2
Number Stack	Operator Stack	Precedence Stack	Entry	Precedence

2. We're back on top of things again. This time, however, the entry IS the equal sign, which terminates the loop. We drop, therefore, to the final battle in step 17.

17. Here we are faced with another While loop. The condition for entry is that the operator stack not be empty. We meet the criterion, so in we go.

18. We compute once as mentioned above. Popping the number stack gives us 3 and 8, popping the operator stack gives us /, so we must divide 8 by 3 (remember, we have to reverse the order since the stack turns things out backward) to get 2. This result then gets pushed back onto the number stack. The result of all this is shown here:

2				
5	+	1	=	2
Number Stack	Operator Stack	Precedence Stack	Entry	Precedence

17. We return to the start of the loop, where we make the test again. We succeed, since the operator stack is not empty, and reenter.

18. Another computation, this time with 2, 5, and +. Adding these gives us 7, and memory becomes

7			=	2
Number Stack	Operator Stack	Precedence Stack	Entry	Precedence

17. We return to the loop test but fail this time. Therefore, we fall through to step 19.

19. We pop the final answer off of the number stack, which is 7. Note that this is exactly what we had hoped the answer would be! Also note that the stacks are now all empty, and we may start another computation if we so desire.

Now that we see how this algorithm works, let's go ahead and adapt it to our needs. We really only need to add two things: an error detection capability and the ability to carry out more than one set of calculations. With regard to error detection, we said that we would only check for two kinds of errors, namely, consecutive operators and consecutive operands. In order to detect such errors, we must be able to compare any two consecutive entries: if they are the same type, then we have an error. This, in turn, requires that we be able to "remember" the previous entry type. We must also make sure that an operator is not entered as the first symbol. We can take care of that by initializing the "previous" operand type (that is, when a new computation is started) to "operator." When an error occurs, we must also clear (empty) all the stacks in order to not have leftover data interfere with a subsequent calculation.

To carry out more than one computation, we can simply enclose this entire program into a loop that asks whether or not we should go again. Recall that we had a special "key" built into our calculator that permitted the operator to enter a c for continue or an x for quit.

This is a fairly extensive program, so due to space limitations, we shall omit the remaining developmental stages. We will, however, examine the finished product and make a few comments concerning it.

STEP 3: CODE THE SOLUTION

The finished program is shown in Figure 16-15. Note especially the use of constants to make the program more understandable. The integers used here actually have no meaning in and of themselves but are only a way of defining symbolic terms that can be used in the program (this actually presages user-defined types as discussed in Appendix A). An additional benefit is that the stacks can be made strictly numeric, whether they are intended to hold numeric data or information about operators and precedences. Let us now take a brief look at the various parts of this program.

Figure 16-15

*Calculator Simulation Program, Which Is Implemented with Stacks
and Permits Operator Precedence in Arithmetic Expressions*

CALC.PAS

```
1     Program CALC (Input, Output);
2
3     (*
4          This program simulates an algebraic calculator. It includes
5          operator precedence and the ability to chain operations.
6     *)
7
8     Const Add = 1; Sub = 2;        (* These constants are defined as codes    *)
9           Mul = 3; Quo = 4;        (* for the possible calculator operations. *)
10          Exp = 5;                  (* Using numeric codes here also permits   *)
11                                    (* a single stack definition for all of    *)
12                                    (* the stacks used in the program.         *)
13
14          Operator = 1;            (* These are codes for the categories of *)
15          Numeric = 2;             (* input that may be accepted by the     *)
16          EqualSign = 3;           (* calculator.                           *)
17
18    Type   StackPtr = ^Stack;
19
20           Stack = Record
21                       Element : Integer;
22                       Next    : StackPtr;
23                   End;
24
25     Var  NumStack, OprStack,     (* These are the three stacks required *)
26          PrecStack : StackPtr; (* by the program.                       *)
27
28          EntryType,                     (* This permits checking of entries to  *)
29          PreviousEntryType : Integer; (* make sure that consecutive operators *)
30                                         (* or consecutive operands are not       *)
31                                         (* entered.                             *)
32
33          Entry, Precedence : Integer;
34          Searching : Boolean;
35          Result : Integer;
36
37          GoAgain : Char;
38
39
40    Procedure GetEntry (Var TheType, TheData:Integer);
41    (* This procedure fetches a single "entry" from the keyboard
42       and assigns it a type *)
43      Var TheInput : Char;
44      Begin
45        Read (TheInput);
46        TheType := Operator;  (* Default, unless we find something else *)
47
48              Case TheInput of
49
50         ` ` : Begin
51                   TheType := Numeric;
52                   Read (TheData)
53               End;
54         `=` : TheType := EqualSign;
55
56         `+` : TheData := Add;
```

Figure 16-15 continued

```
57        `-` : TheData := Sub;
58        `*` : TheData := Mul;
59        `/` : TheData := Quo;
60        `^` : TheData := Exp;
61              End;
62       Readln
63     End;
64
65
66   Procedure Push (Var Top:StackPtr; N:Integer);
67   (* This pushes the data N onto the stack named Top *)
68     Var Node : StackPtr;
69     Begin
70       New (Node);
71       Node^.Element := N;
72       Node^.Next := Top;
73       Top := Node
74     End;
75
76
77   Function Pop (Var Top: StackPtr) : Integer;
78   (* This pops the stack named Top, returning the data
79      and disposing of the node from which it was taken *)
80     Var Temp : StackPtr;
81     Begin
82       POP := Top^.Element;
83       Temp := Top;
84       Top := Top^.Next;
85       Dispose (Temp)
86     End;
87
88
89   Function TopOf (Top:StackPtr) : Integer;
90     Begin
91       TopOf := Top^.Element
92     End;
93
94
95   Function Empty (Top:StackPtr) : Boolean;
96     Begin
97       Empty := Top = Nil
98     End;
99
100
101  Procedure Compute (Var Number, Operator, Precedence : StackPtr);
102  (* This carries out a computation *)
103    Var N1, N2, Op, Pr : Integer;
104        Result, K : Integer;
105    Begin
106      N2 := Pop (Number);
107      N1 := Pop (Number);
108      Op := Pop (Operator);
109      Pr := Pop (Precedence);
110          Case Op of
111      Add : Result := N1 + N2;
112      Sub : Result := N1 - N2;
113      Mul : Result := N1 * N2;
114      Quo : If N2 = 0 then
115              Result := 0
116            Else
117              Result := N1 Div N2;
```

Figure 16-15 continued

```
118        Exp : Begin
119                Result := 1;
120                For k := 1 to N2 Do
121                    Result := Result * N1
122                End
123            End (* Case *);
124        Push (Number, Result);
125        Writeln ('      <',Result:1,'>')
126
127    End;
128
129
130    Procedure Clear (Var TheStack:StackPtr);
131    (* This completely clears a stack, that is, it removes and
132       disposes of any remaining nodes *)
133    Var Stuff : Integer;
134    Begin
135        While TheStack <> Nil Do
136            Stuff := Pop (TheStack)
137    End;
138
139
140    BEGIN
141        Writeln ('CALCULATOR'); Writeln;
142        GoAgain := 'c';
143        While GoAgain = 'c' Do
144            Begin
145
146                NumStack := Nil;
147                OprStack := Nil;
148                PrecStack:= Nil;
149
150                PreviousEntryType := Operator;
151                GetEntry (EntryType, Entry);
152                While EntryType <> EqualSign Do
153                    Begin
154                        If EntryType <> PreviousEntryType then
155                            (* we may continue *)
156                            Begin
157                                PreviousEntryType := EntryType;
158                                If EntryType = Numeric then
159                                    Push (NumStack, Entry)
160                                Else (* We have an operator *)
161                                    Begin
162                                        If (Entry=Add) or (Entry=Sub) then
163                                            Precedence := 1
164                                        Else if (Entry=Mul) or (Entry=Quo) then
165                                            Precedence := 2
166                                        Else (* Entry=Exp *)
167                                            Precedence := 3;
168
169                                        Searching := True;
170                                        While Searching Do
171                                            Begin
172                                                If Empty (OprStack) then
173                                                    Searching := False;
174                                                If Searching then
175                                                    If (Precedence <= TopOf (PrecStack)) then
176                                                        Compute (NumStack, OprStack, PrecStack)
177                                                Else
178                                                    Searching := False
179                                            End;
```

Figure 16-15 continued

```
180                          Push (OprStack, Entry);
181                          Push (PrecStack, Precedence)
182                       End (* Operator Stuff *);
183
184                  GetEntry (EntryType, Entry)
185
186             End (* proceed *)
187           Else (* We have an error *)
188             Begin
189               Clear (NumStack);
190               Clear (OprStack);
191               Clear (PrecStack);
192               Writeln ('ERROR'); Writeln;
193               EntryType := EqualSign (* Mark this calculation as being completed *)
194             End
195
196         End (* While *);
197
198       While not Empty (OprStack) Do
199           Compute (NumStack, OprStack, PrecStack);
200
201       Result := Pop (NumStack);
202
203       Write ('c/x '); Readln (GoAgain); Writeln
204
205     End (* Major Outer Loop *)
206
207   END.
```

Main Program. This is pretty much our original algorithm with the error detection and loop capabilities added. Note again how the constants make the program more readable. One other thing to note is the method by which the While test of the algorithm step 12 is implemented (lines 169 through 179 of the program). Since we cannot assume, in Pascal, partial evaluation of Boolean expressions, the test must be broken up into several If/Else statements.

Procedure GetEntry. This gets the entry from the keyboard and generates the correct category (operator, number, or equal sign) and data (either the arithmetic number or the exact operator read in). There is a certain amount of contrivance here in that the first character read in is used to determine what happens next, but this device reduces the complications of converting a string into a number, which is what would have to happen otherwise.

Procedure Push. This procedure can be used to push data onto any of the three defined stacks. The stack elements were constructed of the same data types expressly for that purpose. This is a straightforward implementation of the algorithm given earlier in the chapter.

Function PoP. This, of course, is the inverse of PuSh and will also work with any of the stacks. There is a variation here with the earlier algorithm in that the possibility of popping an empty stack is ignored, since, given the constraints of the problem, that can never happen.

Function ToPOf. This, of course, returns the current top of any stack without disturbing it.

Function EmPty. This function returns True if the stack under consideration is empty and False otherwise. It is used in conjunction with the loop tests of the main program.

Procedure Compute. This does the actual computations using the stacks. The numbers and operator are popped (as well as the precedence, so that the correlation between operators and their associated precedences remains correct) and then used to compute a value. This value is then pushed back onto the numeric stack for further use later.

Procedure Clear. This clears a given stack and is used to clear all the stacks when an error occurs. Clearing the stack means emptying it.

STEP 4: CHECK OUT THE PROGRAM

A test run is shown in Figure 16-16 (for the sake of compactness, the output is rearranged in a column format; read from top to bottom, left to right to get it the way the computer originally printed it out). The program can be seen to work beyond our wildest dreams! Notice that all the simple calculations and all the chained calculations work and that errors are detected properly.

STEP 5: DOCUMENT

This program is complicated enough so that some rather extensive documentation is required. In fact, the explanations provided in the "code" section above are also really needed for full comprehension. Nonetheless, the program can be understood.

SUMMARY

In this chapter we examined several kinds of one-dimensional linked structures. The first was the linked list, which is a one-dimensional list held together by pointers rather than subscripts. Insertions and deletions are relatively easy, and the structure utilizes the minimum amount of memory necessary to retain data. The second structure examined was the queue, a FIFO structure that permits elements gener-

Figure 16-16

Test Run and Output for the Calculator Simulation Program

```
CALCULATOR       2                3                +
                 ^                *              ERROR
  12            10                4
  +             =                 -              c/x  c
  56                  <1024>           <12>
  =             c/x  c               17           +
      <68>                           /          ERROR
c/x  c           5                 5
                 +                 =            c/x  c
  12             6                     <3>
  -             *                      <9>         6
  56             7              c/x  c             +
  =             =                 16             -
      <-44>           <42>         +           ERROR
c/x  c                <47>         23
                c/x  c             -            c/x  c
  12                                  <39>         45
  *             5                 5                33
  56            *                 *             ERROR
  =             6                 2
      <672>     +                 ^            c/x  x
c/x  c                <30>         8
                7                 =
  56            =                     <256>
  /                   <37>             <1280>
  12            c/x  c                 <-1241>
  =                              c/x  c
      <4>
c/x  c
```

ated at random times to be processed in an organized fashion. Finally, we looked at the stack, whose LIFO properties make it ideal for translating computer programs and keeping track of procedure and function calls.

Having now completed an examination of one-dimensional linked structures, we will look in the next chapter at two-dimensional linked structures. The two structures we will study are the heap and the tree. At the conclusion of that chapter, we will have completed our look at data structures and (sad but true) our complete introduction to computer science.

EXERCISES

CONCEPTS

1. Define or explain the following terms:

Dispose	New
Doubly linked list	Pop

Head	Predecessor
Nil	Push
Node	Successor

2. Discuss how the requirements that queue insertion take place only at the tail and that queue deletion take place only at the head make this data structure useful.

3. Discuss how the requirement that stack insertion and deletion both take place only at the top makes this data structure useful.

4. Show how *recursive* procedure calls can be implemented on a stack. Give an example (as in Figure 16-14) and trace it.

5. Diagram the processes of insertion and deletion on a doubly linked list.

TOOLS

6. Consider the following definitions:

```
Type PtrStuff = ^Stuff;

     Stuff = Record
                 Amount : Real;
                 Rate   : Real;
                 Size   : Integer;
                 Next   : PtrStuff
             End;
```

Assume further that the following information exists:

Start	−[pointer to 1st node]
1st node −	34.76	0.075	325	[pointer 2nd node]
2nd node−175.00	0.125	19	[pointer 3rd node]
3rd node −	1.25	0.030	1776	[Nil]

What actual data corresponds to the following references?

a. Start
b. Start^.Rate
c. Start^.Size
d. Start^.Next
e. Start^.Next^.Amount
f. Start^.Next^.Next^.Size
g. Start^.Next^.Next^.Next
h. Start^.Next^.Next^.Next^.Rate

7. Generate appropriate type definitions in correct Pascal for each of the following:

a. A list of names and phone numbers.

    b. A list of power bills containing Name, Old Reading, New Reading, Previous Balance, Payments.

    c. A doubly linked list of nodes containing the Time and Position of an artificial satellite.

    d. A queue of computer jobs, each of which has a Name, Number, and Size associated with it.

    e. A stack for procedure calls that contains the return address of the called procedure.

PROBLEMS

8. Write a program for a phone book using linked lists. The entries should be listed alphabetically by name. Once the list is formed, it should be possible to input a name and output the corresponding phone number.

9. Rewrite the ARE real estate problem using a doubly linked list.

10. Simulate a grocery store check out. Assume that the store has five check-out stands, and that when the store opens, only one check-out stand is active. The policy of the store is to open a new check-out counter whenever all of the open check-out stands have more than four people at them and to close a check-out stand if all the open check-out stands have fewer than three people at them. Assume that when people are ready to get in a line, they will go to the check-out counter with the shortest line. Further, make the time they require at the check stand proportional to the number of items they are buying. Have the program follow the sizes of all the check-stand lines as time goes by. Generate the number of customers and their purchases via a procedure that queries the operator for the information.

11. Write a program that simulates an RPN (reverse Polish notation) calculator. For demonstration purposes, suppose you wanted to compute the following expression:

$34 + 16 \times 8 - 376 / 9$

With an algebraic calculator, you would simply enter it as written; however, with an RPN calculator, it must be entered as follows:

$34 \ \ 16 \ 8 \ \times \ + \ 376 \ 9 \ / \ -$

In other words, the numbers are entered in the correct order, but the operators are entered whenever it is time to do a calculation. When an operator is entered, the calculator carries out the operation on the two most recently available operands. In the above example, when the $\times$ is entered, 16 will be multiplied by 8; when the $+$ is entered, 34 will be added to the result obtained from 16×8. This goes on until all the data is processed.

12. Write a program that inputs a text, separates the words, counts them, and produces an alphabetical linked list of the words encountered. For example, if the text to be examined is

this is the text which is the input to this problem it is

then the following list should be generated:

input	1
is	3
it	1
problem	1
text	1
the	2
this	2
to	1
which	1

13. Consider a linked list with nodes containing the following:

```
Type PtrData = ^Data;

      Data = Record
                  Name        :String;
                  NextName    :PtrData;
                  SSNo        :String;
                  NextSSNo    :PtrData
              End;

Var   ByName, BySSNO : PtrData;
```

The idea here is to construct two linked lists in one; by starting with ByName and following the NextName pointers, the list will be ordered alphabetically by name. However, by starting with BySSNo and following the NextSSNo pointers, the list will be ordered alphabetically by SSNo!

Hint: First construct the list alphabetically by name, then traverse *that* list and set up the pointers for SSNo.

14. Write a procedure that simulates either recursive or nonrecursive (or both) procedure calls. Input should consist of a program and procedures such as

```
Main
   step1
   step2
   call ProcA
   step3
ProcA
   step1
```

```
      step2
      call ProcB
      step3
      call ProcC

  ProcB
      step1
      step2

  ProcC
      step1
```

And output should consist of a trace as follows:

```
Main
step1
step2
   ProcA
   step1
   step2
      ProcB
      step1
      step2
   step3
      ProcC
      step1
step3
```

15. Rewrite the print queue problem to take into account the possibility that the print jobs may have a priority associated with them. Use only two priorities here, either high or low. All low-priority jobs should be added to the queue just as before. However, any high-priority jobs should be inserted at the head of the queue. Choose one of the following methods:

a. Simply insert any high priority jobs at the head of the queue.
b. Insert any high priority jobs at the point in the queue where the high and low priority jobs meet.

17

Nonlinear Linked Structures:

Trees and Heaps

*H*aving looked at linear linked structures, we are now ready to move on to two-dimensional linked structures. In this chapter we will examine the fundamental two-dimensional list structure known as the tree, and in particular the variants of binary search trees and heaps.

Let's begin by looking at a few examples of trees to help formulate a conceptual understanding. The quintessential example of the data structure called a tree is the family tree, as shown in Figure 17-1a. When drawn in this way, the structure even looks like a tree. However, trees used as data structures in computer science are invariably portrayed upside down, as shown in Figure 17-1b.

Figure 17-1

A Typical Ancestor Family Tree (a) as Such Trees Are Usually Shown and (b) as a Computer Data Structure

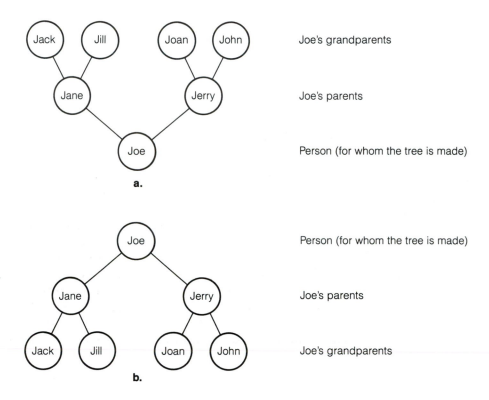

The tree shown in Figure 17-1 is an example of an ancestor chart, in which each person's parents are shown. However, it is possible to represent families and generations in an alternate fashion by listing descendants. Such a tree is shown in Figure 17-2.

Arithmetic expressions can also be represented as trees. Recall from Chapter 4 the method we used to indicate how the operations in an expression are evaluated, for example,

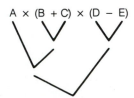

Figure 17-2

A Typical Descendant Family Tree

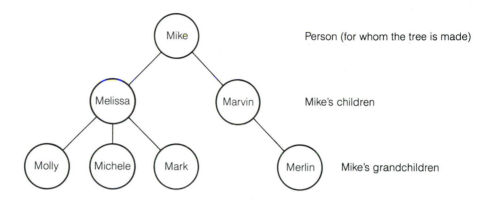

This is actually an example of an upside-down tree structure. If we flip it over and make the variables and operators a part of the resulting structure, as shown in Figure 17-3, the expression can be seen to be a tree. Note that the tree expresses *exactly* how the operations are to be carried out and does so without the need for parentheses!

Another example of a tree can be seen in the table of contents of a book, where the book as a whole can be broken up into chapters, each of which can be subdivided into sections, and so forth. Such a tree is shown in Figure 17-4.

Figure 17-3

An Arithmetic Expression Written as a Tree

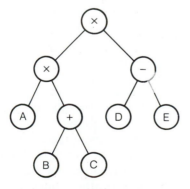

Figure 17-4

The Table of Contents of a Book Represented as a Tree

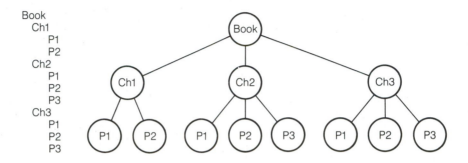

```
Book
  Ch1
    P1
    P2
  Ch2
    P1
    P2
    P3
  Ch3
    P1
    P2
    P3
```

These examples permit us to abstract and generalize the properties of trees. The primary characteristic of a *tree* is that any given element can be descended from *one and only one element*, although any given element may generate any number of other elements. A secondary characteristic of trees is that the only way to reach a particular element is to start at the top (bottom?) and follow a unique path through the elements until the location of interest is reached.

Now that we have seen some typical trees, let's examine a special category of trees, the binary tree.

17-1 *Binary Trees*

All the tree examples we have seen so far can be divided into two categories. The first category is exemplified by the ancestor chart in Figure 17-1, where each of the people listed must have *exactly two* parents so that the resulting tree will always be perfectly symmetrical. The second type of tree, as demonstrated by the descendant's tree and the table of contents, is constructed so that each person (element) can have an arbitrary number of descendants. (In this case there are no constraints on the extent to which the tree can proliferate.) The first type is called a **binary tree,** because each element propagates exactly *two* other elements (or none at all). Such trees can be manipulated efficiently with regard to searching, sorting, and representing data. These are the kinds of trees we will examine in detail in this chapter.

Let us further delineate the properties of trees and introduce some terminology. A typical binary tree (in which each of the important components is labeled) is shown in Figure 17-5. As we expect for linked structures, the individual elements are called nodes. Special names are given to classes of nodes based on their relative positions within the

Figure 17-5

A Typical Binary Tree, with Terminology

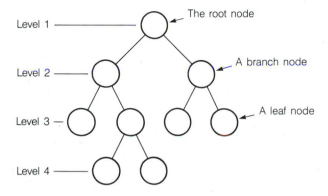

structure. The **root node** is where the tree starts, **branch nodes** (also called interior nodes) are nodes that generate other nodes (there are three in the figure), and **leaf nodes** (or terminus nodes) are nodes that do *not* generate any additional nodes (there are five in the figure). Also, all node connections exist only *between adjacent levels*. A tree structure may *not* have any horizontal or multilevel connections. Owing to this property, the relationships between tree nodes are named much as are the relationships in families. A node is called a parent, mother, or father if it is connected to other nodes and if it precedes these nodes by one level. The nodes so connected are called offspring, sons, or daughters. Adjacent nodes having the same parent are termed siblings, brothers, or sisters. Terms such as "grandparent" and "grandchild" are also used.

We are now ready to present a formal definition of a tree, which can be done recursively (in fact, almost anything you may want to do with a tree can be done recursively):

1. A single node is a tree.

2. A tree may point to an arbitrary number of disjoint (that is, unconnected) subtrees.

If we are referring to binary trees, we may amend the above definition to read "exactly zero, one, or two disjoint subtrees" instead of "an arbitrary number of disjoint subtrees." (It is interesting to note that a linked list is nothing more than a category of tree in which each node may have only one offspring!)

The five common operations of traversal, insertion, deletion, searching, and sorting may be applied to trees. As is true with linked lists, sorting is frequently done using a clever sequence of insertions, and searching can be carried out via traversal. The processes are similar to those carried out on linked lists.

We will begin by considering simple tree traversal. The linked-list counterpart to this operation corresponds to starting at the first node of the list and going all the way through to the last node (as we did in the shopping list problem of Chapter 16, for example).

TRAVERSAL

Traversal, of course, is the means by which we visit (process) every node in the tree. By "process a node" we mean doing whatever is appropriate for the application being considered. Processing can be as simple as printing out one field of the node, or it can be as complex as altering the information contained in the field. There are, in fact, three standard ways in which a tree can be traversed. These are called PreOrder, InOrder, and PostOrder traversal and correspond to traversals in which the root node is processed first, second, or last. All three traversals can be written recursively (and elegantly) as follows:

PreOrder Traversal

1. Process the root node
2. Process the left subtree in PreOrder
3. Process the right subtree in PreOrder

InOrder Traversal

1. Process the left subtree in InOrder
2. Process the root node
3. Process the right subtree in InOrder

PostOrder Traversal

1. Process the left subtree in PostOrder
2. Process the right subtree in PostOrder
3. Process the root node

Let us demonstrate each of these traversals on the tree shown in Figure 17-6. When we process a node of this tree, we will simply write out the node. Note that the tree shown in Figure 17-6 is a representation of the following arithmetic expression:

$$a + b * c / d - e * f$$

InOrder. We begin with InOrder traversal, rather than PreOrder, because InOrder is a little easier to see and more commonly used than the other types. We will trace through this algorithm in detail to see how InOrder traversal works.

Figure 17-6

Sample Tree for Demonstrating PreOrder, InOrder, and PostOrder Traversals

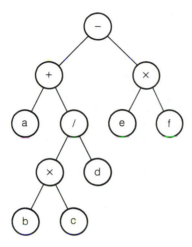

1. Process the left subtree in InOrder

   To do this, we move to the root node of the left subtree, which is (+), and recursively begin the algorithm again.

   1. Process the left subtree in InOrder

      We move to the left subtree in the current node, whose root node is (a).

      1. Process the left subtree in InOrder

         There is no left subtree (it is null); hence, processing is trivially complete! We may therefore move on to the next step at this level.

      2. Process the root node (a)

         The current root node is (a); hence, we process it by writing it out as

         Output → a

         We may now move on to the next step at this level.

      3. Process the right subtree in InOrder.

         This is also null and therefore trivially processed; we may move on.

   2. Process the root node (+)

      We have returned to the root node (+); hence, we process it by writing it out, which gives us

      Output → a +

   3. Process the right subtree

      (At this point, since this is getting rather lengthy, let's abbreviate the remaining explanations.) The right subtree root node is (/).

    1. Process the left subtree (whose root = ×)
       1. Process the left subtree (whose root = b)
         1. Process the left subtree (null)
         2. Process the root node (b)

           Output → a + b

         3. Process the right subtree (null)
       2. Process the root node (×)

         Output → a + b ×

       3. Process the right subtree (whose root = c)
         1. Process the left subtree (null)
         2. Process the root node (c)

           Output → a + b × c

         3. Process the right subtree (null)
    2. Process the root node (/)

       Output → a + b × c /

    3. Process the right subtree (whose root = d)
       1. Process the left subtree (null)
       2. Process the root node (d)

         Output → a + b × c / d

       3. Process the right subtree (null)
2. Process the root node (we're back to root = −)

  Output → a + b × c / d −

3. Process the right subtree (whose root = ×)
    1. Process the left subtree (whose root = e)
       1. Process the left subtree (null)
       2. Process the root node (e)

         Output → a + b × c / d − e

       3. Process the right subtree (null)
    2. Process the root node (×)

       Output → a + b × c / d − e ×

    3. Process the right subtree (whose root = f)
       1. Process the left subtree (null)
       2. Process the root node (f)

         Output → a + b × c / d − e × f

       3. Process the right subtree (null)

This is definitely a laborious process. However, recursion makes the process easy to state, and the computer normally has to do all this work.

    The result of the InOrder traversal is the original arithmetic expression! This may seem like a lot of work to go through just to regenerate the original expression. However, if we define "process a node" appropriately, the traversal can be used to carry out the actual computations. This is in fact one of the methods used by compilers in translating programs.

PostOrder. We move next to PostOrder, because it is the second most widely used traversal and generates an interesting and recognizable result. We reproduce the algorithm here for clarity and then carry out a much abbreviated trace (since we have already gone through one such trace in excruciating detail). It is understood that all the processing is in PostOrder:

PostOrder Traversal
    1. Process the left subtree in PostOrder
    2. Process the right subtree in PostOrder
    3. Process the root node

1. Process left (whose root = +)
  1. Process left (whose root = a)
    1. Process left (null)
    2. Process right (null)
    3. Process root (a)

    Output → a

  2. Process right (whose root = /)
    1. Process left (whose root = ×)
      1. Process left (whose root = b)
        1. Process left (null)
        2. Process right (null)
        3. Process root (b)

        Output → a b

      2. Process right (whose root = c)
        1. Process left (null)
        2. Process right (null)
        3. Process root (c)

        Output → a b c

      3. Process root (×)

      Output → a b c ×

    2. Process right (whose root = d)
      1. Process left (null)
      2. Process right (null)
      3. Process root (d)

      Output → a b c × d

    3. Process root (/)

    Output → a b c × d /

  3. Process root (+)

  Output → a b c × d / +

2. Process right (whose root = ×)
  1. Process left (whose root = e)
    1. Process left (null)
    2. Process right (null)
    3. Process root (e)

Output → a b c × d / + e

2. Process right (whose root = f)
   1. Process left (null)
   2. Process right (null)
   3. Process root (f)

   Output → a b c × d / + e f

3. Process root (×)

   Output → a b c × d / + e f ×

3. Process root (−)

Output → a b c × d / + e f × −

You may recognize this as the original expression written in reverse Polish notation (RPN, also called suffix Polish notation). It permits an expression to be written without need for parentheses yet still preserves the order in which the operations must be carried out. (Some scientific calculators work this way.) Reverse Polish can be used to aid in the translation of expressions written in computer languages.

PreOrder. The PreOrder algorithm is also recursive and follows a pattern very similar to the ones already shown. We will, therefore, omit the details and simply present the results of the traversal, which are

− + a / × b c d × e f

This is our expression written in prefix Polish notation, which is an alternate way of writing parentheses-free expressions.

We can now traverse an existing tree. However, we may well ask, Where do trees come from in the first place? Trees are usually constructed by successive insertions, much as linked lists are formed. Therefore, we next consider the process of building a tree.

INSERTION

To examine the idea of tree insertions, we must introduce another variation of trees, namely, the **binary search tree.** For such trees, the values of the children of any node have a fixed and known relationship to the value of the parent. For example, the value of the left child may always be less (either numerically or lexically) than the value of the parent, and the value of the right child may always be greater than the value of the parent. In these situations, there is an overall order imposed on the tree that is useful when searching and sorting.

A tree is constructed by successively inserting new nodes into the tree. Naturally, the algorithm for doing the insertions is recursive, and the approach is as follows: If there is no tree yet, make the node you wish to insert become the root of the whole tree. If the tree does exist, then check to see if the data in the node to be inserted is less than or greater than the data in the root node. If it is less, insert it into the left subtree; if it is greater, insert it into the right subtree. This can be expressed algorithmically as a procedure:

Procedure InsertTree (Root, Node)
If Root = Nil then
   Root ← Node
Else if Node^.Data < Root^.Data then
    InsertTree (Root^.Left, Node)
Else
    InsertTree (Root^.Right, Node)

Here, `Root` is a pointer to the tree into which insertions are to be made, and `Node` is a pointer to the node to be inserted. `Root^.Left` and `Root^.Right` are pointers to the left and right subtrees, respectively. The method of using pointers here is identical to that used with linked lists; the only difference is that whereas in a linked list only a single pointer is needed, here *two* pointers are required, one to go left and one to go right.

Let's clarify this algorithm by tracing through an example that makes use of it. Suppose we want to construct a tree from the following words:

    computers can be fun

We can build a tree from these words by successively inserting them into a tree following the procedure described above. Initially, of course, we have no tree. We begin by obtaining the first word to be inserted, namely, "computer." This becomes the root node to the tree, since we are just getting started, and the tree is created in the form

computers
/   \

Note that the tree (actually the current root node) has two `Nil` pointers, one going left and one going right, since there are not as yet any subtrees.

Now that the tree has been started, we may go on to insert the next word, "can." Since the tree is no longer null, the algorithm says we must check to see whether the data to be inserted is less than the data in the root node. In this case it is ("can" is less than "computers"). Therefore, according to the algorithm, we call `InsertTree` (recursively), using the *left* pointer of the node we are working with as the root node of the tree we want to insert "can" into. Since the left pointer is `Nil`, we find, on entering the procedure, that we have a `Nil` root! We therefore make this current node the "root," and our tree becomes

```
  computers
  /       \
can
/ \
```

At this point we come to the next word, "be." When we enter the algorithm, we find that the tree is not null and that our data is such that we must insert the word "be" into the left subtree. We consequently call the insert procedure recursively, using the node containing the word "can" as the root node. Since "be" comes before "can," we call the procedure once again (going to the left) and find a Nil pointer. According to the algorithm, we immediately make "be" the root node of this new subtree, yielding

```
      computers
      /       \
    can
    / \
  be
  / \
```

We now get to the last word (so to speak), "fun." Again, entering the algorithm we find that the tree exists, but this time we need to go to the right, since "fun" is greater than "computers". One more entry into the procedure will give us

```
      computers
      /       \
    can        fun
    / \        / \
  be
  / \
```

Now this may not look like much, but if *an InOrder traversal of this tree is made, the words will come out in alphabetical order.* Consequently, not only have we constructed a tree but we have alphabetized the words as well! This particular technique is also very aesthetic. Both tree building and traversal are very elegant recursive procedures.

Let us now develop an application that uses tree insertions to alphabetize a list of words.

Book Title Alphabetization

Let's alphabetize a list of book titles. We will read in an arbitrary number of such titles and alphabetize them via binary search tree insertions.

STEP 1: UNDERSTAND THE PROBLEM

We will alphabetize the titles by way of a two-step process: we will first construct a binary search tree and then print out the alphabetized titles by doing an InOrder traversal of the resulting tree. Processing the nodes will consist of merely printing out the titles.

STEP 2: PLAN THE SOLUTION

The solution, as we said, will consist of two parts. We must first construct the tree and then traverse it. To construct the tree, we will need to read a title, create a node for that title, and then insert it into the tree. The second part of the algorithm only needs to call an InOrder traversal to print out the alphabetized list. We must also incorporate all this into a loop. Accordingly, we can write a general description for the program as follows:

```
While not EOF Do
   Read Book Title
   Create a Tree Node
      New (Node)
      Node^.Left ← Nil
      Node^.Right ← Nil
      Node ^.Title ← Book Title
   InsertTree (Tree, Node)
Print out the alphabetized list
   InOrder (Tree)
```

We have chosen to use an EOF loop to read in the book titles from an external file. Note the simple elegance with which this entire process can be stated! We still need to refine the recursive algorithms for `InsertTree` and `InOrder` and adapt them to our needs. However, with our knowledge of links, this can be done easily as follows:

```
Procedure InsertTree (Root, Node)
If Root = Nil then
   Root ← Node
Else if Node^.Title < Root^.Title then
```

```
     InsertTree (Root^.Left, Node)
Else
     InsertTree (Root^.Right, Node)
```

There aren't many changes at all. The InOrder traversal needn't change much either:

```
Procedure InOrder (Node)
Process the left subtree in InOrder
   If Node^.Left ≠ Nil then
       InOrder (Node^.Left)
Process the root node
   Write Note^.Title
Process the right subtree in InOrder
   If Node^.Right ≠ Nil then
       InOrder (Node^.Right)
```

We must, of course, include the ReadString procedure in order to get the book titles in the first place. As far as the tree nodes themselves are concerned, the Pascal syntax is no different from what we have used for linked lists. We may in fact define the necessary structures simply as

```
Node = Record
          Left  : PtrNode;
          Title : String;
          Right : PtrNode
       End;
```

As we might expect, each node contains a field for the data, a pointer to the left child, and a pointer to the right child.

We now have all we need in order to convert these algorithms to Pascal.

STEP 3: CODE THE SOLUTION

The result of our work is shown in Figure 17-7. The coded insertion and traversal procedures almost seem too easy to believe, but that's because they are expressed recursively. Remember that these procedures require the computer to do a lot of work, but this does not detract in any way from the beauty and elegance of the solution.

STEP 4: CHECK OUT THE PROGRAM

A sample run is shown in Figure 17-8, along with a listing of the input file. We didn't use very many titles here, but the program would work as well with a thousand titles. Be aware that this program doesn't need to address the problem of how many titles may appear. Since we are

Figure 17-7

Program That Alphabetizes Book Titles via Successive Tree Insertions
Followed by an InOrder Traversal.

TITLES.PAS

```
 1    Program TITLES (Books, Output);
 2
 3    (*
 4         This program reads in an arbitrary number of book titles from
 5         an external file and alphabetizes them via tree insertions,
 6         followed by an InOrder traversal of the resulting tree.
 7    *)
 8
 9    Type   String25 = Packed Array [1..25] of Char;
10
11           PtrNode = ^Node;
12
13           Node = Record              (* Tree Nodes *)
14                     Left  : PtrNode;
15                     Title : String25;
16                     Right : PtrNode
17                  End;
18
19    Var   Tree : PtrNode;           (* The tree we are constructing        *)
20          NewTitle : PtrNode;       (* The newly created node we wish to insert *)
21          ThisTitle : String25;     (* The actual title just read in        *)
22
23          Books : Text;             (* External file containing the book
24                                        titles to be alphabetized        *)
25
26    Procedure ReadString (Var TheFile : Text;
27                          Var S : String25);
28      Var k : Integer;
29      Begin
30        For k := 1 to 25 Do
31            Read (TheFile, S[k]);
32        Readln (TheFile)
33      End;
34
35
36    Procedure InsertTree (Var Root, Node : PtrNode);
37    (* This procedure builds a binary search tree by successive insertions *)
38      Begin
39        If Root = Nil then
40            Root := Node
41        Else if Node^.Title < Root^.Title then
42            InsertTree (Root^.Left, Node)
43        Else
44            InsertTree (Root^.Right, Node)
45      End;
46
47
48    Procedure InOrder (Var Node : PtrNode);
49    (* This procedure carries out an InOrder traversal of a tree *)
50      Begin
51        If Node^.Left <> Nil then
52            InOrder (Node^.Left);
53        Writeln (Node^.Title);
54        If Node^.Right <> Nil then
55            InOrder (Node^.Right)
56      End;
```

Figure 17-7 continued

```
57
58
59    BEGIN
60
61      Writeln ('BOOK TITLES');
62      Writeln;
63      Writeln ('Reading titles, constructing the tree...');
64      Writeln;
65
66      Reset (Books);
67
68      Tree := Nil;  (* Start out without a tree *)
69
70      While not EOF (Books) Do
71        Begin
72          ReadString (Books, ThisTitle);
73          (* Create a new tree node *)
74            New (NewTitle);
75            NewTitle^.Left  := Nil;
76            NewTitle^.Right := Nil;
77            NewTitle^.Title := ThisTitle;
78          (* Put the node into the tree *)
79            InsertTree (Tree, NewTitle);
80
81        End;
82
83      (* Print out the alphabetized list by doing an InOrder traversal *)
84          Writeln;
85          Writeln ('Alphabetized Titles');
86          Writeln;
87          InOrder (Tree)
88
89    END.
```

using dynamic list structures, we just use whatever memory we need to get the job done.

STEP 5: DOCUMENT

The program is easily read and understood.

SEARCHING

We next look at how to find something in a tree (perhaps an Apple?). This, of course, corresponds to the operation of *searching*. Binary search trees are ideal for this purpose, because the structure of the tree itself permits a very, very simple recursive implementation of a binary search.

The search process involves checking the key against the current value in the root node. If the key is less than the root node value, we can eliminate the root node and the entire right subtree (aha!) and

Figure 17-8

Test Run of the Alphabetizing Program, Including a Listing of the Input File

```
$ type books.dat

COMPUTER PROGRAMMING
COMPUTER SCIENCE
COMPUTERS AND SOCIETY
COMPUTER ARCHITECTURE
WHO DID YOU SAY IT WAS
ABOUT SPACE AND TIME
COMING HOME AGAIN
YOU CAN'T GO HOME AGAIN
PASCAL PROGRAMMING
ABOUT THE HOUSE
WHO DONE IT THIS TIME
ZEKE THE HORSE
AARON RODE AWAY
ONE MORE TIME
NEVER AGAIN
I LEFT MY HEART IN SF
COMPUTING TRANSCENDENTALS
AT ONCE AND AWAY


$ run titles

BOOK TITLES

Reading titles, constructing the tree...


Alphabetized Titles

AARON RODE AWAY
ABOUT SPACE AND TIME
ABOUT THE HOUSE
AT ONCE AND AWAY
COMING HOME AGAIN
COMPUTER ARCHITECTURE
COMPUTER PROGRAMMING
COMPUTER SCIENCE
COMPUTERS AND SOCIETY
COMPUTING TRANSCENDENTALS
I LEFT MY HEART IN SF
NEVER AGAIN
ONE MORE TIME
PASCAL PROGRAMMING
WHO DID YOU SAY IT WAS
WHO DONE IT THIS TIME
YOU CAN'T GO HOME AGAIN
ZEKE THE HORSE
```

search only the left subtree. If, on the other hand, the key equals the current tree root node, then we've found what we're after! If both of these tests fail, then we merely search the right subtree and eliminate the root and entire left subtree. Note the binary nature of the search: with each test we can eliminate half the tree.

Let us present the algorithm that will accomplish this task:

```
Procedure SearchTree (Root, Key)
If Root = Nil then
    It's not in this tree
Else if Key < Root^.Data then (*it must be in the left subtree*)
    SearchTree (Root^.Left, Key)
Else if Key = Root^.Data then
    We have found it; do whatever
Else (*It must be in the right subtree*)
    SearchTree (Root^.Right, Key)
```

This certainly was easy! Let's go ahead and develop an application to demonstrate the use of binary search trees.

Library Catalog

Suppose we wish to extend the TITLES program so that rather than merely printing out a list of the alphabetized titles after the tree has been constructed, it is possible to search the titles for a specific book. If the book is found, the program should report the call number of the book. If the book is not found, the program should state that the book title is not in the list.

STEP 1: UNDERSTAND THE PROBLEM

Let us begin by defining the structure of the tree nodes, which will be a little different from the structure used in the TITLES problem. We want the node to contain

```
Node = Record
            Left   : PtrNode;
            Title  : String;
            CallNo : String;
            Right  : PtrNode
        End;
```

The overall algorithm itself will consist of a section containing a loop that will read a file of titles and build the tree (just as in the previous example), followed by a section that will read in a title from the keyboard and then search the tree for that title.

STEP 2: PLAN THE SOLUTION

We can borrow most of the algorithm from the TITLES example. Altering it appropriately for our present situation yields

```
While not EOF Do
   Read Book Title
   Read Call Number
   Create a Tree Node
      New (Node)
      Node^.Left ← Nil
      Node^.Right ← Nil
      Node^.Title ← Book Title
      Node^.Number ← Call Number
   InsertTree (Tree, Node)

Read Book Title from Keyboard
While Book Title ≠ 'QUIT' Do
   SearchTree (Tree, Book Title)
   Read Book Title
```

We already have the algorithm for InsertTree, and we just presented the algorithm for SearchTree. Therefore, we have everything we need and may proceed to the next step of the development process.

STEP 3: CODE THE SOLUTION

The final, coded solution is shown in Figure 17-9. It is every bit as elegant as the first example we completed in this chapter.

STEP 4: CHECK OUT THE PROGRAM

A test run of this program is shown in Figure 17-10. We first read in the book titles (which are, by the way, the same as the ones we entered in the TITLES example) and then go on to query for specific books. If a book *is* in the list, the correct call number is produced, and if the book is *not* in the list, an appropriate message is generated.

STEP 5: DOCUMENT

The program is well documented and easy to understand.

Particularly note how much easier the fundamental operations can be carried out when used in conjunction with tree structures. The al-

Figure 17-9

Program That Constructs a Binary Tree of Book Titles and Then Searches the Tree for Specific Titles

LIBRARY.PAS

```
1     Program LIBRARY (BookList, Input, Output);
2
3     (*
4         This program alphabetizes an arbitrary number of book titles from
5         an external file via tree insertions. The program then prompts
6         the user for book titles from the keyboard and searches the
7         alphabetized list, reporting the call number of the book if found
8         or a message to the effect that the book is not there.
9     *)
10
11    Const Quit = 'QUIT                          '; (* Lets the user quit searching
12                                                     for book titles *)
13
14    Type  String25 = Packed Array [1..25] of Char;
15
16          PtrNode = ^Node;
17
18          Node = Record                (* Tree nodes *)
19                    Left   : PtrNode;
20                    Title  : String25;
21                    CallNo : String25;
22                    Right  : PtrNode
23                 End;
24
25    Var   Tree : PtrNode;             (* The tree we are constructing *)
26          NewTitle : PtrNode;         (* The newly created node we wish to insert *)
27          ThisTitle : String25        (* The title just read in *)
28          ThisCallNo : String 25;     (* The call number just read in *)
29
30          BookList : Text;            (* External file containing the book title
31                                         and call numbers of the books to be
32                                         worked with *)
33
34
35    Procedure ReadString (Var TheFile : Text;
36                          Var S : String25);
37    (* This procedure reads in book information from the external file *)
38       Var K : Integer;
39       Begin
40         For K : = 1 to 25 Do
41             Read (TheFile, S[K])
42       End;
43
44    Procedure ReadTitle (Var S : String25);
45    (* This procedure reads in a book title from the keyboard *)
46       Var K : Integer;
47       Begin
48         For K:= 1 to 25 Do
49             Read (S[K]);
50         Readln
51       End;
```

Figure 17-9 continued

```
52
53
54    Procedure InsertTree (Var Root, Node : PtrNode);
55    (* This procedure builds a binary search tree by successive insertions *)
56       Begin
57         If Root = Nil then
58            Root := Node
59         Else if Node^.Title < Root^.Title then
60            InsertTree (Root^.Left, Node)
61         Else
62            InsertTree (Root^.Right, Node)
63       End;
64
65
66    Procedure SearchTree (Root : PtrNode; Key : String25);
67    (* This procedure searches a binary search tree for the key *)
68       Begin
69         If Root = Nil then
70            Writeln (' ** Title not in library **')
71         Else if Key < Root^.Title then
72            SearchTree (Root^.Left, Key)
73         Else if Key = Root^.Title then
74            Writeln ('Call Number : ',Root^.CallNo)
75         Else
76            SearchTree (Root^.Right, Key)
77       End;
78
79
80    BEGIN
81
82       Writeln ('Library Catalog System');
83       Writeln;
84       Writeln ('Reading titles, constructing the tree...');
85       Writeln;
86
87       Reset (BookList);
88
89       Tree := Nil;  (* Start out without a tree *)
90
91       While not EOF (BookList) Do
92         Begin
93            ReadString (BookList, ThisTitle);
94            ReadString (BookList, ThisCallNo);
95            Readln     (BookList);
96            (* Create a new tree node *)
97               New (NewTitle)    ;
98               NewTitle^.Left   := Nil;
99               NewTitle^.Right  := Nil;
100              NewTitle^.Title  := ThisTitle;
101              NewTitle^.CallNo := ThisCallNo;
102           InsertTree (Tree, NewTitle)
103
104        End;
```

Figure 17-9 continued

```
105
106        (* Input a title and see if it's here *)
107          Write ('Enter Search Title> '); ReadTitle (ThisTitle);
108          While ThisTitle <> Quit Do
109            Begin
110              SearchTree (Tree, ThisTitle);
111              Writeln;
112              Write ('Enter Search Title> '); ReadTitle (ThisTitle)
113            End;
114
115      Writeln ('Good-bye')
116
117    END.
```

gorithms and programs are extremely elegant and quite short compared to the methods used for arrays and linear lists. The savings in space and time is significant.

We have now looked at all the fundamental operations associated with trees save one: deletion. This may be the last, but it is by no means the least, so let's tackle this next.

DELETION

Deleting a node from a binary search tree requires, as do all deletions, a search of the structure to first locate the node we wish to delete. Once the node to be deleted has been located, a recursive algorithm exists to remove it from the tree. The algorithm can be stated as follows:

Procedure Delete (Tree, Node)
If the node is a leaf node then
    Delete Node
Else if the node has only one pointer then
    Replace Node by the subtree to which it points
Else
    Replace Node by its InOrder Successor
    Delete the InOrder Successor of Node

"Before" and "after" diagrams, showing exactly what transpires for each of the three possible cases treated in the procedure, are shown in Figure 17-11. Observe that deletion of an interior node (Figure 17-11c) requires that additional deletions occur.

To better demonstrate this, let's examine a problem whose solution makes good use of node deletion in a binary search tree.

Figure 17-10

Sample Run of Library Catalog Program, Including a Listing of the Input Data File

```
$ type booklist.dat

COMPUTER PROGRAMMING      345.TY
COMPUTER SCIENCE          354.G
COMPUTERS AND SOCIETY     TY756.09
COMPUTER ARCHITECTURE     955.WQ
WHO DID YOU SAY IT WAS    Z54.B88
ABOUT SPACE AND TIME      AR4.S321
COMING HOME AGAIN         TG5R44
YOU CAN'T GO HOME AGAIN   RRJ.345
PASCAL PROGRAMMING        321.H
ABOUT THE HOUSE           ER55.BV
WHO DONE IT THIS TIME     590.09R
ZEKE THE HORSE            GT5.N77
AARON RODE AWAY           AA55
ONE MORE TIME             PT22.TY
NEVER AGAIN               9055.H
I LEFT MY HEART IN SF     177C
COMPUTING TRANSCENDENTALS 099.KL
AT ONCE AND AWAY          TTY


$ run library

Library Catalog System

Reading titles, constructing the tree...

Enter Search Title> AARON RODE AWAY
Call Number : AA55

Enter Search Title> ZEKE THE HORSE
Call Number : GT5.N77

Enter Search Title> COMPUTER SCIENCE
Call Number : 354.G

Enter Search Title> ABOUT THE HORSE
 ** Title not in library **

Enter Search Title> COMPUTERS
 ** Title not in library **

Enter Search Title> I LEFT MY HEART IN
 ** Title not in library **

Enter Search Title> AAA
 ** Title not in library **

Enter Search Title> QUIT
Good-bye
```

Figure 17-11

Deletion of Nodes from a Binary Search Tree: (a) a Node with No Descendants, (b) a Node with One Descendant, and (c) a Node with Two Descendants

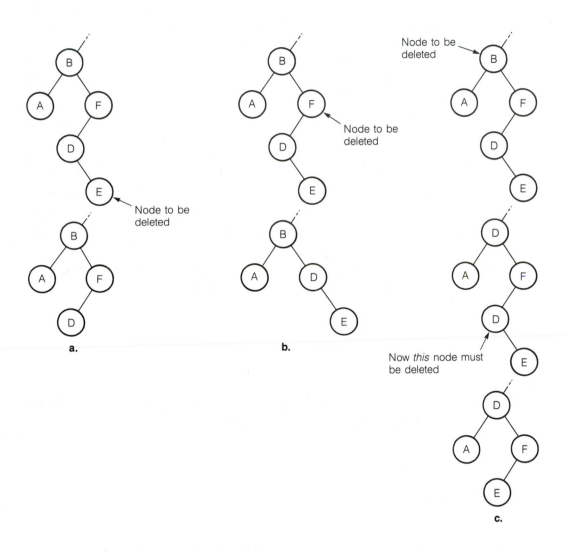

Priority Queues

A priority queue, despite its name, is not really a queue at all but rather a binary search tree. The word "queue" is used in the name because the structure shares many properties with linear queues, such as (in the absence of other considerations) the fact that elements are added at the end and removed at the front. A priority queue operates similarly to the print queue simulation we carried out in Chapter 16. There, as print requests were received, they were tacked to the end of the queue, and as the printer became free, requests were printed out (deleted) from the front of the queue. A priority queue functions the same way *except* that incoming requests may have a priority associated with them. In general, the higher the priority, the closer to the front of the queue the request is placed. Consequently, insertions may occur *anywhere* within the queue. Nodes are *still* deleted from the front, although it is also possible to remove a print request from somewhere in the middle of the queue before it reaches the front (the equivalent of giving up your place after standing in a long line).

To make this clearer, suppose we had the queue shown below. Each element in the queue is a print request consisting of a priority (the first number) and job number (the remaining digits):

7–134

7–135

7–136

If job number 137 comes along and also has a priority of 7, it will simply be added to the tail of the queue to yield

7–134

7–135

7–136

7–137

However, if job number 138 comes along with a priority of 3, it will go to the head of the list:

3–138

7–134

7–135

7–136

7–137

If we next receive job number 139 with a priority of 5, it will go into the middle of the list:

3–138

5–139

7–134

7–135

7–136

7–137

Print requests are still deleted from the front (unless a specific delete request is made), and low-priority jobs are still tacked on to the back.

Let's see how we can implement a priority queue.

STEP 1: UNDERSTAND THE PROBLEM

We want to implement a priority queue in which the following operations can be carried out:

1. Insert a new node

2. Delete any arbitrary node

3. Remove the head node

We must also consider how much of a simulation we want to do here. In this case, let's just implement the procedures and functions necessary to carry out the queue operations. We will have a main program that inputs a code for the desired operation and then calls the proper routines. To see how this all happens, let's include in the options the ability to print out the complete queue. Therefore, we want to implement the following:

1. Insert a new node

2. Delete any arbitrary node

3. Remove the head node

4. Print out the entire queue

5. Quit

What data to include is also a consideration. Since we are more interested in the tree than the simulation, let's work with a job number made up of a single four-digit integer such that the first digit represents the priority and the remaining three digits represent the job number. As we did with the simple print queue, we will have the program assign job numbers. A print request will simply consist of the priority for the job to be queued (rather than a name). And, of course, we want to implement this via a binary search tree.

STEP 2: PLAN THE SOLUTION

We may begin by deriving our preliminary algorithm as follows:

```
Tree ← Nil (* Create an empty tree *)
Job No ← 100 (* Initialize the job number *)
Display a Menu
Read the Option
While Option ≠ Quit Do

  If Option = Insert then
    Read Job Priority
    Job No ← Job No + 1
    This Job ← Priority × 1000 + Job No
    New (NewJob)
    NewJob^.Left ← Nil
    NewJob^.Right ← Nil
    NewJob^.Job ← This Job
    InsertTree (Tree, NewJob)

  Else if Option = Delete then (* Delete any old node *)
    Read This Job (to be deleted)
    Delete (Tree, This Job)

  Else if Option = Remove (* From the head of the list *)
    This Job ← Head (Tree)
    If This Job is Nil then
      Write 'The queue is empty'
    Else
      Delete (Tree, This Job)

  Else if Option = Print then
    InOrder (Tree)

  Display a Menu
  Read the Option
```

There is almost nothing in this algorithm that we haven't already seen before. We recognize the input-controlled loop as the primary control structure. The `InsertTree` procedure is exactly the same as the one we used in the `TITLES` and `LIBRARY` programs. The only thing that may look at all strange here is the method used to generate a complete job number. The priority (that is, the first digit) and the job number (the remaining digits) are merely combined algebraically to yield a single numeric value.

However, we *do* have to implement a `Delete` option. Note that we have set up the `Delete` procedure in such a way that its arguments consist of a pointer to the tree from which the deletion is to be made and the *value* of (not a pointer to!) the node to be deleted.

We also have a Remove option, which works by first calling a *function* that finds the head of the queue and then uses Delete to take it out. Note that, since the queue is really a tree, it is *not at all* obvious where the head (lead node) of the structure really is. In a binary search tree, the first node (lexically speaking) is not necessarily the root node but may be any node, depending on the order in which the nodes were inserted. Also, we must make sure the tree is not Nil before attempting to delete a node from it. Finally, the print option is just exactly the InOrder traversal we used in the TITLES example.

We are now left with the problem of generating two new subprograms, Delete and Head, so let us proceed to do so.

Delete. The delete procedure takes, as arguments, a pointer to the tree from which the deletion is to occur and the *value* of the node to be deleted. As always, the node to be deleted must be located within the structure before it can be deleted. We might be tempted to use the Search procedure of the LIBRARY example to first locate the node and then go ahead and delete it. Although this sounds logical, it won't work. A problem arises in that, although Search will return a pointer to the correct node, we really need to know the predecessor node as well. (Compare this with linked list deletions.) To make matters even worse, we need to know not only the predecessor node *but also whether it is the left or right pointer of the predecessor that points to the node we wish to delete.*

The difficulties appear formidable, but they can be reduced considerably if the Search and Delete operations are combined into a single procedure. Doing so then permits the recursive nature of the search to keep track of the various predecessors automatically.

Let us therefore use the Delete algorithm presented at the beginning of this section and add the Search capability to it as follows:

Procedure Delete (Node, Key)

If Key < Node^.Data then (* We have to go left to find it *)
  If Node^.Left ≠ Nil then
    Delete (Node^.Left, Key)
  Else
    Key is not in the list

Else if Key = Node^.Data then (* We have found it *)
  If the node is a leaf node then
    Delete Node
  Else if the node has only one pointer then
    Replace Node by the subtree to which it points
  Else
    Replace Node by its InOrder Successor
    Delete the InOrder Successor of Node

Else if Key > Node^.Data then (* We have to go right to find it *)
  If Node^.Right ≠ Nil then
    Delete (Node^.Right, Key)
  Else
    Key is not in the list

Note that this algorithm is essentially Search with Delete processes added to it.
    Let's add a few more details:

Procedure Delete (Node, Key)

If Key < Node^.Data then (* We have to go left to find it *)
  If Node^.Left ≠ Nil then
    Delete (Node^.Left, Key)
  Else
    Key is not in the list
Else if Key = Node^.Data then (*We have found it*)

  If Node^.Left = Nil then
    If Node^.Right = Nil then (* The node is a leaf node *)
      Delete this Node
        Dispose (Node)
        Node ← Nil

    Else (* We have only a right pointer *)
      Replace this node by its right subtree
        Temp ← Node
        Node ← Node^.Right
        Dispose (Temp)
  Else if Node^.Right = Nil then (*We have only a left pointer*)
    Replace this node by its left subtree
      Temp ← Node
      Node ← Node^.Left
      Dispose (Temp)

  Else (* We have *both* pointers, and it's a pain *)
    Replace Node by its InOrder Successor
      The Successor ← InOrderSuccessor (Node^.Right)
      Node^.Data ← The Successor^.Data
    Delete the InOrder Successor of Node
      Delete (Node^.Right, The Successor^.Data)
Else if Key > Node^.Data then (* We have to go right to find it *)
  If Node^.Right ≠ Nil then
    Delete (Node^.Right, Key)
  Else
    Key is not in the list

We've used a temporary node pointer to assist in the complete disposal of nodes that have subtrees. This algorithm also includes sections to delete the three kinds of nodes we may encounter: a node with no subtrees, a node with one subtree, and a node with two subtrees. For the last kind of node, the InOrder successor must first be found. Next, the data from the successor must be attached to the deleted node. Finally, the successor node must be deleted. This requires that we be able to find the InOrder successor to a node, so we have had to include a new function, InOrderSuccessor. However, aside from this new function, the algorithm is complete. Let us, therefore, move on to the algorithm for InOrderSuccessor.

InOrderSucc. We notice first that if an InOrder successor to a node exists, it *must* be found by going to the right; anything to the left is a predecessor. Consequently, the argument to the function is the right pointer of the current node. Also recognize that this is a *function*, and it is intended to return a pointer to the successor node.

The procedure algorithm itself is essentially the InOrder traversal algorithm made to terminate prematurely. In fact, it has but two parts, as follows:

```
Function InOrderSucc (Node)
If Node^.Left = Nil then
   InOrderSucc ← Node
Else
   InOrderSucc ← InOrderSucc (Node^.Left)
```

A word of explanation: after we get past the initial node whose successor we wish to find (the successor *must* be to the right of this node), the InOrder successor must be to the *left*. Consequently, if there *is no* left pointer, we must be at the successor; if there *is* a left pointer, the successor must be in the direction of that left pointer.

This, then, gives us all the detail we need for deletion, and we can move on to the problem of finding the head of the queue (tree).

Head. This function is intended to return the key *data* item of (and not a pointer to!) the first node in the queue (tree). Finding the lead node involves initiating an InOrder traversal but terminating it when we arrive at the lead node. Basically, the idea is this: if, on entering the function Head, we find a Nil node, it means that the tree is null. If the tree is null, of course, then there *is* no first node. On the other hand, if the tree exists but there is no left pointer, then *there is no predecessor* to the node we're looking at (any predecessor must be to the left). However, there is only one node in the tree that has no predecessor, namely, the lead node. Thus, the current node must be the lead node. Finally, if there *is* a left pointer, then a predecessor to the current node *does* exist, and the first node of the tree (which has to precede this node) must be somewhere in that direction. An algorithm that expresses all this can be written as

Function Head (Node)
If Node = Nil then
    The tree is null
Else If Node^.Left = Nil then
    Head ← Node^.Data
Else
    Head ← Head (Node^.Left)

Having completed `Head`, we now have algorithms for all the bits and pieces necessary to implement the priority queue, and we proceed to do that next.

STEP 3: CODE THE SOLUTION

The final result, obtained by assembling the various algorithms and coding them, is shown in Figure 17-12. The primary concern here is, of

Figure 17-12

Program That Controls the Functioning of a Priority Queue, Which Is Implemented via a Binary Search Tree

```
PRIORITY.PAS

  1    Program PRIORITY (Input, Output);
  2
  3    (*
  4         This program simulates the functioning of a priority queue. The
  5         queue itself is implemented via a binary search tree.
  6    *)
  7
  8    Type   PtrNode = ^Node;
  9
 10           Node = Record                  (* Tree Nodes *)
 11                    Left  : PtrNode;
 12                    Job   : Integer;      (* Print Job number *)
 13                    Right : PtrNode
 14                  End;
 15
 16    Var    Tree : PtrNode;       (* The tree we are constructing *)
 17           NewJob : PtrNode;     (* The newly created job node *)
 18           ThisJob : Integer;    (* The job we are working with, either to
 19                                    be inserted, deleted, or removed *)
 20           JobNo : Integer;      (* Job number generated by the program *)
 21           Pri : Integer;        (* Job priority *)
 22
 23           Op : Char;            (* Operation chosen by the user:
 24                                     I : Insert a job
 25                                     D : Delete a job
 26                                     P : Display the entire queue
 27                                     R : Remove a job from the head of the queue
 28                                     Q : Quit doing all this now *)
 29
 30
 31    Procedure InsertTree (Var Root, Node : PtrNode);
 32    (* This procedure builds a binary search tree by successive insertions *)
```

Figure 17-12 continued

```
33      Begin
34        If Root = Nil then
35          Root := Node
36        Else if Node^.Job < Root^.Job then
37            InsertTree (Root^.Left, Node)
38        Else
39            InsertTree (Root^.Right, Node)
40      End;
41
42
43    Procedure InOrder (Var Node : PtrNode);
44    (* This procedure carries out an InOrder traversal of a tree *)
45      Var Pri, JobNo : Integer;
46      Begin
47        If Node^.Left <> NIL then
48            InOrder (Node^.Left);
49
50        Pri := Node^.Job Div 1000;       (* Break up the composite Job ID *)
51        JobNo := Node^.Job - Pri*1000;   (* into its priority and its sequence *)
52        Writeln (Pri:1,'-',JobNo:3);     (* number for display purposes *)
53
54        If Node^.Right <> Nil then
55            InOrder (Node^.Right)
56      End;
57
58
59    Procedure Delete (Var Node : PtrNode; Key : Integer);
60    (* This procedure deletes a node from a binary search tree *)
61      Var TheSuccessor, Temp : PtrNode;
62
63      Function InOrderSucc (Node : PtrNode) : PtrNode;
64      (* This function finds the inorder successor to a given node *)
65        Begin (* InOrderSucc *)
66          If Node^.Left = Nil then
67            InOrderSucc := Node
68          Else
69            InOrderSucc := InOrderSucc (Node^.Left)
70        End; (* InOrderSucc *)
71
72      Begin (* Delete *)
73        If Key < Node^.Job then
74            If Node^.Left <> Nil then (*Try the left subtree *)
75              Delete (Node^.Left, Key)
76            Else
77              Writeln ('Job not in list')
78        Else if Node^.Job = Key then
79            (* WE HAVE FOUND IT *)
80            If Node^.Left = Nil then
81              If Node^.Right = Nil then (*This is a leaf node *)
82                  Begin
83                    Dispose (Node);
84                    Node := Nil
85                  End
86              Else                          (* We have a right pointer only *)
87                  Begin
88                    Temp := Node;
89                    Node := Node^.Right;
90                    Dispose (Temp)
91                  End
```

Figure 17-12 continued

```
92              Else if Node^.Right = Nil then (*We have a left pointer only *)
93                  Begin
94                    Temp := Node;
95                    Node := Node^.Left;
96                    Dispose (Temp)
97                  End
98              Else (* We have both pointers and must find the successor *)
99                  Begin
100                    TheSuccessor := InOrderSucc (Node^.Right);
101                    Node^.Job := TheSuccessor^.Job ;
102                    Delete (Node^.Right, TheSuccessor^.Job)
103                  End
104        Else if Key > Node^.Job then
105           If Node^.Right <> Nil then (* Try the right subtree *)
106               Delete (Node^.Right, Key)
107           Else
108               Writeln ('Word not in list')
109       End; (* Delete *)
110
111
112  Function Head (Node : PtrNode) : Integer;
113  (* This function finds the first node, lexically speaking, in a tree;
114     that is, the node that would first be printed out if an InOrder
115     traversal were done. *)
116     Begin
117       If Node = Nil then
118           Head := 0
119       Else if Node^.Left = Nil then
120           Head := Node^.Job
121       Else
122           Head := Head (Node^.Left)
123     End;
124
125
126  BEGIN (* The main program, at long last! *)
127
128     Tree := Nil;      (* Start out without a tree *)
129
130     JobNo := 100;     (* Initialize the job numbers *)
131
132     Write ('Operation (I,D,P,R,Q) : '); Readln (Op);
133     While Op <> 'Q' Do
134       Begin
135
136         If Op = 'I' Then
137             Begin
138                 Write ('Pri > '); Readln (Pri); (* Just input a value for the *)
139                 JobNo := JobNo + 1;                (* priority and attach it to the *)
140                 ThisJob := Pri * 1000 + JobNo;   (* job number *)
141                 New (NewJob);
142                 NewJob^.Left := Nil;                 (*Create a new node for this job *)
143                 NewJob^.Right := Nil;
144                 NewJob^.Job := ThisJob;
145                 InsertTree (Tree, NewJob)
146             End
147
148          Else if Op = 'D' then
```

Figure 17-12 continued

```
149              Begin
150                  Write('JobNo> '); Readln (ThisJob); (* Read the ID of the job *)
151                  Delete (Tree, ThisJob)              (* to be deleted        *)
152              End
153
154          Else if Op = 'P' then   (* Display the entire queue *)
155              Begin
156                  Writeln;
157                  If Tree <> Nil then InOrder (Tree);
158                  Writeln
159              End
160
161          Else if Op = 'R' then           (* Remove the head of the queue, as *)
162              Begin                         (* to print it out *)
163                  ThisJob := Head (Tree);
164                  If ThisJob = 0 then
165                      Writeln ('Queue is empty')
166                  Else
167                      Delete (Tree, ThisJob)
168              End;
169
170          Write ('Operation (I,D,P,R,Q) : '); Readln (Op)
171      End
172
173  END.
```

course, with the procedure to delete nodes from the tree. The main program itself simulates the operations necessary to the correct functioning of a priority queue. Note that the function Head generates a value of zero to indicate that an empty queue has been encountered.

STEP 4: CHECK OUT THE PROGRAM

A rather extensive test run is shown in Figure 17-13. The first several operations involve inserting prioritized print requests into the queue and viewing them as they are added. The insertion works correctly. The next several operations involve deleting specific nodes from various places in the queue, and these operations also work. Finally, the head nodes are removed (as they would be when printed out) in the last batch of entries. The whole system functions properly.

STEP 5: DOCUMENT

Although this is a very complex program, the comments and recursions make it understandable.

With this example we have come to the end of our discussion of binary search trees. We move on to the final topic of this chapter (and of the book!), namely, heaps.

Figure 17-13

Test Run and Sample Output from the Priority Queue Simulation Program

```
$ run priority

Operation (I,D,P,R,Q) : P


Operation (I,D,P,R,Q) : I
Pri > 7
Operation (I,D,P,R,Q) : P

7-101

Operation (I,D,P,R,Q) : I
Pri > 7
Operation (I,D,P,R,Q) : P

7-101
7-102

Operation (I,D,P,R,Q) : I
Pri > 6
Operation (I,D,P,R,Q) : P

6-103
7-101
7-102

Operation (I,D,P,R,Q) : I
Pri > 7
Operation (I,D,P,R,Q) : P

6-103
7-101
7-102
7-104

Operation (I,D,P,R,Q) : I
Pri > 3
Operation (I,D,P,R,Q) : P

3-105
6-103
7-101
7-102
7-104

Operation (I,D,P,R,Q) : I
Pri > 7
Operation (I,D,P,R,Q) : P

3-105
6-103
7-101
7-102
7-104
7-106
```

Figure 17-13 continued

```
Operation (I,D,P,R,Q) : I
Pri > 2
Operation (I,D,P,R,Q) : P

2-107
3-105
6-103
7-101
7-102
7-104
7-106

Operation (I,D,P,R,Q) : I
Pri > 6
Operation (I,D,P,R,Q) : P

2-107
3-105
6-103
6-108
7-101
7-102
7-104
7-106

Operation (I,D,P,R,Q) : I
Pri > 2
Operation (I,D,P,R,Q) : P

2-107
2-109
3-105
6-103
6-108
7-101
7-102
7-104
7-106

Operation (I,D,P,R,Q) : I
Pri > 7
Operation (I,D,P,R,Q) : P

2-107
2-109
3-105
6-103
6-108
7-101
7-102
7-104
7-106
7-110

Operation (I,D,P,R,Q) : I
Pri > 1
Operation (I,D,P,R,Q) : P

1-111
2-107
2-109
```

Figure 17-13 continued

```
3-105
6-103
6-108
7-101
7-102
7-104
7-106
7-110

Operation (I,D,P,R,Q) : D
JobNo> 7101
Operation (I,D,P,R,Q) : P

1-111
2-107
2-109
3-105
6-103
6-108
7-102
7-104
7-106
7-110

Operation (I,D,P,R,Q) : D
JobNo> 7110
Operation (I,D,P,R,Q) : P

1-111
2-107
2-109
3-105
6-103
6-108
7-102
7-104
7-106

Operation (I,D,P,R,Q) : D
JobNo> 1111
Operation (I,D,P,R,Q) : P

2-107
2-109
3-105
6-103
6-108
7-102
7-104
7-106

Operation (I,D,P,R,Q) : R
Operation (I,D,P,R,Q) : P

2-109
3-105
6-103
6-108
7-102
7-104
7-106
```

Figure 17-13 continued

```
Operation (I,D,P,R,Q) : R
Operation (I,D,P,R,Q) : P

3-105
6-103
6-108
7-102
7-104
7-106

Operation (I,D,P,R,Q) : R
Operation (I,D,P,R,Q) : P

6-103
6-108
7-102
7-104
7-106

Operation (I,D,P,R,Q) : Q
```

17-2 *Heaps*

A **heap** is actually a form of binary tree, but its implementation and uses are sufficiently different to warrant separate coverage. The primary characteristic of a heap is that for each node the values of the children are all greater than the value of the parent. (The relationship may be such that the values of the children are *less than* the value of the parents instead; it doesn't matter as long as all parent/child relationships are consistent.) There is, however, no required relationship between the values of the children. In other words, both children must have values that are greater than the parent value, but the left child's value is not required to be greater than the right child's value.

A typical heap of words is shown in Figure 17-14. Notice that a heap is a perfect binary tree in that *every* node (except possibly those at the lowest levels) has exactly two children. Also, for heaps the required relationships involve *only* parent and children; nothing is expressed or implied about any other relationship. An important consequence of this is that *the root node always contains the smallest element*, and herein lies much of the usefulness of heaps.

Let us begin our discussion of heaps by looking at how they are usually implemented.

Figure 17-14

A Typical Heap

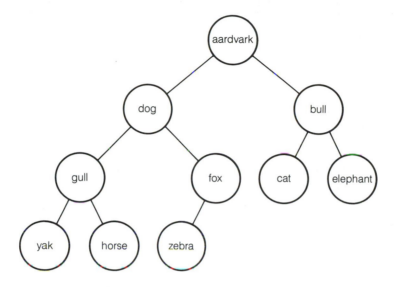

IMPLEMENTATION

A major difference between trees and heaps is that heaps are invariably implemented using arrays. This is due to the fact that a heap is a perfect binary structure; that is, each parent *must* have exactly two children. The links between the nodes are implied rather than explicit and can be easily computed. (Sound like subscripts?) Let us examine the relationships between a conceptual heap and the actual array used to implement the heap. This situation is shown pictorially in Figure 17-15.

The real beauty of this system is apparent if you watch what happens when you go from one node to another. Given a node whose array subscript is k, the following relationships apply:

Parent Subscript	k
Left Child Subscript	$2 \times k$
Right Child Subscript	$2 \times k + 1$

Check this out in Figure 17-15. Node 5, for example, has left child node $2 \times 5 = 10$ and right child node $2 \times 5 + 1 = 11$.

A similar relationship holds when going the other way, namely,

Child Subscript	n
Parent Subscript	n div 2

Figure 17-15

Relationship Between Conceptual Heap Nodes and the Array Elements Used to Implement the Nodes

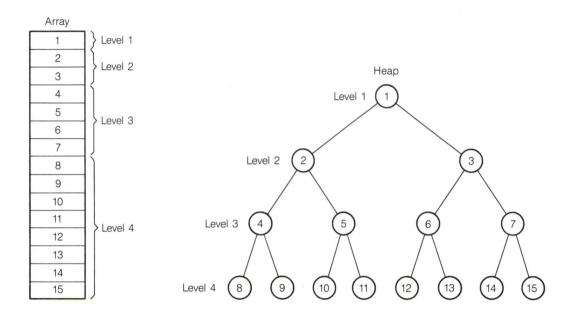

In other words, dividing the *integer* subscript by 2 results in the subscript of the parent. Again, check this out in the figure: node 7 has as a parent node 7 / 2 = 3.

Now that we understand how a heap is put together, let's see what we need to do to build one.

CONSTRUCTION

A heap is constructed much as are other list structures, namely, by successive insertions. Elements are inserted into the heap from top to bottom, left to right. As each is added, it is compared with the parent to ensure the proper greater/smaller relationship. (In fact, this represents the first part of the heap sort introduced in Chapter 15.) Let us demonstrate this process by constructing a heap from the words in the sentence

we will make a heap from this sentence

When we begin, the heap is empty. Therefore, we take the first word and insert it into the first node, giving

we

Since this is the first node, there is nothing else to be done. We then take the second word and enter it into the second node, yielding

```
    we
   /
 will
```

Since this is *not* the root node, we check to see if it has the proper relationship with its parent, that is, it must be larger. Since "will" is in fact larger than (alphabetically coming after) "we," everything is fine and we go on.

The next word is "make," and it is added to the third heap location to give

```
    we
   /  \
 will  make
```

When we check the parent/child relationship here, however, we find that it is wrong: "make" is less than "we." Therefore, we exchange the two of them to make a new heap:

```
   make
   /   \
 will   we
```

This new heap now has the correct relationship, and we move on to the next word, which gives us

```
    make
   /  \
 will   we
 /
a
```

As in the last addition, "a" is in the wrong place and must be exchanged. This gives us

```
    make
   /  \
  a     we
 /
will
```

We note with dissatisfaction, however, that "a" is *still* in the wrong place. It must be exchanged again with *its* parent to yield

Now the heap is correct. Let us continue the construction with abbreviated commentary.

Insert "heap":

Exchange:

OK. Insert "from":

Exchange:

OK. Insert "this":

OK. Insert "sentence":

Exchange:

The heap construction is now complete.

The next item on the agenda is to derive an algorithm for the heap construction process. We can start off with a general algorithm, such as

```
Loc ← 0
Read Word
While Word ≠ Stop Do
    Loc ← Loc + 1
    Heap[Loc] ← Word
    Arrange (Loc)
    Read Word
```

We use an input controlled loop to enter the words. When we read a word, we place it into the heap (array) at the next available location and then call the procedure Arrange to make sure the parent/child relationship is correct. (By making this a procedure, we can defer consideration of the details.) We then input another word and repeat the process. When we exit the loop, Loc will contain the exact number of elements that are in the heap.

This brings us to the procedure Arrange. We can use a recursive algorithm to check the relationships as follows:

```
Procedure Arrange (Child)
If Child = 1 then
    We got it
```

Else
   Parent ← Child / 2
   If Heap[Child] < Heap[Parent] then
     Exchange them
      Temp ← Heap[Child]
      Heap[Child] ← Heap[Parent]
      Heap[Parent] ← Temp
     Now check on the parent
      Arrange (Parent)

This procedure will construct the heap. As we said earlier, the properties of a heap are such that the root node contains the smallest value of all the heap elements. Thus, we know that exactly *one* of the elements (the element at the root) is in order. We can institute an additional process, however, which will permit us to complete a sort of *all* the elements. This is the famous *heap sort* we introduced in Chapter 15.

SORTING

The heap sort procedure consists, from this point, of removing the root node and then reestablishing the heap by going down through the structure. What do we do with the root node when it is pulled off? We can handle this in one of two ways: the node can be placed into another array, or it can be exchanged with what is currently the last heap element. In either case, as the sort progresses, the size of the remaining heap diminishes.

Let's continue to sort the heap we created in the previous section. This is the heap:

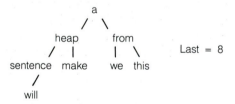

When we start out, we have the whole array to sort. The last element that needs to be sorted is (in this case) element 8. We exchange the first element (node 1) and the last element (node 8). Since element 8 is really no longer a part of the heap, we change the index of the last element to 7:

We then reconstruct the heap by starting with the root node and checking each child. We choose the smaller of the two children and exchange. We continue on with the exchanged child (if there is one) until we get to an index that is beyond the current end of the heap.

In this case we check the children of node 1, which are found in nodes 2 and 3. Since "from" is less than "heap," it is exchanged, giving us

Since there was an exchange, we must repeat for element 3, "will." The children of 3 ("will") are 6 ("we") and 7 ("this"). Since "this" is less than "we," we choose it to exchange, giving us

The next child to look at is "will," whose children *should* be 14 and 15. However, these children are beyond the current end of the heap, and any attempt to continue will result in disaster. Therefore, we will not attempt any further exchanges, and we are assured that the heap has been reformed.

At this point we exchange the first element with the current last element and decrement the current last element, yielding

```
            will
           /  \
      heap      this
      / |       | \        Last = 6
 sentence make   we  from
     /
    a
```

We then continue this process. Eventually, the following will be obtained:

Now the array is in order when it is traversed from the last element to the first!

The major attraction of the heap sort, as opposed to the various list and array sorts we have encountered so far, is in the method used to choose which elements to exchange. In linear sorts we are required to go through the entire array and exchange appropriate elements. However, in a heap sort the path followed in looking for the elements to be exchanged goes through the heap *one full level at a time*. If we have eight elements (as in the above example), the biggest number of elements we will have to look at is four—one at each level. A *linear* sort of eight elements will have to look at eight elements. As the list gets bigger, so do the savings in time. If we have one thousand elements, a linear search will have to examine one thousand elements, but a heap sort will have to examine only ten elements! This is truly an efficient (because it is a logarithmic) process.

Sort. Let's generate necessary and appropriate algorithms for this sorting process. We may begin by defining an iterative procedure as follows:

Procedure Sort (Heap, Last)
While Last > 1 Do
    Exchange Heap[1] and Heap[Last]
    Last ← Last − 1
    Rebuild (Heap, 1, Last)

This is pretty direct! Note that parameters include the array to be sorted (Heap) and the size (which corresponds to Last).

We must now deal with the problem of rebuilding the heap, indicated here as the procedure Rebuild. This procedure takes as arguments the array name and the first and last element to be used in rebuilding the heap. This anticipates a recursive algorithm. Let's look at the details.

Rebuild. The details of this procedure can be gleaned from the foregoing presentation, as follows:

1. Procedure Rebuild (Heap, Parent, Last)
2. Find the Children
3.   LeftChild ← Parent × 2
4.   RightChild ← LeftChild + 1

5. If LeftChild > Last then
6.   We're Done!
7. Else (* We must pursue the rebuild *)
8.   See which Child to follow
9.   If RightChild > Last then
10.   TheChild ← LeftChild
11.   Else
12.   If Heap[LeftChild] < Heap[RightChild] then
13.   TheChild ← LeftChild
14.   Else
15.   TheChild ← RightChild
16.   If Heap[TheChild] < Heap[Parent] then
17.   Exchange Heap[TheChild] and Heap[Parent]
18.   Rebuild (Heap, TheChild, Last)

Let's look at some of the salient features of this algorithm. We test for termination in line 5 of the procedure. If there are no more children to be considered, then we are done. Note that we need only check for a left child. If there is no left child, there cannot be a right child, either.

If we are not done, we must determine which child (path) we have to follow to reconstruct the heap. We arrive at line 9 with the knowledge that there *is* a left child, so we check for a right child also. If there is no right child, then the *only* path available is the one that passes through the left child. Therefore, we mark the left child (line 10) as the one we must pursue.

However, if there *is* a right child, we will find ourselves at line 12, where we know that *both* left and right children exist. In this case, we must compare the values of both children and choose the path that leads through the smaller of the two.

We finally arrive at line 16 and have determined the correct path to follow in reconstructing the heap. At this point we check to make sure that the parent/child relationship is correct. If it is not, we must exchange the positions of the parent and child and then rearrange the remainder of the heap by calling Rebuild again, recursively. This process will continue until either we run out of nodes or we find a proper parent/child relationship.

At this juncture we have all the algorithms we need to carry out a heap sort, so let's develop an application that uses the sort.

Heap Sort

We will write a driver program that simply inputs a list of words, alphabetizes them, and prints them out. The purpose is to encode a heap sort to see what it looks like.

STEP 1: UNDERSTAND THE PROBLEM

We have spent the last half of this chapter trying to do just that, and there is no need for further commentary at this point. We will simply carry out a demonstration of a heap sort.

STEP 2: PLAN THE SOLUTION

We already have the algorithms, so all we need to do is put them together.

STEP 3: CODE THE SOLUTION

The assembled and coded program is shown in Figure 17-16. We have included, of course, our familiar friend ReadString to input the data and also a procedure Exchange to carry out the necessary exchanges.

STEP 4: CHECK OUT THE PROGRAM

A test run is shown in Figure 17-17. The words are, of course, correctly alphabetized. Although there are only 11 words here, there is nothing to prevent us from sorting as many as we like, up to the maximum of 50 defined as the array size.

This particular sort is one of the best for two reasons. First, although it uses the concept of a two-dimensional list structure (heap) to carry out its work, it nonetheless is implemented using arrays. Since arrays are probably the most commonly used data structure for computer applications, the heap sort can be used in just about *any* computer language, not just in Pascal. Further, since arrays use direct access to refer to elements, the actual execution time is relatively fast (compared to other data structures).

Second, the heap sort is intrinsically fast, being on the order of $n \log n$. And, as an additional advantage, it can be implemented recursively in an elegant fashion. Of course, now that we know how it's done, we can adapt it to any program that requires data to be sorted.

STEP 5: DOCUMENT

The documentation is a little more extensive than usual but is sufficient to make the program readable.

Figure 17-16

Program That Uses a Heap Sort to Alphabetize a List of Words

HEAPSORT.PAS

```
1    Program HEAPSORT (Input, Ouput);
2
3    (*
4          This program uses a heap sort to alphabetize a list of words.
5    *)
6
7    Const Stop = 'STOP           '; (* Allows the user to mark the end
8                                          of the list of input words *)
9
10   Type  String15 = Packed Array [1..15] of Char;
11         List = Array [1..50] of String15;
12
13   Var   Word : List;          (* This is the array of words to be alphabetized *)
14         TheWord : String15;   (* This is the current word being read in *)
15         Last : Integer;       (* This is the size of the array, or conversely
16                                  the number of words in the list *)
17
18         k : Integer;          (* Just a loop counter *)
19
20
21   Procedure ReadString (Var S : String15);
22     Var K : Integer;
23     Begin
24       For K := 1 to 15 Do
25           Read (S[K]);
26       Readln
27     End;
28
29
30   Procedure Exchange (Var A,B : String15);
31     Var Temp : String15;
32     Begin
33       Temp := A;
34       A := B;
35       B := Temp
36     End;
37
38
39   Procedure Arrange (Var Heap : List; Child : Integer);
40   (* This procedure takes the word most recently added to the heap
41      and makes sure that it has the correct relationship with its
42      parent. If it doesn't, it is exchanged with its parent and
43      the procedure is called again recursively. *)
44     Var Parent : Integer;
45     Begin
46       If Child = 1 then
47           (* We got it; go back home *)
48         Else
49           Begin
50             Parent := Child Div 2;
51             If Heap[Child] < Heap[Parent] then
52                 Begin
53                   Exchange (Heap[Child], Heap[Parent]);
54                   (* Now check on the parent *)
55                       Arrange (Heap, Parent)
56                 End
57           End
58     End;
```

Figure 17-16 continued

```
59
60
61   Procedure Sort (Var Heap : List; Last : Integer);
62
63   (* This procedure is the actual heap sort, and it operates on the
64      heap after it has been constructed by successive insertions *)
65
66
67     Procedure Rebuild (Var Heap : List; Parent, Last : Integer);
68     (* This procedure reforms the heap after the root node of the
69        heap has been removed *)
70       Var LeftChild, RightChild, TheChild : Integer;
71       Begin
72         (* Find the children *)
73           LeftChild := Parent * 2;
74           RightChild := LeftChild + 1;
75
76       If LeftChild > Last then
77           (* We`re Done! *)
78
79       Else (* We must pursue the rebuild *)
80           Begin
81           (* See which child to follow *)
82               If RightChild > Last then
83                   TheChild := LeftChild
84               Else
85                   If Heap[LeftChild] < Heap[RightChild] then
86                       TheChild := LeftChild
87                   Else
88                       TheChild := RightChild;
89           (* See if we have to do an exchange *)
90               If Heap[TheChild] < Heap[Parent] then
91                   Begin
92                     Exchange (Heap[TheChild], Heap[Parent]);
93                     Rebuild (Heap, TheChild, Last)
94                   End
95           End
96     End;
97
98
99     Begin (* Sort *)
100      While Last > 1 Do
101        Begin
102          Exchange (Heap[1], Heap[Last]);
103          Last := Last - 1;
104          Rebuild (Heap, 1, Last);
105        End
106    End; (* Sort *)
107
108
109    BEGIN
110      (* Input the Array of Words *)
111        Last := 0;
112        Writeln ('Enter the words, STOP to end...');
113        Write ('>'); ReadString (TheWord);
114        While TheWord <> STOP Do                  (* This section of code constructs *)
115          Begin                                   (* the heap by reading in the words, *)
116            Last := Last + 1;                     (* placing them into the heap, and *)
117            Word[Last] := TheWord;                (* then calling Arrange to make sure *)
```

Figure 17-16 continued

```
118              Arrange (Word, Last);          (* the parent/child relationships *)
119              Write ('>'); ReadString (TheWord)  (* are all ok *)
120          End;
121
122      (* Sort the array via a heap sort *)
123          Sort (Word, Last);
124
125
126
127      (* Print out the array, backward *)
128          Writeln;
129          Writeln ('The alphabetized list...');
130          Writeln;
131          For K := Last downto 1 Do
132              Writeln (Word[K])
133
134   END.
```

Figure 17-17

Sample Run of the HEAPSORT *Program*

```
$ run heapsort

Enter the words, STOP to end...
>these
>are
>all
>of
>the
>words
>that
>i
>want
>to
>alphabetize
>STOP

The alphabetized list...

all
alphabetize
are
i
of
that
the
these
to
want
words
```

This completes the introductory section on heaps, and we move on to The End of the chapter and the book.

SUMMARY

This concludes our examination of the two-dimensional list structure known as the tree. We introduced trees in general and then moved on to the special case of binary trees, in which each node may generate up to two additional nodes. We learned of the methods used to traverse trees, namely InOrder, PreOrder, and PostOrder.

We then considered binary search trees and saw how they can be used to carry out the analogy of a linear insertion sort, although in two dimensions. We also examined methods of searching and deleting items from such a tree.

Finally, we looked at heaps, which are implemented with arrays. Heaps provide the means by which a very efficient sort, the heap sort, can be carried out. We examined the necessary processes in detail and used them to produce a program that sorts an array using a heap sort.

EXERCISES

CONCEPTS

1. Define or explain the following terms:

Binary search tree	Parent
Binary tree	PostOrder traversal
Branch node	PreOrder traversal
Child	Root node
Heap	Sibling
InOrder traversal	Tree
Leaf node	

2. Trace through the PreOrder traversal of Figure 17-6.

3. Express the program shown in Figure 17-7 as a tree.

4. Trace the function `InOrderSucc` of Figure 17-11 on the nodes of Figure 17-6.

5. Express the following expressions as trees:

a. a + b * (c − d / e)
b. (a + b) / (c − d)
c. ((a + b) * c − (d − e)) ˆ f

6. Traverse the following tree in PreOrder, InOrder, and PostOrder:

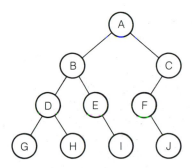

7. Delete the following nodes from the above tree (start with the original tree each time): G, J, D, E, B, A.

8. Build a binary search tree via successive insertions from the following words: dog, cat, canary, cardinal, horse, cow, llama, hedgehog.

9. Complete the trace of the heap sort shown on page 695.

10. Construct a heap by successive insertions from the words in problem 8.

11. Complete a heap sort of the words used to construct the heap in problem 9.

TOOLS

12. Consider the following type definitions:

```
Type PtrTreeNode = ^TreeNode;

     TreeNode = Record
                    LeftChild : PtrTreeNode;
                    Index : Integer;
                    Grade : Char;
                    RightChild : PtrTreeNode
                End;
```

Assume further that the following information exists:

```
Tree      - [pointer to the root node of the tree]
Rootnode - [ptr to left1] 235 A [ptr to right1]
Left1     - [ptr to left2] 167 C [ptr to right2]
Right1    - [Nil]          217 B [Nil]
```

```
Left2      - [Nil]              776 F [Nil]
Right2     - [Nil]               12 D [Nil]
```

What actual data corresponds to the following references?

a. `Tree`
b. `Tree^.Index`
c. `Tree^.Grade`
d. `Tree^.LeftChild`
e. `Tree^.RightChild^.Grade`
f. `Tree^.LeftChild^.RightChild^.Index`
g. `Tree^.LeftChild^.LeftChild^.LeftChild`

13. Generate appropriate type definitions in correct Pascal for each of the following:

a. A binary tree whose nodes contain names and room numbers
b. A descendant's tree (each person may have up to six descendants)
c. An ancestor chart that includes name, date of birth, and date of death
d. A binary search tree of social security numbers

14. A certain problem requires that arithmetic expressions be stored as a tree. Each node may contain either an operator (character) or number (real). Generate appropriate type definitions in correct Pascal for the nodes and pointers.

15. Generate appropriate type definitions in correct Pascal for each of the following:

a. A heap of integer codes (maximum of 1024)
b. A heap of elements containing names, addresses, and phone numbers (maximum of 100)
c. A heap of variable names and their types (maximum of 2000)
d. A heap of characters (maximum of 256)

PROBLEMS

16. Solve one of the following problems using binary search trees:

a. Problem 11 of Chapter 15
b. Problem 18 of Chapter 15
c. Problem 8 of Chapter 16
d. Problem 12 of Chapter 16

17. Solve problem 16 of Chapter 15 using heaps.

18. An alternate method of carrying out a heap sort involves taking the top element off of the heap and moving it to a different array. The heap is then reformed by moving the smaller of the two children up into position and continuing on in this fashion. The heap, of course, gets smaller as the process continues. Assuming we have the following original heap, the process can be shown as

```
        A
      /   \
    L       B
  /   \
 U       T
```

```
        ‾
      /   \
    L       B         A
  /   \
 U       T
```

```
        B
      /   \
    L       ‾         A
  /   \
 U       T
```

```
        B
      /   \
    L       T         A
  /
 U
```

```
        ‾
      /   \
    L       T         A B
  /
 U
```

```
        L
      /   \
    ‾       T         A B
  /
 U
```

```
        L
      /   \
    U       T         A B
```

```
        ‾
      /   \
    U       T         A B L
```

```
        T
      /
    U                 A B L
```

```
        ‾
      /
    U                 A B L T
```

```
        U             A B L T
```

```
        ‾             A B L T U
```

Modify the procedures of Figure 17-15 to carry out the heap sort in this fashion.

Epilogue:

A View from the Top

*I*f you have reached this point in the text by working and slogging your way through, congratulations! You have surmounted a not inconsiderable amount of material and learned a great deal that will stand you in good stead, both academically and professionally. No matter where you plan to go from here or what your intentions are, you have learned the fundamentals of computer science and will be able to apply them to further academic study or to actually programming and working with computers.

Even though we have come to the end of this course and this text, let us nonetheless continue the tradition we have developed by previewing what comes next. This will perforce take us beyond the confines of this book. Assuming that you want to continue your education in computer science, let us see what lies beyond.

Studies that typically follow this first computer science course fall into one of four categories: computer languages, architecture/organization, software systems, and data structures. Although there is, naturally, some overlap, these four categories mostly describe the further undergraduate study you will encounter. As we have always done, let's look at them one at a time.

Computer Languages

The first category is that of computer languages, and it can be divided into two subcategories: *specific language syntax* and *abstract language theory*. Let us examine these separately.

With regard to the specific language syntax, you will encounter courses designed to teach you the specifics of various procedural languages (see Chapter 4). Typically, you will learn FORTRAN, BASIC, and COBOL, although there are many other possibilities. In general, Pascal is superior to such languages, because Pascal contains more structuring elements for both data and control than any of these other languages. However, it is nonetheless possible to write structured programs (in the sense that we have been using this term throughout this text) using structured data types in any of these languages. Your knowledge of structuring concepts will permit you to write good, structured, understandable programs in *any* computer language.

With regard to abstract theory, computer languages generally are a legitimate topic of study in and of themselves. A great deal of useful information can be gained by abstracting the properties and concepts found in various languages. In addition, the representation and description of languages and the theory that pertains thereto are very similar to the method we used to present Pascal in this text.

Architecture and Organization

The second major division of study is *architecture and organization*. These terms refer to the computer hardware aspect of the discipline. The former term usually refers to the conceptual aspects of hardware, that is, what a programmer sees as available resources. The latter term refers to the actual physical implementation of the machine. Although we just barely touched on hardware in this text, we have nonetheless presented enough of an introduction that you can appreciate computers themselves. Further, typical procedural languages (such as Pascal) tend to reflect the hardware on which they are implemented. For example, many Pascal operations have corresponding machine operations. Also, a computer is really nothing more than a hardware implementation of an algorithm! In fact, any problem you can solve on a computer by writing a program, you can (in principle) also solve by building a machine. A computer is nothing more than a physical implementation of an algorithm that carries out general software algorithms!

A related area is that of assembler and machine language programming (Chapter 4). These languages are closely related to hardware. However, a language is a language, and although writing "structured" assembler programs takes a little practice, your background in the subject will make it that much easier for you when you get to that point.

Software Systems

Next we come to *software systems*. We have been writing software all along, and for the most part, further study in this area is a matter of degree rather than of kind. Instead of writing individual programs, the emphasis will be on large interrelated programs (see Chapter 3). The methods for doing this are analogous to the program development process described in Chapter 3, just more formal.

Data Structures

The last category is that of data structures. You have already been introduced to most of the data structures you will encounter throughout your academic career. Further study consists of introducing a few new structures and some interesting new ways to deal with the old ones. In addition, new algorithms and their analysis will be presented, and old algorithms will be examined more closely. However, having already been exposed to data structures and the algorithms to manipulate them, you will find this area of exploration easier.

An extension of the data structure concept can be found in *data base* and *data base management systems* (DBMS). These combine aspects of data structures and algorithms in such a way as to permit sophisticated access to large quantities of data. DBMS is especially useful in the business sphere, where centralization of data and access provides significant efficiency increases (as well as some novel problems).

In addition to the courses that explore these four categories, your future study will lead you to some things that don't fit in quite so neatly. Examples include graphics (using the computer to draw pictures on a CRT or on paper), artificial intelligence (making the computer act smart), and numerical analysis (grinding out solutions to tough math problems). Further theory will also be introduced, which will aid in the description and implementation of these topics.

Conclusion

This concludes the text and our preview of what you will find "out there." Opportunities abound in the field, and you are again to be congratulated on your accomplishments to date. The aim of this text has been to provide a means by which you can become well grounded in the fundamentals of computer science with a minimum of pain and suffering and a maximum of interest and motivation. (Suggestions from students and instructors with regard to ways in which this book can be improved are welcome.) Finally, good luck on your next adventures in the world of cybernetics!

Appendix A:

Scalars, Ordinals, and User-Defined Types

*T*he Pascal language provides a resource that, although not necessary in any fundamental sense, can be used to advantage for simplifying some programming tasks and enhancing the readability of Pascal programs. This is embodied in the concept of *user-defined scalar types,* a kind of do-it-yourself data. Recall from Chapter 4 that Pascal has four basic data types: `Real`, `Integer`, `Char`, and `Boolean`. These are the elementary types (referred to as *primitives* in Chapter 13) from which more complex collections of data can be constructed. Computers are designed, in part, to permit easy manipulation of primitive data. Occasionally, however, situations arise for which it would be nice to have additional data types available. When this happens, Pascal permits you to make up your own types! In fact we have already worked with some user-defined types, namely, arrays, strings, and records.

The purpose of this Appendix is to show you how to define and use your own data types. (A knowledge of control structures is assumed in the ensuing presentation.) Since the way in which Pascal permits data types to be defined is not discussed until Chapter 14 on arrays (and in fact the example here makes use of arrays), it would be best to wait until you've read Chapter 14 before attempting to work through this Appendix.

We'll begin by categorizing the predefined data types via an exposition of their properties. We will then define our own data types in such a way as to ensure consistency with Pascal's predefined types.

Scalars

The first word in the title of this Appendix is "scalar," and in fact all of the predefined data types are scalars. What is a scalar? The term comes from mathematics, where it is used to indicate a quantity that has only a *magnitude* (as opposed to a magnitude and direction). Examples of mathematical scalars include real numbers and integers but exclude vectors and matrices. In Pascal (actually, in computer science generally), terminology and concepts carry over: real and integer data types are also considered to be scalars. Scalars do not *have* to be numeric, but for the sake of clarity let's restrict our discussion to numeric scalars for right now.

We can derive an important property of scalars by considering the above definition a little more closely. Since scalars possess a magnitude, it is possible to *rank* them, or put them in order. In other words, for any two scalars, one of the relationships *less than*, *equal to*, or *greater than* must exist. Consequently, it is always possible to order any two scalars and, by extension, *all* scalars (of the same type).

Scalars can be defined as a collection of objects that can be represented on a line, where the magnitude of any scalar is proportional to the distance on the line. A familiar example is the number line used in algebra. In fact this is the origin of the term "scalar," since a scale is nothing less than a sequence of ordered numbers proportional to distance!

The properties of scalars apply to all four of the fundamental (primitive) data types in Pascal, and therefore all four types can be categorized as scalar quantities. This is easy to see with the `Integer` type, less so for `Real`, and possibly not at all for the cases of `Char` and `Boolean`. Let us, therefore, take a moment to demonstrate that all four types are indeed scalars.

Let's look at an example of integers on a number line, such as

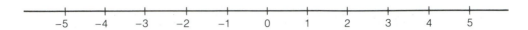

From this we can see that any integer is related by being less than, equal to, or greater than another integer and that the exact position of the integer on the line is linear (proportional to distance).

Real numbers can also be fit into such a scheme, the only difference being that there are many more of them (in fact infinitely more of them). Even so, it is possible to put real numbers on a line, for example,

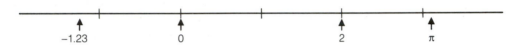

As in the case of integers, it is possible to compare any two real numbers, and their positions on the number line are proportional to their magnitudes. (Keep in mind, however, that in mathematics, integers are just a special case of reals, whereas in computer science, integers and reals are considered two separate and distinct data types.)

When we consider the `Char` type, this scheme may no longer seem to apply. However, in a computer, characters are stored as integer numbers. Consequently, characters must have properties similar to integers. As such, the character set of a computer can be ordered. (See the discussion of collating sequence in Chapter 9 and its expansion in Chapter 15.) For example, a typical ordering of selected characters on a computer (this particular ordering is the ASCII sequence) is

Since characters can be ordered, they can be compared. (`1` is less than `9` is less than `A` is less than `P` is less than `a` is less than `z`.) Note that this table is a number line of sorts. Finally, since characters can be compared, they must be scalars!

Finally, we examine the Boolean data type. There are only two elements of this type, `True` and `False`. However, as with characters, these values are represented at the lowest level as numbers. In this case `False` turns out to be less than `True`, and therefore these are also scalar types.

Pascal makes a further distinction in scalar types and defines a subcategory called ordinals. Let's examine these next.

Ordinals

The ordinal types in Pascal are `Integer`, `Char`, and `Boolean`. These types are called **ordinals** because their respective elements can be ordered very easily. The `Real` type is left out primarily because the order of its elements is not very easy to see. For example, it is obvious that the integer 25634 comes after the integer 25633, that the letter `'S'` comes after the letter `'R'`, and that `True` comes after `False`. However, if we consider real data, the situation is more complex. What real number, for example, would immediately follow 3.14159? Would it be 3.14160? Would it be 3.141591 or even 3.141590001? There is, in fact, only one number that *could* follow, based on the way real numbers are represented in the computer. However, it is not at all obvious *what* that number should be. Consequently, real numbers are excluded from the ordinal types.

Ordinals have wide applicability in computer science. For example, throughout this text we have used integers (an ordinal type) to control counted loops:

```
For Time := 1 to 100 Do
    Begin
      F := R * Time;
      Writeln (Time, F)
    End;
```

However, it is legal to use *any* ordinal type (including those you define yourself) in such a loop. Thus, the following program segment is perfectly valid (provided that the variable counters have been declared to be of type `Char`):

```
For Letter := 'a' to 'z' Do
    For Next := 'a' to 'z' Do
            Writeln (Letter:1, Next:1);
```

This segment will print out all 676 possible two-letter words in English. Since `Boolean` is also an ordinal type, it, too, may be used in counted loops:

```
For a := True DownTo False Do
    For b := True DownTo False Do
        For c := True DownTo False Do
            Begin
              f := a and b or not c;
              Writeln (a,b,c,f)
            End;
```

Another use of ordinal types is in the definition of arrays (see Chapters 13 and 14). The following are valid array definitions:

```
Type Weird = Array ['A'..'F'] of Real;
     SpacedOut = Array [False..True, False..True] of Char;
     Bonkers = Array ['a'..'m', 100..150] of Integer;
```

Data of these types can be declared as

```
Var  First : Weird;
     Middle : SpacedOut;
     Final : Bonkers;
```

Elements of these arrays can be referenced as

```
First ['B'] := 234.567;
Middle [True, True] := '#';
Final ['g', 125] := 1024;
```

As always, of course, variables (of the proper type) may be used as subscripts.

Since ordinals can play an important role in programming, Pascal provides three predefined functions that can be used with them: Pred, Succ, and Ord. We will briefly introduce these.

Pred. The function Pred returns the predecessor of its argument (that is, the element that comes right before). For example, the Pascal statement segment

```
H := Pred ('C');
N := Pred (256);
L := Pred (True);
```

will assign a value of 'B' to H, a value of 255 to N, and a value of False to L. Take note of the fact that Pred(False) is not defined, since there *is* no element that comes before False in the Boolean data type.

Succ. The function Succ returns the successor to its argument (that is, the element that immediately follows). The Pascal segment

```
H := Succ('X');
N := Succ(127);
L := Succ(False);
```

will assign a value of 'Y' to H, a value of 128 to N, and a value of True to L. In a fashion analogous to the Pred case, the function Succ(True) is undefined, since there *is* no successor to True.

Ord. This function gives the linear, numerical order of an ordinal type. The result of the function is not normally used in an absolute sense but rather as a way of getting relative distances between ordinal values. For example, the statement

```
Difference := Ord('H') - Ord('F');
```

would generate a value of 2, since the letters 'F' and 'H' are two letters apart.

Now that we have introduced scalars and ordinals, we are ready to see how to define your *own* data types.

User-Defined Types

In Pascal there are two ways you can define your own data types: you can use parts of what Pascal already has, or you can actually make up your own types. The former is referred to as a **subrange type** and the latter as an **enumerated type.** We will look at each of these in turn.

SUBRANGE TYPES

You can define any *continuous* sequence of an existing ordinal type as a subrange type in Pascal. As we have always done, let's present the Pascal syntax of this via a new definition:

> declaration-section → constants
>   types
>   variables
>
> types → **type** type-definition-list
> | nil
>
> type-definition-list → type-definitions
>
> type-definition → subrange-type-definition
>
> subrange-type-definition → identifier = low-value .. high-value

Let's demonstrate subrange types with an example. Suppose we wanted to use the English letters 'A' to 'Z' as a distinct data type and the digits (in character form) '0' to '9' as a separate data type. Further, suppose we needed positive integers from 0 to 2048. We could define each of these as a separate data type, as follows:

```
Type English = 'A' .. 'Z';
     Digits  = '0' .. '9';
     Numbers = 0 .. 2048;
```

Of course, once we had defined these types, we could then declare variables of these types as

```
Var Letter1, Letter2, Letter3 : English;
    FirstDigit, LastDigit : Digits;
    BigO : Numbers;
```

Note that, whereas you could write

```
Letter1 := `P`;
```

you absolutely *could not* write

```
Letter1 := `p`;  ← WRONG, WRONG, WRONG!
```

because Letter1 is of type English and `p` is NOT a valid element of the English type. You could also write

```
BigO := 1024;
```

but not

```
BigO := 2500;  ← NO, NO, NO!
```

for exactly the same reason.

Once you define a subrange type, you can use it exactly as you might use any of the predefined ordinal types.

We are now ready to move on to what we consider to be the "true" user-defined types, *enumerated types*.

ENUMERATED TYPES

In Pascal you are free to make up new data types and name the elements as you like. Such data types are said to be *enumerated*, because the type is defined in terms of an (ordered) sequence of elements that you must list individually. Using our Pascal syntax we can describe these as

type-definition → subrange-type-definition
                 | enumerated-type-definition

where

enumerated-type-definition → identifier = (element-list);

As we said, you are free to define the elements in any way you choose. Let's look at a couple of examples. Suppose that you are writing a program that involves computer components. You could define a data type that would fit this scheme as follows:

```
Type Component = (Inp, Outp, ALU, Control, Memory);
```

You might then define variables of this type as

```
Var Piece, Chunk : Component;
```

You could then go ahead and write a section of code that uses these, for example,

```
Piece := ALU;
Chunk := Memory
```

or even something like

```
If Chunk <= Piece then
    Writeln ('Wrong Order!')
Else
    Writeln ('Proceed');
```

Let's make sure this is clear: Piece and Chunk are variables of type Component, which means that the *only* values they may contain are the five values Inp, Outp, ALU, Control, and Memory. These latter five names are NOT variables, and they are certainly NOT strings. They are *elements* of a *user-defined* data type. In fact they are *scalars* and *ordinals:* Inp is less than Outp is less than ALU is less than Control is less than Memory. The comparison in the above program segment (that is, Chunk <= Piece) would be False, since Memory does NOT come before ALU in the type definition statement. The ordinal values of a defined type are identical to the order in which the elements are listed in the type statement.

As with the predefined ordinal types, the Pascal functions Pred, Succ, and Ord may be used with enumerated types. For example, Pred(Control) would yield the value ALU, Succ(Control) would yield the value Memory, and Ord(ALU) - Ord(Inp) would give the integer value of 2.

Also, as with any ordinal type, enumerated data types can be used in loops or array definitions, for example,

```
Type Component = (Inp, Outp, ALU, Control, Memory);
     Funny = Array [Inp .. Control] of Char;

Var  Codice : Funny;
     Piece: Component;
         .
         .
         .
```

```
For Piece := Inp to Control Do
     Readln (Codice[Piece]);
```

Enumerated types may be used to enhance the readability of programs and to provide a convenience for special applications. Consider, for example, the program listed in Figure 16-15 (an algebraic calculator simulation). In lines 8 through 10, constants are defined and used as an aid to program readability. As mentioned in the text accompanying the simulation program, however, we may choose to define our own data types instead. This could be accomplished by changing lines 8 through 37 to read

```
Type Tokens = (Add, Sub, Mul, Quo, Exp,
               Operator, Numeric, EqualSign);

     Stack = Record
               Element : Tokens;
               Next    : StackPtr
             End;
Var  NumStack, OprStack, PrecStack : StackPtr;

     Entry, EntryType, PreviousEntryType : Tokens;

     Precedence : Integer;
     Searching : Boolean;
     Result : Integer;

     GoAgain : Char;
```

Note how much more readable and understandable than the original this is!

There is only one glitch in the system: user-defined enumerated types *may not be input to or output from the program in which they are used!* Consequently, a certain amount of contortion may sometimes be required of a programmer to make the connection between the outside world and the internal defined data types. This frequently (but not always) means using a Case statement. For example, if a program makes use of colors of the rainbow, the data may be typed as

```
Type Colors = (Red, Orange, Yellow, Green, Blue, Violet);
```

The variables could be declared as

```
Var  TheColor  : Colors;
     ColorCode : Char;
```

However, when it comes time to input the colors, some kind of code will have to be used (perhaps characters 'R', 'O', 'Y', 'G', 'B', 'V').

These codes would then have to be *converted* to the appropriate data type as follows:

```
Readln (ColorCode);
       Case ColorCode of
'R' : TheColor := Red;
'O' : TheColor := Orange;
'Y' : TheColor := Yellow;
'G' : TheColor := Green;
'B' : TheColor := Blue;
'V' : TheColor := Violet;
       End;
```

Once the conversion is accomplished, the program may proceed. The necessity of conversion reduces the utility of user-defined types somewhat but does not do so excessively. The reward is a program that is easier to read and understand. (In this case, anyway, the end justifies the means.)

APPLICATION

Let's finish up this Appendix by developing a program that makes use of user-defined scalar types. In order to show the full utility of such types, we will consider an example that involves arrays.

Financial Appreciation

Let's look at short-term investments, where both the principle and interest change on a monthly basis. We would like to see how such investments appreciate over time. (The term "appreciate" is used in the sense of increasing value.)

STEP 1: UNDERSTAND THE PROBLEM

We want to enter monthly base (investment) amounts and monthly return (interest) rates for one year. Assuming these same values apply in ensuing years, we want to see how the total value of the investment increases over time. The easiest way to carry out this process involves reading the base amounts and interest rates into appropriate arrays and then using a loop to successively compute new balances. For any given month of any given year, the new balance can be computed easily according to this equation:

New Amount for the month ← Old Amount for the month ×
Interest rate for the month

This, of course, is to be recomputed for each month over the specified span of years.

STEP 2: PLAN THE SOLUTION

Since this is little more than a simple array problem, we can generate an initial algorithm quite easily as

```
Get the Time Span
   Read Initial Year
   Read Final Year
Get the Data
   For Month ← Jan to Dec Do
      Read Base Amount [Month]

   For Month ← Jan to Dec Do
      Read Interest Rate [Month]

Compute the Appreciation
   For Year ← Initial Year to Final Year Do
      For Month ← Jan to Dec Do
         Base Amount [Month] ← Base Amount [Month] × Interest Rate [Month]
Output the Results
   For Month ← Jan to Dec Do
      Write Base Amount [Month]
```

The only thing we really need to watch out for here is the interest rate for each month. If it is expressed as a percent, it must be converted to a fraction. Further, in order to get the actual new base amount (as opposed to just the interest earned), the interest rate must be expressed as 1 + Interest Rate. Making this adjustment gives us the following final algorithm:

```
Get the Time Span
   Read Initial Year
   Read Final Year

Get the Data
   For Month ← Jan to Dec Do
      Read Base Amount [Month]

   For Month ← Jan to Dec Do
      Read Interest Rate [Month]
      Interest Rate [Month] ← 1 + Interest Rate [Month] / 100

Compute the Appreciation
   For Year ← Initial Year to Final Year Do
      For Month ← Jan to Dec Do
         Base Amount [Month] ← Base Amount [Month] × Interest Rate [Month]
```

Output the Results
   For Month ← Jan to Dec Do
      Write Base Amount [Month]

STEP 3: CODE THE SOLUTION

Given this algorithm, we can generate the program. Note that the loops, for the most part, go from one month to the next. This suggests that we should use a data type that consists of months. We can very well use integers here (going, say, from 1 to 12), but the readability of the program would be greatly enhanced if we defined a *new* data type. The definition may be expressed as

```
Type Months = (Jan, Feb, Mar, Apr, May, Jun,
               Jul, Aug, Sep, Oct, Nov, Dec);
```

If we define such a data type, we can actually go ahead and use the months as written with no further changes! This also will enhance the readability of the program and decrease its complexity.

For the sake of exposition, let us further restrict the years over which the appreciation may be computed to 1980 through 2000. We now require a subrange data type, which we can define as

```
Type Years = 1980 .. 2000;
```

Incorporating all this into a full program yields the result shown in Figure A-1. Note that we have defined new data types Months and Years, and, further, in line 14 we have defined an array type whose subscripts consist of elements of the data type Months! We then go on to define appropriate variables in the Var section of the program, including those of type Months, Years, and Amounts. Notice how much more readable the program is since we've employed user-defined data types.

We have also added some "human engineering" to this program in lines 32 through 34, 42 through 44, and 63 through 65. (That is, we have made it easier for the user and reduced the chances of error.) Essentially, what we have done is to allow the inputs to be taken and the outputs to be given quarterly rather than monthly. The order of the months is taken into account here, such that the first quarter of the year is cut off in March, the second in June, the third in September, and the last in December. The program segments that do this look *exactly* like any typical binary decision; the only difference is that we are using our own, rather than Pascal, data types.

STEP 4: CHECK OUT THE PROGRAM

A sample run of this program is shown in Figure A-2. Monthly figures are aligned (during both input and output) on a quarterly basis. The results are also correct.

Figure A-I

Program That Employs User-Defined Scalars to Compute Financial Appreciation

APPREC.PAS

```
1    Program APPREC (Input, Output);
2
3    (*
4      This program uses both subrange types and enumerated types
5      to compute variable investment appreciation over a period
6      of one year.
7    *)
8
9    Type Months = (Jan, Feb, Mar, Apr, May, Jun,
10                   Jul, Aug, Sep, Oct, Nov, Dec);
11
12       Years = 1980 .. 2000;
13
14       Amounts = Array [Jan .. Dec] of Real;
15
16   Var  BaseYear, ProjYear, TheYear : Years;
17        TheMonth : Months;
18        BaseAmount : Amounts;
19        RateIncrease : Amounts;
20
21   BEGIN
22
23     (* Get the initial information *)
24        Write ('What is the base year?        '); Readln (BaseYear);
25        Write ('What is the projection year? '); Readln (ProjYear);
26        Writeln;
27
28        Writeln ('Enter the monthly base figures for ', BaseYear:4);
29        For TheMonth := Jan to Dec Do
30            Begin
31               Write ('   $ '); Read (BaseAmount[TheMonth]);
32               If (TheMonth = Mar) or (TheMonth = Jun) or
33                  (TheMonth = Sep) or (TheMonth = Dec) then
34                      Writeln
35            End;
36        Writeln;
37
38        Writeln ('Enter the monthly rate increases (as a percent)');
39        For TheMonth := Jan to Dec Do
40            Begin
41               Write ('   % '); Read (RateIncrease[TheMonth]);
42               If (TheMonth = Mar) or (TheMonth = Jun) or
43                  (TheMonth = Sep) or (TheMonth = Dec) then
44                      Writeln;
45               RateIncrease[TheMonth] :=
46                      1.0 + RateIncrease[TheMonth] / 100.0
47            End;
48
49     (* Compute the appreciation over time *)
50        For TheYear := BaseYear to ProjYear Do
51            For TheMonth := Jan to Dec Do
52                BaseAmount[TheMonth] :=
53                      BaseAmount[TheMonth] * RateIncrease[TheMonth];
54
55
```

Figure A-1 continued

```
56      (* Tell them what we found *)
57          Writeln;
58          Writeln ('The final monthly values are:');
59          Writeln;
60          For TheMonth := Jan to Dec Do
61              Begin
62                  Write ('    $',BaseAmount[TheMonth]:8:2);
63                  If (TheMonth = Mar) or (TheMonth = Jun) or
64                      (TheMonth = Sep) or (TheMonth = Dec) then
65                          Writeln
66              End;
67      Writeln
68
69   END.
```

Figure A-2

Sample Run and Output from the Financial Appreciation Program

```
$ run apprec

What is the base year?       1986
What is the projection year? 1990

Enter the monthly base figures for 1986
    $ 1200    $ 1350    $ 1100
    $  900    $ 1000    $ 1500
    $ 2000    $ 2200    $ 2100
    $ 1700    $ 1200    $  800

Enter the monthly rate increases (as a percent)
    % 1.5    % 1.4    % 1.2
    % 1.1    % 1.0    % 2.0
    % 1.9    % 0.8    % 0.5
    % 0.9    % 1.0    % 1.1

The final monthly values are:

    $ 1292.74    $ 1447.18    $ 1167.60
    $  950.60    $ 1051.01    $ 1656.12
    $ 2197.36    $ 2289.42    $ 2153.03
    $ 1777.89    $ 1261.21    $  844.98
```

STEP 5: DOCUMENT

As always, documentation is complete at this stage. Note especially how much the user-defined data types add to the readability of the program.

This concludes our presentation of scalars, ordinals, and user-defined data types in Pascal. The techniques demonstrated in this Appendix may be used where appropriate (and when desired) in solving problems presented in the other chapters.

Appendix B:

Sets

*I*n this Appendix we examine sets, which are an interesting and useful but certainly not fundamental data structure. We introduced the concept in Chapter 13 and will now develop it further. The ensuing discussion assumes a knowledge of control structures, and therefore it is recommended that this Appendix not be covered before you have read Chapter 10.

We may define a **set** as an unordered collection of objects. The fundamental property of a set is that it has members, and the primary operation on sets consists of determining whether or not a given object belongs to a particular set. Sets may also be combined in various ways. Let's define a few sets and see what we can do with them. We begin with set N, expressed as

$$N = \{1, 2, 3, 4, 5, 6, 7, 8, 9, 10\}$$

Note that this set consists of the integers 1 through 10 and has been defined by *listing the elements it contains*. This is probably the most common method of expressing the elements of a set.

Let's now define three more sets, E, D, and S, as follows:

$$E = \{2, 4, 6, 8, 10\}$$
$$D = \{1, 3, 5, 7, 9\}$$
$$S = \{1, 2, 3\}$$

The set E consists of all the *even* numbers between 1 and 10, set D consists of all the *odd* numbers between 1 and 10, and set S consists of the smallest three positive integers.

Sets E, D, and S are said to be *subsets* of set N, because every element in each of them is also an element of the larger set. On the other hand, N is *not* a subset of E, since each element of N is *not* found in E. However, every set is a subset of itself.

It is also possible to have an *empty set*, which is a set containing no elements. We can express it as

$$e = \{\ \ \}$$

Let's now look and see what kinds of operations pertain to sets.

Operations

As we already mentioned, one of the primary operations done on a set is to make a determination of whether or not a given element is in a set. We may, for example, ask the following questions and receive the corresponding answers:

Question	Answer
Is 5 in N?	Yes
Is 5 in E?	No
Is 5 in D?	Yes
Is 5 in S?	No

There are other operations as well, namely, *union, intersection*, and *difference*. Let's look at each of these next.

Union. The union of two sets consists of all the elements that are in either or both sets. (An element, if it is in both, is of course only counted once.) In this respect, union is analogous to addition. We can compute the union of some of our sets as follows:

$$C = E \text{ union } D = \{2, 4, 6, 8, 10, 1, 3, 5, 7, 9\}$$

Note that the set C so produced *is exactly the same as set N*. We can say that set C and set N are equal, which means they have *exactly* the same elements. Recall from our definition of sets that they are *unordered;* hence, the fact that the elements of sets N and C are not in the same order has no bearing whatever on their equality.

Here is another example:

$$F = E \text{ union } S = \{1, 2, 3, 4, 6, 8, 10\}$$

We have altered the order for clarity, but again it makes no difference to the definition of the set itself.

Taking the union of a set with itself doesn't make it any bigger or change it in any way:

$$N \text{ union } N = N$$

Intersection. The intersection of two sets consists of those elements that can be found in *both* sets. For example, we may have

$$G = S \text{ intersection } D = \{1, 3\}$$

The elements 1 and 3 are the *only* ones that can be found in both sets simultaneously.

Here is another example:

$$H = E \text{ intersection } D = \{ \ \} = e$$

In this case, there are *no* common elements; hence, the result is the empty set.

Difference. The difference of two sets consists of those elements in the first set that are *not* in the second set. For example, we have

$$R = N - S = \{4, 5, 6, 7, 8, 9, 10\}$$

In other words, you start with the first set and remove (subtract out) any elements in common between the two sets. Note what happens when we reverse this operation:

$$Q = S - N = \{ \ \} = e$$

Sets and set operations are available in Pascal (of course), so we turn to them next.

Pascal Definition of Sets

In Pascal, sets can be constructed out of elements from any ordinal type (see Appendix A). In this Appendix, however, we will consider only sets made up of integers and characters.

Set types are defined via the type statement. The required statements, when used for the purpose of creating sets, are

declaration-section → constants
                         types
                         variables

types → **type** type-definition-list
       |nil

type-definition-list → type-definitions

As you know, there are many kinds of type definitions. In this Appendix we are interested in the *set* type and may proceed to define it as

type-definition → set-type

set-type → identifier **= set of** type

where *type* can be any ordinal type. Of course, once the appropriate set type is defined, variables (sets) of that type can be declared (*must* be declared if you intend to use them) via the Var statement.

For example, suppose we were writing a program that required sets of characters to distinguish upper- and lowercase letters. We can define the appropriate type and variables as

```
Type Letters = Set of Char;
Var  UpperCase, LowerCase : Letters;
```

This would declare two sets named UpperCase and LowerCase, which could contain any possible collection of valid characters.

As another example, consider the sets we worked with at the first of this Appendix. These could be defined and declared as follows:

```
Type Numbers = Set of Integer;
Var  N, E, D, S, Empty, C, F, G, H, R, Q : Numbers;
```

(Strictly speaking, you cannot have a data type that is a Set of Integer because there are too many integers. A subrange is actually required, and these are discussed in Appendix A.)

After these sets are declared, they are all empty sets, regardless of what they are called. The situation is analogous to ordinary variables in that declaring the variable (or set) does *not* give a value to it. These values for both variables and sets must be assigned in the executable section of the program. Set values are assigned by listing the elements to be included in a set within square brackets. If we want to assign values to the first five sets above, it can be done as follows:

```
BEGIN
  N := [1, 2, 3, 4, 5, 6, 7, 8, 9, 10];
  E := [2, 4, 6, 8, 10];
  D := [1, 3, 5, 7, 9];
  S := [1, 2, 3];
  Empty := [ ];
```

Note that the last assignment is really redundant, since Empty is *already* an empty set. It does show how to clear (or empty) a set.

Once we have generated some sets, we can do set operations on them. The Pascal operators corresponding to the standard set operations are

Set Operation	Pascal Operator
Union	+
Intersection	*
Difference	-

With these operators, we may generate the remaining defined sets (as we did previously) by using the following Pascal statements:

```
C := E + D;    (* Union *)
F := E + S;

G := S * D;    (* Intersection *)
H := E * D;

R := N - S;    (* Difference *)
Q := S - N;
```

One thing you *cannot* do with sets is input or output them directly. However, you can input an element and then add it to a set (via the union operation) or check to see whether or not an element is a member of a set and if so print it out. We will see an example of this shortly.

This brings up a question: How does one test for membership in a set? In Pascal this is done by using the operator In. If, for example, we want to see whether or not the value 5 is in set C, we can do it as follows:

```
If 5 in C then
   whatever
Else
   whichever;
```

Normally, of course, we'd use variables for this, such as

```
If SpecialNumber in C then
   whatever
Else
   whichever;
```

There are other questions as well that can be asked about set relationships. These can be summarized as follows:

Relationship	Pascal Operator	Example
Is one set equal to another?	=	C = D
Is one set *not* equal to another?	<>	C <> D
Is one set a subset of another?	<=	C <= D
Does one set contain another set?	>=	C >= D

Let's now go on to look at some program examples that demonstrate the use of sets.

Applications

We will begin by looking at a very common application of sets. Recall that in Chapter 10 we programmed a calculator simulation to demonstrate the use of decision structures. The program was written twice, once for nested If/Else (Figure 10-3) and once for Case (Figure 10–5). Recall also that there was a significant difference between the two: whereas the former could detect an invalid operator, *the latter could not.* Let's alter the Case version of the simulation in order to correct the deficiency.

Calculator Simulation with Sets

We wish to make use of the properties of sets to permit the Case version of the calculator simulation to detect invalid operators.

STEP 1: UNDERSTAND THE PROBLEM

We should already understand the problem, but for the sake of clarity let's briefly review it. The problem is to input an operator and two numbers and then carry out the indicated operation on those numbers and print the result. For example, if we entered a +, 4, and 5, we should expect the sum of 9 to be displayed. The only thing we want to add to this version is the ability to test for invalid operators.

STEP 2: PLAN THE SOLUTION

The solution involves creating a set that contains all the legal operators and then checking to see whether the most recently input operator is in fact an element of that set. If it is, we continue; otherwise, we display an error message.

We can write a high-level algorithm (which, for the sake of brevity, does not duplicate elements of the original algorithm) to display the critical aspects of the process as follows:

Set of Ok Operators ← { + , − , * , / , ^ }

Read Operator
While Operator ≠ 'x' Do
  If Operator is in the Set of Ok Operators then
    Continue as planned
  Else
    Write 'Invalid Operator'
  Read Operator

Only the exact manner in which the set should be implemented remains to be determined, and this is the subject of the next step.

STEP 3: CODE THE SOLUTION

Assuming that the person running the program can hit any key when trying for an operator, let's make the set we use a set of `Char`. We can then define the valid operators as characters and see if the operator that has been input (which is *also* a character) is in the set. These techniques have been used and incorporated into the program as shown in Figure B-1. Note especially the simplicity with which this has been done!

STEP 4: CHECK OUT THE PROGRAM

A sample run is shown in Figure B-2. There is a distinct improvement in this new version over the two original versions. It is now possible to check for an invalid operator *immediately* and not bother to request any data if there is an error!

STEP 5: DOCUMENT

Got it.

Let's go through another example, one that makes more use of the available Pascal set operations.

Figure B-1

Calculator Simulation Program of Chapter 10 Rewritten to Use Sets for Determining Invalid Operators

CALCCASE.PAS

```
 1    Program CALCCASE (Input, Output);
 2
 3    (*
 4       This program simulates a calculator. It inputs two numbers and
 5       an operator, carries out the indicated operation on the numbers, and
 6       then prints out the results. It makes use of the Case statement
 7       to choose among operators and in addition uses sets to check
 8       for an invalid operator.
 9    *)
10
11    Type PossibleOps = Set of Char;
12
13    Var  N1, N2, Res : Real ;    (* Operands and result *)
14
15         Op : Char;                 (* Operator: + addition
16                                                 - subtraction
17                                                 * multiplication
18                                                 / division
19                                                 ^ exponentiation
20
21                                                 x to exit *)
22
23         OkOps : PossibleOps;    (* This is a set which will contain
24                                    all valid operators. *)
25
26    Function PWR (b, e : Real) : Real;
27    (*
28       This function computes exponentiation of a real base (b)
29       to a real power (e); the power is converted to an integer (m)
30       before use.
31    *)
32      Var m,i : Integer; (* i is just the loop counter   *)
33          r : Real;       (* Result of the exponentiation *)
34      Begin
35        m := Trunc (e);
36        r := 1.0;
37        For i := 1 to m Do
38           r := r * b;
39        PWR := r
40      End;
41
42
43
44    BEGIN
45
46      OkOps := [ '+', '-', '*', '/', '^' ];
47
48      Writeln ('Calculator Simulation');
49      Writeln;
50      Write ('Enter operator or ''x'' to end : '); Readln (Op);
51
52      While Op <> 'x' Do
53         Begin
54            If Op in OkOps then
```

Figure B-1 continued

```
55              Begin
56                  Write ('Enter 1st number : '); Readln (N1);
57                  Write ('Enter 2nd number : '); Readln (N2);
58
59                      Case Op of
60              '+' : Res := N1 + N2 ;
61              '-' : Res := N1 - N2 ;
62              '*' : Res := N1 * N2 ;
63              '/' : Res := N1 / N2 ;
64              '^' : Res := PWR (N1, N2);
65                      End (* Case *);
66
67                  Writeln ('Result : ', Res:5:3)
68              End
69          Else
70              Writeln ('Invalid Operator ... Try Again');
71
72          Writeln;
73          Write ('Enter Operator   : '); Readln (Op)
74
75      End (* While *);
76
77  Writeln;
78  Writeln ('Exit Calculator.')
79
80  END.
```

Figure B-2

Output from the New and Improved Version of the Calculator Simulation Program

```
$ run calccase

Calculator Simulation

Enter operator or 'x' to end : +
Enter 1st number : -12.5
Enter 2nd number : 17.9
Result : 5.400

Enter Operator   : *
Enter 1st number : -3.3
Enter 2nd number : 10.5
Result : -34.650

Enter Operator   : #
Invalid Operator ... Try Again

Enter Operator   : !
Invalid Operator ... Try Again
```

Figure B-2 continued

```
Enter Operator    : /
Enter 1st number : 4.0
Enter 2nd number : 5.0
Result : 0.800

Enter Operator    : x

Exit Calculator.
```

Set Calculator

Let's generate a program that does for sets what the previous program did for numbers. In other words, we want to input sets and carry out set operations on them.

STEP 1: UNDERSTAND THE PROBLEM

We want to enter sets and carry out operations on them. The operations we want to do are

Operation	Code
Input the first set	1
Input the second set	2
Take the union of the sets	U
Take the intersection of the sets	X
Take the difference of the sets	D
See if the sets are equal	=
See if the first is a subset of the second	<
Exit	Q

We have associated codes with each operation. Also, for ease of programming, we will limit the possible set elements to lowercase letters only.

STEP 2: PLAN THE SOLUTION

The general solution is identical to the calculator simulation, and we can write it as

```
Read Operator
While Operator ≠ Q Do
   If Operator in Ok Set of Operators then
           Case Operator of
      1  : InputSet (S1)
      2  : InputSet (S2)
      U  : R ← S1 + S2
           OutputSet (R)
      X  : R ← S1 × S2
           OutputSet (R)
      D  : R ← S1 − S2
           OutputSet (R)
      =  : If S1 = S2 then
              Write 'EQUAL'
           Else
              Write 'NOT EQUAL'
      <  : If S1 ≤ S2 then
              Write 'SUBSET'
           Else
              Write 'NOT SUBSET'
      End Case
   Else
      Write 'Invalid Operator . . . Try Again'
   Read Operator
```

Note that we are using sets here for two purposes: first, as the data used by the program, and second as a means of discovering invalid operators (exactly as we did in the previous problem).

We have indicated procedures as a way to input and output sets, so we must consider those processes next.

`InputSet.` This procedure consists of a loop that inputs possible set elements, checks them for validity, and then adds them to the set if appropriate. We will use the sentinel value approach to control the loop. The algorithm for this can be expressed as

```
Procedure InputSet (TheSet)
   TheSet ← [ ]
   Read Element
   While Element ≠ 'Q' Do
      If Element in Ok Elements then
         TheSet ← TheSet + Element (* Union *)
      Else
         Write 'Invalid Set Element'

      Read Element
   OutputSet (TheSet) (* Confirm *)
```

The set is cleared before elements are added, each element is tested to make sure it is valid, and the completed set is printed out for verification purposes.

`OutputSet.` This procedure is a little tougher, since the only way we can print out a set is to go through it one possibility at a time and, if the element is in the set, print the element out. We can write an algorithm to do this as follows:

Procedure OutputSet (TheSet)
   For all possible elements Do
      If the element is in the set then
         Print it out

This is actually easier than it may seem at first, especially since we have limited the possible elements to lowercase letters only. We can in fact use a loop in which the counters are *characters* rather than integers (see Chapter 9 and Appendix A). Trusting that this may be done, we can write

Procedure OutputSet (TheSet)
   For Possibility ← 'a' to 'z' Do
      If Possibility in TheSet then
         Write Possibility

Although this is a bit of a bother, it will work well enough.

This completes the algorithms for this problem, and we may move on to the next step in the process.

STEP 3: CODE THE SOLUTION

The algorithms, in conjunction with our recent discussion about sets, provide us with all the tools we need to convert this solution to a program. The result of all our efforts is shown in Figure B-3. A few points about this program are noted as follows:

Line 22. Note the use of a loop that does in fact use characters for counting purposes.

Line 40. When an element is added to a set via the union (+) set operator, it must be expressed as a set. This is done by enclosing the element inside square brackets, effectively making it a set with a single element.

Line 51. The set `OkOperators` is defined by listing the elements that it is to contain.

Line 52. The set `OkElements` is a little different. Since listing the elements of this set would be lengthy, Pascal permits a set

Figure B-3

Program That Permits Input of, Operations on, and Output from Sets

SETCALC.PAS

```
1    Program SETCALC (Input, Output);
2
3    (*
4        This program permits the construction of and operations on
5        any arbitrary sets.
6    *)
7
8    Type Sets = Set of Char;
9
10   Var  Operator : Char;
11        OkOperators, OkElements : Sets;
12        S1, S2, R : Sets;
13
14
15
16   Procedure OutputSet (TheSet : Sets);
17   (* This procedure outputs the elements of a given set. *)
18     Var Possibility : Char;
19     Begin
20       Writeln;
21       Writeln ('The set consists of');
22       For Possibility := 'a' to 'z' Do
23           If Possibility in TheSet then
24               Write (Possibility:2);
25       Writeln
26     End;
27
28
29   Procedure InputSet (Var TheSet : Sets);
30   (* This procedure inputs set elements and constructs a set
31      from them by successive union. *)
32     Var Element : Char;
33     Begin
34       TheSet := [ ];
35       Writeln ('Enter the set elements, ''Q'' to end : ');
36       Write ('> '); Readln (Element);
37       While Element <> 'Q' Do
38         Begin
39           If Element in OkElements then
40               TheSet := TheSet + [Element]   (* Union *)
41           Else
42               Writeln ('Invalid Set Element');
43           Write ('> '); Readln (Element)
44         End;
45       OutputSet (TheSet)                     (* Confirm *)
46     End;
47
48
49   BEGIN
50
51     OkOperators := ['1', '2', 'U', 'X', 'D', '=', '<'];
52     OkElements := ['a' .. 'z'];
53
54     Writeln ('Set Calculator Simulation');
55     Writeln;
56     Writeln ('Enter set operator or ''Q'' to quit :');
57     Readln (Operator);
```

Figure B-3 continued

```
58
59        While Operator <> 'Q' Do
60           Begin
61              If Operator in OKOperators then
62                     Case Operator of
63                 '1' : InputSet (S1);
64                 '2' : InputSet (S2);
65                 'U' : Begin                    (* Take the Union *)
66                          R := S1 + S2;
67                          OutputSet (R)
68                       End;
69                 'X' : Begin                    (* Take the Intersection *)
70                          R := S1 * S2;
71                          OutputSet (R)
72                       End;
73                 'D' : Begin                    (* Take the Difference *)
74                          R := S1 - S2;
75                          OutputSet (R)
76                       End;
77                 '=' : If S1 = S2 then
78                          Writeln ('            EQUAL')
79                       Else
80                          Writeln ('            NOT EQUAL');
81                 '<' : If S1 <= S2 then
82                          Writeln ('            SUBSET')
83                       Else
84                          Writeln ('            NOT SUBSET');
85                     End (* Case *)
86
87              Else (* we do not have an operator *)
88                     Writeln ('Invalid Operator ... Try Again');
89
90              Writeln;
91              Write ('Enter Operator : '); Readln (Operator)
92
93           End (* While *);
94
95        Writeln;
96        Writeln ('Exit Set Calculator')
97
98     END.
```

made of contiguous elements to be expressed elliptically. In this case the notation means that the given set is to contain all of the lowercase letters ' a ' through ' z ', inclusive.

STEP 4: CHECK OUT THE PROGRAM

A fairly lengthy test run of this program is shown in Figure B-4. Note that all the set operations are carried out correctly and that errors made during entry are all caught and exposed.

Figure B-4

Test Run of the Set Manipulation Program

```
$ run setcalc

Set Calculator Simulation

Enter set operator or 'Q' to quit :1
Enter the set elements, 'Q' to end :
> a
> e
> i
> o
> u
> Q

The set consists of
 a e i o u

Enter Operator : 2
Enter the set elements, 'Q' to end :
> #
Invalid Set Element
> a
> b
> c
> d
> e
> Q

The set consists of
 a b c d e

Enter Operator : U

The set consists of
 a b c d e i o u

Enter Operator : X

The set consists of
 a e

Enter Operator : D

The set consists of
 i o u

Enter Operator : =
          NOT EQUAL

Enter Operator : <
          NOT SUBSET

Enter Operator : P
Invalid Operator ... Try Again
```

Figure B-4 continued

```
Enter Operator : 1
Enter the set elements, 'Q' to end :
> a
> b
> c
> d
> e
> Q

The set consists of
 a b c d e

Enter Operator : 2
Enter the set elements, 'Q' to end :
> a
> c
> e
> Q

The set consists of
 a c e

Enter Operator : =
         NOT EQUAL

Enter Operator : <
         NOT SUBSET

Enter Operator : 1
Enter the set elements, 'Q' to end :
> a
> c
> e
> Q

The set consists of
 a c e

Enter Operator : 2
Enter the set elements, 'Q' to end :
> a
> b
> c
> d
> e
> f
> g
> Q

The set consists of
 a b c d e f g

Enter Operator : =
         NOT EQUAL

Enter Operator : <
         SUBSET
```

Figure B-4 continued

```
Enter Operator : 1
Enter the set elements, 'Q' to end :
> x
> y
> Q

The set consists of
 x  y

Enter Operator : 2
Enter the set elements, 'Q' to end :
> x
> y
> Q

The set consists of
 x  y

Enter Operator : =
          EQUAL

Enter Operator : <
          SUBSET

Enter Operator : Q

Exit Set Calculator
```

STEP 5: DOCUMENT

As we have come to expect, the documentation is sufficient and appropriate.

This concludes our presentation of sets. As with the previous Appendix, the techniques demonstrated here are intended to be used with other chapter problems if and when appropriate.

Appendix C:

Characters, Codes, and Conversions

*R*ecall from the discussion of characters and collating sequences in Chapter 8, Chapter 15, and Apendix A that every character in the computer has a number, or numeric code, associated with it. The assignment of numeric codes to characters is completely arbitrary, but for the sake of conformity a common set of codes is beneficial. In fact, two such codes are in common usage—ASCII (American Standard Code for Information Interchange), which is used primarily on non-IBM computers, and EBCDIC (Extended Binary Coded Decimal Interchange Code), which was developed by IBM and is used almost exclusively on IBM machines. (An extended set of ASCII codes that contains many special graphics characters is used for the IBM PC and compatibles.) Both sets of character codes are listed in this appendix.

Pascal provides two standard (and inverse) functions used to convert characters to their respective numeric codes, and vice versa. The function `Ord`, introduced in Appendix A, converts a character to its corresponding numeric code. For example, if ASCII codes are being used, executing the statements

```
TheChar := 'G';
NumCode := Ord (TheChar)
```

would assign a value of 71 to the variable `NumCode`. Conversely, the Pascal function `Chr` converts a numeric code into its corresponding character. Again assuming ASCII codes, the sequence of instructions

```
Code := 63;
WhichChar := Chr (Code);
Writeln (WhichChar);
```

would generate the output

```
?
```

since the character ? has an ASCII code of 63. The ability to convert characters to numeric code is especially useful when it is necessary to manipulate characters that cannot be easily entered via the keyboard, for example, the Escape key or the Delete key. If you know the correct numeric code, you can generate the corresponding character.

Standard ASCII Codes

Code	Character	Code	Character	Code	Character
0	NUL (null)	15	SI	30	RS
1	SOH	16	DLE	31	US
2	STX	17	DC1	32	(space)
3	ETX	18	DC2	33	!
4	EOT	19	DC3	34	"
5	ENQ	20	DC4	35	#
6	ACK	21	NAK	36	$
7	BEL (beep)	22	SYN	37	%
8	BS	23	ETB	38	&
9	HT	24	CAN	39	`
10	LF (line feed)	25	EM	40	(
11	VT	26	SUB	41	)
12	FF	27	ESC (escape)	42	*
13	CR (carriage return)	28	FS	43	+
14	SO	29	GS	44	,

(continued)

Standard ASCII Codes (continued)

Code	Character	Code	Character	Code	Character
45	–	73	I	101	e
46	.	74	J	102	f
47	/	75	K	103	g
48	0	76	L	104	h
49	1	77	M	105	i
50	2	78	N	106	j
51	3	79	O	107	k
52	4	80	P	108	l
53	5	81	Q	109	m
54	6	82	R	110	n
55	7	83	S	111	o
56	8	84	T	112	p
57	9	85	U	113	q
58	:	86	V	114	r
59	;	87	W	115	s
60	<	88	X	116	t
61	=	89	Y	117	u
62	>	90	Z	118	v
63	?	91	[	119	w
64	@	92	\	120	x
65	A	93	]	121	y
66	B	94	^	122	z
67	C	95	_	123	{
68	D	96	`	124	¦
69	E	97	a	125	}
70	F	98	b	126	~
71	G	99	c	127	DEL (delete)
72	H	100	d		

EBCDIC Codes

Code	Character	Code	Character
0	NUL (null)	45	ENQ
1	SOH	46	ACK
2	STX	47	BEL (beep)
3	ETX		
4	PF	50	SYN
5	HT		
6	LC	52	PN
7	DEL (delete)	53	RS
		54	UC
9	RLF	55	EOT
10	SMM		
11	VT	59	CU3
12	FF	60	DC4
13	CR (carriage return)	61	NAK
14	SO		
15	SI	63	SUB
16	DLE	64	(space)
17	DC1		
18	DC2	74	[
19	TM	75	.
20	RES	76	<
21	NL	77	(
22	BS	78	+
23	IL	79	¦
24	CAN	80	&
25	EM		
26	CC	90	]
27	CU1	91	$
28	IFS	92	*
29	IGS	93	)
30	IRS	94	;
31	IUS		
32	DS	97	/
33	SOS		
34	FS	107	,
		108	%
36	BYP	109	–
37	LF (line feed)	110	>
38	ETB	111	?
39	ESC (escape)		
		122	:
42	SM	123	#
43	CU2	124	@

(continued)

EBCDIC Codes (continued)

Code	Character	Code	Character
125	´	196	D
126	=	197	E
127	"	198	F
		199	G
129	a	200	H
130	b	201	I
131	c		
132	d	209	J
133	e	210	K
134	f	211	L
135	g	212	M
136	h	213	N
137	i	214	O
		215	P
145	j	216	Q
146	k	217	R
147	l		
148	m	226	S
149	n	227	T
150	o	228	U
151	p	229	V
152	q	230	W
153	r	231	X
		232	Y
162	s	233	Z
163	t		
164	u	240	0
165	v	241	1
166	w	242	2
167	x	243	3
168	y	244	4
169	z	245	5
		246	6
193	A	247	7
194	B	248	8
195	C	249	9

Appendix D:

Pascal Syntax Summary

*T*his appendix contains syntax descriptions for those elements of Pascal that have been introduced in the text and is *not* a complete description of the full Pascal language. Although for the most part it is a collection and summary of the syntax descriptions presented in the text, a few items have been added for completeness to make up for the fact that many of the syntax elements, though discussed at length, were not formalized as syntactic categories. The form of the syntax descriptions here is the same modified BNF used throughout the book.

Since we did not originally use BNF to describe expressions, this syntax summary is divided into two parts: (1) a general description of Pascal language elements and (2) assignment statements and expressions.

Pascal Language Elements

program → heading-section
      declaration-section
      executable-section

heading-section → **program** identifier (file-list[1])

declaration-section → constants
              types
              variables
              functions
              procedures
              forward-declaration

constants → **const** constant-definition-list
      | nil

constant-definition-list → constant-definition
      | constant-definition constant-definition . . .

constant-definition → identifier = value;

types → **type** type-definition-list
      | nil

type-definition-list → type-definition
      | type-definition   type-definition . . .

type-definition → array-type-definition
      | string-type-definition
      | record-type-definition
      | pointer-type-definition
      | subrange-type-definition
      | enumerated-type-definition
      | set-type-definition

array-type-definition → identifier = **array**
    [lower..upper] **of** type;
              | identifier = **array**
    [lower1..upper1, lower2..upper2] **of** type;

string-type-definition → identifier = **packed array**
    [1..upper] **of char**;

record-type-definition → identifier = **record**
                    field-definitions
                    end;

[1] May include the standard files **input** and **output**.

field-definitions → field-definition
    | field-definition   field-definition . . .

field-definition → identifier : type;

pointer-type-definition → identifier = ^type;

subrange-type-definition → identifier =
        low-value .. high-value;

enumerated-type-definition → identifier = (element-list);

set-type-definition → identifier = **set of** type;

variables → **var** variable-definition-list

variable-definition-list → variable-definition
    | variable-definition   variable-definition . . .

variable-definition → var-list : type;

var-list → variable
    | variable, variable, . . .

type → **integer** | **real** | **boolean** | **char** | **text**
    | user-defined-type

functions → function-definition-list
    | nil

function-definition-list → function
    | function function . . .

function → f-heading-section
    f-declaration-section
    f-executable-section

f-heading-section → **function** identifier
    (parameter-def-list):type;

parameter-def-list → parameter-definition
    | parameter-definition; parameter-definition; . . .
    | nil

parameter-definition → parameter-list:type
    | **var** parameter-list:type

parameter-list → parameter
    | parameter, parameter, . . .

f-declaration-section → declaration-section

f-executable-section → **begin**
        executable-statement-list[2]
end;

procedures → procedure-definition-list
    | nil

procedure-definition-list → procedure
    | procedure procedure . . .

procedure → p-heading-section
        p-declaration-section
        p-executable-section

p-heading-section → **procedure** identifier
        (parameter-def-list);

p-declaration-section → declaration-section

p-executable-section → **begin**
        executable-statement-list
end;

forward-declaration → f-heading-section; **forward;**
    | p-heading-section; **forward;**

executable-section → **begin**
        executable-statement-list
end.

executable-statement-list → executable-statement
    | executable-statement; executable-statement; . . . executable-statement

executable-statement → assignment-statement
    | input-statement
    | output-statement
    | counted-loop
    | compound-statement
    | conditional-loop
    | binary-decision
    | case-statement
    | with-structure

assignment-statement → variable := expression[3]

[2]Must include a statement of the form function-name := expression

[3]The particulars on the assignment statement are detailed in the next section of this appendix.

input-statement → **read** (input-list)
       | **readln** (input-list)
       | **readln**

input-list → variable-reference
       | variable-reference, variable-reference, . . .

output-statement → **write** (output-list)
       | **writeln** (output-list)
       | **writeln**

output-list → output-item
       | output-item, output-item, . . .

output-item → expression
       | expression:n
       | expression:n:m[4]
       | string constant

counted-loop → count-up-loop
       count-down-loop

count-up-loop → **for** counter **:=** start-expr **to** end-expr **do**
       executable-statement

compound-statement → **begin**
       executable-statement-list
       end

count-down-loop → **for** counter **:=** start-expr **downto** end-expr **do**
       executable-statement

conditional-loop → while-do
       | repeat-until

while-do → **while** logical-expression **do**
       executable-statement

repeat-until → **repeat**
       executable-statement-list
       until logical-expression

binary-decision → **if** logical-expression **then**
       executable-statement

[4]n, m are positive integer constants or variables.

else
  executable-statement
  | **if** logical-expression **then**
   executable-statement

case-statement → **case** selector **of**
    selector-list

selector-list → selection-definition selection-definition
    . . .

selection-definition → value-list : executable-statement;

value-list → value
    | value, value, . . .

with-structure → **with** record-identifier **do**
    executable-statement

Assignments and Expressions

In the first section of this appendix, the assignment statement was defined as

assignment-statement → variable := expression

The assignment statement is the primary method by which data values are stored in the computer for later use by a program. Recall from Chapter 4 the definition of *expression*: a combination of constants, variables, and operators that can be reduced to a single value. This definition is actually somewhat restrictive in Pascal, and the primary condition for successful assignment is that the variable on the left and the expression on the right be *assignment compatible*. In the case of scalar variables (see Appendix A), this condition reduces to the original definition of expression; here we will discuss scalar variables first. Since in Pascal the variable and the expression part of an assignment statement can also be a data structure of arbitrary complexity, we will look at this second possibility as well.

SCALAR ASSIGNMENTS

Assignment compatibility for scalars in Pascal requires that the variable on the left be exactly the same type as the value to which the expression on the right reduces, with one exception: It is permissible to assign an integer expression to a real variable. The components of an expression may be any of the following:

    constants
    variables
    function references
    operators

Rules for generating expressions are as follows:

1. Binary operators must have two operands associated with them, for example,

```
Amt / Time
```

2. All operations must be stated explicitly; for example, if you wish to multiply G and R, you cannot write the expression as

```
G  R
```

Instead, you must write it as

```
G * R
```

3. Unary operators must have one operand associated with them, for example,

```
not AllDone

 -Winnings
```

4. Consecutive binary operators are not allowed.

5. Parentheses may be used but must be balanced (that is, there must be as many right parentheses as left parentheses), for example,

```
F * ((a + b) / (c - d))
```

Further, in Pascal all operators have a precedence associated with them, as follows:

High precedence   `not`

`*   /   div   mod   and`

`+   -   or`

Low precedence   `<   <=   =   <>   >   >=   in`

`not` is a unary operator. The operator `-` may be either unary (negation) or binary (subtraction). All other operators are strictly binary.

STRUCTURED DATA ASSIGNMENTS

In Pascal, any two variables are assignment compatible as long as they are of the same type. Consider, for example, the following declarations:

```
Const   MaxSize = 125;

Type    Counts = Array [1..MaxSize] of Integer;

        Stuff = Record
                    Number  : Integer;
                    Average : Real;
                    Code    : Char;
                    Time    : Real;
                    New     : Boolean
                End;

Var     First, Second : Counts;

        Item1, Item2 : Stuff;
```

Given these declarations, it is permissible to write in the executable section of the program statements such as

```
Second := First;

Item2 := Item1;
```

In the first assignment statement, the value of each and every element of the array `First` is transferred to the corresponding array element of the array `Second`. The assignment statement is equivalent to the following loop:

```
For k := 1 to MaxSize do
    Second[k] := First[k]
```

In the second assignment statement, each and every field of Item1 is transferred to the corresponding field of Item2. This assignment statement is equivalent to

```
Item2.Number := Item1.Number;
Item2.Average := Item1.Average;
Item2.Code := Item1.Code;
Item2.Time := Item1.Time;
Item2.New := Item1.New;
```

Glossary/Index

it with the record data structure. 170, 428–429

array of. *See* **Array of records**

definition, 476–477

Record structure   In Pascal, a data structure in which related but heterogeneous data is collected in one place. 171

Recursion   The situation that results when a subprogram (procedure or function) calls itself. 365–366

complex, 384–409

to implement binary search, 548–549

InOrder traversal and, 658

in QuickSort, 559, 561–562

simple, 370–383

stack implementation and, 631

Recursive definitions, 366–370

Recursive exponentiation, 377–381

Registers   Special fast memory locations dedicated to and located within the CPU. 16

Related arrays   Same as **Parallel arrays**. 467–468

application, 468–475

Relational expression   A category of logical expression in which two quantities are compared to see if one is larger, smaller, or the same as the other. 231–232, 246, 248

Relational operator   An operator that compares two quantities; in Pascal, $<$, $<=$, $<>$, $>$, $>=$. 231–232

Repeat until loop   Posttest iterative structure in which the loop instructions are repeated until the test at the end of the loop becomes true. The number of iterations required is usually indeterminate. 254–259

Return   Transfer of control out of a subprogram and back to the point from which a subprogram was originally called. 123

Reverse Polish notation, 660

Root node, 655

RPN, 660

Run-time error   An error that occurs while the program is executing; the error may manifest itself as a message from the computer or as incorrect output. 98, 104–116

Scalar   A quantity that has only a magnitude; scalars can be represented on a line, where the magnitude is proportional to the distance on the line. In Pascal, the scalar types are the primitives Integer, Real, Boolean, and Char. 711–712

Scientific notation, 66

Searching   An operation on a data structure that attempts to locate the position of a particular element within the structure. 431

algorithms for, 513–514

application to trees, 655–656, 666–672

arrays and, 514–554

Second generation languages, 56

Selection sort, 556, 559, 560, 578

application, 565–573

details of, 562–565

Semicolons

absence in nested binary decision statements, 278

for delimiting statements, 61, 69, 83, 221

errors in usage, 96, 97

Sentinel value   A predetermined value for an input variable read during an iterative process that is used to indicate to the computer that the loop is to be terminated. 242, 280, 534

Sequence   One of the three fundamental control structures; permits sequential execution of instructions. Also called process. 190

Set   An unordered collection of objects. 430, 724–725

applications, 729–740

operations, 725–729

Pascal definition of, 726–729

Side effect   Changing a global variable within a procedure or function. 143

Sin, 340–341

Single quote character, 67

Skip, 448

Software   Programs. 12, 16–25

systems, 708

Solution

coding, 40, 83–86

planning, 34–40, 48–49

Sorting   Operation on a data structure that orders the elements in the structure according to some criteria. 431

algorithm analysis and, 578

algorithms for, 513–514

applications, 565–573

application to trees, 655–656

bubble, 556, 557–559, 578

heap. *See* Heap sort

insertion, 556–557, 578, 592

orders, 555–556

selection. *See* Selection sort

techniques, overview of, 556–562

Source file   Text file (usually on a disk) that contains a source program. 170

Source program   High level version of a program entered into the computer as text. 27

Space, single. *See* Blank character

Space allotment, for output, 80–81

Spurious error   An error message generated by the computer for an error that does not really exist but rather is a result of another error somewhere else in the program. 100